anthology of the best cricket writing, by acclaimed commentator and cor-
spondent Christopher Martin-Jenkins.

Cricket has inspired more writing, in terms of both volume and quality,
than any other sport. A romantic game of skill, patience and heroic deeds,
cricket is also a tough duel between batsman and bowler, unique because the
team battle is dependent on the sum of individual struggles.

Christopher Martin-Jenkins has written about cricket professionally for
twenty-five years, and his personal collection includes well over a thousand
cricket books. His journalism and *Test Match Special* commentaries have won
him the respect of all cricket lovers.

This richly entertaining anthology conveys the sweep of cricket's evolution
from W. G. Grace to Shane Warne, from the sport's origins in the Weald to
the contemporary professional (and increasingly commercial) game. There are
sections on 'A Boy's Game', 'England v Australia' and 'Champions and Char-
cters', and contributions from such luminaries as C. L. R. James and Mike
Brearley, Neville Cardus and E. W. Swanton, Stephen Fry and Edmund
Blunden.

Christopher Martin-Jenkins is the author of *The Complete Who's Who of Test
Cricketers* and edited *The Wisden Book of County Cricket*, two of the most
distinguished cricket books published in the last twenty years. A former BBC
Cricket Correspondent, Christopher Martin-Jenkins commentates on *Test
Match Special* and is currently *Daily Telegraph* Cricket Correspondent.

D1078668

2. 2.

THE SPIRIT OF

CRICKET

A Personal Anthology

CHRISTOPHER MARTIN-JENKINS

faber and faber
LONDON BOSTON

To the memory of John Moody and Norman Smith,
collectors and enthusiasts;
and to Henry Watkinson,
a promising left-handed photocopier.

First published in 1994
by Faber and Faber Limited
3 Queen Square London WC1N 3AU
This paperback edition first published in 1995

Photoset by Intype Ltd, London
Printed in England by Clays Ltd, St Ives plc

Christopher Martin-Jenkins is hereby identified as author of
this work in accordance with Section 77 of the Copyright,
Designs and Patents Act 1988

A CIP record for this book is available
from the British Library
ISBN 0-571-17349-7

4 6 8 10 9 7 5 3

Contents

Introduction

It happens that I am sitting down to write this introduction, halfway between my forty-eighth and forty-ninth birthdays, aching in almost every limb from the effects of playing in a club match at the weekend. It was my first game for three weeks and will probably, from necessity not choice, be my last for just as long. But the weeks of another season are speeding by and the time when I shall be obliged to be merely a passive cricketer must be imminent. Hours spent watching have long since exceeded those spent playing. All too soon, I suppose, the reading and dreaming years will be upon me.

It is, after all, given to only a very few to have the will, fitness and means still to be playing, as Cyril Hollinshead did, in 1992, at the age of ninety. Representing the Gloucestershire Gypsies, he bowled six overs for 16 runs against the Gloucester Clergy and I do not suppose the respect he was accorded had much to do with charity. Certainly not if the Clergy team contained cricketers as competitive as the sometime, long-time Oxford blue, the Rev. Andrew Wingfield Digby, who is as fierce an opponent on the cricket field as they come, as well as being a dauntless proponent of the Gospel.

Hollinshead, who played one match for Gloucestershire (no runs, no catches, none for seven, but a first-class cricketer for ever) became sports editor of the evening paper in Cheltenham and obviously managed his time a good deal better than I do. He may also have been luckier than I in another respect: one of only two three-day games I played in, at Cambridge, was ruled not to be first-class at a subsequent meeting of the then arbiters of first-class status in England, the MCC. The wicket I took on a sunny Saturday, and the duck I scored on a foggy Monday before the match was abandoned, therefore remain unrecorded in the vast *Who's Who of First-Class Cricketers*. Duck or not I should like to have been included, if only to impress my sons.

Cricket enthusiasts fall into two main categories: those who would play rather than watch and those who would do the opposite. A fortunate few are actually paid for doing one or the other. The former group, you would guess, prefer to play because they are quite good at the game, but of course it is not always so. Some very bad cricketers persevere week in, week out for years and years, although they may frequently have no more than a walk-in, walk-out part to play. Some are acutely aware of their limitations or, to put it less kindly, their incompetence. They are the ones for whom the game just occasionally comes up with a blissful surprise, in the form perhaps of a winning catch or the inside edge which secures the unexpected victory.

Most cricketers, however, believe that they are better players than others deem them to be, certainly if the latter are opponents rather than team-mates. Most suffer, in varying degrees, from delusions of grandeur, although all skill is relative and it is perhaps the secret of cricketing happiness to find the level of the game wherein you can excel regularly enough to be an important member of the side. People do it, I know, but I cannot imagine being unselfish enough myself to turn out regularly for a side without being reasonably certain of a bat and, in normal circumstances, of a bowl. Those who do are heroes and so in their way are the scorers and umpires, although they all have the satisfaction of knowing that the game could not proceed without them.

To enjoy themselves, cricketers have not only to feel involved and, relatively speaking, important, but also to know that they are spending large portions of their three-score years and ten in a worthwhile cause. Cricket can be, after all, the most time-consuming sport of all. Paradoxically, to be fun, cricket must be serious.

It is one of the common fallacies about village cricket, for example, that it is a carefree way to spend a weekend afternoon. On the contrary, games between villages were every bit as important to the participants in the days before cars and railways as they now are in well-organized leagues, with points at stake and all the attendant potential for competitive play and ill-feeling. I did not witness at first hand the moment when Dennis Lillee and Javed Miandad came close to a stand-up fight in a Test match and the only time I have seen a bat raised in fury by a batsman within inches of a loquacious wicket-keeper's head was in a Saturday afternoon club match. Again, the first instance of an underarm sneak designed specifically to prevent a batsman scoring a six to win off the last ball of a match was not, as is commonly supposed, in a one-day international between Australia and New Zealand but in an evening knock-out match in Surrey.

James Love got it right – feminists will understand that I am not being chauvinistic – when he hailed cricket as a 'glorious, *manly* game.' That is definitely not to suggest that it should become the preserve of bullies and cheats, but it is to say that much of the romantic, almost spiritual, gloss with which the Victorians imbued it was false. Of course it is a game which inspires heroic deeds and chivalrous ones too, but in essence it is a tough duel between a batsman and a bowler, unique because the team battle is for ever dependent on the sum of the individual ones.

Perhaps it is the very hardness of the core which has attracted some writers of sentimental nature. More to the point is the fact that writing about cricket became fashionable in the twilight era of the British Empire, when the game was seen as a metaphor for life. In many ways, of course, it is, but it is as well not to labour the point, and the best cricket writing is at least tinged with realism.

The immense choice available to an anthologist nevertheless covers mainly only a relatively small part of the game's history, the period which followed the first Test match in Australia in 1877. It is quite a thought that the well-documented heyday of the Hambledon club in Hampshire had occurred a century before and that organized cricket had been in existence at least since the first surviving code of laws was published in 1744. The game had been played less formally since medieval times. Suggestions that it began as a recreation for shepherds, with stick, stone and wicket gate, are perhaps no more than informed speculation but double evidence places the game in England from the very start of the fourteenth century. There in the wardrobe accounts of the Royal Household for the twenty-eighth year of Edward I's reign, 1300, are the words unearthed from their library by the Society of Antiquaries:

> Domino Johanni de Leek, capellano Domini Edward fil' Regis, pro den' per ipsum liberat' eidem Domino sup adludendum ad creag', at alios ludos per vices, per manus proprias apud Westm' 10 die Marcii 100s.

As translated by the renowned classicist, cricketer and cricket historian H. S. Altham, they read:

> To Master John de Leek, chaplain of Prince Edward, the King's son, for monies which he has paid out, personally and by the hands

of others, for the said Prince's playing at creag, and other sports, at Westminster, March 10–100s.

Altham believed 'creag' to be a low-Latin version of the native Saxon word cryce, meaning a stick. He noted also the contemporary illumination to a Decretal of Pope Gregory IX, embellished in England, showing a boy with a straight club and a ball and his tutor demonstrating a stroke, left-handed, with something like a modern cricket stump. If the combination of these two shreds is not conclusive, the famous reference by John Derrick in 1598 that he had played 'creckett and other plaies' at the Free School in Guildford in about 1550 is incontrovertible. By the time of Oliver Cromwell's late boyhood in 1617, there is evidence that he played the game in London and it spread to the extent that Cesar de Sassure, in his *Foreign View of England in the Reigns of George I and George II*, could compare cricket to football as a relatively peaceful game. 'Everyone plays it,' he wrote, 'the common people and also men of rank . . . They go into a large open field, and knock a ball about with a piece of wood. I will not attempt to describe the game; but it requires agility and skill.'

Agility, skill and character. 'Courage is the thing,' said J. M. Barrie to his audience at St Andrew's University in 1922, 'all goes if courage goes.' Sooner or later this is true for every game, but a cricketer's character has to be made of more than just physical bravery in the face of a hard ball: it is also mental tenacity, the determination to do well, to get on top but not to get carried away. 'If you can keep your head, while all around you/Are losing theirs and blaming it on you.' Graham Gooch is not a literary man, but he might well have muttered those words during his period as captain of England during the early 1990s. When Michael Atherton was appointed to succeed him, on his first day in office he paraphrased another of Kipling's *bons mots*: 'Cricket can change so quickly; you should never be overwhelmed by failure, never get too carried away by success.'

Sometimes in professional cricket this mental strength is required simply to withstand the insidious taunting of the sledger or the sneering mockery by which a Dennis Lillee or a Merv Hughes tries to undermine the batsman. Sometimes it is needed merely to silence the inner voice of self-doubt which can be every bit as inhibiting. Often it is needed during a run of failures, or when injury threatens a career. A cool head and a brave heart are as much the essentials of a successful cricketer, at any level, as a quick eye and a nimble body.

It is not just a question of courage, this matter of cricketing character. The game reflects everyone's faults and virtues: the rash and the calm; the faithful and the cynical; the humorous and the lugubrious; the honest and the treacherous; the bold and the cautious; the foolish and the wise.

This is why it is so much fun to write about. And, of course, it frequently confounds the most informed pundit and produces the most unlikely heroes. David Steele was considered by all, even the fellow professionals who respected but did not fear him, to be a run-of-the-mill county cricketer; in 1975 he became the most talked-about national sporting hero in England, after walking out to bat in his first Test innings at Lord's, grey-haired and bespectacled, late because he had gone down one flight of stairs too many in the pavilion and found himself in the gentlemen's lavatory instead of the Long Room. At the age of thirty-three, but looking much older, he scored 50 against Lillee and Thomson at their best and England, 49 for 4 soon after his arrival, ended the day with 300-plus.

Steele's Staffordshire grit served England well for another season against the even fiercer West Indian attack; but they did not pick him to tour India so his was a brief glory. Less brief and less remarkable, however, than that of D. W. Carr. At Oxford he achieved little as a fast bowler, but he enjoyed his subsequent club cricket with the Mote at Maidstone and the Band of Brothers. At the age of thirty-two he began to practice the googly. At thirty-seven Kent asked him to play against Oxford and he took seven wickets. Against Australia at the Oval in the final Test he took the new ball, dismissed Gregory, Noble and Armstrong in his first seven overs and in the whole match bowled 69 overs and took seven wickets. Subsequently, at Scarborough, he took another eight against the Australians, but he never played for England again.

So much lies behind 'going in an open field and knocking a ball about with a piece of wood'. Cricket has baffled those not brought up with it and bored some who have. But it has charmed and enthralled millions of others to the extent that what follows is but a microcosm of the game's literature. If you will, read on; dream on; and, if you are agile enough still, play on.

1

The Spirit of Cricket

It is not easy to define without sentiment. Lord Harris came close to it in his famous letter to The Times, *and the ideal he speaks of is still one to be cherished, for all the cynicism of much contemporary cricket.*

I make no apology for preferring the romantic to the hard reality. Both are part of the game: Cardus's 'There can be no Summer in this land without cricket,' and Rattigan's experience of disillusionment when the great batsman he had gone to watch was out to an ungainly stroke as soon as he had arrived.

The spirit of the game is more than willing; it can be noble. But its flesh is often also weak. Never mind: 'A man's reach should exceed his grasp, or what's a heaven for?'

Foster It, My Brothers

Sir, I appreciate, I assure you, the suggestion that I might like to send a message of good will to all my cricketing friends on my eightieth birthday and I gladly, in the words of Rip Van Winkle, greet them and 'their wives and families, and may they live long and prosper'.

Only there is something a bit ominous about the suggestion. Does it convey a hint that it is time I said farewell to cricket? If so, I have no intention of complying with it. Cricket has been too good a friend to me for nearly seventy years for me to part with it one moment before I have to. I cannot remember a time when it did not convey its friendly welcome. In school at Eton the tapping of the bats in Sixpenny assured me of happy hours to come, and reminded me of happy hours in the past. I have been fairly busy for most of my life, but never so busy that the thoughts of cricket and my companions were not an inspiration to get on with the work that I might the sooner enjoy the invigorating capacity.

And my message includes youth, and I advise them to get all the cricket they can. They will never regret it: I might apply to it Mr Jorrocks's commendation of hunting: 'It's the image of war without its guilt, and 25 per cent of its danger.' And in my message to youth I will repeat what I said to the half-holiday cricketer, 'You do well to love it, for it is more free from anything sordid, anything dishonourable, than any game in the world. To play it keenly, honourably, generously, self-sacrificingly is a moral lesson in itself, and the class-room is God's air and sunshine. Foster it, my brothers, so that it may attract all who can find the time to play it; protect it from anything that would sully it, so that it may grow in favour with all men.'

Thus, Mr Editor, thanks to your kindness I have the opportunity of sending my greetings to all my friends round the world, both those I do not know as well as those I do, for we are all comrades in the world of cricket.

Yours faithfully,

HARRIS

Lord Harris to *The Times* (3 February 1931)

A game of the English Summer

Every summer I travel north, south, east and west to watch cricket. I have seen the game played far down in Kent, at Dover, near the cliffs trodden by King Lear. There, one late August afternoon, I said good-bye to a cricket season on a field which lay silent in the evening sunshine; the match, the last of the year, was over and the players gone. I stayed for a while in the falling light and saw birds run over the grass as the mists began to spread. That day we had watched Woolley in all his glory, batting his way through a hundred felicitous runs. While he batted, the crowd sat with white tents and banners all around – a blessed scene, wisps of clouds in the sky, green grass for our feet to tread upon, 'laughter of friends under an English heaven'. It was all over and gone now, as I stood on the little field alone in the glow of the declining day. 'The passing of summer,' I thought. 'There can be no summer in this land without cricket.'

Whenever I am in love with cricket's beauty and sentiment I always think of the game as I saw it go to an end that day in Kent, as though to the strain of summer's cadence. Cricket, as I know and love it, is part of that holiday time which is the Englishman's heritage – a playtime in a homely countryside. It is a game that seems to me to take on the very colours of the passing months. In the spring, cricketers are fresh and eager; ambition within them breaks into bud; new bats and flannels are as chaste as the April winds. The showers of May drive the players from the field, but soon they are back again, and every blade of grass around them is a jewel in the light. I like this intermittent way of cricket's beginning in spring weather. A season does not burst on us, as football does, full grown and arrogant; it comes to us every year with a modesty that matches the slender tracery of leaf and twig, which belongs to the setting of every true cricket field in the season's first days.

When June arrives, cricket grows to splendour like a rich part of the garden of an English summer time. In June the game is at the crown of the year; from Little Puddleton to London the fields of village and town are white with players in hot action. Batsmen move along their processional way to centuries at Lord's, while in a hundred hidden hamlets far and wide some crude but not inglorious Hobbs flings his bat at the ball, and either misses it or feels his body tingle as willow thwacks leather. Bowlers set their teeth and thunder over the earth, seeing nothing in the world but a middle stump. And when a wicket falls, fieldsmen in the deep give themselves to the grassy earth, stretch limbs, and look up into the blue sky. Now is the time of cricketer's plenty – June and July. Let him cherish every moment as it passes; never will he be so young again.

With the advent of August, cricket loses the freshness and radiance of its heyday. Colour and energy begin to leave the game, even as colour and energy begin to leave the summer itself. Cricketers grow weary; ambition wanes as the sun wanes. The season goes to its end with a modest and lovely fall. It does not finish rhetorically, as football does, vaunting a cup-tie final before a million eyes. One after another the

3

cricketers say good-bye in the darkening evenings of late summer; they fold their tents and depart, and nobody sees them. The noisy crowds have left the game for the new darling with the big ball. Down at Eastbourne (it may chance to be) the season comes to an end on a quiet day, on which the crack of the bat sends out a sweet melancholy. As the cricketer leaves the field, not to set foot again on his game's carpet for months and months to come, he has his moments of private sentiment. He glances back to take a last look at the field as the hours decrease and autumn grows in everything. He is glad that cricket belongs to summer, comes in with the spring, and gets ready to go when the trees are brown. Other games can be played in different parts of the world. Cricket is a game which must always be less than its true self if it is taken out of England and out of the weather of our English summer.

So much for the season and the setting, the time and the place. The game itself is a capricious blend of elements, static and dynamic, sensational and somnolent. You can never take your eyes away from a cricket match for fear of missing a crisis. For hours it will proceed to a rhythm as lazy as the rhythm of an airless day. Then we stretch ourselves on deck-chairs and smoke our pipes and talk of a number of things – the old 'uns insisting that in *their* time batsmen used to hit the ball. A sudden bad stroke, a good ball, a marvellous catch, and the crowd is awake; a bolt has been hurled into our midst from a clear sky. When cricket burns a dull slow fire it needs only a single swift wind of circumstance to set everything into a blaze that consumes nerves and senses. In no other game do events of import hang so bodefully on a single act. In no other game does one little mistake lead to mischief so irreparable. You get another chance at football if you foozle a kick; but Hobbs in all his majesty must pass out of the scene for hours if for a second he should fall into the error that hedges all mortal activity. Many a great match has been lost by a missed catch; terrible are the emotions of long-on when the ball is driven high towards him and when he waits for it – alone in the world – and the crowd roars and somebody cries out, ''E'll miss it – 'e'll miss it!' Years ago, in a match for the rubber in Australia, Clem Hill and Victor Trumper were making a mighty stand, turning the wheel of the game against England. Here were two of the greatest batsmen of all time thoroughly set, scourging the English attack with unsparing weapons. Hour after hour they cut and drove right and left. Wilfred Rhodes, who seems always to have been playing cricket, tossed up over after over, angling for the catch in the deep. And at the very moment when the fortunes of the battle were on the turn, moving definitely Australia's way – at this moment of fate, Clem Hill let his bat swing at a ball for all he was worth in valour and strength. Up into the sky the ball went, and it began to drop where A. E. Knight was standing. All eyes rested on Knight; the vast Sydney multitude were dead still as the ball fell like a stone. Knight held his catch, but as he did so, he was seen to go down on one knee, and bow his head. Some of the English players, thinking Knight was ill, moved towards him. But as they approached, Knight raised himself, made an explanatory gesture, swallowed emotion in a gulp, and said to his anxious colleagues, 'It's all right, it's all right; I was only thanking my Maker.' Cricket can mean much to a man: responsibility can weigh down the strongest.

The laws of cricket tell of the English love of compromise between a particular freedom and a general orderliness, or legality. Macdonald's best break-back is rendered null and void if he should let his right foot stray merely an inch over the crease as he wheels his arm. Law and order are represented at cricket by the umpires in their magisterial coats (in England it is to be hoped these coats will never be worn as short as umpires wear them in Australia, much to the loss of that dignity which should always invest dispensers of justice). And in England umpires are seldom mobbed or treated with the contumely which is the lot of the football referee. If everything else in this nation of ours were lost but cricket – her Constitution and the laws of England of Lord Halsbury – it would be possible to reconstruct from the theory and the practice of cricket all the eternal Englishness which has gone to the establishment of that Constitution and the laws aforesaid.

Where the English language is unspoken there can be no real cricket, which is to say that the Americans have never excelled at the game. In every English village a cricket field is as much part of the landscape as the old church. Everybody born in England has some notion of what is a cricket match, even folks who have never had a cricket bat in their hands in their lives (few must be their number, since it is as natural to give a cricket bat as a present to a little boy as it is to give him a bucket and spade when he goes to the seaside). I should challenge the Englishness of any man who could walk down a country lane, come unexpectedly on a cricket match, and not lean over the fence and watch for a while. Has any true Englishman ever resisted the temptation, while travelling on the railway, to look through the carriage window whenever the train has been passing a cricket field? The train rushes round a curve just as the bowler is about to bowl; in a flash we are swept out of sight of the game, and never can we know what happened to that ball! Cricket is not called the 'Sport of Kings'; it is the possession of all of us, high and low, rich and poor. It was born in a small place and it has conquered all the habitations of our race. Wherever cricket is taken, England and the flavours of an English summer go with it. The game's presiding genius is W. G. Grace, dead and therefore immortal. He gave his heart and soul to cricket, stamped the English stamp on it, and caused it to loom with his own genial bulk in the eyes of his countrymen for all time. To-day, when it is regarded right and proper for the nation to pay honour to all heroes of the open air, Grace would have been knighted. But the very idea of 'Sir W. G. Grace' is comical. You see, he was an institution. As well might we think of Sir Albert Memorial, Sir National Debt, Sir Harvest Moon – or Sir Cricket!

Neville Cardus, *Cricket* (1930)

The Village Game

A thunderstorm is stooping over the old cricket ground in my memory. It is not a date that I can identify, and I do not know who the awaited opponents of our team are – an Estate, a Brewery, the Constabulary, some sort of Rovers, more likely just another village side. It is the fore-noon, and that inky cloud is working round the hill, as black almost as the spinney of firs on the boundary, imported trees which I always suspect of being aloof in their hearts from the scene and its animations. I feel oily splashing drops and doubt if we shall have the promised encounter in the afternoon. The summer seems to have fallen into low spirits, and there is nobody about except the rooks and pigeons – we have heard all they have to say – and a crying woodpecker down under the oak at the river. The storm drifts, the cloud-edges are effaced; but the rain patters steadily on the metal roof of the mowing shed, the gutters gurgle, all the trees are grey with the shower. Past the far side of the field a figure with a sack for a hood drives his cycle apace, never turning his eyes this way for a moment; and no one from the vicarage steps out to see if there is any prospect of play.

Yet the hours pass, and after all the rain has wearied, and stopped.

The smoky-looking day may remain thus, neither better nor worse, and the turf is good. A bicycle is being pushed through the meadow gate by a cricketer in flannels under his mackintosh, and one by one they all assemble. An unlocking of padlocks and shifting of benches in the pavilion, a thump of bats and stumps being hauled out of the dark corners. The creases are marked, and the offer of a bowling screen rejected. Our boys put catapults back in their jackets and affect to know personally the visitors now arriving, pointing out one or two with awe – that one who hits sixes, and that one with the spectacles who never scores less than seventy. There are not many cricket caps on show, and some of the players are observed to feel safest with braces and ties on.

Sawdust wanted! The fielding side have spread themselves about the soaked ground, and all is otherwise ready – even the two batsmen have gone out to their creases, casting rather unhappy looks on their companions in the pavilion, who sit down in a row and brood. It is odd, this serious game; perhaps it is the greyness of the day that causes it to take this mood. Sawdust! A bucket is being carried forth by the groundsman, whose squat shoulders and beard look like the picture of Hudibras; he tips out his two little mounds of sawdust, and marches off to his shed, as who should say, 'That is the end of the match for me. That *is* the match.' The one-armed bowler measures his run, dips the ball into the sawdust, and with three or four sharp steps whizzes it at the opposed batsman; it passes with a wet smack into the gloves of the man behind the stumps. All the fieldsmen attend gravely. This bowler has pace. But no smile.

But the ball won't turn and after a time the batsmen lose their reverence and risk sending it over the head of the little man at point; the score is hoisted, and the bowlers are changed. It is mainly that schoolboy who is the cause of this. His score in the book is inspected, it adds up to 18 already. He looks too delicate to perform among these rugged elders, but he is calm enough. At last a large hand and circling arm send him a ball which sails up very much like the one before which he carted over peering faces into the long wet grass; it falls shorter, hits him on the boot. He knows his offence, and the umpire does not let him off; but his innings has gone far enough. There are several batsmen to follow him, and already the total is one which in these games of strong trundlers may serve – 50 up. The boy who has seen to this matter and accepted the punishment for his single error so immediately goes walking away there, with his hands stuck into his green jacket, as if on Robinson Crusoe's island, to the far parts of the field. He seems to have this cricket business in his pocket. When he was questioned just now as he put his pads away 'what the bowling was like,' he answered slowly and peacefully, 'The fellow from the lower end turns them a little from the off.'

The circuit of the field which falls away to the stream is wide enough for him to be still strolling and watching the blue moths among the sorrel when the downfall of the last of his team-mates arrives. It was not so easy out there as he found it. These men with the ball have a terrible natural skill. Perhaps it is not mere talk, that they can drop it on a threepenny bit placed between the wickets. They can probably hit a rat with a turnip in the light of their lantern before he knows that he is in the way.

But here is the second part of the game, and the relaxation of the interval dies into another period of silent close watching. Only about 75 runs are necessary, but those who are to try for them do not look exactly merry at the prospect. The church clock tolls out again, five o'clock; it always comes to the hour slower, speaks it in a lower tone than that brisk silver-voiced one at the grange. In the pavilion a faint notion goes that 'if we can't get the runs we may make a draw of it'; but half-past six under the circumstances is a good way off. Once again in the sulky light against the gloomy trees the bowlers appear the dangerous persons of the drama as they strike their heels in, start their run and slam the ball at their opponents; the stiff farmer and the patient gardener, though their chins express refusal to be less than British, do not quite treat their bats as natural extensions of themselves. As their admirers the boys look at their narrow escapes, there are inevitable gaspings. Meanwhile someone looks away from the torture for a moment and directs attention to two youths in the next field: youths who ought to have been playing here, and who are credited with ability equal to any bowler's attack in the world; and these are on their way unconcernedly to bream swims with rods and baskets and landing nets. A case of defection, too sad to be dwelt upon, but it all goes with this slow grey day.

The home team is in trouble. The curate from whom (on the old principle 'omne ignotum pro magnifico') at least a few wristy educated shots were expected on his first appearance here, has just had his bails flicked off, very hard luck; and the side is half out. The scoreboard is not our study now. Moreover, Mr Warrener won't get his innings; he has received a message from his master, General Goble, who surely could not have sent for him at this (familiar) crisis except on account of some grave emergency. A boy, however, is walking out to the captain of the fielding side, to supplicate for leave to bat instead of the confidential

8

Warrener. The captain grins, pulls the boy's ear and says yes. The boy comes back with an attempt to be neutral about it, 'It's all in the day's work,' but he feels alarmed, and things all round are grey.

Bert Pilgrim, who has a rich curly head of bronze hair, goes and confronts the bowlers. He takes a bat which is so chewed up – the only spare one too – that only he (it suits him) uses it in a match. He does not use it long, but he operates it much as when he tries his strength at the Flower Show with the maul which drives a block up a tall post, to ring a bell and return the penny if bumped hard enough. He gets one boundary off the dodging umpire's backside and a six in the homely equipage of the old woman selling popcorn, liquorice straps and still lemonade. The score is not improved enough in spite of all this, and Bert comes back again rather grumpy because a very old gentleman, as he sees age, has wrought his downfall with the very kind of bowling he prays for to his heathen gods. The ancient, belted in several faded colours round a massive central contour, first took leave to bowl a few gentle ones up and down aside from the wicket, while the batsman affected indifference. Such was the fashion of those unhaggling days, though it was going. Then to the game again. The ball was coming up so mildly, but it evaded Bert's punitive swing, he glared round, the bails fell, he said something. And another one.

The end is in sight; some restless man begins putting away the tackle lying about – and the boy who bats in place of Mr Warrener finds himself going in. 'Just you stay there.' But 'over' was called. In his neat shoes polished like his locks for the match, the boy stands prepared to run any number of runs. 'Poggy' at the far end puts his bat to the ball – the boy is called: 'no, yes, go back, come on' – and with a little pause of compassion and shame the bowler, ball in hand, breaks the wicket at the boy's end. He pats him on the shoulder, which is Fame enough. The match is finished, stumps are pulled up; players withdraw from the place, leaving two sawdust patches and some tracks of trampled mud for the alighting rook to investigate. And at last the western sky glows into a little colour, like the streaks on the honeysuckle by the glistening hedge which the players and their friends pass on their way to strong tea and plum cake in their homes. We shall not be very well pleased to find the match reported in next week's *Messenger*.

Edmund Blunden, *Cricket Country* (1944)

Mr Merryweather Says

One of the joys of an Oval Test is always the presence in force of the very young; but when on the first morning of this match the great Graeme Pollock tried to sweep Titmus over a gasholder and was ignominiously bowled I was sadly reminded that for fathers and uncles it can also be a curse.

From my seat in the Press box, where the only form of childhood on display is unlikely to be primary, I could still, in imagination, hear a hundred shrill voices indignantly cross-examining a hundred embarrassed adult escorts.

'But Daddy, you told me if I ever tried to cow-shot a straight ball you'd put me over your knee and—'

'My dear boy, that wasn't a cow-shot at all.'

'What was it then?'

'It was a lofted sweep with a horizontal bat, and you have to be as great a batsman as Pollock ever to attempt such a stroke.'

Unconvincing, you'll agree, and it would hardly have got Daddy off his spot for much longer than it takes to crunch a chocolate Crunchie.

'But he missed it, Daddy, didn't he?'

'Yes, he did.'

'Then he can't be such a great batsman, after all, can he?'

'Yes, he can. What's more he is. What you must understand, my boy, is that all great batsmen can have an off day.'

'But why does he have to go and have one when I'm watching?'

An unanswerable question, and one fraught with tragedy. Should that child suffer the supreme misfortune of never seeing Graeme Pollock bat again (I assume that he missed that little masterpiece of his second innings, for if he had seen England bat on Friday he would sensibly have spent Saturday either fishing or coshing, according to his temperament) then sonny-boy will go through the rest of his life convinced that Graeme Pollock is the kind of batsman who potters about for an hour or so for a paltry 12 runs, and then misses a potty old cow-shot.

Still, that misfortune is at least unlikely. Both sonny-boy and Graeme Pollock have happily a long time to go, and their paths are fairly certain to meet again. But consider a more conclusive tragedy – one that happened to me and to my small charge at the Oval Test in 1948.

The dismal happenings of the first morning left him comparatively unmoved. He didn't think Lindwall and Miller particularly fast – 'not nearly as fast as Mr Merryweather when he really lets one go in the nets' – and England's first innings total of 52 was, by his standards, an eminently respectable one. Mr Merryweather, one gathered at lunch, would have been reasonably satisfied at the course of the morning's events, although rather angry with Compton's running between the wickets. (Compton didn't, if you recall, have much running to do, but he did still contrive to drop his bat once in his abbreviated knock, while Hassett very chivalrously threw to the wrong end. Mr Merryweather would have disapproved of that too, it seemed. While against his own boys dropping their bats, if opposing boys dropped theirs his orders were that they should be instantly and remorselessly liquidated. I was beginning to dislike Mr Merryweather.)

After lunch I watched with gloom, and my charge with boredom, Australia's massive opening stand. Then came the first wicket and Bradman's entrance, and we both perked up. In fact, if you remember, we both stood up, along with the other thirty thousand.

My charge had been told that he was going to see the greatest batsman on earth, and the sight of the crowd rising and the English team giving him three cheers impressed him greatly. Perhaps, for once, Uncle Terry hadn't been telling him lies, and perhaps at last he was going to see a batsman just slightly better than Mr Merryweather. He sat down expectantly.

When, two balls later, Bradman was on his way back to the pavilion I had no words. If I had had, I couldn't have said them.

My charge looked at me and saw the reason for my silence. He sympathetically allowed a fairly long pause before he decided to comment.

'I don't think he should have played forward to that.'

I agreed, and awaited in resigned misery the inevitable reference to Mr Merryweather's superiority to Bradman at dealing with short-pitched googlies. Happily I never got it.

The tact of a ten-year-old can be surprising.

But the tragic fact remains that to that ten-year-old (now, at twenty-seven, a kind of Mr Merryweather himself) the name Bradman will always bring a clear image of a batsman who played forward when he should have played back, and got bowled for a duck in consequence.

Returning to the Oval, 1965, and the events of the second day, how, I wonder, would Daddy have coped with this kind of catechism:

'But, Daddy, you said we put the South Africans in because we had to win the match?'

'Yes, I did.'

'Then why aren't we making more runs?'

I think Daddy would allow himself a pause in which to light a cautious cigarette, before replying.

'Well, you see, what we're hoping to do is to bat until about lunchtime on Monday and then—'

Another wicket to a forward defensive prod would almost certainly have fallen at this moment and would have invited the inevitable riposte.

'Well, we're not going to, are we?'

'It doesn't quite look like it, I agree.'

'So why can't we make more runs while we *are* in?'

'Eat your nice Crunchie.'

'No, Daddy. I want to know. Why aren't we making more runs, more quickly?'

'Well, it's the wicket, you see. I heard E. W. Swanton on television . . . yes, that's right. The one that reminds you of your headmaster and got the OBE . . . No. Better than the Beatles . . . No. *Better* . . . Well, don't believe it. Anyway, I heard Mr Swanton say that it was the fault of the wicket. He said it was a good wicket, and a true wicket, but that it's not the kind of wicket that allows the ball to come readily on to the bat.'

Only a single crunch of a Crunchie, I should think, before the final knock-out.

'But Daddy, if the ball won't come on to the bat, why can't the bat come on to the ball? I'm sure that's what Mr Merryweather would ask.'

The towel flutters into the ring.

'Would he? Well, Mr Merryweather, God rot him, would be bloody well right. Now do your nice crossword and forget all about the silly cricket. Daddy's going to have a drink.'

Which is exactly, as it happens, what Uncle Terry was already doing.

Terence Rattigan, *The Cricketer* (1965)

Nets

'On Monday last, with rain threatening, and the wind in the East – that Jarndyce v Jarndyce feeling – I, the greater wading bird, led down my young wadelings to their baptism, some flapping their callow wings with eager and lively hope, some quacking faint but disregarded protest. For twenty minutes we swam about, then came the rain once more, and evening, and soon

Universal darkness buried all.

And that, my boy, was our first day's practice at the nets.'

Thus, some weeks ago, with aquatic and ornithological metaphor, hitting his favourite quotations a customary crack *en passant*, wrote my old friend S—, who, after preliminary skirmishes, has year by year sent forth his juvenile troops to do battle on the green fields, in sun, hail, rain, wind; the left legs drilled to cover-point, the insidious binocular stance exorcised with tempered abuse, the right foot, that strays too easily to square-leg, goaded into orthodoxy, every move in the field attempted, practised, repractised, bungled, ameliorated, almost perfected – the swift return with flick of wrist, the high swerving ballooner, the cruel kick of the 'half-half-volley' to ankles, till their

Young skins became as leather, –

And so he writes, in that study well-remembered, surrounded by the flannelled gladiators of his golden age, Sam Woods, Lionel Palairet, the great Doctor towering in bearded majesty – he always favours the heroes of the West – to tell me that he is doing it all over again, cursing the gathering momentum of youthful degeneracy, the soft hands, the dense heads, the all-too-tardy feet, telling me by letter what he once told me so unerringly by verbal precept, anxiously awaiting the first match, yet calm when its inevitable failures come, a noble workman in a noble craft.

In those days the best net to be in was D—'s; for some years there was a hole, by tradition unrepaired, about three yards from the ground, little more than the size of a cricket ball, in the line of extra-cover: to put a drive through it was the Mecca of D—'s pupils: for several reasons; aesthetically it was a greater triumph than finding a dedans guarded by

Peter Latham at tennis, so small and strait was that hole, and therefore called by some, irreverently I fear, the 'path to heaven': then, the ball, once through the celestial aperture, came to rest either among sweet-peas, which suitably enraged the gardener, or amid the raspberries, which rewarded the finder: again, it irritated D—, to whom any stroke that lifted the ball an inch, was according to the height of the parabola, a bad stroke.

Good Spartan D—! Long-suffering mentor! Stern and inflexible purist! None after you has so plumbed the *foundations* of the game, for ever crying out on the misdirected toe, curtly praising some stray freak of brilliance, never bowling till the bat was raised over the leg stump, gazing resignedly through short-sighted glasses at your pupil, who scours the red-lipped fruitage for the erring ball, who feebly feigns victory in the search,

iam iam prensans

yet another raspberry, with the ball long since in his right trouser-pocket!

Behind D—'s net, a long carry for a boy, was a bank topped with pines, and beyond them – oh bliss! – the roof of the school laundry, on to which sometimes, on red-letter mornings, a young Thornton would crash the guileful delivery of D—, and scarcely suppress his shout of triumph as the slates rattled to the earth. One boy there was, ever after to me, though he now renounces such trumpery with elderly disdain, whom I watched hit three consecutive rockets, two from boys, the last from D— in person, on to that roof, high over the trees against the blue, and D—, almost angry, yet inwardly, I fancy, not wholly displeased, said, 'Dash it boy, dash it, fetch those balls, and don't *grin*, confound you!' Yes, he may renounce it, tinsel of infancy, but I can hear the death-rumble of those slates today.

At Greyfriars we were not popularly supposed to be skilful at cricket. That is as may be. But it was not for lack of practice. L—n, noble sward, was netted more accurately than the codfish on the Dogger Bank, and, in the halcyon days, we could burst forth from the sweat of Danish steel-yards and the prison of paradigms to the field where C—, an old professional of immemorial cunning, sparing yet accurate and benevolent in precept, was waiting with an inexhaustible supply of off-breaks pitched to a length: he bowled them without emotion, deviation or strain, a source of joy and wonder to the unspoilt eye of boyhood; and if he were not obtainable, what matter? Perish the cant which denies value to untutored

14

play! Bradman picked up what passed for a bat, and, unseen of the critical and corrective coach, blossomed into the wonder of the modern world. A coach can guide, but never give: the supple wrist, the intuitive eye, the rhythmic abandon of stroke, these are the gifts of nature, not the learning of man: and if those untutored nets at Greyfriars were not always wholly serious, if after half an hour, the time for experiment set in – monstrous swerves, unearthly googlies, late cuts off half-volleys of a Macartneyesque frivolity, what would you of four boys whose combined ages were scarce more than that of Wilfred Rhodes when he helped England to win back the Ashes and her sliding fame at the Oval in 1926?

Then, in two or three swift-gliding years, came the nets on Green: most beautiful of grounds, with the Hindhead hills in the distance, a glory of varying blue, and M—, true Yorkshireman, bowling away the sunny hours, and with him, the silent G—, left-handed machine, who spun them from leg with horny fingers even on that smooth dureness, and loved to pitch them where the guy-ropes cast a shadow, dire whim that recalls the figure of honest Lumpy seeking out a fair downhill trend for his shooters on the slopes of Broadhalfpenny Down.

Lastly, the nets at Oxford, in the Parks: over the High, past the Bodleian, into which there passes a bent old scholar in cap and gown, burdened with books, loving learning more than the sun: a river-party emerges into the light with cushions and laughter and cheering flagons: the smell of the trees in Parks Road, and soon the urchins at cricket under the trees, irrelevant perambulators, and Tom Hayward, reluctantly retrieving *coups-de-vache* from the longer and the wetter grass.

R. C. Robertson-Glasgow, *The Cricketer* (1932)

The Element of Time

The pivotal tension of Larwood, Bedser, Tyson, Lindwall, Trueman: cumulative rhythm exploding in the fire of delivery. The left arm drags down the sky, the right arm reaches back to draw strength from the earth. Leonardo once drew the dynamics of it. The fast bowler's art is among the most beautiful expressions of the human body; energy, stamina, control, combined in vivid fluency of movement. He is a man of sweat and determination and of necessary hatred in action: off the field a lover of beer, of horses, of women, of sleep. He can be broad of hip and shoulder like Tate, Trueman, Bedser; lean as a whippet like Statham; a nonchalant, fallible, God-created virtuoso like Miller; a model of har-boured resources, perfectly synchronized, exquisitely powered, like Lindwall. He creates silence, envy, fear, destruction. The hips swivel, the arm comes over, and at 90 m.p.h. or more the ball, a spurt of shining red, invades the stumps. Vivid green of grass, whiteness of flannel, the pale honey-coloured stumps and bat: sometimes a click, a roar, and a stump cartwheels yards into the arms of the wicket-keeper crouching far back. It is a matter of pauses, of slowly developing momentum, of sudden split-second action that can create havoc or merely a flurry of air. There are other arts: of flight, of spin, of length as naggingly repetitive as the water-torture. But the great fast bowler's is the final apotheosis, the embodiment of a devilish joy that is at once physical and spiritual, retributive and musical. A rite, a ritual of Chinese inscrutability and subtlety, to which no calligrapher has done justice, an art-form, a balletic background to gossip and drinking, a rural antic, a social event, a conflict reflective of national prestige, a résumé of English taste, habits, maso-chisms, a canalization of the erotic impulse, a species of warfare, the instinctual man's introduction to aesthetics, an aspect of history – you can go on phrase-making till the cows come home, and everything will be true.

Once kings played at it, the rich gambled on it, the high-born used it for displays of personal splendour (where once they had private armies), and Rowlandson painted sexy, hair-awry country wenches, breasts bouncing like peaches, flying between the wickets while languid dandies scrutinised them for future pleasure. It is a far cry from all that to a modern Test match at Lord's between England and Australia, where fifty typewriters, squads of broadcasters and television commentators record the bowling of every ball and flash its result to the four corners of the earth. The village game, under the Sussex Downs or in a Hampshire hamlet, with its shooting pitch, adjacent cattle and scything batsmen, has, it's true, changed scarcely at all. And in the back streets of northern cities, where sun gleams fitfully, if ever, the same chalk stumps are marked on suburban walls, the same skills disposed and passions expended.

For cricket is both metropolitan and rural, a matter of moment or triviality, of exquisite skills or farcical inadequacy. The addiction to it, one would think, is an infection of the blood, an inheritance, the result of a long acclimatization and apprenticeship beside which the labour of Zen masters dwindles into insignificance. Yet Americans fly the Atlantic for a Test match, the Irish stop talking and down their tankards (perhaps only to take them up again in more justifying circumstances), Mr Samuel Beckett hastens to Lord's (perhaps *Godot* is really a cricketing parable?), and lovely, dreamy girls who have never worn a batting glove sit entranced and unplaintive for hours, even days on end. Can it be accounted for in terms of aesthetics or sociology, psychology or group therapy? Probably what starts, as with opium eaters, as curiosity may end as compulsive addiction, a habit that cannot be broken. When will something happen (the answer is, when you are not looking), when will it end (the day after you've gone), what is the point of it (and of life, you may well ask)? It exists, it has mystery, it is in turn languid, comic, boring, beautiful, dramatic; it has the endless capacity to surprise. Like women's faces, or the sea, its rhythms change without warning: blankness and calm are replaced by sudden squalls or tempest. Its decline and dissolution are prophesied with annual glee, yet its cyclical vitality reasserts itself, and has done over 250 years, with triumphant unobtrusiveness. It is a sport without public relations, of monstrous discomfort and inadequate catering, of spartan conditions and no showmanship. The inherited dream survives: of military bands and striped marquees, of chilled hock and heartwarming girls, of deck-chairs or the long, sweet grasses, of salmon and strawberries, of elderly dandies and ghostly reminiscences. But a dream it is, of which only the dandies, stiff-backed, and button-holed, preserve, like effigies, their embalmed flavour.

And, of course, the reminiscences; no sport has produced such anecdotes or images, such fond memories whether of personal prowess or the doings of the great. Cricket at Hove, with Tate bowling and the ball darting off the seam as if possessed, the great lordly days of Fry, Ranji, Duleep, shirtsleeves rippling, the bat an extension of bone, all breeding and elegance; the Roses match at Headingley, Rhodes, Hirst, Verity, the Tyldesleys, Paynter, Bowes, the rough, pawky, knowing talk, the ball on a sixpence and not a stroke too many; Compton at Lord's, darkly handsome, and the runs flowing like gold, sweeps and cuts and cover-drives, an endless improvisation; Hutton, pale, classically correct, withdrawn, all that is meant by single-minded and ascetic, yet when unfettered, and the mood on him, the most lavish of batsman; Laker at Old Trafford, spinning out nineteen Australians with a calculation of length and flight, a variety of angle, marvellous to behold. The canny ruthless genius of

Bradman, devoid of flourish, almost of human fallibility; the lightfooted, caressive brilliance of Harvey, the sleight-of-hand catching of Lock. Newlands at Capetown, with Wardle like a conjuror exploding his googly in the faces of South Africa's batsmen and the clouds trailing like surplices from Table Mountain. Sobers at Bridgetown, Barbados, thrashing the ball through the covers into the flying-fish stalls, Worrell, lazily off-driving, Walcott, Othello-like smiling giant, ferocious in the square cut, and the inscrutable Ramadhin, sleeves buttoned at the wrist, viperishly flicking out his fingers for the leg-break.

An atmosphere, a style; they are never the same, in two grounds or two players. It is from the fusion of the two that the poetry of cricket springs, the cricketer seen stereoscopically in context; the Australian in the steamy heat of Brisbane, or at Adelaide, against the Mount Lofty Hills, the Lancastrian at Old Trafford, Farmer White at Taunton, Bedser at the Oval, Woolley at Canterbury, Tich Freeman at Maidstone, Edrich at Lord's, Hammond and Graveney at Bristol, Walters at Worcester, the place in each case reinforcing the image of the player. Environment, character, style; yet what, over and above what we know it instinctively to be, is style? The moment when aesthetics and power coincide? Poets have tried to define it: Lawrence Durrell, for example. 'The dry bony blade of the sword-grass might suit me better: an assassin of polish. Such a bite of perfect temper as unwary fingers provoke, not to be felt till later, turning away, to notice the thread of blood from its unfelt stroke.' Or Marianne Moore, describing Escudero and Etchebaster, 'There is no suitable simile. It is as though the equidistant three tiny arcs of seeds in a banana had been conjoined by Palestrina; it is like the eyes, or say the face, of Palestrina by El Greco, O Escudero, Soledad, Rosario Escudero, Etchebaster!' Yet one has only to see Hutton or May or Cox stand at the crease, watch Lindwall measure out his run, Evans take Bedser on the leg-side, or Dexter hit off the back foot once, to know the authority of the player, to be aware, as of pure form in sculpture, of an essential rightness, a perfection of technique.

That one can think and write in such terms, without incongruity, is of course one of the fascinations of cricket. It demands a fullness of response, a training in strategic subtleties, as do few other games. You can isolate any section of a drawn, apparently fruitless, match, and to the connoisseur it will be of complex interest.

It is, finally, the element of time that distinguishes cricket, for, as with the stream-of-consciousness novel (James Joyce, infecting perhaps his erstwhile secretary, Samuel Beckett, was a student of it), life is lived on more than one level. There is the game, yes, one might say the actual observing of the ball bowled, the stroke made, the adjustments of field, the change in score, but there is also the sense of place, the pleasure of being out of doors, absolved from responsibility, the eye continually beguiled. There is time to talk without obligation to do so, to listen to the chatter of unknown neighbours (at Lord's, in the pavilion, you can pick up unobtrusively all you could ever want to know about wildfowling, duck-shooting, rose-growing, trout-fishing, troop movements, club finances, wines, tailors, etc.), above all, to think. In other sports, people have no time to think; a cricket match is a storehouse of thought, of thought occasioned by the game itself, by the beauty, wit, or intelligence of one's companion, or simply a private unravelling of problems, personal, political, moral. Fortunately, cricket is slow of exposition, and one never has enough time to think idly or to purpose, anyway. No wonder actors, doctors, barristers, parsons, writers, harassed husbands, recuperating drunks, lonely eccentrics and frustrated cavalrymen make for Lord's with the instinct of homing pigeons. The bars are open all day, you can sit alone or not, as you wish, speak or be silent, doze or roam about. Where else, while watching something else, can you learn so much? Dream such dreams? Evade such entanglements? Pass so many hours doing so little harm to others? So that, batteries recharged, senses stimulated, we can return, as conquerors or victims, to the noisy world in which we are condemned to live.

Alan Ross, *The Boundary Book* (1962)

Village Cricket

... Broiling afternoon ... deck-chairs under the spreading ... the muted coo of pigeons in the immemorial ... delicate tracery etched against blue ... gently undulating emerald velvet sward ... cucumber sandwiches ... distant tinkle of ice in lemonade jug ... satisfying clunk of pad against willow ... distant insistent click of curate's false ... 'Oh, well played, Ronald! ... Run, Doctor, run!' ... Doctor's reflexes not what they were ... short single ... hair's breadth ... flutter of applause ... soporific hum of bees in ... white figures moving in ancient ritual against time-honoured backcloth . . . part and parcel of cherished national heritage . . . warp and woof of very fabric . . . Ronald caught in gully by bounder who looks as though he ought to be wearing braces, black trousers and snake-fastener belt . . . 'Nice little knock, Ronald!' . . . helped put us into double figures, anyway . . . 22 for 3 . . . not bad . . . not bad at all . . . clatter of crockery . . . drowsy murmur . . . shadow's imperceptibly . . . smell of freshly cropped . . . democracy in action . . . squire and labourer toiling side by side for the common . . . glorious uncertainty . . . all sorts and conditions of men . . . regardless of race, colour or . . . young thingummybob in next . . . all pimples and Brylcreem . . . hopeless . . . notice out of corner of eye Mrs Bisset struggling with tea-urn . . . ought to help her . . . magnificent figure of a woman . . . summer dress certainly shows off her . . . wonder what she ever saw in old . . . hypnotic drone . . . stray dog . . . harsh cawing of rooks high in . . . six by young whatsisname . . . sheer fluke . . . plumb through old Granny Murchison's lavatory window again . . . enthusiastic ripple and sporadic . . . distant tinkle of broken glass . . . hypnotic click of knitting . . . satisfying clunk of bat meeting . . . crimson orb setting in . . . wonderful cloud effects . . . just like galleons . . . shadow of church spire imperceptibly . . . white figures moving like ghosts in ancient . . . where else but in England would you . . .

Peter Sellers and Peter Munro Smith, The Boundary Book (1962)

Stolen Hours

It has been my experience, deplorably but I suspect not uniquely, that cricket tastes sweetest during stolen hours. I am not thinking about a day off from the office for 'grandmother's funeral' in order to go to Lord's. It is more subtle than that. Much of the cricket I have watched and still remember from years long past came at times when, glancing at my watch or prodded by a companion, I got a message from my conscience that I ought to be elsewhere. That is the moment when, perversely, the match comes alive, wickets fall or fieldsmen race.

The thought first came to me in the 1950s when I had an informal arrangement with a companion in the House of Commons. When during June or July the House had an all-night sitting (as it did quite often in those years), we would consult in the early morning at Westminster about what was on at Lord's.

We would get out of the Commons around 10 a.m. warned by the whips to be back punctually at 3.45 p.m. – since the Government's tiresome business had not been disposed of – and head for St John's Wood. My companion was Christopher Hollis, then Member for Devizes and a passionate supporter of Somerset. I supported Kent. We tried to avoid matches which involved either county and so might strike a jarring note.

Usually we retired first to our respective homes for a bath and shave; but occasionally we had to give that a miss. They were not fussy about such things at the Lord's turnstiles. Then we would settle down in a stand and let the sunshine take hold of us – it seemed always a sunny day. Around noon we would consult. Would a glass of beer make us any snoozier than we already felt. We always agreed that it could not.

But the magic started to work in mid-afternoon when we looked at our watches. 'Whips want us back!' Whatever the state of the game, the cricket then became compulsive watching. That was the pleasurable hour.

I think I was first corrupted by the stolen hours doctrine while I was still at my preparatory school. My father, not a keen watcher but a dutiful parent, took us to the Oval to watch Surrey in some international match. I was thrilled and before going to bed wrote my reflections on the day, which I showed to my father. By a coincidence, he had invited one of the younger masters at my school to lunch a day earlier at the Hans Crescent Hotel, where we were staying.

Asked what he would like to drink, this innocent fellow chose a whisky and soda. 'And all of two fingers,' (a recognized measure in those days) my father afterwards exclaimed indignantly to my mother. 'I don't think much of a place where masters drink like that'.

So when, tentatively, I proposed a second day at the Oval, though it meant a late return to school, my father replied injudiciously: 'No hurry to go back to that sort of place.' There was a row when I did get back, but that second day at the Oval produced wonderful cricket.

During much of my childhood A. P. F. Chapman, Cambridge, Kent and England, whose sad story was recently chronicled by a biographer, played for my home town of Hythe. Indeed his agreement to turn out for the side, particularly in Hythe Cricket Week, was part of the not very happy compact he made with Mr G. L. Mackeson, who owned the local brewery, was dotty on cricket, and gave him a job.

Percy Chapman, particularly when he was striking against modest club bowlers, was not a man you could leave unwatched. It was simply not possible while he was on the field to fulfil undertakings to be back home at appointed hours. In those days parents had absurdly old-fashioned ideas about punctuality at meals. It was never easy to describe, when you got back in time for the coffee, how many balls Chapman had hit out of the ground.

Stolen hours mix with cricket in many guises. To me the funniest passages in A. G. Macdonell's classic story about the village cricket match in *England, Their England* is not the blacksmith's bowling but the hours frittered away in pubs before the match begins.

I can testify from experience. When some of us joined the editorial staff of the *Morning Post* in the early 1930s, a condition of employment was willingness and ability to play in the newspaper's annual match against the editor's village of Dunmow in Essex. H. A. Gwynne, CH (no less) was strict about this. So strict that before the match some of us would go to the nets then run by an Australian, Alan Fairfax, in the basement of Thames House.

We then undermined this valuable practice on the journey to Dunmow. For in those days the road to Dunmow from London went through Benskins country, and they brewed incomparable beer. 'You fellows must be thirsty after your long drive', Gwynne would say when we arrived suspiciously late for lunch and careful not to try to enunciate a word like 'suspicious'. 'Have a glass of sherry!' That and a glass of port after the lunch wiped out most of the benefits of Fairfax. Mercifully, our side included R. C. ('Crusoe') Robertson-Glasgow, the Somerset bowler, then the newspaper's cricket correspondent. For health reasons, he was supposed not to drink, and he bowled well enough to keep the rest of us our places on the staff.

Then there was a Monday in 1938, when I was persuaded not much against my will to go to Canterbury to watch Kent play against the Australians. This was Frank Woolley's last summer and his final appearance against Australia.

The Australians had spent Saturday scoring their runs. On Monday Kent batted and before we had time to buy a scorecard and settle down, Woolley was out – for virtually nothing. I was due back in London after lunch, but as the Kent wickets fell it occurred to me that a follow-on was possible. I hung on guiltily in that expectation, which was fulfilled.

In the late afternoon light Kent batted again. I forget exactly how many Woolley scored: something like 70 out of 75. Much of the old grace and magic was restored to him for that short hour. When he was out, I see very clearly still the salute the Australians gave him as he left their playing fields for ever.

A year later, 1939, we had the West Indians with us. When they got to the Oval (19, 21 and 22 August) time was running short of all of us. I felt drawn to this match. The difficulty was that on the day I chose to go galley proofs were awaiting my urgent attention in my newspaper office. Why urgent? Because the booklet I had written for them was about air-raid precautions.

From rather a good seat at the Oval I consulted my companion, Miss Rose Talbot, later of Malahide Castle and now resident in Tasmania. She was a matchless cricket-watching companion because she would speak only between overs, and then sparingly. She advised that the proofs ought to wait until stumps were drawn. So I stayed on to see amazing displays by Stollmeyer, Weekes and Constantine. That stolen hour had to last some of us for five years. In bad moments of the war I drew heavily on my memory of it.

Bill Deedes, *Quick Singles* (1988)

Tibby Cotter's Last Bowl

(From the NSW Cricket Association Archives)

I was 'Tibby' Cotter's[1] cobber in the 12th Light Horse and on the night of 30 October 1917 we were at Khallassa, in Southern Palestine, the most remote portion of the southern position. We watered our horses there, and prepared to move off in the attack on Beersheba.

'Tibby' was one of the best foragers in the AIF. He would come to light with a bottle of champagne in the middle of the desert, and the lads in the section all looked at him to turn up with something unusual.

---

[1] 'Tibby' Cotter bowled fast for Australia from 1904 to 1912.

About 1.30 on the morning of the attack, 'Tibby', who had received instructions to report to Echelon on a guard, turned up at the unit. He said to me: 'Bluey, I've skittled a Turk in one hit; and what do you think he had on him? Here it is – a yard of ling.'

He wasn't going to Echelon, he insisted, but said he would treat the boys to a Stammell fish supper in Beersheba, and be damned to the consequences.

We moved off at 4.20 a.m. from Khallassa, and attacked Beersheba that afternoon. 'Tibby' was next to me on one side in the charge, and Trooper Jack Beasley on the other. Rex Cowley was there also. The other three were skittled by a machine-gun, and after we had cleared the Turks out, the troops went back half-an-hour later to bury the dead.

'Tibby' was still alive when I got to him, and he recognized me. 'Blue,' he said, 'you can have the fish supper on your own.' He died shortly afterwards.

He should never have been in the charge. Had he obeyed orders, he would probably have been alive today.

Just before we left Khallassa, 'Tibby' – who, in a bowling competition at Tel-el-Fara, bowled over 18 single stumps at full pace out of 24 – took up a ball of mud, and throwing it into the air, said: 'That's my last bowl, Blue; something is going to happen.'

'Blue,' *New South Wales Cricket Archives* (1917)

2

Sad and Sublime
The Poet's Game

Robert Graves observed that to be a poet was a condition not a profession. There is a remarkable amount of poetry, or verse, or worse, about cricket and I have tried to beware the cloyingly sentimental or verses produced out of duty rather than from the heart.

Here are some famous poems and some seen only once. None moves me more than John Arlott's 'The Old Cricketer'. None more simply emphasizes the difference between success and failure than Siegfried Sassoon's 'The Extra Inch'. None better reminds us that the game is for us all than Jeff Cloves's 'Park Players'.

Dreamers

Soldiers are citizens of death's grey land,
Drawing no dividend from time's tomorrows.
In the great hour of destiny they stand,
Each with his feuds, and jealousies, and sorrows.
Soldiers are sworn to action; they must win
Some flaming, fatal climax with their lives.
Soldiers are dreamers; when the guns begin
They think of firelit homes, clean beds and wives.

I see them in foul dug-outs gnawed by rats,
And in the ruined trenches lashed by rain,
Dreaming of things they did with balls and bats,
And mocked by hopeless longing to regain
Bank holidays, and pictures shows and spats,
And going to the office in the train.

Siegfried Sassoon, *Counter-Attack and Other Poems* (1918)

There Is a Season

Terms and years moved round
Like stars above the western ridge that rise
Ever the same in different fields of light.
In summer still, out on the dazzled square,
All the white custom of the game goes on;
Time hurries or makes sure, the yellow shades
Bring on the evening, till the players seem
A motion in quiet and their play remote
Even from themselves: and still in March the track
Is set, the runners kneel and start, the rain
Leans with them at the bend, and the blown sun
Signals them home.

Robert Gitting, 'Lines written for the Jubilee of St. Edward's, Oxford'

Grace Before Dinner

The Australians came down like a wolf on the fold,
The Marylebone cracks for a trifle were bowled,
Our Grace before dinner was very soon done,
And Grace after dinner did not get a run.

Anon., *Punch* (1878)

Lillee

O Lillee of the valley of the shadow
O shade of the vale of tears and fears
Wizard of Oz – O raging prima donna
accept this bunch of humble belladonna
from the ranks of stricken batsmen – and
with this testimonial and valediction
mark the venomed blackness of the berry
scent the sullen purple flower
clasp them to your lilied bosom – my
how they complement your glower.

Jeff Cloves, The Cricketer (1983)

The Batsman's Betrothed

She walks around the boundaries late
beneath the plane trees by the gate
next the sight screen betimes she waits
from habit or from sorrow.

One summer in the grass she lay
while bowlers toiled and he made hay;
what if my man be called away?
she thought and feared tomorrow.

He was, she paled, the season died,
a letter came, she cried, she cried,
widow am I before a bride
I've lost my dashing fellow.

She walks around the boundaries late
beneath the plane trees by the gate
where the hedge row begins to plait
the briar with the willow.

Jeff Cloves, The Cricketer (1986)

Park Players

We are cricketers here – look
at our creamy flannels our dazzling shirts
the low-ankle boot the cable-knit sweater –
long white hose and those floppy sun hats such
as Empire builders wore
we wear

We are cricketers here – smell
the leather the wood the linseed sweat
and liniment the occasional bitter tear –
oh yes it's not unknown park players we are
but we care
we care

We are cricketers here – observe
the way we strap our pads protect our parts
and glove our vulnerable hands –
you won't see it better done at Lord's
but we play without fear
without fear

We are cricketers here – taste
our teas all freshly made with fondest care
by fiancées families and friends –
visit any county ground you'll never find
teas better anywhere
better anywhere

We are cricketers here – listen
to our changing room chat of batting form
the pitch the turn the bounce the light –
you'll never hear it better told
by commentators on the air
on the air

We are cricketers here – touch
us and you are touched in turn by all
black brown and pink who play in white –

28

unknown park players we are
in parks evermore
everywhere

Jeff Cloves, *The Cricketer* (1987)

Forefathers

On the green they watched their sons
    Playing till too dark to see,
As their fathers watched them once,
    As my father once watched me;
While the bat and beetle flew
On the warm air webbed with dew.

Edmund Blunden, *The Shepherd and Other Poems*
of Peace and War (1922)

Cricket

Where else, you ask, can England's game be seen
Rooted so deep as on the village green?
Here, in the slum, where doubtful sunlight falls,
To gild three stumps chalked on decaying walls.

G. Rostrevor Hamilton

How 'Horatius' Horace Carried His Bat

To every man of cricket
    Time cometh soon or late
When he must face fast bowling
    And square up to his fate.

And this was true of Horace
   That day when he went in
To stand there at the wicket –
   His side's last chance to win.

Nine wickets down! and only
   Nine runs to win, but that
Was far too much for Horace
   Who scarce could hold a bat.

But Horace asked for 'centre'
   With courage bravely feigned
And turned his face to counter
   The five balls that remained.

The first of these came swiftly
   And, taken by surprise,
Instinctively he faltered
   Stepped back, and shut his eyes.

The second ball, a bouncer
   Might well have hit his head,
But Horace, seeking safety,
   To square leg umpire fled.

Next ball he nicked in passing
   With horizontal bat;
It missed the slip as someone,
   Too hopefully, cried 'How's that!'

Both batsman ran – returning
   To where they'd been before,
For Horace – oh! the wonder! –
   Had hit a bound'ry four!

Two balls to go! The bowler
   With bounding run and swerve
Sent forth the hard red missile
   Intending to unnerve.

That ball his pad encountered,
   Appeals burst forth, but failed

And Horace faced, unbeaten,
  The final ball – and quailed!

Last ball! still five runs wanted –
  For Horace much to ask:
A bound'ry six would do it:
  A far-beyond-him task.

With length and speed, aggressive,
  Then came that final ball,
And everyone expected
  To see the wicket fall.

It *missed!* – missed bat and batsman,
  Missed stumps and 'keeper. 'Run!
Come on!' cried Horace, 'quickly!
  We can at least get one!'

Both batsmen, running wildly,
  Between the wickets flew:
The ball was stopped by longstop
  Who, just as wildly, threw.

He threw, too late for stopping
  One bye more on the score,
Too hard – it crossed the bound'ry –
  An overthrow of four!

Five byes! (poor wretched longstop!)
  And so the game was won:
Erratic overthrowing
  The batsmen's task had done.

So Horace was a hero
  And proud not only that
He'd scored four runs (by mishit),
  But carried, too, his bat!

And if you want a moral
  There's this that I must say:
Runs scored by better batsmen
  Bad fielders throw away.

Donald D. Christie, *The Cricketer* (1986)

31

The Season Opens

'A Tower we must have, and a clock in the tower,
Looking over the tombs, the tithebarn, the bower;
The inn and the mill, the forge and the hall,
And the Loamy sweet level that loves bat and ball.'

So a grey tower we have, and the centuried trees
Have arisen to share what its belfry-light sees,
The apple-plats richest in spring-song of all,
Kitchen-gardens and the field where they take bat and ball.

The stream with its moments of dance in the sun
Where the willows allow, runs and ever will run
At the cleft of the orchard, along the soft fall
Of the pasture where tourneys become bat and ball.

And now where the confident cuckoo takes flight
Over buttercups kindled in millions last night,
A labourer leans on the stackyard's low wall
With the hens bothering round him, and dreams bat and ball;

Till the meadow is quick with the masters who were,
And he hears his own shouts when he first trotted there;
Long ago; all gone home now; but here they come all!
Surely these are the same, who now bring bat and ball?

                                            Edmund Blunden

At Lord's

It is little I repair to the matches of the Southron folk,
    Though my own red roses there may blow;
It is little I repair to the matches of the Southron folk,
    Though the red roses crest the caps, I know.
For the field is full of shades as I near the shadowy coast,
And a ghostly batsman plays to the bowling of a ghost,

And I look through my tears on a soundless-clapping host
   As the run-stealers flicker to and fro,
      To and fro:
   O my Hornby and my Barlow long ago!

It is Glo'ster coming North, the irresistible,
   The Shire of the Graces, long ago!
It is Gloucestershire up North, the irresistible,
   And new-risen Lancashire the foe!
A Shire so young that has scarce impressed its traces,
Ah, how shall it stand before all-resistless Graces?
O, little red rose, their bats are as maces
   To beat thee down, this summer long ago!

This day of seventy-eight they are come up North against thee
   This day of seventy-eight, long ago!
The champion of the centuries, he cometh up against thee,
   With his brethren, every one a famous foe!
The long-whiskered Doctor, that laugheth rules to scorn,
While the bowler, pitched against him, bans the day that he was born;
And G. F. with his science makes the fairest length forlorn;
   They are come from the West to work thee woe!

It is little I repair to the matches of the Southron folk,
   Though my own red roses there may blow;
It is little I repair to the matches of the Southron folk,
   Though the red roses crest the caps, I know.
For the field is full of shades as I near the shadowy coast,
And a ghostly batsman plays to the bowling of a ghost,
And I look through my tears on a soundless-clapping host,
   As the run-stealers flicker to and fro,
      To and fro:
   O my Hornby and my Barlow long ago!

Francis Thompson, The Collected Poetry (1913)

The Old Cricketer

He sits alone to watch the men
At cricket on the village green,
And savours calmly, once again,
The life-remembered, quiet scene
That to his ageing sight grows dim,
And then he sees, with clearer eye,
That these men's fathers play with him,
Their fathers' fathers standing by.
He leaps once more, with eager spring,
To catch the brief-glimpsed, flying ball
And quickens to its sudden sting:
The brightness dies: the old eyes fall,
They see, but do not understand,
A pursed, rheumatic, useless hand.

John Arlott, *Of Period and Place* (1944)

To John Berry Hobbs on his Seventieth Birthday

16 December 1952
There falls across this one December day
The light remembered from those suns of June
That you reflected in the summer play
Of perfect strokes across the afternoon.

No yeoman ever walked his household land
More sure of step or more secure of lease
Than you, accustomed and unhurried, trod
Your great, yet little, manor of the crease.

The game the Wealdon rustics handed down
Through growing skill became, in you, a part
Of sense, and ripened to a style that showed
Their country sport matured to balanced art.

34

There was a wisdom so informed your bat
To understanding of the bowler's trade
That each resource of strength or skill he used
Seemed but the context of the stroke you played.

The Master: records prove the title good:
Yet figures fail you, for they cannot say
How many men whose names you never knew
Are proud to tell their sons they saw you play.

They share the sunlight of your summer day
Of thirty years; and they, with you, recall
How, through those well-wrought centuries, your hand
Reshaped the history of bat and ball.

John Arlott, *Of Period and Place* (1944)

Cricket at Worcester, 1938

Dozing in deck-chair's gentle curve,
Through half-closed eyes I watched the cricket,
Knowing the sporting press would say
'Perks bowled well on a perfect wicket.'

Fierce mid-day sun upon the ground;
Through heat-haze came the hollow sound
Of wary bat on ball, to pound
The devil from it, quell its bound.

Sunburned fieldsmen, flannelled cream,
Looked, though urgent, scarce alive,
Swooped, like swallows of a dream,
On skimming fly, the hard-hit drive.

Beyond the score-box, through the trees
Gleamed Severn, blue and wide,
Where oarsmen 'feathered' with polished ease
And passed in gentle glide.

The back-cloth, setting off the setting,
Peter's cathedral soared,
Rich of shade and fine of fretting
Like cut and painted board.

To the cathedral, close for shelter,
Huddled houses, bent and slim,
Some tall, some short, all helter-skelter,
Like a sky-line drawn for Grimm.

This the fanciful engraver might
In his creative dream have seen,
Here, framed by summer's glaring light,
Grey stone, majestic over green.

Closer, the bowler's arms swept down,
The ball swung, pitched and darted,
Stump and bail flashed and flew;
The batsman pensively departed.

Like rattle of dry seeds in pods
The warm crowd faintly clapped;
The boys who came to watch their gods,
The tired old men who napped.

The members sat in their strong deck-chairs,
And sometimes glanced at the play,
They smoked and talked of stocks and shares,
And the bar stayed open all day.

John Arlott, *Of Period and Place* (1944)

Cricket at Brighton

At night the Front like coloured barley-sugar; but now
Soft blue, all soda, the air goes flat over glower-beds,
Blue railings and beaches; below, half-painted boats, bow
Up, settle in sand, names like Moss-Rose and Dolphin
Drying in a breeze that flicks at the ribs of the ride.

The chalk coastline folds up its wings of Beachy Head
And Worthing, fluttering white over water like brides.
Regency Squares, the Pavilion, oysters and mussels and gin.

Piers like wading confectionery, esplanades of striped tulip.
Cricket began here yesterday, the air heavy, suitable
For medium-paced bowlers; but deck-chairs mostly were vacant,
Faces white over starling green. Later, trains will decant
People with baskets, litter and opinions, the seaside's staple
Ingredients. Today Langridge pushes the ball for unfussed
Singles; ladies clap from check rugs, talk to retired colonels;
On tomato-red verandas the scoring rate is discussed.

Sussex v. Lancashire, the air birded and fresh after rain,
Dew on syringa and cherry. Seaward the water
Is satin, pale emerald, fretted with lace at the edges,
The whole sky rinsed easy like nerves after pain.
May here is childhood, lost somewhere between and never
Recovered, but again moved nearer like a lever
Turned on the pier flickers the Past into pictures.
A time of immediacy, optimism, without stricture.

Post-cards and bathing machines and old prints.
Something comes back, the inkling and momentary hint
Of what we had wanted to be, though differently now
For the conditions are different, and what we had wanted
We wanted as we were then, without conscience, unhaunted,
And given the chance must refuse to want it again.
Only, occasionally, we escape, we return where we were;
Watching cricket at Brighton, Cornford bowling through
　　sea-scented air.

Alan Ross, *Poems 1942–67* (1967)

Driving to the Match

The linnets flit from hedge to hedge
The lark exults on high,

37

The cattle, crowded at the brook,
Lift up their dripping heads to look
    As we go driving by.

The hoofs are on the road, boys,
    They sing a merry catch:
O the sun's at noon, and the year's at June,
    And we're driving to the match!

The brown-armed peasants in the hay
    Stand still with shaded eye,
The village children shout with glee,
And mothers leave their work to see,
    As we go driving by.

The milkmaid flings a saucy smile,
    The farmer heaves a sigh,
Our horses' music floods the air.
And all the world is O so fair
    As we go driving by!

The hoofs are on the road, boys,
    Hark to their jocund catch;
O the sun's at noon and the year's at June,
    And we're driving to the match!

E. V. Lucas

Ballade of Dead Cricketers

Ah, where be Beldham now, and Brett,
    Barker, and Hogsflesh, where be they?
Brett, of all bowlers fleetest yet
    That drove the bails in disarray?
And Small that would, like Orpheus, play
    Till wild bulls followed his minstrelsy?
Booker, and Quiddington, and May?
    Beneath the daisies, there they lie!

And where is Lambert, that would get
  The stumps with balls that broke astray?
And Mann, whose balls would ricochet
  In almost an unholy way
(So do baseballers 'pitch' today);
  George Leer, that seldom let a bye,
And Richard Nyren, grave and gray?
  Beneath the daisies, there they lie!

Tom Sueter, too, the ladies' pet,
  Brown that would bravest hearts affray;
Walker, invincible when set,
  (Tom, of the spider limbs and splay);
Think ye that we could match them, pray,
  These heroes of Broad-halfpenny,
With Buck to hit, and Small to Stay?
  Beneath the daisies, there they lie!

Envoy

Prince, canst thou moralize the lay?
  How all things change below the sky?
Of Fry and Hirst shall mortals say,
  'Beneath the daisies, there they lie!'

Andrew Lang, Rhymes à la Mode (1884)

The Catch

Stupendous scores he never made,
But perished ever with dispatch:
No bowling genius he displayed,
But once, in a forgotten match,
  He made a catch.

No doubt a timely stroke of luck
Assisted him to do the trick;
He was at cover, and it stuck:

39

It travelled fairly low and quick –
    The kind that stick.

His friends the proud achievement classed
As fortune's most eccentric whim,
And ere a week or two had passed
The memory of the catch grew dim
    To all but him.

To all but him, for he relates,
With varying ornament and phrase,
The story to the man who waits
Unwilling in Pavilion ways,
    On rainy days.

The catch has grown in splendour now –
He had a dozen yards to run;
It won the match, as all allow,
And in his eyes there blazed the sun,
    And how it spun.

Life of old memories is compact,
And happy he for whom with speed
Blossoms a gorgeous tree, where fact
Has planted, in his hour of need,
    A mustard seed.

Alfred Cochrane, *Collected Verses* (1903)

The Score Board at Lord's

In chequered black and white above the green
This giant register surveys the scene,
And, moving in its own mysterious way,
Above the plot and passion of the play,
Presents the futile or triumphant deed
With cold celerity for all who read.

No quiver of excitement you may trace
In the blank outlook of that sombre face;
No preference in the crisis of the fight
Of Blue and Blue for either Dark or Light;
No shouts, no thrills, no fevers disarrange
That stately process of that silent change.

What though you be the buttress of the side,
The prop on whom the other ten relied,
And, through some antic of malicious luck
Your looked-for century comes out a duck,
No whit does that austere Colossus care,
Your number's vanished and the next one's there.

Nor will it serve that you denounce as bad
The verdict passed on your obstructing pad,
No sympathy it sends, no soothing balm,
But marks the issue with Olympian calm.
A moment since and you were Number Two,
You're the Last Player now – so much for you.

Well may you ask, my disappointed friend,
Is life like this, relentless to the end,
Taking no thought of anything but fact,
Of how men act, not how they meant to act,
Or will it lend an ear to failure's claim,
When accident defeats a worthy aim?

Alfred Cochrane, Collected Verses (1903)

The Extra Inch

O Batsman, rise and go and stop the rot,
And go and stop the rot.
(It was indeed a rot,
Six down for twenty-three).
The batsman thought how wretched was his lot,
And all alone went he.

The bowler bared his mighty, cunning arm,
His vengeance-wreaking arm,
His large yet wily arm,
With fearful powers endowed.
The batsman took his guard. (A deadly calm
Had fallen on the crowd.)

O is it a half-volley or long-hop,
A seventh-bounce long-hop,
A fast and fierce long-hop,
That the bowler letteth fly?
The ball was straight and bowled him neck and crop
He knew not how nor why.

Full sad and slow pavilionwards he walked.
The careless critics talked;
Some said that he was yorked;
A half-volley at a pinch.
The batsman murmured as he inward stalked,
'It was the extra inch.'

Siegfried Sassoon, *Collected Poems, 1908–56* (1961)

The Year Before the War

He carried the score in his head
from radio to radio, like milestones
through the three days. It was
August in the long school break
and the sun shone from Heber Road
to Dulwich Park as it had always done
on running games and trees that
were stepped enough to climb.

And just up the road, a little
further than his boundaries, but
known from the top of a swaying

42

Victorian tram, small white figures
ran on the grass and made history.

The fretwork fronts of the radios
were galleons, or the sun going down
on the Empire: Marconi and Ecko,
Bush and HMV, all tuned to the same
few voices; listening posts on the air
that was making England between eleven
and lunchtime, lunchtime and tea.

Later, the war blotted it out,
as though a cleaver had cut clean
across all that came after boyhood.
But then, when barrage balloons were
not even dreaming, Hobbs and Hammond,
Bradman and Larwood were the names
they claimed to make their games of
chalk wickets and old grey tennis balls.
Hutton had not entered that mythology:
he was the bit of history they bumped into.

*　*　*

Through quiet chinks in a long cacophony
the commentators brought them out. It was
a year of stiff-armed salutes and shrieking voices;
of a father beginning a journey that
did not end, and an iron gate clanging shut.

It was a Saturday at the end of the summer –
break, and the days were tearing away
like a grownup's temper. It was the
Timeless Test: 'What if it lasts a month!'
they said. 'What if it lasts till Christmas!'

He knew Edrich as he knew Hobbs and
Hammond, Larwood and Bradman, from
the backs of the cigarette cards they
read and then flicked in gambling games.
He heard them come out. He heard them begin.
And then he ran in the streets and forgot them.

43

At teatime he eased the sweat-wet shirt
from his back and remembered. Edrich had gone
but England were 374 for 1. He ate bread
and jam, drank tea, grabbed a ball and ran out.
'I bags I'm Len Hutton!' he shouted.

* * *

Sunday was a killjoy day of best clothes
and a thick ear if you tore them. The streets
were empty, so he walked to the dogpond at
Peckham Rye and watched long-haired mongrels
who belonged to no one chase quietly collared
bitches of recognizable breeds. He jumped back
as they shook black-green water everywhere
and brushed splashes from his clothes.

He watched a strange boy leap from the pondside
to a drain six feet out. It was easy. They
did it in turns until his foot slipped and
he sat in the stagnant water. The strange boy
ran away and he walked slowly towards punishment.
The Test was tomorrow and school the day after.

* * *

On his last day of freedom he counted
the lamp-posts, the trees, the telegraph poles
and avoided all the cracks in the pavement.
By the time fifteen men had disturbed
the pigeons at the Oval, the bushes in
Dulwich Park were noisy with schoolboys.

That day names fell from their cigarette
cards on to the Oval grass: Hammond
and Hardstaff, Paynter and Compton.
And calling the names out made them feel famous.

They heard the score shouted by park–
keepers and from shops walking home.
It did not interfere with their playing
but they tucked it away, comfortable

at winning. And, as the day shone on,
even the grownups became excited.

Stumps were drawn as he ate his tea:
Hutton was 300 and Bradman's record 34 away.
He did not believe it would be broken:
Bradman was always, like Bluebird or Tommy Farr.

* * *

After nearly fifty years he remembers
only that it happened when he was there
and that he found it lost among old
dance songs and his short running breath.

Each stroke had sent the present searching
into the past where it was recovered and recorded.
Eleven Australians tried to stop it, there and then,
dead at one moment on a summer's afternoon.
But it went on until it was claimed and written
and talked about and became the year before the war.

Edwin Brock, *Quick Singles* (1986)

A Child's Cricket in Lancashire

I

The past
like a scattering of lost
cricket balls
in the long summer grass.
In the long summer passed,
before boredom and whisky
and work took their toll,
a lad of seventeen
played the game
with the men on the square

of life, at the centre
of the forever oval world.

What has passed
is an urgent innocence
an absolute necessity
to win at all cost;
no one is ever
not out in this game
at the last.

II

One term
at my school I achieved
a half century
of absences. Playing truant
at the nets with cricketers
more able than I
seemed more profitable than geometry or pi.

And I am sure I found
more of life
in those forever dwindling
never ending days in the sun,
more about accepting
an end and how to begin;
and more about
these middle years, how to take
a run out without expecting
justice or a pat on the back.

III

At night in light snow
under sodium lighting
two intent figures
at the nets without nets
in the centre of a road.

To be that dedicated
is the most extraordinary thing
or so it seems to me today.
To be that keen to accelerate
performance, to make the team
and keep one's place
has never been repeated, well
not by me at any rate.
Life then was to drink
from an ever brimming cup.
Now if at first I don't
succeed, I give up.

IV

When Learie
and the black men came
to Wadham Road, they were
the rarest sight
I'd ever seen.
For us all there had never
been such exotic
supple creatures, such explosive
laughter on the green
of our ground, and such
a game.

And I shook
the great man's hand,
he bowled to me
and I to him, never
was there such a net
as that day
or ever since. And he
stayed on, he joined us
and sometimes
he played with the team.
Now of course
all seems but a fading dream.

47

V

Lancashire the county
of the greats,
the greatest exponents
of the game. And Yorkshire?
We tried not to think
about Yorkshire. The red rose
had to grow upon my cap,
no other desire, not even
girls could keep me from it.

The nearest I came –
much later playing jazz
with a horn playing wicket
keeper from Old Trafford;
the best I could do.

And now nothing left
but memories
of a setting sun, sounds
and smells across
the shadowed field,
white on green, my hands
held out for the catch
that never came.

Henry Graham, *Quick Singles* (1986)

Double-Wicket Maiden

Bob twirls his bat like the Sheriff in a nervous town,
as the bowler arches against the whitewashed screen.
He springs down the wicket, slithers to the turf.
The ball lands on his belly, disappears. It rises
in a slow parabola. As it clips the off-side bail
its shadow blinks on his bewildered face.

48

Tom, aged by the umpire's coat, flips pebbles
    from his left hand to his right. He hunches
as the heavy feet grow louder, stiffens
as the ball cuts back, eludes the groping bat.
The black teeth in the spurting mouth
that screams into his face disgust him.

Alan tilts the blade of grass to make the ball
of cuckoo-spit glide the other way. Each bubble
    squirts a beam of coloured light into his eye.
Figures grey behind the stained-glass windows
filter through the fog, seem to wave and shout.
He shakes his head and tilts the blade again.

Sandy, in the outfield, hears the captain's cry,
sees the ball grow small above the trees. His hands
gauge the angle as he totters in vague circles
He dives like a letter through the box. His slide
    ignites the matches in his pocket. He streaks
    for the river like a dragon running backwards.

Walter cracks his knuckles as he pounds back to his mark.
He curves his massive shoulders to shield the alignment
of his fingers with the seam. His shirt, sodden, clings
like a second skin. He charges like a buffalo,
heaves into the final stride. The batsman watches calmly
as the ball swings wide, slams into the keeper's gloves.

Alex, in the gulley, pivots, shades his eyes
as fielders lob the ball along the line. He peers
    past the roller to the cornfield, where Sarah
had been strolling with their second-wicket-down.
Wind sends yellow waves towards the flat horizon.
He groans. The ball cracks hard into his shin.

John Latham, *The Cricketer* (1982)

49

Hamlet's Lament

(ON RETURNING TO HIS FAVOURITE OLD TRAFFORD STAND ON A DAMP SUMMER MORNING)

Oh that this sodden bucket seat were still a bench
Woody and cool, and quick to shed its dew.
Oh that the powers that be had not so fix'd
Their canons 'gainst old seating! O Lords, O Lords,
How sticky, stiff, cramped and ill draining
Seem to me these plastic holèd tubs.
Fie on them. Ah fie, they leave no room
For legs, survival bag or lunch; Gross commercialism
Commends them merely – That it should come to this!

M. Burlinson, *The Cricketer* (1986)

See Off the Shine

Bouncers and bumpers and beamers
Have whizzed round my ribs and my head,
I've faced the fast men and the seamers
Who flourish on balls shining red.

The slips like some vultures have clustered
And silly mid-off hovered near,
I vowed that I would not get flustered
By balls flashing close to my ear.

This fast bowling's really a menace,
I've been hit on elbow and wrist,
I wish that I'd taken up tennis
Or swimming, or snooker, or whist.

The ball has been swerving and swinging
And frequently beating my bat,

50

The bowler's voice in my ears ringing
With strident appeals of 'How's that?'

But now my long vigil is ending –
The spinners are up to their tricks
And any loose balls I'm intending
Dispatching for four or for six!

This off-spinning ball I am sweeping,
Away it balloons into space,
Square leg has the ball in safe keeping –
I'd much rather bat against pace!

Imogen Grosberg, *The Cricketer* (1982)

Hadlee's Victim

Hadlee in, fast beneath
the high arc of his arm,
the ball delivered from his palm.
Then, that soft, sweet click,
and pause, as though a pin's
been pushed in air –
a gap closed over by applause.

Hadlee fluid, Gatting hurried,
Middle stump knocked back,
the bail sent 20 yards behind
where umpire 'Dickie' Bird
walks to fetch it, shaking his head.
He straightens the stump,
knocked askew, so play,
when ready, can resume.

And the England captain trails off
past Father Time on the main stand
who, sickle on his shoulder
takes the bails off, and,
at the same time puts them on,

walks towards the shaded portraits
of the Long Room, his bat,
the drooping of his back
in the verdant shadows
of the pavilion now,
through the gate and up the steps.

Christopher Sykes, *The Cricketer* (1986)

Death of a Cricketer

'If I knew that I was going to die today, I think I
should still want to hear the cricket scores.'
G. H. Hardy, quoted in *Variety of Men* by C. P. Snow

He lay unconscious the whole hot afternoon,
Staring through windows at unnerving clouds,
Noting how still the curtains were, like shrouds,
Thinking 'This afternoon will be my last.'

Through headphones he caught excited chatter,
Clunk of ball on bat, remote applause;
Serious debate of prospects; scores
He thought 'I fifty-three and nearly out.'

Too tired to read the poems that he'd brought,
He tried to hear their echoes in his brain,
But could not through the static of the pain,
Their drugs and drips and dressings that could not ease.

The hours drifted. White, then orange, then red,
The sun watched him with a terrible eye.
'When it sinks behind that rooftop, I will die.'
His last thoughts were how he wished he'd done things.

Differently, though he'd long known that; known too
Knowing was not enough but knowing how,

Beyond him quite. But no more knowing now,
Though he wished he could have known the Test result.

Brian Levison, *The Cricketer* (1987)

Close of Play

How shall we live, now that the summer's ended,
And bat and ball (too soon!) are put aside,
And all our cricket deeds and dreams have blended –
The hit for six, the champion bowled for none,
The match we planned to win and never won? . . .
Only in green-winged memory they abide.

How shall we live, who love our loveliest game
With such bright ardour that when stumps are drawn
We talk into the twilight, always the same
Old talk with laughter rounding off each tale –
Laughter of friends across a pint of ale
In the blue shade of the pavilion.

For the last time a batsman's out, the day
Like the drained glass and the dear sundown field
Is empty; what instead of summer's play
Can occupy these darkling months ere spring
Hails Willow once again the crownèd king?
How shall we live so life may not be chilled?

Well, what's a crimson hearth for, and the lamp
Of winter nights, and these plump yellow books
That cherish Wisden's soul and bear his stamp –
Time's ever-changing, unalterable score-board,
Thick-clustered with a thousand names adored:
Half the game's magic in their very looks!

And when we've learnt those almanacks by heart,
And shared with Nyren . . . Cardus . . . the distant thrill
That cannot fade since they have had their part,
We'll trudge wet streets through fog and mire

53

And praise our heroes by the club-room fire:
Oh do not doubt, the game will hold us still!

Thomas Moult, *The Poetry of Cricket* (1964)

3

A Boy's Game

A little more romance before we get down to the famous players and their deeds. It is childhood cricket that first inspired most of us, and who has not had experiences to identify himself with P. G. Wodehouse's famous description of his schoolboy hero Mike impressing his elders and betters in the nets, or of young Horace, a minor hero in de Selincourt's nostalgic novel The Cricket Match? *Or even with the experience, included here, of John Cleese at Clifton where A. E. J. Collins achieved the most immortal schoolboy feat of all?*

There are many paths to the top in cricket. Sir Donald Bradman describes his first experiences more dispassionately than Jeremy Coney: both went on to captain their countries. But, as others with Raymond Robertson-Glasgow's disease of cricketomania *know, much success has to be in dreams.*

Vitaï Lampada

There's a breathless hush in the Close to-night —
Ten to make and the match to win —
A bumping pitch and a blinding light,
An hour to play and the last man in.
And it's not for the sake of a ribboned coat,
Or the selfish hope of a season's fame,

But his Captain's hand on his shoulder smote –
'Play up! play up! and play the game!'

The sand of the desert is sodden red –
Red with the wreck of a square that broke –
The Gatling's jammed and the Colonel dead,
And the regiment blind with dust and smoke.
The river of death has brimmed his banks,
And England's far and Honour a name,
But the voice of a schoolboy rallies the ranks:
'Play up! play up! and play the game!'

This is the word that year by year,
While in her place the School is set,
Every one of her sons must hear,
And none that hears it dare forget.
This they all with a joyful mind
Bear through life like a torch in flame,
And falling, fling to the host behind –
'Play up! play up! and play the game!'

Sir Henry Newbolt, *Admirals All and Other Verse* (1897)

Collins of Clifton

It seems hard to imagine that the batting exploits of a thirteen-year-old schoolboy in a junior house match would be followed by the nation in the columns of *The Times*, but that was the extraordinary story of Arthur Collins. His remarkable innings of 628 out of a total of 836 developed like a modern soap opera over five days and must have been a welcome distraction to readers of *The Thunderer* as the news pages rumbled with the forthcoming Boer War.

Arthur Edward Jeune Collins began his foray into the record books on Thursday 22 June 1899 when he opened the batting for Clarke's against North Town in a house match at Clifton College. Gradually over the next five days he reached previously unattained landmarks, batting for a total of six hours and fifty minutes. As *The Times* grandly proclaimed part way through the epic, he was 'the first batsman in the world to make 500 runs in a single innings'.

He finished with 628 but had he not run out of partners, who knows what score he might have achieved. Nor did he seem to be in danger of running out of steam. He and Redfern added 183 for the last wicket, Redfern contributing only 13 to the partnership. Although his stay at the wicket was spread out over five days, with plenty of time to rest between instalments, it must still have been a tremendous feat of strength, stamina and concentration for a boy of his age. By the end of the second day Collins had raced to 501 not out, and although rain curtailed play on the subsequent afternoons this 'easy, graceful batsman' did not give up. In all he struck one six, four fives, 31 fours and 146 twos (boundaries on one side of the ground counting as twos), but that still left a lot of running for himself and his partners.

Not content with having crushed his opponents with the bat he also proved a useful combatant with the ball, taking 7 for 33 in the first innings and 4 for 30 in the second. North Town, by now thoroughly sick of the sight of him, just subsided in this less than equal contest and were bowled out for 87 and 61, to give Clarke's victory by an innings and 688 runs. Had it been a boxing match, the referee would have intervened long before the end to save the opponents suffering further punishment as they were obviously unable to defend themselves. The metaphor is not inappropriate since Collins was also a talented boxer, winning the featherweight title at school in 1901 and a bronze medal at Aldershot. A fine all-round sportsman, Collins excelled at racquets, rugby and swimming, as well as cricket.

Collins, who had been orphaned in 1898, the year before his momentous innings, left school and joined the Royal Engineers. Posted to India, where he had been born, army duty limited his appearances on the cricket field, though he often showed that he had the talent, if not the opportunity to succeed in a higher class of cricket. Promoted to the rank of captain he served on the Western Front where he was mentioned in despatches, but the following month on 11 November 1914, at the age of twenty-nine, he was killed in action in the First Battle of Ypres.

Joanne Watson, *Moments of Glory* (1990)

Puerilities

'O joy! that in our embers
  Is something that doth live
That nature yet remembers
  What was so fugitive!'

In the kaleidoscope of infancy such things as goblins in the dark corners of the nursery at twilight, a saw-edged Eton collar, coloured Easter eggs, or the back of the vicar's head in the Creed, are worthy rivals to cricket. But all of them, cricket as well, are fugitive, for memory is a fond deceiver, deigning sometimes on quiet summer evenings to be a friend, yet readily changing with the east wind or a rainy Monday morning to an elusive and rebellious servant. So Nature, mindful of the unequal struggle, has given us eyes as an ally against this rebel. Hence the proud father, watching his son at the nets drive one along the ground 'left foot over, body well behind', is carried gently back to a similar stroke of his own, or more probably to some glorious 'cow-shot', followed by the inevitable crash behind and the not less inevitable bray from in front, 'Oh, if you *will* think you've got a scythe! . . .

And when, proud father, you have gone home again, revolving fair visions of another Grace, some second Tate, whose fame will illumine your declining years, and when you have perused again the half-term report, the memory of which had been effaced by your son's skill at cricket, do not, I beg, repine, do not be amazed!

To repine is useless, for your stern, corrective letter will be answered by a terse statement that 'we won our match on Saturday easily'. To be amazed argues sheer stupidity, for your better judgement should tell you that at this very moment your son is playing Surrey v. Yorkshire, surreptitiously, but with full analyses, in his exercise-book; in spite of the tragic grandeur of John of Gaunt who, like other modern John of Gaunts, is lamenting the passing of the good old days, and in spite of the undeniable truth that Caesar threw his cavalry (wantonly) across the river. Or else, having irretrievably confused the Doldrums with the Gulf Stream, he has issued forth from the lesson unshaken, and is abusing some wretched ignoramus who oils his splice and thinks Chapman plays for Sussex.

'So don't fatigue yourself, I beg, sir!' or meditate correction. Let fall the reproving pen, and comfort yourself with the thought that Grace and Porson both had their points. Nay more, quinine may quell the incipient cold, aspirin may alleviate the sick-headache, potent is the birch for the genuine sluggard; but no triumph of science, no potion, no nostrum, not even hellebore, fabled herb, can certainly cure that sweet disorder of the youthful mind, *cricketomania*. It can, indeed, be arrested and kept with bounds, but only by the skilled cricketopath.

May I assist you, fond parent, to diagnose the symptoms? Some, no doubt, will ring familiar in your ears. Others need for full development the contagion of other small fellow-patients. Let us take one or two, and examine them.

It is the prerogative of the medical profession to make up Latin prescriptions illegible to all but the chemist – and after all, he, poor man, only pretends to read them as he pours in the paint-water – but *cricketopaths* – that is, devotees of *cricketopathy*, would-be healers of *cricketomania* – flatter themselves that they have invented a Latin diction, limited as yet, to keep pace with the progress of the science, and they affirm that the most universal symptom in this disorder is *cacoethes interrogandi*, or *question-itch*. A well-known cricketopath has made an interesting collection of these, some of which I append:

1. Why did Grace have a beard?
2. Would you rather bat left-handed and bowl right-handed, or bowl left-handed and bat right-handed?
3. How old is Grimmett?
4. If there were no County Championship, how would they know who were the best players?
5. Did Wass know Greek?

The leading textbooks on *cricketopathy* lay down that, for this cacoethes, any apathy or neglect on the part of the practitioner is dangerous, as the questions will merely be repeated until they become definitely mechanical and purely rhetorical. At which stage no sedative is of any avail. The prescribed medicine is either *responsio verisimilis*, or if that be unobtainable, *plausibilis evasio*.

There is another symptom worthy of recording, no less familiar to the student of this disorder, which is called by some, quite simply, *cacoethes scribendi*, or *writing-itch*; by others, more technically, *punctiuncula caeca*; that is, a kind of blind stabbing with any sharp instrument, a compass, pencil, or even a new nib. A diagram is drawn, containing wides, sixes, obstructed-the-fieldsman-wilfully, no-balls, bowleds, and other human contingencies. Forthwith, in the imagination of the patient, some team, Middlesex haply, or the local village, take the field, and their fate is decided by a series of (clandestine) stabs. If the patient is fond of the team which he is stabbing, he frequently has to create a new diagram containing more sixes and fours. If otherwise, more bowleds and caughts are born. If even this artifice fails to stab the favoured team to victory, the patient opens his eyes to effect critical stabs. But this is a variation of the symptom, and is more properly termed *punctiuncula semi-caeca*, or even *punctum mendax*. The scores are then duly registered. Quite recently a cricketopath discovered in the possession of a patient, otherwise quite healthy, a fragmentary indication of this symptom, which read as follows:

J. B. Hobbs, bowled Me   .   .   .   .   . o
ME, not out (at the end of Latin)   .   .   .   381

I have been assured that there are only two cures for this form of the disorder, and that even they bring only a temporary alleviation. One is *impositio longa*, the other *confiscation implementorum*.

But, as I have said, it is a sweet disorder. For in boyhood the ball that hits the bottom of the middle stump is not a d— shooter and the groundsman's fault, but a beastly grub, and the action of wayward fate. The loss of a Test match is just 'a swindle', not the crash of an empire or the harbinger of national decay.

In fact, *cricketomania* is never fatal, at least not to the young.

R. C. Robertson-Glasgow, *The Brighter Side of Cricket* (1933)

Father

Our backyard was often a hive of competition – summers of schoolboys, cousins, neighbours and city council workmen who would flock to our tennis court to relive a turbulent tied Test. Even when these crowds deserted us, the family game remained intact. We all had our parts to play. Mother excelled in cries of encouragement from the kitchen window, while my two brothers and my father closed in as they eagerly sensed their turn to bat.

Even now Father is tall; then he was a giant. But a benevolent one. I came up to the bottom of his fly when I was first included in more serious sessions on the court. It wasn't until a further four years had passed that I could look the zipper in the eye.

Armed only with the family bat that dragged awkwardly behind my steps to the crease, I would struggle for perfect backlift. It was too big for me. It was my brother's bat. It had to be swung surely. What is now an instinctive habit was then a determined effort as its weight tugged at my developing forearms.

Once momentum was achieved it was difficult to stop mid-shot. Many times I cursed inwardly as the path of the departing ball flew a gentle arc into the waiting hands of the most disinterested fielder.

Father recognized my problem and altered the rules to compensate for my immature limbs. Yet he too appeared a Goliath, carefully positioned in front of the setting sun, relishing the conditions of bounce and turn with the contented smile of one who knows he is about to secure a wicket.

The enduring impression of that silhouette is of height combined with legendary leanness of Coney form. Father Mantis. A man who needed three sets of shin pads to cover knee to ankle. He played all parts: bowler, fielder, umpire, and threatened continually to become a commentator. Every shot was followed by encouragement or warning.

Generally his comments bordered on profound pessimism and the strategy the bowler should employ to expose the pretender. Each batsman was another challenge, another opportunity to reveal his skill. He always took special pleasure in beating the bat with his unique armoury – the high looping slower ball which when it pitched, spun viciously towards the groin; the quicker 'shin-crusher' that caused chronic bruising to my front leg, and the unsettling 'beamer' that would plunge me headlong on to the cold hard asphalt.

Father's enthusiasm was all-consuming. His raucous appeals for catches behind or lbw often upset neighbours' cats in season, and caused our clematis to become barren the following spring. Under his guidance I learned the basics of playing forward and back, to move the feet, to lean the shoulder, to roll the wrists. He never played cricket himself, yet his devotion was that curious mixture of the aesthetic and the obsessive. We had a routine. Dad would return home, drape his paisley dressing gown on his spare frame and tune up. The violin sat ready and waiting. And as the strains of Beethoven wafted on Wellington air I warmed up myself with a backyard adaptation for single players.

It involved a sacrifice by Mother. In pre-television days when a bout of after-school loneliness struck, I headed for Mother's top drawer. It housed her stockings – the gossamer mesh type so ideally suited to Test matches. A cricket ball could be inserted, and in no time at all could hang suspended from the clothesline. I was lucky my mother was tall. With the combined weight of the ball and the length of the foreleg, it rotated tantalizingly at forward defence height. It was a simple game. There were two sides of international repute. I made myself captain and opening bat, in fact I was the entire batting side. The stocking swung freely when struck with the stump I was given by Uncle Morris. I would watch its return closely and attempt to hit it again and add a further run to the total. A miss meant a wicket had fallen.

The weather played a crucial part in this game. First the wind tended to blow the ball and change its swing dramatically. Secondly, if it was fine, the weight of other clothes on the line encouraged the knot to loosen and periodically slip towards the sheets. This demanded nimble feet, not only to readjust to the wicket a yard to the right, but also to avoid being enveloped by wildly flapping linen.

It was a game I enjoyed immensely, despite words from Mother about the rapid deterioration of her latest silks. These solitary innings filled my afternoons and often the twilight hours of my childhood. Through them I began the process of reading the line, waiting until the last second to play. They were good for self-esteem because there was never a chance of a witnessed failure. The failures were private, and your overwhelming desire to succeed in the company of Test heroes was assured.

On most nights there was time for only one innings. Father swept from the lounge, ready for throw-downs on the court. Every other activity was arrested. The routine was well established. We had until dinner.

Father lived an ordered day. It began with the collection of milk from the gate (a signal for nature's symphony to wake), bus timetables synchronized on his breakfast and neighbours reset clocks as he walked briskly to the train.

Now his day at the Reserve Bank was over he could release any frustrations. I bore the brunt. He mainly threw off-spinners from 10 yards. A background in economics enabled an intuitive familiarity with the game. Cricket merely represented another model, and he manipulated and marshalled his resources to his advantage. The white service line on the court was always just on a length and combined with an elliptical compo ball to create inconsistencies of turn and bounce. He insisted on large apple boxes, multiples of three to be the wickets. His dressing gown sleeves merged with the background, and he often claimed the use of up to fifteen fieldsmen.

Our immersion was total. Sometimes it was so dark I had to listen for the tell tale rhythm of his brogues in a follow through to know the ball had been released. Mother understood this and often delayed the soup long enough for a result, announced by Father's incessant commentary.

He is one of the multitude of fanatical watchers, although he still brings an academic approach to the game. Now many hours are spent analyzing an innings, a shot, a ball. I'm sure this is familiar territory to many. Cricket encourages this kind of intimacy.

Our lives were encapsulated in the one vast playground of our tennis court where we learned and tested our skills. Here were Lord's and Eden Park, where a sixteen-match series of England versus Bert Sutcliffe was played. These inter-sibling battles lasted over days, just as the big games did, and lent an air of reality and respectability to the encounters. They were played with a solemn intensity, being interrupted by only meals and darkness. These were the first day-night games, conceived well before the advent of Kerry Packer. We had been exploiting the twilight hours for years, with apple box wickets and makeshift bowling markers, before he came on the scene.

The only essential items for these games were a ball, bat and wickets, and the rules could be improvised. Unfortunately, when minimum scoring rates were introduced, lifting the ball became a necessary art. I say art advisedly because if the ball was ill-directed, it would pass over our neighbour's boundary fence. Much of my youth was spent storming Mr W's residence to reclaim tennis balls in an attempt to continue a match. This was no easy task.

Mr W lived with his sister in a tidy brown and green weatherboard house. His presence in the street was quiet and unobtrusive. He was in all probability a mild-mannered, gentle-natured man, but to us, as he whisked our ball away, he inspired powerful dread. It was the aspect of silence that made him so forbidding. We were never quite sure if he was watching. He was always potentially patrolling his grounds. We could possibly creep, face blackened at the dead of night, into his garden, only to feel his icy hand creep out from the middle of a rhododendron.

Possibly his vocation heightened his sensory system where children were concerned. He was a teacher. Certainly he was a finely tuned man, locked into Coney wavelength. Like the reliability of modern radar he would rise out of his chair and open the door, just as a mis-hit ball would pass over the wire netting on to his territory. There it would lie, concealed, until his hand plucked it like a piece of freshly ripened fruit. From a distance, four pairs of eyes willed him to turn, smile and toss the ball back, but instead it joined the seasonal crop inside his garage. He became a next-door Sheriff of Nottingham, the reason for stoppages of play, the subject of children's rhymes. The untimely death of a goldfish from his pond widened the gap even more.

When there were no tennis balls left, and Mother threatened to overcome our lassitude by suggesting some domestic chores, a council of war was held and a daring hit-and-run plan was devised. I, being the youngest, would have to lead while my brothers created noisy diversions behind the safety of the hedge. Occasionally such a raid worked, but too many times I had to cower behind a sapling, grateful for my thin frame, yet knowing I was still partially visible. My answer now to those people who find my scoring slow, is, 'Blame Mr W. He made me keep the ball down.'

On the opposite boundary was Mr Bruce. Everyone joined in when we played with him. He was only allowed to bowl underarm, yet the sight of him attacking the bowling crease clad in voluminous shorts, thick legs with ankle socks, was more than adequate preparation for Dennis Lillee. His sedentary occupation had created an underworked cardio-vascular system which, when under stress, caused his breathing to be so loud as to rival the Kingston Flyer.

Most cricket matches appear to the onlooker to be pleasant and gentlemanly, but this is not so. The surface politeness masks the deadly intent beneath. Our feelings, however, were openly hostile; guttural snarls from bowlers delivering catapults from eight yards, howls of dismay from batsmen losing their wickets, and bellows from captains changing the reluctant fielder who was fielding for both sides. It always seemed odd to me that I didn't object to catching out my older brother one-handed, thereby reducing our chances of winning the game, at least until he had me alone behind the coal-box.

This was garden cricket at its best. The subtleties of keeping away from budding flowers, the sublime art of steering the ball between geranium and coprosma. Catching too, was a testing craft when angles of deviation from unfinished block walls and developing cherry blossom had to be calculated immediately. Until the age of ten this backyard shaped my future. It encouraged leg-side shots particularly. Down one side was the hedge that I had to reluctantly trim every fortnight, a major source of runs. It also grew on a gradient difficult to field.

If any girls played, this was the area they would patrol. They didn't often play, only if we were really short. Still we enjoyed them, slipping on the sloping ground, catching their dresses on impudent branches and revealing their under-garments which in those days were quite substantial. Probably the eye contact at those moments was enough to send them indoors, but as I recall there was little opportunity for any other form of contact at any time as they kept a safe distance.

Any stray dogs passing would generally call in for a stint in the covers. Dogs have always treated cricket with studied interest. They like to get the feel of the covers or third man. They have played a part in all levels. From these early private encounters to the most public arena of Eden Park in a Test match they turn up to confirm their curiosity. Sometimes they show a friendly disposition, other times it's graphically menacing.

Our intruder at Eden Park wasn't a dog – it was an alligator. The length of its molars convinced those close to the action that it was no beast to be tampered with. If it wanted backward square then no one else patrolled that area. 'Paddles' told me it could have the entire leg-side if it wanted. In Radella, Sri Lanka, 'Bootsie' Edgar was hounded by a mangy hydrophobic beast. It's the only time I've heard Bruce volunteer to field bat-pad to John Bracewell – at least until the dog's attention wandered to a nearby tea-picker.

From Kaitaia to the Bluff cricket games were interrupted by canine creatures who delight in making their own play, usually beside the stumps in front of a hastily retreating wicketkeeper. It's probably the same dog on a tour of his own, who's mildly amused at these bi-peds who attempt to retrieve balls that have been exclusively dog's-work for years.

Our backyard was eminently suited to their style of play and offered the comfort of Mrs Bett's climbing roses. These fielders had the uncanny knack of catching anything that moved. Countless times my better efforts were ended when, supposedly in the throes of a heavy ablution, they leapt horizontally to pluck a scorching off-drive two inches off the turf. This accounted for the urgent requirement of control and ball on the ground.

The two captains would meet for the toss and settle down to a long Test innings. The air was thick with Fred Trueman and Martin Donnelly. In reality these innings were inevitably shorter, mainly because of the development of new rules that became an extension of the bowler's armoury to remove the intransigent. If someone looked like digging in, the 'half-out' rule came into operation. Not only was he out caught on the full, but also when the ball bounced once and was then caught. Two of these 'half-outs' and the innings was tamely surrendered. Balls, of course, could be trapped in all manner of places – the tray on a trike, lodged in a fork in a tree, in a wheelbarrow, concrete mixer or stuck in the hedge, although it must be added that if it fell while attempts to remove it were being delicately negotiated, it was alive again.

Games were always close and constantly threatened to disrupt meal arrangements. It was here that I first experienced the need to deny the bowler and my developing sense of hunger as Mother's tasty delights wafted on to the pitch. Although if I was at the non-striker's end, a place incidentally where I play my best cricket, I would rush through the hole in the hedge and beg for a morsel at the window.

These games were our 'Tests'. We played till dusk night after night. They provided the opportunity to play out our skills in safety while still remaining competitive.

My memories confirm their social importance but they also are a vital part in a developing love for the game, for success and for building self esteem.

Jeremy Coney, The Playing Mantis (1985)

How I Got Compton Out Twice

'So why should we listen to your opinion on the subject of cricket?' you ask. Well, I'll tell you why. Because I once got Denis Compton out twice in an innings, *that's* why. '*Twice* in an innings?!' you cry.

Now, I should make it clear that I believe that getting Denis out once in an innings would not be that much to write home about. A cause for momentary joy certainly, particularly in 1947, but not something that one would necessarily want on one's gravestone. After all, a lot of people have done it. Lindwall, Miller, Bedser, Laker and Bertie Buse, to name a few. But to dismiss the brilliantined genius twice in one knock is something else. Here is how it happened.

Denis came down to play against Clifton College, a West Country sports academy, in 1958. His son was a pupil there. So was I. I was in the team as a slow off-spinner, because during June I was more or less unplayable. This was because for these four weeks the pitches were in line with a huge red-brick building called School Hall. Being six foot five, my arm cleared the sightscreen easily and so if I bowled the ball from the right end with the right trajectory the batsman was lucky to get so much as a late glimpse of it. During June, this was. Compton came in July.

He'd been in about ten minutes when I was called upon to bowl. He'd not had much of the strike and needed about four for his fifty. He was coming down the wicket in a way I'd never seen before. In first-class cricket I'd seen him leave his crease as the bowler bowled. On this day he was setting off at about the same moment that the bowler commenced his run-up. There was a danger with the quickies that he was going to strike the ball before it left the bowler's hand. I'm very sorry, I'm exaggerating. Let's just say he was as non-creasebound as it is possible to be.

As an off-spinner I had one advantage over and above School Hall. That was our coach, Reg Sinfield, ex-Gloucs and England. He was quite my favourite person at Clifton, funny and wise and kind. I'm afraid he showed most of the masters up dreadfully. Anyway, Reg had told me to bowl very wide at any batsman running down the wicket, so just before my first over I said to the wicket-keeper, one Pickwoad, '*Third* ball, I'll bowl him a very wide one. Be ready for it, we might get a stumping.' 'You can bowl him a wide one if you like,' said Pickwoad, 'but I'm not stumping him. I want to watch him bat.' This was a blow.

I don't remember what happened to my first two deliveries, but they were eventually retrieved. I ran up to bowl the third ball. Denis Compton left his crease and I bowled him a wide one; so wide that it surprised him, passing him yards down the wicket. It pitched, leaving him stranded, and proceeded at a gentle pace and comfortable height towards the waiting Pickwoad. Pickwoad calmly rotated his wrists through 180 degrees, and thrust the back of his gloves at the ball. The ball shot up in the air. 'Damn!' cried Pickwoad towards the master-in-charge, umpiring at square leg. But to my amazement the ball landed, span sideways and bumped against the stumps, dislodging a bail, with the King of the Sweep still yards out of his ground. I'd got him.

Time passed. I became aware of a strange stillness. It occurred to me that no one had appealed. Denis had wandered back to his crease and now stood there, slightly puzzled, Pickwoad was replacing the bail. The other fielders seemed absorbed in their personal problems. Pickwoad picked the ball up and tossed it back to me. 'Bad luck,' he called.

Then I realized I'd blown my chance. If I'd appealed straight away it could have been put down to youthful excitement. But to do so now was cold-bloodedly to spoil everyone's afternoon. I'd got Compton out and no one would ever know. It was a sad moment. I turned, walked back to my mark, ran up and bowled the next ball, a slow high full toss on the leg stump. Spectators started taking cover.

Whether Denis was distracted by the sight of a bowler openly weeping in his delivery stride, or whether he took it upon himself to right this particular wrong, I shall never know, but painstakingly he hit a catch to mid-on. Mid-on was Ken Whitty, playing in his first match for the XI, and consequently the only other man in the ground with an interest in the catch being taken. Had the ball been edged to Pickwoad, it would no doubt have been thrown over the sightscreen for six. Whitty grabbed glazedly at the ball and suddenly stood there triumphant, the ball securely wedged between his chin and his forearm. Compton, D. C. S. c White b Cheese, the *Bristol Evening Post* later announced . . .

P.S. Pickwoad now lives in Canada. Serves him right.

John Cleese, from *The Ashes Regained* by Mike Brearley and Dudley Doust (1979)

Pulpit Cricket

I lost my first real friend and made my first real enemy during a cricket match played in an Edinburgh church on a grey Sunday evening in mid-winter.

Hamish was his name; 'Wee Hamish' to his friends but not to casual acquaintance, for he had a fighting technique closer to the gutters of Leith than the Academic groves nearer Princes Street, and disliked having his small stature noted.

We were staunch members of the Presbyterian Kirk; staunch in the sense that we didn't really know that any alternative existed – certainly we weren't offered any. The services were interminably dreary, or seemed so to us, but even then I could recognize a certain dour professionalism which I miss in my present southern exile. They were at least efficiently, powerfully, and determinedly dreary, and we got full value for our baw-bees – two and a half hours was par for the course. What is more important to this tale, no self-respecting minister would dare offer a sermon lasting a whit less than an hour and a half.

Apart from one joyous hymn (to which our salivary glands responded like Pavlovian dogs, for lunch or high tea lay, heaven-like, just beyond the glad amen), the sermon came last. The proceedings up to that consisted of hymns and psalms sandwiched between long prayers composed by the minister extempore; at least so I was told. For many years I thought (for I had some Latin) that this meant 'dragged out of his past', and being of a charitable nature I assumed this implied before he had picked up much of his no doubt considerable education.

During the preliminary proceedings, there was much upping and downing, which was quite enjoyable on a fairly primitive level. The young know instinctively what is good for them, and praying enriches the soul, while singing does wonders for the wind. But there was no doubt that we couldn't get down to anything really serious until the preacher climbed into the pulpit, and it must have gladdened his heart and raised his pious hopes to see our eager faces peering up at him. I am afraid we were not eager for the salvation he was offering.

We were impatient to get going on one or two major Sunday sports. One was and is a traditional pastime wherever the Sabbath is observed with rigour. I refer to what I might call low-intensity sex, though I understand the level has gone up a bit these days. In my time it involved ogling the girls from our sister school who sat in the pews opposite. We never actually met these girls, unless they were in fact our sisters – which didn't count – and probably the boldness of the eye contact was in inverse proportion to the possibility of any other form of contact. However, we didn't understand these things, and consequently enjoyed ourselves enormously.

The other game was pulpit cricket, which as far as I know is limited to England and other nations where cricket proper is taken neat. How we learnt it I cannot remember. That first winter term I had not yet played the real thing in any serious organized way; cricket in the Clyde valley is not a heavy scene, or wasn't then. But somehow we knew the rules, and we played it with solemn intensity, and, as you will see, serious intent. It knocked the blazes out of flirting, which we tended to employ merely to fill out the slack patches inevitable in even the most enthralling of games. I have to admit that as I got older the emphasis changed, but that is another story.

The way we played (there are local variations), was as follows: each of the two players drew up a team, usually of international repute. The selector normally appointed himself captain and opening bat: false modesty was uncommon, although Squiffy MacFarlane frequently put himself No. 7 with Hutton as skipper. We put this down to an unhealthy passion for Denis Compton and prophetic disregard for the eternal values of amateurism. Squiffy grew up to be a Senior Taxation Officer, obsessed with mere cash values, and he still wears Brylcreem.

The captains drew lots, and the winner submitted his team to the whims of the umpire – not the Great Arbiter in the sky, Who was not, we thought, likely to be entirely sympathetic, but His temporal agent, the current preacher, who was innocently and immediately available. His every gesture was scrutinized as a possible sign of divine decision-making – we assumed that the Good Lord knew Umpires' Standard Signalling Technique.

Thus, a hand raised aloft was a bye, unless the finger was pointed, which meant out, and the next man on the list faced up. Horizontal arm-swings were fours, and I well remember a visiting High Churchman who shocked our Elders to their quivering puritan cores with his genuflections, but nearly seduced us into the arms of the Scarlet Woman by blessing the congregation, and thereby clocking up three four-byes on the trot. I have ever since been attracted to religious symbolism.

On the other hand it may be that my bias against red-hot gospelling was instilled by a Salvationist from Inverness who callously destroyed one of my most promising sides in thirty seconds of a hectoring finger-wagging diatribe on the evils of strong drink. Wee Hamish insisted that each wag was a wicket, and I had to admit he was within his rights. We remained friends on that occasion, for a sportman plays by the rules, but I never buy *Watchtower* in a pub.

One arm held horizontally was a no-ball, and during a particularly accusatorial sermon I had to invite Hamish to take Lindwall off for bowling sixteen consecutive bouncers. He was very firm with Ray, but diplomatic, as any great captain must be.

Short runs were very rare, but we had one visiting preacher who kept hitching up his academic hood, and as a result produced a negative score in a Test between England and Scotland: not so unnatural as it sounds, for Scotland was batting.

Other rules I leave to your imagination, for I must come to the break between myself and Wee Hamish. It was the last Sunday of term, and the evening service. We had started the final and deciding match of a series of seventeen two Sundays previously, but play had been deplorably slow, due largely to the fact that the preacher at every service had been the local incumbent, the Rev. Doctor Zebediah MacTavish, MA, DD, whose theology was divine, but scoring rate diabolical. The match had, however, gradually built up to an exciting climactic position as the reverend gentleman lumbered into his peroration. My side (McKendrick's Cricketing Kings – MCK rather than MCC – subtle stuff), had crawled to 46 all out. Hamish's lot (some idiot name like Toppsex – a bit obsessional, was Hamish) had clawed their way to 41 for nine. It was riveting. It had been riveting for over twenty minutes while the diverse pieces of the sermon were pinned together with great dialectical skill but no sporting significance.

'Amen,' cried the preacher.

Oh no! Not a tame draw after four arduous sessions in the field?

Now came the friendship-shattering event. Some great upsurge of religious fervour seized the normally undemonstrative minister. He flung both hands high towards heaven, and cried again.

'Amen, Amen!'

He stepped back, and fell off the pulpit with an enormous crash.

To some present the immediate question was whether the preacher was damaged: rather more had the same worry about the pulpit, for ministers are two a penny, but repairs cost hard cash. For us, there was only one issue: was it a six, or had he quitted the field of play before completing the signal?

We could not agree, Hamish and I, and the argument twisted and finally killed our once happy relationship. I got a letter from him the other day. It began: 'Dear Sir or Madam.' Perhaps we never knew each other all that well.

Fergus McKendrick, *Pulpit Cricket and Other Stories* (1983)

Practice Makes Perfect

At the back of our house was an 800-gallon water tank set on a round brick stand. From the tank to the laundry door was a distance of about eight feet. The area underfoot was cemented and, with all doors shut, this portion was enclosed on three sides and roofed over so that I could play there on wet days. Armed with a small cricket stump (which I used as a bat) I would throw a golf ball at this brick stand and try to hit the ball on the rebound. The golf ball came back at great speed and to hit it at all with the round stump was no easy task.

To make my game interesting I would organize two sides consisting of well-known international names and would bat for Taylor, Gregory, Collins and so on, in turn.

The door behind me was the wicket, and I devised a system of ways to get caught out and of boundaries. Many a time I incurred mother's displeasure because I just had to finish some important Test match at the very moment she wanted me for a meal.

The open side of my playing area corresponded to the on-side of a cricket field, and therefore I did not have to chase the ball for any shots on the off-side.

This rather extraordinary and primitive idea was purely a matter of amusement, but looking back over the years I can understand how it must have developed the co-ordination of brain, eye and muscle which was to serve me so well in important matches later on.

Another form of amusement, was to take a golf ball into the neighbouring paddock where I would stand some 10 or 15 yards from the dividing fence and throw the ball to hit a rounded rail. My main purpose was to make the ball come back at various heights and angles so that I could catch it. Obviously this also developed the ability to throw accurately, because if I missed the selected spot, it would mean a walk to retrieve the ball.

The playground of the primary school was separated from that of the high school by a fence, but we had the privilege of standing at the gateway. I was frequently to be found at that gateway watching the senior boys play cricket, and once or twice at their invitation managed to have a few hits with them.

Even in the senior school playground, there was no cricket pitch, and our practice was carried out on dirt, which resembled Nottingham marl in appearance. Our wicket was the bell post. A chalk mark indicated the height of the stumps, and many an argument ensued as to whether the post had been struck above or below the chalk mark.

Bats mainly consisted of pieces of wood from a gum tree, fashioned after the shape of a baseball bat. Pads were never worn, and the ball was of a type commonly known as a 'compo'. A boy usually occupied the crease until he got out.

The first cricket match in which I played occurred when I was about eleven years of age. It was at Glebe Park, Bowral; not on a cricket ground but on the football field. The pitch was plain dirt, and was the most level piece of earth we could find.

Bad as it was, I don't think that it equalled the Australian pitch which 'W. G.' described thus: 'There was so much dust on the pitch that the ball sometimes stopped where it was pitched by the bowler.' (Ref. *The Graces* by Powell-Canynge Caple). They must have been slow lob bowlers.

Little did I dream that later a beautiful cricket ground would exist on the same recreational area bearing the name of 'The Bradman Oval'.

In this first match of mine our captain won the toss and decided to bat. For the other side a left-hand bowler obtained a wicket with his first ball, another with his second ball, and I arrived at the crease, a none too confident lad, to stand between the bowler and a hat trick. How I survived the first ball remains a mystery, but I did, and eventually carried my bat for 55 runs.

In the High School there were occasional matches on sports afternoons between scratch teams, and there were only two occasions when I played for our school team against a neighbouring school. In the first of these two matches, against Mittagong School, we played on a concrete pitch covered with coir matting, and out of our team's total of 156 runs my contribution was 115 not out. I was then twelve years of age, and that was my first century.

Naturally I was elated, but my pride was short-lived, for next day we were lined up in the playground at school and the headmaster said: 'I understand that there is a certain boy among you who scored a century yesterday against Mittagong. Well, that is no reason or excuse why you should have left a bat behind.' I was never guilty of a similar offence again.

Don Bradman, *Farewell to Cricket* (1950)

Deceit and Chicanery

Summer's lease hath all too short a date, Hugo old boy, thought Adrian, but your eternal summer shall not fade. In my imagination you are immortal. The man walking beside me is merely The Picture of Hugo

Cartwright, ageing and coarsening: I have the real Hugo in my head and he will live as long as I do.

'I think we'll bat first, sir,' the Narborough captain announced after winning the toss.

'That's it, Malthouse,' said Hugo. 'Knock 'em up and bowl 'em out.'

'Trust me to lose the toss,' said Hooper. 'Sorry, sir.'

'Don't be a dafty-trousers,' said Adrian. 'It's a good wicket to bat second on, it'll dry out all through the afternoon.'

He threw the ball to Rudder, Chartham's opening bowler, before taking his position at the stumps.

'Remember, Simon,' he said, 'straight and on a length, that's all you have to do.'

'Yes, sir,' said Rudder, swallowing.

The ground was in a kind of valley, with the looming Gothic of Narborough Hall on one rise and the church and village of Narborough on another. The pavilion was whitewashed and thatched, the weather perfect with only the faintest of breezes luffing the fielders' shirtsleeves. The grim seriousness of the children preparing to play, the detached amusement of Hugo at square leg, the church clock chiming mid-day, the round circles of fine gang-mown cuttings in the outfield, the sun winking off the roller by the sightscreen, the distant clatter of spiked shoes on the pavilion concrete, the open blue of the wide Norfolk sky, the six pebbles in the hand of Adrian's outstretched arm, this whole monstrous illusion froze, while to Adrian the world seemed to hold its breath as if uncertain that such a picture could last. This fantasy of England that old men took with them to their death-beds, this England without factories and sewers or council houses, this England of leather and wood and flannel, this England circumscribed by a white boundary and laws that said that each team shall field eleven men and each man shall bat, this England of shooting-sticks, weather-vanes and rectory teas, it was like Cartwright's beauty, he thought, a momentary vision glimpsed for a second in an adolescent dream, then dispersed like steam into the real atmosphere of traffic-jams, serial murderers, prime ministers and Soho rent. But its spectral haze was sharper and clearer than the glare of the everyday and, against all evidence, was taken to be the only reality, its vapour trapped and distilled in the mind, its image, scents and textures bottled and laid down against the long, lonely melancholy of adulthood.

Adrian brought down his arm.

'Play!'

Rudder bowled a ball of full length and the batsman swept his bat elegantly forward in defence. But the ball had already gone through him and Rice the wicket-keeper was leaping in glee. The batsman looked round in disbelief to see his off-stump lying on the ground. He returned to the pavilion shaking his head, as if Rudder had been guilty of some appalling social blunder. There was a liquid spatter of applause from the boundary. The school were in lessons and wouldn't be watching until after lunch.

Adrian tossed a pebble into his right hand and smiled across at Hugo.

'I got him, sir!' said Rudder, polishing the ball against his leg. 'I bloody got him. Golden bloody duck.'

'You beat him for pace, old love,' said Adrian, drawing him aside. 'The next batsman will be scared, bowl him two very quick ones just outside the line of off-stump and then a slower ball on middle, but disguise it.'

'All right, sir.'

Adrian wondered if it was a breach of etiquette for an umpire to coach during play. But then he saw Hugo, who had been replacing the bails at the other end, whispering urgently to the incoming number three. Very well then, they would fight it out between them, like First World War generals.

Rudder did as he was told for the first two balls, letting them fly at the new batsman, who played and missed at the first and left the second alone. He came thundering up for the third ball, grunting and stamping like a buffalo. The batsman quaked.

'Subtle disguise I don't think,' Adrian said to himself.

The ball was let go of early and seemed to float in at half the speed. The batsman had nearly completed his defensive stroke by the time it got to him, with the result that the ball was knocked from his bat gently back to Rudder who threw it up in the air with a yell of triumph.

'Caught and bowled! And hast thou slain the number three? Come to my arms, my beamish boy. Two for none, oh frabjous day, calloo callay!'

Hugo was furious at lunch. His side had been bowled out for fourteen runs. He couldn't believe it.

'I'll kill them!' he said. 'I'll castrate them and hang their scrotums from the score-board.'

'Don't worry,' said Adrian. 'We'll probably be all out for ten.'

'I'm going to replace the whole team with boys from the scholarship Sixth. At least they'll have some brains. What good is ball sense without common sense? I mean, trying to square cut a straight half-volley! It makes me want to throw up.'

Adrian was sure that he himself wouldn't sulk quite as gracelessly if it had been his side that had been dismissed for fourteen. But then Cartwright had always been ambitious. He remembered the time they had walked back from Biffen's tea-party and Cartwright had talked about going to Cambridge. That had been the same day that Trotter had hanged himself.

Adrian smothered a sudden desire to rap his spoon on the table, call for quiet and announce, 'This man opposite me here, my fellow umpire, I thought you might like to know that he sucked me off one night in a hotel when he thought I was asleep.'

'Funny old game,' he remarked instead.

'Look,' said Hugo. 'If you do cream us straight after lunch, how would you feel about making it a two-innings match?'

'Well . . .'

'It'll go down as your victory of course, but we do need the practice.'

'All right,' said Adrian. 'I'll check with my team first.'

Hooper was doubtful.

'We've never played two innings before, sir. What happens when we pass their first score?'

'We make as many runs as possible before we're all out.'

'Sir, suppose they can't get us all out?'

'That's when you have to declare, dear. Make sure you judge it so that there's time to put them in again, bowl them out and then pass their total before stumps. We don't want a draw.'

'When are stumps?'

'Narborough's Mr Cartwright and I agreed on seven o'clock. I'll have to ring the school and check with the headmaster. You'll be late for bed of course, but it'll all be the most super-duper fun.'

The whole school turned out to watch after lunch. As Adrian had feared, Narborough's leg-spinner, Ellis, completely baffled his boys. Once they had got used to the ball bouncing and spinning one way, he would send down top-spin and undetectable googlies that made the ball fly off to the waiting close field. Chartham was all out for thirty-nine after an hour and a half of tortured embarrassment. Hugo looked very smug as Narborough prepared for their second innings.

'We're only twenty-five ahead,' said Adrian.

'That's all right, isn't it, sir?' said Rudder. 'If we get them out for fourteen again we'll have won by an innings and eleven runs.'

'If.'

The Narborough openers stalked to the wicket looking determined and confident. They were playing in front of their home crowd now and had experienced the satisfaction of seeing the Chartham team writhe.

Rudder's first ball was a wide. Adrian signalled it, with raised eyebrows.

'Sorry, sir,' said Rudder with a grin.

His next ball was driven to the mid-off boundary, the next was hooked for six. The fourth, a no-ball, was late-cut for two which became six after four overthrows had been added. The next two were both glanced for four. Rudder turned to Adrian to collect his sweater.

'Two more balls yet, Simon.'

'Sir?'

'There was a wide and a no-ball in there. Two more balls.'

'Oh. Yes, sir. I forgot.'

The next two were each smacked for four over Rudder's head.

'What's going wrong, sir?'

'What's going wrong is you're not bowling properly. Line and length, darling, line and length.'

For the next two hours the opening pair batted freely and fiercely, putting on a hundred and seventy-four, until one of the batsmen, the same man Rudder had clean bowled first ball of the morning, retired to let some of his friends enjoy the slaughter.

Hugo's merriment was unbearable over tea, for all the whiteness of his teeth and the sparkle in his eyes.

'Well that's a bit more like it,' he said. 'I was beginning to get worried this morning.'

'Dear old friend of my youth,' said Adrian, 'I'm afraid you've discovered our principal weakness.'

'What, you can't bowl you mean?'

'No, no. Sympathy. My boys were simply devastated by your glumness at lunch, so we decided to cheer you up by letting you have some batting practice. I take it you're declaring over tea?'

'You bet. Have you out of here, tail between your legs, by half past five.'

'Is that a promise?' said a voice behind them. It was Professor Trefusis.

'Certainly, sir,' said Hugo.

'What do you think, Mr Healey?'

'Well let me see . . . two hundred and thirty-nine to make before seven. I think we can do it all right, if we don't panic.'

'Ellis isn't tired, you know,' said Hugo. 'He can bowl for hours at a stretch.'

'My boys were beginning to read him by the end,' said Adrian. 'We can do it.'

'I have just placed a bet with my nephew Philip,' said Trefusis. 'Two hundred pounds on Chartham to win at odds of five to one against.'

'What?' said Adrian. 'I mean . . . what?'

'I liked your entrance papers, most amusing. I don't see how you can fail.'

'Well,' said Hugo, as Trefusis ambled away, 'what a bloody idiot.'

'Oh, I don't know,' said Adrian, popping a sandwich into his mouth, 'smart investment if you ask me. Now, if you'll forgive me, I have to go and brief my platoon.'

'Want a side bet?' Hugo called out after him.

'Right,' said Adrian to his team. 'There's a man out there who is so sure, based on the evidence of what he's seen, that you can do it, that he has bet two hundred pounds that you will blow these bastards out of the water.'

They were padding up in the pavilion, forlorn but brave, like Christians preparing for an away match against Lions.

'But what do we do about Ellis, sir!' said Hooper. 'He's impossible.'

'That's a trough of piss. You step up to him and you cart him all over the park, is what you do. Just don't get pushed against your stumps. Aim for the close-in fielders, if you miss the ball you might manage to belt them with your bat on the follow-through.'

'Isn't that a bit unsporting, sir?'

'Arseholes. Whistle, hum, look unconcerned, look bored. When he's ready to bowl, you step forward and say you're not ready. Disturb his rhythm, demonstrate contempt. Don't forget, I'm out there, and he'll want to bowl from my end because of the slope.'

'You won't *cheat* will you, sir?'

'Cheat? Good heavens. This is an amateur cricket match amongst leading prep schools, I'm an Englishman and a schoolmaster supposedly setting an example to his young charges. We are playing the most artistic and beautiful game man ever devised. Of course I'll cunting well cheat. Now, give me my robe and put on my crown. I have immortal longings in me.'

Out in the middle, little Ellis took the ball and flipped it from hand to hand with the disturbing competence of a born spinner of the ball.

Adrian patted his head.

'Good luck, little chap,' he said. 'Don't get upset if they punish you a bit. It's only a game, eh?'

Ellis looked puzzled. 'Yes, sir.'

A sporting round of applause from the Narborough boys welcomed Chartham's opening pair to the wicket.

'Here they come now. They're both rather savage hitters of the ball, I'm afraid. But if you don't lose your head you should be able to cut it down to ten or so an over. A word of advice, though. Try and do something about disguising that googly of yours a bit better . . . sticks out like a sore thumb.'

Ellis tweaked the ball out of the side of his hand uncertainly.

'Thank you, sir.'

'All right, here we go. Don't be nervous.'

Frowde and Colville, the openers, had certainly taken the game-plan literally. They surveyed the field with lofty disdain and smiled faint patronizing smiles at the short leg and silly point crowded around them, nicely blending admiration for their physical courage and doubt for their mental capacity. They were welcome to stand there and be cut in two, but they had been warned.

'Play!' said Adrian.

Ellis stepped forward. Frowde at the other end threw up a hand and bent to do up his shoe-laces.

'Sorry!' he called. 'Won't be a sec.'

Ellis turned back to his mark and waited.

'All right, Frowde?' said Adrian.

'Fine thank you, sir. Just don't want to get tangled up when I start running.'

'Quite so,' Adrian dropped his arm. 'Play!!' he boomed.

Ellis bowled a full toss which Frowde hooked straight over the boundary. The short leg fielder glared at Ellis: the ball had nearly decapitated him.

Adrian signalled a four to the scorer.

'It was a six,' said Hugo at square leg.

'Sorry?'

'It was a six!'

'Are you sure?'

'Of course I'm sure! It went clean over.'

'Well if you're sure,' said Adrian, signalling a six. 'I didn't want to give ourselves two extra runs. That was a six, scorer!' he yelled, just as Ellis next to him was catching the return from deep mid-wicket. The blast in his ear made him drop the ball. Adrian picked it up for him.

'Try and get them to bounce on the ground first,' he said helpfully. 'That way it's harder for the batsman to hit quite so far.'

Ellis's second was a long hop square-cut for four.

'You see?' said Adrian. 'That's two fewer already.'

The next was on a good length and driven straight to close extra cover.

'There might be a couple here,' shouted Frowde to his partner.

'Genius,' thought Adrian, as they ran one run after the extra cover fielder fumbled the ball in his amazement at the possibility that anyone was going to run at all.

Ellis was made of stout stuff. His next ball was an excellent leg-break that nearly had Colville stumped.

Adrian stepped forward and patted the pitch.

'You must watch your feet after you've bowled,' he said to him. 'You're not allowed to run on in the area between the two wickets. It kicks up rough stuff and helps the bowler at the other end.'

Little Ellis was aghast at the possibility that Adrian might think he had been trying to cheat.

'I'm very sorry, sir,' he said. 'I didn't mean . . .'

'I'm sure you didn't, my dear fellow. That was just a warning, that's all. I'm sure it won't happen again.'

Ellis knocked the next ball from so wide of the stumps that it glanced straight across Colville for four byes.

He was taken off after three more catastrophic overs and retired to long on, blinking back tears and fending off the jeers of his home supporters on the boundary.

Cricket, thought Adrian. It's so character-building.

After the collapse of Ellis the outcome was never really in doubt. The fast man at the other end was competent but soon exhausted. Weirder and wilder alternatives were tried, boys who dropped slow balls from a great height, boys with violent actions like windmills that produced gentle long hops, boys who bowled balls that bounced twice before reaching the middle of the pitch, but to no avail. The openers put on a stand of a hundred and twelve and the fourth-wicket partnership of Rice and Hooper scored the final runs as Narborough church clock struck six.

Adrian watched it all with raised eyebrows and an impartial smile. Hugo boiled and seethed and glared, glancing miserably from time to time at the stony figure of his headmaster who sat perched on a shooting-stick next to Professor Trefusis.

'An instructive match,' said Adrian as he and Hugo pulled up the stumps. 'I thought we were in real trouble at one stage.'

'I can't understand what the hell went wrong with Ellis,' said Hugo. 'I really thought he was the most gifted cricketer in the school. An England prospect even.'

'He's young yet. Temperament is the problem there, I fancy. I tried to calm him down and encourage him to get on with his natural game, but he was a bit overawed. Don't give up on him, he's learnt a lot today.'

'He'll learn a bloody sight more after I'm through with him.'

The Narborough team, hot and limp with exertion and defeat, saw them off in the driveway. Hugo stood with them, sipping at a can of beer.

'Three cheers for Chartham Park,' called Malthouse, their captain, raising his arm with an attempt at casual gallantry. 'Hip-ip.'

'Ray!' murmured Narborough.

'Hip-ip!'

'Ray!'

'Hip-ip.'

'Ray.'

'Three cheers for Narborough Hall,' shouted a flushed and triumphant Hooper, punching the air. 'Hip-Hip!'

'Hooray!' bellowed Chartham.

'Hip-Hip-Hip!'

'Hooray!'

'Hip-Hip-Hip-Hip!'

'HOORAY!'

'Goodbye then, Hugo. See you for the return match.'

'We'll pulverize you.'

'Of course you will.'

A madness suddenly possessed Adrian. With a pounding heart he leant forward and whispered in Hugo's ear.

'I was awake, you know.'

'What?'

'That night in Harrogate. I was awake all the time.'

Hugo looked annoyed.

'I know you bloody were. Do you think I'm an idiot?'

Adrian stared open-mouthed and then burst out laughing.

'You total . . . you complete . . . you . . .'

Trefusis stepped forward.

'Well, young man, you've earned me a thousand pounds. Here's two hundred, my original stake.'

'Oh really,' said Adrian. 'I couldn't.'

'Of course you could,' he pushed a bundle of notes at him. 'Tremendous display.'

'Yes, they're not a bad bunch, are they?' Adrian looked on affectionately as his team climbed into the minibus.

'No, no, no. You!'

'Professor?'

'I knew that the man who wrote those artfully disguised second-hand essays, who disgorged such specious and ill-thought-out nonsense with such persuasive and brilliant flair wouldn't let me down. You've clearly a genius for deceit and chicanery. I look forward to seeing you next term.'

Stephen Fry, The Liar (1991)

4

Pioneers

Hambledon represents not so much the beginning of cricket as the beginning of cricket literature. The players celebrated by John Nyren's observant eye and vivid memory are forerunners of the mighty players of the Test era and Nyren the forerunner of Denison, Cardus, Robertson-Glasgow and many more.

Nyren showed that the game was about characters as well as character and as the first touring team from Australia demonstrated, they come, like Joseph's coat, in many colours.

Hambledon

'If you want to know, sir,' said Beldham to Pycroft, 'the time the Hambledon Club was formed, I can tell you by this: when we [Farnham] beat them in 1780, I heard Mr. Powlett say: "Here have I been thirty years raising our club, and are we to be beaten by a single Parish?"' Now the Rev. Charles Powlett, a son of the third Duke of Bolton and Lavinia Fenton, the original 'Polly Peachum', is not very likely to have been connected with the club before his appointment to the living of Itchen Abbas in the early sixties. Yet Beldham was probably more accurate than he knew in his evidence, for in the year 1750 Hants faced London single-handed, and in 1756 the Hambledon Club, then for the first time mentioned, opposed the strong Dartford side on the Artillery Ground. Eight years later 'the gentlemen of Hambledon, called Squire Lamb's club', met Chertsey, 'with great sums of money depending', and in 1767 Hambledon won two matches by the unprecedented margins of 262 and 224 'notches', a feat that may very likely have inspired the Rev. Reynell Cotton, master of Hyde Abbey School, Winchester, to write his famous 'Cricket Song' for the club:

> Then fill up your glass! – He's the best that drinks most;
> Here's the Hambledon Club! Who refuses the toast?
> Let us join in the praise of the Bat and the Wicket,
>   And sing in full chorus the Patrons of Cricket.

'Squire Lamb' remains an enigma, though there was a Squire Land who was a little later 'Master of the H.H.'. But history is probably right in ascribing to Charles Powlett the chief glory of developing, even if he did not found, the club. He, Dehaney, and some others of the first known membership were Westminster boys in the forties, so would have been in close touch with the 'advanced' London game, and, it may be, were responsible for pruning away such local peculiarities as Nyren's archaeology hints at. Certainly Powlett, as 'steward', was the life and soul of the club for many years, piloted it through at least one crisis, and, when the end came, was the last to abandon the sinking ship.

In September 1768 Hambledon challenged Kent and beat them easily: in that match 'Mr Small, of Petersfield, fetched above seven score notches off his own bat.' One of the most picturesque figures in all cricket history, John Small, was born in 1737, and lived for all but the first six of his eighty-nine years of life at Petersfield, where he was for seventy-five years a member of the church choir, playing the tenor violin until the year of his death. Originally a shoemaker, he later became a gamekeeper, and regularly took his 'seven-mile tour' before setting out for a match. All his spare time he devoted to the making of bats and balls, and hung before his house a painted sign which read:

> Here lives John Small,
>   Makes Bat and Ball,
> Pitch a Wicket, Play at Cricket
> With any man in England.

It was no idle boast, for indeed he was for years the first batsman in the land. Once he kept up his wicket all three days of a match against All

England, while, when 'Lumpy' Stevens clean bowled him in Bishops-bourne Paddock in 1772, it was acclaimed a nine-days' wonder, not having been done 'for several years'! In May 1775 there was played on the Artillery Ground a match between five of Hambledon and five of Kent, each with one given man: it was a desperate game, and when Small, the last man, went in, 14 runs were still wanted. 'Lumpy' Stevens was the given man for Kent, and, naturally, did all the bowling, and at the crisis was in such form that several times he bowled the ball through Small's wicket without touching either of the stumps or the bail. Hambledon got home, but the memory of 'Lumpy's' ill-luck remained, and led soon afterwards to the addition of the third stump to the wicket, and so contributed directly to the 'straight and defensive' style in batting. One of the protagonists of the straight-bat revolution, certainly its finest exponent in that age, Small turned his skill as bat-maker to account (Dark of Lord's was his apostle in the trade), and worked up a straightened and shouldered blade, with which he defied the new 'length' bowling, and continued to execute against it his favourite strokes, the 'draw', and the off-drive, with left leg well across and the wrists in full play. Who knows but that he owed something to the intuition of a woman, for Mrs Small was enthusiasm itself for the game, and any match day at Hambledon you might have seen her hurrying up to the ground from Petersfield: she always carried a green umbrella of enormous dimensions, which she would flourish excitedly in order to signal her husband's hit, shouting the while, 'Run, man, run; you'll be out!'

Small's 'forte' was defence, Tom Sueter's attack. The latter, says Nyren, was the first man to break through the old rule of fast-footed play: he would jump in and hit it 'straight off or straight on; and, egad, it went as if it have been fired'. Sueter, too, was the first man to master 'the cut' which the new bowling had now made possible, but it was as a stumper that he won his greatest fame. 'What a handful of steel-hearted soldiers are in an important pass, such was Tom in keeping the wicket. As a proof of his quickness and skill, I have numberless times seen him stump a man out with Brett's tremendous bowling.'

This Brett, with Richard Nyren, was the club's first bowler, and his pace and accuracy made him a serious rival to 'Lumpy' as the best in England. Nyren was left-handed, slower, but 'always to a length', and the master of every honourable device in the game. He was the unquestioned 'General' of the Hambledonians in all their matches, and with his eye for talent soon marked the possibilities of the little farmer, Lamborn. With the old-fashioned bowling it was quite a common thing for the ball to be given a twist, or bias, as it was then called, from leg to off, but here was a man who could reverse the process – the first 'off-spinner' in history; and when All England played Hambledon 'this new trick of his so bothered the Kent and Surrey men that they tumbled out one after another as if they had been picked off by a rifle corps'!

Such were some of the leading figures in the first Hambledon eleven known to fame, the eleven of the 'Old Players' whom Beldham affected somewhat to despise, but then he can never have seen them in their prime. Somewhere about 1770 the club had a run of ill-success and was on the eve of being dissolved, but they determined to have one more try, met Surrey on the Laleham Burway ground, beat them by one run, and never again looked back. In the next ten years, Nyren tells us, they played fifty-one matches against 'England, etc.', and gained twenty-nine of them: the records of the time, so far as they have proved recoverable, substantially confirm the claim.

'The arena of their glory, the Marathon ennobled by their victories, and sometimes enriched by their blood', was Broad-Halfpenny, a swelling shoulder of down some two miles to the north-east of the village itself. Some twenty years ago it had become plough-land, to the horror of the cricket pilgrim, but now it is back in turf again, safe and secure, we may hope for all time, in the pious keeping of Winchester College. To celebrate its rescue, a match was played there last July between the College Eleven and the Hambledon Club: as one privileged to take part in it, I can myself attest the delight of playing upon that fine and lively turf, as fair a wicket as ever John Small found it, with the cloud-shadows chasing each other over Chidden Down to the north, and the larks singing overhead. Once again Hambledon were victors, captained by Mr Whalley-Tooker, a descendant of one of the original members, and once again the field, we may be sure, 'echoed to the cheers of a soundless, clapping host'.

In the old days there was a 'lodge' erected on the ground 'for the convenience of members', and ladies were catered for by the booths of Barber and Richard Nyren, in which it was hoped that beef, ham, chickens, and tarts would, with the help of the fine down air, stand in the place of 'Marbres, Aspigues, Blanc Manges, etc.'. The true club house, the Bat and Ball Inn, still stands, looking across the road on to the centre of the down: but time has not dealt kindly with it, nor suffered it to preserve even a little of the romance that should properly invest it. The old sign-board is gone – to make fuel, it is said, one wintry night; the first iron gauge for testing the width of bats has gone too, just pirated in quite recent years by some gentleman who 'took a fancy to it', and the last of the old club chairs met an irrevocable fate, when Farmer Someone, 'a very heavy-sterned man', as the landlord put it, sank into it one day and 'came right down'; nor can its cellars any longer yield anything comparable with that immortal viand (for it was more than liquor) on which John Nyren waxed so lyrical, 'Ale that would flare like turpentine, genuine Boniface, that would put the souls of three butchers into one weaver.' Well for John Nyren that he cannot see the change since the days when he was but 'a farmer's pony' to the Hambledon Club, and before his father, its 'head and right arm', had gone to join old Richard Newland in the Elysian fields.

In the early eighties the club found another home on Windmill Down, now a fir-plantation, much closer to the village, and about this time a new generation of players begin to appear in its ranks. Perhaps the beginning of the change is to be found in that defeat of Hambledon by Farnham in 1780 which so shocked Charles Powlett: certainly the greatest figure of the new regime were western Surrey men.

First a word or two on Tom Walker, whose inventive genius does not enjoy the celebrity which it may fairly claim. As a batsman so sound and steady that Lord Frederick Beauclerk, cricketer and divine, would dash his hat down on the pitch and call him 'a confounded old beast', and so successful as to win from his contemporaries the name of 'Old Everlasting', it is yet as a bowler that he should find his niche in history.

'I told you, sir,' said Beldham, 'that in my early days all bowling was what we called fast, or, at least, a moderate pace. The first lobbing slow bowler I ever saw was Tom Walker. When, in 1792, All England played Kent, I did feel so ashamed of such baby bowling; but, after all, he did more than even David Harris himself.' But Walker was far from content with this success. A few years later he came out as the positive originator of the new 'throwing bowling'. What was the exact form it took is difficult to decide, but there can be no doubt that it was the prototype of the 'march of intellect revolution' of 1827–30. Both Beldham and Nyren state in so many words that John Willes, of Kent, to whom the credit of the innovation is generally, and even on his own tombstone, assigned, did no more than revive the style which Walker had originated, but from which he was prohibited by the Hambledon Club, as being 'foul play'.

Of William Beldham much could be written. Born near Farnham in

87

1766, he died at Tilford in the ninety-seventh year of his age. For thirty-five years, without a break, his batting dominated the great matches, and even when he was verging on the Psalmist's allotted span he was 'barred' from inclusion in ordinary county fixtures. He was 'safer than the Bank', says John Nyren, and yet a most brilliant hitter. There was no more beautiful sight than to see him make himself up to hit the ball, and no finer treat in cricketing than to watch him at the wicket face to face with David Harris.

Over the south door of the Long Room at Lord's there hangs a very beautiful picture of him, seated, leaning on his bat, in tall hat and pleated smock: it must have been even so that Mitford found him when, in the evening of his days, he visited 'the great, the glorious, the unrivalled William Beldham' in his cottage home at Tilford, and left of that visit a record which need never fear oblivion. 'It was a study for Phidias to see Beldham rise to strike, the grandeur of the attitude, the settled composure of the look, the piercing lightning of the eye, the rapid glance of the bat, were electrical. Men's hearts throbbed within them, their cheeks turned pale and red. Michael Angelo should have painted him. Beldham was great in every hit, but his peculiar glory was the cut. Here he stood with no man beside him, the laurel was all his own; it was like the cut of a racket. His wrist seemed to turn on springs of the finest steel. He took the ball, as Burke did the House of Commons, between wind and water; not a moment too soon or too late. Beldham still survives. He lives near Farnham, and in his kitchen, black with age, but, like himself, still untouched with worms, hangs the trophy of his victories, the delight of his youth, the exercise of his manhood, and the glory of his age – his BAT.'

Last, and greatest, of the Hambledon bowlers comes David Harris. Born at Elvetham, in Hampshire, in 1754, he was a potter by trade, and perhaps his work lent a peculiar suppleness and strength to his fingers, which would account for the extraordinary life and fire of his bowling off the pitch. Of his generous and warm-hearted nature Nyren speaks with unconcealed affection. 'He was one of the rare species that link man to man in bonds of fellowship by good works, that inspire confidence and prevent the structure of society from becoming disjointed'; and yet, 'I do not mean that he was a *canter*. Oh no! No one ever thought of standing on guard and buttoning up his pocket in Harris's company.' When first he joined the club he was only a raw countryman, and deplorably addicted to bowling full tosses; but old Richard Nyren took him in hand, and preached to him the great principle of 'three-quarter' or length bowling, and David, as one would expect from a man of his parts, set himself to master the art. Many a time, an old cricketer told Pycroft, you might have seen him practising at dinner-time and after hours all the winter through. The result was a bowler who, in grandeur of method, in accuracy of pitch, in devastation of effect, dominated his own generation, was accorded by its immediate successors the isolation of outstanding genius, and remains today, 150 years since he first knew Broad-Halfpenny, one of the few supreme figures in the history of the game.

'He was always first chosen of all men in England,' says Beldham, and Mitford tells the same story. 'There have been a hundred, a thousand orators; there never was but one David Harris. Many men make good speeches, but few men can deliver a good ball. Many men can throw down an enemy, but Harris could overthrow the strongest wicket. Cicero once undermined the conspiracy of Catiline, and Harris once laid prostrate even the stumps of Beldham.'

It seems generally true that bowling is the dominating factor in cricket, determining, that is to say, the general characteristics of the game, and especially the style and method of the batsman. Of course, there are exceptions, as when the genius of 'the Champion', for a time, practically killed fast bowling, and promoted the growth of the off-theory school on the diamond cut diamond principle. But it was the off-theory that emasculated batting of the old leg-strokes, and it has been the swerve and the googly, quite as much as the Jam Sahib's back-play, that have led to the development of 'modern batting'. Even so, it was David Harris's bowling in the last two decades of the eighteenth century that led to the fundamental revolution in batting which determined the whole subsequent development of the game. Now, in Harris's bowling there were three main features – length, accuracy, and 'nip' from the pitch. He was not the first of the length bowlers by any means – 'Lumpy' and Richard Nyren had both shown him the way. In accuracy of pitch he may not have been superior to the former, though we read that where the turf was thin Harris's deliveries would wear a small patch bare of it; but he was the first of all bowlers to combine length and direction with real pace, and, above all, to make the ball 'lift' quickly from the pitch. For this quality his peculiar action, of which Nyren's description is famous, and in which the ball was, as it were, forced away from the level of his armpit, was no doubt primarily responsible: 'Like the Pantheon in Akenside's hymn', says Mitford, 'it was simply and severely great', and Lord Frederick

Beauclerk, one of the very greatest players of the next generation, described it as the grandest thing of the kind he ever saw. Of its effect, then, there can be no question. His balls, says Nyren, were very little beholden to the ground when pitched; it was but a touch and up again. And woe to the man who did not go in to block them, for they had such a peculiar curl that they would grind his fingers against the bat. And again – and here is the crux of the whole matter – 'To Harris's bowling I attribute the great improvement that was made in hitting, and, above all, in stopping; for it was utterly impossible to remain at the crease when the ball was tossed to a fine length. You were obliged to get in, or it would be about your hands, or the handle of your bat, and every cricketer knows where its next place would be.'

To this new problem batting reacted. The 'old players', says Beldham, stayed 'puddling about their crease and had no freedom', and he declared that it was he, Fennex, and Harry Walker who first opened their eyes as to what could be done with the bat, Walker by his cutting, and he and Fennex by forward play. At first their methods shocked the critics: 'Hey! hey! boy! What is this? Do you call that play?' said his old father to Fennex, when he first 'went in and laid down a ball before it had time to rise', and 'You do frighten me there jumping out of your ground', said Squire Powlett to Beldham when he did the same: but Beldham for thirteen years averaged 43 a match, and Fennex was the tutor and model upon whom Fuller Pilch founded his play.

At the end of his little book Nyren enumerates the names of the Hambledon team when it was in its glory, and concludes: 'No eleven in England could have had any chance with these men, and I think they might have beaten any twenty-two.' That this was no idle boast we may surmise from the fact that in June 1777 they met a fully representative eleven of England on 'The Vine' at Sevenoaks and beat them by an innings and 168 runs. It was in this match that James Aylward, a great left-handed batsman, stayed in the whole of two days to make 167: it was also one of the first games in which three stumps are known to have been used. For their 'foreign' matches the eleven travelled together in a caravan, or 'machine', as it was termed in the 'minute' directing Mr Richards, the club treasurer, to see to its purchase; but for their home games they assembled independently, the Surrey contingent regularly riding the thirty-odd miles from their homes and being allowed to debit the 'Horse Hire' to their expenses.

The founding of the MCC in 1787 was really the death-knell of the

Hambledon Club: more and more did London become the centre of great cricket, and steadily the membership declined, and the players were lured away by the golden magnet. Fitly enough it is at Lord's that in 1793 Hambledon played its last-recorded match.

But before we suffer this great eleven to drop back into the mists of memory, let us try to picture once more the turf on which they played, and to people it once again with the figures which still stand out fresh, vigorous, and personal from John Nyren's canvas.

It is a fair June morning, and some twenty minutes before ten, as we mount the gentle rise that leads out of the Hambledon vale on to the sunny shoulders of Broad-Halfpenny Down; wickets will be pitched at ten o'clock, but play will not start for, perhaps, another half-hour, so we have time to look about us.

There, on the edge of the close-cut turf, stands a little group in serious converse, debating, no doubt, as to where exactly they shall pitch the wicket, and discussing their tactics for the day. In the centre is the head and right arm of the club, Richard Nyren, who has been on the ground early, as well he may, for does not his bedroom window look straight over the pitch? He has just 'had words', firm, but respectful, with the great Sir Horace Mann, of Kent, about that rising young batsman, James Aylward, whom Sir Horace is trying to filch away from Hambledon with the lure of a bailiff's post on his own estate at Bishopsbourne (and lure him he did; but the best batsman made but a poor bailiff, we are told). The old 'General' has registered his protest in the 'face to face, unflinching, uncompromising' manner that was second nature to him; he has 'differed from his superior without trenching on his dignity or losing his own', and, that done, turns to the more immediate problem of driving into the thickest skull of Lamborn, the little Farmer, the fact that with his heaven-sent gift of an off-break, it is essential that he should give the ball a chance of hitting the wicket by pitching it outside the off-stump. That 'plain-spoken little bumpkin' has not yet learnt his lesson; an hour or two hence he will miss by a hair's breadth the leg-stump of the Duke of Dorset, and 'forgetting, in his eagerness and delight, the style in which we were always accustomed to impress our aristocratical playmates with our acknowledgment of their rank and station', he will bawl out, 'Ah, it was *tedious* near you, sir,' and so set the whole ground laughing.

Now, while these weighty matters are being debated near the ground's centre, there float out from the open windows of the club-room in the Bat and Ball the notes, true, pure, and strong, of two voices singing in harmony: it is Tom Sueter and George Leer, fit partners in song with their tenor and counter-tenor, for are they not partners in the game? Tom Sueter, as keeper of the wicket, and George Leer, 'sure as a sandbank', at long-stop, who could stand a whole match against Brett's bowling, and not lose more than two runs.

Meanwhile, up the road from Petersfield comes John Small and the first to greet him is the Duke of Dorset, and warmly too, we may be sure, for their mutual respect and liking has lately been pledged in no ordinary manner: the Duke had sent Small a handsome fiddle and Small, like a true and simple-hearted Englishman, returned the compliment by sending his Grace two bats and balls, 'also paying the carriage'. His arrival in the club-room is greeted with a buzz of mingled amusement and admiration, for the story has got abroad how an evening or two ago, when on his way by a field path to a musical party, he was attacked by a vicious bull, and how, 'with the characteristic coolness and presence of mind of a good cricketer, he began playing on his bass, to the admiration and perfect satisfaction of the mischievous beast'. Small is 'Old Small' now, for his son, 'young John', has already made his name, and it is some time since 'Lumpy' Stevens astonished the cricketing world by clean bowling the father. But he is still the straightest bat in England, and is looking forward eagerly to another meeting with his old rival. The latter, of course, is out in the middle, anxiously inspecting the ground, in the hopes of a 'brow' off which his balls will shoot, but with a thought or two for the good dinner awaiting him at the end of the day in the Bat and Ball; for does he not owe his very nickname to the fact that at one of their dinners he once did eat a whole apple-pie!

But who are those posting up to the ground on horses that show some signs of a longish journey? The first is none other than the great Beldham himself, whose crisp, fair hair and fresh glowing cheeks have already earned for him from his clubmates the name of 'Silver Billy', and, by his side, a little keen-eyed man, now past the time for active play, but still an acknowledged judge and tutor of the game, Harry Hall, gingerbread maker, and apostle of the high left-elbow and straight bat; these have been up betimes, for they have ridden from Farnham, and will ride back there again when the match has been won.

But, from further yet afield, from their lands near the Devil's Punch Bowl at Hindhead, come two others, 'those anointed clod-stumpers, the Walkers, Tom and Harry. Never, sure, came two such unadulterated rustics into a civilized community.' Harry was left-handed, and, as hitter, his half-hour was as good as Tom's afternoon, but the brother was, for all that, the greater man. Look at him where he stands with his hard, ungainly, scrag-of-mutton frame, his long spider legs, and his wilted apple-John face; see him run for that ball, he moves like the rude machinery of a steam-engine in the infancy of construction, every member seems to fly to the four winds, he toils like a tar on horseback. Yet this same ungainly Tom will rival even Beldham himself; he will go in first, and as often as not be not out at the end. He will never speak while at the wicket; but, whether at practice or in an innings v. All England, be the same phlegmatic, unmoved man, a very Washington of cricketers. Harris once bowled 170 balls to him for one run, but Walker once made 95 not out and 102 in one and the same match on the White Conduit Fields. Well did Mitford write: 'You might as well attempt to get Wellington from a field of battle, or Bentley from a Greek Poet, as to get Walker from his wicket.'

Last and late upon the ground comes Noah Mann, from North Chapel, twenty miles or more away in Sussex, short, strong, active, swarthy as a gipsy, and the fastest runner in all the club; all eyes are on him as he gallops on to the ground and, leaning low over his saddle, swoops up the handkerchiefs that his friends have tossed down for him – a familiar and ever-popular feat with the now crowded ring.

A few hours hence he will be at the wicket, and woe betide the bowler that tosses one up within reach of those impetuous arms, he will hit it away for ten, as he did one day on Windmill Down; or if the game ends early he will make a match at running with any man on the field, wait on him for half the distance, and then pass him and romp home a victor whom Nyren never saw vanquished.

And so we will leave them, this great eleven, as Mitford left them ninety years ago, with homage on our lips: 'Troy has fallen and Thebes is a ruin. The pride of Athens is decayed, and Rome is crumbling to the dust. The philosophy of Bacon is wearing out, and the Victories of Marlborough have been overshadowed by greater laurels. All is vanity, but cricket; all is sinking in oblivion but you. Greatest of all elevens, fare ye well!'

H. S. Altham, *A History of Cricket* (1962)

Windmill Down

(TO W. A. BETTESWORTH)

This is the place; here is the story told
   Of those first players in that far-off June
That shines still on these Hampshire downs. Behold
   The very turf, the pitch where some high noon
   'Lumpy' would choose his sloping wicket, soon
To rouse deep-throated chorus from the ring,
Vying with Beldham, Walker, Brett, to bring
   Fame to the tales that Nyren's readers con,
Names for undreamt of rhymers yet to sing,
   When primroses are out at Hambledon.

Gone are those days, yet hither, as of old,
   Come players for the game; moon follows moon,
Still the same happy echoes fill the wold,
   Still from the down's deep wood the pigeons croon,
   About the old inn parlour village shoon
(Ale-fragrant still the air) go clattering,
And gardeners bowl and blacksmiths catches fling,
   And bat from ball cracks music, and upon
Green turf the high sun dies to evening,
   When primroses are out at Hambledon.

And so where wickets stand or grass is rolled,
   From Windmill Down to Sydney, the same boon,
Born of the game, continues. Caught or bowled
   The players pass – one law for lord or loon.
   The piper changes; who should change the tune
Le roi est mort. E'en so: God save the King!
For Lockwood's, we shall watch Macaulay's swing,
   Hobbs follows Grace, Holmes Hirst, Tate Richardson,
Carr can still show us Jessop's larruping,
   When primroses are out at Hambledon.

Friend 'tis the end begins. The play's the thing.
We win or lose again, remembering.

We shall find sunlit swards by Acheron,
And toss bright obols, each returning spring
When primroses are out at Hambledon.

Eric Parker, *Between the Wickets* (1926)

The Hambledon Pantheon

Before I proceed with my catalogue of the Hambledon Pantheon, it may be worth while to mention a circumstance connected with poor Noah Mann, the player named a few pages back. As it will tend to show the amenity in which the men of lower grade in society lived in those good old times with their superiors, it may prove no worthless example to the more aristocratic, and certainly less beloved members of the same rank in society of the present day. Poor Noah was very ambitious that his new-born son should bear the Christian name, with the sanction, of his namesake Sir Horace Mann. Old Nyren, who, being the link between the patricians and plebeians in our community – the *juste milieu* – was always applied to in cases of similar emergency, undertook, upon the present occasion, to bear the petition of Noah to Sir Horace, who, with a winning condescension, acceded to the worthy fellow's request, and consented to become godfather to the child, giving it his own name; adding, I have no doubt, a present suited to the station of his little protégé. How easy a thing it is to win the esteem of our inferiors; and how well worth the while, when the mutual pleasure only, resulting from the action, is considered! Sir Horace, by this simple act of graceful humanity, hooked for life the heart of poor Noah Mann; and in this world of hatred and contention, the love even of a dog is worth living for.

The next player I shall name is James Aylward. His father was a farmer. After he had played with the club for a few years, Sir Horace got him away from us, and made him his bailiff, I think, or some such officer; I remember, however, he was but ill qualified for his post. Aylward was a left-handed batter, and one of the safest hitters I ever knew in the club. He once stayed in two whole days, and upon that occasion got the highest number of runs that had ever been gained by any member – *one hundred and sixty-seven!* Jemmy was not a good fieldsman, neither was he remarkably active. After he had left us, to go down to live with Sir Horace, he played against us, but never, to my recollection, with any advantage to his new associates – the Hambledonians were almost always too strong for their opponents. He was introduced to the club by Tom Taylor, and Tom's anxiety upon the occasion, that his friend should do credit to his recommendation, was curiously conspicuous. Aylward was a stout, well-made man, standing about five feet nine inches; not very light about the limbs, indeed he was rather clumsy. He would sometimes affect a little grandeur of manner, and once got laughed at by the whole ground for calling for a lemon to be brought to him when he had been in but a little while. It was thought a piece of finnikiness by those simple and homely yeomen.

And now for those anointed clod-stumpers, the Walkers, Tom and Harry. Never sure came two such unadulterated rustics into a civilized community. How strongly are the figures of the men (of Tom's in particular) brought to my mind when they first presented themselves to the club upon Windmill-Down. Tom's hard, ungain, scrag-of-mutton frame; wilted, apple-john face (he always looked twenty years older than he really was), his long spider legs, as thick at the ankles as at the hips, and perfectly straight all the way down – for the embellishment of a calf in Tom's leg Dame Nature had considered would be but a wanton superfluity. Tom was the driest and most rigid-limbed chap I ever knew; his skin was like the rind of an old oak, and as sapless. I have seen his knuckles handsomely knocked about from Harris's bowling; but never saw any blood upon his hands – you might just as well attempt to phlebotomize a mummy. This rigidity of muscle (or rather I should say of tendon, for muscle was another ingredient economized in the process of Tom's configuration) – this rigidity, I say, was carried into every motion. He moved like the rude machinery of a steam-engine in the infancy of construction, and when he ran, every member seemed ready to fly to the four winds. He toiled like a tar on horseback. The uncouth actions of these men furnished us, who prided ourselves upon a certain grace in movement and finished air, with an everlasting fund of amusement, and for some time they took no great fancy to me, because I used to worry, and tell them they could not play. They were, however, good hands when they first came among us, and had evidently received most excellent instruction; but after they had derived the advantage of first-rate practice, they became most admirable batters, and were the trustiest fellows (particularly Tom) in cases of emergency or difficulty. They were devilish troublesome customers to get out. I have very frequently known Tom to go in first, and remain to the very last man. He was the coolest, the most imperturbable fellow in existence: it used to be said of him that he had no nerves at all. Whether he was only practising, or whether he knew that the game was in a critical state, and that much depended upon his play, he was the same phlegmatic, unmoved man – he was the Washington of cricketers. Neither he nor his brother were active, yet both were effective fieldsmen. Upon one occasion, on the Mary-le-bone grounds, I remember Tom going in first, and Lord Frederick Beauclerk giving him the first four balls, all of an excellent length. First four or last four made no difference to Tom – he was always the same cool, collected fellow. Every ball he dropped down just before his bat. Off went his lordship's white hat – dash upon the ground (his constant action when disappointed) – calling him at the same time 'a confounded old beast'. – 'I doan't care what ee zays,' said Tom, when one close by asked if he had heard Lord Frederick call him 'an old beast'. No, no; Tom was not the man to be flustered.

About a couple of years after Walker had been with us, he began the system of throwing instead of bowling, now so much the fashion. At that time it was esteemed foul play, and so it was decided by a council of the Hambledon Club which was called for the purpose. The first I recollect seeing revive the custom was Wills, a Sussex man.[1] I am decidedly of opinion, that if it be not stopped altogether, the character of the game will become changed. I should hope that such powerful and efficient members of the Mary-le-bone Club as Mr Ward, &c., will determine, not only to discountenance, but wholly and finally to suppress it; and instead, to foster and give every encouragement to genuine, bona fide bowlers – men with a fine delivery.

I never thought much of Tom's bowling; indeed the bowling of that time was so super-eminent that he was not looked upon as a bowler – even for a change. He afterwards, however, greatly improved; and what with his thorough knowledge of the game, his crafty manner (for he was one of the most fox-headed fellows I ever saw), and his quickness in seizing every advantage, he was of considerable service to his party, but he never was a first-rate bowler. He was a right- and Harry a left-handed batter, and both were valuable men. They came from Thursley, near Hindhead; they and their father were farmers, and their land lay near to the Devil's Punch-bowl.

[1] Mr J. Willes. E.V.L.

The next in succession will be John Wells, the Beldhams, Harris, and Freemantle.

Shortly after the Walkers had joined us, John Wells became a member of the Hambledon Club. John lived at Farnham, in Surrey, and was, if I recollect, a baker by trade. He was a short, thick, well-set man; in make like a cob-horse, proportionately strong, active, and laborious. As a bowler he had a very good delivery; he was also a good general field, and a steady batter – in short, an excellent 'servant of all work'; and, like those misused Gibeonites ('hewers of wood and drawers of water'), he was never spared when a wear-and-tear post was to be occupied. In cricket, as in the graver pursuits in life, the willing workman is ever spurred; he may perform labours of supererogation, and his assiduity meets at best with 'mouth honour': let him, however, but relax his muscles – let him but shorten his career to the speed of his fellows, and he instantly sinks below them in the estimation of his employers. Whether in this case the feeling arise from envy or not, it is hard to decide; assuredly, however, in very many instances, the mill-horse-grinder in the track of duty is acknowledged with greeting, while extra merit 'goes out sighing'. John Wells possessed all the requisites for making a thoroughly useful cricketer; and, in his general deportment, he was endowed with those qualities which render man useful to society as well as happy in himself. He was a creature of a transparent and unflawed integrity – plain, simple, and candid; uncompromising, yet courteous; civil and deferential, yet no cringer. He always went by the title of 'Honest John Wells', and as long as I knew him he never forfeited the character he had gained. Little more need be added respecting his merits as a player, for he must be fresh in the memory of all who have been accustomed to see the best playing; suffice to say that, in addition to his level merits as a general cricketer, he was esteemed to possess an excellent judgement of the game, and in questions that were frequently mooted his opinion would be appealed to.

The Beldhams, George and William, come next in succession, brothers, and both farmers. They also, with Wells, came from Farnham. George was what would be called a fine player; a good batter, and generally competent to fill the different posts in the game; but, as he attended the club a few times only during my stay in it, I am unable to discriminate or speak pointedly to his merits. Upon turning, however, to his brother William, we come to the finest batter of his own, or perhaps of any age. William Beldham was a close-set, active man, standing about five feet eight inches and a half. He had light-coloured hair, a fair complexion, and handsome as well as intelligent features. We used to call him 'Silver Billy'. No one within my recollection could stop a ball better, or make more brilliant hits all over the ground. Wherever the ball was bowled, there she was hit away, and in the most severe, venomous style. Besides this, he was so remarkably safe a player; he was safer than the Bank, for no mortal ever thought of doubting Beldham's stability. He received his instructions from a gingerbread baker at Farnham, of the name of Harry Hall. I once played against Hall, and found him a very fair hand, yet nothing remarkable; he knew the principles of the game, yet, like many of inferior merit in performance, he made nevertheless an excellent tutor. He was a slow bowler, and a pretty good one. He had a peculiar habit of bringing his hand from behind his back immediately previous to his delivering the ball – a trick no doubt perplexing enough to an inexperienced batter. In his peripatetic lectures to the young students, Hall perpetually enforced the principle of keeping the *left* elbow well up (this charge was of course delivered to the *right*-handed hitters), and excellent instruction it was; for if you do keep that elbow well up, and your bat also upright (in stopping *a length ball*), you will not fail to keep the balls *down*; and, vice versa, lower your elbow, and your balls will infallibly mount when you strike them.

Beldham was quite a young man when he joined the Hambledon Club; and even in that stage of his playing I hardly ever saw a man with a finer command of his bat; but, with the instruction and advice of the old heads superadded, he rapidly attained to the extraordinary accomplishment of being the finest player that has appeared within the latitude of more than half a century. There can be no exception against his batting, or the severity of his hitting. He would get in at the balls, and hit them away in a gallant style; yet, in this single feat, I think I have known him excelled; but when he could cut them at the point of the bat he was in his glory; and upon my life, their speed was as the speed of thought. One of the most beautiful sights that can be imagined, and which would have delighted an artist, was to see him make himself up to hit a ball. It was the beau idéal of grace, animation, and concentrated energy. In this peculiar exhibition of elegance with vigour, the nearest approach to him, I think, was Lord Frederick Beauclerk. Upon one occasion at Mary-le-bone, I remember these two admirable batters being in together, and though Beldham was then verging towards his climacteric, yet both were excited to a competition, and the display of talent that was exhibited between them that day was the most interesting sight of its kind I ever witnessed. I should not forget, among his other excellences, to mention that Beldham was one of the best judges of a short run I ever knew; add to which, that he possessed a generally good knowledge of the game.

Hitherto I have spoken only of his batting. In this department alone, he had talent enough to make a dozen ordinary cricketers, but as a general fieldsman there were few better; he could take any post in the field, and do himself credit in it: latterly he usually chose the place of slip. But Beldham was a good change bowler too; he delivered his balls high, and they got up well. His pace was a moderate one, yet bordering upon the quick. His principal fault in this department was that he would often give a toss; taking him, however, as a change bowler, he was one of the best. He would very quickly discover what a hitter could do, and what he could not do, and arrange his bowling accordingly. Finally, although his balls were commonly to the length, he was much better calculated for a change than to be continued a considerable length of time.

One of the finest treats in cricketing that I remember, was to see this admirable man in, with the beautiful bowling of Harris.

Having finished with the best batter of his own, or, perhaps, of any age – Beldham – we proceed to the very best bowler; a bowler who, between any one and himself, comparison must fail. David Harris was, I believe, born, at all events he lived, at Odiham, in Hampshire; he was by trade a potter. He was a muscular, bony man, standing about five feet nine and a half inches. His features were not regularly handsome, but a remarkably kind and gentle expression amply compensated the defect of mere linear beauty. The fair qualities of his heart shone through his honest face, and I can call to mind no worthier, or, in the active sense of the word, not a more '*good* man' than David Harris. He was one of the rare species that link man to man in bonds of fellowship by good works; that inspire confidence, and prevent the structure of society from becoming disjointed, and, 'as it were, a bowing wall, or a tottering fence'. He was a man of so strict a principle, and such high honour, that I believe his moral character was never impeached. I never heard even a suspicion breathed against his integrity, and I knew him long and intimately. I do not mean that he was a *canter*. – Oh, no – no one thought of standing on guard and buttoning up his pockets in Harris's company. I never busied myself about his mode of faith, or the peculiarity of his creed; that was his own affair, not mine, or any other being's on earth; all I know is, that he was an '*honest man*', and the poet has assigned the rank of such a one in creation.

It would be difficult, perhaps impossible, to convey in writing an accurate idea of the grand effect of Harris's bowling; they only who have played against him can fully appreciate it. His attitude when preparing for his run previously to delivering the ball would have made a beautiful study for the sculptor. Phidias would certainly have taken him for a model. First of all, he stood erect like a soldier at drill; then, with a graceful curve of the arm, he raised the ball to his forehead, and drawing back his right foot, started off with his left. The calm look and general air of the man were uncommonly striking, and from this series of preparations he never deviated. I am sure that from this simple account of his manner, all my countrymen who were acquainted with his play will recall him to their minds. His mode of delivering the ball was very singular. He would bring it from under the arm by a twist, and nearly as high as his arm-pit, and with this action *push* it, as it were, from him. How it was the balls acquired the velocity they did by this mode of delivery I never could comprehend.

When first he joined the Hambledon Club, he was quite a raw countryman at cricket, and had very little to recommend him but his noble delivery. He was also very apt to give tosses. I have seen old Nyren scratch his head, and say – 'Harris would make the best bowler in England if he did not toss.' By continual practice, however, and following the advice of the old Hambledon players, he became as steady as could be wished; and in the prime of his playing very rarely indeed gave a toss, although his balls were pitched the full length. In bowling, he never stooped in the least in his delivery, but kept himself upright all the time. His balls were very little beholden to the ground when pitched; it was but a touch, and up again; and woe be to the man who did not get in to block them, for they had such a peculiar curl, that they would grind his fingers against the bat: many a time have I seen the blood drawn in this way from a batter who was not up to the trick; old Tom Walker was the only exception – I have before classed him among the bloodless animals.

Harris's bowling was the finest of all tests for a hitter, and hence the great beauty, as I observed before, of seeing Beldham in, with this man against him; for unless a batter were of the very first class, and accustomed to the best style of stopping, he could do little or nothing with Harris. If the thing had been possible, I should have liked to have seen such a player as Budd (fine hitter as he was) standing against him. My own opinion is that he could not have stopped the balls, and this will be a criterion, by which those who have seen some of that gentleman's brilliant hits may judge of the extraordinary merit of this man's bowling. He was considerably faster than Lambert, and so superior in style and finish that I can draw no comparison between them. Lord Frederick Beauclerk has been heard to say that Harris's bowling was one of the grandest things of the kind he had ever seen; but his lordship could not have known him in his prime; he never saw him play till after he had had many fits of the gout, and had become slow and feeble.

To Harris's fine bowling I attribute the great improvement that was made in hitting, and above all in stopping; for it was utterly impossible to remain at the crease, when the ball was tossed to a fine length; you were obliged to get in, or it would be about your hands, or the handle of your bat; and every player knows where its next place would be.

Some years after Harris had played with the Hambledon Club, he became so well acquainted with the science of the game of cricket that he could take a very great advantage in pitching the wickets. And not only would he pitch a good wicket for himself, but he would also consider those who had to bowl with him. The writer of this has often walked with him up to Windmill-Down at six o'clock in the morning of the day that a match was to be played, and has with pleasure noticed the pains he has taken in choosing the ground for his fellow-bowler as well as himself. The most eminent men in every walk of life have at all times been the most painstaking; – slabberdash work and indifference may accompany genius, and it does so too frequently; such geniuses, however, throw away more than half their chance. There are more brilliant talents in this world than people give the world credit for; and that their lustre does not exhibit to the best advantage, commonly depends upon the owners of them. Ill luck, and the preference that frequently attends industrious mediocrity, are the only anodynes that wounded self-love or indolence can administer to misapplied or unused ability. In his walk, Harris was a man of genius, and he let slip no opportunity to maintain his pre-eminence. Although unwilling to detract from the fame of old Lumpy, I must here observe upon the difference in these two men with regard to pitching their wickets. Lumpy would uniformly select a point where the ball was likely to shoot, that is, over the brow of a little hill; and when by this forethought and contrivance the old man would prove successful in bowling his men out, he would turn round to his party with a little grin of triumph; nothing gratified him like this reward of his knowingness. Lumpy, however, thought only of himself in choosing his ground; his fellow-bowler might take his chance; this was neither wise nor liberal. Harris, on the contrary, as I have already observed, considered his partner; and, in so doing, the main chance of the game. Unlike Lumpy, too, he would choose a rising ground to pitch the ball against, and who is well acquainted with the game of cricket will at once perceive the advantage that must arise from a wicket pitched in this way to such a tremendous bowler as Harris was. If I were urged to draw a comparison between these two great players, the greatest certainly in their department I ever saw, I could do it in no other way than the following: Lumpy's ball was always pitched to the length, but delivered lower than Harris's, and never got up so high; he was also slower than Harris, and lost his advantage by the way in which he persisted in pitching his wicket; yet I think he would bowl more wickets down than the other, for the latter never pitched his wicket with this end in view; almost all his balls, therefore, rose over the wicket; consequently, more players would be caught out from Harris than Lumpy, and not half the number of runs got from his bowling. I passed a very pleasant time with Harris when he came to my father's house at Hambledon, by invitation, after an illness, and for the benefit of the change of air. Being always his companion in his walks about the neighbourhood, I had full opportunity of observing the sweetness of his disposition; this, with his manly contempt of every action that bore the character of meanness, gained him the admiration of every cricketer in Hambledon.

In concluding my recollections of Harris, I had well nigh omitted to say something of his skill in the other departments of the game. The fact is, the extraordinary merit of his bowling would have thrown any other fair accomplishments he might possess into the shade; but, indeed, as a batter, I considered him rather an indifferent hand; I never recollect his getting more than ten runs, and those very rarely. Neither was his fielding remarkable. But he was game to the backbone, and never suffered a ball to pass him without putting his body in the way of it. If I recollect, he generally played slip.

The Freemantles. There were two of them, and, I believe, brothers. John and Andrew were their names. One was an acknowledged player long before the other began. I am now, however, speaking of Freemantle the bowler. He, with Andrew, came from some town between Winchester and Alresford. John was a stoutly made man; his standard about five feet ten inches. He delivered his ball high and well, and tolerably fast, yet he could not be ranked among the *fast* bowlers. The best compliment I can pay him is that he was reckoned very successful, and, moreover, that his being a member of the Hambledon Club was sufficient guarantee for his general ability, as those sound and experienced judges would never admit as member any man who did not possess some qualifications above the common level.

As a batter, John Freemantle would have been reckoned a good hand in any club. He would now and then get many runs; yet, withal, he could by no means be pronounced a *fine* batter. As a man, he bore a high character for straightforward, manly integrity; in short, he was a hearty John Bull, and flinched no more from doing his duty than he did from a ball in the field, and this he never did, however hard it might hit him.

Andrew was a shortish, well-set man, and a left-handed player. He was an uncommonly safe, as well as good hitter; and few wickets that I could name were more secure than Andrew's. He would often get long hands, and against the best bowling too; and when he had once warmed into his hitting, it was a deuced hard matter to get him out – an accident would frequently do the business. In his general style of batting he very much reminded me of Aylward, who has been spoken of some pages back. He usually played the long field, and was remarkably steady and safe in this department. But Andrew Freemantle could be depended upon, whatever he might undertake, whether in cricket or in his worldly dealings.

Upon one occasion when I had come up to London, I heard of a match being played in Lord's Ground, and of course made one of the spectators of my beloved amusement. Andrew Freemantle was in, and one of the new-fashioned bowlers, commonly called throwers, was bowling to him. His name was Wells,[1] and I believe he came out of Sussex. He was the first I had seen of the new school, after the Walkers had attempted to introduce the system in the Hambledon Club. Wells frequently pitched his balls to the off-side of the wicket to Freemantle's left-handed hitting, who got in before the wicket, and hit the thrower's bowling behind him. Now, had he missed the ball, and it had hit his leg, although before the wicket, he would not have been out, because it had been pitched at the outside of the off-stump. I mention this trifling circumstance to show the knowledge the latter had of the game.

Andrew Freemantle's fielding was very fair; his post was generally the long field. He, however, must be so well known to many of the Mary-le-bone men now living that I need enumerate no more of the peculiar characteristics of his playing.

Next comes that deservedly esteemed character John Small, son, and

[1] See note on page 97. E.V.L.

worthy successor, to the celebrated batter of the same name. He, as well as his father, was a native of Petersfield. Young Small was a very handsomely made man. For perfect symmetry of from, and well-knit, compact limbs and frame, his father was one of the finest models of a man I ever beheld; and the son was little inferior to him in any respect. Jack Small! my old club fellow! when the fresh and lusty May-tide of life sent the blood gamboling through our veins like a Spring runlet, we have had many a good bout together:

> But now my head is bald, John,
> And locks as white as snow, —

and yours have, doubtless, bleached under the cold hand of mayhap three score winters and more; but the churl has not yet touched the citadel. *My* heart is as sound as ever, and beats regular and true time to the tune of old and grateful thoughts for long friendships. You, I am sure, can echo this sentiment. You are a musician as well as a friend, and know the value of steadiness in both characters. I think we could give some of the young whipsters a little trouble even now. Like the old Knight of the Boar's Head, we might need the *legs* of these Harry Monmouths; but it is my opinion we could bother them yet, at a good stand to our post. They would find some trouble to bowl down our stumps. They say, Jack, you were born with a bat in your hand. I can believe the tale, for I am sure you inherited the craft from both father and mother. She, I think, took as much delight and interest in the game as he. Many's the time I have seen that worthy woman (every way deserving of so kind and excellent a husband) come galloping up the ground at a grand match, where he was to play (for, you know, she always accompanied him to those high solemnities); and no player even could show more interest in the progress of the game than she, and certainly no one, as was natural, felt so much pride in her husband's fine playing.

I do not remember, John, that you were much of a bowler; but I remember that you were everything else, and that your judgement of the game was equal to that of any man. Your style of hitting, to my mind, was of the very first quality; and I can name no one who possessed a more accurate judgement of a short run. By the by – is that account true which I have heard, that upon one occasion, at Mary-le-bone, you and Hammond went in first, when there were only forty runs to get to win the match; and that you made an agreement together to run whenever the ball passed the wicket-keeper: that you did this, and between you got the whole forty runs before you were out? I have been told this anecdote of you both, and, if true, it clearly shows, according to my opinion, that the judgement of the people who played against you must have been strangely at fault, or they might have prevented it; for had but the long-stop been well acquainted with the game, he would have put you out.

I always admired your fielding, Jack: I am not sure that your middle wicket (the post that your father occupied) was not as good as his – though, I dare say, you would not allow this. Certain am I that a better never was put at that post. And now, farewell, my old club-fellow.

Reader! in a few words (now he has left the room), I assure you that in every way he was as complete a chap as I ever knew – a genuine chip off the old block – an admirable player, and a highly honourable man. The legs at Mary-le-bone never produced the least change in him; but, on the contrary, he was thoroughly disgusted at some of the manoeuvres that took place there from time to time.

About the time that John Small had risen into the celebrity I have just been describing, his father and Nyren retired from the field. I cannot do better, in concluding these brief recollections, than enumerate the most eminent players in the Hambledon Club when it was in its glory.

David Harris,	Tom Walker,
John Wells,	____ Robinson,
____ Purchase,	Noah Mann,
William Beldham,	____ Scott,
John Small, Jun.	____ Taylor,
Harry Walker.	

No eleven in England could have had any chance with these men; and I think they might have beaten any two-and-twenty.

John Nyren, *Young Cricketer's Tutor*, edited by Charles Cowden Clarke (1833)

William Lillywhite and David Harris

[Lillywhite] Was born at his Grace the Duke of Richmond's, Goodwood, Sussex, on 13 June 1792, and is consequently in his fifty-fourth year. He stands five feet four inches in height, and weighs 11 stone 8 lb. By trade he is understood to have been for many years a brickmaker, but after he had taken his position as the first bowler of the day, somewhat unwisely, because he could not himself attend to it, he became the landlord of a public house in Preston Street, Brighton, in addition to his proprietorship of a cricket ground.

To these two events Lillywhite may assign his subsequent pecuniary misfortunes. Two years since he quitted these properties, protesting against what he conceived to be the unjust treatment of his landlord, and came up to London—

> . . . to seek his fortune,
> And begin the world afresh,

declaring that nothing should induce him to stand forth again in defence of his county's cause so long as that gentleman retained an interest in the ground upon which

> The fray was fought.

To this determination the little man has strictly adhered. Shortly after his arrival in London he applied to Mr J. H. Dark, the proprietor of Lord's, upon the subject of an engagement, and in a short time we found him one of the Ground.

The name of Lillywhite will ever remain amongst cricketers as that of one of the *three* men, who, in their time, have caused a complete revolution in the practice of the game in reference to bowling; the more so, as by the effectiveness of his style of delivery, although directly opposed to the then received and long-adopted principles, he succeeded in commanding the support of several of the leading patrons of cricket, and, ultimately, after various experimental tests in matches got up for the express purpose in obtaining the sanction of the Committee of the Mary-le-bone Club to its general introduction into their grand matches.

But Lillywhite was not alone in the field at this particular period, seeing that there was *our Jem* (Broadbridge), whose indulgence in the *overhand* delivery was occasionally carried to a far more violent extent than by himself. There were many, however, who were wont in those days to contend that Jem was not higher or more unfair in his delivery than Lilly, and backed up their assertion by adding that, if the latter were as *tall* as the former, the height and position of his hand would become more glaringly apparent, and that every umpire would declare his bowling to be unfair; for the delivery of the ball with the hand over was a no ball. But the law upon this point in those days was even more stringent than at present, because the line of demarcation when Lillywhite came forth, was *below* the *elbow*, and not as now, *not above* the *shoulder*. Fair or unfair, certain it is, that the *Nonpareil* of Sussex caused a thorough revolution not merely in bowling but in the mode of hitting. It may, in truth, be said, that his system paved the course for that which has followed the reception of Mr Mynn's fine lightning pace, namely, much *chance* hitting – brilliant as many of the hits are – instead of the play of *science*.

How different was the effect produced by the celebrated David Harris, who is said to have been the finest bowler that cricket has witnessed, even down to the termination of the season 1845.

William Denison, *Sketches of the Players* (1846)

The Throwing Problem

At the period of Lillywhite's appearance in the field, the author filled the position of sub-editor to a daily journal, and in that capacity devoted many hours of his time to the consideration, and columns of his paper to the discussion of the then and probable future operation and consequences of the new system. He was also the contributor on cricket matters to that old and estimable publication, the *Sporting Magazine*.

It was during this period that Mr G. Knight, an influential member of the Mary-le-bone Club, adopted the high delivery, and who, in consequence of the opposition that was raised to its introduction, formally brought the subject before the Committee of that aristocratic body. Not succeeding, however, he addressed three letters to the cricketing world through the medium of the *Magazine* in question, in whose pages the point underwent considerable discussion. These letters, the author is aware, were seen but by few of the noblemen, gentlemen, and in all probability, not by *one* even of the players, of 1845, and therefore, with a view of informing all upon the subject, and affording them an opportunity of learning how strong was the content in reference to the toleration of the style of bowling which that gentleman was anxious to have recognised by the Mary-le-bone Club – of which style Broadbridge and Lillywhite especially were the illustrators – he presents them, together with the experiment matches, to his readers. Indeed, without those documents, the memoir of Lillywhite would be imperfect.

During the season of 1827, Lillywhite's appearance in the field first created the commotion on the subject, and accordingly a match was played between Kent and Sussex, of which the following notice appeared in the November number of the *Sporting Magazine*:—

'The cricket season has closed with the match between Sussex and Kent, with Saunders and Searle given. Throwing was the order of the day, but, on the part of Kent, there appeared no thrower or bowler, except Mr George Knight. Searle, however, was tried, and luckily performed very well. It is in fielding that gentlemen ought to be superlatively excellent; and though some of the most splendid players of the day are of that class, it is grievous to know that the majority of gentlemen field badly; and for this reason, principally, that in practice their whole attention is devoted to batting, instead of being equally divided between that and fielding. None can excel in fielding that are not fond of it for its own sake. It is a singular circumstance that Lillywhite did not hit a wicket during the whole match, nor was the wicket at which he threw, hit by either of the bowlers on the other side.

'I must now make a few remarks on the system of throwing which has been acted on so much this season, and which Mr Knight and a few others wish permanently continued. At present you are aware it is not allowed by articles of cricket, and I have yet heard no sufficient reason for its introduction. It is agreed that the game is now generally too long; and, it is said, it would be curtailed by the throwing. This I do not admit. I think fewer runs would be obtained, but that the game after a time would be equally long. The fine lively scientific hitting would be lost. There would be comparatively no cutting to the point or slip; and no driving forward. I have bestowed much pains in learning the sentiments of not only performers but cricket spectators, and I venture to assert that nine-tenths of the cricket world are against the proposed alteration of the existing rule.

'The Mary-le-bone Club are looked up to as the legislators in cricket; their authority has never hitherto been disputed; and if they mean to preserve their power and influence, let them, like other wise law-givers, respect the feelings of their subjects. Introduce throwing, and three-fourths of the present lovers of cricket will cease to have an interest in the game. They will be unable to appreciate a style of play they have never learned; and with those advanced in years it will cease to revive recollections of their youthful days, and will produce nothing but disappointment and disgust. The County of Sussex, from throwing being allowed, has attained a celebrity it never before acquired; but even there, the feeling is decidedly against the system. Those who excel in throwing naturally wish the system success; and among these must be reckoned Mr Knight, a very powerful supporter; but he is too liberal, I trust, to force down the throats of the public what is nauseous and revolting merely because it happens to suit his palate; and I am sure his zeal, activity, science, and manliness, will ensure him a sufficient reputation as a cricket player, without resort being had to a system in which he may shine for a time, but where he may be eclipsed next year by many men who know nothing of the principle of cricket, who could never distinguish themselves in a legitimate way, but who may chance to discover a happy knack of throwing a ball. When throwing is once established, Broadbridge and others will show that they cannot be faced on hard ground without the most imminent peril. I despise danger as much as any man, and have no anxiety on my own account – though I confess it would not be pleasant to receive an injury in the month of May that would deprive me of all play for the remainder of the season – but there are many men to whom broken fingers, straight joints, etc., might prove of the most serious consequence.

'The All-England match was purely experimental, and not subject to the rules of cricket as far as concerned bowling. This the players understood, and they acted upon the understanding by playing the first two matches. I believe, Mr Editor, you concur with me in hoping that throwing will not be allowed: rather widen or heighten the wickets, which would induce freedom of play; or even, if necessary, admit the straight-armed bowling, allowing it to go as high as the shoulder, *so that the back of the hand be kept under when the ball is delivered*. But the best remedy that I can suggest is to begin the game at nine o'clock, instead of eleven or twelve, and the grandest matches would then be disposed of in two days, in fine weather. – I am, Sir, your most obedient servant,

A LOVER OF CRICKET.'

William Denison, *Sketches of the Players* (1846)

Alfred Mynn, Esq.

Was born at Twisden Lodge, Goudhurst, fifteen miles from Maidstone in Kent, on 19 January 1807, and is consequently now in his fortieth year.

Personally Mr Mynn is one of nature's finest specimens – he stands six feet one inch in height, and weighs 18 stone; sometimes a few pounds over and at others a few pounds below that standard, and is withal gifted with extraordinary activity. Strictly, the sketch of Mr Mynn ought not to appear in this collection; because it was intended to contain a memoir only of those who are recognized as professional players, and who are regularly paid for their assistance. But as Mr Mynn is one of the brilliant wonders of his day in the game, the author could scarcely have felt justified in sending this work to the world without having devoted a few of its pages to a gentleman who has been so great an instrument in the illustration of the science, and so important a feature in all our matches from the day of his advent.

Mr Mynn is the son of a gentleman farmer who for many years resided at Bearsted, near Maidstone. This farm Mr Mynn himself continued to occupy until last year, when circumstances compelled him to give it up.

For several years prior to Mr Mynn's debut at Lord's the author was in the habit of playing with and against him in Kent and Surrey, and quickly arrived at the conclusion that if Mr Mynn should ever make an appearance at Mary-le-bone, the Powers would covet his aid upon all occasions when it could be obtained. And so it proved. Not merely was he an excellent and powerful bat, but his bowling came upon the mass of the cricket public with startling effect. There was not anything like it either for extraordinary rapidity of pace with the uphand bowling, or accuracy of length and general steadiness. Ere the batsmen who did not know him could oftentimes get their bats down to play his bowling, the stumps were shivered, or the ball was in the hands of, or past, the 'long stop'. There had been no bowling, never any of the same character, for several years, which demanded that vast quickness of play requisite to make any stand against the giant bowler. Almost the only parties who could for some time do anything with him at Lord's were Mr Ward, Pilch, and Wenman. In the case of Mr Ward, the readiness with which he could adapt his play to the *pace*, is thus easily explained. In former years, when he was about to take part in a match where an unusually fast bowler was to be opposed to him, he would for several days previously select one of the most rapid bowlers at Lord's or elsewhere, and practise him at 18 or 19 yards' distance instead of the 22. He would calculate the assumed difference between the paces of the two men and mark out the length of ground for his practice accordingly; so, that when he came to face the actual opponent, his eye and hand were fully prepared for the difficulties he would otherwise have had to combat. It was by these and similar acts of foresight and almost interminable practice that Mr Ward, in his more active days, was enabled to make so invariable a good and effective stand in the numerous matches in which he was engaged. This end has in more recent times been gained by Mr Felix, the Hon. E. Grimston and some others of our best bats by practice at the *Catapulta*. To this practice may be attributed much of the excellence possessed by Mr Felix. Of course it is needless to point out that the great length of Mr Ward's reach, was not the least of his advantages. Hence it came to pass that that gentleman was one of the most successful opponents of Mr Mynn's bowling.

Mr Mynn's prodigious strength and stature, make the velocity with which he propels the ball his *natural* pace. And here it is that the folly of smaller men, who are of course very much more feeble in physical capability, has since *his* introduction into the public matches, become so glaringly apparent. Ere *he* came out, the majority of bowlers had made Lillywhite's 'high delivery' and pace their main object of attainment; but no sooner was it seen that the rapid speed of Mr Mynn's bowling carried havoc that with one consent, as it were, all 'put on the steam', and flattered themselves they were rivalling the subject of their envy. What has been the result? Why, that whilst a man who had confined himself to that which was his natural pace, and therefore having the ball within his control, had been in the habit, if anything of a bowler, of delivering, generally speaking, *at* the wicket; he now by his *over* bowling rarely *approached* the stumps, except by chance, and likewise tended to hazard the match by his liberal contribution of 'wide balls'. It is an egregious error to suppose that every bowler has an equal facility of applying the same set of muscles when in play, with the certainty of achieving that object for the accomplishment of which by another, his envious or emulous feeling has been aroused. The mere act of delivering the ball *before*, or of retaining it an instant *after* the hand has arrived at a given point, will make all the difference. That act, that variance, will either make or mar. Then, the peculiarity of position of the left foot, or the movement of the hand or wrist, at the *instant of delivery*, are matters whereon separately or collectively will depend the ultimate achievement of a particular end in respect to bowling; and unless a man should come forth with equal strength and weight, equal stature, and moreover with precisely the same delivery, and having had as much practice, he may rely upon it that he will never approach the excellence of Alfred Mynn. For some time after Mr Mynn had come out, his bowling was occasionally distinguished by wildness, a vice which he has long since overcome by practice, and a better exercise of judgement: and the result is that whilst in his earlier days, *speed* would appear to have been his first aim of attainment, and hence the 'wide balls', in the last few years his bowling has been constantly *at* or near the wicket, but at a lessened pace, and of course with fewer 'wides'. Nevertheless he is still the fastest of our public bowlers.

As a batsman it has already been stated that Mr Mynn ranks in the highest walk. He is signalized too for possessing one of the most even dispositions that man has ever been gifted with. Rarely has it occurred that his temper could be ruffled; and at cricket, his natural good humour has never been known to have been cast aside. His countenance bespeaks equanimity of temperament, and an inclination to pass through life without a single angry indication, or without offering an offence to his fellow-man. Gratitude for a kindness displayed towards him is a leading feature in his character, and one of the greatest sources of delight to his mind is to give utterance to his thanks, for the attention paid to him by Mr Ward and others of the leading patrons of the game some years since, when he was for several months placed on a bed of sickness, in consequence of the severity of a series of blows received in a match at Leicester, upon his right knee and leg during a long innings. To the futile attempts of other bowlers to rival the *pace* of Mr Mynn is to be attributed the enormous increase in the number of wide balls. There are occasions when the best bowlers may give a wide, but in 19 cases out of 20, with them it will be an accident. With by far the largest majority, however, the same result has its origin in *over* bowling. The parties deliver beyond their natural powers; control of the ball is thus lost, and a wide is the consequence. The bowling from this fact assumes the character of recklessness. These individuals do not appear to copy Mr Mynn in any one feature, except so far as his *pace* is concerned. Were they carefully to watch his bowling, they would discover that he has much manoeuvre in his system, and for this simple reason, that, bowling *within* his power, rapid as is the speed, he has in most cases the command of the ball.

William Denison, *Sketches of the Players* (1846)

William Clark

Was born at Nottingham on 24 December 1798, and is now, therefore, in his forty-eighth year. He stands five feet nine inches in height, whilst in weight he is 13 stone and 11 lb. Clark has for some years been a licensed victualler. He kept the celebrated Trent Bridge Cricket Ground, about a mile out of the town of Nottingham, and has long been known in the matches played in all the Northern and Midland districts of England, as a cricketer of no mean capabilities. Of late years, however, he has become distinguished, and, it may with truth be added, notorious, as about the most awkward bowler with whom a batsman has to deal in the present age. For many years the paces of bowling were in the majority of cases slow, and what may be denominated middle speed. For instance, in the former, T. Walker and Lumpy may be named as the demonstrators; and in the latter, we may name David Harris, and come down to the times of Howard, etc.; but Mr Osbaldeston, and Brown of Brighton, afterwards launched forth as fast ripping bowlers. These, and one or two others were, in the upper classes of the game, almost the only exceptions to the then most general system of bowling which for some time was constantly designated as a good, middle-pace, and the high home and easy. Amongst the leading illustrators of this peculiar style of pace may be mentioned, Lord F. Beauclerk, Mr Budd, and Lambert. In the course of years, however, that which had obtained the designation just referred to, assumed a different character by means of a *round*, instead of an *underhand* method of delivery. The immediate effects of this change in the system of propulsion of the ball from the hand of the bowler were, first, to produce a *twisting* or *working* in the action of the ball as it left the ground after its pitch; and, secondly, where the ground itself was in good order to accomplish a *quicker* and a higher rise, added to a *cutting* operation in the pace notwithstanding the fact, that upon the ball quitting the hand, that pace was precisely the same as the *underhanded*. Whatever difficulty there was then in playing a ball of the former character, it arose simply and alone from the effects of the *round* delivery, and not from any increase in its pace. Matthews and Ashby afterwards appeared, but in their cases, the delivery which previously had been a little round, became raised above the elbow. The elevation of the hand appears to have produced so many good effects, as to have obtained a sufficiency of approbation amongst the Committee of the Mary-le-bone Club to induce that body to alter the rule, so as that such a delivery should be admitted. With many bowlers the delivery was with a *straight* arm. This continued until the season of 1827 when Lillywhite made his appearance at Lord's, and with him the delivery was up to the shoulder, and a *leetle* more occasionally; (what followed upon the *debut* and the subsequent recognition of the little man and his style, will be found in his own sketch). Thus matters went on, almost every person having the least pretension as a bowler, and hundreds who did not possess one single qualification, getting up his hand and bowling over, until some time about 1835 or 1836, when Mr Alfred Mynn was introduced at Lord's, and then another revolution in the delivery ensued. Almost every body now, especially amateurs, put on the steam, and endeavoured to bowl as fast as this new light. It was then, and it is even so now, not an uncommon sight to behold a little man of nine or fewer stones in weight, trying to propel the ball with the same speed as did Mr Mynn of eighteen stone, and the result, as was to be anticipated, has been that the bowling has become in the majority of cases, distinguished for its wildness and almost total want of steadiness.

It is, therefore, with the greater satisfaction, that the present opportunity is seized to call attention to the peculiarities and effects of the style of bowling which has been adopted by the subject of this memoir; and it is done with the hope that others beside that individual and the author of these pages, will have sufficient courage to practise its pace, despite the derision and attempts at ridicule with which a considerable portion of the cricketing world are disposed to visit it. If the only result it should accomplish without gaining the general infusion of slow bowling into our matches, were to induce an abandonment of the random, reckless, and wild bowling – bowling at a pace beyond a man's actual physical strength – and the substitution of a pace concurrent with the powers of the respective bowlers, and hence the almost certain direction *at* the wicket, if no other end were achieved, still, a vast benefit would have been obtained for the interests and well-doing of the game.

Clark's delivery approaches to what Lambert's was, ere he had adopted the straight-armed round bowling, about midway between the height of the elbow and the strict underhand, accompanied by a singular peculiarity of action with the hand and wrist just as the ball is about to be discharged. The effect of this is, if the ground be not in bad order and not heavy, that the ball pitching to the leg stump, or a few inches wide of it, gets up quickly and with a twist that in a majority of cases, if not played, will carry it to the two off, or the off stump alone. This and the slowness of the pace, are the two main characteristics of Clark's bowling. But he does not fail to exercise his head and judgement, and, therefore, as will be readily conjectured he manoeuvres with his adversary. He pitches up, or drops short, he tosses the ball higher so as that the batsman may fancy he is going to have a home pitch, when in truth, he finds that it alights just at the proper length, and so beats him and takes his wicket, or he delivers it about the usual height from the ground. At another time, the pitch is unusually short, well to the leg, and then the batsman makes up his mind that he shall administer severe punishment; when lo, the other is in most cases beaten by the ugly twist, and if his stumps be not disturbed, or he has not put up the ball, he congratulates himself on his escape with an exclamation of 'What stuff! I ought to have hit that to the d—l! What extraordinary stuff it is!' and resolves that, should such an opportunity offer again, he will not miss it. The chance is quickly given, because Clark having observed the difficulty his opponent had been placed in by the preceding ball, calculates that at the second one, of the same character, he may increase that difficulty, and obtain his wicket, either by causing him to give a catch, or by bowling, or having him stumped out. All the players, particularly those who have the more recently come out, ridicule slow bowling as *stuff*, and talk largely before they go in, of what they will do with it – how they will hit it here, cut it there, and drive it forward – but what have they done against it when? And there are others too, who, though they have been much longer in the field, are nevertheless, totally unable to deal with it in a general way, with anything at all approaching to a reasonable certainty. As a proof of this assertion, let the reader refer to the account of the matches in the last two years at Canterbury, between Kent and England. In both of these, Clark, of Nottingham, bowled. All the best of our players completely *muffed* their batting, in the former season especially, as will be guessed by the following detail of their efforts: Pilch scored 3 and 13; E. Swann, Esq., o and o; Howard, Esq., 10 and 5; Dorrinton, 11 and 6; A. Mynn, Esq., 1 and 4; Wenman, 2 and o; Hillyer, 2 and 6; F. Fredericks, Esq., o and o.

It is not pretended that the followers of the game in the present day could not cope with *slow* bowling, but that none of them have had prac- tice at it, and hence their difficulty when opposed to it. But there are two grounds probably why it may take some years ere it be again brought into more general use: first, the want of that moral courage which it is neces- sary to bring forth on the part of the individual who may think proper to adopt the pace as a bowler, to combat the jeers and ridicule which parties are disposed to cast at it; and next, the existing desire there is amongst batsmen to have the excitement of the lightning speed, from which occasionally a splendid hit is accomplished. Moreover, it really would appear from the great anxiety there is on the part of the batsmen to practise the *rapid* bowling rather than the *slow*, that they are afraid of having their powers of patience and capabilities of defence put too frequently to the test. The author, in the course of the last season, took the trouble to note in many of the matches where either Clark or himself were engaged, that there was a very large preponderance in their favour, in reference to the number of balls that would have taken the wicket unless they had been played as compared with those of the fast bowlers having a similar direction. Thus it must be clear that the demand upon the practice of defence was much greater against the *slow* than against the *fast*; in other words, that one of the finest branches of the science was more constantly being called into action by the former than by the latter. But there are many difficulties to be surmounted ere a batsman, however skilled, can successfully oppose a well-pitched, well-delivered, well-working, and, at length, quick getting up slow ball. First, from the want of being accustomed to it, he is deceived by the pace; then he expects, if the delivery be a high one, that the ball is coming well up to him, although it alights at the proper stop; then, he does not anticipate that the pace can carry any effective or deceptive twist with it, and still less does he look for the ball not only twisting a great deal, but rising with considerable velocity to a difficult height to play with safety. But it is necessary, to obtain these results, that the ground should be lively; for if it be wet (as was the case last season) the probability is, that the ball will neither get up nor work. Hence it becomes easy to punish; and therefore it has occasionally happened that a batsman has fetched a long score off it. One of the main grounds upon which the author has so strongly, during the last three years, urged the wisdom of a more general introduction of slow bowling, has been not simply that, if good, it is most effective, but that its success may induce many of those who now *overbowl* themselves, and rarely approach the wicket except by chance, to draw in the speed of their delivery, so as that they may bowl with the ball perfectly under their command. It is manifestly a mistake for a bowler of from 9 to 13 stone, to think that he can propel his ball with as much speed as Mr Mynn, who, for many years, has carried a weight ranging from 17½ to 19¼ stone. Moreover, Mr Mynn not only has the extra power afforded by his natural activity and weight; but his height, six feet one inch, contributes in no small degree to constitute the pace he had adopted, his *proper* and *legitimate* pace. Let not the younger cricketer attempt the very fast bowling, unless he be gifted with those capabilities by the hand of nature which entitle him to assume it. He may depend upon our assurance, that at least 19 out of 20 will fail to become good bowlers if they are *above the pace*. Let him take Hillyer and Lillywhite as models of the slower bowling, unless he be a tall, large, and powerful man. It would indeed be a difficult task to select a more excellent fast style than that of Sir Frederick Bathurst, who, beyond dispute, is the best amateur bowler of the day. To revert to Clark, having personally a strong feeling in favour of slow bowling, the author would urge that the style of the subject of this memoir, and his pace could be most beneficially followed; and he hopes, ere another year shall have passed, to meet with a large accession of converts to his opinion. All that is required to accomplish such an effect, is, that the approaching season may be free from that excessive wetness which, to a certain extent, marred most of the matches in 1845. There was scarcely a contest wherein the *slow* bowling was introduced, which was not spoiled by the rain.

Clark's average for the last three summers was this: In 1843 he played 7 matches; he bowled 36 wickets, giving an average of 5 per match, with 1 over.

In 1844, he played 4 matches, in which he bowled 15 wickets, had 19 caught from him, obtained 13 wickets in one match, and having taken 34 wickets in all, made an average of 8 and 2 over per match.

In 1845 he played in 12 matches, had 18 innings, scored 61 in one hand, the like number in one match, and in all 261, giving an average of 14½ per innings. He bowled in these matches 57, had 49 caught off him, took in all 106 wickets, producing an average of 8¾ per match.

As a batsman Clark is far from an inferior man; but he does not rank in the first class.

William Denison, *Sketches of the Players* (1846)

The Birth of Lord's

Many who are not familiar with cricket believe that the name Lord's has some connection with the peerage:[1] nothing could be further from the truth. The name comes from Thomas Lord, the pivot round whom the formation of the Marylebone Club turned. Lord was born at Thirsk, in Yorkshire, on 23 November 1755, and his father, who was a substantial yeoman of Roman Catholic stock, had his lands sequestrated when he espoused the Stuart cause in the rising of 1745, so that he had to work as a labourer on the very farm that once belonged to him. The Lord family moved south to Diss, in Norfolk, where Thomas Lord was brought up, and from here, on reaching manhood, he migrated to London and found employment at the White Conduit Club as a bowler and sort of general attendant.

This club, only a few of whose scores are extant, deserves always to be remembered affectionately by cricketers as 'the acorn that blossomed into the gigantic oak known as the Marylebone Club'.[2] Formed in 1782, it was an offshoot of a West End convivial club called the 'Je-ne-sais-quoi', some of whose members took to frequenting the White Conduit House and playing their matches in the adjoining fields near Islington.

In 1786 the members were tiring of this site, and the Earl of Winchilsea,[3] a great patron of cricket, and Charles Lennox, later fourth Duke of Richmond, offered to Lord their guarantee against loss if he would start a new private ground. White Conduit played several matches at Marylebone in 1787, but it seems almost certain that at the end of the season the old club was merged into the newly formed Marylebone Cricket Club. The MCC had been born.

Lord, being assured of support, quickly got to work, with the result that in May 1787 he opened his first ground on what is now Dorset

[1] In a recent conversation Mr H. Douglas Bessemer told me that when his nephew Gordon Johnston – a prisoner in Italian hands – was elected a member of the MCC in 1942 Johnston's relatives were able to send him a message through the Vatican. In case, however, the Italian authorities should attach a sinister meaning to the letters 'MCC' the message just stated that he had been elected to Lord's. The Italian interpreter at his camp, apparently unaware of the existence of the well-known institution at St John's Wood, concluded that one of the prisoners had been raised to the peerage. From that moment Johnston was treated with great respect, and was allowed many concessions, much to his own and to his fellow-prisoners' advantage.
[2] A. D. Taylor, *Annals of Lord's and History of the M.C.C.* (Arrowsmith, 1963).
[3] Lord Winchilsea, the ninth Earl (1752–1826), may be considered the founder of the MCC – 'the urbane and loyal Winchilsea', as Lord Frederick Beauclerk called him.

Square, on the Portman Estate. In the Portman Estate Office is a map of 1780 which shows the site of the field of seven acres which Lord secured for his ground. It was at the time leased to one Samuel Adams: whether Lord obtained a sub-lease from him or a new lease cannot be said, as the Portman Estate records all went to salvage during the Second German War.[1]

The first great match at Dorset Square was on 31 May and 1 June 1787, when Middlesex beat Essex by 93 runs in a game played for 200 guineas, and the earliest recorded MCC match was against the White Conduit Club on 27 June 1788, the MCC winning by 83 runs. The first thing Lord did was to put a fence round the ground, thereby ensuring privacy for the Club. It is possible also that no gate money was charged at Islington, and Lord instituted an entrance-fee of sixpence to the public. Lord's quickly became popular, and the matches were well attended,[2] but during its early existence the MCC played very few games. However, all went well with the ground until 1810,[3] when the last game was played on 17 August of that year, the Old (over thirty-eight) beating the Young by 90 runs.

In that year whatever lease there was apparently ended, and the site was let on building leases, with ground rents of over £600 a year, its value during the twenty-one years' tenancy of Lord having reached a figure far beyond his resources.

Lord had foreseen that he would have to leave his original ground, so as early as 15 October 1808, he rented two fields – the Brick Field and the Great Field, at North Bank, on the St John's Wood Estate – for a term of eighty years, free of land-tax and tithe, at £54 a year. The new ground was ready in 1809, and therefore for two seasons Lord had two

[1] In J. Stockdale's plan of London (1797) the ground is shown as 'Prince of Wales's Cricket Ground'. The Rate Books of St Marylebone indicate that Lord was lessee of the Allsop Arms in 1785, which suggests that he acquired the ground adjoining at the same time. However, it was not ready for play until two years later. The Allsop Arms (now called Allsop House) today stands on the corner on the opposite side of Upper Gloucester Place. Moon's garage occupies the site where the inn stood. There is a tradition that the players used to change in the old inn.

[2] 'Colonel Greville had his pocket picked on Monday last at Lord's ground of cash to the amount of £30. The pickpockets were so daring on Monday evening in the vicinity of Lord's Cricket Ground that they actually took the umbrellas of men and women by force, and even their watches and purses, threatening to stab those who made resistance. They were in gangs of between twenty to thirty, and behaved in a manner the most audacious.' – Extract from the Press, 1802.

[3] An interesting and important event took place on 29 June 1799, when colours were presented to the Royal East India Volunteers.

grounds on his hands, the St John's Wood CC using the new enclosure. This club was afterwards incorporated in the MCC.

The new Lord's was officially taken over on 8 May 1811, the turf having been removed from the original ground in Dorset Square, so that 'the noblemen and Gentlemen of the MCC' should be able 'to play on the same footing as before'. The move was not popular with many of the members of the MCC, and the Club did not play a single match there in 1811 or 1812 – and only three during the following year.

In that year another move became necessary, as Parliament had decreed that the Regent's Canal should be cut through the centre of the ground. The Eyre family, on whose estate the second ground was situated, were willing to grant Lord another plot, which enabled the Club to make its headquarters on the site it has ever since occupied. And so Lord once again transferred his turf to his third ground (at a rent of £100), in time for the opening of the 1814 season. He was now a person of some importance in the parish of Marylebone, for he was made a member of the Marylebone Vestry in 1807 and also conducted a wine-and-spirit business.

Four days before the ground was due to be opened there was a big explosion in the 'Cricket-ground public-house', which did considerable damage.[1] Despite this inauspicious start the third Lord's soon began to attract the public, and appropriately enough in the first great match recorded on the new site the MCC beat Hertfordshire by an innings and 27 runs.

Although the ground was a success, Lord was apparently not altogether satisfied with the pecuniary results, and he obtained power from the Eyre Estate to develop the ground as a building site to enhance the value of the sixty-eight years remaining of the lease, and plans for building houses were actually drawn up which limited the playing area to 150 square yards. William Ward, a director of the Bank of England, and later MP for the City of London, saved the situation by buying Lord's interest in the ground for £5,000.

Lord's contact with the famous ground thus ceased in 1825, but he continued to live in the St John's Wood Road until 1830, when he retired

[1] 'A shocking incident occurred on Thursday at New Lord's Cricket-ground public-house, Marylebone Fields. The landlady of the house had occasion to use a small quantity of gunpowder, and whilst in the act of taking the same from a paper, containing a pound weight, a spark from the fire caught it, and it went off with a great explosion. The landlady, her sister, and four little girls were seriously burnt. The two former are in a dangerous way.' – Extract from the Press, 1814.

to West Meon, in Hampshire, where he died on 13 January 1832, aged seventy-six.

In 1835 Ward and his four daughters, who joined in the lease to bind any interest they had in the property, transferred it to J. H. Dark, who, on the advice of Benjamin Aislabie, gave £2,000 for it, and undertook to pay an annuity of £425 to the Ward family during the unexpired term of the lease, which was for fifty-nine years from Midsummer Day 1834, at a yearly rental of £150. In his book *Recollections of Lord's and the Marylebone Cricket Club*[1] W. H. Slatter, whose family had a long connection with Lord's, says that when Dark first leased Lord's there were two ponds, one in front of the centre portion of the present Mound Stand, and the other at the west end of the ground. From time to time these ponds were filled with brick rubbish and gradually disappeared to some extent, but for years the wickets and outfield were very rough. Dark himself lived in a house near the present members' luncheon-room.

Among the early MCC members there is no more striking personality than the Rev. Lord Frederick Beauclerk, DD. He was born in 1773, and in 1787 his father became fifth Duke of St Albans, succeeding his cousin the fourth Duke. Both these Dukes were grandsons of His Majesty King Charles II and the pretty, witty actress Nell Gwyn. Of royal lineage – albeit with a bar sinister – and son of a duke, Lord Frederick was an aristocrat in an age when a deference amounting almost to obeisance was paid to persons of exalted rank, and in course of time he became an autocrat at Lord's. As player and captain he strode the cricket field a dominant figure, and he was equally dominant in the pavilion in the affairs of the Club.

As to his ability as a cricketer, there can be no dispute: he was regarded as the finest all-round amateur of his day. Some thought E. H. Budd a better bowler, but as a batsman Lord Frederick was the former's superior, his play being more scientific, in the then more orthodox style of the professionals, and he never gave his wicket away. He made eight centuries on the first Lord's – a large number in those early days. His highest score in cricket was 170 for the Homerton Club against Montpelier in 1806. He kept up his form well beyond middle age, scoring, in 1824, 99 for the Bs against England, and in 1827, when fifty-four, playing an innings of 78 against W. Ashby, slow right-hand, the best bowler of the day. This score is reminiscent of W. G. Grace's 74 in his

[1] Published privately in 1914.

last Gentlemen v. Players match, at the Oval in 1906, when he was fifty-eight. What the famous Doctor was to a later generation, so was Lord Frederick to his generation.

As to Lord Frederick's merits as a man, he must be judged in the light of the times in which he was born and in which his early life was spent. Anyone who reads the correspondence of that incomparable letter-writer Horace Walpole can see how widespread was gambling in the eighteenth century. At Almack's and White's thousands were won and lost at cards or dice in a night. Nothing was too absurd on which to have a bet. One instance will suffice. Writing in 1756 to Sir Horace Mann, Walpole says, 'Mr Lord Rockingham and my nephew Lord Orford have made a match of five hundred pounds, between five turkeys and five geese, to run from Norwich to London.' It was not to be expected that cricket would be immune from the gambling fever.

In earlier days cricket had been regarded as a game confined to the lower classes, but when men of quality began playing it in increasing numbers matches were arranged for stakes up to a thousand guineas, and there was much betting on the result. At any rate in a cricket match a backer had a longer run for his money than a throw of the dice provided, and as the match proceeded there was the opportunity both for hedging and for side-bets. Lord Frederick was one of the greatest single-wicket players of his day, and it is not surprising that in such an age he sought to turn his cricketing prowess to monetary gain. He frankly stated that he expected to make £600 a season by playing matches for stakes. It must be admitted that matches were sometimes sold. There are whispers that have come down through the years that Lord Frederick was a party to such roguery, and though he did things which would not be tolerated today, there is no evidence of it. One can imagine that when a crucial catch was dropped or a batsman failed to score a disgruntled backer said unpleasant things, and, like all dictators, Lord Frederick had his enemies. When he died in 1850 *The Times* gave no obituary notice, and the *Annual Register* dismissed the event in four lines, from which we learn that he died in Grosvenor Street.

An account of his prowess appears in *Celebrities I have known*,[1] by Lord William Lennox, son of the Duke of Richmond, who was so prominent in forming the MCC. This was the Duke who fought a famous duel with the Duke of York, grazing his head with a bullet, after which he was

---

[1] Four vols; London, 1876–77.

posted to Edinburgh, where he spent much of his time playing cricket with the soldiers, which in those days was considered a great condescension for an officer. Lord William Lennox, with his brother George, had been playing in a cricket match in Goodwood Park, for Boxgrove against Bersted, and as the match reached its end he described the following scene:

A party sallied forth from the house, headed by my father, including Lord Winchelsea, Lord Frederick Beauclerk, Sir Horace Mann, General Bligh, the Honourable Henry and John Tufton, and Richard Leigh. They had quitted the dining-room after imbibing a fair quantity of port wine, leaving instructions with the butler that clean glasses, devilled biscuits, and a magnum of 'beeswing' should be ready on their return from the cricket field . . .

'How stands the match, youngsters?' said Lord Frederick . . .

'Oh, we've beat them by twenty runs,' I responded.

'I suppose you Westminster fellows are in pretty good form.'

Of course we answered 'Yes.'

'Look here,' he added, 'I'll put you to the test . . . if you get me out I'll tip you a guinea.'

We agreed, upon which he doffed his coat, borrowed a bat from Lillywhite, our umpire, and stood manfully up at his wicket . . . Undoubtedly Lord Frederick was the first gentleman cricketer of his day, for although he could not equal David Harris in bowling, surpass Tom Walker in batting, or Hammond in wicket-keeping, he united in his own person all those three great points in the game to such a considerable degree as to be pronounced the Crichton of cricket. My brother and myself soon found that we might as well have endeavoured to bowl down the Monument as Lord Frederick's wicket, and we were in despair that we should never see the golden reward, when fortunately . . . he was caught out, bowled by myself.

'Well bowled, well caught,' he exclaimed, 'there's a guinea apiece for you, you have earned it fairly.'

Lord William adds:

Lord Frederick was one of the best bowlers of his day at Cambridge . . . His bowling, though extremely slow, was very effective; knowing exactly where to pitch the ball, he so delivered it as to cause a quick and abrupt rise. At the period I write of [Lord William was born in 1799] the members of the Marylebone Cricket Club always appeared in their sky blue club dress.

There is something very pleasant about this picture of Lord Frederick, as there is something pathetic about the last picture of him, sitting in his brougham at Lord's, with a nurse beside him, watching the cricket and surveying a scene where for so long he reigned supreme.

Before his last illness, and when his playing days were over, he had his regular seat just inside the wicket of the pavilion, where he sat with cigar in mouth and his little white snappish dog, who barked everyone in and out. Woe betide the hound that ventures today to put even half a nose inside Lord's!

A contemporary of Lord Frederick was E. H. Budd, who was born in 1785. He made his first appearance at Lord's in 1802, and his last for the MCC against Marlborough College, at Marlborough, fifty years later. He was a very hard hitter, and once hit a ball out of the original Lord's in Dorset Square. For this feat Lord had offered a reward of £20, which Budd announced he would distribute among the players, but Lord refused to pay. Budd was also a magnificent fieldsman and a bowler of pace – and a great all-round sportsman.

The honour of the first century on the present Lord's belongs to him – 105 for his eleven against Osbaldeston's in 1816. Budd played with a bat weighing three pounds, which is to be seen in the pavilion today.

William Ward, who 'saved' the ground in the twenties, was probably the most powerful batsman of his day, and his 278 for the Club against Norfolk in 1820 held the record at Lord's for over a hundred years.[1]

So long an innings was an almost unheard-of feat in those early days, but perhaps what is more interesting is the fact that Ward's bat weighed no less than *four* pounds, and that it was used by him for *fifty* years! Many years later Albert Trott ruined his batting by trying to carry pavilions with a three-pound bat like that of Budd's, so Mr Ward was evidently no mean weight-lifter!

Closely associated with Lord Frederick was George Osbaldeston, who played his first match on the original Lord's in 1808. He was invariably referred to as 'the Squire', and Sir Theodore Cook, editor of *The Field*,

---

[1] Ward's record broken by P. Holmes, of Yorkshire, against Middlesex in 1925, with 315 not out. This was beaten by J. B. Hobbs for Surrey v. Middlesex in 1926, with 316 not out, a record in turn eclipsed by Graham Gooch's 333 for England v. India in 1990.

in his Introduction to the Squire's autobiography,[1] recounts the following story. Two old friends met, and *A* mentioned the old Squire. *B*: 'What old Squire?' *A*: 'George Osbaldeston, of course.' *B*: 'What is he Squire of?' *A*: 'Why, he's Squire of England!'

The Squire was the son of George Osbaldeston, of Hutton Bushall, Yorkshire, by Jane, only daughter of Sir Thomas Head, Bart., and was born in Wimpole Street on 26 December 1787. His father was a son of the Rev. John Wickens, Rector of Petworth, who assumed the name of Osbaldeston on his wife Philadelphia, in 1770, inheriting half the estates of Fountayne Osbaldeston, MP for Scarborough. The Squire was educated at Eton and Brasenose College, Oxford, and left without taking a degree. Master of the Quorn from 1817 to 1821, and again from 1823 to 1828, with the famous Tom Sebright as his huntsman, he was later Master of the Pytchley and the Atherstone. There was no finer man to hounds or over a steeplechase course. He was also a great shot – he once killed ninety-eight pheasants in a hundred shots – as well as being an expert fisherman, and was pretty handy with his fists, promoting many a fight. A small man, about five feet six inches in height, he was, however, of great strength, with a tremendous chest, and weighed 11 stone. He had charming manners, and was very good-humoured and gay, and 'never spoke harshly or in an unkind way of any human being'. A great gambler, he is said to have lost £200,000 on the Turf, while he played whist for very high stakes, both on the tricks and on the rubber. In 1831, at the age of forty-four, he made a wager that he would ride two hundred miles in ten hours, and won with an hour and eighteen minutes to spare, using a horse for every four miles.

In 1800 the Squire won a bet of 200 guineas from Lord George Bentinck, but Bentinck, on paying the bet, let slip from his lips, 'This is robbery.' 'This will not stop here,' said Osbaldeston, and a challenge to duel followed, which took place at Wormwood Scrubs. Two versions are given of this encounter – one that Osbaldeston fired in the air, the other that a ball went through Bentinck's hat, missing his brain by two inches.

All Osbaldeston's friends were firm in their opinion that the Squire would never claim the recovery of a dishonest bet, and a reconciliation with Lord George was later effected.

As a cricketer Osbaldeston, though a splendid hard-hitting batsman, was best known as a bowler, said to be the fastest who had yet appeared,

[1] *Squire Osbaldeston: his Autobiography*, edited by E. D. Cuming (Lane, 1926).

and in conjunction with William Lambert he was ready to challenge any other pair in England. He challenged for a match of fifty guineas Lord Frederick Beauclerk and T. C. Howard, to decide who were the stronger pair. Just before the match Osbaldeston was taken ill, and suggested a postponement. 'No! Play or forfeit!' said Lord Frederick. 'I won't forfeit. Lambert shall play you both, and if he wins have the money,' was Osbaldeston's reply. Lord Frederick argued that such a match was nonsense, but Osbaldeston held his ground, and said, 'If you don't play we shall claim the stakes.' In the result Lambert made 56 in the first innings and 24 in the second – total 80. He dismissed Lord Frederick and Howard for 24 and 44 – total 66 – and so won by 14 runs. Lambert, however, showed great guile. Lord Frederick had an irascible temperament, and, wides not counting, Lambert bowled them to him till he lost his temper, and then bowled him with a straight one. Lord Frederick was not too magnanimous, and took a revenge that does not redound to his credit. In a moment of pique Osbaldeston removed his name from the list of members at Lord's. Later in life he came to live at 2 Grove Road, St John's Wood, and sought re-election. Lord Frederick prevented his readmission as a member by his determined opposition, though both Budd and Ward pleaded for his reinstatement.

Sir Pelham Warner, *Lord's, 1789–1945* (1946)

Brighter Cricket

The Aborigines were the greatest exponents of brighter cricket in the history of the game. Although their methods were unorthodox, unlike contemporary cricket they did not rely upon electronic gadgetry for artificial effect, but devised their own special methods. Upon taking the field, they normally put the birds to flight with three rousing cheers and a strident whoop of encouragement for their opposition. Cricketing costume had not yet achieved the drab purity of modern fashion, but even by Victorian standards the Aborigines sported more colour than any team. Even more striking was their ensemble of possum skin and lyre-bird feathers worn during exhibitions of native skills. This was the same costume which they had worn in Sydney on the occasion of their farewell appearance, for which the feathers cost five pounds. Perhaps it appealed to those who hankered after the romantic life of the carefree savage. One spectator who saw them at the Oval believed that 'with a piece of fur wrapped round their loins and a sort of fur cap on their heads, they walked with a proud, elastic step that contrasted strangely with their former gait'. Another onlooker expressed his emotions in dogged verse:

> Arrayed in skin of kangaroo,
>   And deck'd with lanky feather,
> How well you fling the fragile spear
>   Along the Surrey heather.

In his old age, Frank Gerald recounted something of his youthful excitement as he watched five of the Aboriginal matches. Gerald's uncle had just returned from the Victorian gold-fields, sufficiently affluent to take his schoolboy nephew to see the opening game at the Oval. They travelled in a wagonette, supplied with a large hamper and liquid refreshments. As in all the matches which he saw, the Aborigines 'gave a good entertainment and the game was never slow'. They ran barefooted between the wickets, and in their enthusiasm they were 'heard as well as seen. They tore up and down the pitch, screaming and shouting native backchat.'

Gerald recalled that it was usual at the luncheon adjournment for the Aborigines to mix freely with the spectators, who supplied them liberally with 'cakes, biscuits and sweets and sometimes a drink out of a flask'. However, he noted that the management maintained strict control and beverages were limited to dilute sherry or tea. But Gerald's most vivid memory was of the first adjournment at the Oval. Perhaps his uncle deserves to go down to posterity as the initiator of Australian barracking at an English cricket ground. At the interval, his colonial uncle 'gave a loud "coo-ee!" and the players came running over to us. Then he talked to them in their own "patter" and soon they were jabbering round the wagonette like monkeys.'

Other expatriate Australians in England were also drawn to see their fellow countrymen. Mrs Mary Alsop drove her two children in their brougham to the Derby ground on 3 September to see the Aborigines lose their match: 'they did not play very well,' she observed with disappointment. Samuel Winter, from Murndal station, western Victoria, was at Lord's ground in June to watch the Aborigines play the MCC.

Advertisements for their matches are vintage Victoriana. Rochdale readers were enticed by the dual attractions of 'these coloured handlers of the willow' and the presence of the Healey Hall Brass Band to celebrate the first match played on the new ground behind the Bowling Green Inn. For sixpence admittance the spectator on the third day of the Trent Bridge match could listen to the Nottingham Sax-Tuba Band while watching cricket from 11 a.m. until 4 p.m. and thereafter witness the following 'Australian and English sports': 1. 100 yards flat races; 2. Running high jump; 3. Standing high jump; 4. 150 yards hurdle race; 5. vaulting with poles; 6. Throwing the cricket ball; 7. 100 yards backwards; 8. Water bucket race; 9. Throwing the boomerangs, and spears, and kangaroo rats, by the Blacks; 10. Lawrence's feat with the bat and ball; 11. Dick-a-Dick dodging the cricket ball.

At these combined athletic and weapon-hurling exhibitions the Aborigines displayed considerable versatility, although some were specialists at certain feats. The most impressive group activity was a mock battle, involving six or more men. At Nottingham three Aborigines standing some 80 metres distant from three other spearmen were 'completely hedged in' by accurately thrown spears; the effect was made more dramatic by war-whoops. At the Oval, J. G. Wood estimated their distance apart as 75 to 85 metres, and he noted that on most occasions the aim was so deadly that unless the recipient had dodged aside he would have been struck by the spear. These spears and the wooden spear-throwers which propelled them were traditional weapons of the Western District people. The spears measured some two metres in length, the shaft consisting of hard wood, with a tip of reed about 30 centimetres long. Lieutenant-General Pitt-Rivers was attracted to the Oval by these spear-throwing exhibitions. A Crimean War officer and a student of the history of warfare, he was preparing his influential essays on the evolution of technology. He watched closely as spears were cast 100 metres with the assistance of wooden spear-throwers, but he could not vouch for their accuracy. However, at Rochdale throws were definitely on target. It was stated that Dick-a-Dick hurled a spear for 130 metres at the Bootle ground.

John Mulvaney and Rex Harcourt, Cricket Walkabout (1967)

5

England v. Australia

It does not matter how strong the sides may be; to the English and the Australians, there is simply nothing in cricket which matters more than a series for the Ashes and nothing which better demonstrates how cricketers can lock horns with unbridled passion yet retain both respect and affection when the battle is done. It is partly so because of the long tradition, partly because there are blood ties between the two countries. They were close enough in the early days for Australia's first Test captain, Billy Murdoch, to have been talked by his old friend W. G. Grace into representing England later. Five men in all played Test cricket for both countries.

These days the world has become so small that the England team often has several players born overseas. It excites greatest controversy when the land in question is Australia, and there was Australian indignation, in 1993, that one Martin McCague, born to British parents in Larne before they emigrated whilst he was a child, should have been picked to hurl the new ball at their own fair-dinkum Aussies; but it had to be tempered a little when it was pointed out that Michael Slater, who won his first cap against England at Old Trafford, was the son of a well-known Lancashire league cricketer, a fair-dinkum Lancastrian.

It posed the question whether a player who learns his cricket in one country should be allowed to play for another; and whether such a man ever cares quite so much for the land he is representing if he has changed his nationality simply to make a living playing cricket. Well, Tony Greig, once memorably described as 'not an Englishman through and through', was born in South Africa of a Scottish father, played for England and settled in Australia. No one played with much greater passion for England than he did, especially against Australia. The tradition motivates them all.

Le Roi Est Mort . . .

I called out to a very small boy in the village here this evening (24 August) as he was slogging a ball up the street, 'Hello, Bradman!' He replied, 'I'm not Bradman, I'm 'Utton!' I apologized instantly.

Hugh Hunter to *The Times* (26 August 1938)

[On 23 August Hutton's 364 against Australia at the Oval had broken the previous Test match record of 334 by Bradman.]

If It Had Happened Otherwise . . .

One of the most famous close finishes in Test history took place at Old Trafford in 1902. England went into this game one down and two to play. They had been desperately unlucky not to win the first Test after bowling Australia out for 36; the second game was rained off; Australia won the third; the only Test ever played at Bramall Lane, Sheffield. There were some curious battles about the selection of the England team. Against the wishes of MacLaren, the captain, the other selectors picked Fred Tate of Sussex in the twelve, and it appears that, in a fit of pique, MacLaren insisted on playing Tate on the day, although he had no great confidence in him. The whole match was to turn on Tate's performance and it is worth saying that he was, on form, a perfectly credible selection. He took 180 wickets that season and averaged 15 with the bat. Everything went wrong for him in the match. England were getting back into the match after trailing by 37 on the first innings, when MacLaren left Tate to field on the boundary for a single ball (he invariably fielded close in for Sussex) and Murphy's Law dictated that Darling should hit him a catch which he dropped. Then, when England went in to make 124 to win in the fourth innings, there was a collapse and Tate had to come in last with eight runs wanted. To add to his misery there was then a delay because of rain. When the game resumed Tate snicked a four and then was bowled. It wasn't really Tate's fault – several batsmen had failed – but it cannot be denied that if he had held the catch, or stopped the ball which bowled him, England would probably have won.

What if they had? The series would then have been one-all and England would presumably have won at the Oval, as they did in reality. The cricketer most likely to have profited from this would have been MacLaren. Including this match, he had captained England in the last thirteen Tests against Australia, winning only one of them. One wonders why he is to this day regarded as one of England's best captains – he won four matches out of twenty-two – but I suspect his reputation owes more than a little to Sir Neville Cardus's romantic appreciation of his style and panache. However, if he had won the last two Tests of that 1902 series and regained the Ashes, he would have been in high favour and would probably have been asked to lead the first-ever MCC touring side in 1903–04; he was available for that tour but declined to serve under Pelham Warner. England had a strong side that year and it would have been stronger still if MacLaren and not Warner had been in the line-up, for MacLaren generally batted successfully in Australia (he made 1,140 runs in 15 Tests there). We must assume that MacLaren would have brought home the Ashes and who would then have denied him the right to lead England when Australia came over in 1905? This was another series England were destined to win, Australia being a little less strong than in 1902, and at the end of it MacLaren's record as captain would have read something like: won 9, lost 10, drawn 8. This would not have been very impressive, but remember that in those days of no radio or television and few correspondents, English supporters took less account of what happened in Australia. MacLaren would have won two home series in succession, and what a hero he would have been! By contrast, what would have been the effect on Warner's career? If he had not been the winning captain in 1903–04, would he have taken the side out in 1911–12 and would he now be remembered as a great captain? The point of all this is that MacLaren would have remained the same sort of captain that he always was – opinionated and pessimistic by all accounts, but with flashes of inspiration. His (hypothetical) future would all have rested on those two balls at Old Trafford.

Let us now move forward in imagination twenty-four years, and across the Pennines to Headingley. In 1926 the Australians were expected to lose the Ashes and they did. The first Test was almost entirely washed out, the second a batting feast on a good wicket with no chance of a finish in three days. In the third Test Arthur Carr put Australia in on a wet wicket, the selectors having first omitted Parker, one of the best wet-wicket bowlers in England; nobody has ever explained why. Bardsley,

Australia's second-best batsman, was caught off Tate in the first over and Macartney, reckoned at that time the best batsman in the world, was dropped by Carr in the same over. He went on to score a hundred before lunch, Australia made 494, and the match was drawn. The fourth game was ruined by rain, Carr developing tonsilitis and missing most of it. When the team for the deciding fifth Test was picked the selectors dropped Carr, allegedly because he was not fully fit, though he later declared that he had been fit to play. Chapman took over, England won the match and Chapman led the next touring side, winning again and becoming the white hope of English cricket.

Supposing Carr had held that catch? For myself, I think the Leeds match would still have been drawn; the wicket was slow and easy by the third day and even if Australia had been skittled in the first innings it would probably not have happened twice. England would have had the best of the draw, though, and there would have been no reason to drop Carr. He would have been the hero who recovered the Ashes and the leading candidate for the captaincy in 1928–29, when he was only thirty-five and still batting well. Chapman, we would be saying now – who was he?

Consider now the first post-war England-Australia Test, at Brisbane in 1946. We think of that first post-war England side as a weak one but it was one of the strongest batting sides ever sent out. Hutton, Washbrook, Edrich and Compton were all in their prime, Hardstaff, Ikin and Yardley were adequate in support, and it is at least arguable that if the series had been going well, Hammond would have risen above his troubles and showed some of his pre-war form. In the event it all went wrong, but let us look at an incident in that Brisbane match. Australia won the toss on a good wicket and lost Morris and Barnes early. Bradman was still seeking his best form – he had been ill during much of the war – and he started shakily. When he had made 28 and the score was 74 for 2, he chopped at a ball which was caught by Ikin. It was far from clear whether he had played the ball into the ground before it travelled to Ikin; the umpire and Bradman thought he had but few other people on the ground agreed. Nowadays slow-motion replays would be available and, for good or ill, we would all know what had really happened. However, Bradman was not out and there is some evidence that the England side allowed the decision to affect their play. He went on to 187, Australia made 645, then the highest score ever made in a Test in Australia, and England, caught on a wet wicket, were put out twice for 313.

Suppose, now, that Bradman had been given out. Australia would have been 74 for 3 and English tails would have been up. The Australians were a formidable batting side but they could easily have been out for 300. England were, as I have said, a good batting side (the bowlers were a mixed bag) and they scored a lot of runs later in the series. They would probably have made 300 or more on a good Brisbane wicket, and Australia would have had to bat on that appalling sticky in the game's third innings. It is fair to say that Australians usually do worse than Englishmen on bad wickets and I cannot help thinking that England would have won the match. In reality, England collapsed against Ian Johnson in the first innings of the second Test at Sydney, but it is at least possible that they would have done much better if they had gone into that match one up rather than one down. Bradman might very well have decided to retire forthwith if he had failed twice in the first Test; but whether he had done so or not, England could well have won the series if the luck had favoured them. The likeliest result, however, would have been a narrow Australian win after a hard-fought series. If Bradman had played on after the (hypothetical) Brisbane defeat he would possibly have had no more than a moderate series. Would he then have retired? I think it likely. If that had happened Keith Miller would have been called upon for more batting and less bowling in 1948, and we might have seen him develop in the way we all hoped for when we saw him in wartime cricket, as a masterful attacking batsman. Hassett would have captained the 1948 side and I think they would have won, but by no means as overwhelmingly as they did in reality. The sides would have been pretty even and this would have made for better cricket. This is no criticism of Bradman but a tribute to a very great player.

England supporters will see the final incident as one of the saddest since the war. It occurred at Old Trafford in 1961. The details are all too familiar. After a typically Australian recovery, England were set to make 256 in the fourth innings, with time to get the runs but not too much time. Dexter played a magnificent innings of 76 and when he was out England were 150 for 2. They needed 106 at a run a minute and really should have won. May came in and, before he had scored, tried to sweep Benaud, the opposing captain, who was bowling leg-breaks round the wicket. If May had left his back leg in position he could not have been leg-before, but his defensive technique for once was faulty and he was bowled for 0. Close came in; he too tried to sweep and was caught, and England tumbled to defeat. Close has been generally blamed for the catastrophe but I feel that May's misjudgement was the crucial one. Even a few runs from him would have settled the issue, for England had a good batting side and would have been capable of putting together the last 30 or 40, even under pressure.

What was the result of this one misjudgement? The sides were one-all before this match and Australia held the Ashes, so this was the game which decided the fate of the Ashes for another two years. May had returned to the captaincy for the third Test and had won it. If he had won the fourth game also he would have come under strong pressure to carry on as captain and take the next team to Australia in 1962–63, to wipe out the memory of that disastrous defeat in 1958–59. I think he would have gone and that his record would be more impressive even than it is. He won 20 of the Tests in which he did lead England; if he had won that 1961 match, led against Pakistan in 1962 and toured Australia, he might have finished with a record of something like won 28, lost 10 (assuming he had not also toured India and Pakistan in 1961–62). The other results might have been that Cowdrey would have taken over a winning side and that Dexter's chance would have been delayed. This in turn could have meant that Dexter stayed in the game longer; I have always thought that the pressures of captaincy forced him into premature retirement. It is all speculative, for May did get out for 0 and did retire from Test cricket at the end of the series. The England selectors opted for new blood rather than choosing Cowdrey, who thus continued his erratic career in the captaincy which confused England's cricket throughout the 1960s (which was in no way Cowdrey's fault). It would all have been much simpler if May had gone on into 1963, Cowdrey had taken over for five years, and the succession had then passed to Dexter or to whoever had by then emerged as the next choice. England have generally been apt to look for new, miracle-working captains rather than stay with men who are doing the job but in this case it may well be that it all goes back to that one misjudged stroke.

Derek Lodge, *Figures on the Green* (1982)

My Ideal Team

My ideal cricket team is one which presents or sums up all of the game's resources of skill and variety of style, the sort of team of which you would say to somebody fresh to cricket and willing to love it: 'There, now watch these players, and in turn they will reveal to you the game's full and ripe content, with every department functioning: brilliance of strokeplay, solidity of defence, fast and slow bowling, swerve with new ball, spin with the old, expert and beautiful fielding everywhere – and everybody a character living and expressing himself by and through bat or ball.' An artistic team, an encyclopaedic team! – and England has never known one which as closely answered to this description as the one assembled at Birmingham in May 1902: A. C. MacLaren, C. B. Fry, K. S. Ranjitsinhji, F. S. Jackson, Tyldesley, Lilley, Hirst, G. L. Jessop, Braund, Lockwood, Rhodes. Could omnipotence improve on this XI as a Platonic ideal or representation of all the known parts and attributes of cricket, a perfect synthesis? The most majestic of batsmen is there, the most scientific batsman is there, the most magical of all batsmen is there. One of the most aristocratic batsmen in his outlook and manner is there, the Hon. F. S. Jackson, who was also a superb off-spinner. The most incisive stroke player of the period was there, J. T. Tyldesley himself. Lilley was a wicket-keeper who could truly be called an organized batsman. George Hirst, one of cricket's greatest all-round players, was also one of the greatest men Yorkshire has so far given to the world. There was Jessop, too, the most astonishing of all cricketers ever born, a scientific quick scorer, a whirlwind of strokes which revolved round a point of calm ruthlessly punitive judgement. There was Braund, a leg-spinner and a sound batsman, and also one of cricket's most lithe and remarkable slip fieldsmen. There was Lockwood, whom Ranjitsinhji maintained was the greatest of all fast bowlers in his experience. And, in last, was the legendary Rhodes, the finest slow left-hand bowler alive in 1902, excepting only Blythe of Kent, and already a batsman good enough secretly to say to himself 'one day I shall open an England innings', which he one day truly did, to the extent of sharing a first wicket partnership with Hobbs amounting to 323.

The England XI at Birmingham in 1902 was, I say, a kind of image or reflection of cricket's essential and finest attributes; every technical excellent was represented by a cricketer whom in his particular capacity God Himself would find it hard to improve upon; for each of them seemed the fully consummated technical exponent and natural apogee of his particular method.

In more recent years I have seen only one other England team which approached this Birmingham one; bear in mind I am not discussing these ideal XIs according to competitive values alone. England lost the rubber in 1902. I am putting forward combinations of cricketers which revealed the ripeness and variety of cricket at a given period, and revealed the ripeness and variety in a representational way fit to be laid up in heaven, so that after all flesh shall have returned to dust, the angels would be able to understand why, amongst games of the open air, cricket stood first for beauty, skill and the revelation of English character. And here is my contemporary XI to vie with the classic contingent of 1902: Hobbs, Sutcliffe, Hammond, A. P. F. Chapman, Hendren, D. R. Jardine, Geary, Tate, Larwood, J. C. White and Duckworth, a team which played at Melbourne in December 1928. It is not, on paper, as authoritative and convincing as the Birmingham XI; but I can think of no other that sets off to better advantage the qualities of English cricket of a later day. I am therefore tempted to throw in the England XIs at Lord's in 1930, and at the Oval in 1938: (1930) – Hobbs, Woolley, Hammond, Duleepsinhji, Hendren, A. P. F. Chapman, G. O. Allen, R. W. V. Robins, Tate, J. C. White and Duckworth; (1938) – Hutton, W. J. Edrich, Leyland, W. R. Hammond, Paynter, Compton, Hardstaff, Wood, Verity, K. Farnes and Bowes. Maybe these comparisons are odious, but they will illustrate my point; there are more things in the game of cricket than are dreamt of in the economy of the scorers.

A game, like anything else, loses in health and vitality when any part becomes greater, or is made to appear more prominent, than the whole. At the present time, 1955, it is possible to watch a first-class cricket match all day and see little bowling that is not quick or dependent on 'swing' or swerve. It is possible to watch batsmen all day and not see a cut or a full-shouldered straight drive. It is possible to go to a county ground a whole week and not see a really clever leg-spin bowler, unless you are a Kentish man. In the early decades of first-class cricket there was not much to admire aesthetically except the pendulum push forward of the bat alongside the left foot, to pace and off-spin. The game had not yet been subtilized and fertilized by the invention of the 'googly' and the development of leg-spin. Cricket was at its greatest between 1902 and

1930; for during these years every known department of play and skill was practised and brought to the point of fine individual art. Since 1946, decadence has set in, the decadence that occurs whenever specialism elaborates one particular trick or trait to the hurt of the balance of the whole. Until the other day there was hardly a fast bowler in England of unquestionable rank; there are still only one or two slow left-arm spinners. It is all 'swing' the ball 'that deviates from the seam' to use the phraseology of the hour. We hear of green wickets. What was the colour of the Old Trafford wicket in the 1900s, when Tyldesley one summer scored 3,000 runs, average nearly 60, with half his innings played on turf so peculiar in texture that small pebbles came to the surface?

I am not one of those who praise the past and neglect the joys of the present. Much in life nowadays is more happily adapted to human needs than ever before. In the realm of imagination progress is a word with no meaning; none the less it is fair and rational to say that in the technical distribution and ordering of artistic pleasure there has been a vast improvement since most middle-aged folk today were in their twenties. Orchestras play more correctly and musically than of yore. Taste in all directions has lost much of crudity. Books are better written in general than in the recent past. Acting in the theatre is less unnatural and spurious. The Vienna Opera in its palmiest days could not produce women singers as lovely to look at and as lovely to hear as the contemporary Seefried, della Casa, Jurinac, Grünig. I shall not be suspected, then, of the sentimental backward-glance that cannot appreciate quality under one's nose, if I confess that there are only two cricketers of today whom *I* would wish to see in, or could imagine surviving contrast amongst the company of, the immortals of the England XI at Birmingham in 1902. Their names are Compton and Evans. And how could we fit them in? – who throw out for them? MacLaren, Fry, 'Ranji', Jackson, even for Denis? *Who* could choose rightly and happily between Tyldesley and Compton? For functional reasons Compton could not take any of the places held by Braund, Hirst, Jessop, Lockwood and Rhodes. I am not sure, even, that MacLaren or any other England captain of the period would willingly agree to the substitution of Evans for Lilley as a safe experienced wicket-keeper and a really sound batsman into the bargain. If the reader asks why I select Compton from all present day cricketers as the only batsman we could conceivably squeeze into the Birmingham XI, at risk of injustice to a recognized immortal, my answer is, 'Try any other name of today,' and remember that we are dealing with an England team which, second to none, exhibited the multifarious attributes of the game, and enshrined cricket's technical genius fully and proportionately, every player a master in his own way, and an artist. Moreover, bear in mind that this XI was picked to win, if possible, a three-day Test match and to lose it at no cost to cricket's pride in spectacle, its gusto of enjoyment, and its scope for the free play of character. If anybody, properly jealous of individual performance of today or the latest hour, imagines that Tyson or Statham might adequately wear Lockwood's boots as fast bowler he will be chastened to learn that in 1902 Lockwood was not only England's greatest fast bowler but also in the same summer scored a century for the Players against the Gentlemen at Lord's.

It is of course vain if fascinating to compare in the abstract great players of different periods. The environment, technically and psycho-logically, changes; the tools of the game, as we have seen, change also. The modern sceptics argue that W. G. Grace was never called on to cope with the 'googly' or elaborate leg-spin. But he was able to cope with fast 'shooters' on rough pitches; in fact he was easy master of every trick of the bowler's trade known in his day. We must assume that once he had scrutinized the 'googly' he would have found the right answer. It is the fact, none the less, that batsmen of the so-called 'Golden Age' were on the whole called on to solve fewer problems of attack than those pre-sented nowadays in first-class cricket. Grace, Stoddart, Shrewsbury, MacLaren, Hayward and other 'Old Masters' needed only or mainly to deal with speed and off-spin on good wickets. Moreover, methods of defensive and offensive field-placing were not then as flexible and tacti-cal as now. No leg-traps for Ranji's glance; none for an off-spinner even on a turning jumping pitch. Seldom did off-spin bowlers attack from round the wicket. No swerve, or very little deliberate swerve, except from Hirst, who was perhaps a more dangerous bowler when he was bringing the ball back, left-hand, from leg-stump to off. No new ball until the end of the longest innings, unless, as John Gunn has said, 't'owd 'un coom in two'.

Extraordinary talent will in all circumstances find its way; a Hutton will assert his superiority over average ability in any period. But I am not sure that all the old-time dashing batsmen, trusting to long-lengthened hits at the pitch of the ball, would survive for long against ordinary new ball bowlers of today, such as Gladwin, Jackson, Shackleton. They lacked organized defences; they played the game more by faith than by reason – and faith is not certain to move an outswinger out of harm's way. Crick-

eters nowadays may be too theoretical: many of the swashbuckling amateur batsmen of the past lacked fundamental brainwork. Look at the
photos of them, in their pretty blazers. There is no speculation in their
eyes. When Richard Tyldesley saw them coming in to bat, after hours of
sweaty labour spent getting rid of the Meads and Hendrens and Whysalls
and Gunns, he would go to his captain and say: 'Let's have another bowl
at pavilion end, skipper. Coloured caps is comin' in.' The advent of the
'googly' was a death knell in the ears of rabid adherents of the left leg
forward method of batting, the majestic sweep to the pitch of the ball. A.
C. MacLaren and R. E. Foster both expressed apprehension upon the
influence of the new bowling and feared it would ruin 'style' and free play
to the offside. Several fine players, notably Rhodes, changed stance and
moved the right foot over towards the off-stump as a means of providing
a second, sometimes a first line, of defence against the last-second
gyration of the 'wrong 'un'. It is a mistake to suppose – and I make this
point again for the sake of emphasis – that all the master-batsmen
brought up in the Golden Age were at a loss to deal with the 'googly';
even a stylist as beautifully poised as R. H. Spooner scored happily
enough against the South African spell-binders. But Spooner, like Tyldesley, played a good deal from the back foot; both these swift scoring
batsmen were at bottom sound in defence. I spoke once to A. C. Mac-
Laren about J. T. Tyldesley. 'It is amazing,' I said, 'that he can keep it up
on all sorts of wickets, scoring thirty or forty an hour, taking risks.'
MacLaren replied, 'But Johnny is as sound as a rock to a good ball; he is
really a very correct player.' This view of the D'Artagnan of cricket was
not orthodox, but I could see the virtue of the exaggeration. George
Gunn also found the 'googly' an easily soluble problem. He simply
walked out to it and, as he says, 'played with tide'. 'There's a lot of
nonsense said about battin',' he has often told me, 'and really there's not
much to it. If it's a straight ball, no matter how fast, play it with straight
bat. If it turns from off, play it with break to on; if it turns from leg play it
with break t'other way. Hey, dear, batsmen have always made two serious
mistakes, always have made 'em as far as I know; and I began playin'
when Doctor Grace were still in game. First of all, they take too much
notice of state of wicket, pokin' and proddin'. Then – and I thinks this is
more serious still – they take too much notice of bowlin'.'

The influence of the 'googly' has not been at all to the bad. On the
contrary it has enriched technique all round; it has, so to say, added to
cricket's orchestration. It certainly helped to develop on-side strokes and

encouraged close study of direction and flight, making for the delayed stroke. (All great batsmen play the ball 'late'.) Besides, 'googly' bowling when practised by a master is in itself a pleasure to watch. To see a Grimmett at work, a Dooland, a Fleetwood-Smith, is stimulating to the imagination of all lovers and students of cricket; here are personal skill and guile in excelsis. 'Swing' bowling is different and boring to see because it is more or less a mechanical exploitation of tools of the game, the seam of the ball, the 'green' of the turf, and all the rest of the jargon. The great leg-spin and 'googly' bowlers were artists and so much in love with the work of their own prehensile fingers that they would bowl for the delight of observing their own handiwork, whether it was being hit or whether in the materialistic eyes of the scorers it was being 'successful'.

To what extent has 'googly' and swerve bowling been responsible for the decline (if any) of great stroke players? I saw nearly all the renowned batsmen of the 'Golden' or pre-'googly' age – MacLaren, Trumper, Ranjitsinhji, Fry, Tyldesley, Spooner, Palairet, Hayward, R. E. Foster, Jackson. I am not prepared to swear on oath that these players were vastly superior in range of strokes or more fascinating to watch than the following, all of whom had to tackle the new bowling, 'googly' and 'swing' at its best: Hobbs, Headley, Hammond, Woolley, Macartney, Donnelly, Merchant, Kippax, Bradman, Duleepsinhji, Compton, McCabe, Worrell, C. F. Walters, Harvey, not to mention Bakewell of Northamptonshire. Technique in cricket must alter when it alteration finds; it evolves by cut-and-thrust, check and checkmate. Now the batsman is on top, now the bowler. In the development of technical tricks of the trade, action and reaction are equal and opposite. When I was a boy off-theory was supposed to be spoiling the game. Today leg-theory is the bane. The genius of great players will lead the way out of every apparent technical cul-de-sac.

My own view is that cricket can be spoiled temporarily and rendered tedious only by a wrong mental approach on the part of players, spectators and press. If imaginative sport is demanded, with the exponents free to give full play to their natural gifts, the right atmosphere of inducement will be produced in consequence of that demand. If the rewards of competition are the *main* desire, victories in rubbers and county championships, then cricket will respond to materialistic stimuli and incitement. It is as simple as all that.

Neville Cardus, Close of Play (1956)

Jessop's Match

After almost eighty years, Jessop's Match still seems to retain a special sort of fabulous and glamorous reputation of its own . . . [but] now that I come to write about it I find myself faced with the fact that the first two days' play contained some incidents which tickle the memory but few to haunt it.

I am glad now that I watched Trumper starting off the match with a characteristic 42, for it was the only time I ever saw Trumper make double figures. But the latter end of the first day's play produced in me a good deal of lingering resentment and muffled snorting as Trumble persisted in a long and stubborn tail-ender's innings of 64 not out ('pottering about' in my view) and, along with Hopkins and Kelly, put on about 150 for the eighth and ninth wickets. The second morning belonged to Trumble too, as bowler this time, unchanged throughout England's first knock and taking 8 for 65. As a result England were left 141 behind, which was all pretty depressing, but we had a great stroke of luck when Australia batted again. Trumper had only made two when he went for a quick run, stumbled, fell flat halfway down the pitch and was run out. Then Lockwood put in a great spell of bowling and Australia were all out soon after the start of the third morning for 121 (Lockwood 5 for 45). So the second day was a great deal more eventful than the tedious first and I am sure I watched every ball with those hopes and fears which only the cricket-lover can appreciate. But it is no good pretending that I can still give an eye-witness account of all that happened. Some of those for-no-particular-reason incidents survive. I remember one immaculate cover-drive of Palairet's better than I remember any individual cover-drive of Hammond's or Hutton's. Above all, two first-slip catches by MacLaren. They were not difficult catches; they came straight into his hands. It was the manner with which he accepted them. He took the ball and tossed it, not over his head to recatch it, but away into outer space with a flick of the wrist in the most disdainful fashion. 'Take it away: it stinks.'

Trumble and Lockwood must in turn have demonstrated that, ever since the first day, the wicket had got worse and worse. After England's first innings total of 183 and Australia's second innings total of 121, how could we possibly be expected to make 263 to win? We couldn't, of course, but the impossibility needn't have been rubbed in to me so cruelly. That hateful Saunders [who had skittled the unfortunate Fred Tate in the previous Test] immediately came sailing in at the Vauxhall end, slinging destruction. MacLaren b. Saunders 2, Palairet b. Saunders 6, Tyldesley b. Saunders 0, Hayward c. Kelly b. Saunders 7. Jackson, at number five, was not out at lunchtime. Braund had joined him, but only for a very short time (c. Kelly b. Trumble 2).

During the lunch interval I noticed quite a number of disgruntled elderly members gathering up their belongings in the pavilion and departing home, unable to face the indignity of witnessing England's abasement. And I wonder what MacLaren had to say about what was served up to him for his mid-day meal.

So, then – Braund out but Jackson still there and appearing remarkably unruffled. And in came Jessop.

Jessop was a favourite subject for Craig's contemporary rivals as cricket poets. I recall two pleasing lines from an unidentified bard:

> At one end stocky Jessop crouched,
> The human catapult—

Crouched was an obvious description: 'the croucher' was a familiar nickname for Jessop owing to his stance at the wicket. 'Stocky' was descriptive of him too, though I think 'jaunty' would be nearer the mark. I knew, of course, all about his reputation as the biggest hitter in the game, but he had disappointed us in England's first innings (b. Trumble 13). Oh, well – perhaps he might treat us to a good slog or two before the inevitable and dismal defeat.

Again I must stick to my genuine and lasting recollections and impressions. It is obviously impossible to recall that Jessop innings in detail but there are certain features of it, and of its effect upon the crowd, that remain as clearly in my mind as though it all happened yesterday. To begin with, I was struck by Jessop's undaunted, almost it seemed heedless, approach – no 'desperate situation' about it. Jaunty. He was his own aggressive self from the start. Before long he took the triumphant Saunders in hand, to my especial delight, and hit him for two fours off successive balls to the long-on boundary. Darling immediately posted two fielders out there but Jessop ignored them and hit Saunders's next two deliveries between them or round them or through them as well. However despondent the crowd must have been during the morning, Jessop aroused them now to a state of wild exhilaration and Jackson must have been scoring steadily on his own. But I confess that the only thing I can remember about Jackson's invaluable innings is his getting caught and bowled by Trumble when he had made 49 and Jackson's exasperated thump with his bat on his pad as he turned to go.

Oh, damn and blast. Any faint gleam of hope of our getting those 263 runs vanished with Jackson into the pavilion. But the Australians had still another Yorkshireman to deal with. Confidence was the last thing Jessop seemed to require, but, had he needed it, George Hirst was the man to supply it – sturdy, defiant and the best all-rounder in the country in his day. (No one else had ever taken 200 wickets and made 2,000 runs in one season and they never will.) Sure enough, Hirst settled down while Jessop continued as before. Trumble was still on at the pavilion end. Still on? He was never off throughout the whole of England's two innings. Jessop hit him for six on to a canvas awning above part of the members' enclosure. The ball came back only to land on almost exactly the same spot immediately afterwards.

On they went, Hirst unmoveable, Jessop irrepressible. Presently the roars of the crowd subsided and gave way to an awesome, aspiring hush. They had roared Jessop to the verge of his century.

How well all cricket-lovers know that tremulous moment and, goodness me, how often have I experienced it myself, but never, never in my whole life has it meant to me what it meant then.

Hush. Jessop crouched. The bowler started his run. It was just as well for me that my heart was only fifteen years old. The bowler bowled. Bang. Uproar.

The conventional Londoner wore a hat in those days and the conventional hat he wore was a straw boater. As Jessop made that stroke dozens of straw boaters were sent sailing from the crowd like boomerangs. Unlike boomerangs they failed to return to the owners, but who cared?

Like all cricket devotees I have many, many times shared with all around me that infectious, 'breathless hush' tension as a batsman, however well set, however self-possessed, has to face up to the obligation of scoring that hundredth run. He brings it off and, amid the general enthusiasm, one feels a spasm of pleasurable secret relief and a glow of fraternal satisfaction in the case of a batsman one is particularly fond of. I know I was young and almost foolishly impressionable at the time but I have always treasured and still treasure that century of Jessop's above and apart from all the rest.

The frenzy gradually subsided; boaters were or were not recovered;

the crowd settled down. England still had a long way to go; but so long as Jessop and Hirst were there . . . Then, oh no, Jessop mistimed a hook-shot and was caught at fine leg. What a tragedy. But that seemed to settle it; that stupendous effort of 104 was sacrificed. We couldn't hope to win now, could we? Hirst was still battling away and scoring steadily but Lockwood didn't last long. Lilley did, though. Beyond all expectation Lilley stuck there with Hirst. The score crept up – 230, 240 – the whole Oval became almost as intent and intimidated as I was, hesitating to applaud too loudly for fear of inciting Hirst and Lilley to rashness.

Lilley got caught for 16 when the total had reached 248. Fifteen wanted and Rhodes came in to join his fellow-Yorkshireman for a last-wicket partnership which was to become a sort of historic addendum to Jessop's hundred, though the legend that Hirst greeted Rhodes with the pronouncement, 'We'll get 'em in singles', was later refuted by Rhodes himself. They got 'em steadily, a single here a couple there, until they had levelled up the match at 262.

That is the moment – or rather the marathon minute – which remains clearest of all in my memory. Duff was fielding at deep long-on to Trumble, who was bowling, as ever, from the pavilion end. An Australian from his seat in the stand a few rows behind me shouted, 'Never mind, Duff; you've won the Ashes.' I saw Duff turn his head with a quick resigned grin and return at once to attention. He of all the Australians in the field was required to be at attention. Trumble, as crafty a bowler as ever existed, presented Rhodes with a slow half-volley on the leg stump. How could any human batsman resist such a heaven-sent gift? 'Hurrah, here it is and here it goes' – wallop. And the ball would sail high into the outfield and, well within the range of possibility, into the safe hands of Duff. Not Rhodes. Not Yorkshire. Rhodes tapped the ball gently past square leg, ran the safe single and the match was won.

When by some means long forgotten I managed to arrive back home that evening, there was my father waiting to welcome me in the open doorway, his arms outstretched in mutual rejoicing. I felt a bit of a hero at having actually been there on Jessop's Day. I still do.

Ben Travers, *94 Declared* (1981)

On the Way

Life on the ship during the voyage out was not according to my expectations; I began it with some romantic ideas lingering in my mind since my boyhood about the talks and intimacy which would occur amongst a company of cricketers setting forth to play Australia. The team merged with the rest of the passengers until you scarcely knew where they were or which was which; Allen rightly encouraged his men temporarily to avoid cricket. The fun of the voyage was at times not easily to be marked off from the fun of a fashionable hotel on any evening at Folkestone after a day at the September festival. It became boring, and I gladly escaped from it. I even left the captain's table – not disrespectfully, I hope. The captain was charming and a marvel of tact. But the time arrived when I was ready either to laugh outright or become sarcastic at the efforts of the social climbers who each evening vied with one another to obtain the captain's recognition. The snobbishness on an ocean-going liner is appalling. I imagine that most captains in the service would like at times to leave the captain's table. But this is another digression.

When we reached the Red Sea, I decided to begin a diary; I did not keep it up, of course, for the simple reason that on a ship nothing often happens; Mark Twain achieved the perfect summary:

> Oct. 13, Got up, washed, went to bed.
>   "   14, "   "   "   "   "   "
>   "   15, "   "   "   "   "   "
>   and so on and so forth.

My own entries are a little fuller; here they are:

SEPTEMBER 25 ON THE *ORION*

'Passengers may sleep on deck in the vicinity of the forward lounge between midnight and 6.30 a.m.' – so runs, with much confidence, the notice that has today been given prominence in the various premises of the *Orion*. We are in the Red Sea as I write, and there is scarcely a soul on board, not including the ship's cat, who is capable of any form of sleep, either on deck or below the deck, in cabin or under the starry heavens; the Red Sea is at its hottest, its stickiest, its cruellest. There is no air in the world, except fetid breath from the desert; the *Orion* makes not a wisp of a breeze as she goes her patient course. The sun is merciless, and when we escape the chastisement of its fiery rods by going under awnings or inside the lounge or drawing-room or tavern or café, then we are suffocated, or, rather, put under some evil drug of the Orient. There is one place only where we can find momentary release from the torment – in the dining-room (only we don't want to dine), where the atmosphere is marvellously chilled. Here the temperature is 75 degrees, and as we enter it we feel as though we have gone into a refrigerator; we expect, even hope, to see frost and snow appearing over our bodies. When at last we reluctantly leave the dining-room and pass out through its swing doors, we go straight, without a second's break, into an oven.

I have never before dreamed that the world could become so hot, that people could endure such miseries, that nature could go its ways so indifferent to mortal needs. For three days the sun has hurled down on us the light and heat that destroys; for three days the sky has contained not a cloud, nothing but the pitiless blue of endless and indifferent space. And hour by hour the sea has grown hotter, so that at night, after the sun has gone down and a lovely silver horn of a moon has enchanted the sky, even then we have had no peace, for the waters hold the day's scorchings and throw them back. 'Passengers may sleep on deck' – may, indeed! I did not try; I kept to my cabin and hopefully manipulated the device that blows air upon you, risking sore throat, stiff neck, double pneumonia. Anything would be better and more merciful than to 'pass out' from Red Sea humidity, either by oozing away or by going mad and diving overboard with such despair that one hit the floor of the ocean and perished as much from concussion of the brain as from drowning.

The other evening, a quarter of an hour before dinner, I met Captain Howard on the staircase; the manager of the MCC team had only ten minutes ago changed into his dinner jacket. His collar was already a rag; Mr Gladstone, after four hours or so of eloquence, never more drastically reduced stiff linen to this state of shapeless wetness. From the foreheads of all of us waterfalls have descended, splashing and dashing like the cascades of Southey's poem. (Was it Southey? – it is still too hot to think here, though at last we are emerging from the Red Sea and a breeze is stirring, giving us a sense of resurrection of all the world from the dead.) At the first hint of this heaven-sent zephyr R. W. V. Robins stripped off his evening jacket and, regardless of dignity and braces, went to the promenade deck and, feeling the faintest suggestion of a wind, said to me: 'We seem to be cooling as we direct our course towards the Antarctic.' Robins has suffered much and has borne it all with humour and an Alfred Lester sort of fortitude.

Everything that science can do towards the defeat of the Red Sea is done on the *Orion*, but nature, as Mr Squeers said, is a 'rum 'un'. 'She's a lovely ship,' said Hammond, 'but I wish she – well had wings!' I tell of these hardships not out of a desire to present ourselves as martyrs and heroes but to console those we have left at home on the brink of an English winter. 'Lucky you!' they said as we departed from Southampton a fortnight ago; 'oh lucky, to be going into the sunshine, while we shiver in the east winds and hug our hot-water bottles!' At the moment of writing, there is scarcely an English man or woman on the boat who would not cheerfully give pounds and pounds sterling for one hour of Manchester's wettest rain and coldest cold. Happy days are probably waiting for us in Australia – we shall deserve them, for we have suffered in the Red Sea's cauldron. But such is human nature that while we were writhing and dissolving in the Red Sea, we persuaded ourselves that the Red Sea was really behaving with unusual moderation; then the moment we sniffed a wind of the Indian Ocean we agreed unanimously that the Red Sea had broken records in heat and life-destroying humidity, and we went about amongst ourselves distributing medals for patience, endurance, and philosophy, so to say. The probability is that we revealed ourselves as so many comfortable creatures of the temperate zone of the earth; it is said by the knowing ones of these parts that the more intelligent inhabitants of the Nubian Desert sometimes visit the Red Sea to enjoy its bracing climate – to them the Red Sea is the Skegness of the Tropics.

Pleasures there have been for us, of course; lazy days in the Mediterranean, when the sunshine has been friendly and the swimmers in the bathing-pool have splashed about, before stretching themselves luxuriously in the lovely slanting light of the late afternoon. Then the evenings. First the sunsets, and the peacefulness that comes over the ship before dinner; people have retired to dress, and the solitary watcher, leaning on the ship's side, has the sense for a moment that he is being divested of personal identity and absorbed into the deepening beauty of the hour of twilight over the ocean as the evening star appears. At night the dancing begins, and here again it is good to escape from the glitter and animation, to withdraw and watch from a point apart. Then it is possible to feel the pathos of contrast – the light and happy intimacy of life brought together for a moment by chance; and the surrounding and lasting immensity of the Indian Ocean. And while all the laughter of young people goes on, and the elders sit domestically in lounge and drawing-room enjoying familiar comforts, the ship moves on, a beautiful sensitive creature, with the flexibility of a canoe and the power and grandeur of an ocean-going liner; through the night it moves, throbbing with a poised life of its own, making a wake in the water delicate as a chain. At the moment we are well beyond Aden, a sun-cursed pile of brown rock, oleaginous, with the refuse kites flapping in the air – a place where the White Man's Burden, and the Black Man's Burden too, can be felt as a weariness to flesh and spirit. We are following the track of a monsoon, and the ship is rolling. In the middle of the night it is thrilling for the landsman to listen from his cabin to the surge outside, and to feel the whole of the boat's nervous system working; you can hear the heart of it. I have grown to love the ship and the quiet certainty of the men who control its strength, grace, and nobility.

Neville Cardus, *Australian Summer* (1937)

Bradman, Barnes and Brown

August 25, 1948: the first day of Bradman's last match at Lord's and my first and only chance, in the age before TV, to set eyes on the world's greatest batsman. And there I was, clutching my satchel with the sandwiches and the Tizer, and there was my friend Farrant, similarly equipped.

'Hello, Farrant,' I said, greeting him warmly.

'Hello, Norman,' he said. In those days public schoolboys didn't have first names, or if they did it was extremely bad form to refer to the fact.

We scurried along to the back of the queue which stretched away from the Grace Gates and right round the corner and almost to the car park.

And this was not a Test match either – merely the Australians v. the Gentlemen and the Australians weren't even fielding their strongest side: Morris and Toshack weren't playing, neither were Tallon and Bill Johnston.

But it *was* Bradman's last match at Lord's.

And it began to rain.

Farrant and I had barely taken our places in the free seats beside the Tavern, square on to the wicket, when one of those waddling, distended bladders relieved itself all over St John's Wood. I couldn't believe it.

'Farrant,' I said, 'it *can't* rain – not today!' And Farrant agreed with me. Nevertheless it was certainly raining and it continued, nerve-rackingly, to rain – not for very long, I suppose, though it seemed like hours – until at last the bladder gave a contented sigh, fastened its trouser buttons and hurried away. Whereupon the sun came out followed shortly afterwards by the umpires and, to our joy, the Gentlemen.

The Australians had won the toss and Bradman would bat today – though not immediately. First there appeared S. G. Barnes and W. A. Brown, themselves figures of wonder to me.

In those days all my heroes, except Compton and Edrich, belonged most firmly to the 1930s, probably because I had read about first-class cricket far more than I had watched it. It was the literature of the game that had hooked me long before I had seen it played. And in 1948 most of cricket's literature stopped at the beginning of the war.

Barnes, the post-war player, I knew about and grudgingly admired because he scored 234 against England on the 1946–47 tour Down Under. But it was Brown whom I watched with the greater awe as he made his way to the middle because he belonged to that Golden Age of the Thirties when all Test cricketers were ten feet tall and the sun shone every day.

(The first match I ever saw was also at Lord's in 1945: England v. Australia in a Victory Test match. Cyril Washbrook made a century that day and Bill Edrich scored 73. But the man I remember most vividly was Hammond, greatest of all England's heroes of the Golden Age and a man I had scarcely believed existed outside the pages of a cricket book. He came to the wicket, burly and belligerent, a dark blue cap surmounting that pleasantly ugly, froglike face and made 83 in hardly any time at all. I never saw him bat again but on that day he made me realize for the first time what an awesome thing a cover drive could be.)

Now, though, as the Gentlemen took the field there was no Hammond among them, for he had gone into retirement, but still there was his near-contemporary, Brown, and with him the younger Barnes, both of whom had engaged with England's former champion in many a titanic struggle. Another time it would have been thrill enough simply to watch these two bat, but not today. As in turn they took guard and prepared to face the bowling, Farrant and I fervently wished them gone. They were merely curtain-raisers, the cricketing equivalent of a juggling act on a variety bill, charged with warming up the audience before the star appeared. We wanted them out, one of them anyway and it didn't matter which.

They didn't keep us waiting long. Barnes went first, caught by Wilf Wooller for 19 off the bowling of a promising young Cambridge under-graduate named Trevor Bailey. An innings of 19 is not usually memor-able but this one was for the sheer ferocity of Barnes's square-cutting. I have never seen its like since. This was not what passes for square-cutting nowadays, with the bat striking behind the ball in what is more of a square drive. This was the real, classic thing, the bat coming down on top of the ball and smashing it to the boundary with a speed to baffle the eye and a force to break any hand misguided enough to get in its way.

But soon – too soon I think now with hindsight – Wooller held the catch and Barnes put his square-cut away for use another day and made his exit. There was a pause and then everyone in the Members' Stand stood up and so did we all, all of us in that packed ground, clapping till our palms were stinging red and continuing to stand and clap as the object of this veneration hurried to the wicket, tugging by way of acknow-ledgement at the peak of that weird, squat cap the Australians wear and walking briskly as if embarrassed by so much attention.

My first reaction was one of mild disappointment: he was smaller than I had expected, chunky but not tall. Hammond had seemed of appropriately heroic stature (probably a bit on the fat side, if the truth were told), big and imposing. Bradman, by contrast, looked almost slight and as he took guard and glanced around the field it was difficult to believe that such a man of such a build could have averaged 99.96 in all Test matches.

But when he started to bat . . . ah, what a transformation – not so much a smallish man as a giant of limited growth. I wish I could remember a particular shot he played, something as indelible as Barnes's square-cut, but I cannot. All I remember is that he seemed to have every shot I had ever heard of and played them all without favouritism like the father of an enormous family who is equally fond of each of his children and takes care to neglect none of them.

How could you set a field – how could you even set about bowling – to a man like that?

He didn't appear to recognize yorkers; to him they were half-volleys. Bouncers were simply long-hops to be hooked away with a roll of the wrists to the boundary behind square leg. Pitch short and he was immediately on the back foot cracking the ball through mid-wicket or the covers; toss it up and he was already three paces down the wicket, calmly deciding which section of the crowd would have the privilege of collecting this one.

They say that Bradman hardly ever raised the ball above the ground. Well, I can vouch for that. Eight Gentlemen had a bowl at him that day and if he hit a six off any of them I have no recollection of it. What I have in my mind is this image of the ball scorching across the grass as it came every time off the middle of the bat and as it went every time just where the fielder wasn't.

They also say – or rather *Wisden* says – that Brown, who scored 120, 'showed even more freedom than Bradman.' I don't remember that; indeed I hardly remember Brown at all except as a necessary figure at the non-striker's end. Elegant, yes, I believe he was that – graceful, too, and immensely competent. But essentially he was a foil, Horatio to Bradman's Hamlet.

'There are more things in heaven and earth, Horatio, than are dreamt of in *your* philosophy' and, crack, there went another drive that only Bradman could have played.

From the start we knew – Farrant and I – that he was never going to get out until he wanted to. Not much more than a week previously he had made a botch of his last Test innings, and positively ruined his overall average, by untypically allowing himself to be bowled for a duck by Eric Hollies. Therefore, if anything at all was certain in cricket it was that he would not make an equal mess of his last appearance at Lord's.

At the Oval against Hollies he had shown human frailty; today he was infallible and so when his 50 came and later his hundred they were attended by such an air of inevitability that we greeted them like confidently expected guests, with pleasure but no surprise.

Somewhere along the line he achieved another record to add to the multitude he already owned by becoming the only overseas player to score more than 2,000 runs on each of four tours of England. And a little after that he reached 150, and with a neat sense of timing decided to call it a day.

Freddie Brown was bowling to him – Freddie Brown who, throughout the Australian innings trundled with honest endeavour through 27 overs without achieving a single maiden – and perhaps Bradman took pity on him. In any event slowly and gently he lofted the ball into the air, so slowly and gently that it could have been deliberate, so slowly and gently that, whatever the batsman's motive, it was almost sadistic, an under-lining of the fact that the only man on the field that day who could get Bradman out was Bradman.

Martin Donnelly moved easily to the catch but well before he took it Bradman had removed his gloves, tucked his bat under his arm and begun walking back to the pavilion as briskly as he had left it.

Once again we all stood up and applauded and cheered, and for a long time after he had gone through the gate and up the steps and vanished for ever from our sight we were still clapping and cheering and Farrant beside me said: 'Gosh,' and I said nothing because suddenly I realized I was weeping.

Farrant said, accusingly: 'Norman, you're blubbing.'

I said: 'So are you, Farrant,' and so he was and so were most of the people around us. But they were all smiling, too, as if they couldn't quite work out which emotion had them in its grip.

Well, as we settled down and blew our noses and cleared our throats the game went on. Hassett, who had already shared a century stand with Bradman and eventually made 200 not out, was now joined by Keith Miller and these two put on another 100-odd for the fourth wicket. At close of play the Australians were 478 for three, but though I stayed to the end and watched every ball I have not the slightest recollection of either Hassett or Miller.

I just remembered that Bradman had come to Lord's for the last time and scored 150. And I had seen it.

Barry Norman, Quick Singles (1986)

The Typhoon Strikes

When we flew out of Brisbane on 2 December 1954, having just lost the first Test match to Australia by an innings and 154 runs, there was one irrepressible voice among many that were subdued. It belonged to God-frey Evans, who was as incorrigible in defeat as he was cheerful in victory. 'Not to worry,' he kept saying, 'we shall be there at the finish.' There was a tired, rather touchy smile from Len Hutton who, a few days before, had made the memorable mistake of inviting Australia to bat. None too soon the flight was called.

Two months later, to the very day, England retained the Ashes on the Adelaide Oval, and Evans made the winning hit. Looking back on it, this seems an even more remarkable transformation than it did at the time. From being a confident and united team at Brisbane, with one overwhelming victory in the bag, Australia were demoralized by speed. The first signs of this came in the second Test match, played on the Sydney Cricket Ground, in a finish of unbearable excitement. The rubber was saved by 38 runs, and by a display of fast bowling that was unmistakably heroic.

To start the story it is necessary to go back to Lord's some months before, when I watched Frank Tyson bowl for the first time. Although only twenty-four he was already bald. He was broad in the shoulder, but he had a stoop in his walk. He looked as much like a wrestler as a cricketer. Born in Bolton, he had been turned down by Lancashire when he went to Old Trafford for a trial. Northamptonshire were glad of him, and in this match at Lord's he impressed everyone with his speed, though not with a rather crude, slinging action. Bill Edrich, one of the great hookers of the day, was taken to hospital after being hit in the face hooking at Tyson. Edrich was back next day – hooking at Tyson. They had both made their point – Tyson that he was uncommonly quick and Edrich that he was uncommonly fearless.

When, in September, Tyson sailed for Australia with a copy of Wordsworth's poems under his arm (he was in the throes of reading for his degree at Durham University), he had fewer than 100 first-class wickets to his credit. No batsman likes searing pace, and it was because of this rather than any intrinsic ability that Tyson was chosen for the tour. The first match, against a Western Australia County XI, was at Bunbury – appropriately enough, so far as Tyson was concerned, on a rodeo ground. Frank was still 'unbroken', and he bowled so wildly that there were those who feared that he would be a liability to the side.

By the time of the first Test match he had been persuaded to cut several yards off his run in order to increase his control, and he was fortunate to have in Hutton a captain with a faith in speed. In the first Test match Tyson took 1 for 160 in 29 overs. Alec Bedser took 1 for 131 in 37 overs, and Brian Statham 2 for 123 in 34 overs. These three could not get out of Brisbane fast enough on the morning of Evans's jocularity.

Before the start of the second Test match a fortnight later, Tyson took six wickets against Victoria at Melbourne, on a pitch which carried the cracks of a jigsaw puzzle and on which the ball kept very low. On the evidence of this, and in spite of a grassy pitch to question his wisdom, Hutton confounded the cricket world by dropping Bedser before the start of the game. Bedser, with well over 200 Test match wickets in his great career, read of his omission when the team was posted on the dressing-room door. Not surprisingly the Press flew at Hutton for discarding a trusty servant, and by the end of the first day England had been dismissed for 154. The pitch was so green that not a spinner bowled: and although by the close of play Arthur Morris had been caught off Bailey at the start of Australia's innings, we went to bed that night feeling we knew better than Hutton and believing that Bedser should have played.

I shall pass quickly over the next three days of cricket. Australia had a permanent advantage; but England, by unyielding effort, never allowed them to develop it conclusively. From 100 for 2 at luncheon in their first innings, Australia were all out by the close for 228. From being 55 for 3 in their second innings, England recovered to make 296. With the ball Trevor Bailey showed the others where to bowl; with the bat Peter May and Colin Cowdrey added 116 in a partnership between Cambridge and Oxford, Quidnunc and Harlequin, bridegroom and best man, Charterhouse and Tonbridge, and Surrey and Kent. Colin was 'nowt but a boy', as George Duckworth used to say, and he had yet to become embroiled in the technicalities of batting.

On the fourth evening of the match Cowdrey was caught at mid-off, trying to lift Benaud for four. Before a large crowd and at a critical time he had been batting with May since before luncheon, and there was now only a quarter of an hour left before the merciful respite of a night's sleep. I remember Cowdrey saying that he thought the clock on Sydney's pinnacled pavilion had stopped in the final hour. Next morning Duckworth, with the team as baggage-master and major-domo, saw Colin in the team's hotel, returning to his room. 'Been to confessions?' he queried, with the candour for which he was known and loved. The point was made, the allusion accepted. Colin had not got himself out, but he had missed the chance of his first 100 against Australia, which he was to make a fortnight later.

Next morning May reached 104 before being beautifully bowled by Lindwall and the new ball, and England left Australia to make 223 to win. When the fifth day started, Australia seemed to be home and dry. The pitch which had been so lush to start with was by now the colour, not of sprouting, but of ripening corn. It was still quite fast, it is true, and it would seam a little; but Australia, with eight wickets standing and needing only 150 more, carried all the money as we drove on that sunny morning to the Sydney cricket ground, where the flags were stiffened by the breeze. It was to be a stirring day, fit to stand with any, and marked by one of the finest innings in history and some of the most indomitable bowling.

Tyson's third over of the day was of paramount importance. By bowling Burke and yorking Hole, beneath the flourish of the latter's backlift, he settled doubts upon the Australians and gave England hope. From then on it was a terrific battle. By lunch, when Australia were 118 for 5, Benaud had been caught by Tyson off Appleyard, a mis-hit flying high enough for Tyson to have time to stagger anxiously underneath it, like a man on the verge of collapse. In the morning only 46 runs were scored in 90 minutes for 3 wickets, when Australia had been expected to storm to victory. In the early afternoon Archer was bowled by Tyson, and Davidson marvellously caught by Evans off Statham. By half past two Lindwall had been bowled by Tyson and Langley by Statham. In three hours' cricket, in fact, England had closed their ranks and achieved unbelievable success. But the agony was yet to come.

At 145 for 9, Bill Johnston joined Neil Harvey, who had made 65 with a subservience to the bowling that was inconsistent with Harvey's assurance of survival. To his third ball from Statham, Johnston looked to all the world to be leg-before-wicket, which produced a stoical reaction from the England side. Harvey, seeing that the time had come to take every chance, proceeded to do much as he pleased. He cut and drove and hooked and glanced without doubt or hesitation; he took the strike when he wanted it, as he bounded through the eighties. He was at large – a batsman of infinite daring and ingenuity. When he hooked Tyson to long leg, Bailey misjudged the catch; and when Bailey came on to staunch the flow of runs Harvey drove him hard and high for four. England's lead was being not so much whittled as spirited away.

Johnston, all arms and legs in comic discordance, kept out the few balls that Harvey set him to receive. Deserted by the Olympian detachment which is supposed to govern one's judgement in the Press box, I felt ill and began to walk distractedly about. Tyson was on his last legs, and even Statham, the most whole-hearted bowler of the post-war years, admitted afterwards that once he had been replaced by Bailey he would have been hard put to it to summon the effort to bowl really fast again that day, even with the new ball, due at 200, to encourage him. At 180 Hutton asked Tyson, who had been running up the slope to bowl, whether he could manage another over, and Tyson, seeing Johnston at the striker's end, said he could. Before the over started Statham walked over to Tyson to advise him to bowl at Johnston's legs, and Johnston, thrusting his bat skittishly at Tyson's first ball, deflected it for four. He missed the second and was acrobatically caught by Evans off the third, Godfrey diving far to his right to hold another blind but hopeful glance. Exhaustion had taken its toll of Tyson's length, the same exhaustion that made Statham physically sick from time to time on the tour. Hutton believed in driving his fast bowlers almost to the limit of their endurance.

Given another twenty minutes, or even less, I have no doubt that Harvey would have won the match for Australia, and virtually the series with it. Instead, Statham and Tyson on that fateful day saved it for England. To achieve full destruction one fast bowler needs another as a partner: Gregory and McDonald, Larwood and Voce, and Lindwall and Miller had been the three most recent examples of that. And now Tyson and Statham were complementary to each other. That day at Sydney they bowled almost without a break. Tyson had the wind because of his greater speed; Statham, bowling into it as it blew from Botany Bay, was no less of a hero. Tyson took 6 for 85 in 18.4 overs, Statham 3 for 45 in 19 overs. Tyson was the more erratic and to the Australians the more frightening; but as Tyson would be the first to admit, Statham was the greater bowler. Statham, having been born to bowl, always had rhythm; Tyson, born to be strong, discovered his own rhythm here in Sydney and retained it through the weeks that followed. Statham was very fast, and yet, as Arthur Morris used to say, Tyson seemed painfully faster.

That night we crossed the road to a night club now extinct, and we drank a toast to Statham and Tyson, and we blessed Harvey for his genius. At Melbourne a fortnight later the contours of the third Test match were much the same. In Australia's second innings Tyson took 7 for 27, and Statham took seven wickets in the match. And at Adelaide Hutton beamed the enchanted smile of complete victory. As a captain he had done much to create the dominance of Tyson and Statham, from the day at Bunbury when Tyson was so rough-hewn and raw. He saw at Sydney that they were a key weapon and he used them like a shrewd tactician. By the end Hutton was mentally spent and inwardly satisfied. The celebrations he left to the younger men, and to Godfrey Evans whose confidence was never shaken. As he had said we would be, we were there at the finish.

John Woodcock, from *The Cricketer's Bedside Book*, edited by Ron Roberts (1966)

Headingley, 1981

Botham was not the only one to have booked out of the hotel that morning. I would have done so too, except that since Middlesex were due to play at Old Trafford on Wednesday, I would be staying in the north. It was a pleasure for him to book back into the hotel on Monday night, and for me to unpack my bag again for the 10.30 start on Tuesday. So, how did it happen?

Botham started relatively quietly, scoring 39 in 87 minutes before tea. He said afterwards, tongue in cheek, that he was playing for a not out! It was Dilley who at first played more aggressively. His method was to plant his front foot somewhere near middle stump, and swing the bat hard at anything to the off-side of where he stood. He hit – and missed – very hard. After tea, Ian hit even harder. I remember some outrageous strokes, a wind-up aimed at mid-wicket that sent the ball way over the slips, and another that went off the inside edge behind square leg for four. (He was using Graham Gooch's bat, who claims the patent for the off-drive that the Fearnley inside edge speeds away to square leg. 'He hadn't used it much during the match,' said Ian later, 'and I thought there were a few runs left in it.') Overall, Ian played wonderfully. He was particularly severe on Alderman, who was kept on until he was exhausted. Botham drove him over mid-off, through extra-cover, past gully. He went down the pitch and hit him splendidly straight for six.

In the dressing-room, we started to think of making Australia bat again – this target, 227, we reached while Dilley was still in – and of lasting out until the next day. It might easily rain on Tuesday, after all. Gradually, our hopes became more ambitious. If Dilley could stay with Botham until the close . . . At a quarter to five, however, he was out for 56, playing on to Alderman who was by then bowling round the wicket to give the batsman less room for his shots. This was his first Test fifty; the stand was worth 117 in 80 minutes. Since tea, the pair had added 76 in 44 minutes.

Despite this exhilarating stand we were in effect only 25 for 8; our elation was, realistically, for two magnificent individual innings. Willis said, fiercely, to me, 'Make Chillie *play*!' We sent Old on his way with a mixture of pleas, exhortations and threats, the latter largely from Willey. Chris is a talented striker of the ball, but one of those batsmen whose initial movement against quick bowlers is back towards square leg. However strenuously he orders that left foot to stay its ground, it always rebels. On the television screen, inside the pavilion, Willey wedged a bat handle against Old's bottom, trying to keep it in place. Chillie did his best, and so did his back foot. Together they accompanied Botham as he reached his hundred – off only 87 balls – and added 67 runs against an increasingly desperate side reduced by this fierce onslaught from magnificence to mediocrity. The desperation was highlighted by two beamers in an over from Lawson to Botham, after which umpire Evans spoke to Hughes. The beamer has been universally condemned by cricketers as an unfair delivery since the best batsmen have been unable to pick it up even in bright sunshine when well set.

What could Australia have done? I know well the feeling of impotence that Botham can engender; we have felt it often enough at the hands of Richards. However, I did feel the Australian seamers went on too long bowling their orthodox line just outside off stump. Admittedly, Botham, Dilley and Old were all liable, even at times likely, to be caught off the outside edge. But they were often hitting the ball hard or missing altogether and the edges cleared the rapidly diminishing number of slips. And despite my reluctance to bowl Willey I was surprised that Bright did not come on at all until the score reached 309–8. I should have wanted to try him much sooner, though with a defensive field. When he did bowl, he came within a hair's breadth of hitting Botham's off stump.

The dismissal of Old was not the end, either, for Botham protected Willis so well that he had to face only 5 balls in the last 20 minutes, and we added another 31 crucial runs. At the close we were 351–9, 124 runs ahead. Another 60 or 70 runs, we felt, and we would actually be favourites!

Afterwards, I made the mistake of going into the Australian dressing-room. I had been there on Saturday evening, when they were cock-a-hoop. Perhaps I went too soon, for in the few seconds that I stood there I sensed thunderous silence, like the moment of Doom, everyone frozen in postures of dejection. Not even Hogg responded to my arrival. At last someone, I think Peter Philpott, the team coach, asked me if I was looking for anyone in particular. I went out again. Certainly the last thing I wanted to do was crow or appear to gloat.

Ian was keen to avoid the reporters. He asked me to tell them that he didn't want to talk. We escorted him through the crowds with a towel gagging his mouth. One newspaper made the best of a bad job with the caption 'Actions speak louder than words'. Half a dozen of us went to Bryan's Fish and Chip restaurant up the road from the ground. We got a round of applause – a rare thing, I imagine, for the friendly but staid clientele of this splendid eating-house. Like a group of John the Baptists we were preparing a path for one greater than ourselves – for Ian and his family came in soon after. Poor Liam Botham, probably overwhelmed and excited by his long stay at the cricket, got a bone stuck in his throat, and his day ended in tears.

Back at the hotel we had a provisional celebration. I offered to buy Ian a glass of his favourite brandy. First I gave him a measure of their worst cooking brandy and asked him to guess its age. 'Twenty years', he said. The Hine Antique turned out to be orange liqueur, but he did recognize that. I remember asking Graham Gooch where he would, ideally, choose to bat in a Test match. He said that he must have the best chance of personal success at No. 4, but obviously was happy enough to bat in any position. We also talked to Goose.[1] He suggested that in the first innings we had been too concerned to bowl a good length and let the pitch 'do' the rest; should we, and he in particular, bowl faster and straighter? I agreed. 'Zap'[2] underlined the point; 'Even Gatt's harder to bat against when he really runs in,' he said. 'And you'd better forget about no balls,' I added. They too had made him tentative. On a pitch with such uneven bounce the harder the ball hits it the more devastating the variations will be. Moreover, bowling tomorrow would be an all or nothing affair, a huge effort without thought of conservation of energy.

We were due to start at 10.30. This time we all booked out. We exercised at 9.40, and commented regretfully on the weather. It was a warm sunny day, better for batting. At 9.50 we had some catching practice. I had decided to go back to first slip myself. In the first innings I left Gooch there, mainly because I was not fully confident having recently dropped two or three slip catches for Middlesex. What worried me most was not that I had dropped them, but that on one occasion I just did not react at all. By now Botham must have been feeling utterly confident and relaxed; I would keep him at third slip, and have Gooch at second from which he would not have to move when Botham bowled. Graham was quite happy to move away from first slip as he had had only two chances there in 2½ Tests and had dropped both. We would keep Gatting at short-leg, the position he had taken over from Woolmer. Willey was the

[1] Bob Willis.
[2] Graham Gooch.

specialist gully, and Gower could go back to the position he excels in, cover-point. I was glad to settle on this pattern. I like to captain from first slip; the players become accustomed to looking for me there, and I can see how the bowler runs in and what the ball is doing. The chopping and changing of slip fielders that had gone on in the first innings and in the other Tests is undesirable; it reminded me of Yallop's problems in 1978–9. Slip fielders need to be comfortable with each other, to learn each other's habits. Willis had a brief batting net. We have given up attempts to coach him, and now leave him to his idiosyncratic ways.

Hughes took the new ball at once, and put all the fielders except for two slips back for Botham, who declined singles. The field came in for the last two balls, and Botham was unlucky not to strike a four or two. We had scored only five more runs when Willis was out. Botham was left not out on 149. It was one of the greatest innings ever played, even though it was to be surpassed only two Tests later.

I said a few words to everyone. 'More aggression, more adrenalin, more encouragement for the bowlers. The Australians will be nervous now'. I also told the four seam bowlers which of them would be starting. Clive Lloyd always gives the new ball to the same pair out of his four quick bowlers. I found it harder to decide. Botham still owed us six wickets, as I reminded him. After all that had happened since Friday morning, I thought that he was most likely to create another miracle so I gave him the new ball. His first ball was a long-hop, the second a swinging half-volley: Wood hit both for fours to leg – hardly a propitious start. At the other end, I went for Dilley. His batting, too, should have lent him confidence. I also thought that if the match became tense it would be impossible to bring him on for a first spell when we had few runs to play with. I would give him two or three overs in which to click; if he didn't, I would bring Willis on early.

In the third over of the innings we had a stroke of luck. Wood drove at a full half-volley, edged, and was caught by Taylor. I appealed only half-heartedly, wondering if the ball bounced after hitting the bat. TV replays showed the umpire to be right. 13–1. Botham had his first wicket, but Dilley was still struggling, it seemed. In two overs he was hit for 11 runs, without bowling badly. He would have to come off. He was, moreover, feeling a strain in his thigh. I sent him to have Bernard Thomas look at it; he was back on the field within a few minutes with the message that he could bowl through the injury if needed.

For the sixth over, I gave the ball to Willis. He said to me, 'Faster and straighter, right?' I nodded. At once he bowled well, up the hill. Botham wanted the other end to help swing the ball; but in the bright sunshine it was swinging little. Chappell and Dyson struggled on, beaten from time to time, but still there. We kept a third man and square leg to stop the edges going for too many runs. After he had bowled five overs, Willis said to me, 'Give me a go at the other end.' Still thinking of Old's possible outswing from that end, my reaction was, 'You mean you've had enough of coming up hill into the wind?' This acknowledged Bob's problem, without committing myself. He said, grumpily, 'Okay, I'll carry on here then.' I put the question to Taylor and Botham during Old's next over. They both thought I should give Willis the end he wanted. Ian said, 'He's looked our most dangerous bowler.' I agreed. We would give Willis his head. To switch them, and to see how the pitch would respond to spin, I tried Willey at the bottom end. I still thought we might miss Emburey's ability to put pressure on the batsmen with close fielders on each side. After three overs of Willey I went back to Old who, like Willis, bowled with more aggression than earlier in the match. In fact, his contribution as the accurate, mean foil to Willis proved invaluable. Until Bright took 10 off his last over, he was hit for only 11 runs in 8 overs.

Meanwhile Bob was steaming in downhill. At last his – and our – luck changed. The change coincided with the return of the clouds, though no amount of cloud cover could explain the reversal that followed. First Willis bowled a perfect bouncer at Chappell, not too short and dead straight. Chappell, protecting his face, could only lob the ball up for Taylor. Next over, Old twice hit Dyson painful blows on the hand as he pushed tentatively forward. There was nothing tentative about the bowling or the fielding now. Willis summoned up all his energy for his last over before lunch. The first ball, not too short but lifting, just outside off stump, was to Hughes. It may have straightened marginally off the pitch – Bob's natural inswing action sometimes causes the ball to move off the seam towards the slips. Up on tip-toe, Hughes was not quite over to the ball, or over it, and edged it low to Botham's left at third slip, where the 'old' Botham took a fine catch.

The score was 58–3. Len Hutton once said that in 1954–5 he first thought they had a chance when Neil Harvey, playing for New South Wales against MCC, had to take his pad off to rub his leg after being hit by a ball from Frank Tyson. 'It must have hurt,' Len said, musingly. I first thought we had a real chance at Headingley when Hughes was out for nought. A few minutes before, Taylor, Gooch, Botham and I were talking about the frustrating near-misses of the past fourteen months, twice at Nottingham, and then at Lord's when the loss of four hours for bad light had been crucial. We agreed, being realistic, that, as at Trent Bridge, Australia would probably scramble home by four or five wickets. (I don't incidentally, believe that predictions like this imply defeatism or loss of aggression.) There was now less than five minutes to lunch. We roused Bob still further; he must fancy getting Yallop this time. 'Short and straight,' we said. Three balls later Yallop had gone, beautifully caught at short square leg from a nasty, kicking delivery. 58–4. We lunched – most of us in the dressing-room at such a crucial stage – knowing that the odds must be down from 500–1 to 6–4.

We spent some time guessing how the remaining Australians would play. Marsh might well 'have a go'; in the first innings at Nottingham he had slogged a quick 19 before being caught off a skier at long-leg. Dyson, Border and Bright would 'graft'. Lawson and Lillee, if we got down to them, might have a swing, especially if we pitched the ball up. One thing was clear: we must keep running at them, harrying their batsmen.

Old struck next, thirteen minutes after lunch, knocking Border's leg stump out of the ground. 65–5. Next over Willis dismissed Dyson. In the previous over the Australian opener had hooked Bob easily for four. Now he tried the same stroke to another bouncer and, a little unluckily, gloved the ball. He was through the shot too soon. 68–6. Two overs later, Marsh too tried to hook Willis, top-edged, and Dilley judged the awkward catch perfectly, taking it a few feet inside the boundary. 74–7. Between overs, Bob came up to me to tell me that umpire Evans had told him not to bowl bouncers at Lawson, the new batsman. I was amazed. 'Forget it,' I said. 'But don't bother with an out-and-out bouncer at first – short of a length, rib-height.' Next over, with his first ball to Lawson, he put an end to all debate, having him caught behind for a single. 75–8. Willis had taken six wickets in six overs; Old had taken the other. In 58 minutes seven wickets had fallen for 19 runs on a pitch playing little worse than in the first innings, when, against the same bowlers, the same batsmen had amassed 401 runs.

The extraordinary match still had an unnerving twist or two in its tail. Australia may have been 75 for 8; but they still needed only 55 to win. In four overs, Lillee and Bright scored 35 of them. When Willis dropped short, Lillee stepped back and half-cut, half-poked the ball way over first slip for four (a shot he must have learned from bowling at Knott). At once

I put a man back in that direction. Again Lillee found room to cut, this time beating Dilley at wider third man. When Willis bowled more to leg, Lillee flicked him uppishly but safely behind square on the leg-side for three, then cut him for another four. Bright weighed in with two solid blows over mid-wicket off Old, and suddenly we were back on the defensive, on the brink of defeat. Gatting made a good point. 'It doesn't matter too much what length Goose bowls to Dennis,' he said, 'provided that it's straight.' Sure enough, Willis bowled a straight half-volley and Gatting himself took his second excellent catch, as Lillee, trying to play more conventionally, contrived to spoon the ball towards mid-on. Gatting took a second to judge how far the ball was coming, then raced in, dived, and caught it just off the ground. 110–9. I took Old off, and brought Botham back. We gave Bright a single. I asked Ian if he wanted a third slip or a gully. 'Third slip,' he said. Agonizingly, two sharp chances went to Old in exactly that position. Perhaps it was as well that the recipient was a Yorkshireman. The crowd would have been less patient had it been Keith Fletcher. It did cross my mind at that time that a Test could go down in history under the name of the man who dropped a crucial catch. Remember Fred Tate's Test in 1902!

A few moments later it was all over. Appropriately, Willis finished it with the perfect, most emphatic ball – a middle-stump yorker which bowled Bright. Australia were all out for 'Nelson' – 111. It was the second time in Test history that a side had won after following on. Bob Willis had come back from the borders of oblivion to set the Ashes alight.

My Harrogate friend cut work for the first time in twenty years, and arrived at the ground when Australia were 56 for 1. He told me that he had never before left a cricket ground hoarse.

Soon after the close I received a telegram from Doug Insole which read, simply: ILLOGICAL STOP CLOUSEAU.

Mike Brearley, Phoenix from the Ashes (1982)

The Two Gs

On a brilliant day of high summer and high batsmanship, Graham Gooch and David Gower effectively regained the Ashes for England at the Oval yesterday, and knocked out of the 1985 Australians whatever stuffing they might have had left.

The day began with a triumph for Craig McDermott and finished with a wicket maiden for Murray Bennett, but in between Gooch and Gower caused utter mayhem. At the close England were 376 for three, Gooch was still there with 179, Gower was out for 157. They put on 351 for the second wicket, the Gower-Robinson stand of 331 at Edgbaston being passed as the sixth highest in English Test history after just ten days.

There are other mind-blowing statistics. But Gower and Gooch did not beat the kind of record people normally trot out on routine days – the highest for the second wicket for England against Australia on this ground. The Hutton and Leyland stand of 382 in 1938 still reigns supreme.

That match (England 903 for seven declared, Hutton 364) is usually regarded as the apogee of English batting. But it was achieved against a weaker Australian seam attack than this, at a time when Australia had already won the Ashes, and was scored far more slowly. England, having kept up a remarkable 3.6 an over all series, were about four an over yesterday.

It would take a very committed fogey to insist that the performances of Gower and company this summer do not rank among the all-time great English batting feats. And there has surely never been a series when England's batsmen have so dominated Australia's bowlers; what people thought would be the great confrontation of force versus object has been wholly one-sided since Lord's.

The first good news of the day for England yesterday was that Botham was fit, and the team was left unchanged. I am still not certain they were right to do without Agnew, but Botham was irrelevant yesterday, so Agnew certainly was. What did matter was Border calling wrong for the fourth Test running (it must be Gower's 10-franc coin again) and allowing England to take first strike on a pitch as dry and fair as the groundsman, Harry Brind, had promised.

Australia's bowlers might have been able to use the pace to trouble England. And Robinson, missing out for once, soon lost his off stump to an in-swinging yorker from McDermott. But their reshaped team soon proved as inadequate in these conditions as they were on the slow pitches of Manchester and Birmingham.

ENGLAND'S HIGHEST TEST PARTNERSHIPS

411	P. B. H. May and M. C. Cowdrey	4th wicket v.	West Indies, Edgbaston 1957
382	L. Hutton and M. Leyland	2nd wicket v.	Australia, The Oval 1938
370	W. J. Edrich and D. C. S. Compton	3rd wicket v.	South Africa, Lord's 1947
369	J. H. Edrich and K. F. Barrington	2nd wicket v.	New Zealand, Headingley 1965
359	L. Hutton and C. Washbrook	1st wicket v.	South Africa, Johannesburg 1948–49
351	G. A. Gooch and D. I. Gower	2nd wicket v.	Australia, The Oval 1985
331	D. I. Gower and R. T. Robinson	2nd wicket v.	Australia, Edgbaston 1985
323	J. B. Hobbs and W. Rhodes	1st wicket v.	Australia, Melbourne 1911–12

McDermott, straining for more yorkers, soon began producing half-volleys, and Lawson, alas for Australia, continued weary and sickly, if staunch. The newcomer, Gilbert, bowled straight, and Gooch drove him straighter, while the slow left-armer, Bennett looked a very slow left-armer indeed. With the ball not turning, he was cannon fodder.

But it could have been different. Gower began as though the weird sisters had said that no harm would befall him until St John's Wood come to Kennington. Most of the shots in his first 50 were speculative, and he might have been caught in the slips on two and on 31, though the only chance that actually went to hand or finger was one to Wessels at cover on 137.

After lunch – perhaps the captain had had a word with himself – he was as majestic as at Edgbaston, playing every shot you could wish for (except the reverse sweep) until, tired, he slashed to backward point after

5½ hours. By then Gower had taken his total for the series to 732, the fourth highest by an Englishman (behind Hammond, 907, Compton, 753, and Sutcliffe, 734). I think I can say with some certainty that it is the highest total by a batsman who was as dispirited and as close to the plug hole as Gower was only three months ago.

Gooch did not give a chance. He already has his first Ashes century, after fourteen frustrating games, and his highest Test score. This morning, perhaps, he will have a double century.

And one trusts no one will demand an apology and a promise not to do it again. He mixed power with delicacy; his sweeps against poor Bennett had touches of impertinence. After tea, when he finally moved convincingly ahead of Gower, Gooch looked unstoppable. Maybe the new Hutton is amongst us.

There were several symbolic moments. After one Gower hook McDermott simply stood and stared hopelessly at the ground for ages. Later the Fosters balloon, which looked the weediest of the various advertising stunts attempted by competing Australian lagers, broke loose from its moorings to become a hazard to aviation, and the fielders stared as if hoping to hitch a ride. Then a group of pigeons waddled across the pitch on a fast bowler's length, perhaps imagining that it was the safest route.

Even the good news had a bad side for Australia. In the last over Bennett turned one past the outside edge of Gatting's bat and induced a slip catch. It brought in Emburey as night watchman. Gatting and Robinson thus become analogous to Edrich, Compton and Paynter, who made 13 between them in Hutton's match. But turn, with England 376 for three? Emburey should have gone to bed last night almost as happily as the day's two heroes.

Matthew Engel, *Ashes '85* (1985)

Peter Who?

Incredibly, unbelievably, the gamble worked. Peter Taylor, the unheralded off-spinner, whose selection had been greeted with headlines saying 'Peter who?' has bowled England out.

Taylor took six wickets for seventy-eight runs, including those of

Lamb, Gower, Botham and Emburey. In part this was a fluke. Taylor was bowling on a turning pitch, a rare luxury in Test cricket these days, and all his wickets were taken when the batsmen played erratic shots, a second unusual event in Test cricket. Nevertheless this was a splendid piece of bowling by Taylor, who with his high arm was able to flight and bounce the ball. At the end of the day spectators were again asking why it was that this man, in a time of limited spin resources, had only played six games for New South Wales. They might also, had they known, have wondered why Steve Whitfield, Taylor's spinning partner at the Northern Districts club in Sydney, had not played at all. Taylor says that Whitfield is the best spin bowler in Australia, and having batted against him, I can support his opinion. Yet Whitfield is thirty-six, and though he has been in the Shield squad, he has not played in a single Shield game.

Probably England did take Taylor too lightly. Botham had tried to hit him off his length yesterday and had failed. Taylor is inexperienced at this level, but he is not young in the craft of spin bowling. This morning he dismissed Gower, who played one of those dreamy off-drives that signify he is content to be a minor batting genius, happy enough to tootle along in his sports car, sipping champagne, like some latter-day Percy Fender. The ball to Gower did dip, falling short of his foot as he moved in to drive, but it was a careless stroke.

At this point England had sunk to 232–6, and were in peril of giving a handsome lead to Australia. Then Emburey joined Richards, and the two hard-headed men of London (actually Richards was born in Cornwall, but he has some cockney characteristics) began to repair England's innings. Richards, a twittering, nervous wreck in Brisbane, has been one of the revelations of this remarkable winter, 'keeping splendidly in Melbourne and batting with astonishing fortitude in Perth. Here he was resolute, defiantly cracking boundaries through the covers whenever Taylor dropped short and wide. Emburey, England's vice-captain, chose the right shots to play; awkward as ever, he collected some runs. He says he loses his wicket when he goes beyond his frugal range of strokes (a sweep, a block, an off-drive and a second sweep) and so he rejects ventures into the unknown. He is by no means a copy-book player, unless the copy-book was written in some rude fish market in the back streets of London.

These two practical fellows added seventy-one runs, to Australia's immense frustration. Sleep, Border's second amateur spin bowler, still on leave from his council job in Adelaide, did not pitch his leg-spinners accurately enough to trouble the batsmen, as they rebuilt England's reply, and there was nothing much in the pitch for the faster men. England lost another wicket only when Richards drove to Wellham, who had been positioned square of the wicket to cut off Richards's favourite shot. This was good captaincy by Border, who has begun to be aware of batsmen's strengths and weaknesses, has begun to realize the need to winkle batsmen out when he is otherwise stuck.

After that England lost wickets regularly, as batsmen struck out at Taylor. Edmonds edged to square leg. Small played some exotic shots, in partnership with Emburey, and then missed a heave, and finally Emburey's alert resistance ended when he hit across the line and was bowled. Taylor left the field in front of his colleagues, near to tears. His career, his years in obscurity, his years without much hope or ambition, had taken an unexpected turn. It was all difficult to adjust to, even for so sane a man.

Curiously Taylor did bring a sense of maturity to this Australian eleven. In Melbourne and Perth spectators had to endure silly antics from McDermott and Zoehrer. Upon taking a wicket McDermott grimaced, punched the air, pointed to the pavilion and appeared to shout like some Sioux Indian at a war dance. Zoehrer was foolish in Melbourne (greeting Edmonds with vulgar remarks) and petulant in Perth, where he exchanged words with Pakistan's Qasim Omar on the subject of a drink of water being sipped by a Pakistani tail-ender. Unnecessary deeds such as these had marked Australian cricket ten years earlier, and Border has done much (as have Gower and Gatting for England) to discourage them. Players had kicked one another, men had been run out for backing up too far, and slowly the lie had been perpetuated that success on the field demanded arrogance and vitriol. Despite the many impressive heroes which sports have bestowed upon us, excuses had been offered whenever a crude, adolescent sportsman had a tantrum. Border has done cricket a great service by not spitting or snarling, by not railing about umpires or shrieking about bad luck. He has blamed no one but himself and his colleagues for losing this series. His conduct on the field has not suffered, and he had brought no indignity upon the game. Marsh, Waugh, and Reid are others who have played cricket with fierce spirit and in disciplined manner. They seem to have managed perfectly well.

This Australian team is not hyped up, is not as subversively aggressive as some of its predecessors. Taylor fits into this new pattern. He appears composed and intelligent on the field, as if he is blessed with an astute cricket brain. He is a responsible cricketer, a reliable elder, a man to whom Border can turn. For once, Border is not surrounded by hysterical young men but by mature adults.

Peter Roebuck, *Ashes to Ashes* (1987)

6

A World Game

Englishmen may have started it, and Australians may have become the opponents English cricketers most want to beat, but cricket was a legacy to every country where the British dwelt for any length of time, and some would say as valuable a gift as any bestowed on the citizens of the Empire. In many lands the game has become just as much an obsession and a part of national life as it has in, say, Yorkshire or Kent.

I have lost count of many of the references I have read or heard in lands once painted red on the map to 'pupils teaching the masters how to play the game'. Clyde Walcott, for one, said it in his capacity as President of the West Indies Cricket Board at a dinner in Jamaica at the start of England's tour under David Gower in 1986. He was not to know – could only guess – that the West Indies would win the series five nil. A 'blackwash' it was called, the second such in a row, and for many the term was used with peculiar relish. People once down-trodden by those brought up to believe that their colour made them superior cannot believe or understand the degree to which England, which in cricket means 'Britain', has lost its self-confidence since the Second World War.

As the world has been shrunk by air travel, so the greater opportunities for talented cricketers overseas to gain experience faster have levelled standards in the world game. Much the same happened in England with the advent of rail travel in the nineteenth century. Natural ability in countries like India and the West Indian islands is now combined with professional expertise. In 1992–93 England achieved the singular humiliation of being beaten in a one-day competition (the World Cup) by Zimbabwe and a five-day Test match (not to mention two one-day internationals) by Sri Lanka. In the days when the former was Northern Rhodesia and the latter Ceylon, anyone suggesting that a full-strength

*England team would lose to such minnows would have been told to go and lie
down in a dark room.*

*Unabashed, the MCC was encouraging further potential humiliations in
1992 by sponsoring a European Cup in England, inviting the champions, who
turned out to be Germany if you please, to play against them at Lord's.*

*Patriotism is the last refuge of the scoundrel and only the small-minded
would disapprove the spread of the cricket gospel to all parts of the world.
Trevelyan suggested that if the French* noblesse *had been capable of playing
cricket with their peasants, their châteaux would never have been burnt. Considering the common royal family, the notion may be fanciful, but had the
Germans been playing Test cricket in 1914 we might never have gone to war
with them. On the other hand, considering their efficiency in most areas of life,
they would probably be almost permanent holders of the traditional trophy for
Anglo-German cricketing series, the Sackcloth.*

An Addict from Quetta

I was pointed towards the rail superintendent's office, where a handsome
old Baluch stood guard on the door. Everything about him was spotlessly
white except his skin, which was the colour of tanned leather; otherwise,
it was white pugri, white beard, white kurta, white shalwar. He took me
by the arm and in fatherly fashion guided me down a corridor to a large
room where activity was much more sedate than in the Karachi version.
Men were dealing quietly with paperwork without the constant interruption of visitors and supplicants. The old chowkidar showed me to an
empty desk at the bottom of the room and indicated that I should sit
beside it. I had been there only a few minutes when a tall figure
appeared, a moon-faced almost bald man with a pullover on top of his
shirt. I rose to offer him the seat, but he waved me down again and pulled
up another chair. I explained what I wanted and he said, 'No problem.
You from England?' Then it was 'Whereabouts?' I told him that I lived in
Yorkshire.

He beamed, and the corners of his big brown eyes crinkled with amusement. 'What do you make of Boycott, then?' I nearly fell off the chair in surprise.

To anyone who hasn't the slightest interest in the game of cricket, the next few paragraphs will be extremely tedious, but that can't be helped because this chance encounter with Anwar Ali was to shape most of my time in Quetta, and cricket dominated my impressions when I came away.

Anwar Ali was, I think, the most obsessive cricket enthusiast I have ever come across; and I have known quite a few who can even bore me, who has been devoted to the game since childhood, with their interminable talk about it and nothing else. It very soon became clear that he was not exaggerating in the least when he said, a little wistfully I thought, 'You know, cricket has been my whole life. I've passed up promotions because of it, because I preferred to play a game instead of studying for exams. So here I am, forty-four years old and still a railway clerk.' When Anwar Ali looked at his watch and said that he must get back to work, I assumed that I probably wouldn't see him again. But he asked me whether I had anything planned for that evening. I hadn't. 'Would you like to come and watch some of the boys working out, then?' His chief cricketing activity, now that he was getting past match play, was to coach the pupils of the St Francis Grammar School in Quetta, a missionary establishment whose headmaster was Dutch, and whose staff was a mixture of Christians and Muslims, though the pupils were mostly sons of Islam. He told me how to get there by four thirty, when the nets would begin, and for the time being we parted.

The interest of Pakistanis in cricket would have been apparent to any visitor to the country who kept his eyes open, whether or not he knew anything about the processes by which Englishmen had spread their national game to this and many other corners of the globe in the course of their imperialism. In Karachi you could scarcely move a mile in any direction without seeing a game in progress, usually on waste ground with improvised equipment, or with proper gear on a school playing field. Sports shops were abundant there, and all displayed large numbers of bats, pads, boxes of balls, gloves, caps and the like. Some of this stuff was imported from England expensively, but most of it was made in the Punjab, in the town of Sialkot, sometimes comically counterfeiting the English brands. Bats bearing the almost identical trade mark of Gunn & Moore were labelled 'Gain More'; blades crimsoned down the back like those coming from the workshops of Gray-Nicolls had emerged from the craftsmen of Sialkot under the name 'Ray-Nicoles'; and so on. As well as seeing so much evidence of the game itself, it was impossible to avoid noticing the popularity of its current local hero, when Imran Khan's countenance was plastered across shop windows wherever you went, as well as on a lot of commercial objects which had nothing whatsoever to do with cricket, down to Japanese motorbikes like the one I had ridden in Sibi. Such was the obvious passion for the game that, in a moment of fantasy, I had come to the conclusion that, were someone to be threatened with attack by a hostile crowd here, he just might be able to stop them in their tracks before they hurt him by bellowing 'Not Cricket!' and holding up his finger like an umpire giving the batsman out: which certainly wouldn't provide him with an escape route in most of the world's unruly places.

I had not at all been prepared, however, for the commitment to the game I was about to encounter in Quetta. When I reached the school playing fields later that afternoon, the nets were up around two concrete batting strips, and a couple of dozen boys were already at it, bowling in relays to the pair of batsmen occupying the creases. Anwar Ali stood between the bowling stumps, keeping an eye on bowling actions, then switching his attention to the strokes the batsman made. From time to time he made some comment, but most of these lads seemed to have very good technique already. Their stroke play was classical, and they showed a marked appetite for hitting the ball hard and often, not at all in the manner of Boycott. As I came up, a kid of maybe twelve years old danced up to the wicket and bowled leg spin on a perfect length which must have turned eighteen inches. On a concrete strip that was very impressive indeed.

'You've got another Abdul Qadir, I see,' I remarked as I drew alongside the coach. He turned and smiled. 'Not bad, not bad.' But the next bowler sent down a long-hop, and the batsman leapt at it eagerly, hitting it so straight and high that the ball sailed over a shed on the edge of the field. '*Dekho*! Watch it!' Anwar Ali shouted to a lad positioned on the boundary to search and retrieve in cases such as this. He spoke to the lads all the time in this mixture of Urdu and English, moving from one to the other as though they were the same tongue. They mostly used Urdu among themselves, with cricketing terms in English popping out now and then. And this rhythmical movement of boys in white flannels and shirts, this graceful mixture of aggression and subtlety which had been part of my life since childhood, went on for two full hours before Anwar Ali indicated that it was time to pack up and go. In the clear spring air of Quetta, we might easily have been 4,000 miles away, taking net practice before the English season began; except that no English cricket ground, not even any of the beautiful village pitches in the dale where I lived, would have had such towering mountains as these in the distance beyond square leg.

'You must come and meet the boys, now,' Anwar Ali said as we went to collect his bicycle, which was propped against the boundary shed. 'We always meet at six thirty after work, to chat and maybe have something to eat. They're all cricketers, too.' I inquired what he meant by 'always'; how often he spent the early evening coaching those pupils before meeting 'the boys' for a chat and a meal. 'Every night,' he said coolly, 'from now till the beginning of October, when the season ends and it's too cold for cricket up here. Only not if there's a match on, or if it rains. Then we call it off.' That was six whole months of the year; about 180 evenings when cricket didn't leave much time for anything else. I had never heard of anyone in England, not even a professional cricketer, who spent so much of half a year on the game. It wouldn't have been tactful to ask what the wives of Quetta made of this.

We crossed a couple of streets and came to the Café Sadiq, whose windows were misted over with steam on the inside. We walked out of sharp air straight into fug, partly produced by cooking and tobacco smoke, partly by the heat from a large metal stove which stood in the middle of the room and had been stoked up so fiercely with coal that the flue running up to the ceiling was all but glowing. We sat down at a table with a gingham plastic cloth laid across it, which was matched by curtains sagging round all the steamy windows. We ordered some tea and food, and then half a dozen men came in, greeted Anwar Ali, drew up chairs and joined us. Within a quarter of an hour our party had increased to sixteen; so many that we were spread around three adjacent tables.

I was introduced to each newcomer in turn, but almost at once forgot their names and the cricket clubs to which each belonged, which went with the introductions – the Quetta CC, the Crescent CC, the Customs CC, the Marker CC, the Wapda CC, and others. One small group lodged more clearly in my memory because their leader was a very tall man with hooded eyes, who wore a cricket sweater over his kurta and under a Western jacket, and a Swedish-style cap unbuttoned above the peak; a very good fast bowler, I was informed. He and his four friends were all coal merchants who played together in the Sheikh XI, which was just another of the twenty-two cricket teams that Quetta regularly turned out. Soon, everyone was tucking into beef tikka or seekh kebab, whose succulent pieces of meat came straight off the spit like rolled-up brandy snaps. But eating wasn't at all the principal reason for the evening muster in the Café Sadiq. These chaps had simply come to gossip about their addiction, like men who have been starved of a drug for some time, though it couldn't have been more than twenty-four hours since they'd had their last fix.

They all wanted to know what I *thought* about various aspects of the game: what I thought of Pakistan's chances in the World Cup, how long I thought Willis would continue to captain England, whether I thought the lbw law would ever be changed to give the spinners more of a chance, what I thought of the Englishmen, the West Indians and the Sri Lankans who had lately gone to play in South Africa in defiance of their cricketing authorities. They were after opinions, not facts, and it soon became apparent that they needed no information from me. Primed by the same intelligence that made Anwar Ali such a perambulating encyclopaedia, they knew quite as much as I did myself about what had lately happened in English cricket, and a great deal more about the game overseas. I was fairly sure that most of them knew more than I about the history of the English county championship.

I was recalling Harold Gimblett's 210 against Sussex at Hove in 1947, when a polite voice at the next table said, 'No, sir. I believe it was at Eastbourne, and I think you'll find it was in 1948, not 1947.' I was certain then that I had met my match. I imagine that any one of them could easily have answered the trickiest cricket quiz question of all, the one about who were the seventeen county captains in the first season after the war, including such obscurities as Fallows of Lancashire, Murray-Willis of Northants, Singleton of Worcestershire, and the fellow from Derbyshire whose name I can never remember however hard I try. The truly pathological significance of Anwar Ali and his friends was that they discussed no other topic even when I was not involved in conversation. This was not merely a case of enthusiasts making the most of a rare chance to share their infatuation with a stranger. While we were eating, there was no cross talk between the tables, but I could overhear what was being said at the other two. '*Ajkal syrf* Brisbane *me ys jaysa* sticky wicket *hay*.' The talk all around me was consistently in piebald sentences like that.

It was well after nine o'clock that night when the party broke up and Anwar Ali rode me through the dimly lit streets on the crossbar of his bicycle. When he left me at the door of my hotel, he said, 'You'll come to nets again tomorrow?' There was little choice; I was already incorporated into a local eccentricity. A pattern had been sketched for my time in Quetta from late afternoon onwards, and deviation from it would have been perverse. For the next three days, each evening was a repeat performance of the first, and I don't believe there were ever fewer than a dozen of us subjecting cricket to intensive care behind the steamy windows of the Café Sadiq. Each time, beforehand, I had watched my moon-faced friend coaching his young charges at the grammar school.

On the third day I wandered into the playing fields a bit earlier than usual, to find only one boy already there before me. He was doing press-ups on the boundary when I arrived, but came over to talk when he saw me. I complimented him on his batting the night before, for he was a genuine stylist with an excellent eye and a very good pair of shoulders. 'Thank you, sir,' he replied, so deferentially that he made me feel like Mr Chips. We chatted about his cricket, about what he wished to do with it, and of course he wanted to be an international star like Imran Khan. But that, he said, would mean that he would have to go away. I assumed he meant going away from Quetta which, I had already learnt, was a backwater so far as professional cricket was concerned; mostly because its cricket season, due to the high altitude climate, did not coincide with the season in Karachi and Lahore, and therefore the top players rarely performed in Baluchistan. That, however, wasn't the point he was making. 'I'm a Christian, sir, and there's too much competition for us.' All the best jobs in the country, he said, went to Muslims and no Christian had a hope of getting anywhere in cricket – 'not like India, where Roger Binney has made the Test team'. He was a boy who knew he had a talent, and he was sadly reconciling himself to a fact of life that would prevent him from exploiting it properly in his native land.

Geoffrey Moorhouse, *To the Frontier* (1984)

Cricket in the Hindu Kush

Overhead a falcon suddenly chattered in alarm as it quartered the bleak broken landscape. The utter silence was broken. At 10,000 feet in the foothills of the eastern Hindu Kush, loneliness and tranquillity frequently go hand in hand, and apart from the occasional glimpses of tribesmen hundreds of feet above me trekking into Afghanistan, I thought I was quite alone.

But the sense of isolation was breached by a familiar sound. The soft solid thud of ball hitting bat came through thin air. Looking at the hostile, rock-strewn countryside, relieved by the odd clump of rough spiky vegetation, I immediately diagnosed a dose of high altitude hallucinations. Again the sound reached me followed by cries of encouragement. Intrigued now and curious, I pinpointed the noise down the valley out of sight behind a sharp ridge. Following an animal track I walked down to the ridge and looked at the scene at my feet.

A group of local tribesmen, dressed in the pyjama-like garb of the North-West Frontier complete with a soft flat hat, were playing cricket on the only flat bit of ground I had seen in the mountains. Cleared of rocks about the size of golf balls, the ground scarcely accommodated the half-dozen or so fielders who, for obvious reasons, were guarding a boundary which marked the edge of a sharp drop into a stream some 2,000 feet below. A string of incomprehensible dialect sandwiched the universally recognized 'good shot' as the batsman sweetly cut the ball square from a delivery hurled down the pitch by an acrobatic bowler trailing yards of billowing cloth and leaving puffs of dust with every step.

For men used to playing a suicidal version of polo with a goat carcass, this must be an abject substitute. However, the sight of two armed tribesmen either side of the scorer seemed to sum up the seriousness of the game being played. Could vendettas include cricket matches, I asked myself?

There was a brief pause as I approached. A curious player came over.

'*Salaam alikum*,' I said in greeting.

'*Alikum salaam*,' he replied. 'Do you know this game?'

'Of course, my country invented it.'

'Are you real English?' (English-speaking *ferengi* are generally known as English whatever their nationality.)

I could see no possible danger in admitting I was a *real* English.

'You will play,' he said with just a hint of the interrogative. 'We stop when the sun goes down.' As this was in four hours' time, and I was still breathless from the walk down, I decided I didn't want to be cricket's first martyr buried in the eternal snows of the Hindu Kush. Anyway those armed spectators might not take too kindly to an infidel who dismissed their star player, whoever he might be.

Abdul whats-his-name swept another ball perilously close to the boundary of no return. The scorer entered a four next to a collection of hieroglyphics that could have been the local cure for diarrhoea. The next delivery vanished into the batsman's voluminous pantaloons, and a roar from the bowler suggested that anywhere else in the cricketing world, an appeal for leg before would have been just a formality. However, as there were no umpires, and a black look heavenwards elicited no help from Allah, the batsman stayed put.

Behind the bowler's arm the glittering 25,000-foot peak of Terrich Mir towered into a cerulean sky – an unbelievable sightscreen. Vast shadows crept across the valley, accentuating the deep defiles, as the sun moved westward. Chukkor, a kind of mountain partridge, started calling high above us. A sudden crack echoed from hill to mountainside as an unseen marksman shot at something or other. A breath of icy wind reminded me it was time to climb back to my hut.

As the improbable scene disappeared behind the ridge, a muffled 'Howzat' proclaimed the possible end to Abdul I-never-learnt-the-rest-of-his-name's innings.

I pondered on the aerodynamics of a sphere of leather at 10,000 feet and felt I understood the Corinthian spirit at last.

Tony Deane, *The Cricketer* (1985)

Tragedy at Thunderpore

One winter's evening while following the fortunes of the MCC in India my eye fell on the venue of their next match – Thunderpore. That's not the real name of the place but near enough to awaken poignant memories.

When I went to India the side was captained by Lionel Tennyson, one of the richest characters of his age. He is lovingly remembered by a vast number of people as a great personality, who by his enjoyment of life gave great enjoyment to all who met him. He belonged ideally to another age, as even the now spacious-seeming days of the twenties and thirties hardly offered full scope for his infectious gusto and gaiety. His heart was in proportion to his sturdy frame and stuffed full of courage and kindness. His conceits were enormous, unaffected, and endearing, a sitting target for the shafts of his friends, whose unrestrained badinage was the sincerest gauge of their affection. If he should occasionally appear in a somewhat undignified light in what I have to tell, I can truly say it stems from the same source.

As the good ship *Viceroy of India* was nearing Bombay our captain convened a meeting in order to arm his inexperienced team against the perils of the Orient. The first part of his address was devoted to the appalling consequence of any indiscretion in diet or other matters in tropical countries. This message, endorsed by the resounding medical terms the speaker had filched for the occasion from the surgeon's manual, made a most powerful impression.

The ensuing part of the talk was a timely reminder of the standard of behaviour expected of us as a touring team in a foreign country. There would be mistakes on the part of umpires, said our leader, but these must be accepted with the traditional stoicism of the sportsman and a big happy smile. His sixteen listeners almost longed for an opportunity to exhibit these manly qualities.

As the tour went on, however, the mistakes in umpiring were singularly few, while the health of the side, although jealously guarded, at times gave much cause for anxiety. Later on when we arrived in the fateful field of Thunderpore strains and dysentery, in varying degrees of severity, had robbed us of half our numbers, and we were hard pressed to raise eleven mobile, if not able, bodies. But the die being cast, that is, having lost the toss again, we tottered into the arena, and the match got under way.

The first few overs delivered by Alf Gover, then recently risen from a bed of sickness, were uneventful. During the third only the most acute observer would have been alarmed at the tense expression on his face as he started on his long, hustling run. It was when he shot past the crouching umpire and thundered down the pitch with the undelivered ball in his hand that it became obvious that something was amiss. The batsman, fearing a personal assault, sprang smartly backward, but the flannelled giant sped past looking neither to right nor left. Past wicket-keeper, slips, and fine leg in a flash he hurtled up the pavilion steps in a cloud of dusty gravel and was gone. That he has never received full credit for this record is due to the lack of timing apparatus and the distance, from the start of his run to his uncomfortable destination, not being a recognized one.

As, in the tight-lipped precipitation of his flight, he had been unable to give any hint of his future movements, fine leg, after a moment's thought, followed up the steps and, having rescued the ball from the bowler's convulsive grasp, announced that we had better start looking for a substitute.

The choice fell on a junior groundsman, and there followed another pause while he was forcefully persuaded to wear boots. Whether pigskin offended his religious tenets or whether he just objected to the discomfort of wearing any type of footwear for the first time, we never did discover.

During this pause another disaster befell us. I was idly bowling the ball to and fro with George Pope, our one remaining bowler of any consequence, when unfortunately something distracted his attention. The ball took him rather below his grievously upset tummy, and to my horror he went down with a terrible hissing sound. When I reached the other end he was in the arms of several helpers who had heard the thud, sweating in a fearful manner and showing the whites of his eyes.

When at this moment the Lord turned to ask him to bowl he was astonished and infuriated to see his one remaining hope apparently writhing in his last agonies. As the victim couldn't speak and no one else had seen the incident, no answer was forthcoming to his testy demand as to what the hell had happened now. Personally I thought that a tactful silence would be best in the circumstances, so without more ado poor old George was carted off to be erroneously treated for a sudden heat-stroke.

Just when it seemed that we might as well pack up altogether, mingled sounds of applause and primitive plumbing announced the heroic reappearance of Gover. At this the game was resumed and he bowled jolly well, admittedly aided by the batsman's uncertainty as to what he was going to do on arrival at the crease.

But they say that misfortunes come in threes, and we didn't have long to wait.

The Lord, bent with sorrow, was standing in the gully in a somewhat broody attitude when a brilliant piece of play lit the gloom like a fork of lightning against a sombre sky. Alf, slightly depleted but ever game, sent down a ball of whizzing speed outside the off stump of India's fairest cutter, Mushtaq Ali. The bat flashed in those blued-steel wrists to catch the ball 'twixt wind and water' and send it ray-like to the paling – but no, that's not quite right. The captain's leg happened to be in the way.

The ball caught him a smack on the shin that would have snapped off a lesser leg like a piece of rotten matchwood. As it was, the results were spectacular, and we beheld another record burst asunder. With a shrill trumpet of agony our captain's mighty bulk rose vertically to a height of eleven feet nine inches, where it appeared to remain suspended for several seconds. It was the nearest thing we saw to the rope trick in India, and on regaining terra firma his agility and eloquence completely eclipsed the efforts of all the nautch girls and impassioned orators we had endured in the course of our travels.

The minor setbacks of the rest of the innings were but pin-pricks against this majestic background, but old Miss Fortune had not yet ceased to leer.

When we started our innings in chastened mood, for the first time in India Umpire Blunder raised his hideous head, or rather his disrupting finger.

Things were indeed desperate when the Lord hobbled out to save the day. Four stinking decisions had easily counter-balanced a friendly attack, and feeling ran high or low according to temperament. But here was the man for the occasion. He had taken just about as much as any man ostensibly engaged on a day's pleasure could be asked to endure, apart from being in some pain. What of it? Had he not made 63 in a Test match with one hand?

The first ball he saw bowled was met by Smith (P.) in the middle of the bat and deftly deflected to fine leg. Up went a great shout, and simultaneously Umpire Blunder's finger. The batsmen had changed ends when this diabolical decision was eventually borne in on them. Smith left stunned, and after a moment's stupefaction his partner advanced on Umpire Blunder. Now was the supreme test. Remembering his teachings on the ship, we awaited the outcome breathlessly. Would it be the big happy smile? If the same thoughts crossed the captain's mind he brushed them aside for something a whole lot better. He made Umpire Blunder a short address which blew him backwards, bow-legged.

I cannot give you the exact text of that immortal message, that is Umpire B's copyright, but stripped of its stupendous embellishments, it boiled down to a straightforward inquiry as to whether, having started blind, he was now also bereft of his hearing.

It is not surprising how long the recipient took to find his voice, considering how small it was when found. The snag was that the next striker had arrived by the time he had reversed his decision, so the point was lost.

But when all is said and done, I doubt if even a smile as happy as Lionel's would have helped in the circumstances. Anyway, every psychiatrist will tell you he done right.

Ian Peebles, *Talking of Cricket* (1953)

MCC in the Far East

The second ball of MCC's tour of the Far East destroyed Geoff Boycott's wicket in the presence of 10,000 Ceylonese partisans at the Colombo Oval. The roar was said to have brought down coconuts from trees all over the island. The response was only slightly less when Keith Fletcher dragged one on from the same bowler, Kehelgamuwa. For the first time in their cricketing history, Ceylon went on to take a first innings lead against MCC, but MCC recovered poise, got better acquainted to the blistering heat, and won a match which was played with talent by the Ceylonese and with much determination, if I may be allowed to say so, by MCC.

A mere glance at the style and technique of the Ceylon players suggests very real understanding of the game. Alan Smith, who had time in Colombo to visit the schools, confirmed that the enthusiasm and effort put into the game at schoolboy level are a firm platform for improvement and can lead to Ceylon becoming a more prominent international force.

Experienced as Syd Buller is, not even *he* could start the unofficial Test on time. There were no bails on the ground. A car had to be sent back to the city to get some. It was not the only unusual aspect of the match: I was asked which roller I would like by the head *groundswoman*. (I must get my wife to work on Sophia Gardens!)

Syd Buller spent his time umpiring, coaching and lecturing. At St Joseph's School in Colombo, he met former Worcestershire player, Laddie Outschoorn, who is the National Coach. Stanley Jayasinghe, formerly with Leicestershire, Ian Pieris (Cambridge) and Dan Piachaud (Oxford) met the team frequently.

Syd Buller was delighted by the keenness of umpires everywhere. The main failing is that umpires in the Far East do not even consider front-foot appeals.

Everywhere social occasions were memorable, lavish, and generous to a fault. Royal occasions were exotic and incredibly grand. At Seremban (Malaysia), his Royal Highness the Yang di Peruan Besar entertained MCC at the palace. It was a brilliant night which immediately breathed informality and humour. One of the match umpires, widely known as the singing postmaster, was coaxed to take over the microphone from the official group of musicians. He did not have the royal permission, but the Yang jokingly said he would not have the postmaster executed if Don Wilson and John Hampshire responded for MCC with the Black and White Minstrel songs. News travels fast from Middlesbrough to Malaysia!

Singapore was hot and dry. Fielding for Singapore on the first day was a torrid business as testified by Roy Stevens, the well-known Navy cricketer of the past ten years or so. Concentration when batting was also a testing experience but it was characteristically overcome by Geoff Boycott (149*) who put on 102 for the first wicket with Alan Jones (67) and 202 for the fourth wicket with Keith Fletcher (96*).

It was that night, Saturday, that Alan Jones, Don Shepherd and I attended the St David's Day celebrations at a dinner-dance. Wales had defeated England in dramatic fashion at Twickenham; it was a night for singing and indulging in rugby success as Welshmen always do!

Coaching sessions were held along the line. Many people in Singapore believe that cricket will die out when the Services withdraw in 1971. The Ceylon Minister for Planning and Development, a former Cambridge man, believed not. Ninety-six youngsters turned up for four nets. That sounds enthusiasm enough to keep the flag flying on one of the most pleasant grounds in the world.

I write now from Ipoh in the north of Malaysia. We were rather aghast when the Secretary met us and said, 'We have a wonderful wicket. No one has ever played on it before. It is brand new.' But even as I write, Boycott and Jones have put on 120 without being parted.

The East is indeed charming. Places which capture imagination, generous, cricket-loving hosts. The wailing call to the mosque floating across the cricket field; cars blow horns as oxen still tug the laden cart. Sikhs, Australians, Malaysians, Muslims, Ceylonese and many others take guard against us and MCC, shirts carefully buttoned against the sun, noses peeling, wet handkerchiefs around the neck, dusty boots and soaking shirts, share in the obvious enjoyment.

MCC v Ceylon Colombo Oval February 20–23
MCC 132 (Lewis 37) (Kehelgamuwa 4 for 19 Tissera 2 for 18) and 302 for 7 (Jones 112 Fletcher 48) (Sahabandu 5 for 86)
Ceylon 134 (Reid 40) (Wilson 6 for 35) and 127 (Reid 30) (Wilson 8 for 36)
MCC won by 173 runs
MCC v Yang Di Peruan Besar's XI Negri Sembilan, Seremban February 26 and 27
MCC 305 for 8 dec (Hampshire 67, Gilliat 66, Boycott 60, C Navaratnam 5 for 90)
Yang's XI 110 (Shepherd 4 for 22) and 163 for 7 (A C Smith 4 for 19)
Match drawn
MCC v Singapore Singapore Cricket Club February 28-March 1
MCC 315 for 3 dec (Boycott 149* Fletcher 96* Jones 67) and 106 for 4 dec (Lewis 32)
Singapore 178 (W Dougan 60, Wilson 4 for 51 Pocock 3 for 49) and 122 (Dougan 36 Wilson 6 for 45)
MCC won by 121 runs

Tony Lewis, *The Cricketer* (1970)

Five Barbadian Heroes

Barbados is an island. It is a small island, pear-like in shape, the most easterly of that long straggling chain of islands which together form the West Indies. It is far from the largest of them, nor has it the most inhabitants, though it is, I think, the most densely populated. Still, a quarter of a million is not a lot. In English terms it has roughly the population of Coventry, just as in size it compares with the Isle of Wight. Yet in terms of cricket it looms like a giant, its players giving both the backbone and the inspiration to one generation of the West Indies teams after another. Its influence on West Indies cricket exceeds, I suppose, that of New South Wales on the Australian scene, and even of the consolidated North, Yorkshire, Lancashire and Notts, on the English. In short, Barbados cricket is both a legend and a phenomenon.

This is not so much an essay on the theme of Barbadian cricket as a reminiscent note on a few of the great players who have come to light there. But I must at least put the characters into their setting. Barbados cricket has roots more than a century deep, for it was in 1863 that the island first entertained, and duly defeated, a team from overseas. That team from the South American mainland was Demerara, which became British Guiana, and the growth of the game in the West Indies derives from the old triangular competitions between these two territories and the intervening island of Trinidad. (Jamaica, far distant, did not come into the argument until very much later.) In Barbados, perhaps because it was so small, partly through pride of ancestry as Britain's oldest Caribbean possession, patriotism always ran specially high. The land is flatter than most of the West Indies, which meant that good grounds could be more easily made. The climate is ideal all the year round for cricket, and – well, when the islanders are not gathering the sugar crop there is plenty of time to practise. The canes, by the way, are harvested roughly between Christmas and Easter, a fact which prescribes this as the normal close season for cricket, except when Barbados receives a team from abroad.

Not least important in the evolution of Barbadian cricket has been the personality as well as the skill of the chief performers. Sir Harold Austin brought early West Indian teams to England, a man of great substance on the island, an excellent cricketer and indeed by all repute for the first quarter of the century its uncrowned king. Of him I cannot write first-hand, but of the other Barbadian hero of his generation I just can, for it happens that the visit of the first West Indian team to play Test matches in England, that of 1928, coincided with my modest emergence as a cricket writer. George Challenor then, at forty, was past his best, and could not quite match his batting five years earlier when with 1,556 runs in the summer he emerged third in the English averages. But even to this youthful, untutored eye, he was a player of pedigree, an off-side stroke-maker in the classical tradition.

As C. L. R. James has pointed out, the development of West Indian cricket is unintelligible unless it begins with the batting of Challenor. Coming to England as a boy of eighteen in Austin's side of 1906 he absorbed the methods of the golden age of batsmanship: of Ranji and Fry in their heyday, of MacLaren, Johnny Tyldesley, Spooner and Jackson. Back home Challenor developed his own play on the lines of the masters, founded indeed a school of his own. To quote James once more, George Headley recalls Challenor's play against MCC on a wet wicket at Bridge-town as late as 1930, when at the other end to Derek Sealy he showed that young man how to play Rhodes and Voce. As a schoolmaster at Combermere he taught and influenced Frank Worrell, upon whose style, more than any other, modern West Indian batsmanship is based. Thus the influence of Challenor persists today.

But it is time to move on, and we must take a big leap through the thirties which was not a specially rich period in Barbadian cricket even if one recalls several good players who toured England at that time, and notably, besides Sealy, the fast bowlers, Herman Griffith and 'Manny' Martindale.

When G. O. Allen's team sailed for the West Indies at the turn of the year in the third post-war winter of 1947–8 their landfall, as it should be for all touring teams, was Barbados. In due course we had our first sight of the excellent Kensington field with its modest pavilion, the thick palm grove at one end, the solid new Challenor Stand at the other, the long, white concrete walls forming the sight-screens which, with the hard, true pitches and the clearest light from pale blue skies, help to make a batting paradise. John Goddard, the Barbados captain, called up a strong, stocky young fellow just going out to have a net, and said, 'This is Everton Weekes. We hope he'll make a few runs against you.' Thus I met my first member of the trinity of Ws destined so soon to burst upon the world of cricket. Frank Worrell was twenty-three when this first post-war West Indian series took place, Weekes was twenty-two, Clyde Walcott twenty-one. There was in fact a little less than eighteen months between the oldest and the youngest, and all three were born within very short range of the Kensington ground. They are hard to separate in point of skill and achievement, different though their physiques and methods have been. Here for instance are their respective batting figures in Test cricket:

	INNINGS	TNO	RUNS	HIGHEST	AVERAGE	HUNDREDS
Walcott	74	7	3,978	220	56.68	15
Weekes	81	5	4,455	207	58.61	15
Worrell	87	9	3,860	261	49.48	9

If Worrell's batting has been just a little less prolific it is no doubt because he played less frequently against the weaker countries. Six of his nine hundreds were made against England, another against Australia. He was also a left-arm swing bowler good enough to take 69 wickets in Test cricket, while Walcott apart from his batting had 65 victims as a wicket-keeper. In performance they cannot decently be divided though Frank's triumphs as a captain set him apart, just as they account for the fact that whereas Everton and Clyde are Officers of the Most Excellent Order of the British Empire his services to cricket have been rewarded with a Knighthood.

The trio are associated so inevitably as household names today one had almost forgotten that but for that little bit of luck which even great sportsmen need the three might just possibly have been two with Everton trailing quite a long way in the rear. His captain's hope that he might make 'a few runs' against us in 1947–8 was literally accurate until, having played in the first three Tests, he squeezed into the last of the four because someone fell out through injury and therein made his first hundred for the West Indies. Later the same year he went to India, getting hundreds in his first four Test innings, so making a world record with five in a row. But for a run-out when he had scored 90 it would in all likelihood have been six. From that point he never looked back, but if chance had not given him his last opportunity against England on 'Gubby' Allen's tour he might not have been chosen for India.

Everton's only other setback, if such it could be called, was his eclipse in the Tests in Australia of 1951–2, but in that he went on playing with a damaged thigh that only rest could cure it is an episode that redounds to his credit rather than otherwise. Fortitude was always a great element in his play and I have little doubt that of all his innings he is proudest of the 90 against England on the fiery Lord's wicket of 1957 when he finally emerged bruised and battered from head to toe. It was this same groggy limb that led to his retiring first of the three. Whereas Clyde played last for the West Indies in 1960, Frank in 1963, Everton did not offer himself for Test selection after 1957–8. He did all his great deeds, in fact, in eleven seasons though he continued to play for and captain his native island, of which he now is the official coach.

If Worrell's batting was the epitome of grace and Weekes was the stocky executioner, Bradman-like in the clean efficiency of his cutting and hooking, Walcott in form was the most exciting player of the three, and, I think, in West Indian conditions the most devastating. Whereas Weekes' physique encouraged him to practise the back-foot strokes, so Walcott's height and weight of frame proclaimed him as a driver. He made twelve of his fifteen Test hundreds on home pitches, and five of these at Kingston where the straight boundaries seemed so short when he was in full cry that mid-off and mid-on, fielding to the fast bowlers, were usually right back on either side of the sightscreen. One stroke there sticks in the mind as an illustration both of his power and of the psychological effect that can be produced by a single blow. In the first

Test of 1953–4 Len Hutton overloaded his attack with fast bowling (as he was apt to do) giving Alan Moss of Middlesex his first game for England to the exclusion of Laker. Moss duly appeared second change with instructions to keep them quiet if he could. In his first over he bowled something a little over a good length to Walcott. As Moss was still following through the ball came whistling past his head like a bullet, hit the concrete wall that forms the screen and flew back more or less at the bowler's feet!

Walcott's greatest triumphs came on the first Australian visit to the West Indies wherein he averaged 82 in the series without a not-out, including five hundreds. Twice he got two in a match. If a testimonial were ever required as to Walcott's stature as a batsman it would be given with enthusiasm by Lindwall and Miller who on that tour were on the receiving end. The West Indian performance in that rubber was a disappointment but Walcott's magnificent play, and especially his driving, made up for much.

Worrell, as I say, won the palm as a stylist. He was the most complete batsman of the three, and the most adaptable. With him timing and execution made up so thoroughly for a relative lack of power that several of his best innings were scored faster than anything achieved by the other two. On the other hand his concentration was such that when a long rearguard seemed to be called for he did the job magnificently. One thinks particularly of when, in answer to a vast English score, at Trent Bridge in 1957, he played through the West Indies innings for 191 not out and so saved them from defeat. He was better suited temperamentally for this sort of effort than either of his great contemporaries.

But it is Frank's leadership of the West Indies on the two tours in Australia and England of 1960–1 and 1963 which gave him a place in cricket that can never be challenged. He went to Australia at the age of thirty-six, the sole survivor of the triumvirate, ripe in experience and in the philosophy of the game, and the response he evoked from his side helped to make the tour a triumph, alike for cricket and for himself. There must have been the strongest possible temptation after so brilliant a climax to retire rather than undertake the rigours of a six-day-a-week tour of England more than two years later. But he shouldered the job and achieved another success scarcely less spectacular than that in Australia. Such was the legacy that Frank handed on to the last of the five Barbadians in my story.

Garfield Sobers as a lissom loose-limbed boy played for the island against India at the age of sixteen and for the West Indies against England a year later, the youngest cricketer bar Sealy ever to do so. That was in the spring of 1954 when Gary was a slow left-arm bowler of the orthodox method and no more than a promising lower-order batsman. In the intervening time he has played in more Test matches and made more runs than any of his countrymen, gathered around 60 catches, and for good measure has become the fourth West Indian to take 100 wickets in Test cricket. All this and he is (at the moment of writing) not yet thirty! The greater frequency of Test tours nowadays, coupled with the fact that the war delayed the entry of the triumvirate, means that Sobers, granted good health, will probably amass a statistical record that is near unsurpassable. Not, of course, that he is a cricketer who invites figures as a yardstick of quality.

In all but forty years of watching cricket I rate Gary Sobers as the greatest of all the all-rounders who have graced the scene in my time. One thing is quite sure: he is the most complete, for he can bowl to Test requirements in *three* styles – a virtue without precedent in itself – and though most frequently seen fielding close to the wicket, where he has no superior, he can acquit himself equally well anywhere. Add to these items the scoring of fourteen Test hundreds, including the world record score, and the catalogue is all but complete, except for the not insignificant fact that, succeeding Frank Worrell on his retirement from the captaincy, he has also led the West Indies to their first rubber victory over Australia.

Gary has played cricket all over the world – except, of course, in South Africa – and wherever he has been he has added to his already formidable technique. By the age of twenty-one his batting had so developed that he was the leading run-scorer on the English tour of 1957. A few months later he extended the first of his Test hundreds to a matter of 365 not out. He was now a League cricketer (as the three Ws had been before him) and in his five seasons in Lancashire with Radcliffe learned to use the new ball and to acquire such pace that he can when the mood takes him bowl really fast. On a tour of India and Pakistan he first practised left-arm off-breaks and googlies in the manner of the Australians, Fleetwood Smith, Walsh and Tribe. Perhaps the final and not the least important stage of his development was the three seasons he played in the Sheffield Shield for South Australia following the tour of Worrell's team in 1960-1.

Australian cricket tightened up his game that vital little bit in all directions without in any way inhibiting its inherent genius. One fact alone is required to illustrate his impact on the Australian scene. The Australian cricketer in a domestic season can only play in eight first-class games: when there is a touring side he may play in as many as a dozen, including Tests. On this allotment no one in the same season – not the Nobles, the Armstrongs, or the Gregorys, the Millers, the Davidsons, or the Benauds – had ever made 1,000 runs and taken 50 wickets. In 1962–3, playing ten matches including two against MCC, Gary did this and just to emphasize it was no fluke he did it again the following year incidentally carrying South Australia to only their second Sheffield Shield victory in a quarter of a century. Can virtuosity go further?

E. W. Swanton, *The Cricketer's Bedside Book*, edited by Ron Roberts (1966)

Ashes on the Continent

And if I suffered at Lord's, what of Headingley? Do you remember a film in which Naunton Wayne and the ever-lamented Basil Radford wandered round Europe, worrying in a delightfully ridiculous way about what was happening in the Test match at Manchester? Like so many misfortunes that occur to other folk, it seemed funny at the time. I waited until the Manchester Test was safely over. (If I didn't have a heart attack when Australia finished at 35 for 8, I shall live to be a hundred.) That should have been good enough. Before the 1953 Leeds Test came along I was determined to stand no nonsense. I was going to visit romantic Austria and moonlit Venice, Bride of the Adriatic. Surely, after Wardle had taken 4 for 7, a man might be allowed to relax for a fortnight. What a fellow wants is to get away from the atom bomb, the cold war and the imminence of national bankruptcy; in short, all the dull routine of every-day life, and soak his soul in peace and beauty. Though, of course, it was difficult for the soul to be at rest, with Hutton suffering from fibrositis . . .

I deliberately turned my back on my own country. All went well at first. The sea was calm, the journey across Belgium and Germany was full of interest, and there was pleasure, not to mention instruction, in seeing Turin, Milan and the long causeway that leads to Venice . . . That first glimpse in the soft evening light of the Grand Canal has an enchantment that age cannot wither. Byron saw it. The Brownings saw it. The passenger in the gondola abreast of mine saw it, leaned forward to wonder at it and, as he did so, accidentally dropped his hat in the water.

He said, unexpectedly and rather loudly, that it was a fair cow, and this peculiar ejaculation, rather than any marked accent, stamped him as a citizen of the great Australian Commonwealth. When I retrieved his hat for him, we discovered that we were being paddled to the same hotel. He was an amiable companion and our relations from the beginning were extremely pleasant. I was determined not to be the first to mention the Test match. He talked to me of mediaeval glass, the magic of San Marco and Ruskin's *Stones of Venice*. I talked to him about Bondi Beach, Chips Rafferty and the ornithorhynchus or duck-gilled water-mole. I hope I appeared witty and nonchalant. It was hard work.

'Never mind,' I said to myself, 'I'll find an English paper tomorrow.'

But I was unlucky. The following day I searched Venice from the Bridge of Sighs to the Lido (pavilion end), without even finding out whether England had lost the toss. (I need not have worried about that. Hutton never won the toss that year.) My Australian friend, whose name was Martin, kept slipping away on the pretext of posting postcards or buying some Venetian glass to send to his wife, but he always came back without (I suspected) having found what he wanted. Before he left Venice he was beginning to have a haggard look. I had, I think, lost several pounds myself.

We came back from Italy to Austria by coach over the historic Brenner Pass. The majestic Dolomites were wreathed in clouds, and Martin and I were wrapped in silence. It was in the Customs shed at the frontier that I first saw an English newspaper. It was stuffed under the straps of a rucksack worn by a big bony citizen in the crowd in front of me. I had virtually to stand on my head to see it and what I saw played havoc with my blood-pressure.

'Feeling faint?' asked Martin considerately.

'If I can read upside down,' I murmured, 'Hutton has got a duck.'

'Ha-ha – I mean, sorry. You'd better have a stiff peg of slivowitz. That should pull you round.'

For the next four days my agony was less in extent but more concentrated. Hampered though we were by the ignorance of foreigners, we managed to ascertain the score once, or nearly once, a day. We had to fight for every paper just as England was fighting for every run. In Innsbruck I followed a respectable old gentleman the length of the famous Maria-Theresienstrasse under the impression that he was carrying the *Manchester Guardian* only to discover that he was really a German professor, flourishing the *Frankfurter Zeitung*.

(England 167, Australia 161 for 3). At the moment when we obtained the news, from a kindly American, who little knew how he was turning the dagger in my wound, that Australia had filched – you couldn't call it scored – 48 for the last wicket, we were standing in front of the great cathedral at Salzburg, listening to Mozart, a man whom, in my less agitated moments, I have always considered as good as Victor Trumper in his own line. We were actually hanging by a bit of wire in the hair-raising cable railway car five thousand feet above the Hungerburg plateau, like peas in a matchbox, when we learned, from a sympathetic fellow-pea, that England's fate hung equally in the balance. Hutton was out in the second innings, too, but Edrich and Compton, old campaigners both, were making a fight of it. But we never heard another word that day.

It was on the way home that Fate began to turn the screw. We set off on a long railway journey, through a corner of Germany, back to Austria, and then into Germany again. Leaving the train we boarded a steamer, like a Mississippi showboat, to sail between castled crags and vine-clad slopes along the poet's 'wide and winding Rhine'. It was while passing the notorious Lorelei rock that I learned that five English batsmen had been lured to their doom and that my beloved country was only about 70 runs on. Why did I ever leave home? I should never have strayed all this way from Headingley, much less from my own wireless set.

Martin slept well. I know I did not. The train roared through the darkness. It was three o'clock before I dozed off. When I woke we were at Cologne. I stumbled out sleepily on to a darkened platform. By some miracle there was a bookstall right in front of me and, what was more, an English paper. I flung the boy a mark (about one and eightpence) and bundled back into the train. What was this? There was only one event in contemporary English history which interested me, and I could find no mention of it. Our return journey had brought us in front of schedule. This was Thursday's paper. I had missed the result, which would have been published in Wednesday's. In quiet despair I tumbled asleep.

When the train stopped next, it was at Aix-la-Chapelle; now it was Martin's turn to forage for a newspaper. I watched him toddle down the windy platform, a flapping overcoat over his pyjamas. I watched him as he located the paper-trolley.

He laid his hand on the newspaper, but, before he could open it, a frolic wind snatched it from his grasp and whisked it, provokingly, exasperatingly, maddeningly along the tracks. As he dashed after it in frenzied pursuit, our train moved off, quietly but inexorably, towards Ostend. I suppose a draw is a fair result.

And of course, we did win at the Oval. I never saw Martin again. Such a nice fellow.

A. A. Thomson, *Cricket My Happiness* (1954)

Prudential Cup Final

LORD'S: SATURDAY, 21 JUNE 1975

West Indies beat Australia by 17 runs

WEST INDIES

R. C. Fredericks	hit wicket, b Lillee	7
C. G. Greenidge	c Marsh b Thomson	13
A. I. Kallicharran	c Marsh b Gilmour	12
R. B. Kanhai	b Gilmour	55
C. H. Lloyd	c Marsh b Gilmour	102
I. V. A. Richards	b Gilmour	5
K. D. Boyce	c G. S. Chappell b Thomson	34
B. D. Julien	not out	26
D. L. Murray	c & b Gilmour	14
V. A. Holder	not out	6
Extras (lb 6, nb 11)		17
	Total (8 wkts)	291

Innings closed.
Did not bat: A. M. E. Roberts.
Fall of wickets: 1–12, 2–27, 3–50, 4–199, 5–206, 6–209, 7–261, 8–285.
Bowling: Lillee 12–1–55–1, Gilmour 12–2–48–5, Thomson 12–1–44–2, Walker 12–1–71–0, G. S. Chappell 7–0–33–0, Walters 5–0–23–0.

AUSTRALIA

A. Turner	run out	40
R. B. McCosker	c Kallicharran b Boyce	7
I. M. Chappell	run out	62
G. S. Chappell	run out	15
K. D. Walters	b Lloyd	35
R. W. Marsh	b Boyce	11

R. Edwards	c Fredericks b Boyce	28
G. J. Gilmour	c Kanhai b Boyce	14
M. H. N. Walker	run out	7
J. R. Thomson	run out	21
D. K. Lillee	not out	16
Extras (b 2, lb 9, nb 7)		18
	Total	274

Overs: 58.4

Fall of wickets: 1–25, 2–81, 3–115, 4–162, 5–170, 6–195, 7–111, 8–231, 9–233.
Bowling: Julien 12–0–58–0, Roberts 11–1–45–0, Boyce 12–0–50–4, Holder 11.4–1–65–0, Lloyd 12–1–38–1.
West Indies won by 17 runs.
Umpires: H. D. Bird, T. W. Spencer.
Man of the Match: C. H. Lloyd.
Adjudicators: R. Benaud, K. F. Barrington, J. B. Stollmeyer.

All honour and glory to the West Indies! The fortnight's jamboree has ended with a royal handshake for Clive Lloyd, leader of the winning side, and the handing over of the Prudential Cup by HRH Prince Philip, the President of the MCC.

When struggles are tense between these two countries, it is often thought that the flint-hard cussedness of the Aussie outlasts the extravagance of the West Indian. But is that a fancy myth? Who will ever forget the glorious first Test at Brisbane in 1960–61, the popping-creases were alive with Australians diving in to snatch heretic singles to win the match in the final over. Four runs to win in four balls, Hall barges into Kanhai as he is about to catch Grout. Next ball Grout grovels in sweat and dust, run out by the coolest possible throw from the boundary by Conrad Hunte. Two balls to go, one to win. Kline and Meckiff rush off for a quick single, Solomon swoops one handed and throws down one stump, the only one he could see, in a single movement. The famous tie, and the truth is that tense moments in cricket turn the legs of every human being to jelly from time to time.

So it was that Ian Chappell's Australia strained after the West Indian total of 291 on this hot summer's day. One minute they were calm, the next almost demented; many batsmen took quick singles which their partners had not agreed to take. Five of them were run out!

As a final it was all one could ever have hoped for a brave new venture in sponsorship. Two hours before the start, spectators gushed out of the underground station at St John's Wood, queues snaked right around the walls and cars filtered slowly into the park at the Nursery end. A capacity crowd and another hot shirt-sleeved day, completing the meteorological miracle which has blessed every single moment of this competition with blue skies and sunshine.

Ian Chappell won the toss for Australia and sent the opposition in to bat though there was nothing in the air that remotely sniffed of Heading-ley. Chappell had in mind, more likely, Lloyd's habit of 'inserting' others.

It had been West Indies' formula for victory all through the tourna-ment so now, before a ball had been bowled in anger, perhaps Chappell had snatched away their good luck charm.

Gilmour, scourge of England, was no-balled three times in the first over, making it clear where the strongest West Indian encampment was. Bells rang out alongside the Tavern and flags were waved. The hubbub died down as Fredericks and Greenidge prepared to take on Dennis Lillee.

Fredericks is a compulsive hooker, sometimes a little chancy, especially with the shot that goes down to the fine-leg region. With typical West Indian lavishness he is happy to gamble, just to see the ball sail for six and will consider himself hard done-by if a fielder hangs on to a skier on the boundary fence. Well, this time he responded to Lillee's bouncer (one of the few in the match) with a mighty swing of the bat. The ball cleared the fielder this time; all eyes followed it, yet there was a trick to the eye which fooled almost everyone. As he spun around in the crease, Fredericks had lost his foothold and slipped against the stumps, dislodging both bails . . . hit wicket bowled Lillee 7. West Indies 12 for 1. There was a certain amount of bad luck in this dismissal for the batsman, and good fortune for the bowler. It was a well judged bouncer putting Fredericks under pressure but possibly the crucial factor was that Fred-ericks was wearing boots with rubber soles. Most professional players would not dream of going into a match which starts as early as eleven o'clock in the morning, when some moisture may still be retained in the turf, without spiked footwear.

To the hero's acclaim, out strode Kallicharran to face bowlers who could not have felt too happy about his treatment of them a week before at the Oval. His innings began with the confident ring of the bat, but perhaps he was lured into the trap of over-confidence. To a ball from Gilmour outside the off stump he tried a square cut, a flicked shot, feet out of position, the ball too close and bouncing reasonably high off a smooth slow surface. Marsh accepted the snick behind the wicket. 27 for 2 bringing Kanhai to the crease to join Greenidge.

They were now edging from a defensive corner and there was obvious unevenness of bounce which the height of Max Walker emphasized when he came on to bowl. Frequently he struck the splice of Kanhai's bat. Kanhai got well and truly stuck in a defensive rut and even lost Greenidge, caught low down by Marsh from a slower ball by Thomson.

Then Clive Lloyd loped into the arena wearing cap, spectacles and a quizzical look on his face. How often has he contradicted his studious appearance with thoughts of violence! Lillee was immediately brought back, but in easy, destructive style, the West Indies captain hooked a colossal six; then off the back foot, coaxed Walker through the cover field. To this point Ian Chappell had persevered with two slips and a gully, but the time had come to dream up defensive patterns. Men were dispatched to deep positions on the mid-wicket and square-cover boundaries. Edwards dropped him at 26. Meanwhile at the other end, poor Kanhai limped on, eleven overs passing without his scoring a run. Experience told him that as long as Lloyd was plundering on he must persevere. The partnership realized 149 in 36 overs and this was the record stand for the whole competition.

Lloyd's hundred came in 82 balls, and if figures alone do not persuade the world that something very special was happening, the inhabitants of London NW8 will tell how the mere sound of his bat, hammering out the music sweet to West Indian ears, destroyed their afternoon sleep!

It was an innings of surpassing talent and power. When Lloyd is at the crease, mid-on and mid-off automatically withdraw ten yards or so. His defensive pushes roast the hands like a lesser man's drives. Although his back foot wanders involuntarily in a small circle as the faster bowlers rush at him, he quickly beds it down on or around middle-and-leg and then levers off it into his strong front-foot attack. There is no shot he cannot play but one or two are not played by any other with the same ease. At his most vicious he 'picked up' balls from Walker, just a fraction short of good length in line with the middle and leg stumps. These he flipped to square leg off the front foot, and sent the ball with a few bounces into the rails, just like sending a flat pebble hopping over a calm sea. Of course his long reach upsets the bowler's length. Without doubt he is one of the most dangerous batsmen in the world because he can change the drift of a match within such a short space of time. Ideal for one-day cricket, and it was yet another stroke of fortune for all who watched that he reserved this great innings for the final.

Gilmour eventually came back with a tight spell of bowling which swung the game marginally back Australia's way. He got rid of Kanhai, Lloyd and Richards – 209 for 6 in the 46th over.

One sadness was that Lloyd's innings should end in argument and confusion. Marsh 'went up' with Gilmour for a catch down the leg side. Gilmour prolonged the appeal, stared expectantly at umpire Bird, even though the adjudicator had turned to stone; but then after conferring with umpire Spencer, Bird gave Lloyd out. Kanhai took off his hat for more than the heat; Lloyd left his verbal mark on the 'middle' and a few missiles entered the arena from the terraces.

However, Australia's grip was promptly cracked open. One of the more unpredictable West Indians decided that the moon was in his quarter that day, and straightaway the bowlers felt the lash of Keith Boyce. Julien supported with Murray and when you think of it, the strength of batting is limitless when you have Deryck Murray, who has opened in Tests, lurking away at number nine. 291 for 8 was the total. To have beaten that would have set a record for the competition.

Just think how close Australia came! They began securely enough even though there is nothing in the styles of either Turner or McCosker to excite aesthetes. McCosker particularly got turned round to work the ball through mid-wicket and when the score was 25 Boyce produced just the ball to penetrate. It swung away, found the outside edge of the bat and landed safely in the eager fingers of Kallicharran at second slip. It was low and beautifully caught. Turner's authority increased while Ian Chappell quickly showed that he was at his belligerent best. Then came the first of the run-outs. A complete misunderstanding left Turner racing for safety. Only a direct hit would beat him and that is exactly what Richards produced in underarm style.

The Chappell brothers then put on 14 with mounting certainty until the plague returned – Greg was run out. Ian ran the ball out square on the off side. Greenidge and Richards could not agree over who was to field it. Greenidge relaxed, Richards turned and recovered the ball, then on the pivot he threw down the only stump of three which he could possibly see. Luck was going with the West Indies.

The third run-out was beyond all comprehension, especially as it saw off the captain himself, and would you believe it, Richards again was the destroyer. He first fumbled the ball, persuading Australia to break the golden rule 'Never run for a misfield', then spun around and fired the ball just above the bails like a rifle shot. Lloyd, the bowler, clipped off the bails.

Australia were well in with a chance before this latest casualty because Walters had settled in to play handsomely. Perhaps they misread the situation; the outfield was as fast as glass, they could well win. Or possibly they wanted to hustle before Roberts came back.

Whatever the causes the slide was started. Walker was the fourth man to be run out and Thomson the fifth.

It is often agony at the end of the day to weigh up the mistakes. The turning points, camouflaged then, stand up and mock you. Will Ian Chappell recall his superb innings or the five run-outs when he remembers this day? His side required 130 runs off the last 22 overs – very possible in fine batting conditions; then 76 off 10 with 4 wickets standing. Gilmour skied, Edwards too, but the character of the side came through when Lillee and Thomson embarked on a last-wicket partnership of bravado, surprising judgement and humour too. They came in at 233 with 52.5 overs gone. Within minutes their cutting and carving had West Indian fielders perched on the boundaries conceding the singles. The score mounted; 21 wanted from 2 overs. It *was* possible, and even more so when Thomson struck a no-ball in the air to Fredericks at cover. Fredericks threw at the bowler's wicket for a run-out; no one backed up and Lillee and Thomson raced the overthrows. Suddenly the field was full of West Indian spectators who, not hearing the call for no-ball, believed Thomson caught and the match won. It was an incredible sight. Fielders were knocked flying in the avalanche, the ball disappeared altogether, but calmly in midfield Lillee and Thomson ran their runs. Could they run 21 off one ball if the ball was not returned?

'Dead ball' was called by the umpires, 3 runs given. Within a minute Thomson was properly out. He played and missed, the ball went through to Murray. Thomson believed Lillee was going to chance running to the wicket-keeper, but instead he was sent back, and it was a fitting summary of Australia's innings to see Murray throw down the wicket without any trouble at all, while Thomson lay covered in dust, a few inches out. This final gallop by the demon fast bowlers revealed that Australia knew how to lose with humour. A game which begins at 11 a.m. and ends at 8.42 p.m. inevitably kills and rekindles hopes by the minute and by the hour; it chars the nerve-ends, bringing, eventually, the delirium of victory for one and that unwelcome stoicism to the other. To the Australians' credit, they charged to their defeat with style and without a single bleat about one-day cricket not being to their liking. Yet as Ian Chappell confessed when asked to comment on the competition, 'Enough is enough' – and I am sure he was right. Meanwhile, none could deny the West Indians the right to wear the first Prudential crown, nor could there be any argument that their captain, Clive Lloyd, was the Man of this unique Match.

Tony Lewis, *A Summer of Cricket* (1975)

7

They Also Serve

The essence of cricket may be someone bowling a ball to a batsman but it takes twenty-four others to make a game: twenty players more, two umpires and two scorers. It helps to have some spectators too and, if it is an important game, some reporters.

This is a chapter about fringe players and the elements; about some forgotten names; and some normally unconsidered aspects of the game.

Not Only a Wicket-keeper

The seaside resort of Clacton on the East Coast in Essex might seem an unlikely venue for record-breaking achievements. Yet, in August 1965 the holiday crowd witnessed an unusual bowling feat when the visiting Warwickshire 'keeper Alan Smith took off his pads and performed the hat-trick.

Few would have earmarked the match of special interest when it began: neither county was challenging for the Championship title, and most of the country's attention was at Trent Bridge where England and South Africa were playing the second Test. With the Warwickshire skipper M. J. K. Smith on England duty, his namesake, Alan, had taken over the county captaincy. The opening two days of the game had been evenly balanced, and when Essex began their second innings with a little over two sessions of play remaining, they had been set a target of 203 for victory in 3 hours 55 minutes. The wicket had been helpful to the seam bowlers on both sides but when Essex started their chase, Warwickshire were handicapped by the absence through injury of their opening bowler, Dr Rudi Webster.

The Essex openers survived the first few overs without any difficulty, and it was then that Smith, keen to get a breakthrough before lunch, exercised the captain's prerogative and decided to turn his arm over for a few overs before the interval.

Alan Smith, or A. C. as he is popularly known, was by no means an unknown quantity as a bowler. During his army service in the mid–1950s he had bowled regularly, and he had a best analysis of 5–32 while playing for Oxford University. It was all a far cry from his school days when he had been banned from bowling in the nets, not because his action was illegal but because, in his own words, 'it was so grotesque'. His whirl-wind, chest-on, apparently wrong-foot delivery, would certainly not have won any points for artistic impression. Aesthetic considerations apart, however, his high action did enable him to get plenty of bounce, and he was always capable of making the ball swing. Smith's style, reminiscent in his own view of Mike Procter or Froggy Thomson, was to yield devastating results on this occasion.

The wicket, so helpful to the seamers during the first two days of the match, 'still had a bit in it', and Smith decided that if he was to bowl at all then, with half an hour to go before lunch, this was the right time. Dennis Amiss took over behind the stumps and Smith, arms flailing, bowled his first overs of medium pace that season. His opening over brought no reward. Then, as he remembers, 'off the fifth ball of the second or third, Gordon Barker was the first man out. Barker hooked the ball and was caught at long leg by Roger Edmonds. The batsmen crossed and off the next ball Geoff Smith, the other opener, was caught at leg-slip trying to play the ball away on the leg side.' That marked the end of the over, so Keith Fletcher had to wait anxiously at the other end before he faced the hat-trick ball. With the entire Warwickshire side crouched round the bat, the twenty-one-year-old Fletcher seems to have been a victim of nerves. 'It was a perfectly straight, good-length ball, and he scooped it up and was caught at short square leg. It was an odd stroke, almost as if he'd made up his mind what shot to play before I'd even bowled the ball – perhaps he expected something short.' With the new ball still swinging,

Smith claimed four wickets in 34 balls for no runs, his last victim being Essex skipper, Trevor Bailey, caught behind by the makeshift 'keeper, Amiss. Bailey's verdict is concise: 'At first we were surprised, then very annoyed.' Unfortunately, despite Smith's success Warwickshire still did not win the match, for Essex held on for the draw, thanks mainly to Robin Hobbs. Smith eventually finished with 4–36 from 21 overs. A. C. looks back on his achievement with great pride, particularly as it was 'the top order' that he bagged.

His feat was greeted, however, with incredulity by those who were lucky enough to see it. He himself describes it as 'just one of those freaks, but entertaining at the time. People were frightened of getting out to me because I wasn't regarded as a bowler and because it was such an awful death to get out to an action that many thought shouldn't be allowed on the field!' As a token of his achievement, Smith was presented with the ball, inscribed to remind him of his unusual hat-trick.

Joanne Watson, Moments of Glory (1990)

Of the Late Frederick J. Hyland

The *Wisden* of 1965, chronicling as usual the deaths of the year before, has a melancholy little entry whose very sparseness of content is the occasion for unlimited wistfulness. Tucked away among the usual compact lists of familiar and half-familiar names for whom this note constitutes in most cases a last salute, this inconspicuous embodiment of obscurity might be slid over by nine readers out of ten without engaging a moment's attention; but for no explicable reason it chanced to catch my eye, and like the lady in the poem, compelled my imagination many days.

'Hyland, Frederick J.,' says *Wisden*, not knowing or not caring what the J. stood for, 'who died in February, aged 70, played as a professional in one match for Hampshire in 1924. Cricket in this game, at Northampton, was limited by rain to two overs from which Northamptonshire scored one run without loss. Hyland later earned a reputation as a nurseryman in Cheshire.' That is all. Nothing else whatever. Boundless and bare, the lone and level sands stretch far away. No sooner did Mr Hyland come than he went, not only by that same door but almost in that same breath. *Le silence éternel des espaces infinis m'effraie*, said Pascal; the monumental brevity of this cricketer's career does the same to me.

Now this entry in the *Wisden* obituary is, of course, by no means the shortest or even the least warranted. Dozens of players who had played less first-class cricket than this simple character, which is virtually to say that they had played no first-class cricket at all, have been granted this last dignity and no questions asked. Earlier editions I have known devote endless entries to worthy clergymen who were in the eleven at Winchester in 1885 and 1886 and though described in *Scores and Biographies* as a fair bat and a useful long-stop, failed to get further than the Seniors' Match at Oxford or Cambridge; and there are many similar enthusiasts who are recorded there as having been born in Brooklyn and been President of the New York Veterans' Cricket Association, or as being well known in Metropolitan cricket circles as the wicket-keeper of the illustrious Mitcham club and an influential figure in local speedway racing affairs. (I pass over other characters who appear never to have touched a bat or ball in their lives but to have attained a variety of other distinctions ranging from the Throne of England to the post of engraver at the Mint at Philadelphia.) Against these the late Mr Hyland has little chance; in some little ways they all were born to greatness, or achieved it, or had it thrust upon them. Not so Mr Hyland; he had no greatness recorded of him at all, at least in the cricketing sense. He was no doubt an excellent nurseryman, but that on its own would hardly have got him into *Wisden* in the way that, for example, tenure of the Throne of England would have done. The distinction that he can wave in the teeth of all competitors (and for all I know he may have done so and more power to him if he did) is an indisputable and a proud one, which nobody will grudge him. He had played first-class cricket; and even taking into account the length of cricket history, the expansion of the first-class game and the thickness of *Wisden*, what kind of proportion of genuine cricket-lovers can say the same?

In the eyes of an emulous and romantic schoolboy (and I will continue to assert, under duress if necessary, that all cricket lovers retain to the end of their days much of that schoolboy's quality for good or ill), the man who has played first-class cricket is marked for ever apart, by an indefinable aura of honour, distinction, achievement if you will, from his less fortunate though equally dedicated fellows who have not. To have appeared, even on one occasion only, for Surrey or Hampshire or whoever, by whatever curious mistake of fortune at however remote a time, invests a man with a *cachet* that must make him for the rest of his life, however dishonourable or unrewarding, the envy of those of lesser attainment or fortune. I knew a man once, a keen and able cricketer of good club standard, whose life was blighted by his tantalizing failure to attain this subtle and almost inexplicable honour. He was a shrewd appraiser of his own worth and never assessed his capacities over-highly; at Oxford in the early 1920s he appeared in a preliminary trial with no success, and was never surprised to be left far off striking distance of the University team. (Small wonder, when such paladins as Jardine, Stevens, Bettington, Hedges, and Robertson-Glasgow already filled out its ranks.) This never disturbed a temperament of admirable equanimity; but a week or two after the abortive trial, when all sense of urgency had departed with his never very realistic hopes, he found himself in the pavilion at the Parks on the opening morning of a match against Somerset, and became aware, some half an hour or so before the game was due to begin, of the tumultuous arrival of the great John Daniell announcing with appropriate adjectival qualifications that two of his Somerset side had failed to turn up and demanding impressment from the highways and byways. (This situation, one has gathered from the writings of Robertson-Glasgow and others, was nothing unusual for Somerset in the 1920s.) I cannot remember for the moment what directed the great man's questing intelligence to the instinctive appraisal of my friend, who was just standing about, as an active and willing cricketer; but apparently the next thing my friend knew was that Daniell had seized him in one huge hand and said, 'You! You come from Somerset, don't you? Will you make up for us, then? Get changed!', and had disappeared, blaspheming dreadfully, into the chaos of the Somerset dressing-room. On wings of delirious delight my friend, who had been born in Oxfordshire and had never to his recollection stepped inside Somerset in his life, but for purposes of record had a maternal grandfather living in retirement near Weston-super-Mare, sped off to get his cricket bag, dreams of long days of idyllic gaiety and success combating in his perturbed mind with conflicting doubts of his ability to perform at all adequately in such august company. Alas, when he returned, breathless but braced to the task, it was to find that in the interval of his absence the two missing members of the Somerset eleven had arrived. No doubt John Daniell was disarming in his apologies; but the deflation of ambition was a sore blow. He put his cricket bag into a corner and the match went on without him, just as half an hour ago he would have expected it to, and never until this day when he must be getting on for seventy, did he play first-class cricket for Somerset or anywhere else. It is an episode in his life which he recalls with a wry and amused pleasure which overlays what cannot be disguised as a rueful and indelible regret.

But Mr Frederick J. Hyland, in most ways, I feel, no less obscure than my friend, went to his grave I hope contented in a way that my friend never can. He had played first-class cricket; and if in his long after-years of efforts and success as a nurseryman in Cheshire he had at times those inevitable periods of recession and despondency that attend upon the worthiest endeavours, he had perpetually the memory to comfort him of the day that marked him out from other nurserymen in Cheshire, the day when for the first and indeed the only time he trod the first-class cricket field in his own inalienable right. What his previous cricket history had been, what his subsequent cricket history was, *Wisden* does not tell me and for the purposes of these meditations I do not need to know; he remains for me an epitome of the life of man as illuminated long ago by the Venerable Bede, the sparrow flying into the banquet-hall, fluttering for a moment in the light and heat, and then flying forth at the far door into the wintry darkness. 'So tarries for a moment,' says the chronicler, 'the life of man in our sight, but what is before it, what after it, we know not' – and, he implies, it would spoil the story if we knew. F. J. Hyland may have been a brilliant and successful performer in and about his native county (or was it his adopted?) and on his relapse into obscurity he may have fluttered anonymous dovecotes the length and breadth of the country until, arriving in the fullness of time in Cheshire, he became a nurseryman and lived happily ever after; but of this we know nothing. His lamented death in 1964 we know about, and three days forty years earlier; but around these minuscule illuminations the blanket of the dark descends.

The fitful light gleamed at what must be called its brightest on Wednesday, 11 June 1924. Hampshire presented themselves to time at Northampton, fresh from a horrible walloping by Kent, who had cleaned them up in two days at Southampton and left them a blank Tuesday in which, under the guidance of their eloquent and illustriously connected captain, they might meditate on their sins. The accident of the English summer weather confined them drearily to the pavilion for the day's early stages; and the young Hyland, who took over one of the two or three vacancies in the side occasioned by the unavailability of several amateurs, one of whom was R. Aird, had plenty of leisure to observe his new team-mates and his new surroundings. The adventitious and unheralded nature of his appearance, on which no comment of any kind is discoverable, rather suggests to the thoughtful historian that he was a last-minute substitute in some unexpected emergency, illness, or injury. Whatever the reason, here he was with his equipment; and here, in company with such renowned warriors as Philip Mead, George Brown, Alec Kennedy, Jack Newman, Walter Livsey and Stuart Boyes, not to mention the Honourable Lionel Tennyson if fraternization was in those stratified times permissible, he ate his frustrated and nervous lunch and tea. Soon after tea the perverse weather cleared a little; and by half past five, for what good it would do, the teams were ready to make a beginning. Hampshire were in the field; and the young Hyland got into his flannels with the rest.

I cannot think that there could have been many spectators present that damp and washed-out end of a rainy Wednesday; I picture a deserted grey field overlooked by gaunt dark houses with glistening slates in relief against a lowering sky. Against the inhospitable wind that drove in over the abandoned benches, the Hampshire team, as they picked their way across the treacherous slippery outfield towards the piles of sawdust which must have constituted the highest lights in the landscape, were no doubt huddled into two or even three sweaters each. Tentatively they moved, as if on eggs, to their allotted places, the young obscure Hyland obediently among them savouring glumly the cold bleakness of his baptism into the county game. I see him a little lonely and aloof, silent in an awed unfamiliarity. As the Northants batsmen, flexing their shoulders, approached the wicket, glances no doubt went up on all sides at a still untranquil sky, and low clouds coming in on the wind sent an ominous spit or two before them.

Alec Kennedy, no doubt going gingerly among the sawdust, bowled the first over, and off one ball, I do not know which, W. H. Denton took a single, I do not know how. Whether his partner, Frank Woolley's brother, Claude, was required to take strike at all is recorded no doubt in the score book, which I have not taken the no doubt virtually insuperable trouble to get unearthed. What we do know is that one run came to Denton off Kennedy's over, and that Jack Newman, opening up as usual at the other end, bowled a maiden; at the conclusion of which, or probably I should think well before the conclusion of which, the aforesaid spits became a shower, the shower became rapidly an intolerable condition in which to play cricket, and the players one and all picked up their heels as smartly as they could and raced for the pavilion and the dry.

What a pitiful waste of time and talent. The Hampshire team were adorned with such great names as I have already listed; sitting in the Northants dressing-room were divers performers of note like Murdin and Thomas, Bumper Wells, Vallance Jupp, Fanny Walden and an inexperienced left-handed fast bowler named Clark, years later to play often for his country. Yet for none of that illustrious company was one more moment's play possible; the ground on the next day, when there were ironic intervals of sunshine, was without question or argument in no fit state; and at about half-past one on Friday, the game was abandoned (Hampshire, minus Hyland, then went off to a horrible walloping from Notts). Young Hyland, rushing off the field with the rest at five minutes to six on Wednesday evening, had rushed for ever out of the first-class game into which he had walked, with what confidence and hope we can only guess, ten minutes or so before. We can never know whether in the whole of his first-class career he touched the ball once. It is very probable indeed that he did not.

Why he never played again is almost as inexplicable as why he ever played at all in the first instance. We lose him, as I say, in all but impenetrable night until, a retired nurseryman of some repute in Cheshire, he dies forty years later. But for all his life he had the comfort that nobody could ever take away from him; he had played in a first-class match, he had gone on the field while registrable balls, to the number of twelve, were bowled. If Hampshire had batted and not fielded, he would have been recorded the honour of a first-class appearance even if he had never set foot on the turf; but a strangely empty honour it would have seemed. As it is, he appeared, he walked the field, he played, and *Wisden*, forty years after, thought it proper to recall it. I am glad that it did; and it prompts me to inquire of learned cricket statisticians whether any man can be traced to have had a shorter career in first-class cricket.

The distinction is perhaps one without a difference; in fact, it may be entirely illusory, and to those who have once stepped across the magic line there is no glamour at all. Be it so; let this exordium remain as a mild, but heartfelt, tribute from one of the keenest but humblest of the outsiders to one who may or may not have been keen but who was certainly one of the humblest of the insiders. Multitudes there have been who have scraped across into the number of the favoured with one appearance (and may I parenthetically honour here the memory of N.

Callaway, an Australian youth, who in 1914–15 played his first and only innings in first-class cricket, a little matter of 207, before packing his kit and going to a war from which unhappily he never returned); but Frederick J. Hyland may here stand toast of them all. He retired, after the fashion of all good philosophers, to cultivate his garden; but by his ten wet minutes on the first-class field he had as irrevocably joined the ranks as W. G. had, whose playing life in that region spanned forty-four years. In the sight of the eternities in and beyond history forty-four years and ten minutes are as one; Frederick J. Hyland, cricketer and nurseryman, may, in the sight of all us envious idealists beyond the pale, stand kin to Grace in honour. Of his kind is the game given its enduring strength and fascination.

> . . . And then they die,
> Perish, and no one asks
> Who or what they have been,
> More than he asks what waves
> In the moonlit solitudes mild
> Of the midmost Ocean, have swelled,
> Foamed for a moment, and gone.

> Ronald Mason, *Sing All a Green Willow* (1967)

Yabba

The green slope of the Hill at the southern end of Sydney Cricket Ground is intersected by a diagonal streak. The streak is a footworn track, beginning at the asphalt path at the foot of the Hill and leading up the couch-grassed rise to the concrete scoreboard towering in the far corner. The pilgrims who trudge up this track are not the short-sighted, seeking a closer view of the names and figures on the scoreboard, but the thirsty, bound for the bar tucked away under the informative façade.

The bar, the track and the green stretch down to the ringside benches close to the white-lattice sightscreen lay in the domain of Yabba.

Australian barrackers are known as masses of people, silently intent, talkatively bored or noisily angry. Yabba was the only one who stepped forward from the ranks of the chorus, so to say, and established himself as an identity. This colloquial wit had a comedian's sense of timing. He had an old soldier's vocabulary, dating back to the South African War, for which he enlisted while on a visit to that country in his early twenties.

On a sleepy afternoon, watching J. W. Hearne break a long scoreless spell with a sudden single, he bellowed: 'Whoa, he's bolted!'

Though nothing was known of his playing experience as schoolboy and youth, he had a knowing appreciation of the game. From his viewpoint almost in line with the wicket he could tell when the batsman was not to blame for slow play. Persistent off-theory or leg-theory bowling soon brought him to full cry as spokesman for the resentful crowd. Sarcastically he thundered at one Victorian medium-pace bowler: 'Your length's lousy but you bowl a good width.' Midway through an over in which a bowler consistently pitched the ball well outside the off stump Yabba yelled: 'Wide.'

Again, next ball (louder): 'Wide.'

Next ball (fortissimo): 'DOUBLE wide' (in a tone implying that the bowler had committed an error like a double-fault at tennis).

He would not rhapsodize about fast scoring if batsmen were gathering runs by the armful on an easy wicket. 'Can I go in with a walkin'-stick?' he would ask.

Yabba was credited with having originated many of the sayings from which tedious repetition has since drained all humour. When two batsmen in long partnership had the fielding side in despair everybody laughed when he suggested sending for the fire brigade to put them out, or calling for a nurse of shady reputation. He became more widely known in Sydney than many members of Parliament. Cinesound made a newsreel about him. A 14-stone man, about five feet ten or eleven inches tall, he used to walk through the turnstiles carrying a hamper and a couple of bottles of beer. Lolling or standing on the Hill he would soon be surrounded by a cluster of admirers who made sure his throat never ran dry. His face was fleshy, with more than a hint of a double chin, and his expression was that of a man enjoying himself. He dressed for the part in an open-neck shirt and sometimes a white coat, like a barman who had temporarily deserted his post to steal a peep at the play. On hot days the coat was discarded, exposing his braces. He wore a cloth cap, or a felt hat pushed back.

His voice, coarse and penetrating, had a brassiness which rang through the nondescript yells and mutterings of the mob like Harry James's trumpet above the noises of the band. On Saturdays when there was no first-class match he watched the Glebe club, and was a loyal supporter of the Cricketers' Arms, of Warren Bardsley, the left-hand opening batsman, and of Albert Cotter, the fast bowler.

To add to the discomfort of a batsman facing the dreaded Cotter, Yabba would bawl: 'Give him one on the big toe, Tibby!' One afternoon when Cotter was running through North Sydney's batsmen a tail-ender had his middle stump smashed first ball. The crowd laughed unfeelingly. As the shamefaced batsman retreated to the pavilion Yabba consoled him with: 'Don't worry, son; it woulda bowled *me*.'

A harsher note was heard in his voice in an Annandale pub late one winter afternoon in 1940. As he raised a pint from the counter somebody bumped his elbow, spilling the beer on the floor. In righteous wrath, Yabba blasted the clumsy oaf with tavernacular invective, including words which, though some of them appear in the Bible, are forbidden out loud in a public place. For the language, Glebe Court fined him £1 in default 48 hours. Yabba served only one of the 48 hours. He described his liberation in these words: 'It was the longest hour of me life. Also the quietest. When the juice went around that the One and Only was in the clink some of the boys in the village had a zack in the tit-for-tat to get me out.'

By occupation he was a dealer who hawked rabbits. In every street and back lane between Long Nose Point and Iron Cove they knew his two-wheeled cart, with its row of disembowelled rabbits hanging by their tied hind-legs, white tails bobbing to the pony's gait. All the cats in Balmain trooped behind his cart; he threw them rabbits' heads. When a customer hailed him Yabba would hitch a rabbit's hindlegs around a hook, expertly peel its skin up to its neck with a flick of the wrist, behead it with a blow of his snickersnee and slap it on to the housewife's plate almost in one action, like a fieldsman picking up and returning a ball. He would drive on, standing up in his striped apron with his vest open to the breeze, calling his wares: 'Rabbie – wild rabbie!' A corruption of his call gave him his nickname, Yabba. Watching one of his cobbers, Alan Bowen, playing football for Balmain, he combined comment and advertisement in one breath: 'You ought to eat my rabbits!'

His voice was not always as bold as brass. One day a batsman was having a sightscreen moved, and umpire George Borwick was holding an arm aloft as a signal to the attendant to keep pushing. The operation took some time. Yabba stared at the umpire's upraised hand and piped up in a schoolboyish falsetto: 'It's no use, umpire; you'll have to wait till playtime like the rest of us.'

The Hill at Sydney has hardly been the same since Yabba died in 1942, at the age of sixty-four, a grandfather. He was a first-generation Australian, born in the inner suburb of Redfern, son of an Englishman and a Sydney woman.

Yabba's name was Stephen Harold Gascoigne. His father was a store-keeper who migrated from that centre of learning, Oxford.

Ray Robinson, *From the Boundary* (1950)

I Was Larwood – and Voce

On summer evenings in the late 1920s, after his work for the day at Trent Bridge was over, Harold Larwood frequently dismissed the entire Australian side for less than twenty runs. His action during these triumphs would not have been recognizable to Neville Cardus. Even with the coal-place door open in the back-yard of Number 10 Watnall Road, Hucknall allowed insufficient space for a run-up and he was bowling slow, underarm leg-breaks, but they were more than Woodfull, Ponsford, Bradman and their team-mates could cope with. They seemed to have no defence. If the ball missed the rather vaguely defined area of the brick wall which represented the wicket they were allowed one run, but a slightly more accurate delivery meant they were out. Sometimes if, say, McCabe seemed to be offering resistance, Bill Voce would be called on to take over – usually with instant success.

This was the beginning of my career in cricket and I was off to a flying start. I was Larwood. And I was also Voce.

These were Camelot cricket days when it seemed almost never to rain till after sun-down, but if it did there was still no escape for the Australians. There was always book-cricket involving the use of a code which translated the initial letter of any page of *Just William* or *Treasure Island* into cricketing terms, R = 1 run, S = stumped, Y = bowled, and so on. I suppose the scorecard might more fairly have read: 'O'Reilly c Richmal Crompton b R. L. Stevenson' but it never did. It was always 'c Voce b Larwood' or 'c Larwood b Voce'. And I was always Larwood. And I was always Voce.

And my success had been achieved without coaching. Miss Molloy, Headmistress of Beardall Street Infants School, did not include sporting activities in her curriculum, and I never saw Miss Piggin or Miss Webster padded up.

So I was not well prepared when I moved eventually to a senior school with grass and nets, and an expectation of overarm bowling at a wicket twenty-two yards away. I tried to reproduce the leg-breaks that had been so successful against the Australians but, delivered from round the back of the neck, line and length were not easy to control. However, my first ball completely beat the bat of Mr S. R. Revill (History and Sarcasm) and I thought it was ungracious of him, as he handed over the two pennies I had knocked off his stumps, to tell me: 'I don't call a ball that bounces about six times, a ball at all, Bailey.' Further discouragement came from Mr H. (Nemo) Newitt (Latin and Sadism) and it became clear that if I was to proceed with a career in cricket I would have to approach it obliquely; round the wicket in fact.

Local walks took me often past the houses of my heroes: past Butler's Hill to Bill Voce's, up to Annesley Road to Harold Larwood's; and eventually through arrangements made by Paddy Griffin the High Street barber (Men's haircut 6d, Boys 3d) I was invited to the Voces for tea and sat beside the great man as he showed me his silver-plated trophies.

I went to Trent Bridge as often as I could and sometimes to the pretty ground further down the Loughborough Road owned by Sir Julien Cahn who used to bowl, as someone once described, not so much 'up and down' as 'to and fro'; at the same time wearing a cap, two sweaters and a blazer. I saw him leading a team of distinguished players, sometimes choosing to open the innings and sometimes to close it but invariably scoring runs and always, but always, winning.

It was indirectly through Sir Julien that some years later my cricketing career took another step forward. He had developed a second cricket-ground at Stanford Hall, his country home near Loughborough. He had added to the Hall an extra wing to accommodate and indulge his two particular pleasures which were conjuring and cricket. So the ground floor was a theatre where he would perform his tricks for the delight of his captive guests and the upper storey was divided into twelve rooms for the team and presumably an umpire, whose night's accommodation, I suspect, might well have been dependent on the generosity of his decisions during the day. All I had to do to win two weeks of luxury at Stanford Hall was to contract appendicitis while on war-time leave from the Army, by which time the wing had been given over to the Red Cross and the only guests wearing white were the nurses. So, although I never quite made Sir Julien's team, I did spend a fortnight in one of their beds – and how many sporting journalists could boast as much?

To advance my career still further I decided to marry into cricket. My prospective bride had told me that as a small girl she had been waltzed round a dance-floor by Herbert Sutcliffe. So, in the manner of the Herbert Farjeon song, I can claim that I've danced with a girl, who danced with a man, who danced down the wicket with Hobbs.

So far, so good; but I was ambitious and progress was slow. I had to make another positive move if I was ever to be invited to tour Australia. I decided to take up work in the theatre.

For some years it seemed that the covers might never be taken off again as far as my career was concerned. Not a ball was bowled, for instance, during a run of *Murder in the Cathedral*, and while many other dramas opened and closed, Play never Commenced.

Eventually, however, my strategy was seen to be working, and in Melbourne, during a theatrical success, I was asked to address the sixth form of a boys' school. I reported to the Headmaster's office and read the name on the door: W. M. Woodfull. I believe I was tactless enough to mention the name 'Larwood' but was careful to avoid any reference to my many moments of triumph in unrecorded battles long ago.

In Sydney I had invited guests to a performance of *My Fair Lady*. Since they were no ordinary guests they came to the dressing-room before the performance, and when he heard the traditional call of 'Five Minutes Please' Mr Larwood said to Mrs Larwood: 'Come on, then. Let's leave him to it. I know what it's like. It's like looking out of t'pavilion windows and watching them umpires going out in their white coats, and you get them butterflies.' I felt I was back on course.

There were many other visitors to the dressing-room during that time and none more welcome, of course, than the Australian cricketers and visiting teams from the West Indies and England. One of the visitors lingered one evening after a performance and eventually asked me would I, as a personal favour, stress a particular final consonant. How could I refuse? Others have abandoned the reverse sweep and given up flashing outside the off-stump for the same man. Yes, Peter. Of course, Mr May.

Perhaps it was due to such contact with the hierarchy of the MCC, and my willingness to co-operate, that I finally played for England. It wasn't at the Gabba or the Oval, nor at Perth or Headingley. It was on the lawn of a house in Kent where I was the guest of Mr P. E. Richardson of Worcestershire, Kent and England. Following a Sunday lunch, Peter's sons and their friends were fitted with Australian caps collected in the course of various Test series, and Peter and I wore England caps. I played two quite distinguished innings and finished with an average of 8.5, which was rather higher than the average of the opposing side. Of their ages I mean.

Since then I have to admit there have been fallow periods such as most cricketers suffer, but the strong survive.

My activities in television have lately been much concerned with the 'summer game' in the adopted persona of Peter Tinniswood's Brigadier and as Hugo Lovelace Charters arguing about *Wisden* statistics with his friend Mr Caldicott. I don't feel I can claim any personal cricketing credit on that account, but I do claim this – only last year I travelled up four floors of a Manchester hotel with Mr I. V. A. Richards. As I stepped out of the lift, I heard him distinctly say: 'Good night.'

That's what I call success.

Robin Bailey, Quick Singles (1986)

The Art of Being Captained

Have you noticed how often cricket books contain a chapter on captaincy? Whole books are given up to all that strategy nonsense, yet nowhere will you find a chapter entitled 'The Art of Being Captained'. On the face of it this is a surprising omission since there are ten of us to one of them, but then cricket always was a bosses' game.

The chapter I have in mind would include advice on how a bowler gets to bowl at the best end; how to slip down the batting order when the wicket's a shade too green; and how to drop catches off the captain's bowling and still stay in the team. Nobody could doubt that these skills have more relevance to a cricketer's enjoyment of the game than rolling the wrists or bracing the left leg into the delivery stride.

True, most coaching manuals suggest that players should keep an eye on the captain, but only because he may want to change a fielder's position in the outfield. This is an extremely naïve notion since a fielder will often pick his position with singular care – close to a hospitality tent for example or a pretty face, or away from that patch of the outfield plagued with ridges, craters and broken teeth. In such cases keep an eye on the captain by all means but first make sure that you don't catch his. Recommended is a head-bowed, eye-cocked position. Using this method (a cap helps) an outfielder can observe the captain trying to attract his attention. At first the captain will use the grand arm's-length semaphore, then the vexed handclap, finally the short crude gesticulation. A captain so trained will soon give up and start fiddling with someone else, leaving the outfielder to patrol his chosen terrain in peace.

Once mastered, the technique of getting into the captain's blind spot is extremely useful – when he's looking for a nightwatchman for example, or someone to bowl with a wet ball. One of the most common applications is sidling unnoticed away from catching positions. Sidling has a huge membership. For a close-to-the-wicket fielder this means standing so that the ball always bounces safely in front of him. On the boundary edge the sidling fielder is the one who hates waiting underneath a catch. When a batsman comes in who favours the rustic heave-ho to the leg-side, the fielder will ignore the captain and sidle towards the sightscreen. By doing this he ensures that instead of the skier straight into and possibly out of his lap, he has to gallop desperately round the boundary – whereupon he will either pluck a catch out of thin air to the surprise and plaudits of spectators or invite their sympathy for a gallant effort made in vain.

A chapter entitled 'The Art of Being Captained' would also tackle the sinister practice of brainwashing. For example, unless a player is very careful, a captain may seek to 'get the best out of him'. Now there are days, frankly, when a chap doesn't want someone getting the best out of him. Of course, he could bowl batsmen out and score runs if he wanted to, but sometimes he just prefers to be left alone to have a good sulk.

The captain trying to get the best out of a player can be spotted in a number of ways. If he approaches a bowler pretending to get some shine on to a very old ball, the bowler should move in the opposite direction, ideally with a limp. The key word to listen for here is 'brake', as in 'Just put a brake on the run rate, old son'.

Batting with the captain can be a particular minefield. Watch out for the observation from his end that you appear to have the measure of the raw West Indian quickie who is enthusiastically discolouring your torso by numbers. The giveaway word here is 'middle', as in 'Your bat seems all middle today, so I'll stay down this end while you see him off.'

Players should beware of such appeals to their self-esteem and recognize that the captain himself may be vulnerable on that flank. If, after a mix-up when running between the wickets, a batsman finds the captain standing alongside, he should suggest that the PR value in him 'walking' would far outweigh the cost of his wicket.

Admittedly such a ploy never worked for me, but then I came from a hard-bitten North Midlands tradition where the captains tended less to the Brearleyan persuasion and more towards the 'do it or else' school of thought.

My first captain had a face as rough as a coalminer's kneepad and he could spit a lot further than some of the England team. These were invaluable assets for leading a junior school side and he was a great success until the teacher discovered that every time a coin was tossed he demanded the money with menaces.

Much as I would have enjoyed a reputation for being 'difficult' to handle, the opportunity never really presented itself. After my first hundred in league cricket the captain responded to my triumphant return to the dressing room with the greeting: 'If you die tonight, we'll manage.' I think he must have been the father of my junior school captain. Anyone who spoke his mind in that team spoke it in the privacy of the pavilion's outside loo. Nobody ever challenged the captain's right to play sheet anchor in a run chase and he never went on holiday for fear of a coup. Irrespective of the state of the wicket, if he won the toss he always put the opposition in to bat so that our batsmen could get their eyes used to the light. In every match he bowled the same two seam bowlers for ninety minutes whether they were getting wickets or a whopping. The spinners would then come on for fifteen minutes whereupon the seamers would return. The captain's mind ran so often down the same track we called him ASLEF.

In many ways playing under ASLEF was the best possible grounding for the first-class game. Here the captain presides over a team living together as a 'family' with all the mutual recrimination and lack of communication implied by that term. The non-stop first-class diet of cricket, travel and hotels means that the art of being captained extends beyond the cricket ground and into every waking moment.

During the evenings away from home the captain will tend to be either a nanny or a nighthawk. The nanny sits with notepad and pencil in the hotel bar after ten thirty, wearing a dressing gown and pyjamas. The nighthawk is the one who wakes a player at two in the morning to tell him it's his turn to be chauffeur.

In the morning the captain can be categorized as a dosser or a sunbeam. A dosser is so monosyllabic and lifeless at breakfast that uncapped members of the team are rostered to help him take the top off his egg. A sunbeam is the one who asks players to go to the ground with him three hours early in order to inspect the wicket. He particularly enjoys crawling under the covers to accomplish this task. Players can avoid all these types by booking into a different hotel.

In essence, then, the art of being captained is a variation on the time-honoured technique of keeping oneself scarce. Always remember, if you go looking for advice the chances are you'll get some. So, to recap, on the field of play remember to stand with the weight nicely balanced between both feet, the body alert but relaxed, arms free to move at all times, head still, keep your eye on the captain and above all keep moving. Oh, and don't forget to limp.

Peter Gibbs, Quick Singles (1986)

The Epithets

The strain of captaining a side such as my own distinguished XI, Heartaches CC, can leave its mark on the most relaxed of leaders if he is not careful. More often than not it is the problems of selection rather than the worries on the actual field of play that age the amateur skipper – these can take days rather than minutes to resolve and an ill-judged selection (or rejection) can wreck friendships, million-pound business deals and/or marriages (many a cricketer's home life has been put to the severest of tests when the call of family duty is put up against the call of the willow). Small wonder that in the winter months I spend many a happy hour selecting teams whose members never complain, let me down, abuse, misuse or confuse me – mainly because these sides are imaginary only; often dominated by players from the past or from fiction. Let me tell you about the Epithets.

All cricket lovers have chosen their World XI team to play Mars and since the days of Fuller Pilch and John Wisden literally millions of other intriguing but non-existent teams must have been picked by selectors of all ages and of all times. Teams consisting of men whose surnames begin with a particular letter of the alphabet, teams of men all born under one astrological sign, teams from one particular era, or teams whose members share some unusual characteristic, such as those who turned out (a real match, this) in the fixture reported in the 1868 *Wisden* (p. 86), One Arm v. One Leg (match drawn); these and many more colourful combinations have flickered to and fro across the daydreams of gentlemen and players, and always will. The most fascinating side I have ever selected is the Epithets – and as you all know, the *Oxford Dictionary* defines an epithet as a 'significant appellation'.

I have a good friend in the music world called Mike Batt, a distinguished composer whose most famous song is probably 'Bright Eyes'. Although recently married to an Australian, Mike has shown little interest when I have suggested that he becomes part of a cricket XI that I have been trying to organize for some time. This is a team of players whose every member's name is either a crucial item required for a game of cricket, or a vital aspect or skill of the game. Mike Batt (spelling inconsistencies are permitted) is a natural choice for this side, if not for the captaincy itself (this is earmarked for a German friend of mine named Franz Lieder). I have several other chums who would qualify for this bizarre assembly, but like Mike, they seem to have been put off cricket for life by the close association with the great game forced upon them from day one as a result of an accident of birth. A colleague from my schooldays was called Padd (presumably, he still is) and I have shared an office in my time with both a Mr Slipp and Mr Court. These men are as one with Batt in their loathing for cricket.

It is therefore likely to take me some time to get this team together. I am forced to turn to history and here my task is easier, but not that much more easy for there have been comparatively few cricketers of distinction who would qualify for this wacky outfit. I have decreed that the team should be exclusively English and drawn only from those who have played first-class cricket. The English rule is a bit rough on eminent foreign internationals such as G. M. Guard (India) and J. B. Plimsoll (South Africa) who would have been a useful, if not sensational, opening pace attack, but I am afraid I can only bring myself to dedicate my selectorial time to Englishmen. Anyway I am sure experts will agree that there would be no room for both a Boot and a Plimsoll in the side.

Here are the Epithets, as selected – the result of many hours of research and painstaking deliberation: Green, Studd, Legge, Bowling,

Box, Bale, Ball, Major (capt.), Close, Fielder, Boot. Twelfth man: Remnant. Umpire: Judge. Scorer: Scorer. How would this lot fare against (say) a similar side from India, selected by Contractor? Let us examine the form and background of the chosen few.

There would be nothing wrong with the opening partnership. The Green chosen to begin the Epithet assault is one of over a dozen Greens to qualify for selection. There are also several Greenes and Greenfields jostling for attention but the man I have chosen to represent the first essential of any game, viz. somewhere to play it, is D. M. Green of Lancashire and Gloucestershire. This excellent opener was extremely unlucky never to have been chosen for England during his career, particularly in 1965 when he scored 2,000 runs without the aid of a single century and in 1968, when he averaged over 40, scoring his seasonal best total of 2,137. Still, it is far harder to win a place in the Epithets and I trust that this honour will more than compensate for the injustices meted out to him by the England selectors. His partner has to be the indestructible Brian Close, of whose breathless hush Sir Henry Newbolt waxed poetic. Close's career as an inspired and fearless all-rounder has spanned four decades and is not finished yet (1985). Now at last he has a side for whom he can go on playing for ever.

After this scenic start, we come down to less picturesque but still vital components of cricket. At the critical position of number three, C. T. Studd (Middlesex) is chosen to remind us that even the tiniest details of the game are of crucial importance. No man in this side will slip as he turns for a quick second run. It would have been possible for me to have picked nine Studds, nearly two Boots' worth, but I did not want to skimp in my coverage of other departments of the game. C. T. was the most talented of the Studd family, topping the first-class averages in 1882 and playing five times for England, which is why he is the Studd I have collared.

Above Studd on the body but one below him in the order is G. B. Legge of Kent and England, who lost his life in the Second World War. This stylish batsman will, I'm glad to say, live on at number four for the Epithets. His slow bowling and alert slip fielding will also be invaluable. It did not take long to decide that Legge was a better bet than any of the three Legards who could have been chosen. Besides, leg-guard is now an obsolete term. (No first-class Padd exists.)

Following Legge is K. Bowling of Lancashire. His selection is a bit of a long shot, but so was Tyson's in 1954. Bowling only played once, for

Lancashire, in that very same year, 1954. Confusingly, he played as a batsman but scored only seven runs in his two knocks. Lancashire never asked him back but I, remembering such successful shock selections as Washbrook v. Australia in 1956 and Steele v. Australia in 1975, have. No Bowler* qualifies for selection, and the two potential Bowles are not quite right – I am looking for nouns rather than verbs.

It would be a rash man indeed who embarked upon an innings without a Box, and I am not about to break with tradition. Thos. Box played for Sussex, Surrey and Hampshire for more than thirty years in the middle of the last century, and so adds a wealth of experience to his crucial protective role. He was a fine wicket-keeper and middle-order batsman. However I do not propose to burden him with work behind the timbers; his job for the Epithets is to score well at number six.

I have every faith in my first six batsmen to get us off to a good start, and indeed it is vital that they do, for there is not a lot left after the opposition have got past Box. At number seven, perhaps batting a little above his station, is Frank Bale of Leicestershire. He was considered an all-rounder of great promise in the early 1920s, but he never quite fulfilled the hopes others had of him. Maybe in these new colours he will feel more relaxed and able to show his full potential. He is the second left-handed batsman in the order (Close of course being the other) and his left-arm slows will be handy.

Several Balls are available; none, sad to say, a leading player of his time. But so vital is a Ball to any game that a place must be found for at least one and the Ball chosen in the hope that he will last for a whole match is K. J. of Northants. He made only twelve first-class appearances, in 1921, but even that is more than any other English Ball.[1] He was a middle-order batsman and a change bowler who might just come good at number eight, one ahead of his captain, L. H. Major. Major is a little lucky to lead the Epithets in that there has never been a first-class English Captain or Skipper, and the only other qualified Major was a professional and thus clearly unsuitable for the leadership of a side such as this. Still, L. H. was felt to be a 'useful' bowler when he made his debut for Somerset in 1903. A pity that his first match was also his last – until now.

At number ten is (at last) another Test player, Arthur Fielder of Kent. He toured Australia twice, in 1903–4 and 1907–8. He played six Tests in

[1] Peter Bowler of Leicestershire and Derbyshire established himself too late for inclusion; likewise Martyn Ball of Gloucestershire.

all, and took all ten wickets in an innings for the Players v. Gentlemen in 1906. A fast bowler of undoubted quality, he once scored a century batting at number eleven which is why I have no hesitation in promoting him now to the dizzy heights of number ten.

The career of the number eleven, Jesse Boot of Derbyshire, is in stark contrast to that of Fielder. But where would a Fielder be without a Boot? Not only that, Boot is the side's stumper, having kept wicket in his one match back in 1895, holding two catches. I am sure many more await him as an Epithet.

The twelfth man has to be a Remnant and George Henry (Kent) just gets the vote over his son, Ernest Richard, and over the aristocratic duo of the Hon. Peter Remnant and the Hon. Robert Remnant. The latter became the second Baron Remnant in 1933, but even this up-market achievement cannot oust G. H. from the substitute's bench. The favoured Remnant was not only a competent fast round-arm bowler in the late nineteenth century but also lived well into his own nineties, an indication that he possesses stamina and patience in spades. The team's umpire has to be the only Judge ever to have graced the first-class circuit, the Middlesex pre-Second World War amateur, P. F., and for Scorer one need look no further than R. I. Scorer (Warwickshire 1921–26). The baggage master would be the brilliantly christened C. C. C. Case who played 255 matches for Somerset from 1925 to 1935 as a defensive middle-order batsman.

There is no Batt, Batsman or Batter in this squad, and players such as Hooker, Driver and Pullar narrowly miss selection because their names are too specialized. Similarly, players who describe merely particular styles of bowling such as Sloman, Speed and Shuter are, with reluctance, deemed ineligible. A fielder such as Spiller would be a bad choice on several counts. Nonetheless I feel the Epithets would give a reasonable account of themselves against most other teams of the imagination; maybe an XI of Hs (Hobbs, Hendren, Hammond, Hutton ...) or Bs (Bradman, Barnes, Bedser, Botham ...) would be a tough proposition, but I would back the Epithets to slaughter Heartaches CC any day.

Tim Rice, *Quick Singles* (1986)

Brian Johnston

Like Ol-Man River, the irrepressible B. J. rolls into the commentary box every spring, fresh as a primrose and bright as the willows in their early-season-green. The game would not be the same without him and to me, often coming back from a wearying tour, his cheery return to the BBC box is an annual tonic. I am sure it is the same for the listeners.

Brian bubbles with enthusiasm, both for cricket and for life. He is frequently a source of interesting gossip about cricketing friends and although at his age he could be forgiven for being a little out of touch with some aspects of the modern game, he is, in fact, always on the ball, up to date with any changes in the regulations (especially the tea regulations) and well informed about promising players.

He remains very much on the ball in his commentaries too. His listeners get a bonus every time: not just the passage of each ball bowled, but a hundred and one additional titbits, which add spice to the main meal. The vast majority of his listeners appreciate the quick-witted puns and the ready recourse to a deep fund of cricketing stories and it is mainly to Brian that *Test Match Special* owes its reputation for friendliness and fun. Like Cleopatra, 'age cannot wither him nor custom stale his infinite variety'.

'Infinite variety' may, actually, be stretching a point, although there is almost no statement that B. J. cannot turn into a pun, and no situation, cricketing or otherwise, in which he cannot find some humour. To criticize Brian, as some have done, for excessive levity or frivolity is unfair. If all the fun and light-heartedness which he brings to his commentaries, greatly to the enjoyment of most of his listeners, were at the expense of telling the story of the game in progress, the criticism would be merited. But it is not. Listeners can rely on a fair and accurate description of the match as well as an entertaining one.

No one loves cricket more than Brian Johnston and few know the game better or do more to enhance its good name. Seventy-five in June 1987, he seemed then about as likely to retire as Mrs Thatcher. When he eventually does, his marvellous sense of fun and peerless gift of the gab will be missed both by his colleagues in the box and his listeners.

Christopher Martin-Jenkins, Cricket Characters (1987)

Cricket in the Bones

Harold Dennis Bird, known hereinafter as Dickie Bird, is exactly as you would expect him to be. He is caring and highly strung; he counts his blessings and lives for cricket; he has never married and is a bit of a card.

At the moment he is in Barbados, umpiring, in his inimitable style, the second Test match between West Indies and Pakistan, pretending to be worried stiff but really enjoying every minute of it. To him has fallen the distinction of being the first 'neutral' umpire to stand in a Test series in the Caribbean.

Dickie Bird is a Yorkshireman, and sufficiently proud of it without being boastful. As a player, much his most glorious achievement was to score 181 not out, going in first for Yorkshire against Glamorgan at Bradford Park Avenue on 19 June 1959. Although, like a true Yorkshire-man, he played a dour game, he was in the side on that occasion only because Ken Taylor was away playing for England. When, for the next match, Dickie was dropped, he was understandably aggrieved, though when informed of it he said, respectfully, 'Very well, Mr Sellers.'

I wrote about a Dickie innings or two, and it was a little like writing about chess by post. His greatest sadness was never to be awarded his Yorkshire cap. He did win a Leicestershire cap, after leaving Yorkshire, but earning a living as a county professional was always something of a struggle for him.

He was probably more at ease opening the Barnsley innings with Michael Parkinson ('You'll know Parkie, I expect') and playing in the Yorkshire League, or coaching the boys of Plymouth College, which he did between finishing with Leicestershire in 1966 and joining the umpires' list in 1969. He umpired his first first-class match in 1970 and his first Test match in 1973.

Cricket is a game that is in people's bones. Some who may not them-selves be great exponents of it, understand it by instinct. Others, although they might be outstandingly effective as players, hardly know the first thing about it. There have been England captains who have been blind to many of its possibilities. Dickie, for his part, has a good *feel* for cricket. This, together with a disarming personality and a complete lack of arrogance, accounts for his success.

He was sixty last Monday, having just stood in a Test match in Trinidad in which he and his fellow umpire, Steve Bucknor from Jamaica, gave seventeen batsmen out leg before wicket, an unprecedented haul. Preferring to be thought of as a 'not outer' rather than an 'outer', Dickie lets it be known that of the decisions given in the bowlers' favour, he was responsible for six and Bucknor for eleven. He describes it as a match played in an exceptionally good spirit, though there are times, perhaps, when he sees no evil and hears no evil because he likes it that way.

He drinks very little, never smokes and does his exercises every morning in the bathroom. If he wanted to, he could go on umpiring in first-class cricket until he is seventy, and he would be quite lost without it. Alex Skelding, another umpiring character of his time was seventy-two when he packed it in. More recently, John Langridge was seventy. Umpiring is both Dickie's hobby and his livelihood. He goes all over the world doing it.

He stood in the World Cup in India and Pakistan in 1987, and before that in the women's World Cup in New Zealand. He has done the Asia Cup in Sri Lanka and adjudicated under a glass roof in a stadium in Toronto. Earlier this winter he stood in the first three Test matches played in Zimbabwe. He has been to Nigeria and Holland, and no sooner will he get back to England a fortnight tomorrow than he will be heading for Hove, to make the acquaintance of Allan Border's Australians and to expect some gentle ribbing from the senior ones among them.

At Bulawayo in November, Dickie beat Frank Chester's record number of Test matches umpired. Chester had been a batsman of high promise for Worcestershire before being badly wounded in the Great War. He umpired his first Test match, with trilby hat and artificial hand, at Lord's in 1924 and his forty-seventh and last at Lord's in 1955. Bird's today is his fifty-second. Among overseas umpires, Tony Crafter heads the Australian list with thirty-three and Douglas Sang Hue is the senior West Indian with thirty-one.

The fastest bowler 'through the air' that Dickie Bird has umpired was Frank Tyson, the best was Dennis Lillee, the most prodigal appealer was Abdul Qadir, the cricketer he has had the most fun with is Allan Lamb. During the tea interval in a championship match Lamb once slipped his portable telephone into the pocket of Dickie's umpiring coat, without Dickie knowing it. After an over or two, to Dickie's astonishment this telephone rang, and he answered it. It was Ian Botham from the Worcestershire dressing-room, saying: 'Could I speak to Mr Lamb, please!' Dickie is not, however, quite the butt he might sometimes appear to be.

If he were, the best players would not like and respect him as much as they do.

His days of seeming to want to get off the field as soon as the sun went behind the clouds or it started to spot with rain are behind him. His experience at Lord's during the Centenary Test match against Australia in 1980, when he and David Constant were jostled by MCC members who felt play should have been in progress, helped to cure him of that. The tag was probably a little unfair anyway: Dickie has always been, if anything, too ready to give his fellow umpire the casting vote.

He lives, as the crow flies, a mile from Chateau Boycott in Barnsley. 'Aye,' he jokes, 'the rich man in his castle and the poor man at his gate.' Dickie was Barnsley's star batsman when Geoffrey Boycott first played for them as a boy. Before opening the innings, Bird, hands shaking, would go to Boycott and say: 'Put me gloves on for me, will you, Gerald?' To this day Dickie calls Boycott 'Gerald', and 'Gerald' believes that then, as now, Dickie put his nervous energy to advantage. 'He likes people to think he's an easy touch,' Boycott says, 'but he's not. Deep down he's quite strong and very fair.'

Boycott is to be seen driving round Barbados at the moment in the white Rolls-Royce that purrs in and out of the Sandy Lane Hotel. Dickie is happier in his white coat and white sun-hat or white cap, or at home at White Rose Cottage, built in the seventeenth century and where John Wesley once slept. His married sister, who lives not far away, does some cooking for him and some cleaning and some washing. He seldom cooks himself, preferring go to the Talbot for a bite of lunch.

On his way home, he calls on his friend, the butcher, who puts him up a couple of sandwiches, to be eaten for supper in front of the telly with 'a coop o' tay'. A man of humble tastes and honest opinions, tempering justice with mercy, presiding at great cricket events, a born worrier yet happy in his work – that is Dickie Bird, and if you ask him to your cricket dinner, he'll give good value there as well.

John Woodcock, The Times (24 April 1993)

The Press Box at Sabina

The Press Box at Sabina Park must rank high among the most uncomfortable on Test match grounds. With perhaps eight present it might be bearable; we mustered around twenty. The chairs were hard and each time any one of the seven in each row wished to remove himself for any purpose, the remaining six needed to tilt or cower and hold their breath. For the more bulky among us it would have been little more difficult to go through the eye of a needle. Similarly, the passing of a cable from inscriber to messenger required a relay operation that the most experienced chain-gang worker would have found taxing. Very often one would have to pass a cable for someone in mid-sentence, only to find, on return to composition, that the idea had flown. Doubtless, some very complex and weighty images foundered.

It was also a box so hot and airless that a pressure-cooker could scarcely have been less inviting. Lunch had to be fetched from the pavilion a long way off, and the ordering of this presented problems of its own. For instance, after several failures in giving verbal orders to the waitress, we composed a daily list. The first time we were two cokes short and two cakes to the good; the thirst-maddened coke-less ones could be persuaded neither to eat nor pay for the cakes. 'I thought it was a hay not a hoe,' said the understandably disgruntled waitress. By the time the match was ending we had a fine service of ham sandwiches, hot rotis and beers in operation. I don't know if the cakes were ever eaten.

There was danger in the box too. Glasses crashed to the ground, beer bottles got crunched underfoot, and once Brian Chapman, bumping his head for the fifth time on the overhanging wooden shutter just above it, sent a thermos cascading on to my forehead and cutting it open. Many American Purple Hearts were less valiantly won.

There were compensations, however. We were directly behind and above the bowler's arm, and so near that Trueman could wink or scowl at us on his walk back. Wesley Hall almost disappeared from sight under us as he turned at the end of his run. Ahead were the hazy slopes of the Blue Mountains, with the military hill-station of Newcastle glittering 2,000 feet up under its customary cottonwool cloud packing.

There were few incident-free days within the box, though I am happy to say that the British and West Indian camps warred within rather than against each other. On one occasion, the *Barbados Advocate*, incensed at Kanhai's running out by a Jamaican, wrathfully flung down a pocketful of dollars in front of the *Daily Gleaner*'s sports editor and called upon the neutral British to support his own allocation of responsibility for the misfortune. 'Only a Jamaican could have done a thing like that,' he fumed.

It was a sartorially colourful box; from the dapper Mr O. Seymour Coppin of the *Barbados Advocate*, zoot-suited and tie-pinned, to Mr L. D. (Strebor) Roberts of the *Gleaner*, whose cynical, amused and cigarette-holdered profile was offset by shirts of daily more dazzling hues. There were blue shirts, canary shirts, even a long, unidentified youth in crimson shirt with gold-braided collar. There were cigars, cheroots, cigarette-holders, and, I don't doubt, marijuana going. The aromas of rum and scotch vied with those of beer and curried goat. Sometimes the girls' school in the garden behind burst into piping song, preparing, it seemed, for next year's carols.

At times it was like an overcrowded raft, with tempers frayed, sailing through equatorial waters out of all touch with the outside world. Barry Osborne, in charge of cables, would come in and announce unavoidable delays (which were usually quickly cleared, but which – with Jamaica five hours behind London time – created anxieties and problems). Agreement could not be reached between us then on whether the ordinary or urgent rate should be used by all, and this caused the most heated controversy of all.

No, there was never a dull moment, but I sometimes think we were lucky to get out of it in one piece.

Alan Ross, Through the Caribbean (1966)

The Captain and the Media

Before the war, press coverage of Test series was minimal. On D. R. Jardine's tour of Australia in 1932–3, only two correspondents accompanied the team. One was a lawn-tennis writer, the other the 'ghost' for Jack Hobbs's daily reports. There was no TV, and scarcely any radio. Jardine could achieve a reticence, not to say secrecy, that would be unthinkable today. Far from announcing the team to the world on the day before a Test, he would not inform even his own players about the side until twenty minutes before the match, when, according to Harold Larwood, Jardine would hang up the list on a hook in the dressing-room and everyone would cluster round to see who had been selected. (Larwood also said that no one from the press would have dared ask Jardine if he was considering leaving himself out of the team, for fear of a punch in the face.)

The attention paid to the modern captain's every word does have its advantages. In the first place, many correspondents are players manqués. Tom Clarke, himself the sports editor of a national daily paper, once described sports writers as 'the eunuchs at the harem'. Court writers, he added, do not typically identify with the rapists or frauds; whereas sports writers usually love the game they cover and, on the whole, wish the players well. (English cricket writers also wish England well, and tend to become jittery when we bat!) Secondly, the publicity is no doubt of benefit to cricket as a whole. At a press conference, the captain may be able to get across his no doubt excellent reasons for a particular course of action. It is an opportunity to educate the public via the media. Moreover it is hard to know what actually happens on a cricket field. It is amazing how often expert witnesses, close to the scene of the crime (the fielders), disagree about, say, which side of the bat a ball passed, or whether a batsman edged a ball. How much harder for a writer, a hundred yards away, perhaps over extra-cover, to have much clue about the finer points? He needs help, and the captain can offer some.

I admit that I enjoyed press conferences, even when we had lost (though, watching Graham Yallop wriggle on the hook in 1978–9, I would have anticipated hating them as much as he did). I found it interesting to try to put my finger on the differences between the two sides, or on moments when a match was lost and won. I was glad, too, to be asked each question once, rather than time and again, as happens when there is no formal conference. My policy was never to say anything I thought to be false, and to tell as much of the truth (as I saw it) as possible. You don't *know*, most of the time, what's going to happen, so why pretend? Yet if some awkward cat is out of the bag, don't deny it. I tried not to put down our players, or criticize the opposition in anything but a restrained and courteous way. It is best, morally and prudentially, to be generous to them whoever is on top. And I, like most England captains before and after, made it a rule never to criticize the umpires. These meetings with the press were, in fact, games in which one tried to keep one's balance like a cat on a wall without falling off either on the side of indiscretion or on that of vapidity.

For my own peace of mind, I had to impose clear limitations on the times at which I was available. At Tests, I would see journalists once on the day before, once on the rest day, and once at the end. We usually arranged for either the manager or the chairman of selectors to visit the press-box around tea-time each day, in case there were any matters of information that we could pass on.

Since Jardine's day, press coverage has become not only more widespread but also more intrusive. Television has intensified this pattern. The style of its coverage has also changed, in the direction of more explicit presentation of the personality of a sportsman. There is greater use of close-ups of a player's face, both under the stress of the game, and while being interviewed. The viewer has an illusion of intimacy with him: the public figure becomes a member of the family, a regular visitor in the living-room. Alan Knott noticed this change in the mid–1970s. Suddenly, like other cricketers, he was recognized far more frequently in streets or restaurants, and his quirks had become public property.

Players are in a position to turn the media's interest to their own advantage, whether through columns of their own or through the opportunities in advertising that familiarity offers. Sponsorship and promotion have expanded enormously, and much of the reason has been the style and matter of the television coverage.

Another aspect of World Series Cricket was that players, umpires and commentators were all employed, *qua* performers, by the same company that ran the game – Packer's Channel 9. Here, the game's administration was too much at the mercy of the commercial interest that supported it, and the players paid for their wages with lack of independence.

The media have, then, contributed to cricket's survival and to players' incomes. Nevertheless, exposure does involve risk, especially to captains, whose responsibility it is to act as spokesmen for the team and themselves. The danger lies as much in their own misjudgements as in misrepresentation or unfair comment. One *faux pas* may haunt a captain who, as cricketer, did not embark upon his profession with public speaking in mind, nor did he have any training in the process.

Some become excessively cautious. Illingworth in his book on captaincy tells of a game at Bournemouth when he bowled a tight spell without luck. Afterwards, the correspondent of the *Yorkshire Evening Post* asked him whether the ball was turning. Illingworth writes: ' "A little," I answered, only to be contradicted by Len [Hutton], who later told me, "Never say it is turning when you have not taken any wickets." ' Illingworth rightly says that Hutton's denial of a plain fact was 'petty and needless'.

But Hutton also had a masterly way with the press. Cowdrey describes the initial press conference in Perth in 1954, when Hutton 'dazzled the toughest and most cynical journalists with a performance that would have outshone Bob Hope . . . The Australian press, I suspect, were expecting a lot of bravado, even bombast. They received the opposite . . . It was all underplayed. "Noo, we 'aven't got mooch boolin'. Got a chap called Tyson, but you won't 'ave 'eard of 'im because 'e's 'ardly ever played . . ." '

A single remark can be costly: it can be used as ammunition against yourself. It was premature of Botham to announce, early in the Trinidad Test in 1980, that 'you couldn't get a result in ten days on this pitch, let alone five' and on the rest day that 'heads would roll' if his side were defeated. West Indies won by an innings and 79 runs despite a whole day being lost because of rain. Greig's choice of words in promising in 1976 that England would 'make the West Indies grovel' would have been tactless from any source; but in the mouth of a blond South African it carried an especially tasteless and derogatory overtone. I imagine that it was this remark that Hutton had in mind when, a few months after this series, he gave Greig a piece of advice on the eve of the tour to India. He kept us waiting a few seconds for the words of wisdom, before saying, laconically, 'Don't *say* too much.'

Crowds and media *are* at times hostile. Peter May's retirement from Test cricket was said, by Illingworth, to have been hastened by press comments on his ability. However, cricketers, including captains, may perceive them as more unfriendly than they in fact are, and react with anxiety or rage. Unfair or malicious responses *do* hurt. But a measure of insensitivity in this direction can help: I once had a letter complaining of my 'having a skin like a rhinoceros's', which I took to be, in this context, a tribute.

One of Botham's main shortcomings as captain of England in 1980-1 was, as I have mentioned, his touchiness about criticism, and his tendency not to be able to differentiate between its types. Thus Viv Richards has described how in the Caribbean Botham would, in the later overs of a one-day match when he might be fielding near the boundary, edge around the fence trying to pick out anyone who was harassing him. On

231

the journey home, Botham threatened Henry Blofeld of the *Guardian* and the BBC who, he thought, had been malicious. But he also saw malice where there was none: what was meant as helpful comment from members of the team could strike him as threatening and disloyal if it happened not to coincide with his own views; so he came to cut himself off from the most powerful and helpful source of advice and constructive criticism available to a captain.

The fact is that there is an essential divergence of point of view between spectator/critic and performer, and a real conflict of interest between any journalism (but especially the trashy kind) and the players. Some friction is inevitable, in sport as in other fields. Sometimes the friction has a vicious edge. Kim Hughes, the Australian captain, in a speech shortly before the final Test in 1981, agreed that his team deserved criticism. But, he went on, some of the things said about them were such that, 'If you were walking along a street and a fellow said that to you, if you had any "go" about you at all, you'd deck him!' Three years later poor Hughes finished his Test captaincy in tears, unable to read through his prepared statement of resignation.

Spectators look for spectacle, drama and excitement; players for security. Onlookers want heroes and villains; performers want to be understood and loved, whatever their failings. Writers are subject to their own pressures (of deadline, competition and bloodthirsty editors); players feel that writing about a game is easier than playing it. Journalists seek quotes; most players will at best speak off the record. (And some in each category manage to muddle the situation, as when, in Australia, Tony Francis, of ITV, quoted some remarks made by Geoff Boycott that were disparaging to me; the former was convinced that they had agreed that the conversation was *on* the record, while Boycott's version was that it was informal and private.)

But the press need not be, and often are not, uncreative and obsessively down-putting. As literary critic and novelist Walter Allen said about the world of books, 'The main function of a critic is to encourage people to read. I've been pretty excited by many books. All I want to do is communicate this excitement to others.' The same can be said of most cricket commentators.

I cannot remember a player who was indifferent to what was shouted, printed or broadcast about him, or who was not more sharply struck by a sentence of blame than a page of praise. As Maurice Leyland said about facing fast bowling: 'None of us likes it, but some of us shows it more than others.' It is up to the captain to make the best use he can of the media, and to establish as much trust as possible.

Mike Brearley, *The Art of Captaincy* (1985)

Is Batting All that Meets the Eye?

Cole Younger was an intelligent outlaw. Being an outlaw, he needed to shoot, and being intelligent, he knew that to survive, he needed to shoot straight. This he did with relative success, as the record of his death in bed from old age indicates.

However, there is, for all ball-players, a relevant piece of evidence which emerges from a study of his life. His concern that a colleague, presumably on whom he might be professionally dependent, could literally not hit a barn door at fifteen paces, but in fact missed it regularly by the same distance, prompted a simple experiment. He discovered that this colleague missed the door when firing right-handed, but, with his left hand, which he rarely used, he was more accurate.

He had revealed a particularly notable case of left-eye dominance in a right-handed gunman, or failed gunman. Undeterred, Younger reasoned that attempting to acquire comparable skill with the left hand would be less profitable than redesigning the sights of the gun, to enable the right hand to shoot where the left eye focused.

However, the implications of the existence of the same imbalance between right and left eyes, as between right and left hands, have perhaps been overlooked in other sports. Great ball-players, who have emerged in defiance of the coaching manuals and the 'orthodox' approach, have been described as 'brilliant but unorthodox', as though their exceptional skill has been acquired in spite of the fact that their style is not the classical one. Denis Compton, for instance, was a batting genius. The accurate ball, on the stumps or just to the leg, was dispatched with equal abandon.

Film of him provides overwhelming evidence of this. He did play the wider ball outside the off stump, but rarely with the same consistency; yet commentators were often inspired to marvel at his apparent nerve at sweeping the ball outside the off stump to leg. A possible explanation is that neither his genius nor his unorthodoxy was a conscious rejection of orthodoxy, merely an instinctive recognition of the unusual relationship between his dominant eye and his dominant hand.

Consider, for a moment, that Compton was left-eye dominant and left-handed, learning for some reason to play right-handed, with a classic side-on stance at the wicket. His dominant eye would be 'on the ball', which was bowled on or around his legs; the short ball outside the off stump was of less use to him, once he had allowed it to be level with his body, facing towards cover-point. The jump from his dominant left to weaker right eye precluded consistent cutting off genuine fast bowlers, though against slower bowling, when there was time for the eye to follow the ball, he was a delightful late-cutter.

The majority of individuals are right-handed and right-eye dominant. In cricket, 'orthodoxy' appears to be based on that statistic, and the placing of the feet and the movement of the head in the playing of all strokes depend upon it. A good eye is essential, but more important, surely, is the answer to the question, 'which one is it?' The placing of the feet is recognized as fundamental to the successful execution of any stroke, but it must depend upon the relationship between hand and eye dominance. The feet must be positioned in order to allow the dominant eye to remain on the ball until contact. The right-handed, right-eye-dominant batsman is naturally an off-side player, and will off-drive and cut more successfully than he will on-drive and pull, especially against faster bowling. Coaching manuals tend to indicate the position that such a player must adopt, in order to play the shot in the classic style, as Hobbs and Bradman did. What in fact, they are suggesting are feet and head positions, which correspond with the requirements of right-eye-dominant and right-handed players, thereby catering splendidly for the majority.

It may, therefore, be helpful to explain the difference in players' ability to play off- and on-side shots, in visual, rather than physical terms. A right-handed, left-eye-dominant player is invariably stronger on the leg-side; Richards and Botham, for instance, are unlikely to be anything else. Similarly, left-handed batsmen combine more commonly with a dominant right eye, which might explain, in part, the predominance of good leg-side players among the great left-handed batsmen. The least common is the left-handed, left-eye-dominant batsman; the absolute exception would be Compton, if in fact he was left-dominant in both hands and eye, yet batted right-handed.

In all sports, though cricket is the only one that really matters, before any decision as to what position the feet should take, in order to execute a stroke effectively, consideration of eye dominance is essential. It is also considerably less expensive than a coaching lesson: simply point a finger at any mid-distance object with both eyes open; then close one eye. If your finger remains focused on the object, then the open eye is dominant; if not, vice versa.

David Akers, *The Cricketer* (1985)

Nineteen-thirties Characters

Julien Cahn was a conspicuous figure in the cricket world of the 1930s with his own team and two superb grounds, one more or less in Nottingham at West Bridgford, the other in front of his house, Stanford Hall, Loughborough. The wickets were perfect, and the outfields were like bowling greens. Hospitality was on a lavish scale with no shortage of champagne; but there were those who took undue advantage of a bountiful host, and latterly therefore drinks had to be signed for. He had a first-class side, most members of which were accommodated in his furnishing business when they were not playing for him either at home or abroad. He took teams to Jamaica, to the Argentine, to Denmark, to Canada, USA and Bermuda, to Ceylon and Singapore and to New Zealand. His purse was apparently bottomless, and, of course, he gave a vast deal of pleasure to very many people, even though his sides were much too strong for most of their opposition. This didn't worry 'Sir J.' – he was first knighted and then accorded a baronetcy for 'service to agriculture and a number of charitable causes' – whose idea of a good game, I suspect, was to see his stars make three or four hundred and then bowl out the enemy quickly enough to avoid too long a spell in the field.

For he played himself, in a manner of speaking, bowling when he felt inclined and sometimes putting himself in first. As a bowler his style is best described as parabolic. It can perhaps be imagined from John Gunn's answer – or it may have been 'Tich' Richmond's – to the question how Sir Julien was bowling that year: 'up and down, I suppose?' 'Not so mooch oop and down, I'd say, as to and fro.' When I took Crusoe to play once at Stanford he remarked that the chief evidence that Cahn was bowling was a faint whistling in the trees. He was probably hit higher and further than any bowler before or since, runs, of course, being no object as there were always hundreds to play with. But sometimes he got a wicket, and high was the merriment.

The brilliant players who surrounded him made some astonishing catches, one of which at London, Ontario, comes back to me as I write. The batsman hit the cricket equivalent of a full brassie shot, low, down wind, and practically straight. Walter Robins – I think one of the best half-dozen all-round fielders I ever saw – came sprinting in full pelt from the sightscreen as the stroke was made and took the ball right-handed down by his boots. Done in a Test at Lord's it would have won imperishable fame.

It was said, no doubt erroneously, that when the side's averages were made up at the end of the season the scorer by a simple manipulation of the decimal point brought the captain up to the top of the list.

He was the sort of man around whom revolved many such stories. For instance, his pads, which were very large, were said to be blown up with a bicycle pump. The ball certainly bounced readily off them for leg-byes which the umpire sometimes conveniently forgot to signal; but I never saw them inflated, though I did once see the butler, who was in attendance to accoutre Julien in the changing tent at Stanford, rush out with the fielding pads which he had forgotten to strap on. Not a bit abashed, his master paused from leading his team on to the greensward, pulled up his trousers and allowed the matter to be rectified.

Even with his legs thus encased it has to be admitted that Julien was not a brave fielder as many will remember. But if this little weakness is mentioned I must add that as Master of the Pytchley and of the Fernie it was said that no fence was too high for him, and that his intrepidity in the hunting field cost him several broken bones. He was, in fact, even more of a mixture than most of us, with an innately kind side to which many a cricketer was indebted, myself included.

Thanks to him I made this first tour of seven weeks, sailing from Southampton in the *Empress of Britain* across the Atlantic and up the St Lawrence river to Quebec, proceeding south down the eastern seaboard of Canada to Chicago and New York, and thence to the climax of the expedition in Bermuda; a week's cricket there, return by sea to New York (through a hurricane, the worst thirty-six hours I ever spent in a ship) and then home in a dead calm all the way in the old *Aquitania*. Our side had four Test cricketers, R. W. V. Robins, I. A. R. Peebles, D. P. B. Morkel (South Africa) and R. C. Blunt (New Zealand) and one to become so, P.

A. Gibb; G. F. H. Heane and S. D. Rhodes, soon jointly to lead Notts, and seven others all of whom either before or subsequently played vary- ing amounts of first-class cricket, C. R. Maxwell, H. R. Munt, F. C. W. Newman, T. B. Reddick, E. P. Solbé, G. F. Summers, and myself. Plus, of course, Julien Cahn.

We won sixteen matches (all one-day) and drew four, most of the North American games being eleven against either twelve or more. In the States there was a preponderance of West Indians against us, this being my first close acquaintance with people from the islands one of which, many years later, was to become a second home. I write as one who has scored fifties in Ottawa, Chicago and New York, but to tell the truth the difficulty on our side was not so much in making runs but in getting in.

Until we got to Bermuda. The excitement that greeted the first Eng- lish side to visit England's oldest colony was, to us, staggering. Our first appearance on the Prospect ground, proceeding round the field in carriages (no cars were allowed on this microscopic mid-Atlantic speck until in war it became of major strategic value) was like a royal pro- cession. And it was at once evident that on a lively pitch of matting over concrete we might be hard pressed. The climax came with our game against Somerset, the champion side, when in front of five thousand people crammed into the little ground (about one in five of the total population) we were bowled out for 85. The chief destroyer was a fast left-arm bowler called Arthur Simons, who on this surface was like Bill Voce and 'Nobby' Clark of Northants rolled into one.

Neither in the West Indies nor Australia have I known a greater hubbub than this whole game was played in, the noise growing, if possi- ble, even greater as the Somerset score ticked up against Robins and Peebles. By the time the ninth wicket went down for 62 the half-battalion of Northumberland Fusiliers who had backed us to a man, on English reputations, at odds of three to one, were feeling a little easier. But they had plenty of shocks to come. Another Simons, Obrien by name, chanced his arm, and the score rose by startling leaps to 82. At this point a well-hit straight-drive looked like going for six when George Heane from long-on dashed across the sightscreen and leapt up to make a marvellous catch, two-handed, above his head. Whereat the crowd thronged the field, and the soldiery threw topees into the air, and carried George shoulder-high to the pavilion, where Julien also was seized, somewhat to his alarm, and borne aloft likewise. Walter Robins always said this was the most thrilling game he ever saw or played in. I think I got 5 before falling to the Voce-ish Simons, and held a catch at extra-cover amid a noise like that which greets a goal in a Cup Final or the winning try at Twickenham.

It was more than twenty years later that the chance came to visit Bermuda again, when I captained my own side there on our way home from the West Indies, in 1956. The Bermudians were rather more sophisticated then, having had various visits including that of Len Hutton's MCC side *en route* to the West Indies. Nor did our game quite match the excitement of that earlier one. But one felt an echo of it when Frank Tyson, indubitably the world's fastest bowler, was hit for six for the first time in his life, it was said, and then for another, by a character rejoicing in the name of 'Cheesey' Hughes.

So much – or almost – for Julien Cahn, though I pass on with reluctance from this eccentric open-handed figure who (according to E. E. Snow, the historian of Leicestershire and also of a slim book, *Sir Julien Cahn's XI*), being something of a hypochondriac, thought nothing of ordering a special train to bring from London the King's physician, Lord Horder, and who took his barber with him round the world. His grounds contained a golf course as well as lawn-tennis and squash courts, bowling and putting greens, swimming pool, besides a lake well-stocked with trout, and – sublime touch! – a performing seal pond. The last addition to the house before war brought such vanities to a halt was a luxurious theatre seating 350, complete with Würlitzer organ.

He purchased from F. S. Ashley-Cooper, the distinguished historian, the best cricket library ever collected, but thereby hangs a melancholy tale. At his death Lady Cahn offered MCC any items they did not already have, which was a generous gesture considering her husband had enjoyed no more than two years of membership. Later the balance of this unique library was put up for auction, the sale being due to begin at eleven o'clock. However, a considerable collection advertised for sale earlier in the morning was withdrawn at the last moment, the Cahn sale began early, and, before serious purchasers arrived, much irreplaceable material went dirt cheap to dealers and has never been located.

When the Australians came, after all, in 1934 they were exuberantly received at the Savoy luncheon given by the British Sportsman's Club, though distinctly less so later on by the crowds at Trent Bridge and Headingley. A word about the BSC, which exists chiefly to greet in this way teams of all kinds from the Commonwealth before the serious business of their tours begins. Its members form a distinguished cross-section of British sporting life, with a chairman of appropriate eminence. At present it is the Duke of Norfolk, with Lord Wakefield of Kendal, the famous 'Wakers', as his deputy. The foundation of the BSC owes itself to the great drama of the sending-off at Twickenham of C. J. Brownlie in the England–New Zealand match of 1924. This happened in the presence of the Prince of Wales, who at half-time is said to have attempted in vain to bring about Brownlie's return. The All Blacks were so angry and upset that they refused to attend the Rugby Union dinner that night. Accordingly with the Prince of Wales's encouragement a luncheon was hurriedly arranged before their departure. Sore feelings were to some extent mollified at this, and the organizers thereupon formed the British Sportsman's Club.

At one period the chair was occupied by someone less at home in sport than politics, and when he remarked what a great honour it was for us to have the famous Sir Jack . . . with us his memory went, and he kept repeating Sir Jack . . . Sir Jack . . . as though a gramophone record had got stuck in its groove. At last someone had to call out 'Hobbs'. Generally these are the smoothest occasions with all the right notes struck.

This is not a Test match chronicle – few readers, if any, would face the daunting prospect of digesting 230-odd of them – but they must have their place. After all they have occupied upwards of a thousand of my working days: the best part of three years' concentrated watching time! England lost the first Test since Bodyline at Trent Bridge by 238 runs – and ten minutes.

There followed Verity's match at Lord's in which after a thunderstorm he took fifteen wickets in a day, and that was that. The Australians are always nervous, and naturally so, when they have to face the music on a pitch on which the ball stops and turns, but when they arrived on the Monday morning with 192 for two on the board it never occurred to them that they would not make the 99 more they needed to save the follow-on. They missed the target by seven runs, and those seven runs meant the match.

The Old Trafford Test was the one in which England made their then highest score against Australia, yet failed to win. One recalls O'Reilly getting England's first three wickets in four balls – those of Walters, Wyatt, and Hammond – and the uproar when Gubby Allen's first over was elongated to thirteen balls. In those days the groundsman was not empowered to renovate the foot-holes during a match, and Bill O'Reilly whose large feet and strong final stride were apt to dig deep holes had bowled 59 overs in the English innings. So what with running wide to avoid the pits and finding a ball that swung a lot, Gubby, in between a few legitimate ones, bowled four no-balls and three wides. He says the over also contained a couple of chances but they seem to have escaped historical notice. He also maintains that he missed a cushy hundred because he misinterpreted a wave from Bob Wyatt on the dressing-room balcony. He though it meant the captain was going to declare, and so had a dip (he made 61, bowled McCabe). Perhaps Bob was just fanning his face – the heat was like Melbourne at its worst. He did finally declare, at 627 for nine, just before tea on the second day of the four-day match, but England never looked like winning.

Altogether it was an ill-fated year for England, with Jardine in the press-box, Larwood also unwilling to play, some ill-balanced sides chosen by Messrs. F. S. Jackson, T. A. Higson and P. Perrin, and a final calamitous match at the Oval lost by 562 runs. For me the final indignity was, after Les Ames had been crocked, to see Frank Woolley in the last of his 64 Test matches keeping wicket.

Sussex have never won the Championship, but 1934 under Alan Melville was one of the years when they very nearly did. They had a last chance when Lancashire came down to Eastbourne at the end of August 1934; but a draw was all Lancashire wanted, and amid spasmodic barracking they set out to achieve it. I remember arguing with Peter Eckersley, the captain, about the methods he had used, and being quelled by his reply, which was to the effect that in that age of low wages he knew how hard-pressed some of his chaps were in the winter and how much the bonus they'd get for winning the Championship would mean to them. That was a lot more important to him than pleasing a lot of holiday-makers sitting round the Saffrons. Not an easy attitude to refute! Strangely enough, I remember Arthur Richardson, of Derbyshire, also at Eastbourne two years later taking very much the same line when his side were fighting to win their only modern Championship.

In those days the best amateur captains, especially those of the largely professional sides of the North and Midlands stood in a somewhat different relationship with their sides from that obtaining today. They were very much the guardians of their flocks even though they were probably junior in age to half the men they led. Melville, Eckersley and Richardson were all still in their twenties at this time, as also were Brian Sellers, who brought Yorkshire six titles in eight years, and Walter Robins of

Middlesex, Tom Pearce and Denys Wilcox of Essex, R. H. Moore of Hampshire, Charles Lyttelton (now Lord Cobham) of Worcestershire, and Maurice Turnbull of Glamorgan.

The fact that most of the captains in the 1930s were roughly of an age with myself meant that I knew most of them pretty well and so got a good idea of what was going on. Among those slightly older were A. P. F. Chapman (Kent), E. R. T. Holmes (Surrey), R. E. S. Wyatt (Warwickshire) and G. F. H. Heane (Notts). Looked back at through the rose-tinted spectacles of time they seem a capable and attractive bunch – which does not mean, of course, that they escaped the perennial criticisms that county cricket was dull and going to the dogs. It always has been, sometimes faster than others.

The diary tells me I moved along the coast that early August of 1934 from Hove to Canterbury, and I need no reminding of what I saw there. There had been a thunderstorm the night before Kent played Notts in the second match of the week, and Percy Chapman thought some while before deciding to bat. He did so, moving up Frank Woolley to No. 1 with the idea of rattling the bowling. Sure enough the ball flew at the start. It flew off the pitch, and it flew off Frank's bat – all ways. The quicker bowlers made the cardinal error of digging the ball in short, which suited the master perfectly. He hooked, of course, and he cut – how he cut! Along the ground, but also over gully's head; for that matter over cover's head likewise. Imperious, disdainful, commanding. The superlatives were never so quickly used up as when Woolley was in the mood.

This sunny day (all August days in the 1930s were sunny) and on this awkward wicket he and Bill Ashdown made 109 for the first wicket in under the hour. 'Actually starting with 52 runs out of 71 in 33 minutes,' says *Wisden*. 'Woolley with sixteen fours got 101 out of 155 in a hundred minutes.' 'Dazzling', they called it. I wonder what description would fit the case in the 1970s when a man is said to have 'flayed' the bowling when he reaches his hundred not twenty minutes before lunch but somewhere around tea-time. Of course, the Notts bowling having been demoralized, Kent plundered at will – 445 for six before the close. Next day 'Tich' Freeman had seven wickets, 'Father' Marriott eleven, and all was over.

When, watching with Frank at Canterbury a year or two ago, I reminded him of the innings he couldn't recall it. If this seems extraordinary remember that he did make 145 hundreds, and, for that matter,

35 scores in the nineties. Perhaps the innings would have stuck in his mind if Notts had bowled a little better. By the way, the older he grew the more he liked going in first, saying that the red one was easier to see. He was forty-seven in 1934, and had still four more summers to go.

Descending with a vengeance to lesser cricket matters I this year began qualifying for membership of MCC by playing. After your cricketing qualifications had secured your acceptance as a candidate you engaged for either ten or twelve days' cricket spread over two years. Assuming you made a few runs or took a few wickets, and behaved with reasonable decorum, you were then elected. The whole process from the time of being put up took four years – as opposed to merely waiting passively, which took about twenty or thirty. I was proposed by Major E. G. French and seconded by D. J. Knight, and on 9 March 1936, in a document from Lord's, the Secretary, W. Findlay, had the honour of informing me of my election and assuming I would 'have the goodness to sign the subjoined order upon your Banker or Agent' he remained my obedient servant. A red-letter day!

But here I was pushing off to Wisbech in late April for a two-day match with a dance in the middle and much hospitality and all things civil, except the weather. For the wind that blows over East Anglia seems sometimes, as I discovered in the early days of the war, to sweep straight from the Urals. We had three Gilligans, no less, and several Cambridge undergraduates, and the captain of Lincolnshire, one Major C. Wilson. Why I specially remember the last-named is because on the second morning, after a notable party overnight, our manager and captain, H. D. Swan, set him to bowl uphill and into the piercing wind. Now 'Swannie' was one of those captains who made his changes by the clock, and it so happened there was no clock. He was forgetful when there was a clock, and much more so without it. So the gallant major went on and on, breasting the wind and the slope, while we gave him a little facetious encouragement and avoided the captain's eye. At last when collapse from a combination of exhaustion and exposure was clearly imminent the wind grew full of sleet, and we all gratefully retired.

'Swannie' was one of quite a collection of middle-aged men who between the wars helped to run wandering cricket. They had plenty of money and leisure, and great zeal for the game, and much kindliness to the young – and were no earthly good whatever. Some of them had been once: others never had. They used to proceed to the nets at Lord's with red and yellow scarves to keep their trousers up, and the ground-staff bowlers used sometimes to amuse themselves with bets as to who would hit the stumps most often. 'Swannie', a large and heavy man, used to field at mid-on very straight, so that he was almost behind the bowler's umpire. There was no question of his running after the ball, and he used to convey the impression that it was well out of reach even when it was whistling past his boots. He went in, when he had to, at No. 11, and I never heard or read of his making double figures. In short he was distinctly the worst cricketer I ever saw, and since both he and his charming wife are long since dead, and were without issue, there is none to take this judgement amiss. He collected strong sides, and went to endless trouble, and loved the company of good cricketers. I expect the happiest time of his life was when he accompanied Archie MacLaren's MCC team to New Zealand and Australia as honorary manager.

Another of a like kind was Captain T. H. Carlton-Levick, who went with MCC to the West Indies, to Canada, and to South America, paying his way in a similar capacity. Carlton designed his own blue cap with the letters MCC entwined on the front, and is to be seen wearing it, and complete with 'co-respondent shoes', squatting at 'Plum' Warner's feet in the MCC South American group of 1926–7. It was said that Carlton used simply to arrive to catch the boat train at Euston or Waterloo and say, 'Hullo boys, I'm your manager.'

Gerry Weigall was in that side of 'Plum's' and was of similar vintage, except that he hadn't a bean to take himself anywhere and moreover had been a good cricketer when young. The Weigall saga is as rich as that of Rockley Wilson, with the difference that Rockley was both a wit and a scholar. Apart from some fondness for the horses Gerry's life was rooted utterly in cricket which he played whenever possible and talked 365 days of the year. He was never without a walking-stick or umbrella, since one or the other was in constant use to illustrate his remarks. He always had a few pet bees buzzing around in his bonnet, and used to inveigh against the criminal folly of selectors and authority generally if their views did not match his own. When in 1928 Woolley, despite making 3,500 runs, was omitted from Percy Chapman's team to Australia his anguish was terrible to see. To think that they had preferred that 'cross-batted village-greener', Maurice Leyland!

He used to inflict on *The Cricketer* articles in which the golden deposit of truth was apt to be obscured by grammatical difficulties and an absence of punctuation. Remonstrating gently with him on this account 'Plum' Warner said 'Gerry, you ought to take a course of Macaulay.'

'What, sir,' he exploded, 'the Yorkshire bowler?' Christian names were scarce with him; everyone was 'sir'. He pronounced various rules or axioms. 'Never eat veal and ham pie for lunch' was followed by 'Never cut in May', and 'Never run to cover on a fast wicket.' The Kent 2nd XI which he captained knew these don'ts well enough. One day young Leslie Todd was in with Gerry and going nicely, when the latter hit one to cover and called for a fatal run. As poor Todd passed him ruefully on his way to the pavilion, the captain consoled him with, 'Only shows you, sir, only shows you!'

Altogether running between wickets was rather a sore point, for although G. J. V. Weigall in the University Match of 1892 took out his bat for 63, the score-book also records that three of the best Cambridge bats were run out while he was in, including his captain, the immortal F. S. Jackson. When from Gerry's square-cut, half-stopped, it was likely that one of them would have to go Gerry is supposed to have sacrificed his partner with the words 'Get back, Jacker, I'm set.' Apocryphal, no doubt. George Fenner, a splendid character himself, who was a stalwart of Kent 2nd XI before he became head pro at Lord's was a repository of Weigall stories, and they were warm friends. On one of the Minor County grounds one day they were surveying a very dubious wicket, Gerry having won the toss, and wondering what to do. 'I think I'd bat, sir,' said George, 'before the flowers come up.'

To the reader who never knew Gerry Weigall he may well sound a rather preposterous fellow. To such I can only say that every cricketer was his friend, and that he never spoke an unkind word about anyone.

E. W. Swanton, *Sort of a Cricket Person* (1922)

Early Laws

Umpires' duties began to grow. In 1787 *The Times* published a dry little piece put in, unusually, by the umpires of a game. It highlights the growing importance of umpires amid the strain and chaos of public reaction to cricket, and serves as a reminder of how much public reaction there was.

A few days ago, two Justices of the Peace sent their mandate to stop a game, which was playing for an evening's amusement, at cricket; but the messenger was desired to return with the players' humble service, and if they might depend upon justice being done them, they would be glad if the worthy Magistrate, for the sake of the peace, would do them the honour to be umpires.

In a period like the late eighteenth century when the game was developing fast, homespun cricket experts abounded, discoursing to umpires on the ins and outs of the new rules, the London game (the game according to the new rules), the rough game (the game according to local rules) and the club's traditions. Umpires who were on the receiving end, especially in areas ambitious for a sophisticated reputation, sometimes sighed for what Nyren called 'the remote and unfrequented villages of England, where the primitive manners, customs, and games of our ancestors survive in the perfection of rude and unadulterated simplicity'.

The simplicity was getting more adulterated all the time. Along with length and rising bowling, straight bats and new strokes, lbw entered umpires' lives to bring cricket's crude innocence to an end. Nyren's friend Tom Taylor was 'a most brilliant hitter, but his great fault lay in not sufficiently guarding his wicket'. He was often bowled while attempting the cut, the new, stylish stroke, because he could not resist cutting at straight balls. On one occasion he and another Hambledon batsman called Ring were what Beldham described as 'shabby' enough to protect their wickets with their feet. 'The bowlers found themselves defeated and the law was passed to make lbw out.'

The 1774 definition and prohibition of lbw was not a direct result of Tom Taylor's or Ring's action. It was becoming common practice to block with feet as well as bat. Accordingly, a batsman was to be given out if he 'puts his leg before the wicket with a design to stop the ball, and actually prevents the ball from hitting his wicket by it'.

Lbw has been a thorn in umpires' sides and a psychological burden from that day to this. In Nyren's time, no one knew which was more despicable – using your feet to guard your wicket or being given out lbw. It was the clause about intention which rankled and always led to the batsman accusing the umpire of either ignorance or slander. The next set of laws, brought out by the newly formed MCC in 1788, relieved the umpires of having to judge the batsman's intention by simply stating that he was out if he was hit by a ball which 'pitched in a straight line to the wicket, and would have hit it'.

Even so, it was not popular. It did not appear on any surviving score-cards until 1795, though this does not mean that umpires were abstaining from lbw convictions; rather that scorers were not distinguishing lbw dismissals from bowled out, any more than most of them distinguished stumped out, 'catched out' and run out from bowled out. The official lbw virgin was the Hon. J. Tufton who, batting for England against Surrey at Moulsey Hurst, was lbw, bowled Wells in the first innings. There is no record of the umpire's name.

Lbw is one of the decisions that can only be decided by the bowler's end umpire. In that respect, it stood out among the 1774 laws, which went a long way towards defusing suspicions that decisions went accord-ing to which umpire gave them by abolishing the absolute jurisdiction of each umpire over decisions at his end. It meant that umpires could consult each other on difficult decisions and ones where they were unsighted. One of the simplest causes of distrust was removed.

Oddly enough, one of the most common causes of trouble was 'cat-ched out'. The 1774 laws do not mention umpires' jurisdiction over decisions about catches; it was taken for granted, and a permanent source of argument. There were furious altercations about whether fielders had caught balls with the help of their clothes, by knocking batsmen out of the way, or with hidden help from the ground. Good catchers were highly prized, especially in country cricket, where good clean catchers were umpires' favourites.

A report survives of one important match between Kent and Surrey in July 1762, for 100 guineas 'and thousands depending', which is a good indication of how easily 'catched out' decisions provoked arguments and how easily arguments could flare up into violence. Whether or not slop-ing ground was a contributory cause of this argument is not clear. This 'great match' was 'not decided' because of a dispute about a player 'catched out' in the first innings when Surrey were fifty ahead. The dispute quickly became a fight, with 'blows and broken heads and a challenge between two persons of distinction'.

There was so much 'confusion' that bets had to be withdrawn. It must have been very bad indeed if bookies agreed to refund bets.

Nyren rated all fielding highly. He described Hambledon's best field-ers darting all over the field like lightning and running swift as hares. Fielding was invaluable when playing on Windmill Down, to which the club moved when some of its players complained that the original ground, Broadhalfpenny Down, was too bleak. Windmill Down was, said Nyren, 'one of the finest places for playing on I ever saw', which means it had a flat pitch. But 'the ground gradually declined every way from the centre: the fieldsmen therefore were compelled to look about them, and for this reason they became so renowned in that department of the game'.

The umpires were unable to see what happened over the brow of the hill, even if they could confer. Trying to see over slopes such as Hambledon played on, and many far worse, was a routine problem for eighteenth-century umpires.

With matches commonly coming to an abrupt end because of disputes, a useful but dangerous tactic for umpires was to set a time limit for any team or player refusing to play, and if the game had not re-started when the time was up, the side refusing to play lost the game. From 1774 on, umpires only had to call play once, not three times, before awarding the match to the team that was willing to play. Even so, sides continued to walk off and sit down in protest with monotonous regularity. Usually they took their umpire with them but they might leave him behind if he proved unusually reluctant to support their action.

The overall impression given by the 1774 laws is one of keenness to improve umpires' relations – all relations: with each other, with players and with spectators. Troublesome matters such as deciding who should choose pitch and innings were eased off the umpires' shoulders. Visiting teams chose both, though if the game was played on a neutral ground, the leading bowlers tossed for innings. Still, London laws notwithstanding, it took a long time to change local customs on such issues.

It was not all easier going for umpires. They were expected to call short runs, which they had been doing for years unofficially. It was now an official, nerve-racking duty, and one local paper reported with evident relief and high spirits the foolishness of one of its umpires in calling a short run when the batsmen had only taken a single.

For the first time notches were called runs in the laws. The two names were about equally common at this time, notches being favoured by more traditional teams like Hambledon.

One of the simplest of the new laws was that, for the first time, the umpires could not be changed simply because both sides wanted them changed. In a way, this was a proclamation of umpires' independence from team and patronal pressure, like their emancipation from having their jurisdiction limited to one end. But how much notice country clubs took of this new rule is open to question, as is the difference, if any, it made to relations between players and umpires.

Nyren's book was purposely eulogistic: he gave a picture of the club he loved in its golden age, which had now passed it by, leaving it resplendent in his memory. Even so, the incidents he recounted do make it sound as if Hambledon matches, including important and tense ones, were cheerful.

> There was high feasting held on Broadhalfpenny during the solemnity of one of our grand matches. Oh! it was a heart-stirring sight to witness the multitude forming a complete and dense circle round that noble green. Half the county would be present, and all their hearts with us – little Hambledon, pitted against All England was a proud thought for the Hampshire men . . . How these fine brawn-faced fellows of farmers would drink to our success!

Nyren waxed lyrical on the ordinaries everyone consumed afterwards at the Bat and Ball. He was a musician and liked the singing as much as the ale and beef. 'Little George' Leer, Hambledon's best long-stop, used to celebrate the day's cricket in duet with Sueter, the wicket-keeper:

> I have been there, and still would go,
> 'Twas like a little heaven below!

It would be nice, though probably unrealistic, to think that the Hambledon umpires went to these ordinaries and festivities.

Just a hint of the problems of umpiring, even at games as idyllic as Nyren described, can be found in his description of Sueter. Unlike Yalden, his opposite number in a team they often played, he did not 'shuffle and resort to trick'. Everyone respected him so much 'that I firmly believe they would have trusted to his decision, had he ever chosen to question that of the umpire'.

Teresa McLean, *The Men in White Coats* (1987)

Retirements, etc. (Law 33)

It has been seen that there are a considerable number of ways in which a batsman's innings can be cut short, but there are still a few more, most of which come under the heading 'Retired'. Among these variations of retirement is the one and only occasion when a batsman has been given out because he has taken more than two minutes to arrive at the wicket. The circumstances were very dramatic: Sussex were playing Somerset at Taunton in 1919, and in the second innings the scores were level and 9 wickets were down. The remaining Sussex batsman, H. J. Heygate, was known to be crippled with rheumatism, but with the game in such a tense position he was persuaded to make an effort to come to the wicket. In his crippled state he took some time in coming, and having at last arrived, he was given out. It seems that one of the Somerset players, L. Braund, had appealed to the umpires about Heygate's delay: consequently, they had timed him, found that he had exceeded the limit, and so gave him out. The game remained a tie (under the old ruling), but high controversy raged over the incident. Here is a note on it taken from the Sussex score-book, made at the time by the scorer:

> With regard to Street's decision that Heygate should not bat, the time was 4 o'clock, so still 3½ hours to play. Heygate was ready to play and was at the wicket when Street decided that as he had exceeded the two minutes he could not bat. He was ready to play and the umpire did not call 'Play'.

Though this is the only time a batsman has been out like this in a first-class match, there must have been other occasions when an appeal could have been made. When the South Africans first toured England in 1894, and were playing Gloucestershire, a sudden fall of wickets found the South African E. A. Halliwell unprepared, and it was a long time before he came out. W. G. Grace protested at the delay and remarked that he thought the South Africans had come here to learn the game. Halliwell's reply to these gibes was to score a century.

Quite possibly, if Grace had made his appeal early enough, Halliwell might have been given out, but it must be remembered that the two minutes must be timed from the moment of the appeal. On one occasion, however, in the Varsity match of 1901, when Oxford were trying most desperately to play out time, one batsman took as long as six minutes to arrive at the crease. The umpire, Jim Phillips, who was always a great stickler for Law, thereupon informed the Cambridge Captain that if he were to claim the match, he would be quite ready to uphold the claim. The Cambridge Captain refused this rather unorthodox offer, but there is no doubt that the batsman had transgressed the two-minute Law. It may be of interest to note that the report of the 1937 Findlay Commission refers to a variation of this Law by which on some grounds play was stopped if a wicket fell within five minutes of any interval, thus allowing a batsman five minutes grace instead of two – often a very useful concession. The report rightly suggested that any such local rule should be abolished, and it was.

Another incident connected with this Law concerns the dismissal of T. E. Sidwell in the Surrey v. Leicestershire match at the Oval in 1921. Sidwell had scored 1* overnight, but turned up late next day, and not being present when play was called, was ruled out. As the Law stands now, a batsman delayed other than by illness or injury may resume his innings out of due order if the fielding captain gives his permission. The choice lies with him, and in the circumstances of Sidwell's absence, P. G. H. Fender, the Surrey Captain, did not give his consent for Sidwell to come in later. A similar incident occurred in the Northants v. All India match in 1932. V. W. C. Jupp, who was not out overnight, was late next morning, and though the Indian Captain was ready to allow him to come in again later in the innings, the umpires (rather high-handedly) declared Jupp out. Perhaps it would be better if the man was automatically out, and the opposing captain had no choice in the matter. A change in the Law would certainly rule out possibilities of unpleasantness.

The two instances just quoted are concerned with cases in which the batsman's absence was not due to injury or illness. If he should be delayed for these reasons, permission is always granted for a delay, but he cannot, of course, resume his innings except after the fall of a wicket.

Sometimes a side's innings has been very much curtailed. In 1890, when playing against Yorkshire, three of the Kent side arrived at the ground so late that the innings was over after 7 wickets had fallen. Kent were thus 'all out' for 46. A similar curtailment seemed likely in the Hampshire v. Essex match at Bournemouth in 1921. Hampshire batted first and soon lost 6 wickets for 21 runs. Mead was then hurt, and as the rest of the team had not arrived, the innings was really finished. By the kind permission of the opposing captain, a ten-minute delay was granted, by which time the late-comers had turned up, and the total was raised to 71. On another occasion J. H. Parsons was 'robbed' of his innings through the collapse of his colleagues. Warwickshire won the toss in the match v. Worcestershire at Worcester in 1921, and their innings began well enough for Parsons to decide to go back home to fetch his spectacles, which he had left behind. After he had left the ground, a collapse set in, and by the time he got back Warwick were all out, and Parsons had to be content with the entry, 'absent . . . 0'.

Apart from these instances, there have been one or two other 'absentee' dismissals. The score-sheet of the Surrey v. Notts match at Trent Bridge in 1878 includes the strange entry: 'Boardman, not arrived yet . . . 0', and the Varsity match of 1841 provides a similar curiosity. Oxford needed 120 runs to beat Cambridge and lost the match by 8 runs. The bald account says: 'They batted only ten men because, with nine runs to win and one wicket to fall, Lord Ward could not be found.' The entry, 'Lord Ward, absent . . . 0' conjures up all sorts of pictures. Another match lost by the absence of some of the team was when Cambridge University beat H. D. G. Leveson-Gower's XI by 8 runs in 1914. In the last innings, Leveson-Gower's XI wanted 172 runs to win, and after they had scored 92 for 1 wicket, two of the team, C. U. Peat and Leveson-Gower himself, left the match, assuming that they would not be needed. A collapse set in, the team was all out for 163, and the game was lost – a result which no doubt surprised the truants. In somewhat similar circumstances MCC lost a match to Middlesex in 1872. The margin was only 9 runs, and the decision might well have been reversed had not two MCC players – C. I. Thornton and J. W. Dale – been unaccountably absent for their second innings. The MCC Committee published a statement 'expressing their surprise and regret' at this, and added a reminder that 'all matches at Lord's, unless otherwise specified, are continued on the third day'. There have also been other occasions when a batsman has shown a reluctance to bat, and it is said that old William Lillywhite once refused to go in when his turn came.

Other deliberate sacrifices of a wicket include those strange cases when a batsman has left his wicket assuming (quite wrongly) that he is out. By the ruling of the 1947 code, umpires are requested to recall a batsman who walks out under this misapprehension, but this clause has not always existed, and here are a few examples of batsmen whom no one has stopped from walking away. They include that of J. Southerton, who in the Surrey v. MCC match at the Oval in 1870 assumed he was caught, and walked out. This dismissal is recorded as: 'J. Southerton, retired, thinking he was caught . . . o'.

The circumstances were as follows: he cut a ball hard to W. G. Grace at point, who picked it up on the rebound, and did not throw it up as if he had made a catch. Nobody except Southerton thought he was out, but he walked away, and when recalled, refused to come back. A similar dismissal came in the Sussex v. Lancashire match in 1919. A. H. H. Gilligan appears in the score-book as 'st Boddington, b Tyldesley . . . 2', but the umpire later said that Gilligan was not in fact stumped (as the scorers supposed), and indeed was not really out at all. Here is a note on the incident by the Sussex scorer:

An unfortunate incident occurred with reference to Mr A. H. H. Gilligan. The scorers saw the wicket-keeper break the wicket, and Mr Gilligan come out, so naturally assumed he was out stumped. What really occurred was: Mr Gilligan, beaten by the ball and hearing one of the fielders say, 'Well bowled,' looked round, and seeing the bails on the ground, thought he had been bowled, and came out.

J. Shuter had a similarly unfortunate demise in the South v North match at the Oval in 1889, as also did J. Painter in the Gloucestershire v Notts match of 1886. He thought he was 'ct and bld', and walked away. In the 1881 Varsity Match C. F. H. Leslie was more lucky. He returned a hard shot to the bowler, A. F. J. Ford, who threw the ball up. Thinking he was caught, Leslie retired, but his partner, W. H. Patterson, put in an appeal which was answered in Leslie's favour. He was recalled from the pavilion and carried his score from 18 to 70. It is not often that a batsman puts in an appeal.

All these misunderstandings are very different from the few occasions when a batsman has deliberately retired from reasons other than for injury or illness. This is not uncommon in Trial matches, but it does not often occur in first-class games. In 1920 P. F. Warner left an innings of 22 incomplete against Essex, as he had to attend a selector's meeting, and in 1944–5 V. M. Merchant, having taken his score to 201 in a match against a Service XI in India, ended a third-wicket stand of 382 with Hazare by deciding he had been in long enough. He thus appears as 'retired . . . 201'. The 1947 code makes it clear that an innings thus deliberately ended must be considered as 'out' for purposes of compiling averages.

Sometimes illness or injury has sadly hampered a side. The worst epidemic was when, in the game v. Notts at Trent Bridge in 1935, Hampshire had three batsmen absent in each innings – a total of absentees suffered in one innings by Somerset v. Yorkshire in 1911, and by Leicestershire v. Surrey in 1920. In the latter match Surrey also had two men away, so the game produced as many as five casualties. Almost as devastating was the luck of the MCC Australian XI when playing The Rest at Folkestone in 1929. They had two batsmen absent in each innings, and in their second innings two of the nine batsmen left had to employ runners. It is just as well that absentees' innings do not count against a player's record. It would be especially hard if F. Buckle (in a Middlesex v. Surrey match of 1869) was regarded as having earned 'spectacles' with entries which read:

> First innings: not sent for in time . . . o
> Second innings: absent unwell . . . o

Not a very good match for Mr Buckle.

Despite the rigours of the game, serious injuries have not been common, and in first-class cricket in England perhaps the only fatality was that of G. F. Summers, who in 1870 died a few days after being hit on the head by a fast ball. Alfred Shaw says in his book that Summers did not properly carry out the doctor's orders for treatment and rest. Some readers may remember the terrible blow on the head received by H. B. Cameron in a Test match of 1929 – a blow which made him unconscious for several days.

Sometimes batsmen have a very uncomfortable time. In the Surrey v. Lancashire match of 1909 at the Oval W. S. Lees was hit four balls running by deliveries from W. Brearley – after which he retired from the match. In recent times Ikin and Hutton had a severe battering from the South African fast attack in the match at Old Trafford, but nothing so unpleasant as the time experienced by the MCC team when playing New South Wales at Sydney in 1920–1. I quote this Australian report on part of the first day's play.

Gregory was bowling very fast and making the ball bump a good deal. He hit Russell on the shoulder and caused him to drop his bat in pain. When he came on again he was greeted with applause. His second ball hit Hobbs on the thigh, but he managed to limp a single. The next ball hit Hendren, who was momentarily hurt. Shortly after

Gregory knocked Hobbs' bat out of his hand, and struck him on the wrist, causing him to dance about for some seconds, leaving his bat where it fell. The next three balls, rising to over six feet, made Hobbs duck to avoid them. In trying to hit him to leg, Makepeace, who made 8, was struck in the chest by a rising ball.

Not even the 'wicked' days of bodyline twelve years later produced such a dangerous picture. In fact, very few batsmen were damaged by the rising ball, possibly because of the massive padding worn by some of them, padding which would no doubt have amused players of the past, including Alfred Mynn, who once played a great innings in acute pain from frequent knocks by fast bowling on his unpadded legs. Bumping balls have indeed hit batsmen occasionally, but a good many of the worst injuries have resulted from the ball coming up off the bat. In a few matches in 1933, Hendren appeared in a cap which had three defensive peaks. This was more probably a joke than anything else, and nothing like it has been seen since. When a batsman is hit there is usually no attempt to lay any special blame on the bowler, but the following entry in the score-sheet of a match between Kent and Sussex in 1873 – the County Cup match in fact – states the circumstances without hesitation. George Humphreys of Sussex is put down as: 'Retired hurt by Mr Coles' bowling . . . 32'. This wicket is not credited to Mr Coles in the analysis!

It is possibly more dangerous to field than it is to bat, and the range of injuries varies from a fielder spiking his hand with his own boot studs to colliding with a colleague when going for a catch. The most injuries come to those who field in the leg-trap. The courage of such fielders is admirable, but they sometimes pay for it. The close fielding of S. G. Barnes in 1948 excited some comment – some said that he was illegally close – but after being seriously hit by a stroke from Pollard, he kept a more sensible distance. Barnes was hit in the back, and was probably more fortunate than D. J. Knight, who, after a hit on the head in 1921, was seriously ill for some time. Let us take off our hats to all close-in fielders, and especially to a catch made at point-blank range by Jack Oakes when he caught S. M. Brown off Jas. Langridge in the Middlesex v. Sussex match at Lord's in 1949. This was a full-blooded drive at face height, which Oakes, at very silly point, stood his ground to, and took without a murmur – a wonderfully courageous catch.

It is really most remarkable that players' careers have not suffered more from injuries. Perhaps the most frequently damaged player has been the redoubtable R. E. S. Wyatt, whose breakages have been extensive, but in spite of them his enthusiasm has persisted.

Though this chapter has been chiefly concerned with absentees, there have been some occasions when serious illness or injury has not prevented a batsman from playing his part. At least two notable innings have been played in Test matches by batsmen using only one hand. Gripping the bat with right hand only the Hon. L. H. Tennyson made scores of 63 and 36 against the speed attack of Gregory and McDonald in the third Test match of 1921, but more recently in the first Test match against the West Indies in 1950, Hutton, also using one hand only, showed that batting is essentially something to be done with the left hand. Other 'heroes' of the sick-bay include Paynter in 1932–3, and T. E. Bailey in 1950–1, both of whom played Test match innings when it was not expected that they would have a chance of batting. In early days, William Lillywhite, in a match between Kent and England at Canterbury, was once carried to the wicket in order to play his innings, and even earlier history relates how Harris the great Hambledon bowler, when crippled with rheumatics, sat down in an armchair on the field when not actually bowling. No doubt, if hit, the armchair would have brought the batsman the 'five-run' penalty.

Finally, let us consider the last possible way in which batsmen can have their innings cut short – namely, by being left 'not out', because they have no partner left to assist them. Some batsmen have a proportion of 'not out' innings much higher than others. H. C. Snary, of Leicestershire, was left 'not out' in 41 per cent of all his 250 or so innings in first-class cricket – a very high proportion. In his first two sessions, C. W. Cook of Gloucestershire batted 65 times and was left undefeated in as many as 45 of them, a fact which suggests that he deserved a better place in the order. Strudwick was another with a high proportion of 'not outs', and in the season of 1910 had had as many as 27 of them. Another wicket-keeper, W. Cornford, once batted ten times in succession without losing his wicket, a record surpassed only by that of J. J. Burrows of Canterbury, whose first-class career, covering the years 1926–7 to 1932–3, consisted of 12 innings, in all of which he remained 'not out' – an astonishing performance. A. H. Fabian had the distinction of playing five innings in Varsity matches without losing his wicket.

Though 'not outs' tend to be the prerogative of batsmen rather low in the order, great players have at times had spells of batting success when they have proved quite invincible. In 1898 W. G. Quaife played six innings and was then out for 3 in a seventh, by which time he had compiled 471 runs before losing his wicket. Even more remarkable was the form of K. C. Ibrahim, who began the Indian season of 1947–8 with scores of 218* and 36*, 234* and 77*, 144 – after which his average stood at 709.

Once really set, the innings of some great men have been cut short only by time or lack of a partner. One in three of all the individual scores of over 100 made by Messrs Mead, Holmes and Wyatt were left 'unfinished', and other good batsmen with a high proportion of 'not outs' include Woodfull, Jardine, C. B. Harris and James Langridge.

When we come to really big scores, we find that of all the 70 individual triple-centuries ever made no less than 35 have been left 'not out'. The highest is Bradman's 452 not out. Who knows to what limits that score might have gone if his captain had not declared? On the whole, I have little sympathy for those makers of unfinished triple-centuries who regret that they cannot go on any longer, though possibly B. B. Nimbalkar had some cause for complaint when, with his lunch score at 443 not out against Western India States at Poona in 1948–9, he had some hopes of breaking Bradman's world record score, only to have his chances denied him when the fielding side refused to take the field again. This was bad luck for Nimbalkar, but it is probably more just that Bradman should keep the record. I feel more sorry for P. R. Johnson, who in the Somerset v. Sussex match at Bath in 1910 suffered such poor support from his colleagues in each innings that he was each time left not out – with scores of 98* and 96*. These were innings of great merit which fully deserved the distinction of a century.

Gerald Brodribb, *Next Man In* (1952)

Parson's Play

One notable Vicar of Esholt in the West Riding of Yorkshire was undoubtedly a practitioner of Christianity as interpreted by the Church of England, and his primary calling was to service of his Master and parishioners; but he did like his cricket.

Sunday matches were beyond his reach but only the most pressing of counter-claims was likely to forbid him a midweek indulgence within reasonable geographical range. He was not, though he might have been, the cleric involved in the story of the Dales farmer who sought from his vicar a mutually convenient time for burial of an aged relative. After various possibilities had been considered and rejected the farmer concluded:

'Tell thi what, Vicar; we'll up-end him in t'church porch and tha can side him when tha's time' – 'side' being the vernacular for 'put away'.

The Reverend C. E. D. Crane had precisely the qualities to maintain, stabilize and glorify those loosely bound associations formed to bring cricketers together entirely for the purpose of cricket; clubs, usually of fanciful title, demanding the minimum and yet the maximum of qualification for membership. They ask not who you are or what you do, where you live or how you live, but would you like to play, with kindred spirits, for such satisfactions as the day might bring.

Parson Crane, as I knew him in the 1930s, found such satisfactions with the Craven Gentlemen CC. The parish of Esholt never was in the Yorkshire district of Craven but, then, the club was people, not residences, and quickly spread beyond its area of origin. It had no clerical basis of membership and, by circumstantial evidence, was open to heathen or heretic. It played in no league or competition, found fixtures where it was welcomed and, in its capacity as host, borrowed or hired a ground.

Opponents were as varied as its own representation. The CG touched the fringes of first-class cricket in meetings with Sir Julien Cahn's XI and did battle on village greens with equal enthusiasm and delight. Schools were visited and 'home' matches at Ilkley and Harrogate gave welcome to such travelling sides as the Frogs from Kent and the Catamarans from London's coloured community. The CG played where and when they could arrange a game and rarely, in my recollection, attempted to turn out the same team twice. Selection was by call for volunteers and when the fixture list appeared in Spring there was eager thumbing of business diaries.

S. M. J. Woods, captaining Somerset on one occasion, is reputed to have surveyed the team-sheet presented to him and remarked: 'Well, I don't know him, or him, but I've heard of him – he's a helluva fine golfer.' CG captains-for-the-day were frequently left in the same confusion.

Unfamiliarity sometimes evoked misunderstanding. In one match approaching climax with a few runs wanted and only one wicket to fall I was supposed to be the batsman in charge, responsible for protecting a number eleven who had bowled well but had disclaimed any batting ambition or competence. On the last ball of an over I called for the tactical single and made my running in continuation of the stroke. From half-way down the pitch I saw my partner immobile and cupping a hand to his ear.

'I beg your pardon,' he was murmuring in the quiet tones character-istic of the deaf. 'What did you say?'

Parson Crane epitomized the purpose and character of the Craven Gentlemen of the 1930s. He would play whenever he could, in minor engagement or major. His enthusiasm was unquenchable and his author-ity in the captaincy invariably bestowed on him was benign. He wanted everybody, including himself, to do well in every match; he sought always 'a summer of roses and wine' and by exercise of imagination and remi-niscence he could contrive high holiday from a wet day.

I never knew him offer a harsh or a hasty word and, heaven knows, there was scope for both in some of the CG techniques. Seen through Crane's spectacles all cricket was sweetness and light and the failures of today were considered only as balancing factors for successes in prospect tomorrow. Parson Crane was at this time about sixty years old.

White hair wisped from beneath his multi-coloured cap and his tackle preserved a flavour of bygone custom. His bat was dark with oil and age and tenderly bandaged. His pads were short and narrow and ventilated, as Ranjitsinhji had favoured, and 'Ranji' represented Crane's pride and sorrow mingled. 'I think I might have got a Blue,' he told us, without a trace of arrogance, 'but Ranji came up at that time.'

On the field Parson Crane's benevolent captaincy sometimes extended to the opposing side. Once when CG had lost the toss to St Peter's School, York, Crane led out his team saying to the accredited bowlers, 'I think I had better have a few overs myself to start with. We don't want to press the boys too hard.'

The sky was cloudless, the pitch perfection, and one of the incoming batsmen was named N. W. D. Yardley. I believe we struggled to an undignified draw after the School declaration.

In my recollection Crane's personal batting was orthodox in method, optimistic in approach and self-mystifying in effect. In match after match he played forward by the textbook and, pondering in the pavilion, he would muse: 'I can't understand how I was bowled; I was sure I played straight.' The technique had stayed with him but the years had taken toll of his timing.

Parson Crane appreciated cricket in terms of Sarah Battle's 'rigour of the game', but he also recognized social obligations implicit in playing host or visitor. He wanted to win, but certainly not at any cost. Gamesmanship, had he been able to understand it, in his team would have hurt him more than an epidemic of dropped catches. His was happy though sometimes haphazard cricket.

One midweek afternoon of August he took a team to play against the staff and resident patients of a private hospital in Wharfedale. The playing area was a lovely sweep of lawn that fronted the mansion. Circling the boundary were trees, shrubbery and flower beds and behind long-on was a wooden summerhouse, furnished with a table and wicker chairs. The weather was sunny and exceptionally warm.

Before the contented captain led his team out to field he suggested that, in view of the heat and the general intention of the occasion, bowling strategy should be based on division of labour. 'We'll bowl two or three overs in turn,' he said, 'and spread out the field a bit.' The plan was accepted with unanimous approval.

After the first changes of bowling in the agreed routine our captain betook himself to the long field where he initiated conversation with the hospital superintendent, who was strolling at the boundary edge. The bowler of the moment, having completed his third over, looked towards the distant leader for relief and further instruction. No sign being returned, the bowler delivered a fourth over, and in the absence of any signal, a fifth. By this time a few wickets had fallen and the master-plan was in confusion.

More careful observation indicated the absence of the CG captain from his last-known fielding position. Calculation proclaimed him absent from the field altogether. At the fall of another wicket search exposed Parson Crane and the hospital superintendent sharing discussion and long, cooling drinks in the shade of the summerhouse. 'The game,' said the unrepentant captain, 'seemed to be going on all right.'

The game was, indeed, on the turn. A tottering innings was cemented by a confident and beautiful batting display that developed undisturbed through bowling changes both formal and of urgent necessity.

The batsman would have been remarkable without his performance. He was small, middle-aged and detached in manner. He was immaculately dressed in well-fitting flannels that looked brand-new; pads and boots were dazzling in the sunshine. The incongruity was a pair of obviously much-used and gaudy-coloured braces.

J. M. Kilburn, *Overthrows* (1975)

8

Storms

We hear and read too much these days about controversies in cricket. They have always existed, but the power of television to give people and events instant and vivid notoriety has given the impression that the sport is far less tranquil than it once was. This leads to newspapers following up stories and sometimes to absurd exaggeration. For day upon day in 1992 one tabloid in London pursued the Pakistan touring team like the hound of heaven, plastering their back pages with banner headlines as they sought to prove that their players had been illegally tampering with the ball. So seriously did the Daily Mirror *take the story that it was equated with the Watergate political scandal in America. Even in the world of politics there are only a few scandals of genuinely historic significance, events which bring down governments and reverberate for decades. The two in my lifetime which come instantly to mind are the Profumo affair and Watergate itself. In cricket there may be one such historic upheaval in a generation, although there are any number of minor eruptions.*

Bodyline and the Packer revolution are the two major stories of the century. I have something in common here with my journalistic mentor, E. W. Swanton, who was a rising young cricket reporter for the Evening Standard *when Percy Holmes and Herbert Sutcliffe broke the world's highest first wicket partnership record against Essex at Leyton in 1932. It was, of course, a great cricket story, but telephones in press-boxes are in short supply even now, let alone then. There was only one in the Leyton press-box, Swanton was beaten to it by a rival and missed an edition. His sports editor decided that if he couldn't dispatch something so hot from the edge of London, he would have little chance of doing so from Sydney. It was a poor piece of judgement and the result was that the* Standard's *tennis reporter, Bruce Harris, went to Australia instead. With no great feel for cricket, he reported the events of the most explosive of all cricket series without the critical eye which might have condemned the English tactics. Suitably chastened, Swanton seldom looked back.*

With more of a nose for news I might myself have been the man to break the Packer story, possibly several weeks before the Daily Mail's *brilliant columnist Ian Wooldridge. His inside source was thought to be Richie Benaud, whose advice helped Packer to hijack the professional game. My source might have been Tony Greig, if I had been more alert to what he was trying to tell me when I went to interview him on the day after the Centenary Test match in Melbourne in March 1977. Always a most personable chap with whom I got on well, it would not have taken much for me to have wrung from him the details of the conversations he had just been having with a Mr Packer. He dropped several hints about the whole game being shaken up and players making amounts of money they had not previously dreamed about. I kept my ears and eyes open after that, but failed to pin anything down before the story broke on the evening in May when Greig was giving a party at his home near Hove for the Australian touring team.*

At the time I was more interested in the cricket than the cricket politics, my chief concern in my then role as BBC cricket correspondent being to find out what Tony thought about England's chances in the Ashes series the following summer. I like to think I might be a little more news conscious these days but there will never be another cricket event as significant as that in my lifetime.

Of shorter storms there have been plenty; a few of them follow, but this is deliberately a relatively short chapter since we read about trouble often enough simply by picking up our daily newspapers.

The Night the Selectors Came to Blows

I beg to state that I convened a meeting of selectors for Saturday evening, 3 February, for the purpose of selecting the Australian eleven to play in the fourth Test match, and also to select as many players as could be agreed upon for the Australian eleven leaving for England in March next.

I was the first to arrive at the rooms of the NSW Cricket Association, getting there about 8 o'clock. Mr Iredale arrived about ten minutes later, and I informed him that the other selectors had not arrived; so he stated he would wait for them at the front door. In the meantime Mr Joe Davis, of the *Sydney Morning Herald*, came into the small room, and was chatting with me on various matters connected with cricket. Mr Sinclair rang up on the telephone about 20 past 8 to say that Mr Hill had left Manly, and to ask the other selectors to wait for him. Mr Hill arrived about 10 minutes to 9, and the other selectors came upstairs immediately afterwards.

The three selectors and myself were seated at the table, Mr Hill on one side, Mr McAlister and Mr Iredale on the other, and myself at the end whilst Mr Davis was standing up near the door.

The conversation was started with regard to the match being played in Melbourne on that day, Mr Hill remarking that it was strange that one of the best bowlers in Australia – Mr Laver – should have been omitted from the State team, and one who should be playing in the Test matches. Mr McAlister then remarked that in his opinion Mr Hill had not sufficiently used Messrs Kellaway and Minnett in the bowling department, so as to rest Messrs Cotter and Hordern. Hill stated that he considered that neither the bowlers in question were any good on the Melbourne and Adelaide wickets. Mr Davis in answer to a question from Mr Hill, also participated in the conversation and remarked that whatever Frank Laver may have been on English wickets, he did consider he was a good bowler on Australian wickets, and quoted that gentleman's averages for the last nineteen years, and at the same time informed the selectors that he would be only too pleased to go down to the office and bring his assistance to them in their work. He also remarked that he considered Minnett was a splendid bowler in so much as he had seen of him on New South Wales wickets. In view of his remarks, Hill informed Mr Davis that he did not consider that he was any judge of cricket.

The discussion again got round on the captaincy question, when McAlister reiterated his statement with regard to the using of Kellaway and Minnett. Hill remarked that McAlister had better take over the captaincy, and that he was quite prepared to hand his resignation to the Hon. Secretary at once. McAlister stated that he was not giving his view as a captain, but as a judge of cricket.

At this stage, Mr Davis, at my request, left the room. I had some telegrams ready to show the selectors with regard to Mr McLaren being available for the fourth Test match, and was only waiting an opportunity to give them this information before leaving the meeting myself.

Hill then asked McAlister where he got his experience as a captain, and he (McAlister) stated that he had captained teams in Australia, and also captained several matches as vice-captain of the Australian Eleven in England, and he considered that he had done all that was necessary. Hill remarked, was it not a fact that Warwick Armstrong had refused to play under him as a captain in the Old Country. This McAlister denied, and Hill asked him to name any match in which Armstrong took part, and in which he (McAlister) acted as captain. McAlister replied that he played under him as captain at Lord's on one occasion, when Mr Noble had to leave the field, but that he did not play under his captaincy in other matches because he always stood down when Mr Noble was not playing. Hill then asked McAlister what matches he had ever won as captain and asked him to write them down on a sheet of paper. McAlister numerated several, and Hill remarked that they were very second-rate matches. McAlister said, 'At all events, I did quite as well as Victor Trumper had done in captaining the Australian Eleven against Gloucestershire, when he almost made a hash of things.' Hill then said, 'Fancy you comparing yourself to men like Trumper and Armstrong.' McAlister replied, 'At all events, I consider I am as good a skipper, if not better, than the two players you have mentioned.' Hill then informed McAlister that he had no idea of captaincy, and McAlister replied, 'At all events, I reckon I am a better skipper than either Trumper, Armstrong, or yourself.'

Hill got up from his chair and informed McAlister that he had better take the position of captain and pick the team himself. Hill then sat down again, and informed McAlister that he knew absolutely nothing about skippering a side which brought forth a retort from McAlister that he (Hill) was the worst skipper he had ever seen. When this remark was passed, McAlister was leaning with his two hands in front of him, and Hill immediately jumped up and said, 'You have been looking for a punch in the jaw all night and I will give you one,' immediately leaning across the table and dealing McAlister a violent blow on the side of the face. McAlister was somewhat dazed, but jumped up and rushed round the table to where Hill was standing, and a fight ensued, both selectors grappling and trying to punch each other in the small space between the table and wall. McAlister sat down between the telephone-box and the table and Hill leant over him but did not strike him whilst on the floor. I eventually managed to separate the two combatants, and I might state here that when the scuffle first took place the table slewed round and Mr Iredale was jammed into the corner, and thus powerless to act. I urged

Hill to get out of the room, but he went to the other end of the table near the door. As soon as McAlister got on to his feet I tried to stop him from rushing at Hill, but they again got to holts. The furniture was knocked all over the room, the pictures were broken, and Hill grappled with McAlister and forced him on to the table and window-sill – another couple of feet and both selectors would have been out the window into the street, three floors below, but this was prevented by Mr Iredale leaning across and catching McAlister by the arm, whilst I pulled Hill off by the coat-tails. As soon as I got Hill away, I at once shoved him out of the door, and told him he 'had better stay outside'. Mr Iredale and myself holding McAlister he shouted to Hill: 'You coward! you coward!' Blood flowed from McAlister's face copiously, and it presented a sorry spectacle. My clothes, collar, hat, etc. were covered in blood. After getting McAlister to sit down, I went outside and interviewed Hill and told him that he had better go home. He said, 'Syd, I will not remain a member of the selection committee any longer, as I refuse to sit with McAlister as co-selector.' I replied that I could not take that as official, but if he would put the matter in writing, I would place same before the board. He said he would write it out at the hotel, and I would call for it. I then gave Hill his hat, papers, etc., and he said that he had had enough the day before at the board meeting, when Colonel Foxton practically branded him a liar in connection with the publication of the telegram he received from McAlister on the eve of the third Test match.

I might also state that during the disturbance, Hill accused McAlister of being drunk, but in my opinion neither Hill nor McAlister was intoxicated.

The two selectors were very heated in their arguments before the climax was reached, and the language was anything but gentlemanly . . .

Mr Iredale and myself took no part whatever in the arguments, but endeavoured in a joking way to try and get the two selectors into a better humour, but without avail. I regret exceedingly that this report has been necessary, but can positively state that this is a true account of the proceedings.

Syd Smith, Report by the Secretary to the Australian Cricket Board of Control, 1912, first published in *Bat and Pad*, edited by Pat Mullins and Phillip Derriman (1984)

Jardine and Warner

It is getting on for forty years since, during the visit of D. R. Jardine's MCC team in Australia, there occurred the extraordinary explosion of feeling that, for those old enough to remember, is recalled by the word Bodyline. It was in fact forty years ago this summer that the first seeds of the idea were sown. There is a full, well-documented, definitive book that covers the whole momentous episode, from its hazy origins to its full translation into practice, and the dramatic consequences, written from first-hand by J. H. Fingleton.

His *Cricket Crisis*, published in 1946 by Cassell, is a notably thorough and objective story, and as such, of course, a valuable contribution to cricket history. Several others in close proximity to the scene have published their impressions, including Hobbs, Bradman, Mailey, Freddie Brown, Bowes, Moyes, and, not least, the founder of *The Cricketer*, 'Plum' Warner. And I must not forget Sydney Southerton's fair and forthright editorial analysis of 'The Bowling Controversy' in the 1934 *Wisden*. There is no lack of literature on the subject, with Jack Fingleton's account the fullest and best.

The average young cricketer of today, however, may have no easy access to such sources, and I hope therefore that the following reflections may have some interest and also perhaps some present value as showing how in the heat of international sporting conflict passions can cloud cool judgement, and blur the boundaries that limit the confines of fair play. The biggest of all sporting rows has a moral and a lesson surely for the players and administrators of today.

The first signs of what came to be known as Bodyline bowling were to be observed, probably, around 1930 when two lusty young men of Notts, Harold Larwood and Bill Voce, were sometimes spurred on by their captain, A. W. Carr, to drop the ball short and make it fly round the ears of county batsmen.

There was, for instance, the incident, recorded with much relish among cricketers at the time, of the Somerset batsman, C. C. C. Case, who, endeavouring to avoid a ball that rose head-high, simultaneously lost his grasp of the bat and trod back on to the wicket. Such was poor 'Box' Case's confusion that, according to *The Times*, he returned to the pavilion 'carrying one of the stumps instead of his bat'. With Carr's active encouragement the Notts fast bowling was inclined occasionally, shall I say, to become a little 'rough'.

Nineteen-thirty was the year that the youthful Bradman first came, saw, and conquered, aiming at and achieving targets not hitherto considered, and in so doing destroying the English dominance of the later 1920s. At the Oval when Bradman was pressing on towards his thousandth run of the series – he did not quite get there, and no one has come near such a target before or since – the placid pitch suddenly grew lively after rain had moistened the top.

While Archie Jackson withstood Larwood in these conditions by classically straight, correct defence, getting right behind the rising ball, Bradman hopped about, using his exceptional speed of foot to keep out of harm's way. One recalls so clearly the contrast of method. Whether or not he really disliked the situation, the little man looked as though he did. Mental notes were made, and the evidence stored up for future use.

MCC were due in Australia in the winter of 1932–33. Whoever had ambitions to lead that side must have seen his first and crucial problem as the containing of the batsman who had begun to set three new run-getting standards. Who were the candidates for the job? Well, there was A. P. F. Chapman, who had led England with such flair and success; but in the last Oval Test he had been superseded by R. E. S. Wyatt. There was Wyatt then, and among other amateurs with Test experience there was also D. R. Jardine, who had had a successful tour of Australia in 1928–29 but had been little seen in first-class cricket since. When the selectors met in May 1931 to name England's captain against New Zealand they had to acknowledge that Percy Chapman, only a year before literally and in every sense the blue-eyed boy, had just come home from an unfruitful tour of South Africa wherein he had altogether failed as a batsman. There was Wyatt and there was Jardine, playing again now with some regularity for Surrey, and if they were not to go back to a much older man – for instance P. G. H. Fender or J. C. White, both forty or thereabouts and a little past their best – there was no one else of comparable qualifications. (The captain had in those days, of course, to be an amateur.)

Wyatt was now captain of Warwickshire, whereas Jardine had had no experience of leadership since leaving Winchester twelve years before. The appointment, however, went to Jardine, and in view of the consequences it is important to note that it was made by the new selectorial triumvirate due to serve much together in the 1930s – 'Plum' Warner, T. A. Higson and P. Perrin.

As was to be expected Jardine sailed through the 1931 New Zealand series, and the following year at Lord's in the one Test accorded to India, redeemed much otherwise paltry England batting by scoring 79 and 85 not out. His position was now secure, and to the public it seemed a mere formality when he was duly named as captain of the MCC team bound for Australia. Douglas Jardine was too aloof to commend himself in the same way as the gay, ever-boyish Chapman. He made no concession to popular sentiment: rather the reverse. The Harlequin cap he almost invariably wore seemed a conscious badge of superiority. Yet in the mind of the average follower a tough fighter was needed to play the Australians at their own game – and the new man was certainly that. To this extent at least the choice was widely approved.

It was only Jardine's contemporaries and those who had been closest to him who had doubts. The Oxford XIs of the early 1920s had seldom broken through a certain sardonic reserve, and had accordingly never considered him as captain. The MCC team of 1928–29 had chiefly noted in him, beside his habitual fierce determination, a particular antipathy for the Australians. In pavilions and dressing-rooms the better-informed were asking one another whom MCC had let themselves in for.

Rockley Wilson, who as master in charge of cricket had come up against Jardine's inflexibility when he was captain of Winchester, delivered the prophetic verdict: 'Well, we shall win the Ashes – but we may lose a Dominion.'

In the summer of 1932 the Notts bowling had elicited a few more grumbles, as had that of Bill Bowes for Yorkshire. I recall watching him bowling at the end of August at Bournemouth in the match that won Yorkshire the Championship. He let go some fast bouncers at the Hampshire captain, Lord Tennyson, who (then aged forty-two) was manifestly not amused, and ostentatiously marched up the wicket and smacked at imaginary marks around half-way.

A more significant protest had been made earlier in the month at the Oval when Yorkshire played Surrey, in a match I didn't see. Bowes bowled fast and short at Jack Hobbs, who protested both on the field and in print. So, too, in emphatic terms did 'Plum' Warner, who actually combined the chairmanship of selectors with the cricket correspondentship of the *Morning Post*.

Warner, who thus early declared his hand, was not only chairman of selectors but was to be manager of MCC in Australia. Hobbs was to travel, too, complete with 'ghost', as correspondent of the *Star*. One wonders whether Jardine, now captain of Surrey, speculated, during that Oval scene and its aftermath, of probable conflicts of view lying ahead.

Whatever premonitions anyone might have had, MCC sailed in September with four fast bowlers, Larwood, Voce, Bowes, and, to the surprise of the critics, G. O. Allen. As luck would have it they started well in their planned subjugation of Bradman by getting him twice on a wet wicket at Perth for 3 and 10. Bradman had made a royal progress by train from Sydney right across the continent. Fingleton, also on the trip to the west, says 'No prince could have had a more regal entry into Perth. As the long and dusty eastern train jolted to a halt thousands crammed the station, the adjoining roofs and buildings, the exits and the streets outside. Police had to force a passage for Bradman, and the Palace Hotel, where we stayed, was in a constant simmer by day and night.'

Such was the atmosphere surrounding Bradman in Australia: needless to underline the implications of success and failure – or, surely, to point the danger to peace and harmony of employing against him tactics in any way suspect.

Jardine brought his fast bowlers gradually into top trim, and against the Australian XI at Melbourne in November, Woodfull was hit by Larwood with a short, fast ball. Larwood here had three short-legs and one back on the boundary for the hook. At Sydney, Voce's leg-trap was increased to four or five, and a press picture showed Fingleton full length with a dozen cricket balls indicating the places, from thigh to shoulder, where blows had struck.

Jack Fingleton says that the MCC bowling in this game took the majority of the New South Welshmen completely by surprise. By the first Test on the same ground the Australian team must have had more than an inkling of what lay ahead, and Warwick Armstrong, the day before the series opened, sent this in a cable to the London *Evening News*.

> As to England's attack I say frankly that I fear there will be trouble if the fast bowlers go for the body instead of the wicket . . . In Australia bowling at the batsman is generally considered unsportsman-like.

Well, Larwood and Voce in the first Test took ten and six wickets respectively, alternating between orthodox methods when the ball was new and the short, fast stuff to a strong leg-side cordon. Stan McCabe, showing the utmost courage and supreme hooking skill, played one of the great innings of history (187 not out in just over four hours), but England won by 10 wickets, needing to score one run only in their second innings.

From Jardine's point of view there was in that conclusive victory only one note of discord. Before the game he asked Allen, who had previously declined to bowl to the leg-side field, whether he would now do so. Allen again said no, and as a result of his refusal did not positively know he would be playing until shortly before the start. Gubby Allen, unlike most of the protagonists in the affair, has never put his views on Bodyline in print: on the other hand he has always maintained in conversation his unequivocal objection to it. What is not perhaps generally known is that he jeopardized his Test place by his refusal to co-operate.

For the second Test, as history records, England, with Bradman due to oppose them after dropping out of the first Test through illness, underlined their intentions by augmenting their fast bowling strength to four, bringing in Bowes and dropping Verity. I suppose that Larwood, Voce, Allen, Bowes and Hammond made up the worst balanced attack ever to take the field for England until Bedser, Statham, Tyson, Bailey and Edrich comprised the bowling against Australia at Brisbane in 1954. However, the Melbourne curator, whether by accident or design, produced an unnaturally slow pitch for the second Test, the result being, of course, less resort to the short, fast stuff, and, incidentally, the best game of the series (Australia won it by 111 runs).

The scene moves to the fair city of Adelaide where, in the third Test, rancour reached its climax, and whence the sad exchange of cables was begun by the Board of Control's first unfortunate volley:

> Bodyline bowling has assumed such proportions as to menace the best interests of the game, making protection of the body by the batsman the main consideration. This is causing intensely bitter feeling between the players as well as injury. In our opinion it is unsportsmanlike. Unless stopped at once it is likely to upset the friendly relations existing between Australia and England.

It is easy in the light of history to fault the text of this grim pronouncement, and in particular the use of the word 'unsportsmanlike' which MCC seized on and, inevitably, repudiated. One must, however, try to imagine the circumstances of the moment in the heat of the battle – and that is the word. Larwood and Voce were whistling the ball round the batsmen's ribs, shoulders and head. Both Woodfull, twice, and Oldfield were hit, and though Woodfull was struck while Larwood was bowling to an orthodox field, as soon as the batsman recovered and play was resumed Jardine at once switched his men across to the leg-side placings – this being the incident which did more to damn him in the eyes both of Englishmen and Australians than any other. The spectators were in constant uproar, while outside the ground behind the long pavilion stand mounted troops waited in readiness in case the field should be invaded. What those in authority feared above all else was that Bradman should be laid low.

The Board's cable set more than the cricket world by the ears. In England as in Australia it was the news of the day, and at home it was only natural that the criticisms were bitterly resented. There were only two Englishmen with the team as correspondents, Jack Hobbs (assisted by Jack Ingham of the *Star*) and Bruce Harris of the *Evening Standard*. The latter, a well-respected member of the paper's staff who had scarcely even seen any cricket before being sent out on this assignment, stuck staunchly by Jardine – who for his part was shrewd enough to see in him a valuable ally. Hobbs, far from repeating his Oval criticisms of a few months earlier, refrained, while the tour was in progress, from any hint of censure, and indeed sent back from Adelaide an almost superfluous plea to those at home to remain loyal to Jardine.

The only other regular cables from the spot came to the *Evening News* from Warwick Armstrong – a notable authority certainly, but scarcely *persona grata* with an English public which remembered his hostile demeanour as Australia's captain in 1921. The morning papers, almost a day behind with the news, had to make do with second-hand comments from old players such as MacLaren, White, Tennyson, and Chapman which, read retrospectively, were generally miles wide of the mark. MacLaren before the third Test, for instance, was saying that the English bowlers would have to pitch the ball further up in order to save themselves punishment from Bradman's 'telling back-play'.

While it was not easy for those far away to appreciate the perils presented by Larwood's great speed and accuracy when he dropped the ball short, there were a few percipient remarks from well-known personalities. Nigel Haig said he was glad that Allen had taken his wickets 'without resorting to intimidation'. A. E. R. Gilligan said that 'cricket is supposed to be fair, and this does not savour of it in the least'. He proposed that leg-theory should be investigated by an Anglo-Australian committee.

Neville Cardus was highly dubious, and asked why, if there were no valid objection to the bowling of Larwood and Voce, Australia's protests had not been emphatically denied by those on the spot. He could only have been referring to Warner and his co-manager R. C. N. Palairet.

Not least the Jam Saheb, K. S. Ranjitsinhji, pronounced: 'Although the batsman has a bat with which to defend himself I disapprove strongly of the concerted leg-side attack. I would rather lose the rubber than win over the bruised bodies of opponents.'

But such sentiments found no echo at Lord's. Although by this time Warner must have reported back, the MCC reply was a complete disclaimer:

We, Marylebone Cricket Club, deplore your cable. We deprecate your opinion that there has been unsportsmanlike play. We have fullest confidence in captain, team and managers and are convinced that they would do nothing to infringe either the Laws of Cricket or the spirit of the game. We have no evidence that our confidence has been misplaced. Much as we regret accidents to Woodfull and Oldfield, we understand that in neither case was the bowler to blame.

If the Australian Board of Control wish to propose a new Law or Rule, it shall receive our careful consideration in due course.

We hope the situation is not now as serious as your cable would seem to indicate, but if it is such as to jeopardize the good relations between English and Australian cricketers and you consider it desirable to cancel the remainder of programme we would consent, but with great reluctance.

As Fingleton points out, the suggestion of the tour being cancelled with two Tests still to go caught the Australian Board in a tender spot. Whatever the unpleasantness, big profits were accruing. The Board's next cable was mighty close to a *volte-face*. It protested that the sportsmanship of MCC was not in question, and in continuing bitterness therefore the tour dragged out its length. England won the last two Tests, and when it was all over not a single Australian player bade them farewell. No record is available of what Woodfull and his team said or thought when, on the rubber being decided, the MCC manager, quoting Lord Roberts, declared that 'the men were splendid', while the captain turned to Kipling.

What of the aftermath? First the MCC Committee – who in the

estimation of all had won the verbal contest hands down – called certain of the principals to testify: Warner and Palairet, the managers, Jardine, the captain, and the two bowlers chiefly concerned, Larwood and Voce. The views of Palairet, the Surrey secretary, a taciturn man, have never been disclosed, so far as I know. His function on the tour was largely financial, but his nature was in some ways akin to Jardine's, and on the tour he is known to have developed a somewhat unlikely friendship with young Bill Voce – the latter surely a good boy led astray, if ever there was one, who has done admirable service to cricket since. Of the five interviewed Warner probably spoke with a lone voice.

But whose opinion was not invited? Firstly that of the vice-captain, Wyatt, who while remaining loyal to his captain, as all were, disapproved of the tactics in question; secondly Allen, the remaining fast bowler, who had refused to use them. Nor was Herbert Sutcliffe, the senior professional, brought in. Nor Jack Hobbs. No one likewise wanted to hear what Walter Hammond felt about it all – though they were to know, as it happened, very shortly. If with the lapse of years the MCC minutes were one day to be made available to some responsible historian the result might be illuminating. Meanwhile the impression must remain from the available evidence that the anti-Bodyliners in the team – who formed a strong majority – were given the minimum of attention. It might have been different had not the fourth Lord Harris, that shrewd, fair-minded autocrat of cricket, died in harness as Treasurer the year before.

However, a more or less chance event was to open people's eyes in England that following summer of 1933, for on an Old Trafford pitch vastly slower than those of Australia, two West Indian bowlers somewhat less fast and accurate than Larwood, Learie Constantine and E. A. Martindale, gave England a dose of their own medicine. Hammond retired with a cut chin, and on returning was soon caught in the leg-trap. He announced without prevarication that if this was how Test cricket was going to be played he wanted no part of it.

Jardine, however, whose courage, either moral or physical, was never in dispute seized a heaven-sent chance to prove his point by batting as steadily as a rock for 127, his only Test hundred. I can see him now playing the dead-bat back stroke with the utmost coolness as those two fine bowlers strained every effort to get some response from the docile pitch – and it was an academic point noted only by the experts that Jardine's methods could scarcely have availed him against Larwood in Australia since from those classical back strokes the ball would have carried to the short-legs. To succeed in 1932–33 an Australian batsman needed to possess the hook in his armour – and Jardine was never a hooker.

Gradually, in the 1933 summer, what was involved in the contentious phrase Bodyline (invented, by the way, almost accidentally by an Australian journalist using 'telegraphese') came to be appreciated by men in authority, and in the winter MCC ruled:

That the type of bowling regarded as a direct attack by the bowler upon the batsman and therefore unfair consists in persistent and systematic bowling of fast short-pitched balls at the batsman standing clear of his wicket.

This amounted to a directive to the umpires to act under Law 46 (Fair and Unfair Play), and it made the way easier for Australia to agree to come to England according to schedule in 1934. But the doubts as to their coming were being debated with equal intensity at both ends of the world, and it was not until 12 December 1933 that a final cable from Lord's made it clear that Australia would be welcome. And the text of that message was passed, as 'Plum' Warner indicates in the following letter, by only eight votes to five. That is how near it came to a rupture of relations. The 'Sandy' to whom he wrote in Adelaide was Sir Alexander Hore-Ruthven, afterwards Lord Gowrie, at that time Governor of South Australia. He had been in England during the Bodyline tour, but when on returning to his post he gauged the strength of Australian resentment, and the deep sense that a just case had been unfairly presented in England, he had sought in the summer of 1933 to put the record straight with J. H. Thomas, the Dominions secretary, asking him to use his good offices with the principal London editors.

In fact the English press had already begun to show the other side of the picture. Hobbs, once the team was home, condemned the bowling tactics roundly, as among others did Reg Bettington, a formidable Anglo-Australian figure who wrote as 'a very close and valued friend' of Jardine's.

CONSERVATIVE CLUB.
Jan. 3rd 1934.

Dear Sandy,

Thank you very much for your nice and very interesting letter, and for your good wishes for 1934 which I heartily reciprocate. Well, I am delighted 'the row' is over – but cannot imagine why after 8–5 in favour of Peace, the chairman allowed the Minority to run the show. Much comment on Oxlade's CBE in the New Year Honours. Personally I think it will do good. It is a gesture, but fancy they don't much like it at Lord's, think it a little premature. Some construe it as saying Board were right in their view though everyone here is certain that their original cable was a terrible blunder. Anyway Australia will no doubt take the CBE as a friendly gesture. The Press and Public will give the team a good reception and a circular (entre nous) will be sent to all the Countries urging them to stop at once any sign of barracking of which there may be some danger in Yorks (Bowes) and Notts (Larwood) if he is able to bowl fast again, which I doubt. The real trouble is Jardine. Is he to be Capt? At present I say 'No' unless he makes a most generous public gesture of friendliness and then I am not sure I would trust him. He is a queer fellow. When he sees a cricket ground with an Australian on it he goes mad! He rose to his present position on my shoulders, and of his attitude to me I do not care to speak. It is hoped he may retire at the end of the Indian Tour, but in many quarters here - where they do not know the truth – he is a bit of a hero. If he is captain in First Test and is not friendly he will not capt. in the 2nd. but I would not have him at all . . .

We start a New Year here on a wave of optimism – things look good – and they say Income Tax will come down. I trust so.

[There follows an invitation to Hore-Ruthven to dine on his visit to England in the summer and remembrances to several Australian friends including Robert Menzies, then Attorney-General and Deputy Premier of Victoria, and Clem Hill. Oxlade, by the way, was chairman of the Australian Board of Control.]

Yours ever

PLUM

In the event Jardine later that winter cabled from India, where he was leading MCC in their first Test tour of that country, saying that he had 'neither the desire nor the intention' of playing against Australia in the summer, and forthwith signed to write about the Tests for the *Evening Standard*. Wyatt led England, and Australia regained the Ashes by winning the concluding Test at the Oval. The tour passed off without much untoward incident except at Trent Bridge where Voce's bowling and the behaviour of the Notts members caused a furore, and for the former the county were required to apologize to the Australians by the Advisory

County Cricket Committee. The scars of Bodyline were far from healed. Jardine forsook first-class cricket for journalism, while Warner continued to write for the *Morning Post*, and after its decease for the *Daily Telegraph*, and to act as Chairman of Selectors.

From Warner's letter his agony of conscience in Australia, when he had to watch a team under his authority carrying through with ruthless efficiency tactics which he so abhorred, can well be imagined. At Adelaide, if not before, where on entering the Australian dressing-room to commiserate upon Woodfull's injury he was coldly snubbed, he must have considered resigning the managership. To have done so – as it appears at this distance – would almost certainly have caused the tour's abandonment, and relations so severed would not have been easily restored. The irony was that the founder of *The Cricketer*, a man of peace if ever there was one, should have been embroiled in the most momentous row in the game's history by the man he himself appointed.

E. W. Swanton, *The Cricketer* (1970)

Local Parishes

With relief we got down to the job of playing serious cricket with two matches against Jamaica, an island which had never been beaten by the MCC. We promptly shattered them by an innings in the first match and drew the second. This was a happy start, particularly as Willie Watson and I slammed into the slow left-handers of Alf Valentine, just to disturb any optimism he might have about the forthcoming Tests.

The second match proved of considerable interest. George Headley, that master batsman of the 1930s, had been brought back to Jamaica on a wave of sentiment, backed by £1,000 in subscriptions from the public. He had missed the first island match through being hit on the elbow during the MCC's loosening up fixture against Combined Parishes. Now he was in the side and it was completely obvious to everyone, including the West Indian selectors, that whether he did anything or nothing, Headley had to be in the side for the first Test. The West Indies Test sides always manage to find room for the local hero of the island on which they happen to be playing their match. Had Headley not been included, it was an open secret that the match would either be boycotted or there would be a riot. In view of what happened later, I am inclined to think that the rioters would have held sway.

As it was, Headley by revealing himself still a useful player if not a great one – he still had a taste for the hook, which our bowlers used to their own advantage – made the selectors' job reasonably easy by defending for four hours for half a century.

Less significant at the time was the fact that J. K. Holt was allowed to stay at the wicket after he had been quite patently caught when in his early twenties. I speak not on my own authority, because I was not playing in the match, but on that of just about all the MCC players in the middle. There was never any suggestion that it was anything more than an umpiring error, yet Holt went on to complete 152 and play himself into the first Test.

The first Test was played at Sabina Park, the ground where MCC's quick bowlers had ruined Jamaica's record. On the basis of that game and with the wicket shiny and seemingly fast, Hutton dismissed all his spinners except Lock, and called up pace men Brian Statham, Freddie Trueman, Alan Moss and Trevor Bailey to carry the England attack. It was a gamble Hutton was to make again at a later date in Australia, and each time the result was disastrous. To our dismay the Sabina Park pitch possessed little pace and the West Indies made a good score.

The England first innings was about as reassuring as a fall down a lift shaft. Ramadhin and Valentine quickly showed us that what they did in England in 1950, they could do equally well in the bright light and on the easy wickets of the West Indies.

When our innings ended we began to get some real idea of the texture of a West Indian crowd when it was roused. Because Valentine was nursing a split finger and his quick bowlers were tired, Jeff Stollmeyer decided not to enforce the follow-on. Uproar greeted this news when it reached the crowd, and their equanimity was not improved when the England bowlers started to plough through the West Indian batting. Everton Weekes and 'Lucky' McWatt rescued the innings and England were presented with the far from impossible task on this pitch of making 457 to win.

By the end of the fifth day England had reached 227 for 2 and the crowd was making it apparent on every possible occasion that Stollmeyer's future was very uncertain. Before Stollmeyer made his bat-on decision, I was of the belief that the toughest skippering job in cricket must have been in captaining a weak England soon after the war. At Sabina Park I revised my opinion.

By the time England reached 277 for 2 the ground was a vat of unrest. Then the desperate Stollmeyer did just what Hutton had done in the first innings and switched to leg theory with Esmond Kentish bowling to a leg-side field of seven.

Just before lunch I was at the other end to Peter May when the future England captain shaped to play at a ball outside the leg stump, changed his mind and as the ball flicked his pads was given out caught behind the wicket. This decision was nothing less than terrible. At no time was May's bat within a foot of the ball.

At lunch-time a hundred extra police were drafted into the ground to keep Stollmeyer's critics at a distance in the event of England winning. At the airport airline officials carefully searched the plane in which he was to leave the island after the match.

As it happened, these precautions were unnecessary. In the circumstances England's batsmen turned out Stollmeyer's best friends and West Indies won comfortably.

But worse than the taste of defeat in our mouths was the broad hint that we had received as to how we could expect the umpiring to be conducted in the tour.

In the first innings Holt was promising to make good in his first Test with a hundred. He was 6 runs off the target when umpire Perry Burke, a sound official, adjudged him lbw to Statham. As reward for this decision Burke's wife, who was in the crowd, was punched in the face by a man (probably a gambler with money on Holt's hundred), and his father dropped in the docks. After that the umpiring deteriorated.

We Englishmen often complained about the umpiring, but perhaps my judgement would err sometimes if I were an umpire whose family was likely to be terrorized. I think I would rather be a popular umpire than go home to a wife who has been beaten by a mob!

The logical way round this problem is to bring umpires from outside the West Indies, possibly Australia, and say go hang the cost, and if that is impossible the MCC should request that Barbadians umpire in Jamaica, Jamaicans in Barbados, and so on, so that there is never the possibility of a local man being victimized. But I imagine the main obstacle to suggestions of this sort would be the fierce local pride that burns throughout the islands.

Against Barbados in the match before the second Test we won by one wicket, the final runs coming when Alan Moss, who found it difficult to contact the ball with his bat, placed his faith in his pads and collected three leg-byes.

Ken Suttle, the sprightly Sussex left-hander, scored well in each innings, yet was not included in the Test side. Instead a place was found for player-manager Charlie Palmer on the strength of his being an all-rounder, and while the West Indies were scoring nearly seven hundred runs in their two innings he was asked to bowl only five overs – one less than Denis Compton. It was an illogical piece of selection.

The first innings of the Barbados Test was rock bottom as far as England were concerned. From the moment that innings ended, we gradually improved as a side until, by the time the last two Tests arrived, we were a formidable unit.

We started the match well enough with the first three West Indians out for 25, and then Clyde Walcott dumped us on our backs with a double century. During this innings Walcott hit the ball harder than any other man I have played against in a Test. It almost seared the fast outfield, and what a contrast it provided to the English batting to follow.

We got stuck in one of the crawls that periodically mars our cricket. We stayed at the crease like a bunch of strokebound chumps while Ramadhin and Valentine wheeled down over after over on that perfect pitch and the crowd howled derision and demanded 'cricket'. My own contribution was 15 runs scraped together in over two hours, easily the worst innings I have ever played.

This nightmare effort started with my receiving two half-volleys which I hit hard to mid-on. Whereupon Hutton came down the wicket and said: 'Not too many shots. We'll play this one carefully.' And we did, although careworn would be a better way to describe it.

Like all nightmares, my innings ended on an unforgettable note. Ramadhin bowled me a slow full toss outside the leg stump which I put straight back at him off the outside edge of the bat. Never shall I forget the effect that flaccid dismissal had on Hutton. He practically slumped over his bat, sheer disbelief and despair written in every line of his body. For over four hours he had defended, subduing all his own great strokes, in his determination to follow the plan he had set for England. I do not think it ever occurred to him that while the plan suited his own talents, it was alien to those of some members of his side.

As I walked dejectedly back to the pavilion, I left him at the wicket looking like a man betrayed. And when he started batting again, it was as if he had suddenly gone berserk. He raced down the wicket, hitting and swishing at everything, almost as though a note of hysteria had crept into his batting which, for so long before, had been dour and canny.

The happiest moment in the England dressing-room came when our first innings ended and we knew that never again could we play as badly. From that point onwards we began to look like world champions, even if it was too late to save the second Test.

The West Indies set us 495 to win and we set about the job like a side jealous of its reputation. We played strokes this time, Hutton, May, Compton and myself, and although we went down to defeat I like to think that we produced batting in that fourth innings fit to stand with anything that the brilliant West Indians had produced.

The umpiring was good in this match, except for one deplorable decision, and again I was in a particularly good position to see as I was batting at the other end. This time Denis Compton was the victim within 7 runs of what would have been his first Test century since playing against the South Africans in 1951. As often happened when England were going well, Stollmeyer came on to bowl his mixture of leg-breaks and googlies. To Compton he pitched a googly well outside the off-stump and the ball hit the batsman's pads as he reached across. Stollmeyer made a noise in his throat, not a proper appeal but the sound non-bowlers make when they beat a batsman who is going well. As much as anything it is an intimation to their sceptical colleagues in the field that they have performed a notable feat.

Well, Stollmeyer made this noise and Compton was given out lbw to a ball that could never possibly have hit the wicket. For some moments there was considerable embarrassment in the middle.

After the Barbados match we left for Georgetown knowing that we had to win the third Test to give ourselves a chance. With three Tests left, there was still in front of us the jute matting of Port-of-Spain, a match which even the optimistic West Indians would not bet on being anything but a draw.

So in preparation for the grand assault we took on British Guiana, a poor side, and thrashed them, Willie Watson and I putting on over four hundred together. Incidentally, Hutton gave another example here of his tremendous shrewdness in assessing a match. When he came back to the pavilion he said to me: 'You'll get a bucketful of runs here.' Yet he himself had scored 0 and only been at the crease a few minutes.

I think one of the reasons for the feeling against the MCC among some of the crowds was that we were too successful against the island sides. We treated them as no other touring side had treated them before, and their supporters did not like to see their heroes tumbled. Among these volatile people that dislike grew into a positive feeling, although I would say at once that the hospitality and friendliness away from the cricket grounds was overwhelming.

As we had determined, the third Test proved us with our triumph. It also produced the Georgetown riot, which was not nearly so acceptable.

After winning the toss for the first time in eight Tests, Hutton manoeuvred our batting into an impressive position. This was one of his great Test innings, and I describe it thus realizing all the implications. He batted for nearly eight hours, chancelessly, rigid in defence, perfect in stroke play. This was the great cricketer, the cool master of every situation that arose.

Hutton's batting was equalled in excellence only by Statham's bowling. On that shirt-front wicket he sent back Worrell, Stollmeyer and Walcott for 10 runs, bowling Stollmeyer with a ball that pitched on the leg stump and hit the off. It rained after that, and so interrupted the West Indian batting slide until the next day.

Their batting was dominated by Everton Weekes who deserved a hundred but just failed to reach it. He was bowled by Lock, and it is a strange thing that no matter what his bowling form may be against anyone else, the Surrey man invariably performs well against Weekes. With Weekes a good cutter and fierce hitter of the ball with almost any stroke, this is not easy to explain.

Yet explosion point came when McWatt and the inevitable Holt were making the West Indians' last ditch stand and doing it pretty well. They had reached 98 and were going for the second run to complete the century stand when Peter May's throw ran out McWatt by a couple of yards. There was no possible doubt about umpire Badge Menzies' decision, yet it still sparked off the Georgetown riot.

Whatever was behind this shameful and frightening outbreak of violence I shall never know. Rum, politics, gambling – all the theories were aired. All I know is that someone threw a bottle, and in the next second it was raining bottles and chunks of wood. Peter May came steaming into the middle, the first refugee from the boundary. We gathered in the centre of the wicket, fifteen fearful men in white in that cauldron of anger. Mounted police and the riot squad appeared. So did a West Indian official who suggested to Hutton that anything might happen and that he had better lead us off the field. The answer was pure Yorkshire: 'We'll stay. We want a couple more wickets tonight.'

So we stayed. And we did the right thing, for as tough as it was I shudder to think what might have happened had we made a move towards the pavilion with the riot at its height. Gradually the hubbub died down, the tension greatly eased by that wonderful clown Johnny Wardle who kept picking up the empty bottles, pretending to drink out of them and then staggering away 'pickled'. Wardle's humour was never more welcome.

But from our point of view the brightest moment in all that trouble came when an uneasy peace had been restored and a boy went round the playing area clearing the bottles. Some joker in the crowd threw another at him, whereupon he started flinging them back as fast as he could pick them off the ground. He peppered that section of the crowd with bottles – with a lovely left-hand throw, too.

We got the wicket for which we risked our necks. When play restarted Ramadhin appeared at the wicket, but showed little interest in staying and we trooped off at the end of a hectic day, forming a bodyguard for umpire Menzies.

Poor Menzies went in fear of his life, for he was one of two umpires introduced to the game after Hutton had objected to the original choice. The police cordoned his house for three or four days.

As a footnote to the match I would add that J. K. Holt was twice caught at the wicket by Godfrey Evans standing back to the quicker bowlers, and each time given not out. He went on to score 48 in the first innings and 64 in the second. The job of bowling to Mr Holt was becoming rather trying.

The inevitable squall was not far away and it blew up in the fourth Test on the Port-of-Spain matting with myself unfortunately playing the starring role. Denis Compton was given the ball for the last over before lunch on the first day and immediately hit a successful streak. Stollmeyer lofted a catch straight back at him. Weekes took a single to get off the mark, and there was Holt at the receiving end. Off the last ball of the morning session he tried a square drive to a googly pitched wide of the off stump, and edged the ball gently into my hands at slip.

I pocketed the ball gratefully and in the same movement started to walk to the pavilion for lunch. After a few paces I realised that I was alone, so a little uncertainly I looked over my shoulder to see that Holt was still at the wicket. I could hardly believe my eyes. I called to him:

'Come on, then,' but still he stayed. Hutton walked in from mid-off, disbelief etched on his face, calling to umpire Achong: 'What about it, Ellis?' Compton joined in the dialogue saying: 'Give him out, Ellis.'

Then Achong made his important contribution. He said: 'No, not out.'

For the first and, I hope the last time, I lost my temper on the cricket field. I flung the ball down, called to Holt: 'That's the fourth bloody time,' and stalked off to lunch to the hissing and booing of the crowd.

Tom Graveney, Cricket Through the Covers (1958)

Genesis of a Cricket Revolution

These are not professionals . . . they were invited to play and if they don't like the conditions there are 500,000 other cricketers in Australia who would love to take their places –

SECRETARY, AUSTRALIAN CRICKET BOARD[1]

Each September, fourteen grey-suited men assemble around a large mahogany table in the committee room of Cricket House in Sydney's busy, downtown George Street. They meet to discuss weighty matters: the administration of cricket in Australia. These businessmen, solicitors, stockbrokers, tax assessors and retired gentlemen of leisure gather in a clubby atmosphere and occasionally issue terse press releases which tell little about what actually takes place inside the dusty, book-lined chamber.

The Australian Cricket Board is an essentially secretive organization. Comprised of representatives of the six Australian State cricket associations, it decides policy, arranges tours and disperses the hundreds of thousands of dollars in profits made on international cricket matches involving Australia. Its constitution, annual report and accounts are strictly confidential. Since 1905 its members, a collection of honorary officials, have directed the destiny of Australia's national sport in their spare time. Even today, their average age exceeds sixty. And until only

---

[1] The secretary of the ACB, Mr Alan Barnes, was commenting on claims by Australian Test players that they deserved increased match payments; 8 January 1975.

very recently, their attitude towards the players under their control has been openly paternalistic and supercilious.

It was against this background that the seeds of discontent were planted. For decades, unrest and dissatisfaction brewed quietly among Australia's leading cricketers as a result of the attitude of these elderly men and the acolytes who followed their instructions. Years of paternalism, of meagre money rewards and of refusing to allow players any say in the running of the game nurtured the seeds of discontent.

By the mid–1970s cricket in Australia was riding a wave of unprecedented financial success. Crowds were pouring into grounds at near-record levels, sponsors were beginning to plough big money into the game, televised cricket was booming. In season 1974–75 the five State associations grossed $1.5 million in revenue; by 1975–76 this had soared to $1.9 million.

The inspirational leadership of Ian Chappell, the brilliance of fast bowlers Dennis Lillee and Jeff Thomson and the classic batsmanship of Greg Chappell all helped lift Australia to the top of the cricket world. Media coverage of the game rose accordingly and the game which five years earlier had been described as moribund was now everyone's favourite.

It was in this euphoric atmosphere that Australia's leading players began to agitate, often publicly, for more money and a better deal. Arguing that they were world-class entertainers who deserved incomes on par with those earned by leading golfers and tennis players, the cricketers found little response to their complaints from the administrators who sat around the table at Cricket House. But as public opinion swung behind the players, some increases were granted. However, they were still doled out in a contemptuous manner which told the players in no uncertain terms that even if there were a few more dollars, there would be no basic change in the master-serf relationship between cricketers and administrators. By 1975, Australian players were earning $400 a Test in basic pay – or $66 a day. This was the reward for reaching the pinnacle of achievement in cricket in a year in which six Tests grossed almost $1 million in gate money in Australia.

Money had suddenly become one of the biggest issues in cricket. Resentment among the players was increasing and the administrators either failed to see it or preferred not to recognize it. In his autobiography *Chappelli*, published in late 1976, Ian Chappell wrote:

Off the field, money is probably the most controversial issue in modern-day cricket. Already it has prompted several head-on clashes between players and officials in Australia. I can see more collisions coming. Administrators don't seem to understand the players' arguments about why we should be better paid. They seem to think we're only interested in bleeding the game dry, without worrying about the consequences it would have on future cricketers.

... The Board has responsibility to see that the leading Australian cricketers are satisfactorily rewarded. To my mind that means an annual salary for top Test cricketers approaching $30,000, plus increases each year to cope with inflation. As a result, I think it's time the Board carefully considered the principle of binding the leading Australian players to full-time contracts, in much the same way as other sportsmen, businessmen and celebrities are contracted.

Unwittingly, the Board had created a potentially explosive scenario. Its treatment of players had aroused intense bitterness; its lack of imaginative promotion alerted professionals to the untapped market available; all this at a time when the game was booming.

The situation was ripe for a promoter's picking and by late 1976 the Sydney media entrepreneur Kerry Packer was quietly eyeing the cricket promotion field and starting to make the necessary arrangements to enter it. Packer had already attempted to have dealings with the men at Cricket House. In late 1975 he asked if he could negotiate for TV rights to first-class cricket for his Channel Nine network. The Board wrote him a polite letter back agreeing to negotiate, but did not actually do so until six months later. By then TV rights had already been sold to the Australian Broadcasting Commission for three years and Packer was informed only commercial rights were available. He said he was interested only in exclusive rights and offered $500,000 a year for five years – for exclusive TV rights. It was more money than the Board had ever dreamt of, but they told Packer they couldn't possibly break their agreement with the ABC. Packer was convinced he had been the victim of 'the old boys' network', as he called it, and it was then he decided he would promote international top-class cricket himself in competition with the Board – and naturally give his network the exclusive rights.

It would be another eight months before the scheme which shook cricket at its foundation stones was publicly unveiled, but his Melbourne television station GTV Nine was already beginning to make preparatory arrangements. In September 1976, a GTV executive wrote to the Melbourne Cricket Club applying for use of the Melbourne Cricket Ground to stage 'a series of matches in December, January and February 1977–78'. MCC secretary Mr Ian Johnson wrote back requesting dates and details of the proposed matches; he never received a reply.

A month later a report appeared in the sports pages of the Melbourne *Age* claiming that Channel Nine network was working on plans to stage a televised series of matches featuring the world's best cricketers. There was no follow-up to the story, but clearly things were moving.

On 27 October Bob Cowper, the former Australian batsman who is now a senior executive with the Henry Jones IXL food group in Melbourne, wrote to his good friend Ian Chappell informing him that moves were afoot involving the Packer organization. In his letter, Cowper told Chappell:

I have been in constant touch with a leading sports sponsor in Australia, Channel 9 [the Packer organization], and it is worth relating the following.

Packer met with Parish some months ago and offered to put many millions of dollars into cricket over the next five years. This would have led to contracts for Test players at between $20,000 and $30,000 for a 12 week period during January and February of each season. An absolute bonanza for the players and the Board and it would have enabled the Board to fulfil obligations both here in Australia and overseas outside this 12 week period.

Needless to say, nothing eventuated as Parish's attitude to say the least was unco-operative and Parish's statement that the Board wanted to pay the players what they can afford should be extended to include the proviso that the players will get what the Board can afford provided the power base of the Board members is retained.

In any event Packer is still prepared to put millions of dollars into cricket over a five year period, starting 1977–78 season, and is looking for support. You just might reflect on the thought of 12 week contracts between $20,000 and $30,000 and let me know your reaction. In my view the players should be right behind it but would have to fight for it to be passed by the Board. If the Board does not want to get involved with Packer at least they should match his offer.

At about the same time as Cowper was talking to Packer, two would-be impresarios were beginning to think seriously about the possibilities of privately promoted TV cricket. John Cornell is a pint-sized television producer and part-time TV comic; Austin Robertson is a lanky, former Australian Rules football champion and ex-sports writer. The two had become friends years earlier when they both worked as journalists on Perth's dull afternoon tabloid, the *Daily News*. Cornell soon tired of small city newspaper work and moved on to TV, where he helped launch the now-defunct daily programme *A Current Affair*. He later teamed up with the 'ocker' comedian Paul Hogan, appearing on television as Hogan's dense side-kick 'Strop' and managing Hogan's business affairs. When Robertson also became fed up with being a newspaper hack, he joined Cornell in a venture to manage the business affairs of leading Australian sportsmen, under the banner of the Cornell-Hogan company J. P. Productions (J for John, P for Paul). Among their first clients were cricketers Dennis Lillee, Rod Marsh and David Hookes.

One evening in mid-November 1976, Cornell and Robertson were talking to Lillee and some other cricketers in a Sydney bar during the Western Australia-NSW Sheffield Shield match. After a few convivial drinks the conversation got around to the sensitive subject of payments to cricketers – always a popular gripe in players' drinking-time discussions. The players informed the promoters in no uncertain terms what they thought of the money they were getting, and the stingy administrators who were doling it out.

Cornell and Robertson sat and listened as some of the most talented cricket practitioners in the world unleashed their furious attack. It was that night's conversation, according to the 'official' story of World Series Cricket later published in *The Bulletin* magazine, that convinced the two promoters they would have little difficulty in signing on the world's best players and setting up a private cricket series. 'The night after Robertson and Cornell had talked to the two Australian players they stayed up until dawn discussing ways of getting a better deal for cricketers', wrote Trevor Kennedy in *The Bulletin*:

> The disaffection with the present system of payment was, Cornell and Robertson believed, widespread. But they didn't realize that it was quite as widespread and deep-seated as it ultimately turned out to be. They felt that they, and the players, could prosper with the right idea. The only thing needed was a catalyst. The promoters and the players needed a backer. They decided to approach someone

they already knew. Kerry Packer, chairman of the Television Corporation group, had lured Cornell and Hogan from Channel Seven to Channel Nine. Packer had also shown what could be done in television and sport with the W. D. & H. O. Wills-*Bulletin* Australian Open Golf Championship.

Cornell, at a meeting with Packer in the media group's headquarters in central Sydney, immediately struck a responsive chord . . . Cornell put to Packer the possibility of a series of Tests and one-day matches to be played along the lines of the Cavalier matches in Britain.

Packer countered: 'Why not do the thing properly? Why not get the world's best players to play the best Australians?' They kicked it around and more or less came up with the formula which is likely to prove international cricket's most enormous success.

With Packer's enthusiasm and financial backing, what could have remained just another bright idea was converted into a 'goer'. Cornell and Robertson had found themselves the millions, the television and a big-time entrepreneur. All they needed were the world's best cricketers.

The two promoters worked through the hot Australian summer of 1976–77 planning their cricket revolution. With Dennis Lillee as chief advisor and assistant, the pair secretly contacted many leading Australian players to test the temperature of the water. The response they received confirmed all their earlier advice: Test players like Lillee, Ian Chappell, Rodney Marsh, Doug Walters and Ian Redpath reacted enthusiastically.

Elated by the verbal commitments from players, Cornell and Robertson turned to the money side of their ambitious venture. Using ACB crowd figures as their base, and assuming several millions' worth of sponsorship, they came up with cost projections which showed there was money, possibly big money, to be made in the private promotion of top-class cricket.

It was all they needed. After further consultation with Packer they decided it was time to act. 'What are we waiting for? Let's go out and sign 'em up,' Packer told the pair of ex-journalists.

And so they did. On 10 January, during the Sheffield Shield match between Western Australia and South Australia in Perth, Dennis Lillee became the first Packer rebel, signing a contract worth $105,000 to play with the revolutionaries. On the same day Lillee, bowling at his best, snared five South Australian wickets for 44 runs.

Ten days later Austin Robertson secured his second piece of cricket flesh. Former Pakistan captain Intikhab Alam, touring Australia with the Pakistan side, signed a curious letter to Robertson in which he agreed to 'join your cricket tourists next year'. It was a letter which provided the promoters with striking evidence, if they needed it, of how favourably their scheme would be accepted by cricketers. Intikhab wrote:

> The price for my services, as you have already pointed out, is negotiable, but I am sure we can reach satisfactory agreement.
>
> Hopefully, you can arrange your schedules to fit in with the various Cricket Boards of Control, but if not, I would still be prepared to join your tour.[1]

On 16 February, after agreement was reached on the broad financial costings, Packer and the two promoters officially consummated their deal. The next day Packer's trusted off-sider and the financial controller of Consolidated Press, Harry Chester, was told of the details in this memorandum:

> Briefly, the idea is that we contract the 30 top cricketers in the world – 15 Australian and 15 overseas players – for a series of five Test matches: Australia versus the Rest of the World, and four two-day limited over matches plus some country matches. The series would be televised live on the Nine Network throughout Australia.
>
> We have already secured the St Kilda football club ground – capacity 50,000 people – which already has top-class wickets. At this stage it appears we can also get a ground in Perth and another in Adelaide. We are currently investigating Sydney. A series of secret discussions with top Australian and overseas players indicate we can get them to join us. But we must move quickly, as most players are about to commit themselves for the next season ... We will attempt to confidentially sign the key Australians in New Zealand next Thursday.
>
> The costs enclosed are self-explanatory and from them you can see that an average Test attendance of 5,000 would cover expenditure. If we were to equal attendances of the recent Australia v.

---

[1] Although he was one of the first 'recruits', and signed an open-ended letter of agreement, Intikhab in fact never played for WSC. Two months after Intikhab signed the letter, Tony Greig became the selector of the WSC World team – and presumably decided there was no room for the experienced Pakistan all-rounder.

Pakistan series (average 20,000 per Test day), the estimated profit would be extremely handsome.

The great cricket revolution was still little more than a clandestine plot hatched in executive suites, but it was on its way. Within months news of its existence would leak out, casting the Australian Cricket Board in the unseemly role of Captain Bligh.

With Kerry Packer's imprimatur stamped on the cricket revolution, Cornell and Robertson left for New Zealand where the Australians were playing a short Test series. Their aim was to secretly sign up the cream of Australian cricket . . . the raid was on.

The pair elicited tacit agreement from most members of the Australian team. Their movements in New Zealand were conducted in secrecy, but after a while a couple of alert Australian cricket writers travelling with the team wondered why this 'odd couple' was spending so much time with the Australians. When the Press started asking questions, Cornell said he was in New Zealand negotiating on behalf of his client Dennis Lillee to join the TV programme *A Current Affair*.[1]

While in New Zealand, Cornell and Robertson conducted an impromptu experiment which illustrated just how money can motivate some top-class cricketers. Prompted by the fact that they were planning to pay $100,000 prize money to the winners of their private series, Cornell and Robertson tested the question of pecuniary motivation on Dennis Lillee during the second Test against New Zealand in Auckland. According to this account published in *The Bulletin*:

At this stage New Zealand was doing pretty well and Lillee was shortly due to go in and bat. Cornell said 'I'll tell you what, Dennis, I'll give you $50 for every run you make over 20.' Lillee talked to Greg Chappell, the Australian captain, and convinced him he should be promoted in the batting order. He was – by one. When he got to the crease he took guard and shaped up – then slogged a magnificent six off the first ball. He turned and grinned up at the grandstand. He went on to make 23 not out . . .

Cornell said: 'When they came off the field Austin told Dennis that we had to leave to catch a plane back to Australia in 40 minutes. We would give him $100 for every wicket he took before we left. I

[1] Lillee did in fact sign a contract to appear on *A Current Affair*, after announcing his unavailability for the 1977 Australian tour of England.

wandered out to have a look at the pitch . . . it looked in pretty good shape. Austin went down to the dressing room and said we'd make it $200 a wicket. By the time we had to leave the ground to catch the plane Lillee had taken four wickets for 19 runs. It was a bit expensive but a very worthwhile exercise'.

Cornell and Robertson returned to Australia carrying a signed contract with Greg Chappell Promotions Pty Ltd – worth $175,000 over five years to the Australian captain – and pledges from the best cricket talent in Australia. But it was back in Australia that the real recruiting started. Former Australian opening batsman Ian Redpath, who now runs an antique shop in Geelong near Melbourne, signed for only $16,500 on 3 March. A few days later, Western Australian swing bowler Mick Malone put his signature to a Packer contract – only hours after mesmerizing the touring MCC side in Perth and virtually assuring a berth in the Australian team to tour England. His prize: a contract worth $57,000 over three years.

While the promoters were surreptitiously going about their recruiting work, the cricket world was preparing amid excitement for the momentous Centenary Test celebration, marking 100 years of Test matches between Australia and England. All eyes were on Melbourne, where the Test and a gathering of hundreds of former star players was to take place. It was the perfect crowded scene for Cornell and Robertson, who were gearing themselves up for their biggest swoop yet.

Two days before the Centenary Test got under way, three members of the Australian Cricket Board met with the five Australian State captains: Greg Chappell (Queensland), Doug Walters (NSW), Richie Robinson (Victoria), Ashley Woodcock (South Australia) and Rod Marsh (Western Australia). The idea of this meeting, the second in three months, was to establish greater rapport between players and administrators and give the cricketers the sense of having some say in the running of the game.

At an earlier meeting in December, the State captains had asked the Board to take over all Australian team sponsorship and reviewed plans to improve the terms of players' retirement benefits. Now, on 10 March, the eight men discussed many things, among them details of the Benson and Hedges Company's sponsorship of Australian cricket and the conditions which went with it – including the players' obligation to assist in the promotion of Benson and Hedges products and not enter into other agreements which would cut across the sponsorship. The players readily agreed to the conditions and accepted the obligations. Yet of those five State captains, one (Chappell) had already signed a contract to play with a rival promoter, another (Walters) was to do so within a week of the ACB meeting and two others (Marsh and Robinson) signed within the next six weeks.

As the Centenary Test unfolded in brilliant sunshine, the 247,873 enthusiastic fans who crowded through the MCG turnstiles were blissfully unaware it was the last time they would be seeing many of the star players performing in Test cricket. During the match Cornell and Robertson added seven more players to their books – Australians O'Keeffe, Walters, McCosker, Davis, Walker and Edwards, and South African batting champion Barry Richards, who was in Australia playing Perth club cricket and was visiting Melbourne for the great event.

Another of the MCG heroes to come under their spell during the Centenary Test was England captain Tony Greig. The tall, effusive all-rounder was informed of the proposed revolution at a private meeting with Kerry Packer. Greig was not given any details until he agreed to promise not to repeat a word to anyone. 'I put him in a pretty tough situation by making him promise to say nothing until the official announcement,' Packer later said of their conversation. Greig agreed to keep it quiet and was given a full run-down of Packer's plans and offered a prime position in the new regime – captain of the World XI, selector, recruiting agent, advisor and, the icing on the cake, a long-term association with the Packer group of companies after he retired from cricket. Greig was enormously impressed and it took him barely a week to accept the TV tycoon's offer, worth $90,000 over three years plus a further $10,000 annual consultant's and captain's fee.

While all this furtive activity was going on behind their backs, the Australian cricket administrators were busily basking in a not inconsiderable amount of glory over their efforts in organizing the hugely successful Centenary Test. They watched the crowds pour in, noted the extraordinary media coverage, thrilled as Australia went on to win by exactly the same margin as it had won the first-ever Test, sipped whisky in the Melbourne Cricket Club and Victorian Cricket Association committee rooms. It had all the symptoms of a classic lull before the storm.

Ironically, the administrators' one big complaint during all this euphoria concerned a swift deal which had just been pulled by an Australian TV network to outbid the ABC from providing direct satellite coverage of the 1978 Australia-England Tests from Britain. In the committee rooms at the MCG during the Centenary Test, Australian officials berated their English colleagues for agreeing to such an offer and privately cursed the network boss who had pulled the 'swifty' on the ABC. His name: Kerry Packer.

Packer had negotiated his first major cricket coup by offering the English Test and County Cricket Board $150,000 for the rights – twice the asking price – then proceeding to woo the English officials. 'We were subjected to high-pressure salesmanship,' TCCB chairman Mr Doug Insole explained to the angry Australian officials at the Centenary Test. He said they were given 'a lavish dinner and so on and so forth'.

The Australian Board members were so incensed at Channel Nine's bold swoop, they decided to alter the system under which TV rights were sold. In future, they brusquely informed English officials, the ACB itself would handle rights negotiations for all Tests involving Australia. This meant that 'outsiders' could be kept out – and Packer knew it. That was the final blow which convinced him the only way he'd ever get top-class cricket TV would be to produce it himself. 'Three times the stiletto went in, and at the end of the third time, I said, "that's it".'

Eric Beecher, *The Cricket Revolution* (1978)

Cracking up in Karachi

Having taken every trick of the series to date, Pakistan produced the ace of trumps for the final Test: utterly unbiased umpiring. England were completely floored. Their mental condition was so close to paranoia after the attentions of Shakeel and Shakoor that they were unable to recognize umpiring of international standard when it came along. England's batsmen by now half-expected to be given out if the ball hit their pad. Only if they knocked the stumps out did England's bowlers think they would be granted a wicket of their own. In Karachi the umpiring was not like that. Quite the reverse. But this only served to confirm my suspicions. It disproved the theory which some still held, that Pakistani umpiring was simply inherently incompetent.

The difficulty in assessing umpiring, which is partly based on personal interpretation, is the shortage of objective evidence. There is, however, one test: the frequency with which umpires give home and visiting batsmen out leg before wicket. Bat-pad catches, stumpings, run-outs and fine edges to the wicket-keeper can also be areas of dispute, and so can leg-before appeals which are turned down. But one objective, indisputable fact is the number of lbw appeals which are upheld. In the case of Pakistani umpiring over the years, the figures are illuminating.

By the time of the Karachi Test, 101 Pakistani batsmen had been given leg before wicket in home Test matches by their own umpires, against 196 visiting batsmen. Before the Test, Mike Gatting declared: 'I've been here three times and it's got progressively worse.' If by 'it' he meant the trend against visiting batsmen, he was correct. The ratio was never 1:1, but it was not outlandishly unequal until 1977–78 when England toured, shortly after martial law – it may not be coincidental – had been reimposed. From then until the Karachi Test ten years later, 58 Pakistanis were given lbw by their own umpires, compared with 131 visiting batsmen. Surprisingly perhaps, England was not the country to have the worst of the deal, until Shakeel in Lahore at any rate. Ever since Gary Sobers was given lbw in his first three Test innings in Pakistan and vowed never to return, West Indies have always had twice as many of their batsmen leg before. Sri Lankans and Indians are more than twice as likely to be given lbw as home batsmen. Australians seem to suffer most of all: 32 of their number have been given lbw, against 12 Pakistanis. There is no difference, however, in the profile of such decisions within each side: that is, there is no statistical evidence to suggest that Pakistani umpires have singled out the top-order batsmen on the touring side, and simply given out Pakistan's number eleven. Right down the order, each visiting player is roughly twice as likely to be given lbw as his home counterpart.

When I tabulated these figures, my reaction was that they were conclusively damning. Nothing could account for the disparity, or could it? Over the last decade, when the disparity had increased, Pakistan's most effective bowling has been done by Imran Khan and Abdul Qadir, and their inswinger and googly respectively might account for this disproportionately large number of decisions in Pakistan's favour. But no: neutral umpires were brought in from India to stand in two Test matches between Pakistan and West Indies in 1986. Imran and Qadir were both playing; and the number of lbw decisions given against each side in those two neutrally umpired Tests happened to be ten-all.

We have also the case of Khalid Aziz. He spoke out after umpiring in a match against West Indies in Karachi. Again, he had been a first-class player himself, who had graduated from Punjab University and taken a job in a chemicals firm in Lahore. He was one of Pakistan's four World Cup umpires, but he stood in only one match. His nerves were said to be still bad. The ban he had received in 1980–81, for saying the Pakistan Board had put pressure on him to make Pakistan win, had not been lifted until early 1987. Ijaz Butt had supported Aziz, a colleague of his at university, in his criticism of the Board and had been suspended too for several years.

A former Pakistan Test player, with a fine record and long experience of English cricket, told me quite explicitly: 'The Board puts pressure on its umpires. It says to them that Pakistan have to win a particular match, and that if Pakistan don't, they won't be umpiring any more Test matches.' An article on the features page of *Daily News*, published in Lahore, was no less candid. Until it appeared, the views expressed in the government-influenced English-language papers had been purely Cyclopian. One might have expected as much from newspapers whose five or six leading 'stories' would invariably concern what the President and Prime Minister had for lunch the previous day, who they met and where they went. Feature articles would eulogize the long-standing brotherly relations between Pakistan and Transylvania, whose despot was about to make a state visit. Imagine our surprise, therefore, when this piece of objectivity appeared, no doubt partly to grind some personal or political axe but also to reassure us that the apple was not entirely rotten:

> That one man's vindictiveness could ruin the game of cricket should not surprise anyone since it was evident, and foretold, by the events in the English tour. In the aftermath of the current series there will emerge only one winner – Mr Hasib Ahsan. To his satisfaction everything is happening exactly according to his plan. With the help of his puppet umpires Hasib has frustrated the English team enough to behave in a manner they seemed incapable of.
>
> The controversies started from the England tour or for that matter, as soon as Hasib was made the manager of the touring side. Amid all the controversies – Pakistan's time wasting tactics, use of substitutes, Saleem Yousuf's catch, David Constant – Hasib never did or said anything to ease the situation; in fact, his statements only sprinkled salt on the wounds. The British Press rightly made a mockery of the streetwise slandering of our manager. His cheap tricks to prove his nuisance value pleased none. It was then that he

planned to take on the English team in Pakistan and teach them a lesson. Meanwhile the pressure kept building up even during the World Cup when Javed Miandad got involved in a customary brawl with Mike Gatting at Rawalpindi. An Anglophile Hasib Ahsan is not and no further proof is needed if he himself admits: *Angrezon ko marnain ka to maza he aur hai.* Well, the way things are, Mr Ahsan is close to physically beating them with the help of his aides in white coats.

As long as Imran was there these matters did not affect the team. A fair minded person of some integrity, he never became a part of these bickerings as long as they did not interfere in his selection or strategy of the team. With Imran's departure the veil of victories has also dropped, displaying quite a few, hitherto hidden, ugly faces.

Enter Javed Miandad. Hasib's perfect partner, the two smallest minds in collusion with the umpires set out to thrash England. This pair is a perfect example of the maxim that give a small man power and he will show you how small he is. That is exactly what is happening.

The standard of umpiring witnessed in the current series is deplorable. Even victory has left behind a bad taste. Losing to a better side in a fair game is not disgraceful but such dubious victories borne out of personal vendetta are unwanted. In Lahore Abdul Qadir would have run through anyway, the unfair assistance only undermined his feat. It only proves that the aim of the establishment is not only to win at all costs but to frustrate the opposition by blatant cheating. Umpiring in Pakistan has always been a controversial issue mainly because dishonest and characterless umpires are manipulated by the captain and the officials. Gary Sobers left this country promising never to come back. Upon wished better luck next time Greg Chappell is attributed to have said: there won't be any %"%*O next time. Very soon Mike Gatting's name will also appear on this list to leave us playing test cricket against Sri Lanka and other second rate teams. The umpiring issue had never been so hot. In this campaign the public is being fooled by a systematic barrage of accusations from all quarters against the visiting team. Constant's name constantly appears in discussions. It can actually be proved with the help of videos that umpiring in the English series favoured Pakistan. The group of commentators and writers who mislead and instigate the public opinion are a part of Hasib's team and, probably, like the umpires, on his payroll.

To say that the English umpires do not know the difference between Qadir's googly and flipper is nonsense. A lamest of excuses. Doubtless, they are the best umpires in the world who make their fair decisions to the best of their ability. One simple statement about the lbw decision. The umpire and only the umpire can judge about a leg-before decision. Even the most sophisticated cameras transmit a two dimensional image in which distance is impossible to discern. A batsman who plays forward is nearly seven to eight feet ahead of the stumps. Now if he is struck on the pad a half an inch turn/deviation in the ball would become a one foot movement by the time it reaches the stumps. But still the camera shows a lot. I shudder to imagine the plight of visiting teams if the cameras were removed. Shakoor, Shakeel and Co., would guarantee any side on any wicket in less than a hundred.

Even Dickie Bird has now advocated an international panel of umpires. There aren't any guarantees but it should be tried since there is hardly any other choice. We have a few umpires worthy of that panel, obviously, none of them is of Hasib's liking.

What happened between Gatting and Shakoor Rana was not over an all important issue. It was bound to happen sooner or later, the intense heat developed over the last few weeks finally blew the lid off. In the torture of Herr Hasib's concentration camp Mike Gatting finally cracked.

Hasib or Miandad are incapable of realizing that in this crusade all are losers – England, Pakistan and cricket. Our own boys are totally disillusioned by these sad events. Selection of the team is unfair, wickets prepared are minefields and umpiring atrocious. One month ago we had the best pace attack in the world, in Faisalabad, Mudassar and Aamir Malik shared the new ball. Shoaib is a permanent member of the team now although in two matches he hasn't bothered the scorers. Even the time in and time out columns show the same thing. Imagine the frustration of Mujtaba or Aamir Malik's first match on a nightmarish wicket. Who is benefiting from this cricket? Miandad's approach has always been petty and negative. Nobody becomes the most hated cricketer in the world just like that. Garbage in, garbage out.

Lastly, one thing which has always puzzled one is that why aren't we more tolerant of these moral aberrations by the umpires and Hasib. One reason could be that this is televised corruption. The moral uprighteousness, character and integrity that we demand from them is unfair. Even the judges of our superior courts would fail this test. Hasib and Co., are part of our system. We keep our eyes closed and remain mute while the whole nation goes down the corruption drain, so why not in this case. *Is hamam main sub nange hain* (In this bath, all are naked).

I assume the presence of the two leading officials of the Test and County Cricket Board encouraged the Pakistan Board to play it straight in the Karachi Test. Raman Subba Row, the chairman, and Alan Smith, the chief executive, arrived two days before the start to explain to England's angry players the reasons for their directive to fulfil the tour. Not that it was the Pakistan Board's original intention to bestow on the Third Test the best umpiring at its disposal. To English incredulity the names forwarded to Peter Lush on the last day of the Faisalabad Test were those of Shakeel Khan and Khizer Hayat. This was some effrontery: that the man who had brought about the most acrimonious relations in England's touring history should have been reappointed for the final Test showed there was no limit to the unscrupulousness of the Grand Vizier.

Hasib Ahsan's reply was, just as typically, charming. He suggested that England's management should appoint whoever they liked. They proposed Indian umpires, and Hasib said he would do his best. He telexed the secretary of the Indian Board and asked for V. K. Ramaswamy and P. D. Reporter, the 'neutrals' who had stood in the two Tests between Pakistan and West Indies. But Reporter had been appointed to stand in the Bombay Test which coincided with the Karachi Test. In any case, I cannot believe there was any possibility that two Indians could have obtained visas and flown to Pakistan at thirty-six hours' notice. In the same way, the practical difficulties made it inconceivable that either Tony Crafter of Australia, Steve Woodward of New Zealand or David Archer of West Indies could ever have been able to stay on in Pakistan for six weeks after the World Cup to stand in the series against England. The Grand Vizier was able to make all his approaches, and gain merit for being seen to do so, safe in the knowledge they could never be accepted.

England settled for Khizer Hayat and Mehboob Shah, the president of the Pakistan Umpires Association who had officiated admirably in the World Cup final. Nobody would question for a moment the integrity of

Mehboob Shah, MA, LLB, unless he were in a paranoid state of mind, as England were. Their captain promised before the game there would be no dissent even under provocation. We saw plenty of dissent, unprovoked.

For the first three days England kept themselves under control and played in better heart if not form. Their discussions with Subba Row and Smith had been unexpectedly amicable in the two days prior to the Test. Gatting said that his lads had 'got a lot off their chests'; Subba Row had been manifestly sympathetic to their distress and admitted he now viewed the Shakoor-Gatting incident in a different light, though his directive to carry on would have been the same. The TCCB chairman had resolved to obtain a reciprocal apology from Shakoor Rana via Safdar Butt, if it was the last thing he did in Pakistan. But the last thing he did was to receive a letter expressing Shakoor's regret in the most conciliatory tones (Subba Row had himself drafted the letter), but with the actual words of apology deleted.

Dust was being wiped from the seats in the main stand of the National Stadium quite unnecessarily, as the match began. Public interest in the most unwatched series was on the wane. The dust came from the expanse of sand around the Stadium, which was built in the desert near the road leading to the airport. The foundations had been rushed up in two months in time for the fifth Test of Pakistan's first home series, against India in 1954–55 (when the Tests were all of four days and all drawn), and stands had been added at subsequent intervals until its capacity had grown to about 45,000. Behind the scenes a typical dispute was going on: the BCCP had allotted the match to the Karachi municipality, not to an irate Karachi Cricket Association, before changing its mind half-way through the Test. If England had been able to look beyond their own troubles, they might have been reassured to see the Pakistan Board had as many internal arguments as external. During the Karachi Test they were also busy reviewing one of their many life bans, this one on the Test batsman Qasim Omar. Younis Ahmed and Sarfraz Nawaz kept receiving almost as many life bans as Test caps during their turbulent careers.

England's attempt at bonhomie was first spoilt by a complete failure of their specialist batting. Given the best pitch and umpiring of the series, and further luck with the toss, they stumbled to 85 for six. Wasim Akram took two wickets before limping off with further trouble in his chronically weak groin. Abdul Qadir followed up with the remarkable feat of bowling three batsmeń on a flawless pitch in the first hour of the afternoon. Athey, finally given the chance of a long innings and attuned by lunch, went to cut the first ball after the interval and was clean bowled by a googly. Chris Broad, Graham Gooch and Gatting had at least seized one opportunity in the series: would Athey never break through?

Gatting went adventurously back to pull Qadir, who was happier than in Faisalabad if not the bowler of overwhelming bounce that he had been in Lahore. The captain was bowled off a deflection for two. I don't think it was possible to pull Qadir off the back foot, so quickly did he hasten through off the hard pitches, and never did he bowl a long-hop. Neil Fairbrother's dismissal was more disturbing. He had been included ahead of Tim Robinson, whose batting was suffering from anaemia. Salim Jaffer bounced a ball at Fairbrother, who half-ducked and half-fended, his bat and gloves raised instinctively for protection. Someone who is bounced out in bright light in Karachi by a left-handed fast-medium bowler has a problem.

The ceiling which was threatening to cave in was held up by David Capel, who thus allowed John Emburey scope for his idiosyncrasies. Capel read Qadir as readily as Linear B, which made his 98 the more admirable for its defiance. Micky Stewart conceded after the series: 'The programme we have at home is not conducive to producing an all-round Test side', and indeed what sort of finishing school can county cricket be when its products go out into the world without any experience of leg-spin? Against Qadir, Capel eked out the odd squeeze either side of point, and had made 41 to Emburey's 70 when his partner upper-cut the second new ball to third man near the end of the first day.

After 374 minutes Capel was no more certain about Qadir's intentions and was bowled driving at one of a sequence of googlies. Much of his hard labour was then undone by England's new-ball bowlers who bowled short, wide and 'orrible. Pakistan reached 100 for 1 off twenty-five overs, Mudassar having been given leg before to one of the few balls pitched up. No doubt Graham Dilley and Phillip DeFreitas were spurred on not only by their captain's support, but also by the mood of the whole party to try and hit as many Pakistani heads as they could, in revenge. Here was a lack of discrimination, on two grounds. Cream is lapped up by cats no more eagerly than erratic pace bowling by Rameez Raja and Salim Malik. Secondly, the first three batsmen in Pakistan's order were the most amicable members of the home team. They had humour and therefore they had perspective; or else, perhaps, being international cricketers of some experience, they had perspective and therefore humour. Either way, they conversed with the England players on the field and shared the odd joke. At the opposite end of the scale were those one might call the vernacular Pakistan players. They were earnest individuals, full of pride, their chests puffed out with patriotism. To the western eye they appeared very immature men. But what was their perspective? I suppose they saw themselves as representatives of a new nation seeking to make its way in the world. They may have felt some inferiority when they looked at Big Brother India on one side and the materially advanced West on the other. They were religious almost to a man; yet, in terms of sportsmanship, unethical. Perhaps they thought any means were justifiable so long as their country, through its cricket team, won a higher standing. From this perspective, humour must be difficult. If humour and professionalism bind the England team, pride and patriotism more seriously unite Pakistan's.

Dilley, playing instead of Neil Foster who had twisted his left ankle, obtained his hundredth Test wicket, but his delight must have been tempered by the realization that the wicket of Ashraf Ali – one of the most vernacular players – had come at greater cost than it was worth. Against England's spinners, Pakistan laboured to score 69 off forty-five overs at one stage, and they lost three wickets in two overs on the second evening. Javed Miandad's was one of the wickets, when he padded up to one of those off-breaks that Emburey turned abnormally at a new batsman, and Mehboob gave him leg before for only the third time in Javed's Test career in Pakistan. Akram disturbed the somnolence by hitting two sixes off Nick Cook, who was experimenting with a shorter, more purposeful run-up; and Qadir later drove four sixes off Emburey during an innings which sealed for him the man-of-the-match and Pakistan's man-of-the-series award. Pakistan's late-order rally, even more far-reaching than England's had been, was led by Aamir Malik, whose forward defence was impressive and whose shots against the pace bowlers were dashing. Pakistan had a lead of 51 and two wickets left at the end of the third day, which was followed by a rest day that did nothing for England's humour.

Initially England's players were cheered by the news from Subba Row that he had seen fit to award them a bonus of one thousand pounds, in addition to their Pakistan tour fee of five thousand pounds. Without consulting the rest of the TCCB, which later reproved him, Subba Row made the award as a hardship payment on the third evening of the match as he was about to fly home. It was a generous, clumsy gesture, the right thing at the wrong time, and a mistake of timing which the Sublime Porte would never have committed (the Grand Vizier, in similar circumstances, would have waited until his players returned home and then have greeted them with the news and flamboyant embraces on the aircraft steps). England's reactions to events in Pakistan had so far been based upon high-minded principle: this award now laid them open to the accusation that the players had only agreed to complete the tour because of the extra money. The thousand pounds acquired the taint of thirty pieces of silver. Moreover, the Masada complex was revived, after a brief feeling that the English side, players and administrators, were together.

On the fourth morning Aamir Malik snicked a low catch to Bruce French who caught it on the dive. Khizer Hayat couldn't see as French had rolled over the ball and, fairly enough, after consulting Mehboob Shah, he gave the batsman not out for lack of evidence. Nor could he do anything else if the batsman refused to accept the keeper's word and walk. But DeFreitas dissented, and Gatting, arms ostentatiously on hips, went down the pitch as if to demand of Hayat what was going on, and there were grave shakings of his head. When England batted a second time, the first three batsmen to be dismissed all waited for an unacceptably long while before departing. Yet Broad acknowledged later that the leg-break he missed would have hit his stumps; Athey looked back towards the keeper after he had played his stroke, which is always a telltale sign of guilt; and the square-leg camera revealed that Gatting's front foot had advanced no more than four inches towards the ball from Jaffer. Until these last two days of the series England had nothing of which to be ashamed; if they had displayed human weaknesses, their reactions had been less culpable than the original Pakistani acts which had provoked them. This 'moral high ground' was forfeited when England's patience snapped without justification.

England's managers, I'm afraid, allowed themselves to be dragged down too. They could not guarantee good cricket from their charges, but they had promised civilized behaviour for the final match, and these aberrations should have been disciplined. But they were not even recognized. Gatting expressed himself 'amazed' at the fuss over England's dissent. Instead of stamping out the boorishness, Stewart spoke to the umpires and established that they had no formal complaints to make. I'm sure that if most of the dissidents looked back in later weeks, they vowed never to do anything similar on a Test match ground at home.

There was more incivility to come from England, as if they thought the whole country was set against them and not just one or two individuals in white coats. The cheer when the aeroplane took off from Karachi for London was too subdued to be offensive. But it was embarrassing to see one of England's opening batsmen fold his arms together and refuse to shake the hand of the guest of honour – a government minister – at the end of the Karachi Test. (He deserved his later punishment.) England also refused the Pakistan Board's invitation to a farewell dinner on their last evening, on the poor excuse that they had too much to do, after six weeks in Pakistan. True, the invitation arrived belatedly, like all communications from the BCCP, who had forever been altering the venues and rest days of England's matches.

England had still to bat for over a day, at least until lunchtime on the last, for the match to be saved. The specialist batting responded by seeing England to 61 for four. Gooch stayed, however, with Capel as his first partner of substance. The young all-rounder, the cut of whose jib had pleased everyone when he hit three consecutive sixes in the Karachi international, now took another six off Iqbal Qasim, who somehow did not find the same support here as in the first two Tests. Emburey was Gooch's second partner, thanks to being dropped by Miandad in the gully when on three. All round Miandad did not have a distinguished series and after the match he resigned as captain. He cited his poor batting form, but he must have already noted that the wind had turned in favour of recalling Imran Khan from retirement.

Crowds on the fourth and fifth days in Karachi were the largest to date, their several thousands taking the total number of spectators for the series to about thirty thousand (no official figures were, of course, announced). How did the Pakistan Board pay for the series without eating into their World Cup profits? In Pakistan there are no accounts. Indeed, there is no such thing as accountability. A law had even been passed to the effect that nobody could be held responsible for anything which had happened under martial law, even though the Holy Quran says we are all accountable. Another defect, simply in the system of Pakistan's cricket, seemed to be that too many strings are held by too few hands. There are no checks and no balances. Hanif, to take one innocent example, not only supervised the preparation of the Karachi pitch but was also a television commentator on the game: in what position was he to criticize the pitch? It would be healthier if each person wore a single hat.

Scyld Berry, *A Cricket Odyssey* (1988)

9

County Cricket

County cricket has evoked more 'romantic' writing about cricket than has any other. Even today in the age of tracksuits and coloured shirts and advertisement-strewn boundary boards it maintains a special hold on many of us. People are right to care desperately how the county game develops: the debate about the rights and wrongs of four-day cricket, intensely carried out in bars and news-paper columns for a long time before it submerged the three-day game, for at least three years but probably for ever in 1993, showed how much many people do so. The reason is that the county cricket is chivalrously yet toughly conducted between players who greatly respect and enjoy playing with one another. The county game has its own folk-lore and its own code of honour; those who have experienced it know it is unique.

The sometime Australian Test cricketer, now headmaster, John Inverarity, spent two seasons with the Kent team as their coach and mentor and concluded that the combination of competitiveness and honourable behaviour in the county game put his own Sheffield Shield – in which he was himself an absolutely outstanding captain, leading West Australia to four titles – in the shade. Another overseas visitor, passing through for a very successful season with Middlesex in 1980, Vincent Van der Bijl, wrote that 'county cricket is an incredible learning platform – the variety of the cricket, the opposition, the wickets, etc. have created a boundless opportunity of gaining a wealth of cricket-ing experience which must be unequalled . . . this variety in England is to me the county system's strength'.

Van der Bijl was talking as a player, but as a spectator too there is a real delight in the idiosyncrasies of every ground and the people who habitually dwell there on match days. The atmosphere is always friendly. Even the notorious

*gatemen, the pensioners who seem sometimes to have more interest in keeping
you out than letting you in, usually have a bark worse than their bite. Who
would want to spend all day by a gate, anyway, especially as the cricket is usually
tantalizingly out of their sight?*

*Large volumes have been devoted to county cricket, so what follows is a mere
pot-pourri, including a mixture of clubs and eras. I commend to you especially
Geoffrey Moorhouse's description of an ordinary day at an ordinary match: the
bread and butter of professional cricket.*

Flat Out

16 July

West Indies 150 for 4: Hooper 54 not out　　　　　　　　　　*Tour Match*

I bowled flat out today. Faster than I have bowled at any other time this
year, and probably last as well. My pace accounted for the wicket I took.
I clean bowled Desmond Haynes after a razor sharp bouncer nearly
decapitated him. I followed that with a slower ball, and then ripped his
off stump out with his feet all over the place.

A large contingent of West Indian supporters enjoyed my spell. 'Hey,
Agnew! Peter May's watching you.' I gestured that I could not see him
anywhere. 'He's over here, disguised in dreadlocks!'

I used to bowl that pace all the time, but I realized that I would only be
physically able to play about half of the championship matches. I would
strain muscles, and be sore and stiff, so that is why I settled for the
shortened run up, and concentrated on swinging the ball. Today though,
the ball did not swing, and so I really let go.

The rain came at about three o'clock and when we got off the field
Andy Roberts was already in the dressing room brandishing a pack of
cards!

Cowdrey's first Test team is being picked as I write. I wonder . . .
Martin Johnson had me in his twelve in the *Independent* today. I was
disappointed that there was no sign of a Selector at the match. I find that
amazing. Apart from myself, there is Philip DeFreitas and David Gower

to watch, although Gower did not play in the end. I know that I made the Windies take note this morning when I was bowling. It would have been nice if a Selector had been there to observe. Gower did. He said that he really enjoyed watching it. I expect Neil Foster and Gladstone Small to get a Test recall. With Cowdrey as fourth seamer that would mean no place for me. Again.

17 JULY

West Indies 370 all out: Greenidge 75; Hooper 62; Dujon 51; Agnew 2 for 114 Leicestershire 33 for 4

Today we witnessed at first hand the terror of the West Indian fast bowling machine. Waiting in the dressing room, knowing that sooner or later the missiles which are currently being hurled at someone else's head will be directed at yours, is terrifying. You question your ability to get out of the way. 'Will I see it clearly? Will I see it early enough? Will I react in time?' All batsmen, from the openers down to number eleven, feel exactly that way. There is none of the usual banter. Just a gasp or moan as another ball flashes past someone's head or smacks into already bruised ribs. It is easy to see why some of England's batsmen appear to have had enough of it.

There was quite a demand for protective gear today. I was padded up by the close and, apart from pads and gloves, I had a thigh guard on my left leg, another on my right thigh, a shin guard strapped to my left forearm, and a thick chest pad strapped over my heart. Plus of course, my helmet. These guys mean business and will let everyone have short pitched balls. It is a far cry from how it used to be, when bowlers *bowled* tailenders out. Tomorrow I will be their human target, just as the others in the team are. It is not a nice thought.

David Gower left before our innings started. That did not go down very well with the batsmen who had to go in and face the music. The majority of the team are not exactly delighted that Gower has pulled out anyway. He says he has nothing to gain by playing against them now. He has just finished a Test, and there is another starting next week.

I bowled a stack of overs today – 29 to be exact. So much for an easy three days. Lloyd Tennant turned up today to watch. He would have loved a game. So much for the theory that the members look forward to the tourist match more than any other in the season. Barely a couple of hundred turned up. There was a smaller crowd than for a run-of-the-mill Sunday league match.

It will be interesting to see whether Viv Richards enforces the follow on tomorrow if we are bowled out cheaply or just goes for more batting practice. The way things went today, if we avoid the follow on by scoring at least 220, it will be a miracle. If they want to bat again I think we should protest by not using our regular bowlers. I certainly do not want to bowl again. I am tired after my efforts today, and we have a vital week of cricket coming up.

Not selected for England. Disappointed, yes, because I feel that if I had been watched yesterday I might have been picked. Apparently it was between me, Pringle and Radford. Pringle won because of his batting.

I found a picture of me bowling Des Haynes in the *Sunday Express* this morning. I cut it out and slipped it in his kit bag before he arrived. It went down very well with their boys, and Desmond enjoyed it, but he did enquire if I remembered the fifth Test at the Oval in 1984. Of course I did. Des scored a hundred and won them the match. He said he will put the picture in his scrap book. I offered to sign it for him. He grunted his disapproval!

18 JULY

West Indies 370
Leicestershire 90 all out: Agnew 8; Patterson 4 for 44; Benjamin 4 for 20
and 103 for 6

Match drawn

Laurie Potter today scored the best 16 not out I have ever seen. He batted for over two hours, did not give a chance, and took everything the West Indies's fast bowlers could throw at him. It was an innings of the highest courage and determination, and on another day it would be worth a century.

I got my innings over and done with before lunch. I batted for over half an hour, and fended a few off my nose. The most painful moment was when a Patrick Patterson full toss missed my pad and hit me on the left calf. I had shooting pains down my leg to my toes, and it was agony. That ball must have been travelling at at least 80 miles per hour, and did not hit the ground to slow it down. It thudded straight into my unprotected leg. Higgy found that hilarious. I was wearing more armour than a jousting knight, and then got pinned on the one bit that was not covered by foam or something similar.

Eventually Winston Benjamin got his revenge for my getting him out yesterday when I edged him to Viv Richards at first slip.

I enjoyed the contest generally. At the time it was hardly pleasant, but I did not give them my wicket. They did not have to work quite so hard to dispose of Suchy – an edge for two, then a straight ball cleaned him up – or Les, who won the toss with Suchy and therefore earned the right to go in last! In our score of 90, his was the only duck. Before going out to bat he ordered Peter Hepworth, today's twelfth man, to go and fetch him a cheese roll and a packet of smokey bacon crisps. 'If my number's up I might as well go with a full stomach,' he said. It was like watching a condemned man eating his last supper.

Then it was a case of trying to save the match, which we did, thanks to Potter and Whitticase, who stayed together for three quarters of an hour. I was due to bat next, but was spared another encounter with Patto. Instead of dnb (did not bat) alongside our names on the second innings scorecard, Suchy reckoned that it should be Agnew, Such and Taylor, dnf – did not fend!

Unfortunately, very little positive emerged from this encounter with the strongest team in the world, except that Laurie showed his courage. The batsmen who were out of nick, are even more so now. I bowled 29 overs in their innings, and am now very stiff. Whitticase has aggravated his back strain, and Suchy has gone in the leg.

19 JULY

Day off. Spent the afternoon in the casualty department of Leicester Road Infirmary. My hand is still very sore, and I find it very difficult gripping things. I struggled batting against the West Indies yesterday, and decided an X-ray was called for. It confirmed what I had suspected. My little finger is cracked between wrist and knuckle.

Fortunately, there is no real treatment. I say fortunately, because it means I can still play cricket. It will just be very sore for the next six to eight weeks. I phoned Craig this evening to tell him the news, and I told him that I do not want anyone else to know. It would be too easy to use as an excuse if things go badly, and I certainly do not want the England Selectors to find out.

20 JULY

Britannic Assurance County Championship
Derbyshire 348 for 4: Barnett 200 not out

What an awful day! Mind you, Kim Barnett played well. He faced the first ball of the day, attacked everything, and blocked the last one to still be there tomorrow morning.

I cannot work out what has happened to the green seaming wickets we played on earlier this season. This one is easily the flattest pitch we have had at Grace Road all season. There is not a blade of grass on it, and it's very hard. Why have we now decided that our seamers cannot compete with Derby's? OK, they have Michael Holding in their team, but he is only one. The last result wicket we had here was the one against Kent, the second match of the year. We will not win the Championship if we keep playing on wickets like this one. Derby are fourth from the bottom of the table. They are no threat to us. We should have taken a gamble and taken them on. We desperately need a victory to stay in touch with the leaders.

I am completely knackered this evening. Jaded probably describes it better. I bowled another 21 overs today, and felt stiff all the time. The West Indies match really took it out of me. That was the first time that I have bowled consistently fast for a long time, and my body is not used to it. Unfortunately we are still in the field tomorrow morning. I cannot say that I am looking forward to it.

Jonathan Agnew, Eight Days a Week (1988)

Last Wicket Stand

When I first saw the St Lawrence Cricket Ground, Canterbury, in August 1939, my attention was distracted from its beauties by having to make a ticklish decision.

If Middlesex beat Kent, we still had a fair chance of winning the championship: so, as captain, I had to move with caution.

There had been a good deal of rain overnight, and the pitch lay lush and green under a strong but fitful morning sun. I had won the toss, and the question was – to bat or not to bat. Being no judge of turf, I found it a hard one to answer. Eventually, finding opinion amongst the bowlers divided and not having a weather prophet handy, I decided to play safe and take strike.

That great and unique pundit, Gerry Weigall, strongly disagreed with my decision. Never a man to underclub himself in the matter of words, he describes it variously as 'criminal', 'lunatic', and 'pusillanimous'. This reminded me of one of Gerry's admirers, who, having listened to a similar denunciation, said he always regarded him as the most consistent authority he knew on cricket matters. The grateful light in Gerry's eye faded slightly when his friend added: 'I have only to reverse your opinion diametrically and I can't be very far wrong.'

Accordingly, I replied that whatever doubts I might have had were completely at rest now that I had heard his views. This sally he took, as ever, in good part, telling me to 'Wait and see, sir.'

As a matter of fact, I watched our progress with a good deal of anxiety. We had several awkward moments, but the first innings score had reached 200–odd when the ninth wicket fell. It was not brilliant, but a gamble might have proved disastrous, and I felt if we could scrape a few more runs my policy would be justified. This depended to some extent on myself, as it was now my turn to bat.

At the other end was Smith (J.), not out 3. He was not, at first sight, a much more likely batsman than I was, on a turning wicket with quite an array of spin bowling. The most entertaining batsman in the country, his technique was fundamentally confined to one stupendous stroke. The left leg was stretched massively in the direction of mid-on, and the bat (5 lb plus) whistled through the air with a powerful and remarkably supple swing.

The direction the ball took if struck, depended entirely on its length, width, and any unforeseen variations in pace from the bowler. Thus the long-hop to the off might be struck, flat batted, over extra's head or, if laggardly from the pitch, come straight back like an anti-tank shell.

The good-length straight ball was Jim's favourite, as this could be driven off the rise far over long-on. But it was when he struck too soon at this type that the customer got the maximum value for his money. The ball would then hiss vertically into the stratosphere while an agitated gaggle of fielders would gather underneath to perform every manoeuvre in drill book and ballet in their efforts to estimate its point of descent.

A frantic captain, if not actively engaged in the mêlée, would seek to gauge the likeliest catcher and make himself heard above the tumult of 'yours' and 'mines'. If he kept his head there was always ample time to summon up the wicket-keeper, but as often as not, the ball would descend with a thud in the middle of a circle dizzy from their exertions.

On this occasion Smith played his natural game, and it was soon apparent that it was his day. After several balls of a particularly good over from Watt had passed the stumps by a tiny margin, the last flew over the big tree at square leg. This was largely the pattern of things to come, and soon the score was progressing by regular instalments of four or six a time.

At the other end I plied the 'dead bat', but was by no means idle. Backing up was not a matter of making a yard down the pitch but of gaining sufficient elbow room to take violent evasive action. To avoid loss of limb, or even life itself, one had to resort to the zooming vertical climb or the undignified crash dive, while averting collision with a bowler and umpire similarly employed.

Canterbury has seen bigger and altogether better stands, but surely never one so packed with improbable action. The ball whined and hummed to every point of the boundary, not excluding the screen directly behind the striker. Fielders, one moment breathing expectantly down the back of my neck, were next belting back to the very edge of the ground. If, at any time, the field bore a slightly orthodox pattern, it did so in deference to tradition, rather than to practical requirements. The captain must have sighed for the orderliness of Hammond or Bradman.

Watt bowled, Wright bowled, Davies bowled, and periodically rain fell, possibly summoned by the ball's frequent excursions into the cloud belt. Eventually the momentous possibility dawned on all present – Smith was going to make a hundred. It was certain that this possibility would in no way affect his tactics, and there would be no question of 'nervous nineties'.

The climax was fittingly dramatic. At 96 Smith received a ball rather short and wide of the off stump. He gathered his eighteen stone and let fly with that mighty bat, only to find the ball on him rather sooner than he had expected. The ball, meeting the flailing blade early in its arc, resulted in a square cut as good as anything John Tyldesley could do. Third man had no time to move. Jim, grinning hugely, had the nerve to look as if he had meant it.

We had added 116, of which Jim had made 98. It was not the fastest hundred of the season, because of the rain, a highish percentage of complete misses, and the time it took to fetch the ball back or find another in similar condition. Still it won us the match, if not the Championship.

The last word, however, lay with the delighted and unabashed Weigall. He dismissed our effort as a 'prostitution of the art of batting'.

Ian Peebles, *Talking of Cricket* (1953)

From Harris to Cowdrey

There is rural Kent, where the heart of Kent cricket first beat: there is industrial Kent, with its paper mills in the north, its factories in the Medway towns and light industries scattered through the county: and, encroaching steadily on both, there is suburban Kent, full of people who depend on London and who have their backs to the county. Kent cricket is the scion of rural Kent, where its roots are still buried. Mr G. Colman (*The Poor Gentleman*, 1802) described Kent as 'rich in pheasants, cherries, hops, yeomen, codlings and cricketers'. Nowadays, it is equally rich in motor traffic, housing estates, commuters and shop stewards. The story of Kent cricket lies in the unwilling accommodation of a countryman's sport to the townsman's way of life.

However, the first recorded cricket match in which one of the sides played in the name of Kent took place far from the hop gardens in the heart of London on Lamb's Conduit Fields. It was assuredly a remarkable encounter. In one of its editions for May 1719, the *Weekly Journal* reported on the curious circumstances surrounding a fixture between Kent and London:

> Last week a trial was brought at Guildhall before the Lord Chief Justice Pratt between two companies of cricket players, the Men of Kent, plaintiffs, and the Men of London, defendants, for sixty pounds played for at cricket: and after a long hearing, and near £200 expended in the cause, my Lord, not understanding the Game, ordered them to play it over again.

And play it again they did, possibly the only match ever arranged by order of court. It would have been interesting to know whether the dispute arose from an episode occurring on the field or merely from the losers' failure to hand over the agreed stake. The will to win was certainly there – at any rate in court – for £200 in 1719 was the equivalent of £1,650 now, or thereabouts, for with the crisis of the South Sea Bubble only a year away, it was a shaky time for the currency. However, his Lordship's judgement seems to have dispelled animosity between the parties. For in the replay when, with four wickets standing, one of the Kent side was taken ill, the game was broken off to permit his recovery and was not resumed until two months later on a different ground, White's Conduit Fields, where Kent lost by 21 runs.

Lord Harris's epic work on the history of Kent County Cricket bears witness to Kent's prominence in eighteenth-century cricket. Kent beat All England by one run in 1744 on the Artillery Ground in Finsbury: and in the palmy days of the Hambledon Club, Kent were one of their most formidable rivals. Even the sketchiest acquaintance with cricket history brings to mind the Kent of Fuller Pilch and Alfred Mynn, of Wenman and Hillyer, in the period following the introduction of round-arm bowling and preceding the acceptance of the overarm delivery. Representative cricket seems to have been a long-standing institution in the county. How is it, then, that in 1970 we celebrate only the first centenary of the county club, rather than its second or even its third?

In the eighteenth century, and well into the nineteenth, cricket rested on the patronage of prosperous landowners who were prepared to spend money on the game and often to employ or to find employment for the promising young cricketer. In Kent there were also both local and regional clubs, but they seemed to survive without formal co-ordination. It is difficult to discover just how a county side was picked and maintained under these conditions. Doubtless, the influential gentry and some of the officers of the clubs acted as an informal selection committee. It was only when inter-county cricket became more regular, when the northern counties wanted to engage the southern counties, when the clubs grew numerous and diverse, when the scale of operations outstripped the landowners' capacity to pay, that the system cried out for an overhaul.

In 1870, not much farther away from Canterbury than Old Trafford, the Prussian and French armies were locked in a one-sided struggle. But in East Kent it was a diplomatic battle that was being joined. A county club had already been established in 1859 under the Presidency of Lord Darnley, but it lacked adequate funds and, still worse, it was never accepted by important sectional interests which valued their independence. In particular, there were rivalries between East and West Kent; and Canterbury Week had its own 'managers' who regarded the Week as their private enterprise. By amalgamating the existing county club with the Beverley Kent Club in Canterbury, by making Canterbury the official headquarters, by providing on the committee for equal representation from East and West Kent, Herbert Knatchbull-Hugessen, a negotiator respected by all parties, reconciled the conflicting interests and laid the foundations of the present club.

'SILENCE, HAWKE!'

But, if Knatchbull-Hugessen gave the club a start, it was largely Lord Harris who steered and shaped it. He captained the county from 1875–89 and thereafter occupied an authoritative position in the direction of its affairs. The county side was not at all strong in the early period of his captaincy, but in his final two years came second and fourth in the Championship table. The groundwork was laid for the golden era of Kent cricket in the years immediately before and after the First World War. In particular he believed that counties should not rely too heavily on professionals but should develop their amateur talent and create a tradition of service in the first-class game. Before his time amateurs treated their links with the county rather casually. Lord Harris was not a man who took kindly to casual treatment.

He was strong-willed and autocratic, but he also had vision and foresight with a capacity to work for long-term objectives. He was extremely formidable as a person with an air of authority before which opposition and criticism melted away. I remember a Kent supporter saying to me, 'When his Lordship told someone to follow him, he didn't have to look round. He knew his man was there.' To bowl a bun, instead of the match ball, to Lord Harris on his own ground first delivery after lunch, as Eric Hatfield once did, required a degree of audacity which it is hard for us in these easygoing times to imagine. The story is told that Lord Harris was once chairman of an *ad hoc* tribunal set up by MCC to investigate some unfortunate incident on the field in which Jack Durston, the Middlesex fast bowler, was involved. Hauled before the tribunal, Durston began, at the chairman's request, to give his version of the story. Lord Hawke, also a member of the tribunal and himself no slouch in terms of status and personality, ventured to whisper a comment to his neighbour, whereupon Lord Harris rounded on him: 'Silence, Hawke! Durston is addressing the chair.' The story may be apocryphal, but it is in keeping with Lord Harris's character. He was well able to carry off such behaviour.

It was near the time of the county club's foundation that inter-county fixtures were sufficiently regularized to justify some kind of national competition. That this competition took the form of a championship table was due more to the press, who began to print unofficial tables in the newspapers, than to the counties themselves. In 1873, however, the counties formally adopted the system, which has persisted without interruption.

Let us now review Kent's performance through this period of ninety-six years. I have extracted from the late Roy Webber's comprehensive digest of the Championship records the relevant material as it affects the county. If we divide the time into the periods which he himself favours, the following results emerge:

Years	No. of Matches	Won	Drawn	Lost	No. of competing counties	Kent's place
1873/87	140	44(32%)	22	74(53%)	9	7
1888/94	106	38(36%)	28	37(35%)	9	6
1895/1914	459	218(48%)	117	118(26%)	14/16	4
1919/39	579	264(46%)	162	150(26%)	17	4
1946/56	300	70(24%)	99	130(44%)	17	15
1957/69	360	105(30%)	146	98(28%)	17	8
	1,944	739(38%)	574	607(31%)		

The numerate reader will have noticed that the sum of the wins, draws and losses falls short of the total number of matches by twenty-four. The balance were ties, matches abandoned without a ball being bowled or other games affected by circumstances which officially ruled them out of the category of drawn matches.

These results show that Kent were a weakish side in Lord Harris's day, the losses comfortably outnumbering the wins. About 1890 they began to improve, but the great days were deferred until 1904. In the eleven seasons leading up to the outbreak of the First World War, Kent were four times champions, twice second and three times third. Since then they have never again won the Championship, though they have been runners-up on four occasions.

From 1919 onwards, Kent were still a fine side. Between that date and 1935 they were never lower than fifth in the table, except in 1929. In the years just before the Second World War they dropped to the middle of the table and, when cricket was resumed in 1946, after two reasonably successful seasons they declined further and during the 1950s had the unhappiest experience of the club's existence. In all but one of these years they were well down in the lower half of the table, though they were never actually bottom. (Kent have been bottom only once, in the 1870s.) Then in the early 1960s they began to move up again to the middle of the table and suddenly, in 1964, they emerged as the side we know today, well led by Colin Cowdrey.

Certain peculiarities of Kent cricket are familiar to all followers of the game. Over the years what Kent have lacked in rigour and solidity they have made good in style and spirit. They have tended to go for a result rather than to play safe, to press on with the game rather than let it congeal, to give rein to individual expression rather than to cramp it. Perhaps this is why they have had their ups and downs more often than such a county as Yorkshire. Perhaps it is the legacy of the amateur approach which Lord Harris sought to cultivate. But in fact, the county has most prospered when the panache of its great players has been supported by a few less obtrusive but dependable colleagues of good calibre.

The public is also well acquainted with Kent's wealth of high-class wicket-keepers. For one county to produce almost in succession three such stars as Leslie Ames, Godfrey Evans and Alan Knott is remarkable. When the same county can also point to Huish, Hubble, G. E. C. Wood, Levett and Catt, its record must defy challenge.

BOWLING LIMITATIONS: FAST AND OFF-SPIN

But if we look for limitations other than a slight want of concentration among Kentish batsmen, they are to be found in the curious absence of high-class fast bowlers and slow off-spinners. Kent have never had the counterpart of a Tom Richardson, a Larwood, a Farnes, a Statham. Indeed, they have seldom had a bowler of real pace, whatever his quality. The best fast bowler Kent have had was probably Arthur Fielder, who opened for the county in the side that won the Championship. But he was not truly fast. For someone approaching England class you have to go back to W. M. Bradley, who played at the turn of the century and was several times picked for England. In recent times David Sayer had genuine pace, but was not quite in the top class.

A list of Kent's finest bowlers would comprise Alec Hearne, who took over 1,000 wickets for the county in the 1880–1900 period, Blythe, Freeman, Woolley, Wright, and Underwood – three slow left-handers, two leg-spinners and one stock medium-pace. In D. W. Carr and C. S. Marriott there were two more leg-spinners of more than ordinary merit. The other bowlers who have given Kent reasonably successful service were, in the main, medium-pace seamers or slow left-handers. None of their slow off-spinners has ever taken 100 wickets in a season.

J. G. W. Davies, *The Cricketer* (1971)

Please God, Let Me Play for Sussex – Regularly

It's mostly old codgers like me who get confused about generations, dates and events (usually whether before or after the war. Yes, I know, and 'Which war?' my friends will ask.) I'm always being mistaken for my father, 'Old' George, and I'm 'Young' George. I know I'm getting to a ripe old age and my pips begin to rattle if you shake me, but I'm not that old.

It was in 1953 and Sussex were playing Lancashire at Aigburgh. Cyril Washbrook and Winston Place, I think it was, scored a lot of runs on the first day and the Sussex captain had run out of ideas by tea, so I suggested I might be able to help and was given a few overs (cap off) and they finished the day with I don't know how many runs. On the third day I received a letter from a James Entwhistle of Preston – and I have it on the wall of my dressing-room now. It said 'Dear Mr Cox. How good to see you still playing cricket. I remember you in 1899 when Sussex played Oxford University at Hove.' He had obviously gone home and looked up the scoreboard that he'd kept and reproduced it. Ranji, Fry, Relf, Tate, Cox, Jessop were all playing. He finished, 'How good to see someone still playing cricket who played in the 19th century. Wishing you many more years of cricket . . .' and the least I could have been, then, in 1953, was seventy-two! Silly old fool. Of course it gave my colleagues a lot of pleasure, and I must admit, me too. But that's only about thirty years ago and the Editor wants my memories of 1921, sixty years ago when I was but ten years old. So I'll give them to him.

We lived in the village of Warnham just north of Horsham and we were six children in the family. Mother and Father were devout church-goers and so were we all, although one or two of us at the end of the line had to be pressed into attending Evensong on glorious summer Sunday evenings.

I said my prayers nightly and I remember after 'Gentle Jesus . . .' and 'God bless . . .' I always added 'Please God let me play cricket for Sussex regularly.' I added the 'regularly' because I thought the Almighty might fob me off with an odd game against Oxford or Cambridge. Hubert Doggart's son, Simon, was more selfless than I and prayed 'Dear God, let the England selectors, when they meet tomorrow, act wisely', and wasn't it Lord Birkett who, when a young Surrey supporter, went right down through the team and said 'God bless Hobbs, God bless Hayward, God bless Hayes, God bless Hitch' and finished with 'God bless leg-byes.'

I was in the church choir and the vicar, Canon Felix Farebrother, was a good friend of mine and I adored him for he loved cricket and captained the village side. (He was canonized, we hear, because he was captain of the Sussex clergy, too.) Even at that age, or it might have been a little later, I was quite a useful bat and, as all boys do, we hung around the pavilion in the hope of a game or at least a 'field'.

I went to the local grammar school at Horsham and I remember I had a pair of white flannels with a Cash's name tape inside with the magic name of A. E. R. Gilligan. A. E. R. had obviously said to Father in the dressing room, 'These any good to your lad, George?' and had thrown them over to father to catch gratefully.

Mother had cut a few inches off the legs and taken them in around the waist which gave me a bit of a baggy seat (something like John Warr's) but I was proud of them and the envy of the whole school. At the same time it made me conscious of my own name and envious of those with exciting initials like A. P. F., P. G. H., A. H. H. and A. E. R. and even J. W. H. T. I'd have been more envious of R. C. Rought-Rought, H. G. O. Owen-Smith, R. C. Robertson-Glasgow, A. C. D. Ingleby-McKenzie and C. D. A. Martin-Jenkins. Cox G. was so insignificant (but I believe Cash's were cheaper by sixpence a hundred for three-letter names). All is not finished though, because I see in the social columns of *The Times* every now and again there is a gentleman with the name of Lt Col G. G. Cox-Cox.

I was proud to be 'Old' George Cox's son. I had an entrée into all the Sussex grounds and even into the pavilions. In 1926 Warwickshire came to Horsham to play in 'the week'. Father was still playing and bowling his flighted left-arm spinners at the age of fifty-three and W. G. (Willie) Quaife was still making runs for Warwickshire at fifty-four. Father had a very good match, taking 17 wickets for 106 runs, a world record then, with fifteen others, mind you, until Jim Laker ruined it all by taking 19, and in a Test too. Living nearby father invited Willie Quaife to supper at home and I can remember these two old men in the garden discussing the day's play and ribbing each other; and apparently W. G. had shouldered arms to what he thought was a leg-spinner and it had 'come on with the arm' and he said to father: 'You old devil', and father replied, 'Oh! it must have hit a dandelion', and as a naïve schoolboy I thought, 'Fancy having a dandelion on a County pitch.'

Talking of Arthur Gilligan, I was on the County Ground at Hove only last summer and watching the cricket from the bottom of the ground underneath the Gilligan Stand (they'll never be able to name a stand after me, will they?). I found myself sitting next to a very old man who talked about the past and how he'd 'seen 'em all' – Ranji, Fry, Cox, etc. The friend I was with, a Sussex Committee Member, said, 'This is Old George Cox's son and he's ninety-five' and he paused and thought for a minute and said, 'I suppose he must be . . .'

Silly old Fool!

George Cox, *The Cricketer* (1981)

Inside the Oval – a Boy's Eye View

It might have been different had we lived closer to Lord's, where conditions for the unprivileged are so very much more comfortable than they are in the concrete austerity of its ugly sister. But we didn't live closer to Lord's, and altogether saw comparatively little of that great ground, though we made a ritual point of attending the Middlesex and Sussex match at Whitsun, usually on the third day, when there was often a considerable finish. No, we were conditioned to spectatorship among the blown dust and orange peel of the inhospitable Kennington benches. There was no shelter when it rained and no shelter when it shone; it was impossible to attain a vantage point from which you could see, as it were, down into the field of play as distinct from across it (much less get behind the bowler without paying extra to sit in the Vauxhall stand, where you were so far away from the game that you might just as well have been in Vauxhall Station); your view was consequently *across* the field, and you saw the ball move dizzyingly before a confusing backcloth of spectators' faces and bodies and legs on the other side of the ground. This would result before the day's play was half over in the beginnings of a headache or a series of exasperating moves to find more advantageous positions. The situation deteriorated so badly that we at last began to direct the envious eyes, which we had for some time been casting on the great tiered pavilion that overhung us all, towards the more practical question of the immediate main chance; and in 1928, early spring, we persuaded our several parents to indulge us to the extent of schoolboy membership of the county club.

We were enrolled as members as early as the February; and words cannot express the pitch of anticipatory excitement to which the imminence of the new season was to bring us. In addition to the obvious luxury in which we were henceforth destined to enjoy the spectacle of our first-class matches, we had the prized privilege, which we were not going to be behind-hand in exercising at the earliest possible instant, of practising under the eyes of county coaches on the holy turf itself. Half-way through April the schoolboy members were invited to avail themselves of this scheme; and alternating arrangements for practice at school (which also took place for the favoured few in the school holidays) with carefully spaced dates at the Oval, we organized our pre-season cricket into a very tidy and attractive pattern long before the tiresome spring term was over and the sports and other irrelevances out of the way. Thus it was that I entered the Oval pavilion as a player before ever I occupied it as a spectator; that is, if I may stretch a point. I suppose I may be allowed without taint of *suggestio falsi* to count my advance from the pavilion in flannels, carrying bat and pads, as a prelude to functioning on the Oval as a player; but that is about all I have to boast of. In actual fact my début in the pavilion cost me (as my débuts everywhere tend to do) a wealth of humiliation that took a considerable time to pay off; for arriving late and alone, and mistaking a hurried direction, I began to change on my own in the wrong dressing-room, surprised at the lack of company but too scared to embark on any further foraging trips; and being discovered by some official or other when half-dressed was bundled with an armful of hastily snatched-up gear into a dressing-room full of my curious and watchful contemporaries. That I have since found reason to believe that the room into which I was thus pitchforked is the historic chamber where England elevens assemble for Test matches is no consolation at all. It took me two or three sessions at the nets to recover from the prickly heat.

The practice was in the hands of a mild-mannered and tentative retired Army officer named Major Luther, tall and willowy with a shock of grey hair on a handsome head that swayed engagingly as he walked. Under his direction, and no doubt concentrating upon taking a rise out of him whenever possible, was a posse of junior professionals, among whom Bob Gregory was by far the most active and encouraging. He would dart down the pitch to demonstrate a stroke, fly back to the wicket and bowl up a suitable ball – and as soon as you had dispatched it into the net with what had seemed to your innocence a reasonably satisfactory wallop 'Look at that *toe!*' he would yell, capering frantically in three directions at once and rushing upon you, tearing at his scanty hair in eagerness to begin the demonstration all over again. Around him his dutiful colleagues wheeled up their routine deliveries. I found some of them painfully fast, notably those of a certain Lock, now the admirable groundsman who has given the Oval wicket its new and characteristic bite; and I later felt more than ever ineffective and insignificant when I came to see these terrifying bowlers in a real match and observed from the shelter of the pavilion how slow and innocuous they seemed. At the nets they were polite but perfunctory; regarded no doubt the whole business as a depressing chore (to this the ebullient Gregory appeared to be an exception); and made occasional shadowy gestures with their hands and arms to show you how you should have placed the last one that bowled you, without (and this always excepts Gregory) translating their commentaries into intelligent speech. Half in and half out of the picture pottered the amiable Luther, in flannels and a curious long white overcoat, hugging the book with the elaborate time-tabled entries regulating our schedule of innings. Part clerk, part player, part organizer, part waif and stray, the good man threaded his way through these manoeuvres without ever seeming to have full control. Once in a while he would bowl, a nice ballooning half-volley as often as not; once he batted for a spell with two or three professionals whacking down all they had at him. I cannot remember how he shaped; to do him justice, I think he had been not so long before a creditable cricketer enough at the Minor County level; and his batting so far as I remember it showed traces of quality and style. We boys laughed ribaldly at him behind his long swaying back; to us he was just another raggable schoolmaster, not a middle-aged man selflessly giving up his time (whether he was doing this for love I do not know) to organizing for a parcel of boys a pleasure and a privilege that they would never entirely forget.

It was an attractive, exciting time. Some of the genuine first team men would occasionally appear, and we would rub shoulders breathlessly with Barling or Garland-Wells. Brooks, the new wicket-keeper, kept in a net one day; another day Fender came, a long beaky figure in mufti, meeting his professionals for the first time that season with friendly and welcoming handshakes. 'Hello, Tom, how are you? Ah, Bob, nice to see you, how are you keeping? Yes, very well, thanks, very well indeed' – and so on all round the affable circle. And across the middle the mowers and the hoses were out, and one of the scoreboards was being painted, and men were astride the awnings on the pavilion roping the canvas – all the buzzing preparations for another summer, in which we, we felt, were to participate, in our access of privilege, in closer proximity to the fountain-head than ever before. Standing on the balcony in our shirts – that same balcony from which just over a quarter of a century later Hutton waved acknowledgements to the crowd that surged at his feet when the Ashes had at last been regained – we could look down to where the glorious springtime greenness flowed away from under us to wash against the far confines of the Vauxhall stand. A dressing-room full of boys behind us, an empty pavilion about us, a great space of green with a flurry of busy activity in the corner by the scoreboard under the gasometer; the eye could take all this serenely in and travel up the road with the clanging trams to the dim arch where the main line runs through Vauxhall Station, away beyond the housetops to the gulls above the river, and overlooking us all, to the left of the gasworks, the Victoria Tower with the flag flying over it, and Baldwin and MacDonald and Lloyd George below.

The pavilion itself yielded up its treasures more slowly. It came to life more readily when the season opened and its members began to fill it, when cricketers at stated intervals went in and out of it and the tobacco smoke rose around and above it in hanging pervasive clouds of blue. At practice time it seemed an echoing shell, expectant of occupants perhaps, but for all that unreal; but on the day of the first game it acquired an organic life and purpose, and we annexed it for our own on that day in a sense in which we had not found it possible to do so before. The first game was a trial game (my life's climacterics seem to hinge themselves on Surrey trials), the earlier and lesser of the two that Surrey laid on before the season began. What notice they took of the form there displayed I do not know; the earlier gave to the unfledged colts, both professional and amateur, a chance to loosen their shoulders and partake at least of the illusion of a match; while the later of the two deployed the whole strength of Surrey, Hobbs, Sandham, Fender and all, together with the most promising of the juniors.

Perfunctory and unimportant as the play was bound to be, it was our first taste of cricket seen from the Oval pavilion, and bright and early on the first day we all arrived with our sandwiches for a full-day session as keyed up and critical as if it had been a Test match. I am not going to recite in order the details of the day (historically it may be said to be of interest as the first appearance on the Oval of an England fast bowler, Alf Gover); it was chilly and dull throughout, and our emotions were concentrated mainly upon the spectacle of the good Luther captaining one of the sides with all his vague courtesy and amiability. In the second over of the game he put a dolly catch on the floor at slip, scrabbling at it as it dropped with a frantic despair which gave us inexpressible joy and contentment; and when later in the day he went in to bat, and in the course of a gallant little innings of something over a dozen he slid for five or six yards on his bottom when going for a quickish single, we reverted to despicable type and were once again the snotty little boys hugely amused over the physical discomfiture of an elder and better.

But the day remains memorable less for the cricket than for our first entranced exploration of the pavilion itself, storey upon dark storey of hushed corridors and great landings opening out into wide and lofty rooms, bars, dressing-rooms, offices, reading-rooms, writing-rooms and the Lord knows what beside. Every room and every corridor was hung with paintings, prints, photographs, posters, of every conceivable quality and size. A vast photograph of W. G. Grace, a beautiful action snap of Hobbs jumping out to drive, an elaborate painting of one W. E. Roller going in to bat in the year 1886, vied for impressiveness with an execrable delineation of the entire membership and staff of the Surrey County Cricket Club in 1910, depicted as standing in and around and in front of the pavilion and embellished with a key diagram indicating the identity of every single member of this very considerable crowd. Up and down the walls were innumerable score cards of historic matches – the Triangular Tests, the match in which Victoria[1] scored 1,107, the match in which Hobbs equalled and beat W. G.'s record number of centuries – printed on silk and framed. We gazed at these treasures for hours, gazed at the photographs of the Australian eleven of 1905, of the Gentlemen's eleven of 1911, of Lord Hawke and Lord Harris, of Digby Jephson and Morice Bird, of Lillywhite and Wisden and Caffyn and Alfred Mynn. A plethora assailed us and we tottered about during the intervals in a quiet stupor; we read every paper in the reading-room; we wrote letters on the note-paper most bounteously provided in the writing-room. In the long central chamber, corresponding to the Long Room at Lord's, we stood awe-struck before the beautifully designed board showing the state of the matches simultaneously playing up and down the country; down in the basement we contemplated, with an even more dizzying sense of the wonders of applied science, the busy little tape-machine which fed it. (In our maturer wisdom we tumbled to it that this little device was cherished by the membership and staff, not only for the readiness of its cricket information, but for the racing results as well. I have seen a batsman walk straight off the illustrious Oval amid the applause of the congregated crowd, and walk straight down into the basement without separating himself from his cap, bat, pads or gloves, to satisfy himself at the very earliest possible instant of time of the result of the 3.30.)

What with finding the best vantage points for watching, and making ourselves acquainted with every available nook and cranny in the place from the clock under the flagstaff to the basement bar, and incidentally noting for future reference all those points in the game which we considered the finer, and they were legion, our first day in that pavilion passed like a fleeting dream. I remember I wrote at least two letters on club notepaper in the intervals of all my other activities; and Victor was button-holed, not for the last time either, by an elderly member who qualified in our minds as Crackpot Member Number One. As this match was a mere perfunctory trial, the attendance was naturally slender, though I dare say there were several hundred old buffers there all told; and it was not long, in terms of weeks and months, before we began to know a number of these characters very well indeed by sight. Some of them to our certain knowledge came every day there was a match on, and for all I know when there wasn't (one or two of them contrived to convey

[1] The State, not the Queen

the impression that they would hardly have noticed the difference). Most of these familiar frequenters were hale, snuffy, genial old men in their sixties and seventies, taking retirement very easily indeed and using it in a way I still have half a mind to emulate myself, when my time comes; and they sat and gossiped in their worn tweeds, bringing out their sandwich tins and their lemonade bottles at the intervals, their old brown hands manipulating the field-glasses with the teased leather straps – patently enjoying the endless variations of this game they could no longer play. A quiet, inoffensive, slightly cracked company, they came and went, a sober background to our naïveté and enthusiasm; and so familiar did they become to us as part of the furniture of the place that it comes as quite a shock to me now – did, in fact, two minutes ago, as I was writing this very paragraph – to realize that, as this time I speak of was well over twenty-five years ago, it is very probable that they are all dead. The pavilion and the pictures are there; the game process on the everlasting green before them; but the background members have imperceptibly changed.

They were there in force on our first day, however, or at least the solid nucleus was there, to build themselves all unconsciously into our minds. Three characters were to impress themselves particularly on our dual consciousness during the three seasons or so while we served our fascinating apprenticeship before becoming blasé full members with the privilege of introducing Tom, Dick and Harry – three characters who, I regret to say, rendered their images indelible with me by reason of their several infirmities. One was a large heavy man, not by pavilion standards very old (probably in his late fifties or early sixties) who for some unhappy reason carried his great head perpetually on one side, projected forward as if he had his chin painfully impaled on a spike. He had a gloomy, contemplative expression, as well might be worn by one in that awkward situation, and was frequently to be observed making one of a small group at the bar in earnest discussion of some imponderable problem, holding his head judicially poised, as always, and carrying in his hand a glass of something short. My memories of him are utterly passive and static, a ruminant figure of an appealing and melancholy fascination; whereas the second of the three, even more pitifully visited by infirmity, provided an active contrast to the first brooding Titan. This man was small, birdlike, eager, and incurably palsied. He trembled intensely and constantly; he smoked a pipe and it beat a fierce tattoo on his teeth as he removed or replaced it; yet he was cheerful, interested, assiduous in following the cricket both at the Oval before him and on the bulletin board; and never far from friends with whom he engaged in gusty discussion. The third, most portentous of all, was the public Crackpot Number One to whom I have already alluded. A tall rangy man with a ginger beard and an eye of an Old Testament prophet, he prowled ominously among the spectators seeking whom he might devour. He cornered Victor in the reading-room on the first day, and I, hovering on the outskirts, came in for most of it. Some time later he cornered me, this time in the lavatory, and I had it all over again. His theme was mystifying and apparently quite irrelevant; I do not understand it and I doubt if I ever shall; but at some time in his life he had conceived an unbounded admiration for the skill at amateur soccer of the celebrated brothers A. M. and P. M. Walters, famous figures in the game in, I should say, about 1890; and solemnly in 1928 in a pavilion dedicated to a game quite other than soccer he would hold us with his glittering eye until he had delivered a short encomium on the outstanding merits of these two players.

Ronald Mason, *Batsman's Paradise* (1955)

Champions of Notts

The two new players introduced into the Notts side during 1928 were both to play a large part in the cricket of the 1930s. C. B. 'Charlie' Harris was born in Underwood in 1907. His brother George had joined the Trent Bridge staff in 1923 and Charlie followed two years later. George never played for Notts, but left Trent Bridge and joined the police in South Wales. He much later played briefly for Glamorgan. Charlie Harris, a right-hand batsman of extreme moods and, occasionally, a very useful bowler, gained a regular place in the Notts team in 1931 and soon became associated with Walter Keeton, as Notts' opening batsman. Robertson-Glasgow paints the picture:

> For Harris is a dreamer. He is a strange addition to Walter Keeton as they walk out to open the innings; Keeton strung up, concentrated, quick-glancing; Harris serenely distrait, revolving idealistic strokes against an attack that will never occur; lagging sometimes a pace or two behind, like a boy with a parent on an unwilling Sunday walk.

Harris was a joker. The stories about him abound and, unlike fishermen's yarns, which grow in the telling, most of those concerning Harris seem to be true: balancing his false teeth on top of the wicket as an added attraction to the bowler; coming out to bat with a lighted candle when he felt the light too poor; putting on a false moustache and posing as a reporter, then conducting an in-depth interview with some poor cricketer making his first-class debut. The crowds loved his batting habit of playing dead bat strokes to a succession of deliveries as if the wicket was treacherous, then for no apparent reason launching into several delightful boundary shots, before going back to his dead bat existence.

His final match was against Hampshire in 1951, but his last season or two was marred by increasing ill-health and he died in August 1954 aged forty-six, deeply mourned by his admiring public.

The second young debutant was George Gunn's son, usually known as Young George. He was destined to play in his father's shadow. He joined the Trent Bridge staff from Nottingham High School in 1925 at the age of nineteen and was a right-handed batsman and leg-break bowler. After some good performances with the second eleven, his chance came against the West Indies at Trent Bridge in July 1928 – during this match King George V and Queen Mary visited the ground and were introduced to both teams. It was the first time since the days of the Dafts that a father and son had played for Notts in the same side. As young George came in to bat the report noted:

> It was an ordeal for the boy, for he had to face Constantine with the new ball, but his responsibilities seemed to rest very lightly upon him. He stayed only ten minutes and made only six, but he was there long enough to show us a nice straight bat, wielded with a sense of touch, an unruffled mien and some of the dear familiar mannerisms of Gunn the elder.

Young George gained a regular place in the County side in 1932 and remained until the outbreak of war. He reached 1,000 runs five times, usually batting at number five, but his leg-breaks tended to be expensive. He did not return to Trent Bridge after the war, save for one game in 1950, and acted as a coach at various schools. He died as the result of a motor-cycle accident in 1957 aged fifty-two. His father said of him: 'If he was half as good as he thought he was, he would have conquered the world.'

Larwood and Sam Staples were chosen to tour Australia with the

1928–29 MCC side; Staples was struck down with muscular rheumatism soon after arriving in Australia and returned home without playing a match. Larwood began the tour well, but the hard wickets gradually took their toll and against a formidable batting line-up, all the England bowlers worked hard for their wickets. Fortunately the Australian attack was made to work even harder and England won the series. Whysall and Lilley went off to Jamaica with Julien Cahn's side; George Shaw the Trent Bridge dressing room attendant went along as well to look after the baggage. The team were away from England for most of February and all of March and played six games in Jamaica.

Playing an almost unchanged side for the third year running, Notts finally clinched the Championship. The regulations had been altered compared with previous recent summers and in 1929 all counties had to play 28 matches. This eliminated the need for percentages: counties still played more than 28 games if they wished and these extra games were 'friendly first-class matches'. Two defeats were suffered, the first at Lord's in late May and the second at Bramall Lane in mid-June. Derbyshire took an early lead in the table, but Notts came to the front in June and from then on were there or thereabouts. Gloucestershire moved ahead in mid-August; Notts, having a match in hand, soon rectified this and they went to Ilkeston for the final match on 31 August as leaders. The combination was slightly altered from the position before the fatal Glamorgan game of 1927. This time, in addition to Notts having to avoid defeat, Yorkshire had to win their match on the same dates. As it happened Yorkshire were defeated, and the rain forced a draw at Ilkeston, so Notts took the crown.

The Lord Mayor of Nottingham invited the Notts team to come to the Council House straight from the match at Ilkeston and a large crowd gathered in the Market Square as the bus conveying the team arrived. Carr, using a megaphone made an impromptu speech:

> Ladies and Gentlemen, it is most awfully nice of you to come and welcome us like this, and we appreciate it very much. We have tried very hard this year to win the Championship and if you only realized what a great strain it has been, you would not ask me to stand here and speak much longer.

The bowling strength was the reason why Notts won the title, the advance of Voce being the most marked individual factor. He used both styles of bowling according to the circumstances, at times fairly fast, swinging the ball, at others using his height and spin to great effect. His wicket tally in Championship matches nearly doubled compared with 1928 and his average fell by eight runs per wicket. In the overall first-class table Voce came fourth, behind Richard Tyldesley, J. C. White and Goddard. He took 120 wickets at 17 runs each. His best return was 14 for 43 against Northants at Trent Bridge, but he also took ten wickets in a match against Worcestershire and Warwickshire. Larwood felt the effects of his winter in Australia and as he also missed several games due to representative calls, he managed only 80 Championship wickets at 18 runs each. Barratt took over 100 wickets and though he was now fairly bulky he still bowled with pace and made the ball get up alarmingly on occasion. Sam Staples had happily recovered from his winter illness and took 75 Championship wickets at 22 runs each; his brother improved beyond anything he had previously achieved and took 64 wickets at 21 runs each. The County therefore had five bowlers, all with averages below 23. In addition the young Shrewsbury bowler, R. D. F. Bland, was given an opportunity when Larwood was unavailable and looked a useful asset.

Whysall stood at the head of the batting, making over 2,000 runs in Championship cricket at an average of 54. His best innings was 244 against Gloucestershire at Trent Bridge when nearly everyone else failed – the total was 396 and Walker the only other player to exceed 50. Payton, now aged forty-seven, missed several matches due to a strained thigh muscle, but came second to Whysall and his 169 against Lancashire, a faultless innings against a strong attack, was the highest of his career.

George Gunn remained remarkable. He celebrated his fiftieth birthday with an undefeated innings of 164 – it was the 54th hundred of his career and he and Whysall added a century first wicket for the 35th time. The match was at Worcester. A week later Worcestershire came to Trent Bridge and George Gunn was formally presented with a variety of gifts from the Lord Mayor, the County Club, his fellow players and the captain. Gunn hit 1,532 Championship runs at an average of 40.31. Walker also completed 1,000 runs.

As was the custom Nottinghamshire went to the Oval at the end of the season to play the Rest of England. It was a great finale to the year, Notts losing by just eight runs.

NOTTS (Champion County) *v* THE REST OF ENGLAND

Played at The Oval, 14, 16, 17, 18 September 1929

REST OF ENGLAND WON BY EIGHT RUNS

REST OF ENGLAND	FIRST INNINGS		SECOND INNINGS	
J. B. Hobbs	*c* Larwood b Barratt	2	b Bland	68
A. Sandham	*c* G. Gunn b Larwood	82	lbw b Larwood	15
F. E. Woolley	b Barratt	106	*c* Whysall b S. J. Staples	15
J. O'Connor	*c* Bland b Larwood	6	*c* G. V. Gunn b Bland	10
*Mr R. E. S. Wyatt	*c* Barratt b S. J. Staples	85	b Barratt	11
M. Leyland	*c* Whysall b Bland	17	*c* and b Bland	75
†L. E. G Ames	*c* Whysall b S. J. Staples	15	b Barratt	0
Mr R. W. V. Robins	b Bland	37	st Lilley b S. J. Staples	45
M. W. Tate	*c* Carr b Bland	32	*c* Whysall b S. J. Staples	7
T. W. J. Goddard	b Larwood	13	not out	13
E. W. Clark	not out	1	*c* Lilley b S. J. Staples	16
Extras	b 1, lb 2	3	b 2, lb 5	7
Total		399		282

1st inns; 1–5, 2–159, 3–170, 4–209, 5–244, 6–272, 7–337, 8–383, 9–397
2nd inns: 1–31, 2–77, 3–105, 4–114, 5–135, 6–135, 7–242, 8–246, 9–260

BOWLING	O	M	R	W	O	M	R	W
Larwood	18	3	54	3	15	1	73	1
Barratt	21	1	83	2	18	2	50	2
S. J. Staples	36.1	7	146	2	18.5	2	63	4
Bland	24	2	106	3	13	0	75	3
G. V. Gunn	2	0	7	0	2	0	14	0

NOTTS (CHAMPION COUNTY)	FIRST INNINGS		SECOND INNINGS	
G. Gunn	b Tate	8	b Robins	96
W. W. Whysall	b Clark	97	*c* O'Connor b Goddard	50
W. Walker	*c* Tate b Clark	1 (4)	*c* Sandham b Robins	0
*Mr A. W. Carr	b Woolley	91 (5)	b Goddard	6
W. R. Payton	*c* Ames b Clark	21 (6)	*c* Hobbs b Robins	32
†B. Lilley	*c* Tate b Clark	10 (7)	b Goddard	5
F. Barratt	*c* Wyatt b Woolley	54 (8)	*c* Sandham b Clark	45
G. V. Gunn	st Ames b Robins	6 (3)	lbw b Robins	17
S. J. Staples	lbw b Robins	21	not out	18
H. Larwood	st Ames b Robins	11	*c* Woolley b Robins	11
Mr R. D. F. Bland	not out	15	*c* Woolley b Robins	1
Extras	b 17, lb 10, nb 2	29	b 14, lb 13, nb 1	28
Total		364		309

1st inns: 1–21, 2–35, 3–204, 4–229, 5–256, 6–265, 7–300, 8–336, 9–339
2nd inns: 1–88, 2–114, 3–122, 4–141, 5–200, 6–209, 7–271, 8–279, 9–299

BOWLING	O	M	R	W	O	M	R	W
Clark	25	5	69	4	25	5	73	1
Robins	26.1	6	108	3	27.3	3	89	6
Tate	21	2	64	1	13	4	38	0
Goddard	14	2	52	0	23	5	56	3
Woolley	9	0	42	2	4	0	12	0
Wyatt					4	0	13	0

Umpires: J. Hardstaff and J. Stone

Bland was the only new player to come into the side. An eighteen-year-old left-arm medium-pace bowler, he played for Notts Amateurs and was a regular member of the Notts second eleven for several years, but his first-class appearances, apart from one game in 1934, were confined to 1929, 1930 and 1931.

The tourists in 1929 were from South Africa and five Tests were staged, though Edgbaston, rather than Trent Bridge, was the venue for the first. Larwood played in three matches and Carr led England in the last two games.

Peter Wynne-Thomas, *The History of Nottinghamshire CCC* (1992)

Derbyshire's Year

Derbyshire's victory over Kent gave them a comfortable lead at the top. A drawn match with the Indians at Derby gave them valuable respite before two more crucial encounters against Yorkshire at Sheffield and Nottinghamshire at Ilkeston.

Yorkshire won the toss and put their opponents in. Derbyshire owed everything to Stan Worthington, who opened the innings and exacted due revenge on Jacques, who had caused such havoc at Scarborough a year earlier. He hit 21 fours in making 135 out of 216, the next best score being 17 by Skinner. Copson struck early, getting rid of Sutcliffe for a duck and by the close Yorkshire were 102 for four. Rain washed out Thursday's play and the battle now centred on first innings points. Yorkshire just scraped ahead, being all out for 218, Copson taking six for 60 and Alf Pope four for 58. So Copson's remarkable run of success continued. Poor health had dogged his progress in 1935 and the club had sent him to Skegness to recuperate. Specialists dispelled doubts about his condition and it was found he was suffering from a strained sacro-iliac joint at the lower extremity of his back. As part of the treatment for this Copson trained with Chesterfield FC and his form in 1936 fully justified the efforts both he and the club had made to get him fully fit.

Derbyshire faced another severe test against Nottinghamshire at Ilkeston, both sides being weakened by Test calls, Nottinghamshire supplying Hardstaff and Derbyshire Worthington to the England team for the second Test against India at Manchester. Invited when Leyland withdrew from the side, Worthington made the most of his opportunity by scoring 87. Retained for the final game at the Oval he became the first Derbyshire batsman to score a century in a Test, hitting 128, most of his 19 fours being scored in front of the wicket, and sharing in a fourth-wicket partnership of 266 with Hammond. It was a magnificent display in which at times he outscored Hammond, driving and pulling to good effect and square-cutting perfectly. Both Worthington and Copson were selected for the MCC tour of Australia in 1936–37 under the captaincy of G. O. Allen and each had their finest season in 1936.

Had he been able to maintain his 1935 form Denis Smith would surely have been in contention with Worthington for a Test place. He had been dropped down the order for a time after an indifferent run but was restored to open the innings at Ilkeston. He stayed nearly three hours for 59, Derbyshire being 154 for six by the close. On Monday they were all out for 187 and then came a thrilling battle for a first-innings lead, won by Derbyshire, with Nottinghamshire getting within five runs of their target, Mitchell taking six for 87. Smith (36) and Alderman (53) gave their side a good second-innings start, the score reaching 94 for two. But the last eight wickets crashed for 31, Voce taking six for 43 and Larwood three for 29 and Derbyshire were all out for 125. Needing 131 to win Nottinghamshire began shakily but they survived several missed chances and won by six wickets. The defeat left Derbyshire still with a clear lead at the top of the table but their neighbours and nearest rivals had narrowed the gap.

Derbyshire ran into more trouble at Chelmsford against the Essex pace attack. On Saturday half the side were out for 29 and the innings was over in two hours for 80. Essex took the lead for the loss of only two wickets, making 219 in all and leading by 139. Alderman held his side together in their second knock against the leg-spin of Peter Smith, but he was out shortly before the close on Monday, Derbyshire ending the day at 195 for seven, a lead of only 56.

On the last morning Alf Pope hit well but Essex needed only 102 to win. They reached 51 for three without looking in any difficulty but an amazing spell by Tommy Mitchell turned the whole course of the match. In 30 balls he took six for 25, Essex being all out for 81. Derbyshire's 20–run victory, their eleventh success in twenty-one games, became all the more significant when it was learned that Nottinghamshire had won at the Oval.

Again Derbyshire had demonstrated an ability to come from behind and win at a crucial time. Defeat at Chelmsford would not have cost them the leadership but it would have made them vulnerable. As it was they maintained a comfortable margin ahead of Nottinghamshire, with Yorkshire now third and Kent fourth.

Mitchell was again in good form at the Oval, where Denis Smith made his first hundred of the season and Alderman took a superb one-handed catch on the boundary to dismiss Barling in a drawn game. Elsewhere Middlesex and Yorkshire won, Nottinghamshire had to be content with first innings points but Kent, now on the slide, had dropped to fifth place, being overhauled by Middlesex.

Again, though, Derbyshire's response to the challenge was positive. A crowd of 7,000 watched them dismiss Leicestershire for 117 at Derby and eventually go on to win by nine wickets after more good bowling from Copson and Mitchell. The game ended in two days, the third occasion this had happened in four Championship games at Derby. It was their twelfth win in twenty-three games, Yorkshire now being in second place and Nottinghamshire third. At this stage Derbyshire needed 51 more points from five games to be certain of winning the Championship.

They were hot favourites but faced a crucial match against Nottinghamshire at Worksop in their next encounter. Worthington was absent at the Oval – his place taken by George Langdale, a forcing left-hand batsman who made his County debut as a twenty-year-old amateur. He later played for Somerset and became a Bassetlaw League official. Nottinghamshire were without Larwood, Voce and Hardstaff and Derbyshire had the best of the match, setting a target of 337 on the final day. But a chanceless display by Keeton and Harris, who shared an unbroken opening partnership of 215, saved the game for Nottinghamshire.

ESSEX *v* DERBYSHIRE

Played at Chelmsford, 1, 2 and 4 August 1936

DERBYSHIRE WON BY 20 RUNS

DERBYSHIRE	FIRST INNINGS		SECOND INNINGS	
A. E. Alderman	*c* sub b Farnes	0	*c* Wade b Farnes	79
D. Smith	b Stephenson	8	b Stephenson	15
T. S. Worthington	*c* Wade b Stephenson	13	*c* Wilcox b Smith	42
L. F. Townsend	*c* Wilcox b Farnes	0	lbw b Smith	8
Mr A. F. Skinner	lbw b Nichols	19	lbw b Smith	7
C. Elliott	b Farnes	4	b Smith	4
H. Elliott	lbw b Stephenson	11	b Smith	14
Mr A. W. Richardson	b Nichols	2	*c* Wade b Stephenson	14
A. V. Pope	lbw b Farnes	9	b Stephenson	33
T. B. Mitchell	b Farnes	0	*c* Wade b Nichols	6
W. Copson	not out	9	not out	3
Extras	b 1, lb 4	5	b 7, lb 4, nb 4	15
Total		80		240

BOWLING	O	M	R	W	O	M	R	W
Nichols	9	2	27	2	18	3	51	1
Farnes	13	6	20	5	27	5	56	1
Stephenson	11.3	4	27	3	18.5	4	56	3
Eastman	3	2	1	0				
Smith					24	3	62	5

ESSEX	FIRST INNINGS		SECOND INNINGS	
Mr L. G. Crawley	b Copson	6	b Copson	1
Mr D. R. Wilcox	lbw b Pope	9	lbw b Townsend	15
M. S. Nichols	lbw b Copson	21	*c* Townsend b Pope	10
J. O'Connor	*c* Alderman b Townsend	87	b Mitchell	21
Mr B. H. Belle	b Mitchell	0	lbw b Mitchell	10
Mr C. T. Ashton	lbw b Copson	10	lbw b Mitchell	0
P. Smith	b Pope	6	b Townsend	8
Mr J. W. A. Stephenson	b Townsend	20	lbw b Mitchell	0
L. C. Eastman	*c* Mitchell b Copson	31	lbw b Mitchell	6
T. H. Wade	not out	6	*c* Skinner b Mitchell	8
Mr K. Farnes	*c* Alderman b Pope	11	not out	1
Extras	b 10, lb 1, nb 1	12	lb 1	1
Total		219		81

BOWLING	O	M	R	W	O	M	R	W
Copson	31	8	64	4	13	6	20	1
Pope	27.1	11	40	3	7	1	16	1
Townsend	19	7	38	2	15	8	19	2
Worthington	5	2	5	0				
Mitchell	11	1	60	1	5	0	25	6

Umpires: H. G. Baldwin and G. Brown

The game was highly significant. Derbyshire, who took five points to Nottinghamshire's three (in drawn matches there were five points for the side ahead on first innings and three for the other side), extended their lead over their neighbours but Yorkshire closed the gap with a crushing win over Somerset at Sheffield. Tension was mounting and it showed in Derbyshire's visit to Eastbourne to meet Sussex. Eighty-eight behind on the first innings Derbyshire lost half their side for 125 and only stubborn batting by the two Elliotts saved the game and three points. The title moved a little nearer and now Derbyshire faced what was on paper their easiest game of the summer against Northamptonshire at Chesterfield.

Northamptonshire were at the beginning of a spell in which they failed to win a match between 14 May 1935 and 29 May 1939, during which they lost 61 out of 99 games. But they gave Derbyshire a real fight after being 65 behind on the first innings. Bakewell and Brookes then shared a fourth-wicket partnership of 211, Bakewell scoring a magnificent 241 not out. It meant Derbyshire needed 347 to win and nerves took over.

It was now that Arthur Richardson, who had not had a particularly good season with the bat, played one of his most vital innings for the County. Points were vital and it was a time for survival. His unbeaten 27, with 41 from Skinner, plus support from Alf Pope, helped Derbyshire recover from 54 for five to 173 for seven, five more points being earned.

Tragedy stalked the game. Mitchell suffered a broken thumb, which put him out for the remainder of the season, but infinitely worse was to follow. Returning home from Chesterfield R. P. Northway and A. H. Bakewell of Northamptonshire were involved in an accident when the car in which they were travelling overturned near Kibworth in Leicestershire. Northway died and Bakewell's right arm was so badly broken that he never played first-class cricket again, his epic display at Queen's Park being his final innings.

Yorkshire, restricted to three points at the Oval, and Nottinghamshire, beaten at Clacton, fell away and Middlesex, their title bid coming a little too late, beat Kent. By the evening of Tuesday 25 August 1936 Derbyshire were assured of at least a share in the Championship. They had 224 points from 26 games (57.43 per cent), Yorkshire having 210 from 28 (50 per cent). Middlesex were now third and Nottinghamshire fourth. It meant that Derbyshire needed only three points from their remaining two games to become Champions. If they lost both of these and Yorkshire won both their remaining matches the two counties would be level at 53.33 per cent. Only Yorkshire could equal Derbyshire, who had led since 7 July and been in second place since June.

So, needing only to avoid defeat to become Champions, Derbyshire travelled to Wells to meet the unpredictable Somerset team. Yorkshire met Sussex at Hove. On the Wednesday Derbyshire were all out for 216, Smith making 93, but as the match progressed they took a firm grip. Alf Pope (five for 35) and Copson reduced Somerset to 146 all out and then 50 from Richardson helped leave Somerset a target of 271 on the final day. Half the side were out for 140, but Arthur Wellard, missed off Armstrong when he had scored a single, turned the game Somerset's way. He drove Armstrong for five consecutive sixes and scored 86 out of 102 in 62 minutes, including seven sixes and eight fours; 74 in 15 scoring strokes. Although Copson took six for 81 in 30 overs of sustained pace (Armstrong had one for 64 in eight overs!) Somerset won the game by one wicket to perform the double over Derbyshire.

It was a disappointment, but the news was received that Yorkshire, who had led by 103 on the first innings, had failed to beat Sussex, so on Friday 28 August 1936 Derbyshire became the Champion County. They had crowned a glorious period in their history and were now at the summit of county cricket.

Defeat at the hands of Somerset, while a fate not unknown to Champions, was not, perhaps, the best way of winning the title but it had been a magnificent game of cricket at Wells. Derbyshire, who had failed to win any of the last four matches, sealed the title in style with an innings victory over Leicestershire in their final game at Oakham. Replying to a total of 151, Smith (169) and Worthington (102) shared a second wicket partnership of 209, their side winning by an innings.

In all matches Worthington made 1,519 runs for the County (average 37.97), his full first-class record being 1,734 (41.28). Leslie Townsend (1,454 runs, 34.62), Smith (1,333, 31.73) and Alderman (1,145, 26.02) were the others who exceeded a thousand runs.

Copson, with 140 Championship wickets and 153 at 12.54 each in all Derbyshire games, led the bowlers. In all first-class cricket he took 160 wickets at 13.34, with only Larwood and Verity ahead of him in the national averages. Mitchell (121 at 21.42) and Alf Pope (99 at 18.13 and 13th place in the national lists) were other key bowlers, while Townsend finished with 63 wickets at 20 apiece. That magnificent attack, minus George Pope for most of the season, was supported by Elliott's splendid wicket-keeping. The fielding, perhaps, was not quite at its best, *Wisden* saying it left much room for improvement, but the close catching of Smith, Worthington, Townsend, and when he was available, Alan Skinner, played its part in the success.

In a wet summer the batsmen did not reveal the same powers of runmaking as in recent seasons but they usually ensured an adequate total made at a pace quick enough to enable the bowlers to do their work. Five of Derbyshire's victories were by an innings, a mark of their superiority, and there were four doubles.

Will Taylor lost no time in making arrangements for a civic reception:

> It was suggested to me that when the Championship was won there should be a public reception for the team on their return to Derby following the match against Leicestershire at Oakham and I immediately set to work.
>
> The Drill Hall was booked and I made contact with our president, the Duke of Devonshire, who was grouse shooting at Bolton Abbey and who came post haste to Derby. The Mayors of the five towns in the county where we played were invited and were present. All arrangements were made for refreshments, and always having the financial position in view, the band of the Sherwood Foresters was booked for a dance after the reception of the team and a charge made to non-members of the Club. Everything went according to plan and we had a wonderful evening.

The reception was held on the Tuesday evening. Arthur Richardson said that whenever he had asked the team for extra effort in a crisis he had always received it. Will Taylor read one or two of the handful of telegrams he had received – congratulations from Brian Sellers, captain of Yorkshire, and one from Maurice Turnbull of Glamorgan on a success gained without having to use them as fodder. The Welsh county finished second from the bottom and Derbyshire did not meet them in the mid-1930s, possibly because of the distance they had to travel.

Wisden said that Derbyshire's triumph was gained on sheer merit:

> Their cricket, reflecting as it always did the true spirit of the game, caused delight to thousands of enthusiasts up and down the country.
>
> Magnificent bowling – they possessed probably the deadliest and best varied attack of any side in the country – team-work rather than individual brilliance, and a will-to-win spirit no matter the position of the game, were the salient factors which made Derbyshire stand out head and shoulders above most of their rivals.

Richardson recalled the Championship side in an interview with Gerald Mortimer, of the *Derby Evening Telegraph*, thirty-five years later:

> Copson and Tommy Mitchell were at the heart of the Championship victory. Two killers, both positive bowlers and both likely to run through a side. Their personalities were as different as their bowling styles.
>
> Bill gave nothing away. Tommy was always tempting them with his leg spinners and was liable to be hit. But he was equally liable to get wickets and get them quickly.
>
> Unfortunately, we lost George Pope in May of 1936 with cartilage trouble after he had really developed during the previous two seasons. But his brother, Alf, did wonderfully well.
>
> He was a most willing player. I would sometimes tell him that he might have to bowl until close of play and he would just say: 'I like bowling, skipper,' and come bounding in for hours.
>
> I wanted Leslie Townsend to make runs, so I did not use his off-spinners nearly as much as Guy Jackson had done. He became a perfect complement to Stan Worthington.
>
> Stan enjoyed fast bowling; Leslie was infinitely happier against spin. I pushed Stan up the order and, therefore, he did not bowl much. I was more interested in specialists rather than all-rounders.
>
> Stan Worthington was a wonderful cricketer. There were times, watching from the edge, when it was hard to tell if it was Stan Worthington or Wally Hammond at the crease. I cannot pay a bigger compliment than to compare him and Hammond.
>
> Denis Smith was a most beautiful hitter. He was inclined, like all hitters, to be erratic, but his record over the years provides an answer to that.

So, with Albert Alderman an unassuming opener and a fine fielder, the top batting was good enough. With Copson and Mitchell in the side, we did not need too many runs and, as a result, the games were always open.

Alan Skinner has never been given the credit due to him. He did not win a blue at Cambridge, but he was one of the best amateur cricketers in the country.

He scored a lot of his runs down to third man and those who did now know him thought he was snicking the ball. In addition he was a superb catcher. I owe him a great debt for the way he filled in when Harry Storer went off to manage Coventry City.

Harry, I am sure, would have played for England if he had not always had football at the back of his mind. He and Arnold Hamer are the only two complete players I have seen play for Derbyshire.

Harry Elliott, of course, was a great wicket-keeper and a wonderful influence on the side. Think of the best regimental sergeant-major you have ever known – that was Harry Elliott.

It was a privilege for me to play in company with such fine cricketers and such wonderful people.

The professionals shared the feeling. They presented him with a silver cigarette case inscribed with the signatures of the Championship team and the simple dedication: 'To the skipper, from the lads.'

John Shawcroft, The History of Derbyshire CCC (1989)

Brian Sellers

In the years immediately after the war the Yorkshire side was a mighty and formidable entity. It would be wrong to say it did not need captaining, but, like a massive mechanism, it did not need driving, only starting and steering. Of the several Yorkshire captains between Lord Hawke and Brian Sellers, all were gentlemen and players of merit, though not of equal merit, and it can be said without disrespect to any of them that Sellers, during the 1930s, was an outstanding leader.

Sellers came to the captaincy after the first half-dozen matches of 1932, when that dashing bat and daring close field, Frank Greenwood, was obliged to resign for family and business reasons, and at once he made his mark, not spectacularly but steadily. He was the son of Arthur Sellers, a notable opening batsman of the 1890s, and he took steps to improve his batting but, from first beginnings, he had something else to bring that was of greater moment than sound batsmanship, important as that may be. Force of character is easy to recognize, but hard to describe. On the silver screen it may be portrayed by glaring eyes, corrugated brows and a voice like the bark of a neurotic bulldog. Anybody who has ever met true force of character knows what a ludicrous travesty that is, for force may go with a quiet voice and good manners.

Cricket is a game, but in Yorkshire they follow the scriptural injunction: whatsoever thy hand findeth to do, do it with all thy might. You naturally keep the laws and play fair, but within the game's written and unwritten rules, you strain every nerve to win. If you are the sort of person who couldn't care less whether you win or not, you are poor in spirit, but undeserving of any beatitude. You are paying your honourable opponents a poor compliment if you cannot be bothered to beat them. Without the will to win on both sides no game would be worth while. Sellers was a solid symbol of that will to win to a degree only surpassed (and I would not take two great names in vain) by Grace and Bradman.

Coming into what was an almost terrifyingly powerful eleven, he first took pains to make himself a capable member of it. Every day, at the wicket or on the field, he was learning something. Soon he had turned into a more competent No. 6 batsman and passed the ordeal by intimidation with honours to qualify as a first-class 'suicide' fielder. By the end of his second season the Yorkshire committee were thanking him for his 'splendid example set in the field'. This was something considerably more than a perfunctory compliment to success. They do not very much go in for compliments in Yorkshire, anyhow.

Since the turn of the century, Yorkshire had been a fine fielding side. Gone was the slap-happy period of the early 1890s. In the first decade of the twentieth century Hirst was the finest mid-off, while Tunnicliffe vied with Braund and Denton with Johnny Tyldesley as the greatest slip and the greatest long-field, in the world. Who is the finest mid-off in the world today? I wish I could think of more than two or three batsmen whose off-drive is hard enough and frequent enough to care. The most brilliant fieldsmen of today – Lock, Surridge, Milton, Watkins – are all 'hip-pocket' men.

Tight as was Yorkshire's fielding in the first decade, in the third the grip became even tighter. Some of Yorkshire's young captains of the period, notably Alan Barber and Frank Greenwood, were gallant close fielders; with them fielding was a fine art. In the 1930s Sellers carried the business one step further: from a fine art to a form of psychological warfare, legitimate but loaded with menace. It was, as the fieldsmen might have explained, perfectly easy. 'All right, lad, if you want to shift us, you *shift* us!' But Sellers and his associates were seldom shiftable.

Leading his side out to field, Sellers somehow gave the impression of the buccaneer captain leading his cut-throats aboard the captive brig. Perhaps it was his walk or his expression of cheerful determination, but that is how he always looked to me. His pirate mate was Arthur (Ticker) Mitchell and the other villain was Cyril Turner, a particularly friendly soul, who never snatched an 'impossible' catch off the bat's edge, except in the way of kindness. The effect of this lowering, threatening vigilance was that opponents coming out to attempt a quite moderate fourth innings total were bundled out for scores woefully below their reasonable hopes. A hypnotic influence was in the air. It was as though an invisible choir was ceaselessly chanting: 'You'll never get 'em, you'll never get 'em . . .' When Verity bowled on a wicket that gave him the slightest help, the ball would fly, as though under magnetic compulsion, towards Mitchell, who seemed to have as many arms as a Hindu deity. The batsman was virtually like Lazarus, bound hand and foot with grave-clothes.

In the eight pre-war years when Sellers captained Yorkshire he led them six times to championship victory. In 1946, the extremely difficult season after the war, he stayed on and led them to one more, which made seven out of nine. In the whole period Yorkshire played 258 championship matches and won 154. Only 24 games were lost. These figures, unlike most, are worth remembering. He had a magnificent side to lead: Sutcliffe, Leyland, Mitchell, Barber, and a young lad named Hutton; as bowlers, Bowes, Macauley, Smailes and the incomparable Hedley Verity. But no one can deny that it was magnificently led.

People have said that Brian Sellers was hard. Of course he was hard. So are diamonds. Also like Sellers, they are rare. Of all the captains of all the counties in this or any recent period, and there have been many admirable ones, none has ever matched Brian Sellers for force, for fire, and for the refusal to accept dominance from anybody on earth. For me he will always be the friendly buccaneer, the pirate who weathered the storm.

A. A. Thomson, *Pavilioned in Splendour* (1956)

Washbrook's Lancashire

With the retirement of Nigel Howard as captain after the 1953 season, Lancashire had no alternative to Cyril Washbrook as his successor. And it would have looked silly if they had tried to find one. The only amateur other than Howard to have played in the 1953 season had been twenty-year-old Colin Smith, who was to win a Blue in the following four years at Cambridge University. Lancashire could have gone outside the club as they did in 1962 when Joe Blackledge was appointed, but with a player of the stature of Washbrook on hand, it would not only have been folly to have looked outside, it would have been insulting. Washbrook's appointment met with general acclaim and he was to continue to hold the position for six years, until he was forty-four years old. When he took over Lancashire, the team was still in such capable hands as those of Alan Wharton, Geoff Edrich, John Ikin, Ken Grieves, Winston Place, Malcolm Hilton, Brian Statham and Roy Tattersall. A year after he had handed over the captaincy to Bob Barber, only Grieves and Statham of those stalwarts remained and Lancashire were looking to a new, young breed which included such talented players as Barber, Geoff Pullar, Peter Marner, Jack Dyson, Ken Higgs, Tommy Greenhough – all of whom were brought along and capped during Washbrook's captaincy – and Geoff Clayton, capped in 1960. Lancashire finished tenth, ninth, second, sixth, seventh and fifth under Washbrook.

Washbrook was one of the most respected players in the game, a loyal, honest man who believed in the game's customs and disciplines. He had been brought up on stern control and believed in it and it would seem that he had problems bridging the gap with the young players bursting with life and ambition. Life in England had changed dramatically since the war. Men had given their lives for their country and were no longer prepared to be subject to the grave, and often unfair, disciplines of pre-war England. The meek submissiveness had gone and bodies, like cricket clubs, that tried to run their organizations on pre-war lines invariably ran headlong into trouble. Lancashire, unfortunately, continued to run along in this fashion until the committee was overthrown in 1964. Two fine examples of change in outlook were provided by Alan Wharton and Geoff Edrich, who had served in the war. If one word had to be found to sum up the feelings of men such as these, it would be equality.

Wharton came from a strong socialist background and found difficulties adjusting to the conservative world of a members' club in first-class cricket. He had also served in the Royal Navy and it was probably inevitable that he would take on authority when he felt authority was wrong. He became a barrack-room lawyer, capable of standing up for himself . . . and for other people. An incident early in his career illustrates perfectly the change that came over cricket – and life – after the war. He was in a game at Gloucester early in 1946 when he fielded as twelfth man through a long, exhausting Walter Hammond innings. He left the field feeling shattered and as he walked into the dressing room, Dick Pollard called out 'Get me a bloody cup of water, Wharton.' Wharton told Pollard he could get his own cup of water and was probably not surprised when he was later called before a three-man committee for showing insubordination to a senior professional. Wharton pointed out that he could make more money as a teacher and a league professional than he was earning at Lancashire and his suggestion that he was prepared to leave ended with the committee telling him there was no question of discipline. Just a suggestion that he might be more tactful in future. Ten years earlier, and Wharton might not have played for Lancashire again. But now, it was a triumph for the working man, the sort that was to be repeated throughout life in England, especially in industry, for many years after the war. Wharton was as good as anybody and wanted the same respect as the next man.

Geoff Edrich had a similar experience during a match away from home when the players were invited to a Saturday-night dance. There was no cricket on Sundays in those days, but at midnight Pollard started to line up the players, ready for checking before returning to the hotel. Edrich told him he had been a prisoner of war for three and a half years and nobody was going to tell him how to spend his Saturday nights. It took time for those with authority, those brought up on the teachings of pre-war England, to come to terms with the way of things after. Pollard had learned his cricket in the hard school and like others around him no doubt believed it was the right way. So the gap was wider than that of a mere generation; it was one deep-rooted in equality, in fairness of mind. It bred bloody-mindedness, too, and the ability of worker and boss to sort it all out was tested to the full.

John Kay, who was the *Manchester Evening News* cricket writer who followed Lancashire around in those days, wrote:

> Washbrook had been through a hard school and demanded the same sort of dedication, discipline and self control he himself had always practised. He never once spared himself in the cause of Lancashire cricket and expected his men sternly to follow his example so that he became, in a sense, a bogey man to the many newcomers Lancashire fielded in those rebuilding days. He tried desperately hard to see the point of view of the new generation, but instead of becoming a father figure, he assumed, undoubtedly without being aware of it, the role of all-demanding schoolmaster.

Eric Todd, who wrote for the *Manchester Evening Chronicle*, said Washbrook was a lonely man after Place and Ikin retired. 'I have nothing in common with this team,' he once told Todd, who added 'This might have explained why Lancashire won nothing under Washbrook's captaincy, although being unpopular or feared did not affect his own performances.'

Certainly, Lancashire had a good enough side to have won the title, particularly in his final year when Geoff Pullar, Ken Grieves and Alan Wharton all exceeded 2,000 runs with Bob Barber and Peter Marner getting 1,000, and Brian Statham, Ken Higgs and Tommy Greenhough all taking 100 wickets. But Lancashire were fifth that year, 20 points behind the winners, Yorkshire, which was exactly the same margin between themselves and Surrey when they finished runners-up in 1956.

Cyril Washbrook was born in Barrow, the village near Clitheroe, on 6 December 1914, but by the time his cricket was developing sufficiently to attract the interest of Warwickshire and Worcestershire as well as Lancashire, he was attending Bridgnorth Grammar School. He nearly did not join Lancashire. He failed to get into Birmingham University, where he would have taken a degree in brewing, only because he had not done a written paper in art. If he had, and had gone to university, he would have joined Warwickshire as an amateur. Instead he went straight from school to join Lancashire as a professional.

When Washbrook arrived at the railway station for Old Trafford in

April 1933, he was making only his second visit to the ground. A tall man, carrying a bag, had also left the train and the eighteen-year-old Washbrook asked if he could tell him the way to the ground's main entrance. The man said he was going there and would show him the way. 'What are you, a batsman or a bowler?' he asked Lancashire's latest groundstaff recruit. 'A batsman,' said Washbrook. 'There's not much chance for batsmen here,' grunted the man who turned out to be Sydney Barnes, then sixty years old and a bowling coach at Old Trafford. Nevertheless, Washbrook made the sort of immediate impact that must have left the likes of Buddy Oldfield, still waiting for his debut after four years on the staff, scratching his head in wonderment. He scored 202 not out for the second team against Yorkshire, was thrust into the first team, and in only his second game there he scored 152 against Surrey at Old Trafford. He was sitting in the junior players' dressing room later when Barnes came in, patted him on the shoulder, pointed out to the wicket, and said simply 'Well played.'

Washbrook went on to become the county's finest post-war batsman and an opener to stand alongside Archie MacLaren in a Lancashire team of all time. His career spanned twenty-six years and his total of runs for Lancashire – and in all first-class matches – stands third behind only Ernest and J. T. Tyldesley. But for the war he would have been Lancashire's most prolific run-scorer. In the five years up to the war he scored nearly 8,000 runs for Lancashire alone; in the five years after he scored more than 8,000. A similar volume of runs in the six years of the war would have taken him to over 36,000 for Lancashire – against the 27,863 (34,101 in all matches) he scored – and would have given him a hundred centuries. Washbrook scored seventy-six centuries – fifty-eight of them for Lancashire – and believes he would have reached 100 regardless of the war if he had not become captain. 'I began to bat a little lower in the order to strengthen the middle of the batting,' he said. 'At that stage we were either in the cart or not going quickly enough, and I got out a number of times after getting 50 when normally, as opener, I would have gone on to a hundred.' Washbrook scored six centuries in his first two seasons as captain, but only one, against Hampshire in his last season, in the last four years. 'I was very proud to be captain of Lancashire,' he said. 'But it was a position I never coveted. I enjoyed it but I'm not sure I wouldn't have been happier just to have continued opening and scoring more runs. But I was a lucky captain. I had a decent set of chaps and I was the Boss and they knew I was the Boss.'

When Washbrook retired, he had completed exactly 500 games for the county, a figure exceeded only by Jack Sharp, Ernest and J. T. Tyldesley. He regards the high spot of an illustrious career, which included thirty-seven Test matches with six centuries and 2,569 runs for an average of 42.81, as being asked to tour Australia, which he did twice. And one of the greatest moments of his career, naturally, was the 98 he scored against the Aussies in 1956 when he was recalled to the team at the age of forty-one and after a six-year absence. He was a Test selector himself at the time and was asked by the chairman, Gubby Allen, to go and order the beer while they discussed him. 'He told me I had been chosen and I said "Surely the situation isn't as desperate as all that." But you don't refuse to play for England and I don't appreciate players today opting out of Test matches. I was very glad to get to 98 in that Test match but another two wouldn't have done any harm. But I was pleased not to have let my co-selectors down.' Washbrook became a member of Lancashire's committee soon after his retirement as a player and, apart from a two-year break, stayed on until 1988 when he was elected President, only the second professional player after Len Hopwood to be so honoured.

Washbrook was a magnificently aggressive batsman in the Golden Age mould, one who took the attack to the bowler, and was one of the finest cover fielders in England, following a great Lancashire tradition. He would have made just as good an amateur player as he did a professional, perhaps even better if he had been totally released from the reins in which professionalism naturally held him. He once said he would like to be remembered by people because he provided entertainment. He can rest assured he did that.

Washbrook launched his six years as club captain by scoring a century against Glamorgan at Old Trafford in the opening game of the 1954 season. By July, he had moved down the order, and apart from a game against Surrey as opener on a difficult Oval wicket in 1958, that was where he was to stay. It was a wet summer. In fact, four of Washbrook's six seasons as captain were wet and miserable. In 1954, nineteen full days were lost, eleven of them at Old Trafford where two complete games were washed out. Lancashire played at Bath again this year, scene of the one-day match the previous year when Bertie Buse's benefit was ruined and Roy Tattersall took thirteen wickets for 69 runs. Somerset were bowled out cheaply again in 1954, for 173 and 119 . . . but Tattersall, who took 113 wickets this year, did not take one at Bath.

This was the period when Surrey dominated the championship with seven successive title wins and in Washbrook's first five years of captaincy Lancashire lost six of their matches against Surrey with the other two drawn. Games against Surrey always put Lancashire firmly in their place and the 1955 game was a fine example where Lancashire lost by an innings and 143 runs after winning the toss and being dismissed for 94 and 108. Surrey, meanwhile, lost only three wickets with Peter May and Ken Barrington scoring centuries.

Washbrook's highest score as captain came in the 1955 match against Worcestershire at Old Trafford when he scored 170 in the eight-wicket win. A last-wicket partnership put on 73, with Roy Tattersall scoring only 5 of them. An outstanding innings from Brian Statham, who scored only five half-centuries in 647 innings, was a rare occasion. And the one to savour most came against Leicestershire at Old Trafford in 1955 when he scored 62 in 31 minutes with twelve 4s, two 6s and two singles, before taking four for 34 in the innings win. Statham recalled it as a good, old-fashioned slog. 'I thought for a minute I was a batsman,' he said. 'But Cyril wasn't too impressed. "Tell that silly young bugger to get out now," he said. He wanted me to bowl for the last half hour.' Another swashbuckling innings that year was provided by Malcolm Hilton who scored his only century, 100 not out in two hours, to take Lancashire from 218 for seven to 372 for nine declared at Northampton. His bowling after that was not quite as impressive as Statham's. He took one for 137 in sixty-one overs.

Brian Bearshaw, *From the Stretford End* (1990)

Daffodil Summer

In the fading August of 1948, on a day by the southern seaside, J. C. Clay, the gentleman of Glamorgan, bowled a measured off-break which struck Charlie Knott, of Hampshire, on the pad. The story has it that Dai Davies, the umpire, a brown, beaming man, raised a dramatic finger and, unable to contain himself, bellowed at Knott: 'You're *out* – and *we've* won!'

Glamorgan had indeed won. Not only a remarkable match, but the County Championship, and for the first time. On that dun afternoon in Bournemouth the pavilion trembled with Welsh singing, voices that floated over the English regular roses, causing raised eyebrows among the gardens and where the band was playing by the sea.

For Johnnie Clay, the lean, grey man, wise as a heron, the triumph had come in his fiftieth year and after seasons of failure, disappointment, even ridicule, for his beloved county. I remember that day, trotting on my trivial rounds as a junior reporter on a local newspaper in Essex, hearing the wonderful news on the radio while I was cross-examining a lady about the thrills and spills of the Women's Institute flower arranging contest. 'Why,' she asked briskly, 'are you grinning like that? Flower arranging is *no* laughing matter.' 'I'm sorry,' I remember saying, knowing she would never understand. 'I'm doing it because I'm happy.'

Happy indeed I was, along with a throng of others. Of the four hundred telegrams sent to Arms Park, Cardiff, the next day was one from an exile in Paris. The news, he said, had made him decide to return home to Wales. What, after all, had Paris to offer?

For me the love affair was new. It is a confession I hesitate to make, even after these years, but, brought up in wartime Newport, I hardly knew of the *existence* of cricket, until I was gone twelve years. Then, after the war – after I had heard about it and was growing in love for it – one day in 1947, I went for the first time to Lord's and had scarcely had time to place my spam sandwiches and myself on one of the free seats (as they were loftily called) below the heads of the trees at the Nursery End, when I witnessed the most exquisite sight of my youthful life. Willie Jones, small as a button, batting against Middlesex, leaned back, folded his body like a spring, and square cut to the boundary. The ball hit the boards with an echo I can hear now. It was as though he had waited for my arrival, after all those unknowing years. From that moment – and although I had left the Land of my Father's and my birth – I had Glamorgan written on my heart.

The trials of the early days of Glamorgan County Cricket Club are nowhere better contained than in a tale told by Jack Mercer, eighty-odd now. He was a Glamorgan player when almost anyone who owned a bat could get a game. 'We had six captains and five wicket-keepers in one season,' he recalled. 'The oddest people used to turn up and get in the side. A great big fellow was in the team one day and Johnnie Clay, being a gentleman, didn't like to ask him whether he was a batsman or a bowler. So John asked me and I didn't know either. "Well," said Johnnie, "we'll put him in the slips. Even if he can't catch, he's a big chap – something might hit him." '

J. C. Clay, the dear man, the quiet cricketer, in the phrase of Wilfred Wooller, was a member of the side which first played in the County Championship in 1921. The application for first-class status had been grudgingly approved. Cricket authority sniffed and intoned: 'If you can get eight other clubs to play you, then you are accepted.' Glamorgan got six and Lancashire and Yorkshire agreed at the last moment to join the list. Certainly the Roses Counties never overrated the urchin Welsh team. 'Yorkshire only ever booked a hotel for two nights when they came to Cardiff or Swansea,' sighed Wilfred Wooller.

The team amazed itself and everyone else by winning the opening match against thoroughbred Sussex. From then on it lost. *Wisden*'s comment that Glamorgan's entry into first-class cricket 'was not justified by results' was honestly echoed by the county's annual report which related sadly: '. . . Glamorgan were like no other side; some say it was not a side at all.' The main bowlers were Harry Creber, who was forty-seven and Jack Nash who was forty-eight. In that first season Nash only just missed his hundred wickets.

The sickly infant years were slow to go. After two seasons in county cricket Glamorgan not only had a solitary specialist slip fielder, they were also £6,212 in the red at the bank. But John Clay believed and others joined in his faith. Cricket had never been considered to be a 'Welsh game' but now, from the valleys and the sandy seaside towns of the south, men who could play took tentative steps towards Cardiff. Dai Davies, the man who, as umpire, played his part in the fateful day many years later, Emrys Davies, a staunch opener, Arnold Dyson, a poetic batsman, and, momentously, a man called Maurice Turnbull.

Turnbull, as captain and secretary, pulled Glamorgan up by the laces of its cricket boots. He organized both the bowling and the finances, he made centuries and friends, he was as articulate in the chair as he was in the field. He was the first Glamorgan cricketer to play for England and then – outrageously – he was killed in the war before all his selfless work came to splendid justification.

In the final seasons before the war the county finished in positions of untold respectability – midway up the table. At that time Wilfred Wooller first walked out to bat, the rugby hero come to the summer game. A big man, combative, unyielding, some said, and still do, too forthright, but a leader born to lead. He was to be Glamorgan's man of destiny. But first he had to wait six years and a war.

They say that when Wilfred Wooller played his first match after his repatriation from a Japanese prison camp and went out to the wicket, tears were running down the cheeks of grown men.

'Like a big skeleton, he was,' an uncle of mine told me. 'And yellow.'

But it would have taken more than the Japanese to daunt Wooller. 'We played a game at Changi prison camp in Singapore on Christmas Day,' he remembers. 'Somehow we found a ball and a bat and we made some stumps. We had an England versus Australia Test match right there in front of the Japanese guards. They looked puzzled.'

Forty years on Wooller is still a big man, tall, unstooping, broad-shouldered, broad faced. He prowls rather than walks. A man like a large leopard. His was the sad but familiar story of a return from years of captivity and privation only to find that life had changed behind his back. His pre-war marriage was quickly over. 'I remember getting in my car and driving from London up the Great North Road – anywhere,' he said. 'I had no idea where I was going.' The road, oddly, led to Africa and a frightening adventure in a crash-landing airplane which made him, abruptly, realize that life was still precious. He decided to do something with his – and returned to Wales to become captain of a Glamorgan team that was to make history.

'At the beginning there was really only half a team,' he recalled. 'The remnants of what we had before the war. But there was a new generation of young cricketers wanting to play, boys like Phil Clift, Gilbert Parkhouse and Alun Watkins, all gifted, all eager. Then we took on some chaps from outside, players that their own counties had decided they did not want.' Three of those cricketers, Len Muncer, Norman Hever and a lad called Eaglestone, were from the richly endowed Middlesex team. With the rag-tag-and-bobtail already assembled in Cardiff they became, under the steely leadership of Wooller, a side of supermen.

It was Johnnie Clay that Wooller patently admired and still remembers with affection. 'He was the most wonderful of men. Quiet, a true gentleman. He loved cricket and lived for it. All the winter he bowled on a practice wicket in his garden. But he was never so serious that his sense of humour would not come bubbling out. One day we were playing against Somerset and C. C. C. Case – "Box" as they used to call him – was batting. He was always a difficult man to get out, he would block ball after ball and never take risks, and on this day Johnnie Clay became so exasperated with the stone walling that he substituted a rubber ball for the cricket ball and bowled that. You should have seen Box's face when the thing took off vertically right in front of his nose.'

Alun Watkins, a Plymouth Argyle footballer, a man built like an arm-chair, but not in the least static, came into the side. He was a pugnacious batsman (I once saw him hit a ball for four to leg – after it had passed the wicket-keeper), a good medium pace left-arm bowler. He was also a fine close-to-the-wicket fielder, one of the clutch which Wooller recruited, taught, inspired, and to whom he gave faith. Wooller says: 'In the season we won the Championship there were plenty of county sides who had far better batting than us, and quite a number with better bowling. But not one had a more brilliant fielding side.'

The county which, only a generation before, had only one man brave enough to call himself a slip fielder, and which had found it necessary to 'hide' four old men in the field, now had a roost of men who were capable of the most miraculous catching feats. Wooller remembered how Ernie Toshack, the Australian, had bowled to a leg-side close field and he employed that in his Glamorgan team. Around the corner the Glamorgan fielders loitered like shop-lifters. 'Our secret weapon,' smiled Wooller. 'In our championship season Watkins, Phil Clift and I took about 120 catches.'

Emrys Davies and Arnold Dyson opened the batting, until the veteran Dyson went to take a coaching appointment at Oundle School, reappearing to play a notable part in the finale to the Championship. Both players from Glamorgan's days of struggle, acquainted with grief, they gave their sober experience to the younger players of the side. Emrys coached the elegant Gilbert Parkhouse and the dapper Phil Clift who became his opening partner. He would stare down the wicket at Clift like a minister in chapel. 'Emrys was a good man, a sober, dedicated fellow, a great father-figure to the team,' said Wooller. Arnold Dyson studied the game every moment, winter and summer. They used to say that he was such a perfectionist that if he touched a catch to slip he always walked even if it were dropped. Morally he was out.

Willie Jones, the bean-sized batsman, topped the county batting averages that summer of 1948, amazingly hitting *two* double centuries but no single centuries. Welsh-speaking Willie had to be encouraged, bolstered. After scoring two thousand runs in a season he was worried in case his contract was not renewed. He never went to the wicket without trembling, scarcely believing that he was capable of doing the things he did. Jones played his favoured square-cut like a man prodding a bear. At Gravesend, against Kent, in June he scored 207. 'When he came in after batting,' remembers his captain, 'his hand was shaking so much he could hardly hold a glass of orange squash. "I'll never be able to do that again, skipper," he mumbled.' A week later he *did* it again – 212 not out against Essex, with Emrys Davies getting 215 in a total of 586 for 5 declared.

They used to call Haydn Davies, the wicket-keeper, the Panda. He was large and dark of head and eye and adopted the stance of that curious, benign and powerful creature. For all his heaviness, both in body and aspect, he was the lively one, the joker, the charmer, the boy for a night out, even when the stern Wooller disapproved. 'He telephoned me one day and said, "Skipper, I've got a broken finger," ' said Wooller. 'I asked him what he intended to do about it and he said, "I'll go on playing. I'll try to keep it out of the way." '

There were others who came in and out of the side as the summer progressed, George Lavis, Jim Pleass, and an absorbing spin bowler from Swansea eponymously named Stan Trick. 'He worked in his father-in-law's garage and he couldn't always get away to play,' smiled Wooller slowly shaking his head. 'But the Swansea wicket was made for him. There he was just about unplayable.' In his first match at the St Helen's ground against Somerset, he took six wickets for 77 in the first innings and six for 29 in the second. But only at Swansea could he do it. They said his sort of bowling didn't travel well.

Of the three imported players, all from Middlesex, the most significant was Len Muncer, a beaming, oval-faced spin bowler, approaching his final seasons. He got through twice as many overs as anyone else, apart from Wooller, and took 156 wickets in the season at an average of 17.12. He was also only just short of a thousand runs. Young Eaglestone batted soundly when he was needed and Norman Hever, the fast bowler, topped the first-class averages for some weeks. At Lord's against Middlesex, the county which had rejected him, he took five wickets for 34. With relish.

But Glamorgan were never players of mere matches. They had the fun and charm and good companionship of a touring repertory company. J. B. G. Thomas, the legendary sports editor of the *Western Mail*, travelled around with them that Daffodil Summer. 'They had an old mangle, the sort your mam used to have at home, and this was transported on the back of a little lorry, together with a pile of tattered, suspicious-looking blankets,' he remembers. 'If Glamorgan arrived at a ground and there had been overnight rain then everybody would set-to spreading the blankets and putting them through the mangle to get the pitch fit for play.'

'They were a lovely bunch of boys. I don't think they quite knew what was happening to them when they won the Championship that summer.' Bryn Thomas would travel by train with the team, sometimes taking his infant son along also. 'We used to be crowded into the compartment, talking cricket, laughing, a whole bunch of us, and little Craig would be up in the luggage rack, staring over the top, taking it all in.' Such an exotic childhood, travelling suspended above those gods, no doubt gave Craig Thomas the seed he needed to become the successful novelist he is today.

The first match of the 1948 season told nothing of the amazements that were to follow over the sunny early weeks. Glamorgan played a friendly game against Thomas Owen's XI, an occasion which, however, was not without its oddities. The year was scarcely out of winter and the conditions were chill, indeed so inclement that Maurice Leyland 'retired hurt' in the visitors' first innings. He had cramp. Emrys Davies, grey as the weather, assembled a painstaking 31 before being dismissed by Len Hutton, a thoughtful bowler in those days, who took two further wickets in the Glamorgan innings at a cost of 22 runs. Sporting declarations in the weather-washed game resulted in Thomas Owen's team being required to score 85 in 45 minutes to win. They were four runs short at the end. One of the umpires was Douglas Jardine. I wish I had seen him. And Hutton bowling.

Another friendly, against Somerset, was played at Newport where once, it was gossiped, the wicket was prepared with more than a touch of witchcraft. Certainly, before the war, the Glamorgan groundsman was rumoured to have prepared a strip of mystic components including silt from the River Taff, coal dust from the River Ebbw and mud from the River Usk 'all boiled up in a Welsh cauldron'. It was forecast that the potion would help the Glamorgan spinners against Gloucester in the summer of 1938. Gloucester made 581 of which Hammond got 302. He liked batting on coal dust.

The 1948 match against Somerset at Newport went better for the Welshmen. Somerset crumpled to the diminutive spin of Willie Jones (who also got 93) and lost by 98 runs.

Essex next were defeated at Cardiff (where the cricket ground was behind the Arms Park rugby stand) by five wickets; then Somerset again at Swansea with Stan Trick from the garage, taking his famous twelve wickets. At Derby, at the end of May, against a strong bowling side, came defeat by the not inconsiderable margin of 301 runs. But there followed three successive triumphs – against Kent at Gravesend (Willie Jones's nervous double hundred) and versus Hampshire at Cardiff, where Hampshire scored a hundred in an hour, going for victory, and were then summarily dismissed in the next hour, mostly by the flighted left-arm bowling of, once again, Willie Jones. 'He made the ball 'ang in the air, aye like a grape,' my old uncle said.

Kent were humbled at Swansea in June, Stan Trick, having more time off from the grease pit, taking ten wickets and Len Muncer eight. More than 30,000 people watched this match over the three days, the multitude that were to follow Glamorgan throughout the season. Wooller, the rugby man, the winter hero, was bringing Welshmen out of the valleys to see a different game, but one which they embraced with hardly less heart and, naturally, with as much singing. It was the first time choral works had been heard at first-class matches.

The uplift was needed, not only in Wales but throughout a Britain bled grey by a war that had finished three years before. Clothes and food were still rationed, there were shortages of almost everything. But the pundits were unimpressed. 'It was not a vintage year,' decided a cricket aristocrat. He was one of many who refused to believe that this unfashionable, even *foreign*, county could actually win. Victory after victory was discounted even when the Welshmen led the table in June, and the setback period which followed in July was acknowledged by those who knew, or thought they did, as only right and to be expected. Lesser counties simply did not ascend like larks. At the end there was a multitude who were not so much surprised as shocked. It was as though the prize had been taken by stealth.

That same season up and down England, in the Test matches and through the counties, went the conquering Australians on their first postwar tour. They scored seven hundred runs *in one day* against Essex at Southend.

At the Oval, England were briskly dealt with: all out for 52. Don Bradman walked out for his farewell innings. He was cheered and applauded all the way to the middle, only to return minutes later in the silence of disbelief – bowled by Hollies for no score. I was there in that throng. I had never seen him bat and now I never would.

On that day Alun Watkins played his first match for England, and received such a battering from Lindwall, that he was too bruised to play in the historic game at Bournemouth which took the Championship.

Meanwhile Glamorgan appeared to have lost their way. They fell to Middlesex and to Leicestershire and there came a faltering series of drawn games, partly through the summer weather turning sour. The game with the Australians never came to any flourish, although with lumpy rain clouds hanging on the Bristol Channel and not an inch of room in the ground, Keith Miller made 84 in the only innings, which came to a stop in a downpour with the tourists at 215 for 3. In another July game Gunner G. A. R. Lock, playing for Combined Services, the only squaddie in the parade of lieutenant colonels, squadron leaders and commanders, took six wickets for 43, a taste of the great days that were to come for him with Surrey and with England.

A victory against Warwickshire, at Neath, kept Glamorgan's nose near the top of the table and then came, in mid-August, with the Welsh weather mending, a wonderful and crucial victory against Surrey at Cardiff. Wilfred Wooller's brave batting, driving and hammering square cuts, ensured a Glamorgan total of 239. Wooller scored 89, his best of the season. Then Johnnie Clay, coming into the team in the absence of Watkins, and having reached the age of fifty, bowled out one of the strongest counties in England for 50 runs. Clay took five wickets and when Surrey followed on took another five. The long, frail, silver man was almost bowled over himself as the Arms Park Welshmen charged across the pitch at the end to acclaim him and the Glamorgan team. The smell of success was in the Cardiff air and very sweet it was.

And so to the final match against Hampshire, at Bournemouth – not the *last* match of the season but the one that had to be won. 'It needed to be then,' remembered Wilfred Wooller laconically. 'Because the last game was at Leicester.' Jack Walsh, the Australian-born spin bowler, played for Leicester and Wooller's team knew they would be pressed to scrape even a draw on the home side's wicket. (So it proved for, having secured the Championship, Glamorgan went to Leicester and were soundly beaten by an innings – the second time that the Midlands county had defeated them that season.)

The habitual champions, Yorkshire, who might have finally overtaken Glamorgan, were engaged against Somerset at Taunton, on the other side of Dorset, and Glamorgan began their innings at Bournemouth with conspiratorial clouds on the sea. Arnold Dyson, on holiday from his school coaching, was asked to play because Phil Clift was injured. Johnnie Clay came into the side instead of the Test-match-bruised Alun Watkins. Both replacements played crucial roles in the events of the next two days.

Emrys Davies and Dyson went forth to bat. Emrys's wife went off to walk around the town. As she shopped she listened for sounds from the ground.

Only ten minutes after the innings had begun dull summer raindrops sent the players to the pavilion and there they remained for the rest of the day, staring out at that most glum of views, the English seaside in the wet.

Sunday was spent wondering. On Monday the skies appeared kinder and once more Emrys and Arnold went to the middle. There now remained eleven and a half hours to win the match. The pair batted steadily as the clock turned, but knowing that the time would come for acceleration. Dyson was out for 51, trying to force the tempo, and at lunch Glamorgan were 99 for one wicket. Willie Jones emerged (tentatively) and, locking up his dashing shots, stared low and anxiously down the wicket at the fiercely advancing Shackleton, one of England's finest pace bowlers.

In mid-afternoon Emrys stroked (yes, *stroked*) a six, an extravagance greeted with almost chapel-like pursed lips from the Welshmen present. Emrys smiled apologetically. Willie sidled his way past his fifty, and when Emrys was eventually out for the most important 74 he had ever accumulated, the unassuming little man from the valleys assumed the mantle, stitched his way patiently through the whole innings while Wooller and Len Muncer and Norman Hever, at the tail, threw their bats. The side were all out for 315, Jones returning, smiling unsurely, with 78 not out.

It was still only early evening and the Hampshire openers, Arnold and Rogers, went out with over an hour left to play. Wooller and Hever bowled. In the captain's second over Rogers played a true leg glance and Gilbert Parkhouse, who had failed with the bat, swooped like a local gull to catch the ball an inch from the ground and no more than three yards from the bat. It was the catch that made Glamorgan really *believe* they could do it. Before the end of play on that brief evening six Hampshire batsmen were back in the pavilion. Glamorgan went to bed looking forward to the morning.

There seemed hardly room or time to breathe on that ground the next day. Not long ago I played in a match there and I sat after the game, in the lemon sun of the evening, years later, trying to imagine how it had been. Wooller, seriously, sent a telegram to Somerset playing Yorkshire at Taunton. The two counties, having for so long been treated lightly, disdainfully, had a mutual bond, and the message 'Hold on to Yorkshire. We're beating Hants' was received and understood. 'Don't worry,' came the reply. 'We're beating Yorkshire.'

With that assurance Glamorgan set about the Hampshire second innings. Every so often a whisper would go from the pavilion around the crowd that Somerset were keeping their word.

John Clay had been out early to sniff the salty air. He pressed his finger tips into the wicket and knew everything would be all right. The information he kept private. He and the oval-faced Len Muncer finished Hampshire for 84. There were now four hours during which to get them out a second time.

Arnold and Rogers batted without any crisis for twenty minutes and four hours began to look a short time indeed. Then young Hever got one under Rogers's bat, pitched right up and moving a shade. Clean bowled. Hope rekindled.

Desmond Eagar, a fine player, charged the Glamorgan bowlers, hitting Willie Jones for a six that came near to disturbing people on the beach. But Muncer and Clay came back and that was enough. Muncer curled one around Eagar's feet to bowl him. The next man Bailey was promptly run out and the two spinners, so disparate in physique and style, whittled their way through the tail. Muncer had claimed five wickets in the first Hampshire innings and Clay three. Now it was the tall Johnnie's turn. The man who had played in Glamorgan's first county match in 1921, bowled as he had never bowled before. By the time he had Knott lbw, and had received the historical affirmative from Dai Davies (Knott swears to this day that the umpire appealed as well!), he had taken six for 48. It was still only mid-afternoon.

So there it was. The miracle at last. They still talk about it in Wales and wherever one Welshman meets another. It was wonderful that time long ago. That Daffodil Summer.

Leslie Thomas, *County Champions* (1982)

Greater than Grace?

Just to see him walk to the wicket was to appreciate that here was majesty. Gloucestershire cricket enthusiasts watched him bat with the same exhilaration and admiration as their predecessors had done for W.G.

Those were the days of midday newspapers which gave the latest cricket scores in the stop press. If they showed that Wally Hammond was batting, many offices and factories and not a few schools suddenly found that some of their members had urgent business elsewhere!

Like all great batsmen he learned the value of each of his repertoire of shots; he reduced the margin of error in those he used most to nil. He never hooked anything but the rankest long-hop, and that was dispatched to some distant roof. His front foot driving, straight or through the covers, was perfection. The ball flashed from his bat literally scorching its track through the grass to the boundary. What must be a true story relates to an energetic young amateur darting about fruitlessly at extra cover trying to lay a hand on any one of his thundering drives. Hammond called out, 'Don't worry, sonny, I won't hit you.' He was just as deadly off his back foot. The ball was hit with the same certainty and force through the gaps.

Bowlers without the surest control were destroyed and right-arm leg spinners were particularly vulnerable. Tommy Mitchell, Derbyshire and Test leg-spinner, was once driven to such distraction that he left the field in despair. Wally Hammond perfected the sweep to leg. Front foot outstretched, bat parallel with the ground, and the best googlies to drop outside the off stump were casually swept to leg at the angle of Hammond's choosing.

Gloucestershire cricket with Wally Hammond in the full flow of his run making was not quite the soliloquy it had been when W.G. held the stage. It must have held good in both cases that often the others tended to be mere cyphers. When batting with him the main responsibility of the other batsmen, besides admiring his superb craftsmanship, was to run when called, generally for two, but above all to learn to count to five and run on the sixth ball of the over to give him strike.

There was an aloof side to his character. Keeping the world at arm's length, like all great batsmen (the same doesn't seem to apply to bowlers) he could become bored with the mundane. Some personal animosity with an opposing bowler or a challenge, perhaps mischievously engineered by Bev Lyon who alone could motivate him; or a great occasion would bring to the fore his competitive instinct.

Wally Hammond made the first of his 167 centuries in 1923. It was his third at the end of the following season in that sensational game against Middlesex when Charlie Parker took a hat-trick in each innings, that gave the cricket world a foretaste of his exceptional talent. In the second Gloucestershire innings he made 174 not out in less than four hours on a turning wicket.

He reserved cricket's greatest ever all-round performance for the 1928 Cheltenham Festival. He had made his first overseas tour to the West Indies during the winter of 1925–26. He contracted a disease there which kept him out of the 1926 season and he spent most of the summer in hospital where one of his visitors was Gilbert Jessop. He celebrated his return to cricket in 1927 with 1,042 runs in May and so emulated W.G's feat of 1895, with the significant difference that all his (Hammond's) runs were for Gloucestershire. The first of the Cheltenham Festival games in 1928 was against Surrey. He made 139 and 143 in the two innings and took 10 catches in the game. Worcestershire followed. In 10.2 overs his cutters and off-spinners brought him 9 wickets for 23 runs. Charlie Parker took the tenth wicket – caught Hammond. In the second Worcestershire innings his analysis was 6 for 105 in 33.3 overs. Charlie Parker was the only other bowler involved. His 33 overs brought him 4 wickets for 31 runs. Wally's batting was almost a failure in the only innings Gloucestershire needed to defeat them; he made 80 out of a Gloucestershire total of 370 for 6 wickets.

In two successive games he had made 363 runs, taken 16 wickets and made 11 catches. That season his tally was 2,825 runs, 84 wickets and 78 catches.

Greater than Grace?

Gloucestershire had now returned to the top echelons of the game. They were fifth in the County Championship of 1928 and fourth in 1929 although in many senses it had been a better year. They had lost their chance of winning the Championship in a one run defeat by Sussex at the Cheltenham Festival. They had won sixteen games. They were second in 1930 and second again in 1931.

In the period 1923 to 1930 two others were to establish themselves as mainstream cricketers. The first was Charles Christian Ralph Dacre, son of the Auckland harbourmaster from nearby Devonport, New Zealand, born 15 May 1899, who came over on that country's first tour as batsman and reserve wicket-keeper. He introduced himself dramatically to Gloucestershire, playing for New Zealand at the Cheltenham Festival in 1927 having already scored 101 and 107 in his first two games of the tour. He opened the innings and in thirty minutes had made 64, including five sixes, out of 82 for the first wicket. This was the very natue of his batting. Small of stature, immensely strong and nimble footed with a devil-may-care approach to both life and the game, he thought only in terms of attacking the bowling. Too often this led to his downfall. He had to serve the stipulated two-year qualification for the County. He made a century, 100 not out, against Oxford University in the first game when he officially joined the County in 1930.

In 1926 the Committee, in its increasingly discouraging search for new talent, set up a Cricketer Nursery at the Fry's Ground. Percy Mills, who was approaching the end of his long career, was the coach. When he moved on to Radley College, Charlie Dacre was temporarily in charge. The Bristol Rugby Club had kindly made its facilities available for the cricket nursery and the gym was used for the indoor nets, with the outdoor in the dead ball area at the club house end of the ground. Charlie Dacre's batting philosophy seemed to be directed entirely to hitting the ball out of the ground. He batted like Jessop must have batted; all exciting, explosive aggression.

Charles John Barnett, born in Cheltenham in July 1910, was the son of C. S. Barnett who had played for the County in 1904 and had occasionally captained the team before his retirement in 1926. From his earliest days Charles had shown himself a cricketer of the greatest potential and made his debut in 1927 when still a boy at Wycliffe College. He never did completely lose the inherent impetuosity that at first led too often to losing his wicket and slowed his maturity. He did not make 1,000 runs in a season until 1930 and his first century in 1933. Having become a professional in 1929 he might be classed as a batsman who bowled and he was at all times a brilliant outfielder. A serious minded cricketer with supreme confidence and a deep perception of the game, in 1930 his greatest cricket was yet to come.

Soon after daybreak on Tuesday, 26 August 1930, spectators began to gather outside the Fry's ground. The Australians were in town and Wally Hammond was 76 not out. Crowded trams trundled up the Gloucester Road and disgorged their passengers who poured off down Nevil Road to join the queues at the entrance. Long before the start of play the gates were closed on the eighteen thousand lucky people crammed inside. They were to live through the most dramatic day's play in the history of the Club.

The Australians had arrived in Bristol cock-a-hoop after thrashing England by an innings and 39 runs in the Oval Test. They had made 695 in their one innings and their brilliant young star, Don Bradman, still only twenty-one, had made 232.

Rain delayed the start on Saturday and play was not possible before 4 o'clock. Victor Richardson, the Australian captain, won the toss and put Gloucestershire in to bat. Two and a quarter hours later, at the end of the day's play, they were all back in the pavilion for 72 runs. The wicket had not dried completely by Monday morning. The great crowd seemed resigned to spend the day watching the Australians amass another great total. Then suddenly their batting began to fall apart. It started when Reg Sinfield brilliantly caught Bradman off Charlie Parker for 42. Tom Goddard then bowled brilliantly, 5 for 52, and the Australians were all out for 157. The wicket became easier for Gloucestershire's second innings. By the end of play they had cleared their deficit and were 147 for 3. Wally Hammond was at his absolute best.

He continued for only a short while on the third morning. Gloucestershire made little headway after he was out for 89. Their innings closed at 202, just 117 ahead.

Bev Lyon opened the second Australian innings with Charlie Parker and Tom Goddard bowling. Jackson and McCabe opened for Australia and soon made 59. The game seemed set for conclusive formality. It is reported that some of their lower order batsmen took the opportunity to change and go down to Gloucester Road for a haircut! Suddenly the score slipped to 67 for 3 wickets. They were hurriedly recalled.

The final drama really began when Charlie Parker bowled the young Bradman. Then, 81 for 6 wickets was soon 86 for 7. Then began an electric battle of attrition between the Gloucestershire bowlers and the Australian tail enders. Slowly the score rose to 108 for 8 before Jim Seabrook brilliantly caught Grimmett for 12. He had batted an hour for his runs. Ten runs and two wickets to go. Each run was fought for. The crowd cheered every successful ball. The ninth wicket fell at 115. Three runs to win. A wicket or a boundary would settle the game. Walker, the last of the Australians, reached the wicket. The batsmen conferred. Bev Lyon set out his fielders. A leg-bye. Two to win. Amid the tension Tom Goddard bowled a faultless maiden. Hornibrook, the other batsman, took a swing at Charlie Parker and edged the shot. They scampered a run. The scores were level.

Now came the real drama. Two balls of that over were still remaining. The buzz of excitement snapped to a frightening silence before he bowled each ball, only to burst out again as each moment of crisis passed. The tension persisted through Tom Goddard's next over, a maiden. Now it was Charlie Parker's turn again.

It was indeed palpitation time. The silences and the explosive cheering greeting each ball increased. The Bristol ground was no place for trembling knees or weak stomachs. Imperturbable as ever he drew on all that experience gained from many a long day's exhausting bowling. A maiden. Fourteen balls had now been bowled with the scores level. Tom Goddard came up for his thirty-fifth over. The first ball rapped Hornibrook's pads. Goddard swung round at umpire Buswell, boomed off his foghorn appeal. Up went his finger with the assured finality that brooks no argument. Pandemonium broke out. The excitement that had been building throughout the day and during those fifteen final balls exploded. The crowd shouted its relief, swarmed on to the field, engulfed the Gloucestershire players, chaired Charlie Parker and Tom Goddard to the pavilion steps. They had bowled every ball of that never-to-be-forgotten final innings.

The crowd gathered in front of the pavilion and demanded speeches from the two captains, who replied suitably, and acclaimed the Gloucestershire players. A memorable day.

It is only right that Bev Lyon should have had the final word. Someone asked him for his impressions of the day. He replied, 'Any captain can win or lose a game against the Australians, but there are bloody few who can tie one.'

Grahame Parker, *Gloucestershire Road* (1983)

From the Nursery End

It was a grey March day in 1932 with the lumpy clouds overhead looking, as a friend of mine once said, 'like school potatoes', that Laurie Gray and I had a trial at Lord's for the MCC ground staff. We had been recommended by Jack Durston, and when Mr Ronny Aird, the Assistant

Secretary, met us he quickly put us at ease with his quiet charm, and asked us to bowl to him. The wicket was matting on concrete, and we bowled away industriously as the cold wind whistled through the tea gardens. After ten minutes of coping most courageously with a very hostile Laurie, Mr Aird invited us both to join the MCC ground staff.

Some weeks later we reported to the ground staff room by the Nursery Clock Tower. Here we were received by our future colleagues with considerably less courtesy than had been shown by Mr Aird. There was no cricket gear in sight, but there were plenty of cloth caps, grey flannels, and old mackintoshes. The place seemed dampish and smelled vaguely of old hymn books – although there weren't any hymn books there.

For us there was very little cricket to begin with, instead we pulled the heavy roller, sold match cards, and became very handy with the besom. You had to prove yourself in the first place under Harry White, the head groundsman. Harry was an old Hertfordshire batsman, and I remember he used to play cut shots with a cricket stump he always carried as we hauled the heavy roller up and down with Ted Swannell, the present head groundsman, 'in the shafts'. Harry's word was law, and, since the clock ruled everything in those days, latecomers, and they were few, got the rough edge of his tongue, and only one man ever defied him. This offender strolled up one morning an hour late – then, watched by the dazed roller crew and an open-mouthed Harry, he prodded the turf with his umbrella and remarked, genially, 'Nice wicket you've got here, White.' The outraged Harry leapt profanely in the air slicing his adjectives all over the square, as 'Doc' Gibbons, the offender, later to become a fine Worcestershire opening bat, moved off to change.

We were certainly not over-coached, and 'nets' were rare, but there was plenty of fielding to be done. As the great county players emerged from the gloom under the Father Time Stand for a go at the nets, they would give a nod or a smile, while still maintaining a certain dignified aloofness. We stared, admired, and wished. The Nursery became a Wonderland as we fielded to the Giants – and cricket had made us its slaves. One of the chances for recognition came with the annual two-day Young Amateurs v. Young Professionals match. How desperately we tried to impress George Fenner the MCC coach!

There was quite a bit of cricket to be had by now, and apart from the Sunday matches I had for the Lord's Nippers (who took their colours from a spearmint packet), and for the Odney Club at Cookham, there were the MCC 'out' matches, Middlesex Club and Ground and the Second XI. That great friend of the young pro, Jack Durston, ran the Club and Ground and the Second XI about this time, and, although we gave him many anxious moments, he saw many of us through to the County side.

Going over to the first-class MCC bowling staff was a great day. Now you lived with the Middlesex side, called them 'Patsy' or 'J.W.', and bowled at the nets to MCC members with the rest of the bowling staff, many of whom were Minor County players. Life 'on the rank', as we called this, certainly sharpened the wits because members had varying ideas as to how long a net should last, *and* the size of the tip that went with it, so it took time to form a mental dossier of this important information. Of course the old pros could tell what they paid, to the nearest sixpence, by the car numbers. The old pros would occasionally put you on to a good 'turn' they saw approaching, but they had to be pretty exhausted themselves to do this.

I can remember seeing the late George Robey, a very good club crick-eter, walking past the gaping 'rank' with two old pros marching protec-tively on either side of him. He was worth ten shillings each, a few funny stories, and a drink at the bar on the way back. It was said that these two pros could see George Robey get into a cab in the West End, and hear him say 'Lord's.'

The bliss of hearing that sentence 'You're playing for the County tomorrow' for the first time cannot be described. I played my first match against Cambridge University at Fenner's. I caught and bowled D. R. Wilcox, and returned to Lord's mighty proud. Len Muncer swears to this day that I never gave him back the two shirts I borrowed for the occasion.

The great C. Aubrey Smith would never miss his net when over from Hollywood. I recall seeing him once striding across the middle towards the Nursery wearing a panama hat, blazer and cummerbund all embla-zoned with MCC colours. He was escorted by two young pros who were on a certain five bob each. That day the net wickets were decidedly 'sticky'. For five minutes, before a big crowd, the great man struggled with the conditions against the medium and slow deliveries. As he played the classic back stroke and cocked the left leg he was struck in various parts of the anatomy. Finally his iron control left him as he was struck in the pit of the stomach. He dropped his bat and roared that he had not travelled ten thousand miles to see how well *they* bowled – didn't they know what a half-volley was?

Getting into the County side in those days was well nigh hopeless unless one was blessed with extraordinary talent. If you did get in, the word of the senior pro was law. Before going out to field against Hampshire, about a year later, Patsy Hendren (he was the senior pro) drew me aside and said that the occasional quick one I bowled was no good against these experienced players and was worth fourpennyworth most of the time, therefore cut it out. I promised faithfully that I would do this.

Eventually I was called upon to bowl by Nigel Haig to the great Philip Mead. The wicket was near the Tavern, and from a group of my relations, enthusiastic applause greeted my first two maiden overs. Encouraged by this I foolishly let my quick one go the first ball of my next over. It went 'up the hill' a little, Philip Mead got an outside edge and the ball flew past Patsy's right knee for four against the Pavilion rails. At the end of the over I was given a dressing-down by Patsy in mid-wicket, watched approvingly by the captain, while my relations thought Patsy was apologizing to me for not catching it!

We still spent a lot of time at the nets, watching the young men who followed us on to the ground staff, and getting used to it all. Altogether life consisted of great companionship, much laughter, and very long winters. There was always a chance to succeed if you stuck to it. On looking back I am proud to have played under F. T. Mann (MCC v. Civil Service) and F. G. Mann for Middlesex and England, and that takes a bit of doing. Middlesex won the Championship in 1947 with a great batting side who always made enough runs for us to bowl at, and Laurie Gray and I are two members of that side who won't forget.

That same summer, nine of us, including Bill Edrich and Denis Compton, were returning from a County match in the days when beer was scarce. We were looking for a certain pub which Bill knew as he was stationed in the area during the war; the pub, according to Bill, was run by the greatest poaching publican in the shires. We found the pub at last and nine of us went in. The bar was lit by oil lamps and the publican, who wore a hairy cap, took a lot of persuading before he began to draw nine pints. As he worked he kept his eye on Bill, saying repeatedly 'I know you.' When recognition came he fairly flung his arms around Bill and the tension and the flow of beer were eased. The old publican pointed to a small wooden urn with a silver shield on it, standing on a shelf in the bar.

'A team from Lunnon give us that for beatin' 'em,' he said proudly, then added with feeling, 'Cricketen – that's the finest game a-goin'.' And nine of us who had started 'Cricketen' years ago 'From the Nursery End' looked at each other and reckoned that the old boy was right.

Jack Young, *The Cricketer* (1964)

Exams in the Middle

For us younger ones demobilization was a long time coming. The war had been over a year before I was sent home at last with some months to wait before going up to Oxford as a twenty-five-year-old student with considerable experience of life and death but rather rusty now on book learning. I had been accepted by Christ Church in the first year of war when it appeared I would not be able to join up until twenty, even if the war lasted that long. After taking the entrance examination I had gone into the viva nervously wondering what erudite questions I might be asked on Latin, Greek or history. The Dean sat at the head of an impressive circle of dons as I waited for the probing queries. There was only one. 'Would anyone like to ask Mr Pawson a question?' asked the Dean after a moment's silence. 'I would,' said one don aggressively. 'Will he please tell us why it is that his father was at Christ Church – but his brother has gone to Magdalen?'

An answer on the lines of 'am I my brother's keeper' went down well with the Dean, and concluded the interview. What a change from the modern world in which, if you are trying for Oxford entry, it is best not to mention any sporting ability which might distract you from work, or any family connection which might evoke fear of favouritism.

My first thought for filling in the summer months was to get as much cricket as possible and qualify for the MCC as a playing member. I had had my name put down at birth, but waiting for an ordinary election was then a long business. So I picked the first possible candidates' match and asked to play in the MCC side against University College. The only instructions sent were to go to Golders Green Underground station, which I presumed to be close to the ground. Arriving there with almost an hour to spare, I found an interminable wait for a bus was the unavoidable next step. The bus ride was long and slow and it was just about start time when I was put off at a crossroads and told the College was a mile down the road.

There I ran with the cumbersome cricket bag rubbing the skin off the inside of my knee. At the porter's lodge I was told this was indeed the College, but the cricket ground was a mile the *other* side of the crossroads. It was over an hour late that I arrived at the ground, breathless, and raced to change. As I hurried out, stuffing my shirt into my trousers, I noticed that the College were already 52 for 8. The captain was not impressed with my apology and ended his lecture by shouting, 'And you don't come to play for MCC looking like a jockey. Put your cap on straight.' Somewhat shaken by the tirade, I had time to drop a simple catch at mid-on before the innings ended. 'I understand you don't bowl and you obviously can't field, so I presume you bat,' said the captain, who then invited me to open the innings. The first ball was a half-volley which I drove smoothly past cover for four. The next pitched a little shorter, came back sharply and knocked out my middle stump. In the bar the captain relaxed when the match was well won. 'I wonder would you be any relation of the Pawson who was a good schoolboy cricketer before the war?' My next match for MCC was almost a year later when I was picked to play at Lord's against Melville's South African side, and at least acquitted myself well enough for any more qualifying matches to be waived. But I would relish reading the report on my only other qualifier.

The change in fortune and level of game was even more immediate. After returning home disconsolate, I found a telegram from Kent inviting me to play in Canterbury Week against Hampshire and Somerset. Canterbury Week then was the highlight of the County's cricket and of its social life and at times, indeed, the cricket took second place. The ebullient skipper, Bryan Valentine, made me very welcome and his refreshing enthusiasm even convinced me I might make some runs. But some clearly thought the privilege I had of playing on this occasion seemed too easily won. As I walked down the pavilion steps for my first innings with the score a comforting 257 for 4, a voice said loudly, 'It's ridiculous the committee allowing untried youngsters to play in Canterbury Week.' I had to face George Heath, the fast-medium bowler, who was the mainstay of Hampshire's attack. Again I struck my first ball sweetly through the covers and again the next came sharply back inside my forward stroke. But, instead of the rattle of the stumps, there was an exclamation of disgust from the wicket-keeper as the ball scraped over the bails. And soon I was enjoying myself against the off-spin of Charlie

Knott. It was with incredulity and delight that I realized I had reached ninety and had a century there for the taking on my debut. Tom Spencer, the Test umpire of recent years, had been keeping me company for a time and encouraging the swift running between the wickets I so enjoyed. Now I fell victim to my own exuberance. Having pulled a ball to mid-wicket, I realized the fielder was an occasional player for Hampshire, F. A. V. Parker, who had been clumsy in his picking up and weak in his throwing. So I called loudly to Ridgway 'easy two' and sprinted for the second without looking. Perhaps the call spurred Parker, but his pick-up was clean and the throw arrowed in over the stumps to leave me a yard short.

Another who did not appreciate my eager running was Arthur Fagg. He was a fine bat but a ponderous runner, who hated being called for the short single, which was the main part of my scoring technique. In a subsequent match I called him for several quick singles, all loudly refused. Finally Fagg came heavily down the pitch and said, 'Look here, Mr Pawson, you've only come into the side in August. I'm tired out playing since May. And if you call me for one more quick single I will make *sure* you are run out.'

After a heady start, it was soon down to earth in the Somerset match because I was twice given out for small scores by Frank Chester, the leading umpire of the day, when I knew the decisions to be wrong. First I was given caught at the wicket hooking at Meyer, and then given out the same way in the second innings when I tangled with my pads, playing at Horace Hazell. A batsman always knows if he has given a catch at the wicket and, though I appreciated there had been a noise to mislead the umpire, I knew I hadn't touched the ball.

That is why I never accept the argument that you should always 'walk'. If you always walk when out and have to walk when not out, you give yourself no chance to even the luck. The fairest method is to leave the umpire to decide all appeals and then to accept his decision without question, even if you know it to be wrong either way. On this occasion, Hazell had amused me as well as dismissed me. He was always talking to himself saying, 'pitch it up'. 'Who's your friend, Horace?' I asked after a time. 'That's Harpic – he's clean round the bend, like me.'

That first score of 90 points two differences between the game then and now. No young batsman today gets the chance to go in at 257 for 4 with as long as he likes to take runs off tired bowling. He usually goes in with a few of the hundred overs left and a pressure for instant runs, or with a crisis score after the more experienced have failed. It was an easier initiation in 1946 and the natural expectations then were for fast runs. I had a limited range of strokes and never thought of myself as a quick scorer by the standards of the time, yet *Wisden* records that on my nervous debut my score took only 105 minutes.

I did not yet feel like a first-class cricketer because such runs as I had made had been plundered from bowlers already worn down by Todd, Fagg, Valentine and Leslie Ames, still a sure punisher of any but the best bowling. But a leading team of that season was Glamorgan and my real baptism came when I went in against them at Dover with the score 34 for 3. Wilf Wooller was not a captain to give any favours to a youngster and for an hour I was hemmed in and hard pressed, but a 71 in such circumstances allowed me to feel I could hold my own in this company. Shortly after, Bryan Valentine, who had shared a partnership of 144 with me against Glamorgan, awarded me my county cap. He was taken aback, but accepted it with his usual good humour, when I told him I should miss the next three matches because I was off for a fishing holiday.

It was as a capped county player that I went up to Oxford, so I was assured of a place in the trial matches and in what would now be called the 'squad' of likely university players. Our captain was Martin Donnelly, the powerful left-hander, who ranks as one of the best batsmen New Zealand has produced. I was entertained by his initial talk to us:

'For those of you who haven't played first-class cricket before, a reminder that you have umpires who won't give you out unless they are certain, and you have good sightscreens at either end. So, if you can't make runs here, don't try playing village cricket! I hope you all enjoy your fielding and work hard at it, because if you play for Oxford you will certainly get plenty of it. And a word about catching. If you miss one, don't worry. It could happen to anyone. Concentrate on catching the next. If you miss that, don't worry. Could happen to anyone. Concentrate on catching the next. And if you miss that, don't worry: you won't be playing for us any more.'

Playing in trials had one unexpected advantage. I missed the start of term 'collections' twice in my first year because both the cricket and football trial games happened to coincide with them. So, instead of several hours of exam papers to be immediately answered, I was given the papers to do at leisure and was able to delve back into my notes. I was, therefore, amused to be told at the end of the year that I had been awarded a Fell Exhibition, which apparently was for the best 'collections' from a freshman. The laugh was on me when I asked what the award meant. 'You get a monetary award from the College, but this is then deducted from your small government grant, so you end up where you started.'

This time I did reach a century on my debut. Oxford's first match was against Gloucestershire and, as the wicket was damp, their formidable spinners, Tom Goddard and Charlie Cook, were expected to be deadly. But the ball came slowly off the sodden pitch and Tom's off-spinners invited the hook, which was my favourite stroke. Cook's left-arm spin also tended to pitch short for such a wicket, encouraging my other main stroke, the square-cut. It was a friendly introduction, but like my Fell Exhibition, it may have looked better on paper than it was in practice. It did impress the selectors enough to pick me for the MCC v. South Africa match at Lord's. This first representative match against the tourists is always a feeling-out of possible Test players.

Waiting to bat has always been the worst part of cricket for me. Once at the wicket, my concentration is so total there is no room for worry and, once the first overs are survived and a few runs on the board, then the tension heightens the enjoyment. Batting at first wicket down I spent a long time watching an entertaining opening stand of 121 as 'Dicky' Dodds and Denis Brookes, adventurous stroke inventor and classic stylist, tamed the new ball bowlers and assaulted Athol Rowan and the other spinner. I had stared at every ball, anxious at first lest either got out, then hoping one would so that I could get some action to still my nerves. I was fortunate finally to go out to face a spinner since I played slow bowling much better than fast. Smith was a simple leg-break bowler with no concealed googly, so I went happily along until the second new ball which put me in instant difficulty. Len Tuckett was the quickest of South African bowlers and on the Lord's pitch he moved the ball disconcertingly off the seam. At the other end was Denis Compton, still playing himself in. That was when I realized the gulf between the good county cricketer and the true Test batsman. The sweat poured from me in the intensity of my concentration as I struggled to follow the darting ball, my muscles tense, my hands biting into the rubber in the fierceness of my grip – and still I found it hard to middle the ball. But from the other end I watched Denis play, relaxed and easy, the ball seeming to home to the centre of his bat. When a ball from Tuckett finally flicked my bail, I was so bemused that I did not realize I was bowled until the wicket-keeper told me. In fact, Denis soon got himself out, too, and for half my thirty-four. But I had seen enough of him at close quarters to realize the difference between the instinctive Test cricketer and the one who would have to fight for every run at that level.

Tony Pawson, *Runs and Catches* (1980)

Surrey's Seven Years

Towards the end of the 1950s big changes were on their way in English cricket. On the whole the game had adapted itself reasonably well to changing times but it was clear that more would have to be done. Nobody had expected the huge crowds of the early post-war years to continue because the counter-attractions were now so numerous. Moreover, the county grounds, mostly dating back to the last century, were badly in need of modernization.

In 1957 MCC had appointed a special committee under H. S. Altham to review the conduct of the game and its future welfare. It covered what was to become familiar ground, the lbw Law, the limitation of on-side fielders, limitation of first-innings overs, preparation of pitches and a possible knock-out competition. These, of course, were proposals only for experiment in English domestic cricket. Some were adopted by the Advisory Committee. The amendment in the lbw Law, designed to reduce padding-up, was to become incorporated in the Laws. Others, such as the first-innings limitation of overs, were tried sooner or later and, like the abolition of the follow-on, were discarded. Whatever else, the cricket administrators of that period can scarcely be accused of not experimenting, even if the counties did not always choose the right experiments to back. There was, however, still a long way to go before the idea of 'marketing' the game took root.

The County Championship was not exactly a help in stimulating interest in domestic cricket, for as the 1950s neared their end there had been only one Champion County for seven years. Familiarity breeds apathy and towards the end of their extraordinary achievement, Surrey's very fine side were being taken for granted.

For the first five years the driving force had been a remarkable crick-eter, Stuart Surridge, who was thirty-four when he took over the cap-taincy in 1952. He was an amateur, a director of his family firm of

371

sports good manufacturers. Among his virtues was the priceless one of enthusiasm. He had come up through the lower levels of Surrey cricket, and since the war, with help from the great coach of the day, Alfred Gover, had developed a bowling action which would not have won prizes for grace but was effective enough to have earned him the new ball with Alec Bedser. That was not all. He was a magnificent fielder close to the wicket and a powerful late-order hitter of the ball.

Under the previous captain, Michael Barton, a pre-war Oxford bats-man, Surrey had been quietly developing into a promising side and had earned a half-share of the Championship with Lancashire in 1950. They had finished sixth behind Warwickshire in 1951 but in 1952 they won twenty of their twenty-eight matches and took the Championship out-right for the first time since 1914. Throughout his five-year reign Sur-ridge had to make do with reserves when Bedser, May, Laker, Lock, Arthur McIntyre once, and later Peter Loader were required for Test matches. In 1952 May, still up at Cambridge, played in only eight Cham-pionship matches.

One always has to be careful not to imply that sides prosper through their bowlers' feats on their home pitches. Figures are usually produced showing that the bowlers took as many or more wickets on opponents' grounds. So it was with Surrey. The Oval in the mid-1950s was a very different place from the ground with the dry fast outfield and the splen-did batting pitches of pre-war and immediate post-war seasons.

Now the outfield was lush and the ball kept its shine. The pitches would soon take spin with a rounded bounce and held something for good bowlers of all types. The other counties might be able to match Surrey in the first innings but it was only very rarely that they also had the spinners who could keep up with Laker and Lock in the second innings. Often it was the speed with which the Surrey bowlers ran through sides that defeated the opposition and the weather. Peter May recounts a match in 1954 when, after Worcestershire had been bowled out for 25, he and Ken Barrington had painfully raised Surrey's reply to 92 for three. At this point Surridge declared. 'We thought he'd gone off his head,' says May. But Worcestershire were then bowled out again for 40 and by half past twelve on the second morning Surrey had earned the points they needed to clinch that year's Championship before the unsettled weather could stop them.

What the Oval pitches undoubtedly did, weather permitting, was guarantee victory for one side or the other. Scores of 300 were rare.

Yet it was on these pitches that Peter May averaged 50 or 60 in the Championship.

Much depended on the strength of the reserves on whom Surrey relied when their Test players were away. Eric Bedser, who opened the innings, was scarcely needed as an off-spinner when the side was at full strength but was an all-rounder for whom any side would have found a place.

Of the other regular players, Bernard Constable was a consistent batsman at number three or four, Tom Clark was a fine driver of the ball, Arthur McIntyre was one of the best wicket-keepers in the country and a quick-footed middle-order batsman. The first Championship was won with the pre-war heroes Laurie Fishlock and Jack Parker, then forty-five and thirty-nine respectively. By the end of the seven years, Micky Stewart and Ken Barrington were established as two of the best young batsmen in the country.

In 1952 Surrey drew away from mid-June and won comfortably. The three matches which they lost were all when their leading players were absent. They had a stiffer task in 1953 when their best players were away recovering the Ashes. Sussex, captained by David Sheppard that year, put in a determined challenge for the Championship which they have still never won and in mid-August Leicestershire suddenly appeared on top of the table for the first time ever. Raman Subba Row, born and bred in Surrey, made a lot of runs after the University season as Surrey came from behind but he had still to do his National Service and when that was over he became captain of Northamptonshire.

Surrey came from even further behind in 1954. Eighth nearing the end of July, they won nine of their last ten matches. When they looked like being thwarted by rain at Cheltenham, Surridge hustled everyone on to the field when the rain temporarily eased and swiftly finished off the match by taking six for 31 himself before a storm soaked the ground.

In the fine summer of 1955 Surrey had the astonishing record of winning twenty-three of their twenty-eight matches and losing the other five. Yet Yorkshire, now a strong bowling side, won twenty-one and only drew two matches. Of the two matches between them, Surrey won at the Oval but Yorkshire won a battle royal at Headingley in June. After being 102 runs behind on first innings, their fast bowlers, Fred Trueman and the left-arm Michael Cowan, reduced Surrey to 27 for 7 on the second evening in a dim light and a frenzied atmosphere which made a Test match seem all sweetness. As usual they finished the season better than anyone, even winning a match at the Oval when the Middlesex fast bowlers, John Warr and Alan Moss, had them 6 for 4 on the first day.

Though they won at Leicester by seven wickets in the middle of May they had been the sufferers from one of the most amazing pieces of bowling in cricket history. They were replying to Leicestershire's modest total of 114 and had reached 42 for 1 with Peter May going well when Charles Palmer, the Leicestershire captain, decided to bowl an over after tea to allow his two spinners to change ends.

In that over he bowled May, so he stayed on and with his accurate medium pace took eight successive wickets without conceding a run. Every time he passed the bat he hit the stumps. Seven of his eight victims were bowled. Surrey were all out for 77 which included a last-wicket stand of 10. Palmer finished with figures of 14–12–7–8. This was on 21 May and until then he had bowled only two overs that season.

The win in 1956 was of more than usual importance to Surrey because it was to be Stuart Surridge's last season. Moreover, no county had previously been outright champions in five successive years. In a season of many interruptions through rain Surrey's ability to dispose of opposition in quick time was decisive.

In 1957 and 1958 Surrey continued their winning run under Peter May, in 1957 by the huge margin of 94 points. They won twenty-one matches against the fifteen of Northants who were second. The win in 1958 was gained in spite of the absence of Alec Bedser through pneumonia in the first half of the season. Peter May was in tremendous form and in the two matches in which Surrey beat the touring New Zealanders by an innings he made 165 and 116 not out. The highest New Zealand total in their four innings against Surrey was 118.

Michael Melford, *After the Interval* (1990)

Oxford Cricket

I have never regarded cricket as a branch of religion. I have met, and somehow survived, many of its blindest worshippers. I have staggered, pale and woozly, from the company of those who reject the two-eyed stance as Plymouth Brethren reject all forms of pleasure except money-making. I have never believed that cricket can hold Empires together, or that cricketers chosen to represent their country in distant parts should be told, year after year, that they are Ambassadors. If they are, I can think of some damned odd ones.

The air of holy pomp started from the main temple at Lord's, and it breathed over the press like a miasma. '*Procul, O Procul Este, Profani!*' We are not as other men. Sometimes I look back at reports of games in which I took part, and I have thought: 'And are these arid periphrases, these formal droolings, these desiccated shibboleths really supposed to represent what was done and how it was done? What has become of that earthy striving, that comic, tragic thing which was our match of cricket?'

University cricket is often written off as a rather advanced schoolboy affair; but the four matches in which I played for Oxford against Cambridge, between 1920 and 1923, produced eight England cricketers, of whom four, A. E. R. Gilligan, A. P. F. Chapman, D. R. Jardine, and G. O. Allen, captained England in Australia. The other four were G. E. C. Wood, J. C. W. MacBryan, G. T. S. Stevens, and C. S. Marriott. Besides these, J. L. Bryan, of Cambridge, was chosen as a member of Gilligan's team in Australia, but was never called on for a Test, and R. H. Bettington, of Oxford, while still an undergraduate, was little behind his fellow Australian, Arthur Mailey, in skill as a leg-break bowler. Nor will false modesty or fear of 'bad form, old chap' prevent me from saying that Clem Gibson and Norman Partridge from Cambridge, and myself, were all, at various times, good enough as bowlers to have played for England without being laughed at. Anyhow, I have seen several worse than us getting a few wickets in Anglo-Australian matches.

My brother Bobs, who had gone to work in a bank in Toronto, wrote to me in spring of 1920 saying, 'I suppose you ought to get your cricket Blue,' and I know I did so suppose. It came on a June evening, in a letter from Frank Gilligan, just as we gathered in the Corpus quad for dinner. Nothing compares with early triumphs. Young success kicks like a mule with a squib under its tail. The years come when friends are not so ready or able to share delight and grief.

Edward Pearce and I went to the pictures that night, in that house where the little manager used to stand at the back of the stalls with imitation diamond-studs in his shirt-front, waiting to restore order, which was almost nightly lost. During the rest of that term, and in the following winter, I liked to walk rather slowly along the High and imagine that other pedestrians were saying: 'Look, that's Robertson-Glasgow, the cricket Blue.' Alfred, Lord Tennyson, they tell us, also liked to be recognized in public. An innocent infatuation. A gift of divination would have diluted my vanity; but I was not yet to know that in four matches against Cambridge I would get only two wickets in 100 overs, for 243 runs. Nor did a batting average of 36 put things right. Few, except myself, cared whether I made runs or not, and, early in that summer of 1920, Frank Gilligan drew me aside in his grave and earnest manner and said: 'I'm not going to let you make runs. You're not strong enough to bat and bowl.' I was pained to think I looked quite so delicate. Besides, I had fancied myself as a batsman.

At the end of April came the Freshmen's match, if match be the word for that trial in which all hope to catch the judge's eye, and none cares which side wins. In their first innings, D. R. Jardine carried his bat for 60. This was the third season in which I had met Jardine. In each of the previous summers I had managed to take his wicket in the Charterhouse v. Winchester match. But in this first innings at Oxford, he made no shadow of a mistake. I had 5 wickets for 23 in 19 overs, mostly with in-swingers.

Douglas Jardine, at nineteen years, was the completest young batsman I have seen, both in method and temperament. It was said that while he was still a preparatory schoolboy, at Horris Hill, he had politely but firmly corrected his master on a point of technique and supported his view by a quotation from C. B. Fry's *Batsmanship*. Tall and well proportioned, he has ever been the perfect example of the orthodox English style. His off-driving, which in Test matches against Australia he was apt to deny himself, was then free and strong, and the bowler who attacked his leg stump was but wasting himself in vanity. But where Jardine excelled was in his back-stroke. It was professional, near to perfect.

I bowled Jardine for 18 in the second innings, which was abbreviated by the leg-breaks and googlies of R. H. Bettington. Reg Bettington, tall, dark of complexion, and of immense power, had come to Oxford with his brother Jack from Parramatta, New South Wales. Both bowled spinners; Jack at a brisk medium to fast, Reg at normal leg-breaker's pace. When Jack could pitch them, he was almost unplayable; but he was erratic. Both were free-driving batsmen. Both were tough rugger forwards, but it was Reg who got the Blue, playing against Cambridge in two years out of his four, largely on the strength of his left-footed place-kicking. Jack was the more finished golfer, Reg the more terrific hitter. Here again it was Reg who played against Cambridge. So Jack, who might so easily have played for Oxford at all three games, landed no Blue at all. He wore his disappointment invisibly. He fell gravely ill not long after returning as a civil engineer to Australia. Then he seemed to recover, but death won. He was as fine a fellow as you could want.

Reg Bettington made the ball buzz like a top, and at the moment of delivery there was a sharp snapping sound. There was another and even sharper snapping sound when he asked for lbw or a catch at the wicket. A Bettington appeal brought all Sydney to the Oxford Parks. Six feet and three inches in height, he took a longish run and bowled with a looping trajectory; not flat, like so many of his sort. I had a fine view of his bowling from short slip. His performance was brilliant that summer. Length, flight, spin, and persistence; he had them all; also a faster ball of vicious suddenness. Years later, when his skill at the leg-break had declined, I saw him bowl a fellow spinner, Richard Tyldesley, with this fast one at Lord's. Poor Dick; he had disentangled the bat-handle from his ample circumference, and stood at the ready, blade in air; but, when he brought it down, the bails had flown.

Greville Stevens bowled leg-breaks and googlies nearly as well as Bettington, and was a distinctly more scientific batsman. Stevens arrived at Oxford with cricket honours already thick upon him. At University College School he had made 466 not out in a House-match. For Middlesex, he had taken 21 wickets at moderate cost in the 1919 County Championship. To crown all, he had played for the Gentlemen against Players at Lord's. As Lionel Hedges said to him: 'Considering these setbacks, you're not a bad fellow!'

Greville had wit and a salty tongue, which some mistook for conceit. When he had walked out to the field for Oxford in his first match, he said to our captain, Gilligan: 'And shall I field in the place that I've made famous?' That was backward point, where he was a fine catcher. 'Yes,' said Gilligan, 'in the deep at both ends.' Myself, I enjoyed his playful remarks; and I recall with delight Greville's comment on arriving in the dressing-room at Lord's for the Gentlemen v. Players in 1924; looking round at some of his fellow cricketers, he said: 'This match isn't what it used to be, and I'm rather tired of it.' Not bad, for twenty-three years old.

Tall and fair, with a face that always made the schoolgirls ask for his autograph, he was yet not of athletic build. His run-up to the wicket was rather prancing and awkward, as if he were glad he hadn't to run any further, which, I think, he was; but he delivered the ball with a high arm, and, unlike so many of his kind, he never lost the potency of his leg-break. In the Freshmen's match, he failed as a batsman. I had him caught in his first innings. He had me bowled in my second. He took four wickets in each innings, twice defeating one H. P. Marshall, from Haileybury, who later was to become known to millions as Howard Marshall, broadcaster. On leaving Oxford, Greville Stevens soon deserted serious cricket for business, becoming a prosperous and astute stockbroker. But he played for England, and bowled C. G. Macartney in that memorable Oval match of 1926 when the tide at last turned against Australia, and Harold Larwood became famous, and Wilfred Rhodes ended his England cricket in clouds of glory.

From Tonbridge, with a name as batsman and cover-point, came Lionel Hedges, bubbling with life and mimicry. Like Stevens, he had been early blooded, having scored 28 and 43 at Canterbury for Kent against Jack Gregory and the Australian Imperial Forces a few days after leaving school. Lionel was at Trinity, which fitted him like a glove. No pleasanter community is to be found in Oxford. Short and strong, he was the best hooker in the side, and at cover-point he was swift to cut off that square single which maddens a bowler. He favoured enormous collars to his cricket shirt and a knotted silk scarf. He was soon into his stride with 86 against Middlesex and 101 not out against Essex. But his nervous temperament was unsatisfied. 'If they don't give me my Blue now,' he said to me, 'I'll make a string of noughts.' He didn't. He played rugby for the University, at stand-off half, on several occasions, but never against Cambridge. Lionel was full of parlour-tricks, including a ride up and down on a fictional hotel-lift. At the end of the first day's play of the Cambridge match in 1922, he bought a newsvendor's pitch and papers in Trafalgar Square and quickly sold out on 'Oxford's deplorable plight'. Later, he went as a master to Cheltenham, and played some fine innings for Gloucestershire. But he died cruelly early, in 1934, from a virulent form of influenza.

We lost the first match, against Warwickshire. It was cold and wet. I took a stinging catch from that craggy old warrior Charlesworth full on the breast-bone, whence it fell to the grass, at mid-off. I took no wickets, but a very long run-up to the crease. Stevens had 5 for 35 in the first innings, Bettington 5 for 48 in the second. Willie Quaife, smallest and correctest of great batsmen, batted a very long time for not so very many, and Jardine was bowled by F. S. G. Calthorpe for 0 in the first innings. A bleak start. But I was asked again for the next match, against Middlesex.

'Plum' Warner was in his last season of captaincy, which was soon to be crowned by that tremendous match at Lord's against Surrey, and the winning of the championship. Warner had taken the England team which beat Australia over there in 1911–12 and whose deeds I had rushed to read each morning at school. And here he was in the flesh, bald as an ostrich-egg under his Harlequin cap, slight, small-boned, pale of face, and with nothing but cricket in his conversation.

In my first innings I was bowled by the foxy J. W. Hearne, and I still had the pride to be very annoyed about it. Then, near the end of the first innings, I took my first wicket in first-class cricket, Captain J. M. S. Love for 0. I also had the towering Jack Durston stumped trying some complicated form of attack. After being led by 24 on the first innings, we ran up 349 for 8 declared. We won, by 139 runs; but that was nothing to me compared with bowling Hendren when he was well set at 50. It was a snifter, though I say it, bending in very late from the off. I walked on air, and would certainly have missed any catch that had come in my way.

We followed this victory by beating Essex by 239 runs. The match was doubly notable; first, because Douglas Jardine, in a spell of seven overs and 3 balls took 6 for 6, including the mighty P. Perrin, bowled for 0. Douglas, with a pensive and halting run, bowled what purported to be slow leg-breaks. Secondly, I acquired a nickname which has stuck ever since. Charlie McGahey and A. C. Russell had put on some 50 runs at the start of their second innings when I bowled McGahey with a full-pitcher which he later referred to as a yorker. In the bowels of the pavilion, Johnny Douglas, the Essex captain, asked him how he was out, and McGahey answered: 'I was bowled by an old— I thought was dead two thousand years ago, called Robinson Crusoe.'

I came to know Johnny Douglas well, and I must have stuck in his mind somewhat, because, when he invited me to stay in his flat at Hampstead later in the summer, I left the bath-tap running while having a drink, and an old lady from the flat below came hustling up the stairs to say that her Persian carpet was ruined and what about it. The incomparable John captained England twelve times against Australia, and after winning four victories to one in 1911–12 he lost all five in a row in 1920–21. You knew, and could often hear, what he was thinking on the field. It was battle, and nothing but, when he walked out, a gladiator, from the wicket gate, thick black hair shining and plastered down, rubbing the new ball on his strong forearm, frowning at some imaginary flaw in its make-up; or else went forth to bat, more grimly yet – for his batting was acquired and his bowling was natural – with strong slow gait, feet outwards, tugging his batting gloves on with his teeth, ready for a week, for a lifetime of that fight which was his cricket, and damn the bowlers and blast the crowd. He won the World Amateur Middleweight Boxing Championship in a fight with 'Snowy' Baker that has seldom been equalled. At the age of forty-eight, in 1930, he was drowned. He had gone below deck to save his father, and the ship, nearly severed by a collision, sank at about midnight in a few minutes.

On Wednesday 2 June 1920, I first met John Daniell, and next day he asked me to play a few matches for Somerset. This was an unorthodox request, as I had no qualification for Somerset, having been born in Edinburgh and living wherever the family, or parts of it, happened to be. Technically, I was qualified for Scotland, but the Scottish selectors have always been rather stuffy about Anglo-Scots, and I was never asked to play for the land of my birth. Not that it matters.

My connection with Somerset was our cousins, the Foxcroft family, of Hinton Charterhouse, of whom Charlie was Member of Parliament for Bath and a High Tory of the utmost spirit and pugnacity. But John Daniell reckoned that this would be good enough. At least I was in the position that no other County could claim me, even supposing they wanted my services. Herein was the mistake made by my friend Leonard Crawley. Being qualified for Durham, he went off to play for Worcestershire, and Durham objected. This little difference led, finally, to a quarrel between George, Lord Harris, Hon. Treasurer to MCC, and Lord Deerhurst, the High Panjandrum of Worcestershire. They met, it was reported, on the Pavilion steps at Lord's, and Lord Deerhurst swept off his grey top-hat and offered Lord Harris a short speech of congratulation on his alleged mismanagement of cricket. Stormy tea-cups long ago.

R. C. Robertson-Glasgow, *46 Not Out* (1948)

Northamptonshire v. Worcestershire

10, 12 AND 13 JUNE 1978 NORTHAMPTON

For more than a hundred years, first-class cricket in England has been founded upon competition for the County Championship, and this is still the contest that ranks above all the rest. I imagine there are people who can recite the list of County Champions since 1864, while being uncertain who won which of the other trophies that various sponsors have offered in the past fifteen years. Grudgingly or gracefully, they have had to accept the fact that the County Championship might now be extinct if the one-day events hadn't drummed up a new army of recruits to the watching of the game, and if commerce hadn't been persuaded to circulate some of its spare cash around the county grounds in exchange for freely advertising its goods: non-smokers can no longer afford to abhor the names of John Player or Benson and Hedges, the bearded must not disdain the attentions of Gillette and, since last season began, the man who likes his liquor neat should not look blearily upon the image of Schweppes. All the same, the johnny-come-latelies must not expect the rest of us to yield too much of our affections simply because social and economic history has at last caught us cap in hand. The County Championship, after all, speaks of something more than cricket, as the briefer county contests do only by extension. This is where deep tribal loyalties of the English have been cherished for generations in the most civilized fashion possible. It is not only Lancastrians and Yorkshiremen who are sentimental about the counties of their birth, whose names and individual characters were forged long ago in the making of this land. I do not think that the grey men who revised our boundaries a few years back, concocting new names and abolishing old ones for their convenience alone, could have felt either cricket or English history in the marrow of their bones. One day my grandchildren, yet unborn, will probably wonder what and where Rutland was; and I would like to think that, if Rutland had ever raised a County Championship team, this might not have been so, in spite of its obliteration from government's map.

There will not be a body at the County Ground this Saturday morning who does not feel such loyalty tugging from his roots. Neither Northants nor Worcester can have any hope of taking the Championship this year unless there is some monumental disturbance of form from one end of the table to the other; with a quarter of the fixtures already played, both are among the bottom four teams. So when Cook wins the toss and decides to bat first, we can be sure that the two or three hundred spectators are here for cricket and ancestral honour alone, and not for the thrill of camp-following a successful side. They are not expecting rapid drama, either, although cricket can provide that any old hour. To a man and a woman they are faithful followers of the Championship match which, played over the course of three days, has been both the nursery and the consummation of the game. I don't think there's any doubt that limited-overs cricket has improved the quality of fielding in this country almost out of recognition, and for that many thanks indeed; otherwise it has subtracted from the infinite variety of skills which cricket evolved and refined in the three-day Championship match, and the virtual disappearance of the leg-spinner is but the most notorious example of this loss. As Vanburn Holder's bow legs gallop to the crease for the first over, an elderly woman passing the West Stand hails a contemporary already in his place. 'How are you?' she asks. 'Oh, not too bad, Mrs Lyman,' he replies, flashing the single peg left in his upper jaw. 'One year older'; and he grins again. Perhaps the pair of them have enough time, these days, to watch a championship match from first ball to last, with its thoughtful passages as well as its dramatic bursts in the maturing strategies of attack and counterattack. And if they don't, this day alone will show enough of technique and grace and character to feed memory and devotion for the remainder of their lives.

There is a fiction that Championship matches start at snail's pace because the players feel they have so much time in hand, but Cook and Larkins are soon giving the lie to that. Almost a run a minute comes in the first half hour as those two men in maroon caps seek to assert themselves against the Worcestershire attack. Cook, having edged a boundary to get off the mark, is the more careful of the two, but Larkins is unbridled from the first ball he receives. He plays and misses Pridgeon once or twice but is not put off by this and turns the bowler off his legs for 4, then square-cuts Holder beautifully to the fence. Within the hour the batsmen are up with the clock and the West Stand sages affirm that this is quite a reasonable start, as Norman Gifford rearranges his bowling to take the first ascendancy away from Northants. Holder gives way to Cumbes, and Pridgeon changes ends. He now bowls with an arc of cars behind him and, beyond them, an expanse of coarse and balding grass which is half the playing area of Northampton Town, an impecunious club whose dilapidated stand crouches along the length of the distant touch-line. The pause for this rearrangement allows the spectators to speculate upon the weather, which could take a hand in this cricket match before it is done. Someone recalls that the long-range forecasters promised us unusual warmth to the middle of June, and here we have yet another dull and chilly day. But people are still sauntering into the ground with their haversacks and their shopping bags laden with thermos and sandwiches; and, between each over, one or two more cars glide round the boundary to join those already behind Pridgeon. I think it is perhaps the spectators more than the players who give Championship cricket a leisurely name.

Cumbes labours for a while from the pavilion end, but in the twenty-fourth over Holder is brought back and the first drama of the match occurs. The West Indian's third ball flies off the edge of Larkins's bat straight to the cupped hands of Turner at slip – and falls to the ground. Holder's hands go to his hips in frustration but his shoulders are resigned. He glares only for an instant at the fieldsman who, at that moment, is emotionally isolated from his team-mates by the size of his error. A difficult catch missed would have got a sympathetic word from the keeper or someone else as close. This one causes the others to look at the floor or up at the sky, anywhere except at Turner, who is rubbing his hands where the ball stung. Then he reaches for his handkerchief and blows his nose in the oppressive silence hanging over the infield. A few minutes later, the Worcestershire spirits rise again when Cook, impatient with his own cautious rate, swings at Pridgeon and is caught by Humphries behind.

'It'll slow up now,' says someone, cocking his eye at the scoreboards's 79 for 1, as Steele's bare head bobs down the pavilion steps. 'Come on, David,' murmurs a less mournful voice, hoping that England's hero of three seasons ago will today emerge from the doldrums of this year. Steele may have been going through a bad patch of late (though he got a few against Essex, someone recalls) but there is still something in his approach to the wicket that would hearten any team in need of runs. It is the bustling walk of the tradesman on whose service you can always rely, and that untimely grey hair above the spectacles only makes Steele look the most dependable tradesman in town. He taps the ground with his bat as he comes eagerly towards the game, and when he is in it, and backing up the bowler's end, he crouches a little, alert and ready to dash forward with whatever the customers may need. Thus he watches Larkins defend for a few balls, practising his own strokes on the side each time the bowler returns; when his own moment comes, he tries to get Holder away to leg several times, but mostly he is going forward to stifle the ball. Then he dabs at one outside the off stump, pulling his bottom hand away at almost the same time, knowing (with a sudden spurt of sweat, no doubt) that he had been lucky to touch that ball past the wicketkeeper for 4. A couple of singles come his way, both of them deflected with the same unease. Then Steele dabs at another delivery that on another day he might have struck soundly off the back foot wide of gully's right hand, but which today he would have done well to leave alone with shouldered arms. This time the dab flicks the ball to Hemsley, who takes it at the second attempt low down in the slips. David Steele has not been in long enough to put his game together again and only a couple of claps are heard as he returned to the pavilion as eagerly, it seems, as when he emerged.

In the West Stand an old chap who has been keeping careful score sighs heavily, closes his book and begins to move off. 'Coming back this afternoon?' asks a crony nearby.

'No,' he says, 'umpiring this afternoon over at Dallington.'

'Oh-ho,' rumbles the other, 'better be careful then'; and, as the one strolls away round the track, the other opens a battered attaché case, brings out pork pie, some salad, knife, fork and proper pot plate, arranges the lot on the closed case across his knees, and begins to take an early lunch.

Larkins has prospered all this time, however, and with his own score, Northamptonshire's has steadily grown. When the cricketers go in to lunch, the two fallen wickets have been exchanged for 122 runs and Larkins stands at 70 not out. The crowd has every reason to be pleased with such a well-founded start and the youngsters are shrill with enthusiasm as they play their own knockabout cricket by the boundary placards advertising this and that. ('Is it 4,' one inquires, settling the ground rules before they begin, 'if it goes past the Burnley Building Society?') Lunch over, Larkins moves on, the tiny figure of Williams at the other end strives, and Gifford again manipulates his bowling to maintain any distraction that the meal break may have begun. He puts himself on at the pavilion end and appeals loudly for lbw against Williams at his very first ball. ''E's at it again,' observes a Northants supporter, who has seen the Worcester captain at work many times before. The ploy doesn't succeed at once, but the general strategy does when Williams, goaded into doing something by Gifford's twirling spin, and his supplication to the gods when the umpires are unmoved, sweeps, misses, and gets his leg in the way of the ball. Larkins has reached 92, and since being missed by Turner he has done nothing dangerously wrong. Almost every over has added to his score and the longer he is there the more commanding he looks. But now a strange pause interrupts his progress towards the century. It takes him one hour and five minutes to move from 92 to 99 and impatience begins to rustle round the County Ground. There is no slow hand-clapping, for Wayne Larkins of Bedfordshire belongs to Northants; he is being given the benefit of all East Midlands doubts, but the impulse to jeer is evidently there. This is misplaced, for the central drama of cricket is emphasized in Larkins's present plight.

This game is at all times a gladiatorial contest between two players, a batsman and a bowler, and everyone else taking part in a match is, at the moment of conflict between those two, playing no more than an auxiliary role. The batsman has his partner, who relieves his isolation with some moral support, but is essentially there for the purely statistical purpose of registering a valid run. The bowler has ten aides in the field, but they are helpless to act until that swift cut and thrust, that intensely private moment between batsman and bowler, is done. This numerical advantage of players to the bowling side, however, creates a situation which is almost unique to cricket. It makes batting, consequently the scoring of runs, an act of defiance by one man against a vastly superior force who control the ball at all times, except in that split second when it touches the bat. Among team games played with a ball, this is also true of baseball alone; but no other sport knows such a heroic stance.

From the boundary today it is hard to see any difference in the playing of the pitch between 2.45 and 3.50. The bowling of Gifford and Patel, Holder, Pridgeon and Cumbes, appears to be no more tantalizing, no more hostile, when Larkins is clearly struggling to defend his wicket than when he was clumping the bowlers aggressively to the ropes. While he is making those seven agonized runs, Willey comes out, knocks up a useful 24 and departs again, and Yardley settles down to some ebullient strokes. The sun begins to beam upon the ground but Larkins stays in the dimness of his own obscuring light. The nervous nineties surely never plagued anyone more than this, and the defiance of a batsman was never more tortured to behold. From a cavalier charge as Rupert of the Rhine, poor Larkins has suddenly been translated into Horatius at the Bridge, and the Etruscans of Worcestershire are hemming him in. The spectators think him a dull dog now but out there, in the middle, it is wits against determination, anxious anticipation meeting the premeditated blow. Gifford, turning at the end of his short run, rolls up his eyes to his aide at mid-on; it is a signal to be ready for a response the bowler will now try to extract from the batsman with this one finely calculated ball. At the striker's end Larkins crouches, not yet knowing the degree of spin Gifford is about to apply, or the trajectory of the missile through the air, or just where on the stubbled turf the ball will pitch. The ball is unloosed by the crafty hand and in the quickness of its flight the batsman summons his eye, his technique, his knowledge and his strength into one co-ordinated movement of his own. As Gifford's delivery pitches fractionally short in a temptingly fulsome arc and turns towards the leg-stump in its upward bounce, Larkins steps forward, left elbow high, bat utterly straight, only the toe of his back foot remaining where he stood, and brings the blade down like a scythe at a precise angle which sends the ball gently along the ground to where mid-on was waiting for a catch. Once more the attackers are defied, in another instant the gladiators will clash again. Larkins straightens up, removes his cap, wipes the moisture of strain as much as warmth off his brow. So the duel between batsman and bowler, the drama of cricket, goes on.

Then suddenly he strikes Holder away for two runs, at 3.56, and he has his century at last. A natty Citroën and a red MG detach themselves from the ring of vehicles at the football end and slip away round the boundary while Larkins is raising his bat at the applause. The drivers are probably content to have seen him reach three figures, but they will miss the best of Larkins today. Having painfully struggled through those last few runs to his hundred he now becomes a different man, even more cavalier than when he plundered the bowling up to 92. He has passed through a psychological barrier, and it is comparable to the effect on track athletes after Bannister ran the first four-minute mile. Citroën and MG are scarcely out of sight before Larkins has belted Pridgeon over the boundary at long-on, where the outfielder eventually has to lie full length to recover the ball from under the Northamptonshire President's car. After tea, Larkins takes the Worcestershire bowlers one by one, and pays them back crushingly for the confinement they had earlier imposed. In just fifteen minutes straddling five o'clock, he hits 35 runs as he rushes from 125 to 160. The sunshine now floods the ground, so that the crickets are dazzlingly white upon the vivid green of the grass, with that solitary maroon cap glowing warmly in its own pool of brilliant light. A couple of hundred people have spent most of their day so far watching the game behind windscreens, but many of them emerge now to enjoy the bright swing of his bat as it cracks the ball this way and that. Yardley is having his fun, too, and Northants are feeling very well when the 300 goes up with three overs left before their innings must close. As almost every local knows, Larkins is approaching the highest score of his life, the 167 he got against Warwickshire a couple of seasons ago. Will he better it now, with only eighteen more balls to be bowled and Yardley glad to be among the runs on his own account? The bowlers are tiring after nearly five hours of work, the outfielders beginning to pant a little from their perpetual chasing since tea. Norman Gifford's pink face looks as if it might be about to boil over from some combustion within. But Worcester are not going to present Larkins with his record on a plate and they have him fidgeting again as he goes for those last few runs. He gets them, though, and when Northants go in at 312 for 4 he is still unbeaten with 170 in the book. It's been a fine innings, with much light and some shade, and I can see why there is talk that he might play for England one day, for there was great character in that score as well as lovely strokes.

Thus Act One finishes, with the likelihood that Northants have already put themselves beyond danger of defeat. Cricket matches, however, are not always settled by the struggles of mortal men alone, and in the course of three days the weather is quite capable of turning certainties, let alone likelihoods, upside down. But Worcestershire's first task must be to build a first innings score close enough to that of Northants to secure themselves at least a draw: the initiative is with the home side and the visitors must wrest it away.

From the outset, Northants set a field to take close catches and be hanged to the incidental loss of a boundary or two; get a couple of wickets tonight and Monday morning will be promising indeed. At third slip Larkins is euphoric, windmilling his arms, chattering non-stop, too excited by his score to keep still or quiet except when it matters, when the ball is being bowled; but then, I imagine, his moustache bristles up at the memory of his fight. Turner must have that somewhere on his mind, too, for the catch he dropped cost Worcestershire nearly 130 runs. He stands at the crease like a slender Regency buck, with his shirt collar upturned so that his chin and his mouth are tucked out of sight inside its sharp points. A neat and stylish batsman, who has been one of the best in the world, and New Zealand cannot be happy that he has decided not to tour England with them in his Worcestershire benefit year. This is the wicket Northants would like to have most of all before close of play and in the first half hour of Turner's innings they twice show that they are terribly keen. First Griffiths, then Lamb, raps him on the pads. Both times there is a strident chorus of appeal and Turner is surrounded by infielders with arms and legs splayed in mid-air, like a war party of Maoris in the last convulsion of a haka before they go for his pakeha blood. Having seen such sights since birth, he is unmoved and steadily forges ahead, hooking Griffiths magnificently for 4 immediately after the first appeal. At the other end the dark and sleek Ormrod, more solid and with less whipcord in his build, thumps singles off the ball and gives the bowlers no change. As the clock on the pavilion moves towards half past six, Northampton-shire's evening ambitions gently die. When the players come in and their long shadows waver into one great dark beam as they merge across the grass, Worcester are 54 runs to the good, with Turner on 33 and Ormrod on 17.

Time was when county professionals put their feet up on a Sunday (though the gentlemanly players might be found out at golf) but that all ended when the John Player League came in and the Lord's Day Observance Society began to go out. This weekend sees these two sides in a one-day tussle over at Milton Keynes, which Worcestershire win. A certain moral advantage is theirs, then, when the cricketers muster at the County Ground again on Monday morning. Half an hour before plays starts on a dull and almost listless day, Cumbes may be seen lapping the football pitch in his track suit, with 'Worcester CCC' in green letters across his back. The rest of the team are finishing their nets by the scoreboard while, on the other side of the field, Griffiths is leading half a dozen lads of the Northants county colts in high catching practice. Between these two groups, the groundsman perched on his orange tractor is mowing the outfield grass and the juice in the clippings sweetens the air with a country smell. The popping exhaust and the grunts and occasional shouts of the cricketers echo in this otherwise empty corner of the town. When Peter Willey, already dressed for play, crosses from the corner shop in the narrow street outside the gates, the sprigs on his boots grate on the stone and can be heard fifty yards away, for there is not another soul in sight. Perhaps twenty-five cars will be drawn up on either side of the sightscreen at the football end when play begins, where on Saturday the traffic was in two rows filling the whole arc. A dozen or so spectators lounge in the pavilion seats which are exclusive to 'Gentlemen members only': it is a small building, not far removed in size or mood from the village green, and a pair of cricket boots with owner attached are propped up on the sill of the Worcester dressing room, a foot or so above a gentlemanly head. A few more figures may be seen elsewhere on the ground and in front of the pavilion sightscreen four boys are batting a tennis ball about. When an old man comes to the pavilion door and shakes a handbell at the world to inform it that play will start in ten minutes sharp, he does not expect this to be a galvanizing noise. Championship cricket in Northampton on a Monday morning begins the way Sunday mornings everywhere generally feel, with occasional pensive movements to whatever the Almighty has in mind.

Geoffrey Moorhouse, *The Best Loved Game* (1979)

10

Champions and Characters

The game, it is often pompously stated, is bigger than the players. In the sense that no one is indispensable and that there always has to come a time when even the great heroes are replaced by new ones, this is true. But in another sense the game is *its players. Their attitude to and interpretation of the game are what makes or breaks it; what makes it competitive or slack; fun or misery; inspiring or dull.*

There is no more consistent cry through the ages than the one from men in the twilight or evening of their careers claiming that 'there are no characters in the game any more'. There are always characters, in fact, in the higher echelons especially. Without character, indeed, in the sense of having fibre for a fight, you cannot get very far in cricket. The word 'character' is a catholic one, however, and cricket has room for men who may be boring but courageous, funny but foolish, witty but impetuous and a hundred other combinations of human virtues, vices and foibles.

No game reveals a man's character more clearly than cricket, with its broad canvas, its long moments of inactivity before the next few seconds of action. See a man at the crease for half an hour and you will be able to tell much about his whole nature. Is he still and calm, or restless and fidgety? Is he tidy, or untidy? Is he talkative, or taciturn? Is he calculating, or rash? Is he nervous, or confident? Here, truly, is one of the game's endless fascinations.

Not every 'great' player is portrayed here, but many are, and some rich characters with them.

The Many-chorded Lyre

There is one great landmark that separates the old batting from the new – the appearance of Dr W. G. Grace in the cricket world. In 1865 W.G. came fully before the public that has admired and loved him ever since. He revolutionized batting. He turned it from an accomplishment into a science. All I know of old-time batting is, of course, gathered from books and older players, but the impression left on my mind is this: before W.G. batsmen were of two kinds – a batsman played a forward game or he played a back game. Each player, too, seems to have made a speciality of some particular stroke. The criterion of style was, as it were, a certain mixed method of play. It was bad cricket to hit a straight ball; as for pulling a slow long-hop, it was regarded as immoral. What W.G. did was to unite in his mighty self all the good points of all the good players, and to make utility the criterion of style. He founded the modern theory of batting by making forward- and back-play of equal importance, relying neither on the one nor on the other, but on both. Any cricketer who thinks for a moment can see the enormous change W.G. introduced into the game. I hold him to be, not only the finest player born or unborn, but the maker of modern batting. He turned the old one-stringed instrument into a many-chorded lyre.

K. S. Ranjitsinhji, *The Jubilee Book of Cricket* (1897)

W.G.: *The hundredth century – 17 May 1895*

This is the batsman Willsher feared, and Shaw,
And Hill, and M'Intyre and Lillywhite;
And Southerton long years since felt the might
Of his attack, and Emmett found no flaw
In his defence. Not Tarrant could o'erawe
Nor Freeman's pace, nor Richardson's affright.
In strife with Lohmann oft he drank delight,
The straightest bat that England ever saw.
Now thirty years have past him by, and still

He takes the field with his first comrades' sons,
And with a boy's heart and a young man's skill
In very wantonness scores thrice the runs
He needs to gain, 'midst plaudits of the skies,
His matchless Century of Centuries.

Anon, *Punch* (1878)

F. R. Spofforth

The victories against the Australians by Cambridge Past and Present and the Players so far restored the public's confidence in our cricket that few people regarded the approaching Test match at the Oval with anything more disturbing than eager interest. The England Eleven was selected by Lord Harris, Mr Burbidge, and Messrs V. E. and I. D. Walker, and the names when published must have read well enough to reassure all but the most determined Jeremiahs. The batting seemed overwhelmingly strong; with the exception of Peate, 24 was the lowest average of any member of the side, and the batting order was so insoluble a problem that No. 10 on the list had perforce to be, in the first innings, A. N. Hornby and in the second C. T. Studd. In bowling, Peate and Barlow could both show remarkable figures up to date, whilst Ulyett in the last Australian match with Yorkshire had taken seven of their wickets for 89, and Steel and Studd had both met with considerable success with the ball in the game with Cambridge Past and Present and Middlesex respectively.

Most important of all, perhaps, was the fact that Palmer, who had bowled with splendid consistency all the tour, was at this time *hors de combat*. Surely, then, as the crowds streamed into the ground on the morning of Monday 28 August, all the omens must have seemed favourable, and few of them can have dreamt that before sunset on Tuesday they would have seen 'the first flight of the winged victory from the White Cliffs of Albion to the long wash of Australian seas'.

When the Australians came down to breakfast in their familiar quarters in the Tavistock Hotel, Covent Garden, the anxieties uppermost in their minds must surely have concerned the weather and the toss. Autumn was hard upon the heels of spring. There had been heavy rain in

London on the Saturday, and more again in the early hours of Monday, and it was morally certain that the Oval wicket could not improve. It must then have been no small relief to them when Murdoch beat Hornby, the English captain, with the toss, and at ten minutes past noon, on a ground already packed thick with eager spectators, Massie and Bannerman went down the pavilion steps to face the bowling of Peate and Ulyett. The morning's play brought to Australia nothing but disaster; at one time six wickets were down for 30 runs, and though Garrett and Blackham then made a plucky stand, only 18 more had been added when the teams left the field for luncheon.

Punctually at a quarter to three the game was resumed, and in the first over young Maurice Read delighted his Oval friends by catching Garrett beautifully at long-off; twenty minutes later the innings was over, and that for 63 runs, the lowest score that the tourists had made in all their thirty matches to date. Certainly the English bowling had been steadiness personified – fourteen consecutive maidens at one period – and Barlow's figures of five wickets for 19 runs in 31 overs were splendid; but the Australian batting was in several cases nerveless and unworthy of them, and they must have taken the field a sadly chagrined team.

When Spofforth yorked the Champion for a paltry 4, and got Barlow caught at forward point with the total no more than 18, their spirits leapt up again; but then Ulyett, after an agonizing first over, hit well, Lucas defended with a cool head and a classically straight bat, and the score crept up to within seven of the Tourists' total, when the Yorkshireman, with something of the light-heartedness that had given him the name and the nature of 'Happy Jack', danced out to Spofforth, missed him, and was stumped. From that moment the tide turned; three runs later Lucas was caught at the wicket, and with Studd clean bowled and Alfred Lyttelton also captured by Blackham off his gloves, six wickets were down and the scores were but equal. Barnes failed, a plucky stand by Steel and Maurice Read then added 26 precious runs, but Hornby only just managed to hoist the hundred before falling to one of the 'Demon's deadliest breakbacks. Peate gave no trouble, and the Australians left the field 38 runs down, but comforted in the knowledge that after their batting collapse of the morning they might easily have had to face twice as big a deficit.

The clouds that were gathering as they drove home afterwards in their hansoms to an anxious meal and an early bed broke during the night, and a heavy downpour, as they were setting out again next morning, made play impossible until ten minutes past twelve. Barlow, in his interesting book of reminiscences, has recorded his opinion that the conditions were at that time unfit for cricket; the ball was like soap, and the mud in the bowlers' holes so bad that the groundsmen had to remove it with a spade before they could be filled with sawdust. It was Australia's great chance, and splendidly did Massie and Bannerman take it; the latter defended grimly, while Massie took his life in his hands and went for the bowling. Runs came fast in spite of bowling changes, the arrears were cleared off and W. G. Grace was seen to be pulling anxiously at his beard. At last Steel induced him to hit across a straight half-volley, and Massie's great innings was over – 55 runs in as many minutes out of a total of 66. Clever bowling changes by Hornby soon got rid of Bonnor and Horan, and with Bannerman and Giffen also gone, England began to breath again, but a little shower eased the wicket a trifle once more, and Murdoch played a captain's innings, only terminated by a brilliant piece of combined work in the field by Hornby, Studd and Lyttelton, and when the last wicket, Boyle's, fell, Australia was 84 runs on.

George Giffen has told us how in the breathless ten minutes that divided the innings the Australians desperately debated their chance, how Spofforth declared that 'this thing can be done', and how they filed down the pavilion steps ready to do or die. A general cheer greeted them, followed by a deeper one still when it was seen that Hornby had elected to open the last innings himself with Grace. Spofforth, at the Vauxhall end, and Garrett began the bowling, and with the score at 15 the 'Demon' beat and bowled the English captain. Barlow followed, only to meet with the same fate his very first ball. The crowd was silent, grimly intent, but the next half-hour saw their enthusiasm and confidence revive, for in that time Grace and Ulyett added 36 priceless runs. Thirty-four only wanted, and eight great batsmen to get them. Surely the bitterness of defeat was past. But at 51 Spofforth, who had crossed over to the pavilion end, whips down his extra fast one at Ulyett, the Yorkshireman plays for the break-back which is not there, just snicks it – Blackham does the rest. Two runs later Grace tries to drive Boyle, just fails to reach the pitch of the ball, and is well caught at mid-off – 53–4–32. Lucas is joined by Lyttelton, who hits a splendid four and the score creeps up to 60.

Now comes the real battle. Boyle and Spofforth set their teeth and bowl as they have never bowled before; maiden follows maiden, four of them, eight of them, twelve of them in succession. Then Spofforth whispers to Murdoch and Bannerman, the latter purposely misfields a hit of Lyttelton's, and he is down at the far end facing the 'Demon', with the dark background of the pavilion behind the deadly arm. Four more maidens and a devastating break-back shatters his stumps; the last act of the drama has begun. Steel can do nothing, and at 70 is sucked out by Spofforth's slow ball and caught and bowled. Maurice Read, who had done so well in his first Test Match innings, is entirely beaten by his second ball and seven wickets are down with 15 runs still wanted. But Lucas is still there, cramped, it is true, by the wonderful bowling, but meeting it with indomitable nerve and resource; surely he and Barnes and Studd can pull us through together? Barnes, one of the most brilliant professionals of the day, and Studd, who has already twice topped the century against these self-same terrors. Five runs are added, precariously enough, and then a gasp goes up all round the ground – Lucas has played on. 75–8–10.

Whether Studd was really as nervous as 'Buns' Thornton subsequently declared – 'walking round the pavilion with a blanket round him' – can never be proved, for the tragic fact is that he never got a ball. Lucas had fallen to the last ball of Spofforth's over, and the first of the next from Boyle jumped up quickly and Barnes was caught at point off his glove. Peate – *spes ultima Troiae* – was a poor, but not a negligible, batsman. He had made 20 in his last innings against the Australians for Yorkshire, and now it only needed one fair hit from his bat and another from Studd's to land England home the winner. Peate, it is evident, means to settle the thing out of hand. He hits his first ball dangerously to leg for two, is all but bowled by his second, plies his bat like a flail at his third and knows that it has been his last.

That accomplished writer, Horan, has told us something of the desperate intensity of that last half-hour, how one spectator dropped down dead, and another with his teeth gnawed out pieces from his umbrella handle; how one English batsman's lips were ashen grey and his throat so parched that he could hardly speak as he passed the writer in the field on the way to the wicket; how the scorer's hand trembled so that he wrote Peate's name like 'Geese'. Giffen relates how, when Peate's wicket fell, the crowd sat for a moment voiceless and stunned, and then broke over the ground in one wild rush to cheer the men who had won the fight.

Spofforth was carried shoulder-high into the pavilion, and if ever a man made cricket history it was he that day. Fourteen wickets for 90 runs was his share of the spoil, and at the final crisis he had bowled his last eleven overs for two runs and four wickets.

AUSTRALIA

First innings		Second innings	
A. C. Bannerman c Grace b Peate	9	c Studd b Barnes	13
H. H. Massie b Ulyett	1	b Steel	55
W. L. Murdoch b Peate	13	run out	29
G. J. Bonnor b Barlow	1	b Ulyett	2
T. Horan b Barlow	3	c Grace b Peate	2
G. Giffen b Peate	2	c Grace b Peate	0
J. McC. Blackham c Grace b Barlow	17	c Lyttelton b Peate	7
T. W. Garrett c Read b Peate	10	not out	2
H. F. Boyle b Barlow	2	b Steel	0
S. P. Jones c Barnes b Barlow	0	run out	6
F. R. Spofforth not out	4	b Peate	0
B 1	1	B 6	6
Total	63		122

First innings / Second innings

	O	M	R	W	O	M	R	W
Peate	38	24	31	4	21	9	40	4
Ulyett	9	5	11	1	6	2	10	1
Barlow	31	22	19	5	13	5	27	0
Steel	2	1	1	0	7	0	15	2
Barnes					11	5	15	1
Studd					4	1	9	0

Fall of wickets: 1–6, 2–21, 3–22, 4–26, 5–30, 6–30, 7–48, 8–50, 9–59, 10–63   1–66, 2–70, 3–70, 4–79, 5–79, 6–99, 7–114, 8–117, 9–122, 10–122

ENGLAND

First innings		Second innings	
R. G. Barlow c Bannerman b Spofforth	11	b Spofforth	0
W. G. Grace b Spofforth	4	c Bannerman b Boyle	32
G. Ulyett st Blackham b Spofforth	26	c Blackham b Spofforth	11
A. P. Lucas c Blackham b Boyle	9	b Spofforth	5
Hon. A. Lyttelton c Blackham b Spofforth	2	b Spofforth	12
C. T. Studd b Spofforth	0	not out	0
J. M. Read not out	19	b Spofforth	0
W. Barnes b Boyle	5	c Murdoch b Boyle	2
A. G. Steel b Garrett	14	c and b Spofforth	0
A. N. Hornby b Spofforth	2	b Spofforth	9
E. Peate c Boyle b Spofforth	0	b Boyle	2
B 6, lb 2, nb 1	9	B 3, nb 1	4
Total	101		77

First innings   *Second innings*

	O	M	R	W	O	M	R	W
Spofforth	36.3	18	46	7	28	15	44	7
Garrett	16	7	22	1	7	2	10	0
Boyle	19	7	24	2	20	11	19	3

Fall of wickets: 1–13, 2–18, 3–56, 4–59, 5–60, 6–63, 7–70,   1–15, 2–15, 3–51, 4–53, 5–66,
8–96, 9–101, 10–101   6–70, 7–70, 8–75, 9–75, 10–77

Umpires: R. Thoms and L. Greenwood

H. S. Altham, *A History of Cricket* (1926)

J. B. Hobbs

Melbourne	1911–12	126 not out
Adelaide	1911–12	187
Melbourne	1911–12	178
Lord's	1912	107
Melbourne	1920–21	122
Adelaide	1920–21	123
Melbourne	1924–25	154
Adelaide	1924–25	119
Sydney	1924–25	115
Lord's	1926	119
The Oval	1926	100
Melbourne	1928–29	142

That is the Test story, in centuries, of John Berry Hobbs – now Sir Jack – against Australia. Twelve centuries, more than those of any other Englishman, against the Great Enemy!

Those centuries, of course, tell only part of the story of the man who, as Australian Test players agree, was the best batsman ever produced by England. You don't judge a cricketer by centuries alone. Quite often such a score is not nearly as valuable to a side as a 40 or 50 made in difficult circumstances – that is, when the strain is on with every pressing minute a test of temperament and resource. And Jack Hobbs was at his very best when the fight was toughest. One other important point: from his first Test match in Melbourne, on 1 January 1908, to his last at his home Oval in Kennington, Surrey, in 1930, Jack Hobbs always opened the innings. He got no easy runs, after the sting was taken out of the bowling. He did his own de-stinging.

Furthermore, that long list of centuries could well have been half as long again. In his first Test innings Hobbs almost made a century. He had scored 83 in three hours of correct batsmanship when Cotter clean-bowled him. He later scored 72 in the same series in Sydney. He made a brilliant 62 not out – scoring twice as fast as the redoubtable C. B. Fry – to push England home to a ten wickets win against Australia in a low-scoring game on a horrible pitch at Birmingham in 1909. In 1926 he scored 88 at Leeds, 74 in the next Test at Old Trafford, 74 at Adelaide in 1929, 65 in his last Test innings in Australia at Melbourne, and 78 at Nottingham in 1930.

It is readily seen, therefore, that Hobbs, given just a little luck, could have added another half dozen or more centuries to his list against Australia.

He played in 41 Tests against Australia and had 71 innings for 3,636 runs at an average of 54.23. He played in 18 Tests against South Africa with 29 innings for 1,562 runs at an average of 60.07. He had only two Tests against the West Indies, for 212 runs at an average of 106.

In all Test cricket, then, with his average not buttressed by games against India, Pakistan and New Zealand, he made 5,410 runs at an average of 56.94. His record number of first-class centuries is 197. He made 61,221 first-class runs at an average of 50.63. Although figures indicate the greatness of Hobbs they don't convey the grandeur of his batting, his faultless technique, and the manner in which he captivated those who could recognize and analyse style. Australians who played against him over the years believe cricket never produced a more correct batsman than Hobbs.

From 1907 to 1930 Hobbs batted against this imposing list of Australian bowlers: Saunders, Noble, Armstrong, Macartney, Cotter, Laver, Whitty, Hordern, Minnett, Kelleway, Gregory, McDonald, Mailey, Arthur Richardson, Grimmett, Ironmonger, Oxenham, Blackie, Wall, Hornibrook, McCabe, Fairfax, and a'Beckett.

They were, too, players who had shrewd captains such as Noble, Clem Hill, Sid Gregory, Armstrong, Collins, Ryder and Woodfull to set fields to the best purpose.

Hobbs took them all in his century-making stride. He played Test cricket until he was forty-eight; he played for Surrey until he was fifty-two.

During tours of England, I used to think fondly of Hobbs, Tom Hayward and Ranjitsinhji as I walked on various mornings across Parker's Piece to the Cambridge ground. It was on the Piece that Hobbs and Hayward first played cricket and it was there, too, that the Indian prince first began to reveal his genius to England.

The Piece must have had much to do with the correct moulding of Hobbs's technique. Provided a young batsman has inherent ability there is no better place to build a solid defence than on a turf that scoots, jumps and imparts abnormal break to the ball. Given too much of it a batsman could form bad habits, such as drawing away from the ball, but the correct amount at a formative time leads to a sharpening of the eyesight, quick footwork and deft wielding of the bat. Such an experience leads the youngster to notable deeds when he finds himself on better, truer pitches.

Hobbs has acknowledged his debt to Tom Hayward in his early days – Hayward introduced him to Surrey – but it is well to note Hobbs's claim that he never had an hour's coaching in his life. He was a self-made cricketer – observing, thinking and executing for himself.

He didn't copy Hayward's stance at the wickets, although there was a similarity. Hobbs improved on Hayward's stance, which was decidedly two-eyed, with the left foot pointing almost straight up the pitch, the two shoulders round and the face practically full on to the bowler. Hobbs, like Denis Compton, had his face, and thus his right shoulder, a little fuller to the bowler than most top-ranking batsmen and herein, as with Compton, could have been the secret of his remarkable prowess in playing on-side strokes. I think that was the case, although, and in this consideration I include Compton again, Hobbs could not have played the cover-drive and the square-drive – both forward – had his body not been admirably positioned to allow of the correct back-swing. Such strokes are immediately denied the 'two-eyed' stancer because he can't swing back through his body.

Hobbs was one of the twelve children of a groundsman at Jesus College, Cambridge. His own first job was as groundsman at Bedford school, where he also did some net-bowling against the schoolboys. His life was thus inseparable from cricket but he had an early set-back when he was recommended to the Essex County Club and found not good enough! Essex turned him down.

Then he tried with Surrey, was immediately accepted and in his second match scored a glorious 155 against Essex. Every run must have given him a special pleasure and, knowing that their club had spurned him, the Essex players must have some galling thoughts at the end of the game – and forever afterwards through Hobbs's great career.

Fittingly enough, for he was years afterwards to displace the Great Man as a scorer of centuries, Hobbs played his first game for Surrey against the Gentlemen of England, captained by Dr W. G. Grace. The game of cricket was to know no greater stealer of a run than Hobbs and, facing up to Grace, he should have got off the mark with a quick single.

Hobbs, very nervous against Grace, played several balls and then played one a few yards up the pitch. He quickly sensed there was a run to be 'stolen' but just as he began his run the quavery voice of the Doctor came down the pitch; 'Thank you, youngster, just tap it back here and save my poor old legs!'

And Hobbs, suitably impressed by the Old Man, who was a terror to the game's newcomers, tapped the ball back to him. He made 18 in the first innings and 88 in the second.

Hobbs played for Surrey against Darling's great Australian side of 1905. He batted beautifully against Cotter, then at his fastest, and had reached 94 when a thrilling throw-in by Clem Hill from the Kennington Oval boundary hit the stumps and ran him out. It was a compliment Hobbs often returned to the Australians. Perhaps the greatest cover-point ever – quick in anticipation, swift to the ball and unerring in his under-the-shoulder return – he had fifteen run-outs on his second tour of Australia in 1912.

No cover-point can ever be considered great unless he has deft, tinkling footwork. As the ball speeds towards him, cover-point must be on the way in to meet it, for a split second thus gained could bring the run-out and, moreover, he should so position his movements in to the ball and throw it to the desired end with one action. A champion cover-point must possess an additional sense. He must sense what the batsmen are doing, for his own eyes never leave the ball. He must, too, be a 'fox', yielding a single here and there to snare the batsman into a feeling of safety and, when his chance comes, cover-point must be able to hit the stumps from side-on nine times out of ten. Jack Hobbs had the lot – all the tricks.

Hobbs's Test career against Australia was preceded by disappointment. A. O. Jones brought the English side to Australia in 1907 with

Hobbs making his first trip. Jones became ill on the eve of the first Test in Sydney and Hobbs seemed certain to get the position. But the selectors did an odd thing, although it was to prove most successful. George Gunn, of Nottinghamshire, had travelled with the team on a health trip and he was asked to play, instead of Hobbs.

Hobbs was not only bitterly disappointed; he thought he had been badly treated, even though Gunn proved the hero of the game, scoring 119 and 74 in a masterly manner in his first Test. Anyway, Hobbs almost equalled the century feat with 83 in the following Test in Melbourne. Gunn headed the Test averages of the tour, 462 at an average of 51.33, and Hobbs was second with 302 runs at 43.14. Together, Gunn and Hobbs put on 134 in the final Test in Sydney. It was a partnership, according to those who saw it, which hasn't been excelled, for classical batsmanship, by any other two Englishmen in Australia.

Hobbs went home to make a 'duck' in his first Test innings against the Australians in England. The Birmingham pitch then was helpful to bowlers. Blythe and Hirst ran through Australia for the meagre total of 74. Hobbs opened for England but Macartney, with the new ball, had him quickly for a 'duck'. But in the second innings Hobbs made a brilliant 62 not out, top score for the match – and England won by ten wickets. His stroke play was classical, so much so that Englishmen described it as the best since Vic Trumper's performances of 1902.

That was a time of outstanding batting strength in English cricket. There were so many men of brilliance knocking at the Test door that those inside could barely afford to fail. Yet, with his own place by no means assured, Hobbs was responsible at Leeds for what Australians thought was a remarkable gesture.

The Captain, M. A. Noble told the story thus:

'Hobbs forced a ball off his back foot between short-leg and mid-on. In doing so he knocked off one of the bails. Believing that it was done in the act of making the stroke we appealed for hit wicket, but the umpire gave him not out on the ground that he had completed the stroke before his foot touched the stump.

'Two or three balls later Hobbs made a weak attempt to play a straight one and was bowled. My impression was then – and still is – that Hobbs believed himself legally to be out and deliberately allowed himself to be bowled. It is a most difficult thing to allow yourself to be bowled without betraying the fact to the bowler or someone fielding near the wicket. It was a match of small scores and the loss then of a player of Hobbs's ability probably had a determining influence upon our success in that game.'

Another Australian captain who spoke in warm terms of Hobbs's outstanding sportsmanship was H. L. Collins. Hobbs gave himself out once at Kennington Oval against the Australians after the umpire had said not out. Few Test cricketers down the years have done that. Most accept an umpire's blunder when it is their way on the principle that they are sometimes given out when they are not and, indeed, some of the moderns stay when an obvious catch has been made in the hope, unworthy as it is, that the umpire will make a mistake!

As I have said, Hobbs's greatness as a batsman lay not only in the fact that he got many runs with incredible consistency but also in the manner in which he made them. He was perfect in the execution of every stroke. His footwork was a model for all players and his style was irreproachable. He was always attractive to watch – a neat, compact figure, faultlessly attired in flannels – whether he was moving along at a fast rate or was on the defensive.

I asked him once which innings he considered the best he had played in Australia.

'Well,' he replied, 'it's a long time since I retired from first-class cricket, twenty-three years, and it was five years earlier that I last played in Australia. Memory grows dim. Quite naturally, I suppose, on being asked which was my best innings I try to recall which was the best of the nine Test centuries I scored in your country. There was that one in 1912 when I made 178 and along with Wilfred Rhodes put on 323 for the first wicket. England won the rubber by winning that match.

Then there was the 122 in the second Test at Melbourne in 1921, made for the most part on a rain-damaged wicket: but we lost that match. Both of those innings gave me a lot of pleasure because I felt that I had played pretty well – if I may, with modesty, say so.'

I put it to him that an achievement that will never be forgotten in Australia was the 49 he made in England's second innings of the third Test in Melbourne of the 1928–29 tour.

'Yes,' he agreed, 'perhaps it would be wise to select that innings as England won the match against all the odds. You would be surprised at the number of Aussies who mention that match when they call to see me in Fleet Street. Just the same as folk here speak about the fifth Test at the Oval in 1926 – another "sticky".' (Hobbs made a brilliant 100 on this later occasion, England winning back the Ashes.)

He continued: 'I well remember waiting in Melbourne for the wicket to dry so that we could continue the match. Australia still had two wickets to fall. I can recall very well how our friends came to the pavilion to commiserate with us, saying what a pity it was the rain came. We thought so too. We considered we didn't have a chance of getting the runs. That old campaigner Hughie Trumble, then secretary of the Melbourne Cricket Club, told us in all seriousness that 70 would be a good score in our second innings. Well, as you know, we chased 332 and eventually won by three wickets. Our success caused quite a stir at home. I remember that a London newspaper cabled out £100 each to Herbert Sutcliffe and myself.'

It was the opening partnership of 105 between Hobbs and Sutcliffe that enabled England to win that match. Not only was it rich in runs but it defied the Australian attack on one of the worst wickets known in Melbourne. Considering the difficulties, that opening partnership would possibly rank as the most outstanding one in Test history.

The wicket was bad all day, going through different phases. Thirty points of rain had fallen and the English innings began in gentle sunshine, increasing in intensity and drying the pitch in patches so that there were spots off which the ball kicked disconcertingly. It was at its most dangerous period from lunch to the tea interval.

The Australians had no fast bowler in this match, the opening bowlers, Hendry and a'Beckett, being no more than medium-pace, but there was an abundance of varied spin in Oxenham (medium off-breaks), Grimmett (leg-breaks) and Blackie (slow to slow-medium off-breaks).

On such a pitch against such spinners, the English task should have been an impossible one, but, right from the beginning, the two great opening batsmen dominated the pitch and the Australians.

For over after over, Blackie bowled around the wicket with a packed leg-side field, but by superb dead-bat play and adept pad-play, together with the most astute judgement in not playing at the ball when it wasn't necessary, Hobbs and Sutcliffe went on for one hour, then two hours and finally came to tea with the score 0–78 – Hobbs 36 and Sutcliffe 32. The whole members' stand rose to them in acclamation.

In effect, the leg-theory tactics of the Australians played into the hands of two such proficient batsmen. Ryder, fast-medium, often hit the body but never seemed likely to hit the stumps. Both batsmen were black and blue on the body – Hobbs was once hit on the head by Ryder – but they never flinched, even though the sharply rising balls yielded many byes off

Oldfield's body. Indeed, one ball from Oxenham rose so sharply off a length that it cleared Oldfield's head (the keeper was standing up to the stumps) for two byes. Three successive balls from Oxenham particularly revealed the conditions – one rose high and went from Oldfield's gloves to the first slip, the next hit Sutcliffe on the shoulder and the next went for a bye off Oldfield's shoulder.

While Hendry was bowling, Richardson, Blackie, Ryder, Bradman and a'Beckett formed a complete circle of under ten yards diameter around the batsman from silly-point to forward short-leg.

The two Englishmen on that day demoralized the Australian bowling, the fielding and the captaincy of Ryder. They gave their usual superb lesson of running between the wickets. One never let the other down. This was exemplified time after time in their calling and acceptance, many of the runs, of a seemingly dangerous nature at the beginning, being completed at a walk. Once, Hobbs walked out of his crease several yards before Blackie bowled and placed him to the on for two.

The century came in 133 minutes. Just before this the old field-marshal, Hobbs, using the stratagem of signalling for a bat, sent a message to Chapman in the pavilion to change his batting order, sending Jardine in next before Hammond.

It was a shrewd piece of advice. Hobbs went lbw to Blackie at 49, but at stumps England were 1–171 – Sutcliffe 83 and Jardine 18. There were 13 byes in that total. Commenting on this in England, Strudwick said: 'A wet wicket in Melbourne is about the worst of its kind, especially for the wicket-keeper. The ball does all sorts of funny things.'

In short, the old firm of Hobbs and Sutcliffe, making their eighth opening stand of a century against the Australians, out-generalled and out-played Ryder and his men. The next day, with three wickets falling for 14 after the match was all but won, England took the honours by three wickets. Sutcliffe played perhaps his greatest innings, 6½ hours for 135 – but undoubtedly it was that opening stand that won the match.

Hobbs found his first great opening partner for England in Wilfred Rhodes and it was fitting that another Yorkshireman, Sutcliffe, should have been his second. Hobbs and Rhodes made a record 221 for the first wicket against South Africa in Cape Town in 1910: and in Melbourne in 1912 they put on 323 against Australia. This still stands on a record for Tests.

Hobbs was at his best in Melbourne, as his records show. In 1926, when Australia had hit up a record first innings tally of 600, one London newspaper announced on its placard: 'Australia 600: Come on Hobbs!' With Sutcliffe, Hobbs batted all the next day, the opening being worth 283. The same newspaper said on its placard next day: 'Thank you Hobbs!'

'Figures,' an admirer once wrote of Hobbs, 'can convey no idea of the Master, of his full-blooded hooking when he was young, of his driving on light, swift feet, of his peerless square-cut, of his leaning leg-glance, of the natural growth of his talents to a quite regal control and superiority.'

There was all that success, too, as I have stressed, when the fight was hardest, when the pitch was cranky. Somebody once aptly observed that it was Hobbs who took the description 'unplayable' out of the category of pitches.

Douglas Jardine, who saw many great batsmen at close quarters, was once asked to name the greatest. He didn't hesitate. 'Hobbs,' said Jardine, 'is number one every time. He was so good on bad pitches.' The interviewer interposed another name. Jardine looked out the window – and refused to answer.

Jack Fingleton, Masters of Cricket (1958)

J. T. Tyldesley

In July 1895 a young cricketer, playing for Lancashire against a strong Gloucestershire XI, batted with an assurance that moved W. G. Grace, in his position at point, to paternal interest and approval. 'Eh, eh,' commented his high voice, 'he's a good lad, and when he learns to play with a straight bat he'll do.' The young cricketer, though he never learned to play with the straight bat (it wasn't in his line), became one of the greatest professional batsmen we have ever had. 'What's his name?' asked Old Trafford on that July day. 'Ty'desley, Tyl-des-ley, Ty'd-dle-sley?' The progress of this cricketer to a popularity with the Old Trafford crowd far beyond that ever known by any other Lancashire player was marked by the changes in the name the crowd knew him by, each change denoting a more and more intimate notion of him. First it was 'Ty'd'sley', then 'J.T.T.', and finally 'John Tommy'. He became one of the county's common possessions – institutional. 'Mornin', Johnny,' somebody would say to him as he stood at his place on the boundary, and when he let it be understood by a glance over the shoulder that Familiarity had not gone out to the winds over his head, then Familiarity preened itself and said to the multitude around: 'Nice feller'.

A lot of people, it seemed, knew him very well – met him on the train from Monton every morning and even went to the same barber's. He really was everybody's business. Mature men, working at grey cloths in George Street on hot afternoons, used to ask, on hearing Lancashire's score was 157 for five: 'How's Johnny gone on?' A great man does not come to this kind of easy familiarity with average folk unless there is nature as well as art in his achievement. Nobody on the sixpenny side ever shouted right from his heart, 'Hello, Charlie!' at C. B. Fry, or 'Hello, Willie!' at W. G. Quaife. Art or high skill refined these cricketers out of the tracks of simple comprehension. Tyldesley was even cleverer than these two batsmen, but his play had in it no austerities, no alienating refinements. His was batsmanship of a sort the average man would cultivate if he could. Technically, of course, Tyldesley's cricket touched an excellence rare even amongst the masters; it is the spirit of his play that is being discussed at the moment, and that was democratic enough – his was batsmanship 'a fellow could understand'.

A bat, indeed, can look an entirely different instrument in different hands. With Grace it was a rod of correction, for to him bad bowling was a deviation from moral order; Ranjitsinhji turned a bat into a wand, passing it before the eyes of the foe till they followed him in a trance along his processional way; George Hirst's bat looked like a stout cudgel belabouring all men not born in Yorkshire; Macartney used his bat all for our bedazzlement, as Sergeant Troy used his blade for the bedazzlement of Bathsheba – it was a bat that seemed everywhere at once, yet nowhere specially. And for Tyldesley a bat was an honest broadsword – a broadsword drawn in no service but the service of Lancashire. This last sentence is not intended as a rhetorical flourish. If we are not to go wrong over the character of Tyldesley we need to know that for him batsmanship was first and last a means to a workmanlike end, which was Lancashire's welfare. The brilliance of his play often blinded one to Tyldesley the canny utilitarian. Art for art's sake was not his cry; his play took the senses by assault, inflamed the imagination, but certain it is he never set himself deliberately to do it. To say the truth, we are at liberty to remark of this wonderful cricketer, who was perhaps the most skilful, the most audaciously inventive batsman of his time, that his philosophy is contained in: 'Be good in service and let who will be clever.' He shed glory over the field unwittingly. A bird that is attending to the hard utilitarian job of building a nest will move us to the artist's delight by poise of swift curving flight. And an innings by Tyldesley, though moving on wings and enrapturing the senses, was always attending to the utilitarian job of building the Lancashire nest. What was an innings of a hundred to Tyldesley if victory did not come to Lancashire along with it? – the man was mocked; the taste of ashes was in his mouth. This, of course, is not the way of the artist. *He* can thrive on an individual achievement because of the wonder in it. He lights his fire that he and others may just be ravished by colour and fine flame: he does not insist that it should be capable of boiling the pot. Tyldesley was certainly not an artist in this deliberate and proud, selfish way. Remember his dourness as he stood over his bat ready for the bowler's attack. He was the image of antagonism, vigilant and shrewd. Tyldesley never seemed, even in his most sparkling innings, to be toying with the bowlers in the manner of the virtuoso, merely to amuse himself and us; he most plainly was checkmating them by courage and opportunism. If he was audacious that was because audacity 'paid' – offence was his best means of defence. He improvised strokes never seen before on the cricket field, not out of the artist's love of doing things in a new way, but because inimical circumstances would not be thrust aside by the old expedients. When he tried a fresh stroke he asked if it 'worked' – like a born pragmatist – not if it was 'artistic'. We all recollect his slash stroke, that upper-cut over the slips' heads. It was not beautiful to see, but immensely fruitful of runs. Had it happened in an innings by Spooner it would have looked like a flaw in a delicate piece of porcelain. But how in keeping the stroke was with the punitive game of Tyldesley!

Again, take his on-driving: he had no objections to lofting the ball, so long as it was lofted warily and profitably. The batsman who is an artist before he is a cricketer has a fastidiousness which is set all on edge, so to say, at the very sight of a stroke 'off the carpet'. Tyldesley had no such compunction. Nor is his lofty on-driving to be taken as evidence that after all he was more than the canny utilitarian, that he liked now and then to live dangerously for the good of his spirit. No; when Tyldesley sent the ball into the air he knew exactly what he was doing; he was not snapping fingers at Providence, nor indulging in quixotry. It is doubtful whether Tyldesley ever hit into the air during a big match out of sheer high spirits. Perhaps the field was set inconveniently for ground hits; very well then, they must go over the heads of the scouts. He could place the ball almost to a nicety. So with his famous cut from the middle stump. Surely, you might object, this stroke was a piece of coxcombry – a display of skill for skill's sake, or, at any rate, a display of skill intended to astound us. Why should it have been? The cut was Tyldesley's master-stroke; he had it under perfect control. 'But,' you may still object, 'why from the middle stump? – nothing canny about an adventure like that.' You may be sure Tyldesley did not cut from the middle stump without a good workmanlike reason. Bowlers knew that he would cut to ribbons anything on the off-side at all short, and they would in consequence keep on or near Tyldesley's wicket. Was Tyldesley then going to let his cut go into disuse? Was his most productive hit to run to waste? Why should he not cut a short ball on the middle stump? Let him only get into position for it – and his foot play was quicker than the eye could follow – and it was much the same as a ball on the off-side, made for cutting. Of course if he missed it the chances were that he would be out. Well, he weighed the chances against his marvellous ability at the cut, and the risk was not palpably greater than the risk a cricketer takes in playing any straight ball – either defensively or offensively.

Macartney used to cut from the middle stump – but for a different reason than Tyldesley's. Macartney would exploit the hit even when it was in his power to make another and safer and even more profitable stroke. For Macartney, though a good antagonist, was a better artist; the spoils of war became in time cheap and tawdry to him. Often did one see disillusion on his face at the end of an opulent innings. Then would he find the challenge of the best bowler irksome: he would throw discretion to the winds in a way that a sound tactician like Tyldesley never did. To refresh his spirit, to save himself from the stale and the flat, he was ready to risk the profitable – to indulge in some impossibly fanciful play of the bat. In this hot quixotic mood his wicket would go to the simplest ball. 'Macartney gets himself out,' was a common saying. How rarely one heard that much said of Tyldesley. A bowler had to work for the wicket of Tyldesley. You might baffle him by skill, inveigle him into a false step; never could you hope that he would give himself away. He wore the happy-go-lucky colours of the care-free soldier of fortune, but they were as borrowed plumes: in the flesh Tyldesley was a stern Ironside, with a Cause – the cause of Lancashire – so sacred that it demanded that a man cast the vanities of art and self-glorification to the wind. This most dazzling of all Lancashire batsmen was, forsooth, a Puritan – a conscript of conscience even, trusting in Lancashire but keeping his powder dry!

There lived not a bowler in his time that did not suffer the scourge intolerable from Tyldesley's bat. Rarely was he to be found not 'ware and waking – on a sticky wicket he was as formidable as on a dry one. At the Oval, or at Edgbaston, his happy hunting-ground, the bowler all too soon would behold Tyldesley's wicket as a wicket a long way distant, his bat a sword of fire guarding it. 'Heaven help me!' the sweaty toiler would appeal to the sky. 'If only he would let one go! I don't ask for his wicket – I've been flogged out of vanity like that – but merciful power can surely grant me a maiden over now and then.' Maiden over, indeed, with Tyldesley in form! He would plunder the six most virgin deliveries you ever saw. It was hard even to pitch a decent length to him. For he knew, unlike the modern batsman, that length is not absolute, but relative to a batsman's reach. And though Tyldesley was a little man, his feet had the dancing master's lightness and rapidity of motion. He covered a larger floor space as he made his hits than any batsman playing today – not even excepting Hobbs. What a disdain he must have in these times for the excuse of timid batsmen that they must needs cultivate patience till bad bowling comes to them! How long would Tyldesley have required to wait for half-volleys from J. T. Hearne, Trumble, Blythe, Noble and the rest? He turned the well-pitched bowling of these masters into the length a punishing hit asks for by swift foot-play. He would jump a yard out of his ground to make a half-volley; he would dart back to the wicket's base to make a long-hop. Two old cricketers once discussed an innings by Tyldesley after the day's cricket was over in something like this language: 'Tha's a reight bowler, Tom. What's thi analysis today – after Johnny'd done wi' thi?' 'Nay, Bill, be fair – tha can't deny I bowl'd well. It wer' t' wicket were too good; I couldn't get any spin on th' ball.' 'Spin, eh? I likes that. Spin on th' ball? Why, I never saw thi' hit th' floor all th' afternoon.'

He was in possession of all known strokes, and, as we have seen, he improvised strokes of his own when circumstances challenged him to do so. His square cut was powerful, and the action of it has been vividly described by C. B. Fry: 'He threw the bat at the ball without letting go of the handle.' Many a day-dreaming point – they needed a point, very deep, to Tyldesley – has been seen hopping agitatedly after the advent of the Tyldesley cut. Sometimes he went on his toe-points to make this stroke. His driving was accomplished by a vehement swing of the bat and a most gallant follow-through. There was no saying whether forward or back play was the mark of his style, he combined the two so thoroughly. He was perhaps the best batsman of all time on a bad wicket. P. F. Warner is never tired of singing the praises of Tyldesley's innings of 62 made on a 'glue-pot' at Melbourne in 1904. England's total was then 103, and Relf was the only other batsman to get double figures.

A great batsman is to be estimated, of course, not merely by his scores, or even by his technique, but also by taking into account the quality of the bowling he had to tackle in his day, and the quality of the grounds he mainly played on. When Tyldesley came to greatness English bowling was in a classic period; he had to face men like Lohmann, Richardson, Peel, J. T. Hearne, Noble, Jones. But not only did he take his whack out of some of the best of our classical bowlers; he was also one of the first batsmen to master the new 'googly' bowling. He passed, in fact, through all the manifold changes in fashion which came over bowling between 1903 and 1919. And whether it was J. T. Hearne or R. O. Schwarz, Rhodes, or D. W. Carr, Tyldesley was always the same brilliant and punitive Tyldesley. Then let us bear in mind as we do honour to his genius that half of Tyldesley's cricket was played at Old Trafford, where in his time the wickets were not above suspicion. What would Tyldesley's record have been had he played mainly on the hard, beautiful wickets of Kennington Oval? But Tyldesley himself never would worry his head over the averages and records, nor need we. His service was all for England and his county – given in happy devoted heart. Think of him as eternally brilliant if you like, but also think of him as eternally modest – if you would have a notion of the real Tyldesley in mind. The man is by nature as discreet and modest as few geniuses ever are, and that modesty and discretion, as one has tried to show, came out even in his most flashing play. Once, in the days when cricketers were asked by a London newspaper to write reports, Tyldesley was the historian of the Lancashire XI. And he wrote his accounts very much in this style: 'Yesterday we had the good luck to get Worcestershire out cheaply, thanks to some good bowling by Mr Brearley and Dean. When we went in the wicket was faster, and Mr MacLaren and Mr Spooner, batting finely, gave us a good start. Sharp did well too, and Mr Poideven had the misfortune to play on after a promising beginning. I also managed to get a few.' And turning to the scores you would read:

A. C. MacLaren b Wilson 41
R. H. Spooner *c* Arnold b Wilson 31
Tyldesley not out 200
L. O. S. Poidevin b Arnold 16
Sharp b Burrows 20
Extras 10

Total (for 4 wickets) 318

The real Tyldesley peeped out in his cricket writings – and he never played an innings that was untrue to his nature.

Neville Cardus, *Day in the Sun* (1924)

George Headley

'Statistics prove—' began a speaker on the wireless the other night, and I turned him off at once. Yet in George Headley's case the bare statistics are the best introduction to his cricket. He was born in Jamaica in 1909, and in 1926 emerged from the village green into good club cricket. Tradition has it that he still wore short trousers. The youthful Bradman, it is related, astonished a big club in Australia both by his batting and by his black trousers. Victor Trumper also banged a Test-match bowler about when clad in other than the regulation white flannel. Some forty years ago Ephraim Lockwood, hastily summoned to fill a breach, went in to bat at the Oval in a check shirt and short pants. The Ovalites were convulsed with laughter. They had a lot of time in which to laugh, for Ephraim made over 80. Constantine relates that his father objected to his coming too early into first-class cricket and would not help him to buy flannels, wherefore he had to save the money sixpence by sixpence. So the material gathers for an essay on 'The nether garments of budding Test cricketers'. Remains only he who wearing none at all, makes his mark in a match: the prospect is not so remote in these nudist days.

The next year, 1927, Headley attracted the notice of the local authorities and earned a place in the Jamaica side against the Hon. L. H. Tennyson's Eleven. Against Clark, M. J. C. Allom, Lee (G. M.), A. L. Hilder and T. Arnott, Headley made 16 and 71, 211, 40 and 71. In the long innings he gave one chance, a hard one, early in the innings, and scored the 211 out of 348.

As is the sad lot of the West Indian batsman, he got no more first-class cricket until the next year, 1929, when Sir Julien Cahn took a team including Astill, Mercer, Durston and Nichols. Headley made 57 and 22, 17 and 43, 41 and 143. He had therefore played in six first-class matches and was not yet twenty-one years old when the MCC team under Calthorpe went to the West Indies in 1930. The bowlers on this team were Calthorpe himself, Voce, Astill, Wilfred Rhodes, Nigel Haig, G. T. S. Stevens. Limited as was his experience, they could do nothing at all with Headley. It was his first trip away to play, and he travelled from island to island for the Tests. In Barbados in the first Test he made 21 and 176; in Trinidad, 8 and 36; and in the British Guiana Test, 114 and 112. Going back home to meet them in Jamaica, he made 64 and 72 and 52; and in the fourth Test, 10 and 223.

In the autumn of that year he went to Australia. He began with 25 and 82 against New South Wales and followed them up with 131 against Victoria on the Melbourne wicket on the first day, batting before lunch. He made 1,000 runs in the season, scored a century in the third Test, and one in the fifth. Last year Lord Tennyson again took a team to Jamaica. Headley made 344 not out, 84 and 155 not out, and 140. His figures to date are 30 matches, 54 innings, 3,507 runs, highest score 344 not out, average 70.14. He has made in all thirteen centuries, including two double and one treble century, and a century in each innings of a Test match.

Whatever statistics may or may not prove, such scoring has only itself to blame if it arouses abnormal expectations. Moreover, he is as great a master of style as he is of runs.

He is a Negro, finely built but short and small, and only a careful judge of physique would notice him in a crowd. But at the wicket no one can miss his mastery. He is of that type which uses a bat as if it is an extension of the arm. Ease, poise and balance, he has them all. Good as his footwork is for defensive play, it is even better in the way he makes ground to the ball. He and Edwin St Hill, the Lowerhouse professional, are great friends, a friendship which began at the nets before the first Test at Barbados in 1930. Edwin St Hill, bowling strong fast-medium, was amazed to see the little Jamaican wristing the good-length ball away between mid-on and short leg or jumping in to drive it. Though he makes all the strokes, these are the two in which he specializes – forcing the ball away on the on side with a back stroke and getting to the pitch to drive. In a bright summer the slow bowlers will be glad to see him go.

As will be noticed from the scores enumerated, he is always in form, and it was noted that he never batted better during the whole of the Australian trip than in the first innings of all – against New South Wales. Hugh Trumble said that the Melbourne innings was one of the best that he had ever seen, and many habitués of the Melbourne ground thought that no finer innings had ever been played there. Headley is a good field. Formerly, he was brilliant, but in Australia, for some reason, the edge of his keenness left him. I have seen him bowl Hendren, well set, three off-breaks and then send one away from the edge of Hendren's bat into the slips, where it was dropped. After that, however, he had shot his bolt.

Headley is a commercial clerk in ordinary life, but is devoted to cricket and is 'a good lad'. If he has to bat tomorrow, he goes to bed tonight. In Australia he failed to get runs against Grimmett. 'I have to make a century against Grimmett,' he told his friend St Hill. Batting very carefully, he made it in the third Test. 'Satisfied?' asked St Hill. 'Not yet; I have to master him now.' In the fifth Test Headley made another century in a little over two hours, playing so brilliantly that even Bradman, Kippax and the rest joined in the applause. 'Satisfied?' asked St Hill. 'Ye-es,' said Headley, hesitatingly. He had been brilliant, but it galled him that he had had to treat Grimmett with some respect. It is the genuine artistic instinct faithful to an inner ideal.

C. L. R. James, *Manchester Guardian* (1933)

'Endren, 'Earne and 'Aig

It is an odd thing, but I cannot remember much about my first visit to Lord's. I know I was staying with Uncle Dick and Auntie Mollie at Hendon. I often would spend short holidays with them – special treats – in the early 1930s. They were both cricket enthusiasts, and would take me with them to Lord's on a Saturday, the *speciallest* treat of all. I was already watching first-class cricket regularly at Leyton, and can remember a good deal about many of the matches I saw there. But the pictures of Lord's are vaguer. I would have guessed that my first match was Middlesex v. Nottinghamshire – I can see Uncle Dick scanning his scorecard with a professional air, and saying disappointedly, 'Oh, Sam Staples isn't playing'; or it might have been Middlesex v. Lancashire, a match in which a Lancastrian called Hodgson (a fast bowler) took a splendid catch in the deep, only a few yards away from us. We usually arrived early, and took seats in front of the Tavern, though on one occasion at least – perhaps there was an especially large crowd, or Uncle Dick had had a rise in pay – we ascended to the Mound Stand. Yet I have studied the scores in *Wisden* for the conceivable seasons, and no detailed memories are stirred.

'PATSY BY NATURE'

But I retain strong impressions of some of the Middlesex players of those years. The strongest – very properly, for a small boy – is of Hendren. He was small, he was nimble, he could catch them in the deep as well as the slips, he could hit the ball like a thunderbolt: everyone knew him as Patsy ('He was baptized Elias and the crowds would have none of it', wrote Cardus, 'for he is Patsy not only by name but by nature'). Once the Middlesex players were throwing catches to one another, at the fall of a wicket. They were fairly languid catches, for it was a hot day. Hendren caught a gentle one near the ground, and in the same movement flicked it smartly backwards to his captain, Haig, who was standing, arms folded, a few yards behind him. It took Haig in the tummy. How we laughed!

Hendren was not one of those cricketers whose apparently brimming good humour on the field was matched by moroseness off it (we can all think of one or two of those). He was a man of wisdom as well as gaiety, what our ancestors used to call a 'thorough' man, the same wherever you sliced him.

Uncle Dick and Auntie Mollie were both Northerners, as I was myself, but like everyone else they yielded to Hendren, and cheered when he made a big score, even if it was against Yorkshire or Lancashire. They had plenty to cheer. I know that a comparison of the statistics of different periods is a vague guide, but he scored over 57,000 runs, average nearly 51, in a career lasting from 1907 to 1938 (not much accomplished before the First World War) with 170 centuries. Only Hobbs and Woolley have scored more runs, and only Hobbs has scored more centuries. It is true that Hendren took some time to get going in Test cricket. This was partly because he was hesitant early in his innings, not a good quality against Gregory and MacDonald. He began the 1921 Test series with 0, 7, 0 and

10. But he would hook the fast bowlers fearlessly when his eye was in and had the footwork to run down the pitch to the spinners, and at the end of his 51 Tests he had scored 3,500 runs, average 48.

We did not – Auntie Mollie and Uncle Dick and I – think so much of Haig, or even Hearne, who after Hendren was the best Middlesex batsman. In the case of Hearne, this was understandable. He was near the end of a long and distinguished career, which had been much handicapped by ill health. He had become a slow, and even dull, batsman, at least to small boys. I have a recollection of even the Lord's boys urging him to get out, so that Hendren could come in. We were unjust to the elegant Hearne, but even Robertson-Glasgow, in a laudatory article, was constrained to write of him, 'So smooth and contained was his method that few spectators, with all respect to them and their shillings, could know how wonderful was the art presented to them.' I was not one of the few, though Uncle Dick, anxious to be knowledgeable, made explanatory comments. Hearne scored 37,000 runs, average nearly 40, so he could not have been too bad; and also took 1,800 wickets, mostly with legbreaks, though we did not think of him as a bowler by the time I saw him.

HS AT THE OVAL

The joke has often been repeated that the Lord was being mischievous when, in the 1900s, he granted Surrey a succession of cricketers whose name began with the letter H. All the talk at the Oval was of 'Ayward, 'Obbs, 'Ayes, 'Olland and 'Itch. But Middlesex (where the aitches are not, apart from the pavilion, much more common than at the Elephant and Castle) were doing well in the early 1930s with 'Endren, 'Earne, 'Ulme, 'Art and 'Aig. Auntie Mollie, who was careful to pronounce her aitches, did not like Haig much. 'Too much of a toff,' she said, and certainly he looked one as he strode down the pavilion steps (the professionals used to come out from their own dressing room, tucked away to the side, a comfortable distance from the pavilion. They need not have done so, but they thought it was not worth the bother of walking round).

Robertson-Glasgow writes more affectionately of Haig than of Hearne. No doubt the men had more in common. Haig was captain of Middlesex from 1929 to 1932, in which years they came nearer to the bottom than the top. He was in one respect a good captain, fond of a chancy declaration. Sussex felt that one season he deprived them of the championship when he made a rash one against Lancashire. In another respect he was a bad one, because once he had started bowling (fast-medium with the occasional out-swinger) he could not bear to take himself off. He played for England against Australia in 1921 – but a great many cricketers played for England in that series. I think Hendren did quite right to smack him in the tummy.

Alan Gibson, The Cricketer (1980)

E. R. Wilson – Yorkshire

In combined accuracy of bowling and of memory no known cricketer has equalled E. Rockley Wilson. As no other, he could drop a ball on the needful spot and his mind on the required incident.

Yet, for a player of eminence, his appearances in first-class cricket have been few. Winchester needed him from May to August, to coach cricket and to teach French in his inimitable and metaphorical manner, and, in August, not even he could command a set place among the pick of Yorkshire. Then, in August of 1919, when he was forty, he came out to show an ignorant and negligent age the meaning of length, taking 36 wickets for Yorkshire at 16.58 each, including Jack Hobbs, when well set, at the Oval.

In 1920 he took 39 wickets at 15.48 each, and remarked, with that jigging push at the knot of his neck-tie, 'I was the discovery of the season.' Anyhow, the selectors noticed him, and he went on his first trip to Australia, under J. W. H. T. Douglas. In the fifth Test match, at Sydney, he took the wickets of Kelleway, Mailey, and Collins for 36 runs.

As a Rugbeian freshman at Cambridge in 1899, he was also a very skilled batsman. In his first match, for A. J. Webbe's team against the University, scores of 117 and 70 suggested that he was playing on the wrong side. He got his Blue, a year too late to receive it from his brother, C. E. M. In his third year against Oxford he scored 118 and 27, and took 5 for 71 and 2 for 38. This season also marked the last of his youthful appearances for Yorkshire. They were far from unsuccessful, but too many were waiting to play. Eleven years later he played eight innings for Yorkshire, and, against Essex, at Bradford, scored 104 not out, 'driving in great form'. In 1922 he took part in a last-wicket stand against Lancashire at Old Trafford during the last over of which that calculating

415

genius, Rhodes, with four runs needed for victory, made no attempt to score from a no-ball, and the match was drawn amid a silence as of the tomb. In this match Geoffrey Wilson fell ill, and Rockley Wilson, assuming the captaincy, led Yorkshire to victory in the Championship.

Throughout these years his art was infused into many generations of Winchester cricketers. As a coach he can have had few equals. He not only knew the game, science and soul, and, to the finest shade, what a young player could be induced to learn, but, like Alfred Shaw, he could pitch the ball pretty well where he liked. 'And now I'll hit you on the toe,' he once said, and hit it. In the middle he was almost certain death to the firm-footed hitter and the shuffling prodder.

The full Rockley Wilson is locked away in the hearts of many friends and pupils, to be brought out, with due and affectionate exaggeration, at reunions and chance meetings. His exquisite wit and impromptu felicities should not wear the dull garb of print; but among the Rockleiana there is one comment too perfect to omit. A noble cricketing lord, whose awful majesty hid a kindly heart, was holding select court in a pavilion, and, seeing Rockley, gave him a shake of the hand. Rockley turned to a friend and whispered: 'Lucky to get a touch.'

R. C. Robertson-Glasgow, Cricket Prints (1943)

L. C. Braund – Somerset

A critic once wrote, with truth and traditional ceremony: 'Braund (L. C.), of Somersetshire, is undoubtedly the most accomplished all-round cricketer of the present day.'

Separating the individual from his profession, I should add that Leonard Braund is one of the characters of England.

He has an air. The tilt of his bowler-hat challenges and easily defeats Fate, who has come back at Braund often, fiercely, and laughably in vain. It is a very smart hat, renewed and therefore, as it were, plural, but of one particular era, and therefore singular; it suggests Romano's and company, and unboastful naughtiness.

He has a slow voice, with a natural and inquiring drawl. When he is inclined to speak on cricket he speaks with long wisdom and a humour that has little respect for persons, and none at all for averages, records, and clumps of figures. He tells of great cricketers, and why they were great; of little cricketers, and why they don't understand their littleness.

He illustrates a stroke with casual cane, or a spin with a snap of the fingers; then suddenly dismisses all with a bout of damnation on coupons, long-hops, of the degeneracy of beer. He may remind you, with a still half-incredulous chuckle, that he refused a second Benefit match at Taunton because he had lost money on the first.

But he will leave you to know or discover that in one series of Tests in Australia he scored a classic century and also took 8 for 81 in one innings, with leg-breaks of nearly medium pace; that on his first appearance for England against South Africa, at Lord's, he made 104, that he once caught the mighty Clem Hill at fine-leg when his official and starting place was at slip.

I count myself lucky to have stood for one August next to Braund in the slips, for the sake of his conversation, for some unlikely catches made so easy, for some easy catches floored with a 'Now, would you believe it?' In batting the style, but no longer the full effect, of greatness was upon him. He had given up bowling; but he would roll a few down between the fall of wickets; and he gave rich advice to the young. Then, they didn't always take it. Now, the advice lives in the mind; its giver in the heart.

R. C. Robertson-Glasgow, *Cricket Prints* (1943)

W. Bestwick – Derbyshire

In the pavilion at Taunton there hung, and, if justice abounds, still hangs, a photograph showing William Bestwick, of Derbyshire, and John Cornish White, of Somerset, shaking hands on the cricket field at Derby. During the two days before, 20 and 21 June 1921, each had taken all ten wickets in an innings – White, slow left-hand, against Worcestershire at Worcester; Bestwick, fast right-hand, against Glamorgan at Cardiff.

In the ensuing match of mutual celebration, White bowled 75 overs and took 13 wickets, Bestwick bowled 58.1 overs and took 5 wickets. They were not of the sort that leans back on a laurel. They were natural men of work. White tilled the face of the earth, Bestwick dug in its bowels; together, they provided good things to eat and a good fire to cook them by.

It is twenty years to this day since Bestwick played in his last match. Among many reasons, technical and social, why he should be remembered, the strongest is that he belonged to the now less fashionable school of faster bowlers, who, having been put on, are left on; or, rather, left alone; not interfered with. He arrived into cricket at that era which was golden for batting and iron for fast bowling.

The art of nursing had not yet come to relieve and insult the toilers under the sun. Bestwick, tall enough, and tremendous of shoulder and arm, didn't need a nurse. A batsman who could fight, an umpire with two out of his five senses, a quart or so of beer at mid-day and sunset, earthy laughter and cursing – these were his game.

His entry into county cricket, at the age of twenty-two, could excite little notice from any but the chroniclers, and, possibly, his own family. He played in eight matches – bowling average 53.75, batting 2.75. 'Other way round, now,' he said to an earnest inquirer, 'and what a laad I'd a'been.'

But Derbyshire, soon to be deprived of both the Davidsons, stuck to him, and in his fourth season he came out top bowler of the bottom county. Three times he had his 100 wickets, then retired, with the encouragement of the committee, to cricket in South Wales.

Here he exercised his strong arm and stronger conversation till, in 1919, Derbyshire, discovering themselves with some to bat but few to bowl, recalled Bestwick, now forty-three, but with native skill unsullied and with native accents unimpaired. He took 89 wickets for them. No one else could do better than 31. Next year, again bitten by the wander-bug, or by some unanalysed form of disgust, he removed his services to the League.

His only bowling that summer for Derbyshire yielded him 7 wickets for 97 runs in 53 overs; his batting, 1 and 5, both not out. But back he came to his own, and to that triumph of 1921; 147 wickets, at 16.72 each, with 7 for 84 against Yorkshire at Hull, including Sutcliffe and Holmes for 13 between them. In 1919 he bowled for the Players at Lord's, but fared poorly. He was less than himself in the London air. But he was considered for England against Armstrong's Australians. 'So was the whole — country,' he used to say.

Now he stayed at home. In his fiftieth year he took 7 for 20 against Leicestershire at Burton, missing victory by one wicket. Some ten days afterwards he played his last game for Derby, fittingly, at Cardiff. Cyril

Walters and Dai Davies were the last two victims of one who, as a lad, had taken the wickets of Brockwell, J. T. Brown, and A. O. Jones.

His bowling being finished and nearly 1,500 wickets taken for under 20 each, Bestwick stood umpire, vastly, for a few summers in county cricket; full of rough comfort and homely counsel for the young imitator.

R. C. Robertson-Glasgow, *Cricket Prints* (1943)

M. Leyland – Yorkshire

'Even at this moment the Sergeant is dishing out rations.' The Sergeant is Maurice Leyland, and these words are from another cricketer. Earlier he had remarked: 'He is quite unruffled, and we consider his aloofness a sort of genius.' And these words brought back to me Leyland standing absolutely still at the crease; not a shift of the foot, not a movement of shoulder or head; while O'Reilly started his odd, walloping, ducking run to the wicket. Leyland's mind, like his body, was still; no fretting, no impatience. He just stood, quietly dishing out defiance.

Leyland in a tight Test match reminded me of the famous four-squarers of ancient or romantic times. He was Horatius on the tottering bridge; Hector, who alone stood between Troy and destruction. He was born to rescue. But he is more dangerous than those who are just stubborn and grim. He has something of D'Artagnan in him; there is a gaiety besides the simplicity and strength; seen in the slight list of the cap, and in a certain jauntiness and optimism of gait.

But solidity is what you most notice in his batting; a breadth of defence most dispiriting to the bowler. His muscular strength is great, and those forearms were well made to destroy a long-hop or baste a half-volley.

In recent years an England Eleven never read well without Leyland's name. If something went wrong early none could so well repair the damage; and it was in the losing matches that you most clearly saw his greatness. He has never said 'Come in, then,' to the knock of defeat; even when the eleventh man joined him and there were 300 more runs to make on a doubtful pitch. His only concession to Fate would be to take guard again and to stare rather more fixedly at the bowler. When runs came easily on a perfect pitch in the sun, and life flowed gaily as the sparkling Thames, you might not particularly notice him. His element

419

was foul weather. He would disappear into the haze of Bramall Lane, where a sterner sort of game was being played under the name of cricket, and entrench himself among the sawdust and smoke and off-breaks and appeals, and do his raw, tough work in silence.

He played an innings of 137 at Melbourne on his first appearance for England. But his great year was 1934, when the Australians won back the 'Ashes' here. He made three centuries in the Test series, and, when all around him was falling, insisted on a century in the disastrous match at the Oval.

He regards his left-hand bowling as something of a humorous feat, sending down broad off-breaks with a broader smile; but he has taken more wickets than you would think, and has baffled the best with his strange twiddlings. I think his ambition is to shove Verity out of the analysis.

His attitude to the bowler may, with slight change, be taken from a letter to Dr Johnson: 'Any violence offered me I shall do my best to repel. I shall not be deterred by the menaces of a ruffian. Your rage I defy. Your abilities are not so formidable. I pay regard not to what you shall say, but to what you shall prove.'

R. C. Robertson-Glasgow, *Cricket Prints* (1943)

C. P. Mead – Hampshire

'Hants wickets fall. But Mead still batting.' Such, in brief, was the history of Philip Mead. There have, doubtless, been greater left-handed batsmen; certainly, there have been more attractive. None could have been further removed from what is, almost unutterably, called a 'glamour-boy'. But what other batsman has there been whose broad back a bowler has so rejoiced to see receding to the pavilion at long and weary last? I should say none in this generation.

He was number four. Perhaps two wickets had fallen cheaply; and there the cheapness would end. He emerged from the pavilion with a strong, rolling gait; like a longshoreman with a purpose. He pervaded a cricket pitch. He occupied it and encamped on it. He erected a tent with a system of infallible pegging, then posted inexorable sentries. He took guard with the air of a guest who, having been offered a weekend by his host, obstinately decides to reside for six months. Having settled his whereabouts with the umpire, he wiggled the toe of his left boot for some fifteen seconds inside the crease, pulled the peak of a cap that seemed all peak, wiggled again, pulled again, then gave a comprehensive stare around him, as if to satisfy himself that no fielder, aware of the task ahead, had brought out a stick of dynamite. Then he leaned forward and looked at you down the pitch, quite still. His bat looked almost laughably broad.

I have known him start poorly, but very seldom. You had to try for a fastish break-back on the off-stump; a leg-break to the left-hander. For his part, he liked to start with a comfortable push to leg; an amiable and natural desire that needed thwarting. He could play all the strokes, without frill or fancy; but, in general, he avoided adventure because he could prosper without it. His off-drive was exceptionally strong.

Risers didn't seem to hurt or harass him; there was, often, a heavy sweater, and some very solid Mead behind it. In defence, he sometimes used a stroke peculiar to himself, correcting an intended forward stroke to a sudden half-cock, which stunned the ball dead in front of his bat. His solid method gave a false impression of slow scoring. Two occasions come to my mind when he was utterly beaten. Once at Taunton, when he ran down the pitch to play, not hit, a ball from J. C. White, and was bowled yards from home. Another time at Weston-super-Mare, when W. T. Greswell made a ball swing in from Mead's leg, pitch on the middle-and-off, and knock out the middle stump. Almost the stick of dynamite.

But mostly, I think of Mead just batting on; a most fearful, interesting, and delightful opponent.

R. C. Robertson-Glasgow, Cricket Prints (1943)

W. J. O'Reilly – Australia

Bill O'Reilly was a fighter. He looked as if, under necessary circumstances, he might have founded or sacked a city. It was a face and form such as you might have seen in a picture of explorers or pioneers. At cricket he would have bowled till his boots burst, and after. If only one cricket ball was left in the world, and that one came to pieces in his hand, he would whiz down a leg-break with the largest fragment. Like Colonel J. W. H. T. Douglas, he had the inspired joy of battle; not the prone hope of the mere sticker, but the last fiery gift of the craftsman. And, with all that, he had gaiety not far latent.

He was a schoolmaster aged twenty-seven when he first played for Australia against England, having done well for New South Wales. It was D. R. Jardine's tour of 1932–33. Through the din of controversy a report, then an idea, reached us here of a new and important figure in cricket; of a bowler who on an Australian pitch could bend them from leg at nearly medium pace, and last all day. In those Tests he twice took 5 wickets in an innings and, in all, 27 wickets at about 27 each.

In 1934 O'Reilly came here under the calm, genial, and astute captaincy of W. M. Woodfull. To a stranger it was a strange bowling action. As with those more florid opponents of legendary heroes, there seemed to be more arms than Nature or the rules allow. During the run-up, a sort of fierce galumph, the right forearm worked like a piston; at delivery the head was ducked low, as if to butt the batsman on to his stumps. But it didn't take long to see the greatness; the control of leg-break, top-spinner, and googly; the change of pace and trajectory without apparent change in action; the scrupulous length; the vitality; and, informing and rounding all, the brain to diagnose what patient required what treatment.

His greatest triumph was in the first Test, at Nottingham. He took 11 wickets for 128 in 78.4 overs, and England lost that remarkable struggle against O'Reilly, Grimmett, and time. At Manchester, in the third Test, when England's total stood at 68 for no wicket, on the cosiest of pitches, he took the wickets of Walters (52), Wyatt (o), and Hammond (4) in four balls. England went on to score 627 for 9, declared. O'Reilly took 7 for 189 in 59 overs. In that Test series he had 28 wickets at 25 runs each.

Against G. O. Allen's team in Australia, 1936–37, his skill was, perhaps, more consistent than destructive, but he topped the 20 wickets. And so, with the wonderful Grimmett now bowling as it were from memory and left behind at home, O'Reilly came to England under Don Bradman in 1938. It was, surely, the most brittle bowling team that Australia has ever sent. It might, and it might not. On the whole, it didn't. But O'Reilly's genius, winning that glorious game at Leeds, kept the 'Ashes' in Australia and disaster at a distance, until that last resounding crash at the Oval.

Here he struggled on, frequently unaided by anything that mattered at all, sustained by his own will and his captain's example. In the total of

903 for 7 wickets he took 3 for 187 in 85 overs of which 26 were maidens. Hard pounding. Here he was outdone. But only once in those Tests did I see him over-matched, and that was when Hammond, in that wonderful 240 at Lord's, made pigmies of all rivals.

Off the course, as they say, he is a man of variety and humour. There is a story, too good to enlarge, of a goat found at midnight in an hotel bedroom, dressed austerely in a waistcoat, watch-chain and an inquiring look. O'Reilly insisted that it was the manager, but of what team or enterprise he would not say.

To end on more terrestrial matters, he was a dangerous left-handed hitter at the tail-end and a prehensile fielder. In all Anglo-Australian Tests he took, in nineteen matches, 102 wickets at 25.36 each. A great heart, and a great bowler.

R. C. Robertson-Glasgow, *Cricket Prints* (1943)

George Cox

George was a man of Sussex, with cricket in his blood and a gift with people of all ages that I have never seen equalled. Wherever he went there was sure to be laughter, a feeling of mellow well-being and a mischievous sense of fun. Crowds sat up in their deck-chairs at Hove and the Saffrons when George walked to the wicket. When his turn came to speak after dinner there would be a ripple of excitement, whether it was at the Hilton or in Ditchling Village Hall. Never, to my knowledge, did George disappoint his audience. No occasion could be too far gone in boredom to be rescued by his wit: his timing and his perfect sense of occasion were alert to every nuance, every sentiment, and it was typical of him that his jokes were almost all at his own expense.

Warnham was his first home and much of his early cricket was played there and at Horsham, where he was schooled at Collyer's School. He told with relish how, as a small boy, playing in his first match for the village, he came upon a bright half-crown on his way down to long-leg. Regarding it as legitimate treasure trove, he pocketed it, only to discover, when over was called, that it was the bowling mark of his captain and vicar, the Reverend Canon Felix Farebrother. It was fitting that only three summers ago George should have stood umpire when Warnham's smart new pavilion was opened by his friend Lavinia, Duchess of Norfolk. He was always faithful to his roots.

He played for Sussex before I was born and I played against him for Somerset in the match in which he scored his 50th century. Not many cricketers gave more pleasure to more people than did George, and most of his finest innings were played against the toughest opposition: Yorkshire before the war, Surrey after it. With August sun beating down on a good wicket, his cap pulled rather rakishly over one eye. George at the top of his form looked an England player. He timed the ball to perfection and seldom hit it in the air. His footwork was swift, his driving and cutting fierce. He ran between the wickets as one would expect of a dashing footballer who had played for Arsenal at centre-forward between the immortals, Alex James and David Jack, in an Arsenal XI which contained seven internationals. Here, if ever there was one, was the true Corinthian athlete. One only had to see him field at cover-point to realize that.

There will always be scores of cricketers who nearly did, or perhaps should have, played for England, but who did not. George always said with a smile that his problem had been that he was 'promising' all through his career. Some words of Maurice Leyland's come to mind about another much-loved county cricketer of the 1920s and 1930s, my old Christ's Hospital cricket coach, Len Bates of Warwickshire, who was, not surprisingly, a friend of George's. 'Len were a good lad,' said Maurice Leyland, 'he'd have played for England, but he played too pretty.' So it may have been with George. Figures didn't much interest him and he had to play his shots. Not for him the pawky prod. He was not, what I believe is called nowadays, a percentage player. In the best sense he was the most amateur of all the professional cricketers, and self-glorification and driving ambition were not a part of his make-up.

He enjoyed success. He could be downcast by failure. Which cricketer isn't? But he had all these emotions under control, though he used to say with whimsical wistfulness that there wasn't a county ground in England in the lavatory of which he had not cried his eyes out having made nought. Nor was he slow to remind us that he had unrivalled knowledge amongst specialist batsmen of first-class ducks; he scored 98 of them. He pointed out that, on balance, it had been very kind of the Sussex Cricket Committee to play him as a professional for the equivalent of two whole seasons without getting off the mark.

His sense of humour showed up even in his bowling, where his seemingly guileless 'drifters' lured many hungry batsmen to their doom. He was the only bowler I came across in first-class cricket who actually apologized to batsmen he dismissed. I remember how pleased he was, after taking four Lancashire wickets at Aigburth, to be mistaken by an old age pensioner for his father, who was, of course, one of the great Sussex bowlers before the First World War and for a decade after it. The old-age pensioner wrote a personal letter to George to say what a pleasure it was to see him bowling again after all those years, and he told George that the last time he had seen him bowl was way back in 1905. Young George worked it out that he would have had to have been at least seventy-seven to have bowled both those spells. That pleased him mightily.

I shall always think that it was the vicissitudes of the game which made George such a superb coach, for as a coach he was peerless. There was a yeoman philosopher lurking inside George. I wonder if any former crick-eter put more back into the game than he did, first at Winchester, where with Hubert Doggart and his beloved Harry Altham he helped to produce a series of remarkable school sides, then with the county side in Sussex and latterly as the President of the Sussex Junior Cricket Festival and President of the Sussex Cricket Society. He saw the game as an educator, a character builder, and he could talk about it with endless fascination.

For me the happiest days of my cricketing life were the Cambridge days and this happiness owed just about everything to George and those late April nets: two weeks of sheer heaven. Somehow in those early 1950s George seemed to bring the sunshine with him. The very cadence of his voice returns. 'Were you there?' when you palpably weren't and had spooned the supposed half-volley gently off to mid-off. 'Lean on it', when you played forward and didn't quite time it; the triumphant 'Yees' when everything was right, and 'Shame' when you played over the top of a yorker and lost your middle stump.

No one ever took a fielding practice quite like George. He had per-fected the art of making the running catch drop an inch in front of one's hurtling dive. We were green from head to foot, our flannels were ruined, we were sweating profusely and we loved it. I suspect that we were actually in danger of enjoying the practice more than the real game. Certainly we were ready for a curry and a talk late into the night when all was done for the day.

In 1949 George took part in a record Sussex partnership of 326 for the fourth wicket with Jim Langridge. It was the second most important partnership of his career. By far the greatest partnership of his life was his marriage to Betty. Their beautiful little cricket ground echoed to the calls of chirpy small boys. Betty was groundsman, George the gardener. They delighted in providing surprises for their guests. I remember the pleasure of finding a coal fire twinkling in the bedroom grate one January night and the sudden appearance with a scuttle of coal of George in his W. G. Grace beard and wig. There was fake iced cake for children's parties that when cut produced a flood of presents. There were exciting drives down hitherto unknown lanes to newly discovered antique shops. There was a Sussex trug filled with fresh-picked green vegetables from his garden for the Secretary of the MCC when he came as his guest through the Grace Gate on the Saturday of the Lord's Test. The old trilby hat seemed set at a specially jaunty angle on such a day as that.

Dennis Silk, The Cricketer (1985)

Bradman v. Bedser

The duels between Bradman and Alec Bedser take pride of place as the most enthralling encounters of post-war cricket. The first time the pair came face to face on the field was in the Brisbane Test, 1946, before the match was a quarter-hour old. Bradman, rather haggard but determined, was winning his way back to health at the time, but Hammond apparently feared him as much as ever. He failed to beset Bradman with the leg-trap which later brought success; as I remember it, only one fieldsman was close up on the leg side and the field was set as for the pre-war Bradman. The drawn-faced batsman, in scratching up five runs in 25 minutes, twice edged Bedser a yard or so short of Voce at second slip, then chopped the big fast-medium bowler just in front of Yardley in the gully. Bedser's great round face was flushed with his exertions in the sub-tropical sun; perspiration glued his black forelock to his shining fore-head. A barracker shouted to him: 'You'll need your brother before you're through.' By the time he was given a spell, after 70 minutes' play, his bolt was nearly shot. Later that day stomach trouble precipitated by his labours in the heat kept him off the field for a while after tea. I do not recall his having brought a frown to Bradman's brow next day, when the convalescent batsman went on to 187 before Edrich bowled him. In the second Test, at Sydney, Bedser was not given a chance early against Bradman in his innings of 234, probably because the new ball was only 41 runs away when the captain entered with Australia 159 for four wickets. The Surrey giant had bowled six overs in the third Test, at Melbourne, before Bradman appeared at 32. He nearly bowled him first ball, and his sixth was so close to yorking him that the ball spun in the blockhole and the batsman made a second stab of the bat to stop it. After one more over Bedser was given a spell. When he returned, Bradman was 57 but was troubled enough to put one ball just out of Hutton's reach at short-leg and to survive an appeal for lbw. In Australia's second innings Bradman was in the twenties before Bedser was brought on against him; he was dropped behind the wicket at 44.

To that point the hefty bowler had not once been rewarded with the most coveted of all wickets. Yet by picking out the Bedser v. Bradman threads, often half-hidden in the general tapestry of the play day after day, we see a pattern taking shape – a pattern outlining the advisability of immediately pitting him against the champion run-getter, with the luck of the game deciding the issue.

The luck swung Bedser's way at their fifth meeting, when he bowled Bradman for 0, ninth ball, in the fourth Test, at Adelaide, where he had the support of two short-leg fieldsmen. In the second innings Bradman came in at 116, was not opposed promptly by Bedser and scored 56 not out comfortably. The fifth Test, on a Sydney wicket that produced exciting cricket, was the first in which Bradman, in at 126, had to start amid a throttling ring of close fieldsmen set by Yardley. In both innings Bedser struck the outer edge of his bat a couple of times, without forcing him to give a chance, and on the last afternoon he caused him, when 63, to mistime a drive up to Compton at cover.

In England, where Bedser bowled with a little less pace and more swerve, Bradman looked as if he had promptly burst the Bedser bubble when he scored 146 against Surrey with forceful confidence. Buried deep under the Australians' total of 632 runs on the Oval wicket, Bedser's part received little notice. In Barnes and Morris's opening partnership of 135 he had bowled ten overs before he was brought on when Bradman was 4, bowled nine balls to him, and was spelled. He had another try when Bradman was 28, then drifted out of the attack until the batting wizard reached 140 in three hours. To that stage Bedser had bowled 25 balls (two maidens) to Bradman and the part of the 140 debited against him consisted of two 2s and four singles. When the big fellow was recalled late in the day for his twentieth over Bradman smacked the first two balls for two and four but the third pierced his forward defence and bowled him.

The pattern was something similar when they met in the first Test at Nottingham. Bedser had bowled twelve overs to the opening batsmen and 80 minutes' worth of shine had been worn from the ball when, at Bradman's entry, Yardley promptly summoned him back. Bedser measured out his run with outsize steps, ending in a long jump. Square-leg came in closer and second-slip slipped across to short fine-leg. Bedser's policy was to have at least a couple of men in such positions to deter the batsman from pushing forward trustingly down the line of the length ball, as could be done if there were no fieldsmen to snap up half-hit in-dippers. With the forward cover so restricted, the bowler could pitch the ball well up, thereby improving the chance of late out-swerve beating the hastened bat cleanly or being edged to wicketkeeper, slip or gully. No man could be spared for silly-point, in addition, without leaving the field so vulnerable to driven fours as to discourage the bowler from keeping the ball up. On the day in question, as they say in the police courts, Bradman's pads saved him from playing Bedser's second ball on, and next over an uppish shot fell safely between short square-leg and mid-on. Near a sketch of the field arrangement, my notebook has a scribbled query that, for the pace of Bedser's bowling to Bradman, the short fine-leg might be better placed squarer. Bedser was rested after four overs, and he troubled Bradman so little in their three later encounters before the close of play that 35 of the Australian's 130 runs were scored off 56 balls from him. Other minds were active about the field-placing, and in the Black Boy Hotel lounge that evening an accidental meeting between Bedser and a couple of Australians led to discussions, as O'Reilly tells in his *Cricket Conquest*. Next morning Bedser took a new ball for the fourth delivery, and three fieldsmen closed in to a remodelled leg-trap which was to become famous – a short mid-on, a forward short-leg and a backward short-leg (Hutton) about seven yards behind the batsman's right hip, rather like a gully thrown up by an earthquake on the wrong side of the wicket. Bradman cover-drove a four, then played a turning shot to Bedser's sixth delivery with the new ball, but its in-dip prevented true connection and Hutton caught it chest-high.

When Bradman came in after about half an hour of Australia's second innings the same fieldsmen grouped at the same end, aft of his legs.

Enough polish still remained on the ball for Bedser to be hopeful of repeating the same dismissal, as if he had been reading *The Postman Always Rings Twice*. For nine balls he pinned Bradman down; twice the batsman started to try to steal runs which his partner, Barnes, thought too dangerous and sent him back. The tenth ball carried a similar dose of swing to the fatal delivery in the first innings, and Bradman played a similar shot which the same fieldsman caught, this time stooping. To paraphrase an Americanism, Bradman had been caught with his glance down.

By now the pattern is plain. We go to Lord's for the second Test knowing this much: Bradman finds it more difficult to get a start against a fresh Bedser bowling a new ball to this three-man leg-trap than against any other adversary he has met. A new ball is an important ingredient; Bedser can make any old ball run away but he needs a glossy one to be sure of bringing it in across the bat. And the poison works most effectively if Bradman can be forced to swallow the dose before he has time to make himself comfortable – as witness the two catches for six runs off sixteen deliveries with new balls in their two meetings in the Nottingham Test.

Nine days later the setting is suitable for another tense duel as Bradman walks in to the Lord's wicket in the fourth over of Australia's first innings. Bowling from the Nursery end Bedser has the pitch's slope and a breeze from behind square-leg to magnify his out-swing and enhance its contrast with the in-swinger. He runs in at an angle toward fine-leg, the aluminium shield on his right boot glinting. To the batsman he looks all boots – and what boots! size 12½ – as he bears down on his victim with mastodonic strides, as if to trample him down if he cannot bowl him out. His light grey-blue eyes bulge beneath their black brows and his forehead is lined with concentration as he launches the ball with high hand.

Bradman plays the bowling warily. An out-swinger beats his bat and off stump, and Evans vainly tries to stump him. Not sure in his timing, Bradman bats half an hour for four runs. Shouts from the crowd prematurely hail his downfall as, twice in four balls, in-swingers glance from his bat a little finer than short square-leg, but they pitch in front of Yardley, who takes them on the bounce. Disappointedly tightening the folds of his right shirtsleeve, Bedser trudges eighteen paces back to his starting-point, wheels to his left, gathers himself in three walking steps, then sets out again on his nine running strides. His arm makes three pendulum beats back past his hip, then his hand makes a preliminary loop by his ear while his determined chin tucks into the shoulder of his raised left arm as it leads his body into the delivery. At 13 Bradman turns another in-swinger waist-high between Yardley and Hutton, fielding finer. Hutton flings himself to his left but the ball is out of reach and goes for a single. On completing the over, his eleventh in 70 minutes' play, Bedser is given his first spell. He walks away, refastening the shirt-button burst open by the effort of delivery. Just before lunch the willing war-horse from Woking is back in harness again, but before then Bradman has quietly inspected the blade of his bat, noting with satisfaction that marks in the middle have begun to out-number red blobs near the edges. Only 19 runs are gleaned from Bedser's 72 balls before the interval, Bradman's share being five singles and an off-driven boundary off 32 balls. Before the Australian captain can get into his stride again after lunch he plays a forward turning shot, at 38, to Bedser's fourth ball, which carries to short fine-leg, shin-high, for Hutton's third catch in the short-leg region in three consecutive Test innings.[1] This staggering sequence sets us dis-cussing how it comes about, as we walk the sunny path beside Lord's pavilion. Bowes identifies the stroke as Bradman's old favourite for clip-ping the ball along the grass in front of square-leg, but now popping it up around the corner. Abe Waddington, the former Yorkshire and Test left-arm bowler, believes it is all a matter of the eye: 'When Don saw the ball quicker he hit that one downward.' Hobbs, taking a line from his own batting after he turned thirty-nine, doubts whether it is sight and thinks it more likely to be one of those occasional faults which develop in the mechanism of a stroke, regardless of a batsman's age. My own eyes tell me that, whatever the cause, Bradman is not making position and timing the stroke as he did against in-swingers before the war; when he contacts this in-dipper from Bedser his bat is pushed farther forward from his legs – out of the inner circle of mastery.

Bradman's own comment as he unbuckles his pads is simply: 'Aw gee, I can't make head or tail of what I should be doing.'

When the Australians bat again the news that Bradman is facing Bedser is enough to empty all the bars at Lord's and to bring white-

[1] It was the fourth time in five consecutive innings in first-class cricket that Bradman had been caught by Hutton in short-leg positions, as this fieldsman held him at backward short-leg off Yorkshire's opening bowler, Ronald Aspinall, at Sheffield, between the first and second Tests. The leg-trap tally became five in ten innings when Compton, in much the same spot, caught Bradman for six off Philip Whitcombe's fast-medium bowling for Middlesex.

badged MCC attendants out from backstage duties, like a posse of sher-
iffs. This time 122 are on the board before Bradman arrives to find the
bails not yet replaced. He scorns this omen by hitting four boundaries in
his first 17. With a worn ball Bedser is hard put to keep him quiet and
goes off at 146 after four overs, making twelve overs for the day. The
most ceremonious welcome ever given a new ball is seen when it falls due
at 155, with Bradman 24. Bedser receives it gratefully for the second ball
of his thirteenth over, first wiping his hands on the grass to avoid soiling
its glistening surface. He fondles it in hands that make it look dwarf-size,
like a red cherry. From more distant stations in the field three men
slowly approach the leg-trap with almost episcopal tread, heightening the
dramatic effect and making the most of the psychological advantage left
by previous success. The first two deliveries with the new ball are outswingers which snap past Bradman's tentative bat into Evans's gloves. As
Bedser walks back we can see a grin on his broad face, usually solemn
with the seriousness of the task. Bradman's concern shows itself in
anxious attitudes and in short walks across to the off between balls, as if
he wants time to think. When he judges that in-swingers will finish
outside his leg stump he breaks a lifetime habit by attempting no stroke
and pushing his padded knees to fend them away. Then Barnes takes
possession of the end facing Bedser for two whole overs while the bowler
worriedly examines the dulling ball. Barnes seldom leaves that end until
the frustrated Bedser is given a spell after a stretch of six overs. In all,
Bradman (35) has made nine of his runs off 27 balls from Bedser. When
he faces this bowler again in the last half-hour of the day he has three
hours' batting under his belt and needs only 11 runs for 100. The ball is
old, the pitch drowsy in the late afternoon sun and the time seems at
hand for the Master to wash away memories of indignities with a flood of
runs. Confidently he cuts at the first ball; it streaks ankle-high wide of
slip, but Edrich somehow gets a hand to it for a catch, rolling over with
his boots in the air.

In the Manchester Test Bedser has only four balls at Bradman in the
first innings and twenty-three on the puddingy pitch in the second
innings, without success.

In the fourth Test the ball is seven overs old when Bradman takes
guard. The most Bedser can do on the Leeds wicket to hasten his
departure for 33 is to strike him in the groin in the first over of the third
morning. The blow jars a nerve centre, causing the batsman to lurch
forward, doubling up. One of a cluster of fieldsmen gives his back a rub,

sympathetic though far from the seat of pain, and play ceases for a minute while he squirms about, limping with his right leg and holding his left side. It might be immaterial, but I think it contributes to Bradman's being bowled next over, playing inside a ball from Pollard which goes straight through to the off stump. In Bradman's second innings of 173 not out on a spin bowler's pitch he collects 26 of his runs from 47 balls from Bedser.

That was their last Test encounter. They met once again at Scarborough Festival but Bedser, under new management, was not pitted against Bradman until he had made a start. Next day, Bedser's first ball to Bradman (33) was glanced waist-high through the backward short-leg position, but Hutton's hands were not there; he was alone, yards away on the other side of the umpire. The stable door was quickly locked by giving Hutton two companions in the leg-trap, but the batsman raised no more hopes or hands in that direction. The great Australian went on blithely to his farewell hundred in England. He was 153 when he tried to blaze a ball into a backyard of a terrace of houses, but ballooned a catch over point, his last stroke in a first-class match in Britain. By some working of chance or higher justice the bowler was Bedser, the catcher Hutton. Toward those 153 the bulky bowler had yielded eight runs off 26 balls.

So cold figures show that in the ten innings in which they clashed in England Bradman scored 807 runs (twice not out). Of his eight dismissals six were by the determined Surrey bowler for a total of 129 runs, made with 69 scoring strokes off roughly 290 balls. Indistinct in the dark abyss of England's defeat, that noble achievement for a hard-working bowler on a losing side was little recognized. From his first triumph at Adelaide, in the last 14 innings in which they were opposed Bedser took Bradman's wicket eight times, a ratio no other bowler ever equalled at straight cricket, though Larwood gouged him out at seven of his last ten opportunities, nearly all in the bodyline Tests.

From Bedser's success rises the question of how this fast-medium bowler and his methods would have fared against the pre-war Bradman. None can say, but I'd have polished up my telescope if, by magically putting one hand of the clock back, we could have seen them at each other when the batsman, too, was under thirty.

Ray Robinson *From the Boundary* (1950)

A. L. Hassett – Poker-face

After Yogi-like meditation over the signature *A. L. Hassett*, an Indian graphologist came up with conclusions about the character of the writer. Linking of the initials suggested a cautious nature, he found, but a long tail-flourish on the *L* and a powerful finishing loop on the *H* inflicted energy. So Hassett would combine caution and energy.

Nothing in the autograph led the expert to mention that with all his other traits Arthur Lindsay Hassett would combine fun – though the way the letters flowed on without pause for full-points might have been taken to mean that he did not know when to stop.

Hassett did know when to stop: at the dressing-room door as he passed out, bat in hand. His long face would be solemnly set, his long top lip dead straight, his eyes rather downcast beneath the big cap-peak. Opponents could learn no more from his face than the Indian did from his signature. Yet on the other side of the dressing-room door team-mates would be gurgling at his parting jest or gesture. Those extremes of private gaiety and public decorum ought to be open to an intriguing explanation, like Africa's Shari crocodile with zebra markings. Yet I think it is simply a sense of duty overpowering a sense of humour.

Hassett playing O'Reilly was a sight worth remembering. In he would walk, his small figure casting little more shadow than his bat. The contest seemed unequal from the start, because O'Reilly, six feet three inches, towered nine inches above him; it would have looked more apt for Hassett to sell him a newspaper than contend with his bowling. Technically, O'Reilly's knack of making some balls pop higher should have troubled short batsmen most. Yet Hassett gained, and deserved, the reputation of being the best handler of the greatest bowler of the age, defying him with his own special combination of dead-bat defence and insolent aggression. Grimmett agreed that Hassett played O'Reilly better than anyone else he saw, and acknowledged his own difficulty in bowling to one so sure in his footwork. Hassett's quick-skipping feet were visible evidence of the speed with which his mind worked to combat the varied pressure of the Master's attack. Often he was hard-pressed by leg-breaks, but when the slower wrong-un curved along he would detect it and on-drive it with lofty impertinence or plonk it to the leg boundary with a stroke that was a cheeky first-cousin to a pull. When a fielder was

433

put deep and square to stop this, Hassett would guide the ball finer. Others found it paid to be silent or civil to 'The Tiger' in the heat of battle, but Hassett would taunt him mischievously. If anything irritated O'Reilly more than being hit it was being edged for runs. One day when his length and flight worried Hassett into scratching several leg-breaks past slip he snapped as the batsman ran to his end: 'Can't you get even one in the middle of the bat?'

Hassett: 'Don't need to with you, Tige.'

Bradman (four times), Macartney, Kippax, Morris and he are the only Australians who have scored a century in both innings of a match twice. Hassett is the only batsman of any nationality who did it in a match against bowling that included O'Reilly. After his 122 in Victoria's first innings at Sydney in 1940 he was rather off-colour when he began his second innings; he looked so woebegone as he trudged his 100 paces from the gate to the far end that some of the fieldsmen laughed at him. He turned the laugh against them by scoring 122 again. That was one of the few times I saw O'Reilly spread the fieldsmen and chiefly use his slower deliveries, with the air of saying: 'Hit that for six or get caught.' In his book, *Cricket Conquest*, O'Reilly acknowledges that Hassett picked his wrong-un better than any other batsman. He writes that Sydney barrackers who wanted to take a rise out of him would call: 'Go easy, there, Tiger, or we'll send for Lindsay Hassett.'

No bat, not even Bradman's, has indulged in such extremes of behaviour as Hassett's. As he awaits the bowler it slopes parallel with his right leg and rests on the line, beside his big toe. Defending, the bat often hangs lifelessly by his shins or is lifted just enough for the bottom to clear the ground as he pushes it forward to lean against the ball. He moves it a few inches for delicate placements. Suddenly the bat comes to life. It flashes up behind his head in backswing for a drive that rocks him up on his front toe in the follow-through; or it clips the ball off his bootlaces toward the leg boundary before the fieldsmen can interfere. On slow ground it provocatively lofts shots over mid-off and mid-on in a way that alarms faint-hearted supporters. When used for a hook, Hassett's bat seems longer than other men's but it takes no longer to smite the ball; the best hook ever played off Lindwall's bumper was by him for Services in 1945 – clean as the parting in his hair. Hassett's bat is at its worst when it goes on the razzle, lurching forward and crosswise in a riotous pull or sweep, in startling contrast with the model rectitude of the rest of his batting. It behaves in this intemperate way only when he is very sure of himself or not sure of himself at all; we have seen it hoist a welcome ball over his shoulder for four and sky an unwelcome one for a catch at short square-leg.

Hassett's bat is most in character when it cuts. He lifts it and drops it on the ball, like the fall of an executioner's blade. On the village green of Titipu he would be the one to come in as Ko-Ko and cut all-rounder Pooh-Bah's most authoritative ball through the Mikado's legs into the orchestra. Cutting square, he chops the ball teasingly out of point's reach. Cutting late, he keeps the slips bending. He is the finest and most-frequent cutter in post-war cricket, the only Australian with faith enough in the safety of the stroke to use it as soon as he comes in.

Hassett stands upright as he cuts; in fact, he is easily erect in all his stroke-play except the sweep, with his right knee down, and the forward stretch, with his nose down. This erectness, his high grip, his quick identification of the ball, his ease of movement and sure balance all combine to produce the powerful shots of 'The Mighty Atom'. With his back heel visible to the bowler, Hassett places his feet about eight inches apart before the front boot begins to creep forward as his attacker approaches. Once the ball is on its way his feet are seldom still. They twinkle in his frequent sallies forward or scuttle well inside the crease when he is driven back. To rising balls he often goes up on tip-toe. Those extra inches of elevation could not save him in the Leeds Test, 1948, when Pollard suddenly made a ball jump lapel-high; it chipped the shoulder off his bat and was caught by Crapp at second slip.

The first time Hassett's sense of duty put aside his normal batting methods Melbourne barrackers passed from incredulous stares to hurt complaints. The crowd knew him as the finest player of a sporting family. At Geelong College he had been captain of cricket and football, 1931 tennis champion of Victorian Public Schools; he had scored a schoolboy record of 2,191 runs in 41 innings (six hundreds) in his five years at the college. The crowd liked his enterprising stroke-play and quicksilver footwork, especially his dancing out to drive with a high grip which put taller men to shame. Australia's selectors were slow to recognize his fitness for Test cricket against Allen's English team. Worse, a temporary patch of failure in club matches had caused Victoria's selectors to leave him out of the State side for a couple of matches (perhaps I can be forgiven for recalling with satisfaction having taken them to task in big headlines for their lack of vision). The aforementioned day when he first infuriated the barrackers came after his restoration. But in their indignation about the hours he occupied making about 80 they failed to give the twenty-four-year-old batsman credit for selflessly camping at one end to keep O'Reilly out, thereby saving the match.

Scraping into the oddly-chosen Australian 16 Bradman took to England in 1938, Hassett soon proved himself the best of his country's newer batsmen. None of the five hundreds in his 1,589 runs on the tour was as valuable as his 33 on the last day of the low-scoring Leeds Test. On a pitch where 10 English wickets had tumbled for 74 that day, the Australians needed 105 to win. England's hopes soared, rocket-like, when the opening pair fell for 9 each and Bradman and McCabe were caught in the mid-teens. Captain and vice-captain could not watch the tense finish. They sat in the room while word was passed through the door from players on the balcony. Merely to stick at the wicket was difficult, much less score. Hassett blinked through the murky light and decided to race a gathering thunderstorm, sink or swim. With page-boy aplomb he hit up 33 while only 8 runs came from other sources. The patter of raindrops bustled his innings to a hurried end, but the storm held off long enough for wicket-keeper Barnett to strike off the winning runs.

In his first match as Test captain he was off colour with tonsilitis when he came in at Johannesburg after both openers were out for ducks. With cubic centimetres of penicillin in his bloodstream he nimbly rallied his side with 112.

Rivalling Hassett's reputation for dependability in time of trouble was his name among cricketers for impishness. When a muddy goat's breathing and movement woke McCabe and O'Reilly in their room at Grindleford, in the Derbyshire hills, the guilt for smuggling it in was never sheeted home, but Hassett's sending a suit to the cleaners next morning was accepted as circumstantial evidence.

As captain of the AIF team in Palestine and Egypt and of the Services' XI in England and India Hassett left loyal friends and grinning acquaintances in many lands. He joked about himself, lamenting the need for a bucket to eke out his height on interesting occasions. As he signed one of the hundreds of photographs handed him by autograph-hunters he noticed that the chin looked dark, as with 5 o'clock shadow. So below his signature he added: 'Always use Gillette blades.' R. S. Whitington tells how Hassett and he were caught in one of the 1945 Calcutta riots. They escaped into a cinema. As they settled in their seats they saw on the screen Ray Milland in the alcoholic throes of *The Lost Weekend*. Said Hassett: 'Let's hop back into that riot.'

Thousands of National Congress demonstrators marched on the field at Calcutta to stop the Services' match against East Zone. As they engulfed the wicket Hassett unconcernedly asked their leader for a cigarette. That act dissolved anger and soon led to the departure of the mob, bearing players' autographs.

There is something incongruous in the sight of husky bowlers going on and off at the behest of the smallest man on the ground, and fieldsmen trotting about at his direction. Without looking around, he would signal an outfielder behind him to a different spot with an inconspicuous motion, as if brushing dust from his sharply creased trousers. An exception was a match at Lahore, where an all-rounder took a few wickets, became indisposed in the heat and retired from the field. After missing him in the hottest part of the day his team-mates saw him reappear late in the afternoon. Hassett ceremoniously waved him to the right, then a little to the left, then motioned him backward – until the fielder found he had been waved back out the gate.

For a welcoming broadcast after the Servicemen were flown from Ceylon to Western Australia, Major W. A. Oldfield spread his typed script on the table in a Perth radio station, then could not read it because he had mislaid his spectacles. Hassett came to the rescue with a funny story, and the pair carried on *ad lib* for ten minutes in a way that had the station staff laughing. Players enjoy refreshers of the same ready wit when they call at his sport-shop in Elizabeth Street, Melbourne.

After watching Hassett practising, one of England's touring women cricketers shyly asked for his bat, autographed. 'Certainly,' replied the State skipper, 'in exchange for a smile and your white sun-hat with the signatures of all your team around the brim.' Some time after the transaction Hassett reappeared with a grey felt hat and obtained the Englishwomen's signatures on it, too. The hat was the one Ian Johnson had intended to wear home.

As in his batting and fielding, assiduous practice has been reflected in the precision of Hassett's one-hand match-lighting act. He takes a match in his fingers, rests the matchbox on the back of his hand, and with one jerk dislodges the box and strikes the match on it as it falls. After lighting cigarette or pipe he rounds the proceedings off by holding the match near his forehead to blow it out with an upward blast.

Before Bradman re-entered cricket after the war and Miller came to the fore, Ponsford was one of several good judges who ranked Hassett Australia's best batsman, just ahead of Barnes. Others fancied Barnes or bracketed the pair, with Brown close up.

The little Victorian with an appetite for oysters and half-volleys was the tenth Australian to pass 40 centuries in first-class cricket and the eighth to score seven hundreds on a tour of Britain. He and Macartney are the only two who twice made three consecutive hundreds on tour. In South Africa in 1950 he took his career total past 12,400 for 227 innings in first-class cricket. Admiring his stroke-play, South Africa's captain, Nourse, said: 'I imagine that if Hassett desired to concentrate on making centuries they would simply flow from his bat.' Even so, in the all-time list of scorers of 12,000 runs in first-class matches by Australian teams, only three (Bradman, Ponsford and Woodfull) have averages higher than Hassett's 61.

Hassett's sense of duty impelled him in several Test matches after the war to stick faithfully to the course laid down for the team, though it meant giving up his natural style of play and brought him a basting from barrackers and critics. At those times he forfeited the crowd's goodwill, earned by other innings. In his first Test in Australia, 1946, he came in when two wickets had gone for 46, to see Bradman edging the ball disquietingly and spared at 28 by disallowance of a slip catch off Voce. Hassett consecrated himself to the task of holding one end safe and husbanding the strength of his partner, who was not fully fit and sometimes limped. He played this supporting role so thoroughly in a record Australian third-wicket partnership of 276 that Duckworth described him as the rock on which Australia's innings of 645 was built. But Hassett screwed himself down so tightly that he was unable to undo the screws and let himself out.

Ray Robinson, From the Boundary (1950)

Denis Compton

Cricket-mad schoolboys in the years after the war had a straightforward choice of idol. If they lived in the north, it was Hutton; and the dashing Denis Compton claimed the rest. There may have been the odd one who put Edrich or Washbrook on a pedestal, but in those days non-conformity was not encouraged and such allegiances were mostly kept a secret. Wicket-keepers, as a breed apart, were allowed to have a soft spot for Godfrey Evans, but without television replays to illustrate their skills, bowlers, except for the bounding leg-spinner Doug Wright, had little following, being simply there to set the game in motion. In our household it was accepted that Gover ran faster than he bowled, though on what grounds nobody explained, and I never had the chance – that is, by watching from behind the arm – to see what a great bowler Alec Bedser was. (Aspiring games-players are so lucky now, being able to soak up techniques a few feet from the television screen, not to mention the practitioners themselves, who can learn what they're doing wrong.)

As a southerner living within an hour or so of Lord's, I was well within Compton's magnetic field. But at first he wasn't even on my short-list. Thinking back over more than four decades, it comes as a surprise that despite coming from a cricket-loving family my first awareness that the game was played on a wider stage than our front lawn seems to have stemmed not from listening but from reading. I'm sure it can't be true. Bradman was too great a scourge of England not to have been a regular topic at the breakfast table, especially in 1936–37 when news of his match-winning efforts in the last three Tests would have been coming through by wireless at about the time we ate. But there it is; like so many conversations since, no doubt including far too many in the last few months, I haven't the faintest recollection of a word of them.

To the best of my belief, then, the source of my new knowledge was the issue of *The Cricketer*, probably the Winter Annual, which contained the report, and still more captivating, the score-board, of the Oval Test of 1938. England 903 for 7 declared, Hutton 364, and Australia beaten by an innings and 579! Conditioned to look on 20 as a pretty useful score, as probably it was against five competitive big sisters and a brother ten years my senior bowling with a cricket ball, the figures made my head swim every time I looked at them, which was often. An innings and 579 – wow! And the fact that Bradman and Fingleton both appeared as 'Absent hurt' did nothing to dilute my pleasure since consciously at least I'd never heard of them. Soon I memorized the score-board's other vast statistics: Leyland 187, Hardstaff 169 not out, Fleetwood-Smith 1 for 298; Heavens, what a rabbit! To begin with, inevitably, Hutton was my god: 364 in an innings lasting 13 hours and 20 minutes were figures hardly graspable. But my father, whose word was law, dismissed him as a mere pot-hunter and Leyland, of whose sturdy Yorkshire qualities he much approved, replaced him as my idol. Hammond's 59 paled into insignificance in that galaxy and as for Paynter 0 and Compton 1 – well, only the fact that they were Englishmen spared them from being lumped with Fleetwood-Smith as palpable no-hopers.

By then, though, it was wartime. Although that *Cricketer* must have been knocking round the house since soon after it was published, it can't have been till 1939 or 1940 that I was old enough to take it in – as far as Test cricket was concerned too late to do anything but dream about it until the war was over. Nevertheless, big cricket of a kind was still being played at Lord's – looking back it's remarkable how much there was of it considering the way the war was going – and finally, on 6 September 1941, the great day dawned. My brother, home on leave, was to take me on the 355 Green Line coach to see Maurice Leyland bat at Lord's.

I never found out which member of the family was to blame for that benighted choice. My record on Green Lines was appalling: I turned green at the very thought of one. Sure enough, I was feeling sick by Radlett and retching by the time we got to Elstree. My brother kept saying 'Only another half an hour to go' but in Mill Hill it was either a scramble for the exit or the technicolour yawn. His face black with hatred, my brother dragged me out. Abused and dazed, I found myself on Mill Hill Station waiting for the stopper to St Pancras when, if someone had been thinking straight, we could have been already there on a fast train from St Albans. How we got to Lord's remains a mystery, except that it can't have been by taxi or I would have vomited again. A. B. Sellers, the Yorkshire captain, was clean bowled by Todd of Kent with the first ball I ever saw there, but my heart was in my boots. Leyland was already out for 42. However, my brother had regained his humour. Sgt-Inst Compton was the one he'd come to see . . . and he was not out 51.

We sat in 'A' Stand, tatty old predecessor of the present Warner Stand, and were among a crowd of more than 10,000 which watched Compton complete a flashing hundred. Then, on one of his innumerable sorties down the pitch, he missed at last and was stumped by Maxwell, bowled Todd for 114. Intoxicating though the innings was – apart from Sellers's first ball the only thing I remember of the cricket – the manner of its ending affected me for years. It wasn't until 1973, when Denis turned out for an old England XI against Rachel Heyhoe's England women in a match organized by the *Evening Standard* at the Oval, that I could watch him bat without an element of terror. Two decades post-knee, plumpish, and well into his fifties, those heart-stopping advances down the pitch were a thing of the past and at last there was no fear of a stumping! It was his first knock for years, but after one rather nervous jab, his bat made its rich noise of his heyday. He scored 29 in six or seven overs and, like Hutton and Reg Simpson, showed that great players never lose their gift of timing.

In the war years, my loyalty had to stand the strain of many strong counter-attractions. Denis had been spirited away to India by some crackpot at the War Office and in his absence Edrich, Hammond, Robertson and Miller held centre stage. Hammond, still majestic, made 100 in each innings in the first match in which I ever saw him play – England versus the Dominions – in the same tremendous game Miller got his 185, including the ferocious, rifled six off Hollies that chipped brickwork above the England dressing-room. Edrich's catapulting bowling action, generating what to young eyes was unimaginable pace, made a deep impression, and it added to his lustre that he won a DFC, flying more missions than any other bomber pilot. However, although it was 1946 before I saw Compton bat again, his 114 had captured me. There was the same infectious gaiety about his cricket, the same warmth and boyishness as Ian Botham has, and before him Gary Sobers. For all three, cricket was, or is, their living. But the secret of their vast appeal was that they seemed, or seem to play the game for fun. Keith Miller and Ted Dexter, both amateurs, were others of the genre. Though there was never any doubting their will to win, nor their courage, determination seldom coarsened into ruthlessness – never in the case of Compton. Even Botham in his basest moments remains a chivalrous opponent.

Nobody could hope to capture the spirit of Compton's cricket more sweetly than R. C. Robertson-Glasgow, writing in the 1948 *Wisden* of the great deeds of Denis and Bill Edrich the year before. 'They seem to be playing not only in front of us and for us, but almost literally with us.' Well, since they shared 7,000 runs that glorious summer, you could say they were entitled to enjoy themselves. But Denis didn't have to be riding on the crest of a wave to communicate enjoyment: of all the times I saw him play, the innings I remember best was a ridiculous 19 against Leicestershire at Lord's in the mid–1950s, when he was past his best. He strolled in when Munden was making runs quite hard to score, bowling slow left-arm spin to slip, gulley and a strong defensive offside field with four men saving singles and another on the boundary. After a cursory inspection, Denis began light-heartedly resetting it. Crack – four to long-off over mid-off's head: one of the offside fielders took fresh station on the boundary. Crack – four to long-on over mid-on's head: gulley was dispatched to plug the hole. Dennis chopped a two through where he'd been, drilled Munden first bounce against the sightscreen before either adjacent fielder could move, picked up a few singles, then missed a straight one and was bowled. It was like sitting down to dinner at the Ritz and being flung into Piccadilly after the hors d'oeuvre. Intensely irritating – but different. A great part of Compton's charm was that no two innings were the same. And it wasn't only my generation that fell under his spell. Ian Peebles's biography might have been written by a doting uncle, while in his *Denis Compton: a Cricket Sketch*, Jim Swanton told a story, so much in character there is no doubt of its veracity, that precisely reflected the hero's sunny nature.

'One afternoon Denis came in from batting at the tea interval and was enduring with his usual indulgence the shafts of genially abusive humour which are a long tradition of the Middlesex dressing-room. Somebody, probably Walter Robins, said: "It's a funny thing a strong chap like you can't drive the ball straight. We never see you hit it over the bowler's head." Denis said: "Yes it is funny; look out for the third ball bowled after tea." A few minutes afterwards the third ball bowled came whistling straight and true into the Members' seats in front of the pavilion, and as the umpire was signalling "six", Denis waved his bat cheerfully to his companions.' There was more than a touch of Botham in that response, though in the latter's case the challenge he would have to answer might be to hit a backhand sweep for six!

Swanton paid Compton the compliment in that sketch of doubting whether 'any game in any period has thrown up anyone to match his popular appeal in the England of 1947–49' and even now it's hard to think of more than three – Botham, Jimmy Greaves and Bobby Charlton – who could be put up as a rival. To his young fans, the years of new-found bliss began in 1946. For though he failed to make a Test hundred against India, he made ten in first-class cricket and with 2,403 runs began making up the six years lost to war. In four home seasons, plus two tours, he scored 14,641 runs with 60 hundreds. The extraordinary affection he inspired in young and old was shown in 1949 when his benefit match, Middlesex versus Sussex in the Whitsun game at Lord's, was watched by 55,000, Denis making 182. Had Middlesex invested the resultant £12,258 with greater wisdom – and the odd horse here and there had justified his faith in them – he might today be almost as prosperous as his friend and fellow scribe Sir Leonard Hutton. Instead, not that it ever seemed to bother him, the bulk of it was lost.

In Australia in 1946–7, MCC's first post-war tour, disappointment was initially rife, tons of runs against the states being little compensation for failures in the first three Tests. With Hammond a shadow of his former self at the age of forty-three, the long and short of England's batting was Hutton, Washbrook, Edrich and Compton, and they were overpowered by the magnificent attack of which Lindwall and Miller were the spearhead. Caught on a sticky wicket, they lost at Brisbane by an innings and 332, and the second Test by an innings and 33 at Sydney, where Bradman and Barnes both scored 234. Though a draw in Melbourne followed, six innings had brought Denis a bagatelle of 116. Then – ecstasy. Demoted a place to number five at Adelaide, he made 147 and 103 not out and with Evans saved the match in the epic stand for the ninth wicket in which the wicket-keeper went 95 minutes before scoring. It was the dawn of Denis's dazzling 1947 when – proof of the marvellous sureness of his striking – he scored 3,816 runs, and 18 hundreds, with one bat, a magic wand of 2 lb 2 oz, to beat long-standing records by Tom Hayward and Jack Hobbs. For the hero, bare-headed and burnished brown by weeks of blazing sunshine, it was one long glorious frolic with the Compton sweep, the Compton cover-drive, the Compton hook, adorning every sports page, while on countless hoardings the handsome Compton features, tousled hair unnaturally becalmed, smiled down as an advertisement for Brylcreem – for a fee of £200 a year! Against South Africa he made four hundreds in the Tests and more than 1,000 runs in all, and one five-week spell in May and June had five hundreds and five fifties in 11 innings – 1,169 runs for ten times out. The sun shone and bowlers of all types became his playthings. The sweep, because it was unique to him – he hit it very fine and with bat nearer straight than horizontal – was his most famous stroke; but his own favourite, and the despair of bowlers, was the cover-drive, which by a late turn of the wrists he could hit behind square as powerfully as to cover's right.

The photograph of a smiling Denis, bat aloft, returning to the Hastings pavilion after overtaking Hobbs's 16 hundreds – inevitably against the hapless South Africans – remains one of the most vivid memories of that perfect summer. Yet even then he hadn't had enough. For Middlesex, the County Champions, against the Rest of England over four days at the Oval, he signed off with a flourish by scoring 246 – the innings in which, slipping as he danced down the pitch to drive Tom

Goddard, he started the long saga of his knee. It went almost without saying that the ball still went for four, clipped to leg as he tumbled to the ground. If the injury lessened his mobility, however, the score-book failed to show it. In 1948 he batted for seven hours at Trent Bridge to score 184 against Bradman's invincible Australians, added 145 at Old Trafford after being hit on the forehead by a Miller bouncer, and on MCC's tour to South Africa that winter put Benoni on the map by making 300 in three hours. As late as 1950, when the knee was to cost him half the cricket season, he played for Arsenal in the FA Cup final and had a foot in the second of Reg Lewis' goals that beat Liverpool 2–0.

If I was probably no longer starry-eyed, I was still prepared to risk my job for Denis when, in 1957, I tarried at Lord's until he reached his hundred in his farewell match. 'And where have you been, might I ask?' inquired my then sports editor as I puffed into the Express building 40 minutes late. I told him, smugly, I'd been watching Compton make his final hundred. 'I could sack you for that,' he threatened. But I was painless. 'Go ahead,' I said, 'it would be worth it.' He didn't. So that story had a happy ending too.

John Thicknesse, Cricket Heroes (1984)

Keith Miller

The picture on the back page of the morning newspaper was probably no more than three columns wide and four inches deep but it seemed to fill the complete area, leaving no room for headlines, stories or adverts. As cricket pictures go these days, it was nothing extraordinary, either, yet the whole strength, personality and magnetic appeal of the man came leaping out. It was taken from fine-leg and showed Keith Ross Miller with his left knee bent, his right knee almost on the ground. The last few inches of his bat could be seen over his left shoulder – those shoulders appeared to fill the whole frame, with broad back tapering down to narrow waist, his face caught in profile as his eyes followed the ball that had cleared the mid-wicket boundary by yards. The photograph was one of many such pictures that could have been taken that day as the 1948 Australians played Leicestershire. They would all have demonstrated Miller's power, for he dominated the Australian innings by making 202 runs, the crowd quickly forgiving him as he strode to the crease at the fall of the first wicket when they had expected Don Bradman, the man they had come to see, to emerge.

Miller became my cricketing hero that day. My love affair with the game had just started to blossom – I was twelve years old with dreams of playing for my country, having just broken into the school second team playing with boys two or three years older than myself. If I was going to have a future in the game as a player, Keith Miller ruined it for me then. Or rather, the picture did. I could bat pretty well, at least good enough to go in at number five in schoolboy cricket. Off-spinning was my speciality, however, until that picture. I never turned another ball after that, even when I went back to off-spinning some three or four years later, having discovered I had no chance of ever becoming another Miller because I could never bowl fast enough, straight enough to copy my hero. But it was fun trying. I became a devoted Miller follower for the rest of the 1948 season although he never produced another innings like the one at Grace Road which prompted me to become a cricket watcher rather than a cricket reader.

I followed his every deed when he returned to England in 1953 and again in 1956, thrilled by the sight of Ray Lindwall; his grace, his pace and his ability to swing the ball when flat out yet annoyed whenever he ran through an England side, denying K. R. the chance to do the same in their new ball partnership as effective as any the game has produced. To me, Keith Miller – born in a Melbourne suburb called Sunshine in November 1919 – was everything a cricketing hero should be – tall, broad-shouldered, handsome, a batsman who could destroy the finest bowling when he was in the mood, a fast bowler who could be as dangerous as any other around at the time when he fancied, a slip catcher with amazing reflexes. A man who lived life to the full. A generous man.

He had long retired by the time I first met him, but he was all the things I imagined him to be when he first captured my imagination. Some years later I took my son – then aged ten – to Lord's, where I was covering a John Player League match. K. R. was reporting the same game and met my son when he called at the Press box to collect me at the close of play. We talked for a few minutes and, as we departed, K. R. suddenly pulled a ten-pound note from his pocket, thrust it in my hand and said 'Buy him a bat from me'. That was typical of K. R., and the bat remains in the Smith home today.

I never asked him the truth about two of the stories I'd heard about his playing days because, had he denied them, it would have shattered the image I had built up as a youngster. One concerned the benefit match for Cyril Washbrook which the Australians agreed to play in 1948 at Old Trafford. The wicket was suspect, the Lancashire batting, with the exception of Jack Ikin's, being wrecked by the Australian attack. Although bruised by more than one delivery that got through his guard, Ikin struggled bravely and stubbornly to build a Lancashire score and had reached 99 when the new ball became due. Bradman, with whom Miller was to clash on more than one occasion, threw the new ball to K. R., who immediately tossed it back again. 'That guy deserves a century. I don't want to be responsible for getting him out now', he said. Bradman instead called up Lindwall who had no such respect for Ikin's gallantry and promptly dismissed him one short of a century so richly deserved.

The other story concerned an incident when Miller had moved from Melbourne to Sydney and was captain of New South Wales in a game at Sydney, a ground he loved in the same way he adored Lord's. K. R. was late arriving, so late he was still tucking in his shirt as he led his team out into the field. He was halfway to the middle when he was reminded by a colleague he had not nominated a 12th man and there were actually 11 players following him out. Without a pause in his stride Miller called out 'All right, one of you guys disappear', or words to that effect.

Even if the events did not take place exactly the way the stories were told to me, I suspect that there is a strong element of truth in both. He wanted to enjoy his cricket and wanted others to enjoy the game with him. He was not a player who took runs or wickets for personal glory or to improve his own statistics. He had no need to. They were impressive enough by the time he finished, his international record establishing him as one of the finest all-rounders the game has produced.

Starting in 1945 against New Zealand, he scored 2,958 runs from his 55 Test appearances, with seven centuries and an average of 36.97. As a fast bowler he took 170 wickets at an average of 22.97, taking ten wickets in a match on one occasion and five wickets in an innings on seven occasions. That is not all. He also took 35 catches in Test matches, making the most difficult appear easy when they were inches from the ground, despite the fact that he often appeared to be standing up straight with his hands in his pockets when the bowler was actually delivering the ball. The most striking quality about K. R. was that things always appeared to be happening when he was on the field of play. You could never ignore him; you could not afford to take your eyes off him for a moment. There was no spite in him although he played hard for his country, angering crowds across the world by delivering vicious bouncers, sometimes on the most docile of pitches and by running only a few yards. That, for me, was the appeal of this man. Cricket was never dull when he was around. It was perhaps because he never wanted to take his fast bowling skills seriously that he could laugh, joke, improvise so successfully. A tennis ball – even a table-tennis ball – was known mysteriously to appear instead of a cricket ball when he finished charging in at the end of a run-up conservative compared with those used today by bowlers half Miller's pace. He claimed more than one Test wicket with a perfectly delivered leg-break, suddenly turning in his trek back to his mark and delivering off half-a-dozen paces. Yet to see Miller coming in off half-a-dozen paces was no guarantee that a leg-break was to follow. With his strength, his bouncer off such a short run could be as vicious as the one from his full run-up. Some people could argue that to turn suddenly and bowl off only a third of the normal run is gamesmanship, against the spirit of the game, but, in those circumstances, batsmen always have the option of pulling away from the crease, claiming that they are not ready. Once they faced up to a delivery from Miller, they had to take the consequences. It was not always pretty. When victory mattered, when his country's cricketing reputation was at stake – as opposed to his own, for he did not worry unduly about figures – he could prove as nasty as any other fast bowler around at this time.

His wartime service in England from 1942 to 1945, flying with the Royal Australian Air Force, left him with a strong affection for most things British – he took the chance to extend his liking of classical music and poetry – as well as many close friends. Denis Compton, Bill Edrich and Godfrey Evans were three of his closest (no doubt partly due to their passion for horse racing which matched Miller's) among the England players he came across, yet he never had any qualms about dishing out bouncers to them, even encouraging Lindwall to do the same in the immediate post-war years when they were both young, fresh and repaid England for the 'Bodyline' tour of Australia in 1932–33.

Yet, strangely, Miller never wanted to be a bowler. He got into the Victoria state side, purely as a batsman, before the Sheffield Shield competition was suspended because of the war, and never attempted to bowl. It was only when the Australian side composed of servicemen played a series of victory matches against England – composed mainly of proven Test players – in England in 1945 and found themselves short of a strike bowler that Miller was encouraged to take up the ball seriously, and only then because others in the side thought he was large enough with his wide shoulders to look the part. They soon discovered he was a natural. For a while he enjoyed the sensation, especially during the early years of his famous partnership with Lindwall, which was first formed against New Zealand in 1945 and lasted until 1956 against Pakistan when Miller's knee troubles forced him to give up. As a partnership, they took 370 wickets in 13 series, Lindwall finishing with 200 wickets – he was to take 228 in all – always having the advantage of the wind.

Yet, after they had destroyed England in 1948, taking 40 wickets between them, Miller began to tire of his role. From then on he was always trying to give it up, starting each summer series in Australia by saying he would like to concentrate on batting, but always persuaded to keep going by colleagues stressing his value to his New South Wales side or the fact that his country needed him. Just how successful Miller might have been; how many more than the 170 Test wickets he finished with would have come his way if he had had the choice of ends is pure guesswork, but a study of his record demonstrates his importance to Australia at the time and supports the belief that he needed a challenging target to bring out the best in him. Of his 170 Test wickets, no less than 100 were batsmen ranked one to five in the order. Tail-enders were not for knocking over – unless they happened to be threatening Australia's control. This theory is also supported by the fact that he took five or more wickets in a Test innings on only seven occasions – a small number when measured against the figures of, say, Ian Botham – suggesting that having played his part in removing the heart of the opposition batting he lost interest, leaving others to supervise the mopping-up operations.

Understandably, for a youngster who grew up under the influence of Bill Ponsford, who lived near Miller in Melbourne, and Bill Woodfull, the Australian captain who taught at Miller's school, batting was his first love. While many wonder just how many wickets he would have taken if he had been the senior fast bowler for Australia, others wonder just how many runs he might have scored if the demands of bowling had not interfered with his batting. He was regarded as a reliable and steady middle-order batsman during his schooldays and on his entry into state cricket via the South Melbourne club.

It was not until after he returned to Australia following the war years, when he lived many of his days expecting them to be his last, that he became known as something of a cavalier, particularly after switching from Melbourne to Sydney, a city he loved just as he loved London. With his frame he was always powerful, almost cruel, on anything that could be pulled through the mid-wicket area although he was never so sure against the bouncers and largely ignored the hook. Yet he could drive the ball through the covers off the front foot as sweetly as anybody else of his day, a stroke of technical perfection.

His love affair with the English crowds in general, and those who flocked to Lord's in particular, started in 1945. He scored three centuries at Lord's that summer, the first for the Dominions against England, the other two in the Victory Test series. He seldom failed at Lord's after that, scoring his one true Test century in England there in 1953 when making 109. He was attempting to concentrate more and more on his middle-order batting then, yet the Australians would never permit him to give up the ball entirely. He was in his mid-thirties when he had one of his most successful series as an all-rounder, helping the Australians beat the West Indies 3–0 in the Caribbean. Miller finished that Test series with 20 wickets, the same number as Lindwall, and also scored three centuries, two of them in Kingston, Jamaica. A year later in England he had his most successful series – in terms of figures – as a bowler, taking 21 wickets although back and knee ailments were starting to worry him.

But Miller's career is not one to be measured in terms of runs scored or wickets taken. His appeal was his personal magnetism. He was a player to be seen in person and not viewed on a television screen, and so he could pull spectators through the gates. People loved him, and he loved people. The friendships Miller made as a player lasted for life. With his ability, he could afford to be generous on the field. When he retired from the game to concentrate on writing and broadcasting, he continued to be generous in life as well.

I remember him in the West Indies in 1967–68 when he was covering England's tour. West Indies fast bowler Charlie Griffith, never a man to rouse any sympathetic feelings as a player, was coming towards the end of his career, struggling to make any impact during the first Test in Trinidad. Griffith's performance deserved criticism and Miller was not slow to deliver it. When he finished his report he went back to the bar at the Queen's Park Oval where Griffith was also having a drink. Miller immediately put an arm round Griffith and said: 'Charlie, don't read me in the papers tomorrow.' That was typical of Miller the man, and my hero. It was the way he always acted.

Peter Smith, Cricket Heroes (1984)

Jim Laker

No cricketer would dispute the proposition that Jim Laker was the finest off-break bowler of his time; and he probably was the best of any age. There have been many in this kind; especially in England where the wet and drying pitches that serve as their killing ground occur more often than in other countries. Until recent years virtually every English county side included one of the species. Men such as Tom Goddard, John Clay, George Macaulay, Jack Newman, Raymond Illingworth, Vallance Jupp, Fred Titmus, David Allen, Bomber Wells, John Mortimore and Brian Langford all had their days when they were all but unplayable. None of them, though, was so complete an off-spinner as Jim Laker. His captain could call on him for any type of operation to be asked of an off-break bowler, on good wicket or bad, and he would do it as well as anyone has ever done.

Six feet tall, powerfully but not heavily built, well balanced and strong-legged, he had all the physical advantages for his craft bar one. He lacked the extremely long fingers which enabled, for instance, Tom Goddard, Athol Rowan, Lance Gibbs, Jack Newman, Peter Jackson or John Clay to spin the ball with relative ease. Laker turned it as much as any of them but, to do so, he had to stretch his first and second fingers so widely that eventually the top of his index finger was bowed into an arthritic condition so painful that at times he simply could not bowl; and finally it ended his playing career . . .

Memory recalls him, fresh-complexioned, strong-shouldered, fair-haired, hitching his flannels as, at a constabular roll, he walked six strides back to his mark; tongue in cheek, casual, relaxed. Then came his run – of four, five, perhaps six, paces; he deliberately varied his approach to defeat the batsman's timing. Always, though, he came up, wrist sharply cocked, profiled, sideways on to the batsman, his left arm high, the hand cupped as if in a votive act. His delivery swing was classically full, the bowling arm driving on down. He changed pace subtly; and even varied his degree of spin by changing his grip – which was based on the tip of the index finger placed across, and not beside, the seam. So, especially on a responsive pitch, he could alter the width of turn from ball to ball. Like all the masters of flight, he could impart a considerable amount of overspin and, consequently, such steep dip as to produce the illusion of half-volley in a good-length ball. He bowled one that went with the arm, which constantly deceived good batsmen, a faster ball, a yorker, and sometimes generated an unexpected amount of bounce. He was always, and essentially, a thinking bowler; and the spectator on the boundary edge, who could not detect his variations at such range, could appreciate them when he saw a batsman play an over of apparently similar deliveries with six different strokes. After he had bowled a ball he used to walk back and, in the moment before he turned, look up into the sky, often with half a smile which he never explained. An over finished, he would take his cap and perch it on his head at a Beattyish angle, peak pointing high, and saunter off, generally to the gully, where he held some good catches.

He took punishment phlegmatically. Hit for six, or when a catch was dropped off him, he would roll his eyes long-sufferingly upwards, and give that finger a gentle rub, and stand tapping his toe on the ground, hand outstretched for the return of the ball. If he took a wicket he turned quietly away; no sign of excitement; at most, some dry, side-of-the-mouth remark. The completeness of his technique was apparent in the difference between his method on a turning wicket, where he went round the wicket and was a parsimonious killer; and on a plumb easy pitch, where, bowling over the wicket, his control and variations imposed care on even the best of batsmen. It would be accurate to say that he was at his best from about 1950 to 1958; though his career might well have continued longer but for that cruelly damaged and deformed finger. Sometimes, while he was waiting to bat, he would sit for hours on end rubbing Friar's Balsam into its tortured rawness. If it was soft, it would bleed; if a callus formed, it would tear away; it was a catch 22, that finger. It was apparent, though, when he returned to play the occasional matches that handicap allowed, for Essex between 1962 and 1964, that his mastery of his craft was as complete as ever. Indeed, until relatively recently, he turned out in charity matches where he could still engage first-class batsmen, and quite outclass those of lesser quality.

John Arlott, *John Arlott's Book of Cricketers* (1979)

Fred Trueman

The life of Fred Trueman is not a single story nor a simple pattern. There is not one Fred Trueman but four – the basic Fred Trueman, Fred Trueman the fast bowler, Fred Trueman the man, and Fred Trueman the public image. He is no one of these four; he is all four of them; and it is difficult to set any order or priority among them. The original Fred Trueman – the miner and son of a miner who, in 1949, set off from Maltby with wonder and hope to play cricket for Yorkshire – still exists, though he is more deeply buried than the usual youthful self that is contained within every man.

Fred Trueman the mature fast bowler was a sharply pointed and astutely directed weapon; Fred Trueman the man has often been tactless, haphazard, crude, a creature of impulse. In Fred Trueman the public image, so many accretions of rumour and fiction have been deposited round the human core that the resultant figure is recognizable only to those who do not know him. The four are not easily reconciled; but they exist within one body – or at least under the roof of one name – and to untwine them is to destroy the essential unity of a composite – but real – character. Of course many of the stories about Fred Trueman are apocryphal; many are not; but even those referring to situations that never existed are ingredients of him, for he is partly a myth – indeed, he accepted a place in mythology with some eagerness. His life is recorded in gossip as well as in *Wisden*.

The lad of eighteen who, after Ron Aspinall was injured, played in four Championship matches of 1949 for Yorkshire would not arouse particular interest now; certainly he would not have done so in the middle 1950s: but 1949 was different. He was not remarkable but he was the uncomplicated, original Fred Trueman. He could not dream that he had come upon his historic cue. All cricketing England was as desperate for a fast bowler to fling back the humiliation imposed by Lindwall and Miller as ever America was for a white hope to humble Jack Johnson. By 1952 that hope had settled upon Fred Trueman and, if the primary Yorkshire character was not destroyed, it was soon encased in a new outer shell of what people wanted to see. He himself was to add fresh layers of behaviour which completed the Trueman of the public image. Even the final picture is not to be defined. A reigning Prime Minister – Harold

452

Wilson, himself a Huddersfield man – described him as 'the greatest living Yorkshireman': while Roy Ullyett made him the subject of his most violently funny caricature.

He played cricket for twenty years at first-class level – until the late 1960s, when he was thirty-seven, far past the fast bowler's normal allotted span, which ends at thirty – and he took more wickets in Test cricket than anyone else has ever done. In that time the bounding energy and fierce pace of youth matured to a semi-instinctive, but also extremely shrewd, technique in handling the fast bowling machine that was a body perfectly constructed for precisely that purpose. For a decade – again much longer than the peak period of even the best of the kind – he was, when the fire burnt, as fine a fast bowler as any.

All this time he was travelling the world, acquiring experience, but still capable of quite boyish brashness; a creature of impulse and emotion who, almost beyond his own control, acquired a reputation – often, but not always, deserved – for violence and four-letter words.

At length that reputation slopped over. There is a histrionic streak in him and, if the men of his own county insisted on seeing him as the archetypal Yorkshireman they themselves wanted to be – blunt, honest, strong, destroying bowler of high speed, smiter of sixes, taker of acrobatic catches, striker of wisecracks, cocker of snooks at authority – he was only too happy – in fact compulsively eager – to play the part. A newspaper column in which, freed from the former control of the Yorkshire cricket authorities, he can state strong opinions; a year round the North country clubs with a vaudeville act which the modest – and some not so modest – found 'blue', have deepened the artificial layers about the original Fred Trueman. Yet, peel it away and, at every level, you have Fred Trueman in varying degrees of his four personalities.

Those four identities, too, are often completely contradictory. He can be uproarious but also – though not often – silent, moody; he can be generous – and mean; he could bowl his heart out – or turn it in; he can be harsh – or gentle; he can be genuinely witty – and horribly crude; almost hysterically funny – and a complete bore; he can be intuitively understanding – and chillingly embarrassing; he can be arrogant – and as uncertain of himself as a schoolboy; he is pulled this way and that by his doubts and his emotions; he wants desperately to be liked and he is, at bottom, lonely. Least of all is it generally understood that, in the urge to succeed at the craft in which he excelled, he lived constantly on the sharpest edge of his nerves.

No one can be sure of holding a true balance between all the constituents of this man of conflicting characters. Indeed, no man can accurately describe another; he cannot even know him because he cannot discover all, while the other, however willing he might be, is not capable of letting anyone else know all about him. No one knows Fred Trueman completely; and none of those who know him at all would agree about him – if only for the fact that no two of them have seen the same Fred Trueman.

The unifying thread running through all the apparent contradictions is that of the fast bowler; not simply a man who bowled fast, nor a man who became a fast bowler, but one who knew from the first moment he considered such matters that he was going to be a great fast bowler. Others of expert knowledge might doubt it: he never did. He realized that there had to be a period – while he grew up – before the rest of the world realized it: but that was the only qualification he allowed. He was not merely a fast bowler in achievement, he was a fast bowler in the mind and in the heart. There is no characteristic fast bowler. Although Trueman and Statham, Statham and Tyson were so effectively complementary, they were, and are, even more different in personality than in bowling method. Fred Trueman was the kind of fast bowler he had created for himself; a larger-than-life-sized figure compounded in the imagination of a boy from the fancies, facts, loyalties, cricket, reading, traditions and all the other influences of a semi-rural, semi-industrial area of South Yorkshire in the 1930s. Whenever he acted in a considered fashion – and he did not always do so at the most important junctures of his career – he acted as that ideal fast bowler who lived in his mind would have done.

John Arlott, *Fred: Portrait of a Fast Bowler* (1971)

Alan Knott

There has never been any doubt about the quality of Alan Knott, who now seems likely to keep wicket for Kent and England for the rest of his active life.

As long ago as 1963, county dressing-room intelligence had it that a young wicket-keeper-batsman in the Kent Second XI was a likely prospect. In the next season, just eighteen, he was brought into the first team for a couple of matches in June and then given a 'run' in August. Against Lancashire at Blackpool he made five catches in the first innings, two in the second; and he turned the course of Kent's last match of the season – with Somerset, who, after dominating the first two days, had reduced the Kent second innings to 58 for 5 and seemed sure to win. Then, with that blend of ability and temperament which characterizes his cricket, Knott – top scorer with 55 – began a revival which carried Kent to 247 and a win by 52 runs.

His predecessor, Tony Catt, emigrated to South Africa soon afterwards, and in 1965 Alan Knott made 74 catches and 10 stumpings; scored 559 runs, including an innings of 49 not out against Sussex, which excited everyone who saw it; was capped by Kent; selected by the Cricket Writers' Club as the Best Young Cricketer of the Year; and was discussed by sound critics as England's next wicket-keeper.

The MCC Under–25 matches in Pakistan, 1966–67, were a proving ground for him; on a dispiriting tour he retained heart and humour, batted with greater purpose and effect than several of the specialist batsmen and kept wicket with skill and joy.

His first Test was the second of 1967 against Pakistan: he made seven catches there, and then five and a stumping in the last match of the rubber at the Oval. He had played himself on to the tour of the West Indies, but not into the England team for the first three Tests. From past experience, Parks had been a calculated selection as a wicket-keeper-batsman on the hard pitches of the Caribbean, but, apart from his 42 in the first Test, he batted unconvincingly and, after three drawn games, Knott was brought in at Port-of-Spain. He kept wicket well, as everyone expected; but, ironically, his previously discounted batting virtually decided the series. West Indies scored 526, and the English first innings was dangerously poised at 260 for 5 when he came in to Cowdrey and stayed to make 69 not out – highest score but one – in a total of 414 from which, after Sobers's declaration, England won the only finished match of the series. He saved the last Test and the rubber with it when he batted four hours for 73 not out, and England held out for a draw with only one wicket standing.

All five Tests against Australia in 1968; a place on the ill-fated Pakistan tour of 1968–69 – on which he had the unique ill-luck of being 96 not out when the third Test was abandoned because of rioting. Last summer he played in all six Tests of the two series, against West Indies –

in which he was John Hampshire's partner in the stand which saved the England batting at Lord's and was given the award for the Man of the Series – and New Zealand. Twenty-four years old this spring, he has now played in 18 Tests, made 52 catches and 8 stumpings and scored 666 runs at an average of 30.

Kent have been fortunate in their sequence of wicket-keepers – Huish, Hubble, Ames, Levett and Evans. Alan Knott faces the records of Leslie Ames, who scored more runs than any other wicket-keeper in either Test or first-class cricket, and Godfrey Evans, who was responsible for more dismissals than any other player in Tests. They will not daunt him.

Dark, quick-eyed, lithe, neat and fast-moving, he is as lively as Evans; though less extrovert, he has the same buoyancy and the same capacity for providing a psychological fillip for his team-mates at trying times. He walks like an athlete, laughs easily, and is a personable reflection of all that is best in the young men of the 1960s and 1970s. He has proved his ability to stand firm at a crisis; his opponents know, too, that he can be courteously generous about their achievements.

He is a wicket-keeper first, an all-round wicket-keeper without distinguishable weakness. His work is economical, he is well balanced, quick to start, and acrobatic in his ability to dive or jump for distant catches. He works close to the stumps to slow bowling, and takes his friend, contemporary and county colleague Derek Underwood with fine understanding; but he also emerges well from the most searching test of a wicket-keeper, which is off-break bowling to a right-hand batsman.

His batting is alert and confident, marked by quick reactions and lively footwork and, though it is informed by an enterprising approach, it is sufficiently correct in its fundamentals, against both speed and spin, for him to play major defensive innings at Test level.

He scored over a thousand runs in the season of 1968, but there was something of a falling away in his batting last season so that at times he seemed too highly placed in the batting order at number three for Kent and six for England. The gifts of a natural batsman, however, are clearly to be seen in him, and he was entitled to the reaction season that even the best players have experienced. Meanwhile he will, no doubt, persevere, in the nets, with his off-spin bowling; we may suspect that he has been told of Alfred Lyttelton, who discarded his pads in a Test and took four Australian wickets for 19 runs.

John Arlott, *The Cricketer* (1970)

Godfrey Evans

Godfrey Evans was, quite simply, the finest wicket-keeper I have seen. At his very best he was capable of making catches and stumpings which no other man would have considered chances. An instance of this occurred in the Test trial at Bradford when Jim Laker ran riot to the tune of eight wickets for two runs. Don Kenyon moved back to a ball that turned and lifted unpleasantly. He played it down and Godfrey managed to catch it one-handed, a full length *in front* of the batsman and equally astonished short legs. I was one of these and had not even moved! On another occasion during a Scarborough Festival match, Billy Sutcliffe glanced a delivery from Alec Bedser wide, off the full face of the bat. Godfrey, as usual standing up to Alec, anticipated, took off and caught the ball one-handed while literally horizontal.

Like so many great players, Godfrey thrived on the big occasion, and it is fair to say that he was normally a better keeper for England than for Kent. For it is not possible to turn in superlative performances every day of the week as a wicket-keeper.

The central figure in the field must always be the man behind the stumps. Not only does he have the opportunity to make more catches than anyone else, but he delivers the *coup de grâce* in the majority of runouts, and he is also responsible for the stumpings. He can transform the whole appearance of the fielding side, camouflaging the poorer returns and adding colour to the proceedings. He is the hub around which the remainder of the team revolves and Godfrey revelled in all this. His bubbling enthusiasm also did much to keep his team going, especially towards the end of a long, hot, unsuccessful day in the field. He was a tonic with his 'We only need two more wickets tonight and we're through them', even though the score at that particular juncture was 330 for 2!

I have played over fifty Test matches with Godfrey Evans and consider the 1950–1 series in Australia his most outstanding. I cannot remember him putting down a catch, or missing a single stumping in five Test matches, while in addition he made a number of 'impossible' catches, especially off Alec Bedser. Godfrey's keeping helped Alec Bedser enormously, and one catch full length down the leg side which dismissed a plainly hypnotized Neil Harvey from a glance off the face of the bat, will always be with me . . .

What was the secret of his success? Apart from sheer ability and a superb eye, it was very largely a matter of vitality. Many people can be brilliant for a short period of time, but it takes a very exceptional person to be just as full of life and just as spectacular an hour before the close of play on a really hot day at Adelaide after five successive sessions in the field. The fact that Godfrey Evans was a born entertainer who welcomed the limelight, and possessed a flair for the spectacular and the audacious, not only made him a universal favourite with spectators; it acted also as a spur to the fielders to maintain the standard he set himself.

In two respects Godfrey was fortunate. He was able to take a swift nap and awake refreshed under the most difficult circumstances. On numerous occasions I have seen him come in at lunchtime, have a drink and then curl up and go to sleep, completely oblivious to the noise of a dressing-room. The other reason underlying his success was his ability to dismiss instantly from his mind any mistake he might make. Many wicket-keepers spend five minutes apologizing for a dropped catch and the rest of the day bemoaning that particular blunder. This may be understandable, but it does not help when the next chance comes along.

Very occasionally he did have a bad day. His worst was at Leeds in 1948 against the Australians, when they turned defeat into victory with a large second innings score on a worn wicket as chance after chance went down. From a purely personal angle I shall remember him dropping Neil Harvey at Manchester. Neil had just come to the crease and managed to get an outside edge. It travelled sweetly to Godfrey, standing back, who was throwing it and appealing when down it went. Throughout Neil's hundred I was haunted by that moment, but not Godfrey . . .

[As a batsman] Godfrey was at his best in a swashbuckling attacking role, for his defence was never sound. He liked to hit hard and often – in addition to the normal strokes he became particularly adept at a shovel shot with which he used to scoop the ball out towards mid-wicket, using plenty of right hand – and to scamper enthusiastically between the wickets. His running was a tonic to the spectators, the fieldsmen, and certainly not least to his partner. He introduced a note of genuine comedy, but never forgot the importance of the stolen single or the advantage to be gained by backing up.

The most significant partnership I had with Godfrey was against the West Indies in 1950 at Old Trafford. The pitch was one of the worst I have ever encountered, a broken beach on which Eric Hollies made the odd delivery rear shoulder high, as well as turn, and the English batting collapsed against the spin combination of Ramadhin and Valentine. When the 'Cheeky Chappie' joined me we were in serious trouble with all the accredited players back in the pavilion and less than 100 runs on the board. Godfrey was completely undeterred. He cut and carved with such impunity that he not only scored a remarkable century, but together we managed to make the record stand for that particular wicket. Before the end the West Indies were not sure where to bowl. England consequently regained command and went on to record our one victory of the series.

The most satisfactory boundary Godfrey Evans ever struck was against the Australians at Adelaide. With only four runs required to win the game and the Ashes I foolishly lost my wicket. In he went, smote the ball to the mid-wicket pickets, and the champagne was waiting for him by the time he returned to the pavilion.

Trevor Bailey, *The Greatest of My Time* (1968)

Ole Blue Eyes

I knew him, of course, many years before he knew me. One summer just after the war I went to Lord's and climbed to what they used to call the 'free seats' under the Father Time clock. Len Hutton was batting at the Pavilion end. I forget the match now, but one over is painted on my memory. To each of the first five balls Hutton played an almost identical stroke, a drive which went either to mid-off or to cover-point. It appeared that he rolled the ball out to them, first one fielder then the other, like a ritual. Neither had to move a fraction; he was just measuring up. The last ball of the over was sent with the same quietness, exactly bisecting the distance between the two men. It struck the boards at the cover boundary with an echoing crack.

It's a long time ago now for both of us. The teenager watcher is middle-aged; the great batsman is long retired to his house and to his memories.

I missed no chance of seeing him at the wicket. In 1951 he made his hundredth hundred against Surrey at the Oval and on the Saturday evening he was not out. Early on the Monday I was in the queue as the sun came up over Kennington. A great crowd was assembled on the bank in front of Archbishop Tenison's school. Boys were standing on the school roof to watch. I had no fear of him failing. The bowler delivered the fateful ball and Len struck it with all his grand and lovely power to the fence.

In 1948 he scored 30 out of an England total of 52 in the fifth Test against Australia. He stood, as though he did not quite understand, as batsman after batsman, Compton, Edrich and all, trudged to the pavilion. It was the first Test match I had ever watched. For years I had waited to see Don Bradman and I only saw him face two balls. Eric Hollies bowled him with the second and I remember thinking: 'Hutton wouldn't have let me down like that.'

Years later I walked into the editor's office at the London *Evening News*, disgruntled and intent on giving my notice. Reginald Willis, a wonderfully wily man who knew the craft of turning away wrath, picked up a cricket bat from behind his desk and said: 'Look at this, Len Hutton made 364 with this in 1938.' He regarded me fiercely: 'Wouldn't like to work with him, would you?'

Of course I did. He had retired from cricket after becoming the first professional to captain England and was engaged to write his comments on the forthcoming series against Pakistan. I was to be his amanuensis. There is a story, and I've never asked Sir Leonard about it, concerning the day he was signed up to give his name to the column (it said: 'Sir Leonard Hutton was talking to Leslie Thomas' in small italics at the bottom). Having put his signature on the contract the great cricketer was led outside the building to be introduced to the motor car that was also part of the reward. I was not present at this ceremony but the tale went that having been shown the plush interior and the shining exterior by a whole pride of directors he smiled his small smile and said: 'Aye, very nice. Where's the wash-leathers?'

Some took this as evidence of extreme Yorkshire thrift and others as part of his methodical attention to the smallest detail which was always a factor in his life on the cricket field. (He once pointed out to the umpires that the pitch was several inches short and they had to prepare another.) Personally I can just see him making the remark about the wash-leathers and I am sure it was one of those moments of mischief in which he secretly delighted and which so many sober and earnest people took for gospel. I never knew him short of an answer. Years after he retired I was enjoying his company at a cocktail party given on the eve of an important one-day international to be played at Lord's. An eager young journalist, pad at the ready (padded up, you might say) asked: 'Sir Leonard, would you have liked to have batted in limited-overs cricket?'

'Oh, yes,' came the careful reply. 'You always have a good excuse for getting out.'

As I got to know him I became familiar with the signs and when I have met him each summer, usually at Lord's, it has been a matter of delight to me that they are still in evidence. Hutton's creased face crinkles up a little, the ongoing effect of the half-smile that issues from the edges of his mouth. He has the most amazing eyes of any man I have ever met, the most riveting blue with flecks of deep humour in them. I have never been confronted with Sinatra but 'Ole blue eyes' can have little on Len of Pudsey.

On the first day I met him, when 'Sir Leonard Hutton Comments . . .' was to be published in the lunchtime edition of the *Evening News*, he did not turn up until the middle of the afternoon. Faced with this important absence I wrote a column on how wonderful it was to see Tom Graveney batting again. (The match was Worcestershire versus the Pakistanis and was Graveney's first game after he left Gloucestershire.) Some time after the lunch interval this long-overcoated figure materialized at the extreme end of the press box. He appeared in no hurry. His back had been bad, he explained. Nervously I showed him my 'Sir Leonard Hutton Comments' piece – a thousand words of thoughts and experiences from a man I had never met. 'Ah, yes,' he nodded sagely. Those blue eyes turned up, smiling. 'That's just what I would have . . . er . . . commented.'

I liked him from that moment and I have never ceased to do so. Once his recurring back pain was so intense that, with help from two England cricketers, I had to carry him to his car. Sometimes I ended up driving it and I remember one occasion when he suggested that we should stop because he had spotted an old lady who wanted to cross the road. Naturally I was the one who got out to perform this chivalry. It turned out that she did *not* want to cross at all. Returning to the car, a little miffed, I told Sir Leonard what had happened.

'Dithering,' he said. 'That's what caused run-outs in Test matches, you know. Dithering.'

During our summer working together I had my first play produced on television. Anxious that it should get as large a recommendation as possible, at least in my own paper, I spent one cricket lunchtime in the press box typing an essay in promise of its excellence. Sir Leonard watched me intently, biting away at a packet of sandwiches as he did so. Eventually, running out of superlatives, I went to the refreshment tent and bought two cups of tea and a packet of crisps. 'Those crisps look all right,' he mentioned.

'Help yourself,' I said busily.

He did. 'They're better with salt', he suggested.

'Isn't there any salt?' I asked, still typing.

'Ah, right, there it is,' he murmured. I was vaguely conscious of his disinterring the blue packet and spreading its contents on the crisps. He sampled the results and pronounced them excellent. While I typed he munched. Eventually when I looked at the packet there were only half a dozen miserable crisps left in the bottom. By this time I knew him well enough to permit sarcasm. 'You might as well finish them off,' I said moodily.

'Oh no, lad,' he said, kindly patting my arm. 'You eat them. They're your crisps.'

He did it for the inward fun of it. I never heard him shout or laugh loudly. The joy was almost secret, shared only if you got to know him. Even now, when someone tells me a Hutton story, I can see the joke protruding, even if frequently they cannot. At Edgbaston, during one of the Test matches we covered together, a young reporter – once again figuratively padded up – approached with diffidence and, nodding at the play, asked: 'Sir Leonard, what do you think they're trying to do?'

With the world's most serious and obliging expression (the lad was from a *rival* newspaper, by the way) Hutton studied the middle for some time and eventually turned. The reporter's pen hovered.

'I think,' said the great man, 'they're trying to get them out.'

And the chap *wrote it down*. The expression of concern and truthfulness that occupied Hutton's face could convince anybody. Once at Trent Bridge I saw him demonstrating to an audience, which included Fred Titmus, John Murray and Barry Knight, how, in 1946, Ernie Toshack of Australia had consistently bowled at his legs. 'I moved over,' said Hutton, demonstrating with a shuffle how he shifted to his left. 'But he was still bowling at my legs. So I moved again, and then again.'

We stood, me and three England cricketers, taking in every word, while, according to the yarn Hutton was standing almost by the square-leg umpire and Toshack was *still* bowling at his legs – with the stumps standing unattended some yards away.

Sometimes when his back was not too bad, he used to bowl to me, in hotel corridors and such-like, with a paper ball tied with string and me with a newspaper as a bat. 'If you could only bat,' he would sigh, 'you'd have made a great tourist.'

His point was that, apart from cricketing ability, you had to be optimistic and resilient to tour abroad, particularly in Australia. He greatly admired Godfrey Evans. 'He'd be keeping wicket all day in Sydney, ninety-five in the shade, and never miss a thing,' he recalled. 'Like the rest he would stagger off the field, have a bath, get dressed, have a drink, sit down at the piano in the hotel and start to play. He was ready for the evening. That's what you need on tour.'

Up at Scarborough last season I told Godfrey Evans this story and he repaid me with one of his own. 'In the 1946 tour,' he said, 'Australia at Brisbane were several hundreds for one wicket. They went on and on piling up the runs and no one looked like taking a wicket. It was as hot as hell too. At the end of one over Len said to me: ' "Godfrey, I think we'll have to get them in run-outs." '

Sir Leonard was one of the adjudicators at that Scarborough match but he was taken ill and had to go home. When I last saw him at Lord's, however, his eye, like that of Moses, was not dimmed. Irving Rosenwater, the cricket statistician, was telling him that his younger son, Sir Leonard's that is, had played in one match recognized as first-class. The figures man revealed it was East Africa versus MCC, at Nairobi on such and such dates, in such and such year, and proceeded to recite from memory the younger Hutton's batting and bowling figures in both innings. Rosenwater stepped back looking rather pleased at his feat.

Sir Leonard's eyes had small lights shining in them. He looked at me and I knew the signs. 'Well, well,' he said kindly. 'You never know what your kids get up to, do you.'

All those years ago when the illustrious batsman and his journeyman scribe were travelling the cricket grounds of England, people would come up to Sir Leonard Hutton, seek to shake his hand and so often say: 'Len – you be given me such a great deal of pleasure.'

And that, too, goes for me.

Leslie Thomas, Quick Singles (1986)

Colin McCool

I first saw Colin McCool play in 1948, when he was over here with the Australians. I had heard of him, as had every other cricketer, a couple of years before, when he had a successful season against Hammond's last England side. In the Tests of 1946–7, he had scored 272 runs in seven innings, which included a century and a 95, and with two not outs, gave him a batting average of 54. But this was not so important, because it was a fairly easy season for Australia to make runs, and he usually went in after Bradman, Barnes and Morris had trampled on the English bowling. What shook us was that he took 18 wickets, at just over 21, and this at a time when Lindwall and Miller, to say nothing of Johnson and Toshack and Dooland and Tribe, were about. Most of McCool's wickets were taken against the best English batsmen. He got Bill Edrich, upon whom he seems to have cast a spell, four times; Hammond twice; Yardley three times; Hutton, Washbrook, Fishlock and Ikin once each.

McCool was, it seemed, the coming Australian leg-spinner, the successor to O'Reilly, the man who would nicely complement the opening assault. Nobody suggested that he was so good as O'Reilly, but he had the advantage of being a batsman, and all seemed fair for him when he was chosen for the 1948 England tour.

It was a grievous disappointment to him. He had a sore spinning finger which would not heal. There were arguments about the best treatment – was it better to rest it, or try to harden it by regular use? Spinners and their captains have often faced this problem: and, as usually happens, neither course was thoroughly followed. Australia kept winning matches anyway. McCool did not play in a Test. It was not, however, the end of his Test career. He went to South Africa with the 1949–50 Australians, and did pretty well. With a match against New Zealand in 1945, and three against India in 1947, he finished his Test career with 36 wickets at 26.61, and 459 runs, average 35.30.

A creditable all-round performance, we thought, and forgot about him. I do not know who was responsible for fetching him from his Queensland milk-round to Somerset. (In case this should meet his eye, I must explain that a milk-roundsman in the remoter parts of Queensland is a very posh chap, selling a great many things beside milk: more like a bloated capitalist than your friendly morning milkman in Somerset.) But he still liked playing cricket, and was tempted back to England to play in the Lancashire League, and qualify for Somerset. There were no instant transfers for overseas players in those days; and while he was qualifying, the regulations were changed, unfavourably for him, so that he had to wait an extra year before he could play in championship matches. It was then 1955, when he was forty years old, and though he had done well in the League, it was three years since he had played in a first-class match. There was much gloomy talk in the bars of Taunton and Bath about investing in an old man.

Nevertheless, he gave Somerset five seasons of splendid service, if not quite in the expected way. Maurice Tremlett, his captain, decided that he needed Colin's batting more than his bowling. He put him at No. 4, and told him to take no silly risks. McCool bore the burden of a frail batting side, and scored about 1,500 runs a year for them, taking nearly 50 wickets a year as well, and holding about 140 catches, almost always in the slips. He felt, himself, that he was not put on to bowl enough – though he always got on well with Tremlett. What was happening, though we had hardly begun to realize it then, was the inexorable and tragic decline of the leg-spinner. When the pitch was thought likely to help spin, it was the finger-spinners who were given the first chance – and Somerset had a reliable one in Brian Langford (I believe he is still the only man to have bowled eight maiden overs in a Sunday League match).

Colin McCool, I am proud to say, became a warm friend of mine during his years in Somerset (and Devon, I must add, not forgetting the Torquay Festival, and some evenings at the Cott Inn, Dartingdon). He did not quite come to terms with the West Country, as Sammy Woods had done, long before, or Bill Alley did, soon afterwards. Woods and Alley settled here. McCool, his five years up, went back to Australia. He missed the sunshine. 'There's no winter,' he said, 'and the beer's better; and the b . . . off-spinners don't turn.'

I think an additional reason was that he found some difficulty in accepting the conventions of English cricket, as it was then. There was a Somerset committee-member, who liked and admired him, and would greet him in the morning with 'Morning, McCool'. The committee-member was seeking to be courteous. He would have thought it pompous to say 'Mr McCool', and impertinent to say 'Colin'. But it infuriated Colin. He thought it was a reflection on his status. He would have preferred something like 'Hi, Col, you old bastard'. The worlds were too far apart.

But I remember him, both for his cricket and his character with deep affection; and so do a great many other people in the West of England.

Alan Gibson, *The Cricketer* (1981).

Tom Graveney

I seldom have nightmares. Say a couple a year. But enough to re-establish my stark fear of heights. Extremely scary. I always wake only a split second before I hit the deck – splat! There's a still fevered moment or two for a shaking hand to fumble for the light switch and a smoke. Then, with relief and realization dawning that I'm both in the land of the living and my pungent pit, I will inhale deeply, smile to myself and, content again, think of . . . Clem Attlee, a former Prime Minister, and George Emmett, a former Gloucestershire bat. And thoughts of George soon turn to recollections of Tom. Ah, Tom. Dear Tom. *Our* Tom.

You need an explanation: in 1946, at the age of eight, I was unaccountably sent the thirty miles from Stonehouse in Gloucestershire to a boarding prep school near Hereford. Now, in spite of his aberration on private education, in all other matters my father, bless him, was as trenchant a socialist as you could ever meet. And you didn't meet many in that true-blue neck of the Randwick Woods unless you bumped into Bert Cole, Ben Parkin, Bill Maddocks or my Uncle John planning the revolution in the Woolpack Inn. Anyway, it so came to pass that, between them, they had won the seat for Labour in the 1945 landslide election. Word of this stunning reverse of the established order seeped even over the county border at about the very same time that I had turned up in Hereford as the most midget, meek and miserable mother's boy even such as Dotheboys had seen. The bigger boys bullied and we namby newts cowered and cringed by day and, at nights, wept and then wet the bed.

Many and varying were the forms of torture. You had done well if you survived a day with only an ear twisted off in the boot room, or a bottom blackened with a scrubbing brush and Cherry Blossom. Most horrendous was 'The Tower', so awful that even the leading sadists only summoned the courage once or twice a year. I heard the dreaded, awful, conspiracy, 'Keating for The Tower tonight; pass it round', whispered through the school on three occasions. The school's church tower was more squat Saxon than tall and fluted Norman. But it was high enough to be absolutely petrifying when you were dangling over its edge held, only by the ankles, by two other boys. The rest of the school would watch the fun from below. I'm still surprised no child ever fell to his death. I am certain it is the reason for my recurring nightmares and my fear of heights. (I can never look out of an aeroplane till it is in the clouds.)

On two occasions I was 'towered' for 'family connections' – that is, every other short-trousered prig in the place was, of course, a Conservative, so when I boasted about my father's and uncle's political affiliations, I did so with my heart in my mouth. I cannot remember exactly why, but I was possibly sent to The Tower when the Labour Party nationalized steel and when they 'sold out' the Indian Empire to 'the wogs'. I was hung as a martyr for Clem Attlee's great radicalism.

The third time was altogether different. In the midsummer of 1948, the triumphant march of Bradman's Australian cricketers had the English selectors in all sorts of panic. For the third Test match at Old Trafford, out of the blue, they selected two Gloucestershire players. I would have got away with it had the only selection been Jack Crapp, our doughty left-hander who had scored a century against the tourists in the county fixture at Bristol. But the wee sprog, George Emmett, was another matter altogether, for he was chosen to replace Len Hutton, revered both in the school and the land as a national institution. So my one-man Gloucester gloat at Emmett's selection had its come-uppance at once. In a seething fury the word went round, 'Keating for The Tower tonight.' I was hung as a martyr for Georgie Emmett. (When he failed in both innings there were threats that I should be 'done' again.)

Here is the point of these rambling recollections: if George Emmett had not been picked for that one solitary Test match, it is quite possible that the world would never have seen Tom Graveney bat. After Bristol Grammar School and National Service in the Army, young Graveney had seemed to have fluffed his apprenticeship as a Gloucestershire cricketer. At the time of that Manchester Test match, which began on 8 July 1948, his 'career' seemed to have ended before it began. On his first-class debut he had made a duck, and followed that with just over 200 runs in 20-odd innings. He was seriously thinking of re-signing for the Army, which he had enjoyed, and taking a PT instructor's course. Certainly he had been demoted to the Gloucestershire Second XI, and looked unlikely for re-engagement.

Then Crapp and Emmett were selected for England. Graveney was hastily dispatched to Bournemouth for the First XI fixture with Hampshire. He made a precocious and calm 47 against the spinners, Knott and Bailey, on a spiteful wicket. In the following match against Somerset at Bristol he scored an undefeated 81. By the time I got home for the holidays, my Stonehouse chums, Peter Beard and Robin Bassett, were filling me in with details of his maiden century, against the Combined Services at Gloucester Wagon Works. It had, they said, been amazingly wizard-prang.

The Cheltenham Festival – nine full days of cricket – couldn't come quick enough. Sometimes we'd catch that chippy little chuffer, the 'Railcar', and change at Gloucester. Other mornings would have us in front of the queue outside Woolworth's in Stroud for the Western National double-decker, over the top past Painswick's yews, and the Prinknash Pottery. We had our greaseproofed-paper sandwiches, a shilling extra for a bottle of Tizer and a pound of plums, a bat and tennis ball for tea-time, and our autograph books. The first time I saw him, Tom made a silky half-century – all coltish, gangly, upright youthfulness, with a high, twirly, backlift and a stirring, bold, flourishing signature in the follow-through – and he came back to the 'gym', blushing at the applause, and signed my book before he went in to lunch. 'T. W. Graveney', neat, joined-up, surprisingly adult.

Next Easter term, I began to feel less of an outsider at school when Dad sent me a present of my first *Wisden*. Even the bully boys asked, nicely, to borrow it. I would show them the Gloucestershire Notes, and the last sentence about the batting – 'A pleasant feature of the season was the form of a newcomer, T. W. Graveney, a product of Bristol club cricket, who showed graceful right-handed stroke play.'

By Cheltenham that August, the young man was actually leading our parade. That in itself was a triumph. Schoolboy romantics do not readily forsake their first heroes. And there had been lots of them about in 'Glorse'. True, Charlie Barnett had gone, off to the Lancashire League; and, sure, we missed the Chalford autocrat's hook of nose and stroke; he smacked bumpers, thwack! as if he was smacking down plaice on the wet slabs outside his fishmongers in 'Zoiren' or 'Chelt'. Then there was the aforementioned Jack and Georgie. Crapp was the calm and watchful leftie; we were never in real trouble till he was out. Unperturbable, he would push his ones and twos to keep the numbers rolling in gentle rhythms, but then, of a sudden, he would break out and hit the thing with a clean, wicked ferocity, then lean placid on his sword, the handle supporting his buttocks like a shooting stick, and he would cross his arms and legs and wait, serene, while the ball was retrieved from miles away. 'Good ol' Jack! Give 'em another one, Jack!' we shouted. But he seldom did it twice in succession. Or even twice in a session.

Emmett was in direct contrast. A tiny man with a nutbrown face and whipcord wrists. He had the twinkling feet of an Astaire, and the same sort of hairstyle. His on-drive singed every blade of grass between the bowler and mid-wicket. His cap was a very faded blue because he wore it everywhere – even in bed I bet, we giggled – and there was always a groan of real sadness when he got himself out. Emmett, and especially Crapp, I learned many years later, were the wise and generous mentors and mother-hens to the young chick Graveney.

In Tom's earliest days, Billy Neale also nursed him in the middle orders. He was a farmer, from Grace country, down Thornbury way. He had gone to school, at Cirencester Grammar, with the county's previous emperor and champion, Wally Hammond, and had always been, they said, the one to understand the moods and melancholy of that great, smouldering genius. They would walk together for hours in the orchards of Neale's Breadstone Farm, talking of this and that; after which Wally was refreshed again. Tom's first captain must have been an influence as well: B. O. Allen was Clifton and Cambridge and once got a double century against Hampshire; he looked as fierce as our Latin master and we never dared ask him for an autograph. He went forth to toss for innings in a brown trilby, like they said Hammond used to do, and he blew his nose with a whopping, red-spotted snuff hankie. And like Charlie Barnett, he used to ride to hounds in winter.

There were other tyros, too, with Tom: Milton was to become a dear favourite; the *Yearbook* started calling him 'Clement' and then 'Charlie' before settling, by public demand, on Arthur. He had the soccer player's bow legs – he remains the last 'double' international – and was the most versatile and thrilling fieldsman I ever saw. And Martin Young, suave and smarmy-haired and always beautifully turned out; his bat always looked pine-fresh new. Arrogant, he had South African connections.

Our bowlers would take up another book: we all tried to copy George Lambert's action – he was faster than Lindwall, for sure. His new ball mucker was Colin Scott, who used to work at the Co-op and had great ten-to-two Underwood feet, and occasionally specialized in sixers. There was Sam Cook (whom the *Yearbook* called 'Cecil' *always*), who was left-arm and reliable and the much-loved apprentice to the very sorcerer himself, our wizard of tweak, Tom Goddard, whose 2,979 career bag of wickets has only been bettered by four others in the whole history of the game. Stumper was Andy Wilson, a tiny tot with massive appeal in every way. He once took ten catches in a match. After all his years keeping to Goddard and Cook, he took bets that he would be the only batsman in the whole land to read Ramadhin's wrong 'un when the West Indies came to Cheltenham in 1950. Both innings Andy shouldered arms to let the little long-sleeved mesmerist's first ball go by outside the off-stump. Both times he was clean bowled. Gloucester were routed that day. Only Graveney made double figures, all blushing uncertainty and middle-of-the-bat, and a man next to me said, 'Our Tom'll be servin' England this side o' twelvemonth.'

And he was. When Denis Compton was injured, Freddie Brown blooded him against the South Africans at Old Trafford in 1951, and on a real sticky he made 15 against Athol Rowan – 'every run full of cultured promise', said John Arlott on the wireless. Tom served England for the next ten years. When George was still King he was taking 175 from the Indians at Bombay; when Lindwall and Miller were still lethal he matched Hutton, stroke for stroke, in a partnership of 168 at Lord's; and a couple of years later he collected a century at Sydney with three successive boundaries; onwards a summer or two, and his massively flamboyant 258 nailed down for ever the wispy mystique of Ramadhin and Valentine, after May and Cowdrey had done the tedious, pad-prod spadework earlier in the month.

Yet while these, and even the shortest innings, were a delight, word was going about that he lacked the cruel competitive edge to take a game and an attack by the throat; he was getting out when the very critical need was just to stay in. He was, horror! playing Festival cricket instead of Test match cricket. Never the twain must meet, and he was dropped for, as someone said, 'being happy only to present his ability, but not to enforce it ruthlessly.'

He had moved from Gloucestershire now. But so had we. And wherever I was in the world, I daresay I wasn't the only Gloucester man to sneak a look first at the Worcester scores to see how Tom had done. For it was soon apparent that there, under the old Norman shadow that matched the mellow architecture of his strokes, his batsmanship had actually become even better. It was still joyous and free of care, but now it was more stable, more serene, more *certain*. The England selectors, of course, seemed oblivious to the fact, and though century followed century and Championship followed Championship, not even the wildest betting man would have wagered on a recall by England. But at last they had to. After his four years in the pleasant backwaters of the shires came an almost tangible rumbling of public demand for Graveney's Test match place to be restored, following another woeful England start to the West Indian series of 1966. They turned to Tom, now in his fortieth year.

And at Lord's too! The full-house standing ovation started as he made his way through the Long Room once again. Hall and Griffith and Sobers and Gibbs . . . he returned to grandstand applause after a magnificent 96. 'It's like a dream come true,' he said as he went back up the stairs, eyes moist with tears. In the next match, at Trent Bridge, England were 13 for 3, Hall's Larry Holmes and Griffith's Joe Frazier both murderously, cruelly, hostile. Graveney and Cowdrey alone had the technique and fearlessness to stand unflinchingly firm. Tom finished with 109, and many still shake their heads in wonder and insist it must have been his very best innings.

But there were still more gems in the old man's kitty. A superlative 165 followed at the Oval; then, next summer, a charming 151 against India at Lord's. A few months later he produced a comprehensive retrospective – 118 runs against the West Indies. 'Any art gallery in the world would have bought that innings,' wrote Henry Blofeld, who was there. He overflowed with fluent strokes and quite outplayed the 1968 Australians, as he did the Pakistanis in the winter, when Karachi saw his last Test match century. When the West Indies rejoined battle next summer he scored 75 in the first Test then, on the free Sunday of the match, played in his own benefit game at Luton. It was against the rules and Lord's banned him for three Tests – in effect, for ever. But Our Tom of Gloucester had become Worcester's Tom, then England's, then the world's.

As this book is a cricket writers' book, it would be nice to quote the retirement panegyric offered to Graveney after his final Test. It can do more justice than I can to a fine cricketer and a fine man. It was written by one of the very best of writers, J. M. Kilburn, who was for forty diligent and creative years the correspondent of the *Yorkshire Post*: 'Graveney may have disappointed some cricketers by playing in Graveney's way, but he has adorned cricket. In an age preoccupied with accountancy he has given the game warmth and colour and inspiration beyond the tally of the score-book. He has been of the orchard rather than the forest, blossom susceptible to frost but breathing in the sunshine ... Taking enjoyment as it came, he has given enjoyment that will warm the winters of memory.'

Yet it might never have happened had George Emmett not been picked for his solitary Test match in the midsummer of 1948. The very same day that Tom was dispatched to Bournemouth and I was dangled, head first, from the top of a church tower in Hereford.

Frank Keating, Cricket Heroes (1984)

Alan Davidson

They called him 'Al Pal', or the 'Mayor of Gosford', and he was one of the finest all-round cricketers the world has seen. Few bowlers could match his late swing and awkward movement off the pitch and there weren't many better fieldsmen in any position in the world. As a batsman he more often than not turned the tide for Australia after the early batsmen had failed.

I first struck him in 1945 when he was playing for Gosford High School and represented Northern High Schools against Combined Metropolitan High Schools in a match at the end of the schools season. In those days he was a hard hitting left-hand batsman and, as always, a brilliant fieldsman, but he bowled left arm unorthodox over the wicket deliveries rather than the ones that later made him famous. We went on our first tour together to England in 1953 and thereafter Davidson never missed a match other than through injury, nor an overseas tour. I played against him for a couple of years in this Combined School cricket and then suddenly he came from Gosford to play with Northern Districts and was an immediate success. So much so that he played his first Sheffield Shield match in 1949, only three years after leaving school cricket.

There are great cricketers in every era and Davidson was one of the greatest Australia has produced, particularly in the period from 1957 to 1963. This was after Miller and Lindwall had left the scene – Lindwall temporarily – thus allowing Davidson full scope with the new ball rather than condemning him to come on when the shine had all but disappeared.

He was injury prone – sometimes real, sometimes imaginary – but he never left the field or stopped bowling for any other than a very real reason. I caught Johnny Waite off him one day in Cape Town in one of those dismissals where fieldsmen and captain work on a certain plan and it happens to come off. Alan had been limping back to bowl and then boring in at the batsmen and moving the ball late, either into or away from them. Then he would limp back and Craig would ask him if he were all right – he would say 'no' and get a sympathetic pat on the shoulder and then bore in again and yet another magnificent delivery.

The Cape Town pitch was very slow and I asked Craig if I could come up three yards at gully for the one that flew off the thick edge and wouldn't normally carry. Davo limped back for the next ball and Waite square drove it like a bullet. I caught the red blur, body parallel to the ground, and was just rolling over for the second time when Davo arrived alongside me, saying excitedly, 'It was the old trap, you know. The old trap.' It had taken him just two seconds to get down and the boys thought it was the quickest he had moved all day.

This was the match where, so much was he on the massage table, that we had a copper plaque engraved and nailed on to the massage table and inscribed 'The A. K. Davidson Autograph Massage Table.'

I saw Waite in South Africa some time later and he recalled this particular incident in the context of Davidson's Test performances and bowling skill. Waite contended that Alan was at his best when not feeling 100 per cent fit. He said the real danger time was when you could see him limping back or looking sorry for himself.

I have never played with or against a more penetrative opening bowler, possibly because of the particular angle in which he came at the batsman, bowling from wide of the return crease to a point just outside the off stump and then swinging late to round about middle stump or middle and leg. He wasn't a big swinger of the ball but he certainly moved it as late as anyone I have seen, and this was one of the prime reasons that he was so successful. He only needed to hold the ball across the seam for variety and deliver it with the same action as for the in-swinger and I will defy any batsman in the world to pick the fact that the ball will continue straight on instead of swinging in.

He used to do this sometimes and at other times he would cut the ball away from the right-hander in a fashion that made him the joy of wicket-keeper Wally Grout and his slip fieldsmen. He and Grout used to refer jocularly to the fact that they had 'made' one another, each pointing out that the other would never have done as well without the benefit of either the bowling or wicket-keeping of the other. There was a lot in this for Grout took some magnificent catches off Davidson, both on the off and leg side, and developed a great understanding with him, as well as the ability to pick the way the ball was going to slant.

Richie Benaud, *Willow Patterns* (1969)

Garfield Sobers

For a few months of 1969, out of sheer weariness, Garfield Sobers ceased to produce the figures of the finest cricketer of modern times. Like all such lapses, his failure prompted little men to berate the great. His lack of success is unquestionable, but it no more detracts from the historic fact of his eminence than some indifferent verses make Coleridge less than a great poet. The only remarkable fact about Sober's bad spell was that it did not occur sooner under the heaviest sustained strain any cricketer has ever known.

No one who has watched him for any appreciable period can doubt that he is the finest all-rounder in the world. Merely to see him come out on the field, his long, hungry stride a strangely tigerish blend of the relaxed and the purposeful, is to recognize a great athlete. Most would agree, too, that he is the most giftedly versatile player the game has ever known. At Test level he has scored more runs than all but five men, all batsmen, pure and simple, in the entire history of the game; only eight bowlers have taken more wickets and three players have made more catches. No one approaches his triple record.

Figures, however, tell only part of the story: they cannot show that he is an excitingly brilliant player yet, also, essentially effective. In six different ways – as batsman, fast-medium bowler, finger-spinner, wrist-spinner, close fieldsman and captain – he has taken up cricket matches and remoulded them to his own design. No aspect of his cricket has been more amazing than his capacity for combining quality and quantity of effort; it is as if a single creature had both the class of a Derby-winner and the stamina of a mule. He is the only man ever to have performed the

474

'impossible' double of 1000 runs and 50 wickets in an Australian season – and he did it twice.

There can never have been such an all-round performance as his in the 1966 West Indies-England series. In the first Test he scored 161, bowled 49 overs for three wickets and West Indies won: at Lord's, where he and Holford, by their long, unfinished sixth-wicket stand made a draw against all probability, he had innings of 46 and 163 not out and one wicket in 43 overs: at Trent Bridge, the second West Indian win, 3 and 94, five wickets in 80 overs: at Leeds, in the match which decided the rubber, he made 174 and bowled 39 overs for eight wickets. When, at The Oval, it seemed as if the side suddenly relaxed after winning the series, he scored 81 and 0 and, in England's only innings, took three wickets. His overall figures for the series: 722 runs, average 103, 20 wickets at 27.25 off 269.4 overs. He made ten catches, and captained the side skilfully and perceptively.

So it was not surprising that, when England went to the West Indies in 1967–68, he decided, after the first three Tests had been drawn, to back himself to bring off another win by his own efforts. At Port-of-Spain he made the declaration which brought down on him the condemnation of all those who bemoan lack of enterprise in the modern cricketer. Everyone remembers that England won the match by seven wickets and took the rubber with it. Not so many recall the efforts of Sobers to draw the series in the final match. He scored 152 and 95 not out, bowled 68 overs for six wickets and pressed England so hard that they held on for a draw with only one wicket standing. He came straight from those matches to England to take up the captaincy of Nottinghamshire. They had been fifteenth in the Championship table of 1967; in Sobers's first season they were fourth – their highest for 36 years: Sobers was first in the batting averages, second in the bowling, took more catches than anyone else except the wicketkeeper – and hit six sixes from a six-ball over.

John Arlott, *The Cricketer* (1970)

Ken Barrington

It seems impossible that it is now three years since Ken Barrington died. He had a vitality which was irresistible and it hangs in the memory like a good tune.

I first saw him batting for Surrey in 1955 when I was only ten and making my first visit to the Oval. Ken was already twenty-five and only now fully establishing himself as a first-class cricketer after eight years on the staff, one of the longest apprenticeships of any great player. But this, of course, was one of the strongest staffs any country ever had, and Ken had been away for years on National Service duty. The discipline learned then, and no doubt already imparted at home in Reading by his father, a regular soldier, served him well through both the difficult first phase of his career and the years of success which followed.

You could, indeed, sense the discipline in his deportment on the field. Everything about him was neat and compact. My memory of that first innings I saw him play for Surrey is a hotchpotch of visual impressions: the black, crinkly hair, bare to the sun as in England it almost always was; an air of purposefulness and bustle; a propensity to chatter and chuckle between overs, with his batting partner (I think for much of that day it was little Bernie Constable) or with opposing fielders; a number of firm drives, through extra cover or wide of mid-on; and one shot in particular, a very late cut, the Stuart Surridge bat coming firmly down on to the ball as it drew level with the off-stump, sending the ball scudding down to where my brother and I sat entranced, between the pavilion and the gas-holders. For some reason that shot, the dark red ball bobbing rapidly over the green turf towards us, and the words of an old Oval pensioner, 'All the way, all the way', remain vividly in my mind.

The match was in August, after Ken Barrington had made his first appearance for England, against South Africa. Looking back this must have been why at this stage he had a special interest for a young spectator. The man who was to score 6,806 runs for England at an average of 58; who was to hit 20 hundreds in 82 Tests; and who was to become the most reliable middle-order batsman of his time started for England at Trent Bridge by lasting three balls – caught by John Waite off the fair-haired, medium-fast Eddie Fuller. Captained for the first time by Peter May, England won by an innings. At Lord's in the second Test he made

34 in the first innings, top score on a lively wicket, choosing to hook Heine and Adcock and having some luck; and 18 in the second. He did not play for his country again for four years. Incidentally, did England ever go through a home season with three more unlikely combinations of opening batsmen than in that 1955 season? Graveney and Kenyon, followed by Bailey and Lowson and Ikin and Close: two all-rounders, one middle-order batsman and three specialist openers who never quite made it at the highest level.

The mid-1950s, despite being highly successful for England, saw a good deal of chopping and changing by the selectors amongst the batsmen, although it was a golden era for bowlers – Trueman, Statham, Tyson, Bedser, Bailey, Laker, Lock, Wardle – all indisputably world class in their different ways. But only in 1959 when Ken Barrington returned to provide the ballast which enabled the sails of May and Cowdrey – and, all too fitfully at this time, of Graveney and the emerging Dexter – to billow out in all their glory, did the good ship England lay firm claim to the blue Riband.

It is worth considering whether England would have been as humiliated as they were the winter before Barrington re-established himself as a Test player if he had been to Australia with Peter May. In theory England were not short of batsmen of class or determination on that trip. But just think how Barrington played in the West Indies the following winter – hundreds in the first two Tests – and in Australia on his first visit in 1962–63, when his last four Test innings were 63, 132 not out, 101 and 94; followed by 126, 76, 47, and 45 in three Tests against New Zealand. Might not he have withstood the menace of Meckiff for longer than some of those who went?

This was the wonderful thing about the mature Ken Barrington: his consistency; Wally Grout's famous observation that he seemed to walk out to bat with a Union Jack trailing behind him was apt enough, for Ken was a tremendous patriot and, well as he often batted for Surrey, he was always at his best for England, when he literally believed himself to be fighting for his country. But there is an element of selfishness in every cricketer, and in the years between his premature elevation to Test status and his return in 1959, Ken Barrington worked out a batting philosophy which, though it often bored spectators and invoked official displeasure, notably when he was dropped for scoring too slow and 'selfish' a century against New Zealand in 1965, nevertheless served him and his country well. In his early days in the Surrey Second XI he had been a batsman with a full array of strokes, hit with tremendous power borne of natural timing and the square-shouldered strength which he carried below that craggy chin and almost de Bergeracian nose. He became frugal with all the strokes which lay within his power, at least until he was fully established at the crease. But often, after reaching 100 (and for a time he acquired a habit of doing so with a six, as a sort of penance for the fastidious care which had gone into the first 94 runs) he would release the pent-up tension and hours of single-minded concentration in a glorious array of drives, hooks and square-cuts.

There were days when he was so out of form that he really would look a strokeless, boring player, days when, as he would have said, he 'couldn't hit the skin off a rice pudding'. But there were many others when one felt that, even when he was allowing himself to loosen the reins and score freely, there was a marvellous security about his batting. The defence was solid and uncomplicated, based more on the back foot against fast bowling than that of many English players, and always resolutely in line against the quick stuff, even though he often looked discomforted by the short lifters of which Hall and Griffith in particular often gave him more than his share. In attack, like all top-class players, he was prolific between mid-wicket and mid-on and, despite the open stance which he developed in mid-career, his off-side strokes were played with textbook positioning and the precision of a drill sergeant. For all his emphasis on defence there was a crisp decisiveness about the attacking strokes and, against the spinners, a willingness to use his feet to get to the pitch of the ball and lift it over the bowler or to mid-off or mid-on.

It was somehow cruelly appropriate that the heart attack which ended his career, and the one which ended his life, should both have been suffered overseas. He was destined to spend much of his time playing on foreign fields and it was on the overseas tours that English cricket supporters often had most cause to be grateful for his solid consistency as England's number three or four. Under a burning sun before an alien crowd Barrington the batsman was in his element. And so he was, too, when the day's work was done, because it was then that the humorist in him was at its most valuable for the morale of his team.

Ken, in fact, was four comedians in one: a visual comic who could exploit something unusual on the field and play on it to the crowd's amusement; a natural mimic who could impersonate some of the characters in the game; a quick wit when it came to dressing-room repartee;

and, perhaps above all, an unconsciously funny man who spread great mirth by getting well-known phrases or proverbs slightly wrong. He would talk, for example, of England 'hanging on by their eyelashes' or a bird in the hand being worth 'two in the basket'. Tony Greig's hundred at Calcutta in 1977 was a 'great innings in any cup of tea' and he assured a gathering of dignitaries in Sri Lanka that they hadn't 'fallen down on any failings'.

Ken's enthusiasm and optimism allied to a willingness to help everyone connected with that particular MCC tour of India did much to help not just the team but the press too. Everyone was greeted with the same cheery grin, jaw thrust out in friendship. But behind the smiles and jokes was a restless, worrying mind. As a player he had smoked too much and had often needed to resort to sleeping pills to stop him from fretting all night about the challenge facing him the next day. As a manager the responsibilities facing him were more varied and sometimes less easy to solve. These things contributed to his shockingly early death in Barbados in 1981. A young and outplayed England team was shattered by the passing of the man they called 'The Colonel'.

Ken was a great batsman, a valuable and under-used leg-spin bowler and a fine fielder with a strong throw and quick reflexes in the slips. He was also one of the most conscientious, dogged and honest-to-goodness characters who ever pulled on an England sweater. And no one ever did so with greater pride.

Christopher Martin-Jenkins, Cricket Heroes (1984)

Brian Close

Bitter-sweet has been the characteristic flavour of Brian Close's cricket career. He has stretched his fingertips to clouds of glory and stumbled in a morass of disappointment and controversy. He has enjoyed the highest distinctions and suffered salt in deep wounds. In twenty years he has known few seasons of quiet content.

He was born at Rawdon near Leeds into a cricketing family and his youthful sporting talent was so pronounced that he was plunged into county and Test cricket at the age of eighteen. Hindsight indicates that too much was undoubtedly asked of him too soon, but true kindness would have involved some cruelty had he been denied the opportunity to score 1,000 runs and take 100 wickets and to play for England against New Zealand in his first season of 1949.

Controversy was thrust on him in 1950 when he was selected to tour Australia during his period of National Service. His mere presence in the side attracted public comment and his performances concentrated it.

He scored 108 not out in the opening first-class match and 0 and 1, in culpable fashion, in his only Test. Long before the end of the tour Close had become a cricketing reject.

His climb to rehabilitation was long and slow and was not advanced by personal decisions that discounted well-meant advice and proved unfortunate in outcome. He hoped for a profitable career in professional football and lost a season's cricket through football injury. He drifted into a state of inconsequential performance verging on the fatalistic. In success he was impressive; in failure he appeared to cultivate indifference.

Occasional undertakings for England failed to stifle misgivings, and a dramatic batting error against Australia at Old Trafford in 1961 seemed to confirm a widespread belief that temperament would always wither the blossom of his talent.

Inherent talent was not questioned. Set against all the left-hand batsmen of his time Close looked comparable with the best in artistry, in power and in potential.

Confining himself within the range of the orthodox he was majestic, but he allowed an impression to grow of accomplishment unharnessed and of immaturity extending far beyond cricketing adolescence. His play suggested that he had not found its purpose.

Yorkshire appointed Close their captain in 1963 because the office was vacant and because professional seniority gave him claim to succession. Within one season he had proved himself brilliantly successful. Clearly exercising authority, shrewd in tactics and leading by example at the crease and in the field, Close not only inspired Yorkshire but invigorated himself. In the five Test matches against West Indies he was a resolute batsman, an innings of 70 at Lord's touching the heroic. At the end of the season Close was a tired cricketer, mentally and physically, but he knew the satisfactions of fulfilment.

He was not required in another Test series until 1966 and then only for the last match of a rubber already decided. West Indies had won three of the first four matches and depression had settled over England cricket when Close was given the leadership of a reconstituted side.

His experience was characteristically dramatic. England won the match and Close's captaincy was rated a decisive factor in the result. A new world of promise was opening to him in his thirty-sixth year.

It was shattered in 1967. As captain of Yorkshire, Close wanted the County Championship and as captain of England he wanted Test match success over India and Pakistan, not only for its own sake but in preparation for a tour of West Indies and for the visit of Australia in 1968.

By mid-August Yorkshire were Championship leaders but only by such a narrow margin that two points from a drawn game at Edgbaston were balanced against opprobrium for delaying tactics in the field when Warwickshire were trying to force victory. Yorkshire's conduct was publicly condemned and on the eve of the last Test against Pakistan Close was held responsible in a formal rebuke.

He was not invited to captain MCC in West Indies and in 1968 he did not lead England against Australia. He had lost foothold, again, on the slippery pathway of esteem.

Through all the vicissitudes of his career he has never lost the appreciation of cricketers for talented performance, for investigation of the game's possibilities and for unflinching physical courage.

Close as a young player raised a thrill of delight in response to his powerful and confident left-hand batting, his easy right-arm action for off-spin or swing bowling and his agility in the field. He was handsome in all his athletic pursuits.

Close in mid-career drifted away to the fringes of distinction because his batting too rarely reflected the full extent of his ability and his bowling talent was not consolidated into artistry under discipline. By the evidence of his best innings no England side should have been complete without him, yet his intermittent appearances could not be counted an injustice.

Appointment to captaincy turned self-assurance into channelled purpose. Close was never a more impressive cricketer, in technique and temperament, than when he assumed the responsibilities of leading Yorkshire.

J. M. Kilburn, *The Cricketer* (1970)

J. T. Murray

John Murray came on the MCC staff as a batsman in 1950, at the age of fifteen. He had learned the game at the Rugby Boys' Club, in Kensington. There were virtually no facilities at school, but the Boys' Club, for whom his father had also played, had a good ground and gave him the opportunity for competitive cricket, football, and boxing. J. T. was also, in those days, a footballer – he was offered terms by Brentford in 1952 – and a boxer – he was the boys' champion of Kensington.

He decided early to concentrate entirely on cricket. He also started to keep wicket. As often happens, the beginning was fortuitous; the regular 'keeper broke a finger during a game, and John stepped in. He had his debut for Middlesex in 1952. From 1953 to 1955 he played for a strong RAF side. He took over from Leslie Compton at the end of 1955, won his cap the next year, and for twenty years has been an automatic choice for Middlesex.

The rest of his career will be well known to readers of *The Cricketer*. He went on all the major tours except to West Indies, and to Australia twice. He played twenty-one times for England; I was surprised it was not more. In my memory he was as much *the* England wicket-keeper of the 1960s as Alan Knott is of the 1970s. This summer he broke the world record for wicket-keeping dismissals.

One of the most striking features of J. T.'s cricket is the stylishness of everything he does. He is completely relaxed, whether taking the ball, or stroking it wide of mid-on. His movements flow; when he is on form he makes it all look so easy. He himself stresses the importance of rhythm and tolerance. Of all his contemporaries as 'keepers he most admires Wally Grout. 'He was never on the ground except when actually diving for a catch.' John's own mannerisms, the tips of the gloves touched together, the peak of the cap touched, give him that feeling of relaxed rhythm that comes across so characteristically.

I asked him if he ever doubted his ability. Yes, he said, he did, right up to 1961 and his first series for England. He had had, after all, very little wicket-keeping experience by the time he became a regular county player. He never worried about standing back. I think he regards the real test to be one's ability standing up. We'd all agree, probably, but it's worth remembering how superlatively good J. T. was (he'd agree that a little of his agility is gone now) standing back.

It is impossible to talk of his career without talking also of Fred Titmus's. Fred is not easy to keep wicket to. For one thing, he bowls very straight; for another, he only really spins some of his deliveries; for a third, he has to be taken half the time at Lord's, where the bounce of the ball has always been uneven. The extent to which they have helped each other is incalculable; perhaps the debt Fred owes J. T. is slightly the greater, since he so often can 'feel' what sort of pace Fred should bowl at, what line, and so on.

My clearest image of John's keeping is of the way he catches the ball. There could be no better model – fingers down, hands relaxed, and a long easy 'give' to one side or other of the body.

His batting has, overall, disappointed many. He agrees that he has never concentrated on it and worked at it as he would have done if it had not been his second string. And it is unlikely that anyone could be both a front-line batsman and a wicket-keeper over a long period in county cricket without losing something of his zest for the former and concentration in the latter job. At his best, he's a wonderful batsman. He often is at his best against fast bowling (he's a fine hooker and driver) and against slow bowling (he uses his feet and hits beautifully over the top). I think that it is characteristic of him that he should be least 'turned on' when playing against medium-pacers, where perhaps grafting would pay.

He is also a man for an occasion, an entertainer. He often saves his best performances for Yorkshire or Surrey, and is less likely to sparkle on a damp day at Ashby de la Zouch.

I asked John about his disappointments in cricket. He has, after all, achieved almost all that an ambitious young man could have hoped for. The one disappointment that he mentioned was that Middlesex have never yet won anything during his career. He thinks the best sides he played for were those of the late 1950s and early 1960s, though he admits that one tends to bring together in memory people who didn't in fact overlap. We have always, however, lacked one or two top-class bowlers to support Titmus and, at different times, Warr, Moss and Price.

Standards of cricket have declined overall, John believes. He is inclined to connect this with the gradual lessening of discipline in cricket and outside. I think that by 'discipline' he sometimes means hardship and knowing one's place. When he came on the MCC staff his place was clear, and very low in the hierarchy. Lord's was then, he says, a way of life. He never resented the fact that he had to sweep the stands, that he had only one session a week reserved for net practice (they had to find time outside working hours for the rest of their practice), or that he was not allowed in the pavilion unless he was actually playing in the game. But the ambition was clearer and stronger; he could see exactly what he wanted to achieve, and what he wanted to get away from. Today, he thinks, it is perhaps too easy for young cricketers, and too many of them think they know too much. And of course you do need discipline to play this game well.

He also believes in enjoying his cricket. At a lunch earlier this season, J. T. said to the younger Middlesex players 'Play properly and enjoy yourselves'. He has done both for twenty-five years. First-class cricket will have lost a landmark when he retires at the end of this season.

Mike Brearley, The Cricketer (1975)

Glenn Turner

In 1971 I found myself flying one morning from Auckland to Sydney in the company of the Australian crew returning home from competing in the One-Ton Cup. Yachtsmen, I concluded after having a good look at them, were picked not only for their physique but for their glamorous exterior and, sitting among these bronzed, muscular film stars, any one of them a strong contender for the next Tarzan epic, I felt somewhat out of place, not least because of the final savage assault of Auckland hospitality suffered the night before.

I was about to close my eyes on this aggressive show of robust health when among the smart uniforms of blue blazers, blue ties, grey flannel trousers and short haircuts, I noticed another intruder, slight, pale and in marked contrast with the Tarzans in every way. It was Glenn Turner, on his way somewhat improbably to play cricket in Kuwait – or was it Bahrain? – and as I lay back again, I pondered with such concentration as I could muster, the diversification of talents among the human race.

This unassuming, relatively unathletic young man, then twenty-three, had already performed some sporting feats beyond the scope of most mortals. He had carried his bat through a Test innings at Lord's, set a new Worcestershire record of ten hundreds in a season and in the previous English summer had scored 150 runs more than any other batsman in the country. Still to come, of course, was the scoring of 1,000 runs by the end of May, a feat which no batsman had been expected to have the chance, let alone be good enough, to do again.

Glenn Turner's success is based inevitably on a sound method. He plays very straight, is a quick judge of length and a beautiful timer who can drive and play square on the off side with a power out of all proportion with his slender frame. In the last ten years I can recall two outstanding innings on turning pitches. One was by Dennis Amiss in Rawalpindi in March 1973, the other was by Turner in the less exotic and less turbulent surroundings of Wellingborough School in 1970. Worcestershire needed 225 in the last innings, which in the context of pitch and previous play, should have been well beyond them, but Turner made 110 not out with great skill and they won comfortably.

Dunedin, with its almost Scottish-type climate, is not the normal breeding-ground for a great batsman and a young New Zealander starts with none of the confident expectation of success of a young Australian batsman. Yet when I first saw him in Wellington, Turner had been picked as a promising eighteen-year-old for the President's XI against Mike Smith's MCC side. He had averaged over 50 for Otago in the Plunket Shield and though on this occasion he was lbw to Peter Parfitt for 5, the selection in itself was an event in a land where batsmen tend to take quite as long to reach maturity as in England.

But at that time New Zealand cricket had an even greater sense of inferiority than usual and it is hard to believe that Turner would have become the batsman he is if he had not decided to come to England. The link between Dunedin and Edgbaston was an obvious one, for at the time of Mike Smith's visit Billy Ibadulla was coaching in Dunedin, and eventually, because Warwickshire could accommodate no more overseas players, Turner came to Worcestershire.

However much natural talent a batsman may possess there comes a point when his success depends on how much he makes of that talent. Temperament has probably played a bigger part in Turner's success than most. One obstacle which he has had to overcome is the traditional doubt at home about the local boy who wins fame overseas. When he went back to New Zealand in 1970, too much was expected of him and he had a modest season, so modest that on their arrival Ray Illingworth's MCC side were astonished to hear suggestions that he might not be in the Test team. He was, of course, picked and did fairly well, though the Auckland

Test, which New Zealand might have won, provided a sample of that strokelessness which sometimes shackled him. His opening stand of 91 with Graham Dowling took over three hours and on a superb pitch lost New Zealand the initiative on the second day. One tended to forget that he was still only twenty-three and was not always sure enough of himself, especially perhaps in New Zealand, to play all the strokes within his range.

However, through the years this has been overcome to the benefit of Worcestershire and New Zealand and I should have thought that few innings by Glenn Turner are a hardship to watch nowadays. Perhaps the most convincing proof of the part played by an equable temperament is the way in which he kept going under pressure to achieve his two most famous feats.

In the last match but one of the 1970 season, against Lancashire at Worcester, he needed one more hundred for the Worcestershire record and, playing beautifully, he reached 99 in the second innings as the declaration was imminent. At this point the Lancashire captain set a field with only one man in front of the wicket on the off side, inviting Turner to take a single there and expedite the declaration. Turner duly tapped the ball on the offside and ran. By some oversight, however, Clive Lloyd had been left as the lone fielder there and, swooping like some great black hawk, he threw Turner out at the bowler's end. Run out 99, a few inches from a historic achievement! It was a cruel blow.

But Turner was undeterred, even by a lively pitch at the start of his innings in the final match, against Warwickshire, and he made 133. In much the same way three seasons later he reached 1,000 runs on 31 May by reaching 93 on a far from perfect pitch when for some days the target had seemed to be escaping him.

Runs are not everything – how and where they are made is usually what matters – but this feat, as Walter Hadlee said, would capture the imagination of schoolboys at home and have beneficial effects for the future of New Zealand cricket. Thus, although Glenn Turner's career is still young, its impact is already considerable.

Michael Melford, *The Cricketer* (1974)

Graeme Pollock

This is the age of competence and solid application rather than of genius and magic, so the presence of Graeme Pollock among the world's great batsmen is all the more striking. Where other successful batsmen eliminate mistakes by not attempting anything outside their proven range, he recognizes few limits and backs his extra ability to see him through.

The easily seen resemblance to another tall left-hander with a full majestic swing of the bat, a certain Frank Woolley, established him at an early age as something out of the ordinary. His remarkable precocity – according to his father he could walk at eight months – the power and range of his strokes and the grandeur of some of his most famous innings have confirmed him as a batsman who would have adorned any age. The bare statistics he will leave behind may not be unbeatable (in six seasons up to the end of 1969 he had played in only 19 Test matches. In the same period Bill Lawry had played in 48), but in full cry Graeme Pollock can make other world-class batsmen look very ordinary mortals.

He was nineteen when he arrived in Australia in 1963, made 100 in Perth in 88 minutes, and played other innings which are reliably reported to have had hard-boiled Australian observers on their feet cheering. The ease with which he took the step to the top was no surprise to those who had seen him already in South Africa and England.

There was mild concern in his family of talented games players in Port Elizabeth when at the age of three he firmly gripped the bat left-handed, for he does everything else right-handed. However, his father, who kept wicket in his time for the Orange Free State, had been similarly inclined. He was in the school side on his thirteenth birthday and, at 16 years and 335 days, became the youngest batsman to make 100 in the Currie Cup. He was no less precocious in other games. One reason for Graeme's early maturity could be that throughout his boyhood he was bowled at by a future Test fast bowler, his brother Peter.

George Cox of Sussex, coaching at Grey High School, was one of those who had the delicate job of guiding the genius in the right direction, and when Graeme Pollock came to England in 1961 with his family, he played a few matches for Sussex Second XI. At about this time he acquired the final two-and-a-half inches over six feet and, as someone who saw him play that summer said, he was a very surprising seventeen-year-old.

A year later he was making 209 not out at Port Elizabeth against the late Ron Roberts' Cavaliers, and a year after that he was in Australia. Of his two Test 100s there, the second was an extraordinary innings of 175. In four hours 43 minutes he and Barlow scored 341, a record stand for any wicket in South African Test history.

His first encounters with the MCC spinners, Titmus and Allen, in 1964–65, were on turning pitches and the honours were with the bowlers. But he finished the series by making 137 and 77 not out in the last Test, and in England a few months later he played what must be reckoned one of the decisive innings in Test history. At Trent Bridge in the second Test he took on the English in their own conditions and, with his brother, who took ten wickets, beat them.

On the sort of damp overcast day on which English bowlers are wont to confound or subdue the best visiting batsmen, he made 125 out of 160 in two hours 20 minutes. In only 70 minutes after lunch he made 91 out of 102. South Africa, who had been floundering at 43 for 4 against Cartwright, were taken to a score of 269 which won them match and series. In sophisticated bowling circles you hear this innings decried as 'lucky' and 'mere slogging', but it transformed the match in a couple of hours. I would have thought that any great batsman would have been proud to have played it against a bowler of Cartwright's skill operating with everything in his favour.

His batting in the present series against Australia, with his greatest single achievement to date, 274 in 420 minutes at Durban, speaks for itself. Against Australia in the great series of 1966–67, Pollock played two innings which especially demonstrated the full range of his remarkable technique. The first was his 90 in 90 minutes at Johannesburg. I remember him moving nimbly down a fast pitch and hitting two 6s and fifteen 4s, mostly off the front foot.

At Cape Town a week later he had a pulled thigh muscle, and on a slower pitch made 209 almost entirely off the back foot. His skill in finding the gaps on either side of the wicket off the back foot brought him 100 in only 139 balls, and only then did he attempt anything off the front foot. A feature of this innings was the ease with which he played a shot to the long-hop, lying back to lift it high and straight, rather than towards mid-wicket where most batsmen will hit it.

He can descend from the sublime to the earthy with a bump. The

Johannesburg innings ended with a fearful swish at a ball which bowled him behind his legs; he has several characteristics reminiscent of Denis Compton: his running between wickets seldom allows his admirers to relax, and he can communicate to them with peculiar clarity his confidence or concern. He can sometimes be prised out through impatience; against accurate spin he will be looking to drive off the back foot anything which is a fraction short of a length. If it does not come, he may get out through taking a liberty with a ball not quite short enough.

Like Denis Compton, too, Graeme Pollock keeps the bowlers interested as well as the public. When they have been struck for 101 in 52 minutes, as was a reputable Barbados attack at Scarborough last September, or if, like one Australian fast bowler, they have to suffer the indignity of an enormous straight drive on to a roof far behind them, they may be lukewarm in their enthusiasm. But at least they are being given a chance in fair and exhilarating combat.

Michael Melford, *The Cricketer* (1970)

Colin Bland

In the Lord's Test of 1965 England were in a flourishing position. They had confined South Africa to 280 in their first innings and had reached 240 for four.

Ken Barrington was at the height of an innings of mounting mastery. He had scored 91 and hit a 6 and eleven 4s. None of the bowling caused him any difficulty.

Batting at the Pavilion end, he played a ball towards mid-on where there was no fielder. Spontaneously he and his partner Mike Smith set off for what appeared to be a comfortable run. He had played the same stroke twice previously and Colin Bland, standing a couple of yards to the mid-on side of the square-leg umpire, had not been able to prevent a run. To a degree he seemed to encourage it.

This time he anticipated the stroke. With a clear start he raced less than ten yards, picked up the ball with his left hand, transferred it to the right and sent it crashing into the stumps at the Nursery end. Barrington was run out.

Later in the innings while fielding more towards mid-wicket, he ran to his right, twisted his body and, as Jim Parks scampered to regain his crease from a reversed call, threw the ball, which remarkably passed between the legs of Parks, and hit the middle stump. He too, was out while scoring with increasing freedom and forcefulness.

From being in a winning position in a match which roused excitement throughout its entire course, England were hard pressed to avoid defeat. At the end of play they needed 46 to win and had two wickets to fall.

Bland, who had made 39 in the first innings, followed it with a top score of 70 in the second.

For a fielder to hit the stumps and, perhaps, achieve a couple of run-outs is not exceptional but in Bland's case the odds were so heavily against him that his feats were well nigh miraculous.

All through that tour and previous tours both in South Africa and Australasia, his accurate throwing and skill in fielding captivated onlookers. Many were drawn to watch the South Africans play, very largely because of the prospect of watching the speed, grace, precision and power which compounded his genius. To me, fortunate to witness all twenty-two of his Test matches, his fielding was a source of recurring exhilaration.

At Lord's he touched a pinnacle of proficiency that has distinguished his whole span of cricket. Through long, lonely hours of dedicated practice, he raised the art of fielding to a new dimension, and his own performances into the realm of legend. It is an academic argument whether, as some maintained, Bland was the greatest fielder of all time but there was no question that his talent far outshone the gifts of all his contemporaries.

It so happened that on the British tour, apart from his first Test, his fielding was not the best he had produced. One reason was because he was seldom placed on the boundary, a position which allowed him to demonstrate his wonderful 'arm' and almost uncanny judgement of distance. He made a realistic assessment of his skill when he said, 'all this publicity has been embarrassing. Apart from Lord's, I haven't equalled my standard at home.'

The New Zealand tour of 1961–62 had been a triumph for John Reid. His powerful batting, combined with a superior number of innings, brought him more runs in the season than more distinguished predecessors in Denis Compton, Neil Harvey, Jack Hobbs and Len Hutton.

He played several devastating innings and with his score at 60 in the fourth Test in Johannesburg he was well set for another such assault. He hit two successive fours off Godfrey Lawrence, then slammed him with all his might deep into the covers.

With a low trajectory the ball travelled too fast for normal human anticipation but, having picked up its flight, Bland flung himself forwards at full stretch, caught the ball in his finger-tips and lay for several moments as though some sculptor had immortalized for generations to come one of the most remarkable catches seen at the Wanderers.

Louis Duffus, *Cricket: Stars of Today* (1970)

Majid Khan

Great is a word bandied around in sport like a shuttlecock, but in reality there are very few cricketers who deserve the label. One I would suggest is Majid Jehangir Khan, former Glamorgan, Cambridge and now the leading Pakistan Test batsman. If in sporting terms greatness can be defined as the ability to outplay all round you, then cricket must surely provide one of the most searching tests. Yet recognition of an individual's brilliance need not necessarily always shine in the spotlight of open competition.

At the windswept, icy county ground in Derby in 1969, Majid put on the most memorable exhibition of batting skill it had been my good fortune personally to witness. It took place in the Derbyshire nets during one of those seemingly endless breaks waiting for heavy overnight rain to drain through a waterlogged outfield. Huddled around the medieval dressing-room brazier thoughtfully provided by the Derby committee to combat the spine-chilling draughts that used to waft through the racecourse ground pavilion, the former headquarters of the county, the Glamorgan team's conversation turned to the art of batting. We had just come from a game against Sussex where Jim Parks Jnr had made a hundred against us on an unpredictable wicket. We agreed that it was the speed and precision of his footwork that had kept us, and Don Shepherd in particular, at bay. At that time, Shepherd was one of the country's most feared bowlers, a man of immaculate length and direction who bowled off-breaks at a brisk medium pace. On a turning wicket he was virtually unplayable, and touring teams in this country had gone away from games against Glamorgan at Swansea with a sigh of relief that the myopic England selectors did not include him in any of the Test series.

While the discussion continued to and fro across the brazier, Majid, never at any stage of his career a talkative man, sat silent, orientally impassive. It was only when we had appeared to have exhausted all lines of debate that he spoke: 'You don't need any footwork in batting, just hands and eye.' In terms of length, this amounted to a major speech from Majid, then in his second season with Glamorgan, having joined on a special registration in 1968, the year after he had toured the UK with Pakistan. The Welsh county committee had no doubt been influenced in their signing of him, by his innings of 147 in eighty-nine minutes against Glamorgan at Swansea and the fact that his father, the distinguished Indian cricketer Dr Jehangir Khan, had been a pre-war Cambridge contemporary of Wilfred Wooller, the Glamorgan secretary. These factors quickly helped to forge a bond which was to last until 1976.

At Derby on that bleak day in June 1969, Glamorgan were on the crest of a winning streak which lasted throughout the season, culminating in them taking the Championship for the second time in their first-class history with an unbeaten record to boot, the first time this had been achieved since Lancashire in 1934. Success is a heady brew and there were many challengers to Majid's claim that footwork counted for nothing.

Within fifteen minutes, three of our front-line bowlers, including Don Shepherd, lined up in a net outside with Majid padded up at the other end about to have his theory demolished. For twenty minutes, on a rough, unprepared, and quite-impossible-to-bat-on wicket where the ball flew, shot, seamed and turned, Majid Khan stood absolutely motionless, parrying the ball as it lifted, cutting or hooking unerringly if it were wide, driving with frightening power if overpitched and swaying out of harm's way when it lifted unexpectedly. Unless he allowed it, not a single ball passed his bat, not a chance was given, not a false stroke made. The bowlers were at full throttle, yet by our own reckoning afterwards that twenty-minute session must have yielded the young Pakistani around 75 runs! He had defied every known textbook instruction, improvised strokes that just did not exist and, without uttering a word, had emphatically made his point. In the presence of genius, no rules apply.

Peter Walker, *Cricket Conversations* (1978)

Dennis Lillee

If he had been created in fiction rather than fact Dennis Lillee would probably have sprung from the earth in the form of a dragon, spitting hell and breathing red flames of fury.

In the BBC's video archives there is a snatch of tape from the 1970–71 Ashes series. Illingworth's men are coming near to their decisive victory at Sydney and the young Lillee, cleaner-shaven and leaner than in his prime, has just cut the ball hard to slip, where he is caught at knee height in a perfectly straightforward way. But he refuses to walk! It needs an umpire's finger to confirm a dismissal obvious to everyone else on the ground. He moves reluctantly from his crease, scowling at all about him; by implication, if not by word itself, he has sworn to get even with his enemy. And time and again he was to do so.

Lillee's fight to regain fitness after the stress fractures in his back which threatened to end a fast-bowling career that had begun with devastating fury and brilliance, is a story of rare courage and determination. He sweated alone in the gym; strode out, equally alone, on long cross-country runs under the harsh, sapping sun of Western Australia. And he emerged as magnificent a physical specimen as has ever bowled fast for Australia, fuelled by what often seemed like a hot anger against batsmen, especially if they had the misfortune to be Poms.

Yet under the mop of hair, dark as night, beneath the brimstone face with its nose like a hawk's beak and eyes like burning coals, was a brain as cool and single-purposed as a snake waiting to envelop a lizard with a flick of its forked and poisonous tongue. This combination of motivation, physical strength and intelligence made him the supreme bowler of his era, at his retirement the most successful of all time and for most of his career the most feared, respected, lionized and reviled.

The man and the bowler were one and the same and cannot be separated. One will remember the bursts of theatrical fury; the petulant, spoiled-boy tantrums; but also the flashing smile and the desire always to please his audience, exemplified often when at the end of a wholehearted over he would accept the proffered autograph books over his shoulders at third-man and sign as many as possible of them between balls, handing them back to delighted owners with a smile and a quip. There was a certain logic, perhaps, in his unexpected production of his own autograph book from behind his back when he met the Queen in the official presentation during the Centenary Test at Melbourne. Officials may have been shocked, but Her Majesty was simply amused. Larrikin he may have been but, usually, a likeable one. He was never happier than when he was stirring the Establishment and throwing down challenges.

But he was at his best and most fulfilled when his mouth was shut and his body was talking. His action was a symphony, rolling melodiously through the long run-up to a glorious crescendo. The left arm swung towards the target as the heavy frame lifted from the ground and the right arm released the ball from its highest point before a power-packed descent and flowing follow-through. He could swing and cut the ball at will, and, whatever he may have said, in much publicized phrases, about bowling bouncers to hurt the batsmen, he did not, in fact, over-use that weapon as so many have done during and since his time. He bowled not to maim people, but to take their wicket in the shortest possible time.

Christopher Martin-Jenkins, *Cricket Characters* (1987)

Kapil Dev

There is something reminiscent of a wild animal in the sight of Kapil Dev on the cricket field. He is a restless figure, erect and alert, saucer eyes darting hither and thither, muscles, it seems, twitching like a deer on the lookout for danger. But it is his opponents who need to beware, for attack not defence is Kapil's constant concern, and for a decade he has been one of the most compellingly exciting cricketers in the world.

He first made a mark as a fast bowler from the then rather unfashionable cricketing area of Haryana, a state he has put on the map in the same way that Richards and Roberts elevated Antigua. The art of pure fast bowling seemed to come naturally to him. He was swift without being lethally quick, but he has always possessed a natural away-swinger with his direct, almost military approach to the stumps after a low walk-back, culminating in a glorious final leap during which the waiting batsman sees the whites of his eyes peeping from behind a high left arm.

Despite his almost stiff-looking back, straight as a shield, he fields brilliantly in any position. He has tended to stand close to the wicket in recent years since sharing the captaincy with the little maestro, Gavaskar.

His batting probably came as a pleasant surprise to those outside his home environment, for not many opening bowlers can also be match-winners with a bat. Kapil has frequently turned the course of a match by bold, clean, supremely confident and fearless hitting. The drive is his special glory, either side of straight and struck with such force that it seldom matters if he hits the ball in the air. His timing, crisp as fresh lettuce, leaves fielders leaden-footed.

He has had some dramatic ups-and-downs as a Test captain, the first of the 'ups' being the 1983 World Cup success in England, made possi-ble only through an extraordinary virtuoso performance by Kapil himself at the lovely Nevill Ground at Tunbridge Wells. There, before the banks of vivid rhododendrons, the underestimated Zimbabwe side had reduced the might of India to 9 for 4 when Kapil came out to bat. Soon they were 17 for 5, but Kapil hit six 6s and sixteen 4s in an innings of 175 not out. India won not only this match but the semi-final against England and the final against West Indies.

If any modern cricketer has had charisma, it is Kapil Dev. India may be inconsistent under his command, but they are no longer considered to be dull.

Christopher Martin-Jenkins, Cricket Characters (1987)

Derek Randall

Derek Randall is a father now, with business interests. His benefit year is already behind him. But he looks as though he ought still to be wearing shorts, with ink stains on his fingers and one of his school socks down by his ankles, the other only half-covering a muddy knee.

Whoever first called him Pinocchio got it just right because, apart from his permanent little-boy look, his limbs seem to move like a puppet's, encumbered by the normal limits imposed by bone and muscle. He has relinquished his right to be Nottinghamshire's regular cover-point – now Tim Robinson has assumed that role – but he still sprints and dives to make stops and catches which not only seem but actually are impossible for the average cricketer. With the possible exceptions of Colin Bland and the young Clive Lloyd he has been the most brilliant, exciting cover fielder of the last generation, a constant source of delight to spectators and as threatening to batsmen as a mamba in the grass.

Randall the batsman now employs the two-eyed stance once used amongst others by Barrington, Parks and Titmus. It helps him to work the ball into the gaps on the leg side with even more dexterity than in his youth, when he preferred the full-blooded boundary to the carefully stroked one or two. But, give him anything like a half-volley on the off stump and he will cream it through the covers all along the ground with a textbook purity. And, having seen the ball bounce back off the fence, he can no more resist a quick conversation with his batting partner now than he could as a nervous twenty-year-old.

Randall has to chat to someone – partner, umpire, opposing bowler – anyone close enough. In the field he will find a spectator to talk to as well if there is one in range. He so wants them to enjoy it all as much as he does. No wonder they love him so at Trent Bridge.

I have been lucky enough to see most of the lows and highs of Derek's career. He was admirably stoic when he completely lost his form and confidence on one tour of Australia. But he was a hero with a capital H at Melbourne in 1977 and at Sydney two years later. Some people, mostly those who were not there, discount the latter match-winning century at the SCG as though Hogg, Hurst, Yardley, Higgs and Dymock amounted to an attack that was not first-class. That simply is not true.

It is certainly true, however, that nothing he has done or ever will do can quite compare with the glory of the Centenary Test. Everyone will recall, no doubt, that after England and Australia had bowled each other out absurdly cheaply, and Australia had then made a big second-innings score, there was an awful possibility that England, tired after their long tour of India, would succumb a second time to end a truly great occasion in premature and embarrassing anti-climax. Her Majesty the Queen, due on the last day of the game after opening her Australian Parliament in Canberra, was in danger of arriving after the game had finished. The Nottinghamshire imp saved the day. Hooking and cutting and driving and, of course, chatting, he stole the show – from the Queen and Dennis Lillee and everyone else.

He has been through many vicissitudes since that day of inspiration – and enjoyed plenty of triumphs too. And Retford's most famous son will know to the day he dies that they cannot take that achievement away. The self-deprecating, slightly barmy youngster who had made his first mark on his first MCC tour by turning a cartwheel during a stuffy soft-drinks reception to the amazement and amusement of his Indian hosts, was suddenly a national hero. The pleasure he gave them and has often given since will long survive his career.

Christopher Martin-Jenkins, *Cricket Characters* (1987)

Richie Benaud

The television commentator, whose face and voice are known to millions in Australia and many millions more in Britain, is *really* known to a very few; perhaps only to his wife, Daphne, who became known to Richie through being the most efficient secretary that the formidable E. W. Swanton ever had.

Richie is pretty formidable too, in his own quiet way. He keeps his own counsel. He does a high-pressure job at a savage pace all the year round literally without blinking an eyelid. Never was a more impassive face, a glassier, more unyielding countenance displayed before a camera. But from lips which barely seem to move, in accents and phrases all his own, come, year after year, match after match, words of pungent authority. His knowledge and his impartiality stand out as strongly as his determination to present cricket and its players in the best possible light. Whatever he may have taken out of the game, he has undoubtedly been good for it. No one else has found such favour with the vast majority of cricket viewers at both ends of the world for so long.

That cool exterior is no mask. Behind it lies a calculating brain and a sharp wit. His organization and self-discipline are as immaculate as his attire. Never a crooked tie; never a hair out of place; never hurried; never late; never ruffled. At the end of a day's commentary he introduces the highlights. The editing of these may sometimes be well, sometimes badly balanced. But the man who introduces them is seldom anything other than shrewd in his appraisal of the events of the day or the position of the match. Not that the highlights mark the end of his day. He still has his column to attend to, and often more stories than just one to write. He drives himself extraordinarily hard.

He was the same as a player, and especially as a captain. Such fastidiousness might have made him a rather dull, utilitarian cricketer. He was actually a bold, attacking one; a daring, handsome batsman; an athletic

497

fielder who at Lord's in 1956 held a catch from the blade of Cowdrey's bat in the gully which knocked him over and took the breath away from everyone who saw it; and a leg-break bowler with a perfect action. It gained him more Test wickets than any other leg-spinner in history.

But it was for his captaincy that he became most honoured. How could England have failed to beat Australia in 1958–59 with a side which included May, Cowdrey, Bailey, Dexter, Evans, Graveney, Laker, Lock, Loader, Tyson, Statham and Trueman? Well, one of many reasons, by all accounts, was that Benaud out-captained May. He was quick to see a gap and to go for it; shrewd in finding the right bowlers for the conditions; adept at intimidating the opposition with hustling fields and aggressive bowling. He had been on losing sides against England in 1954–55 and 1956, and he had every motivation for revenge.

In 1961, with Ted Dexter now his adversary, he famously stole a match which Dexter seemed to have won for England by a marvellous attacking innings. Knowing it was hit or miss, Benaud began bowling round the wicket into the rough and, making light of a damaged right shoulder, he spun England to an embarrassing defeat.

Benaud the opportunist and the competitor. He has shown the same quick-witted eye for the main chance in his working life and maintained an admirable standard. He relaxes by playing golf, approaching the game with the same meticulous care he applies to everything else. His clubs are the best you can find; his swing has a professional's arc and strength. He likes to win, and usually does.

Christopher Martin-Jenkins, Cricket Characters (1987)

Shane Warne

People tend to forget prophecies which fail to come to pass but for spot-on prediction Bobby Simpson's assessment of Shane Warne, made at Worcester well in advance of his matchwinning performance in the first Test at Old Trafford, was almost biblical: 'He'll turn the ball from the first ball of every Test. He's the best leg-spinner of twenty-three I've ever seen.' It was because Warne turned the first ball he bowled at Manchester two feet to bowl a dumbfounded Mike Gatting that England got into a mental as well as technical tizzy against him. If David Gower, not Gatting, had received it, it might have given him a nasty shock, but it would have been very unlikely to have bowled him. Facing Warne out of the rough in the second innings would not have been easy, but neither would Warne have enjoyed having to switch his line, aware that a left-hander pushing well forward would be unlucky to be given lbw, but that to anything pitched straight far more shots would be available than for right-handers.

That England's selectors, well briefed about Warne's prodigious power of spin, should have seen all this in advance does not concern me here. The potential for Warne to lead a wholesale revival of the art of wrist-spin round the world over the next ten years certainly does. When Ian Salisbury becomes a regular member of the England attack, which, with luck, he should and will, four of the nine Test-playing countries will be including young leg-spinners. Sri Lanka should be able to find one with the ease that England once whistled up fast bowlers from the mines, and South Africa, New Zealand, Zimbabwe and even the West Indies will be earnestly on the look-out for one themselves. For batsmen from all these countries, the wrist-spinner, as in England, causes chronic unease borne simply of complete unfamiliarity with the art. We all fear the unknown.

Warne and Salisbury are both twenty-three, Anil Kumble and Mush-taq Ahmed both only twenty-two. Each has different qualities but none gives the ball such a vicious rip as Warne does, and with his blond hair ('not so much of the peroxide, mate, it's natural', he says) and diamond-studded ear, he should attract the young. He may look a playboy, and off the field he has certainly enjoyed himself on the way to being a national hero, but he is intelligent, as his sparing use of the googly and the other variations – top-spinner and flipper – shows. Against Graeme Hick at Worcester he refused to bowl anything but leg-breaks, preferring, appar-ently certain of his Test place, to plant doubt in Hick's mind about the major matches even as Hick was cracking him to all parts of the ground on the way to 187.

For sheer ability to turn the ball, Warne has probably had no equal since 'Chuck' Fleetwood-Smith, who started life as a fast right-armer but became famous as a left-arm googly bowler. The England leg-spin-ner Ian Peebles wrote of him: 'Fleetwood-Smith spun the ball tremen-dously, more than anyone else I can think of, and bowled a very good "boosie". His trouble was, not unnaturally, lack of control, but on his day he could be all but unplayable to all but the highest class.' Peebles recalled how in the match against Victoria in 1932–33, Wally Hammond was commissioned to go out and destroy him. He did so and Fleetwood-Smith was not picked for another three years. A pity for England that Hick's onslaught did not have a similar effect.

One reason is that Warne does not lose control as often as Fleetwood-Smith, or give the batsman respite with a frequent bad ball as Salisbury is still inclined to do. The West Indians noticed a big improvement in this respect during last winter's series in Australia and Carl Hooper says he has 'come on in leaps and bounds' even since the end of the Australian season. 'The tours of New Zealand and now of England are obviously doing him good,' Hooper says. 'When we played him in an early match before the Tests he lacked control and gave us a few too many loose ones. But he bowled very well in Melbourne (1–65 and 7–52) and I was very impressed with what I saw on the television from Old Trafford. I don't think I've ever seen anyone turn the ball more, but he's not too difficult to read. We were lucky to have a couple of left-handers against him; especially Brian Lara who never let him settle – down the pitch to drive or back to pull or cut. I think England's batsmen are lacking a little bit of confidence at the moment.'

Just a little. They were warned – no pun for once intended – by no less a batsman than Martin Crowe, following Australia's tour of New Zealand in which Warne took 17 wickets in three Tests – that he was something special. Crowe's advice, conveyed via Dennis Amiss to Keith Fletcher before Old Trafford, was that he is unusual in that he makes the ball turn across the right-handed batsman, often from outside leg stump, rather than pitching middle-and-off or off stump like most of his kind. Fore-warned or not, Gatting was taken aback by the first ball he bowled – who would not have been? – and although by the second innings the England batsmen had worked out that they could safely put their pads to anything pitched in the same area, Warne was already varying his line better and a ball pitched outside the off stump was not necessarily the googly. Graham Gooch played him with the greatest confidence, but even he did not always get it right and it was worrying that Hick played him better in the first innings than he did in the second.

Warne was brought up in an expensive Melbourne suburb on the sea and says that although he preferred Aussie Rules football at first, 'by the age of sixteen my ambition was to play cricket for Australia'. He won a scholarship to the Adelaide Cricket Academy (government financed) and prepared for life there by playing league cricket in Bristol, acquiring such a taste for English pub fare that he put on two stone. The Academy coaches thought he was a spoilt boy and sacked him but he played his first match for Victoria in 1991 and spent the following summer at Accrington in the Lancashire League.

He had played only five first-class matches and taken only fifteen wickets when the Australian selectors picked him to play against India in the Sydney Test of January 1992. Shades of the England selectors choosing Douglas Carr, the mystery googly bowler, at the age of thirty-seven in his first season in first-class cricket, to play against Australia in 1909. Carr took three prime Australian wickets in his first seven overs and seven in the match but did not play for England again. Warne, after chastening figures of 1 for 150 against India, was given a second chance at the Academy by Rod Marsh, gave up the beer, started early morning running, swimming, gym-work and boxing and lost 28 lb. He also spent the winter practising his bowling art with another ex-larrikin leg-spinner, Terry Jenner.

Picked to go to Sri Lanka last August, Warne took 3 for 0 with his last eleven balls to win a match Australia had looked certain to lose. In all three of the games his country has won since – against the West Indies at Melbourne, New Zealand at Christchurch and England at Old Trafford – he has been outstanding. As Simpson says: 'He is proving to youngsters that leg-spin isn't old fashioned.'

Leg-spinners often become less effective once they become familiar but the England batsmen need to sort him out soon if the beaming face of 'Hollywood' Warne is not to be the very symbol of Australian success this season.

Christopher Martin-Jenkins, Daily Telegraph (12 June 1993)

Ted Dexter

Ted Dexter yesterday added his name to the casualty list of English cricket's calamitous past twelve months. Two weeks after the fall of his captain, Graham Gooch, Dexter resigned his role as chairman of the England committee. Many reasons will be advanced for his going; the most pertinent is that he had lost his credibility.

Dexter, whose contract worth around £30,000 a year extended to next

March, would have faced concerted pressure to resign from a group of county chairmen next Tuesday at a meeting of the Test and County Cricket Board (TCCB). The irony is that this movement was generated by Chris Middleton, who is unlikely to see out the year as chairman of a bankrupt Derbyshire.

Dexter, fifty-eight, had to go because nobody believed in him any more. His input at lower levels of national cricket, worthy and often hidden from view, was unappreciated within the clamour for success at Test level. Under mounting criticism from public and media, some of it malicious and much of it a misinterpretation of his wide-ranging role, Dexter concluded his position was untenable.

During more than four years of office, Dexter presided over 44 Tests, of which England won 9 and lost 21, 11 of them to Australia. They were two hours away from the last of those defeats when Dexter's decision was made known, though perversely it had not been made known to the captain, Michael Atherton. 'I am sorry he feels he has got to go,' Atherton said. 'I'm not aware of the reasons so I cannot comment further.'

Dexter's duties will officially cease at the end of the month, probably after he has confirmed Atherton as captain for the winter tour to West Indies. He will have no say in the selection of the tour party, now likely to be done chiefly by captain and manager.

Speculation has already begun about the identity and job description of Dexter's successor. It is an appointment the board is unlikely to rush. M. J. K. Smith, the chairman of Warwickshire and a man with time to devote to the cause, is a strong favourite. Micky Stewart and Ossie Wheatley are plausible contenders and there is a possibility that Wheatley's present post, as chairman of the TCCB cricket committee, could be merged to produce one coherent position.

There is no immediate threat to the team manager, Keith Fletcher, although the length of his contract and his miserable record to date will be debated next week.

Alan Smith, chief executive of the board, explained: 'We have known since before the first Test that Ted would not be seeking re-election. He has now come to the conclusion that it is best to make the break earlier. It was his wish that the decision should be made known today.

'Ted has been wondering about his position for some time. He is a sensitive person. The team played very poorly at Headingley and I think that was a key factor in his decision, because he was always motivated by how the team was doing.'

Smith stressed that there was no question of Dexter having been asked to go. For the officers of the board, it is harrowing to see the power base of the national team in disarray; to sack the chairman on the day a new captain lost his first game in charge would have been masochistic.

There will be counties, next week, which propose the scrapping of the England committee, set up under Dexter's auspices early in 1989. Their case will be that it has failed in its ultimate aim of producing a strong national team and, on the evidence of eight defeats from nine Tests during 1993, they would be right. But as Smith said yesterday: 'I don't think 1992 was a disastrous year, nor 1991 or 1990. This has been a very disappointing year, that's obvious. But although our system is not perfect, I am personally satisfied that the England committee is working.'

Dexter, who captained England in 30 of his 62 Tests between 1958 and 1968, was to some degree a victim of his personal high profile within a job he elected to make low profile. The most glamorous cricketer of his generation, a face and voice well known, he could hardly expect to operate quietly in the background. People wanted to know what Dexter thought of every Test match and, because many perceived his brief to be simply chairman of selectors, they also expected him to be present every day.

This was not how he intended to do the job and, to his credit, he was never swayed from his vision. He attended the first three days of each Test, travelled to watch the senior, A and under-19 teams for sections of overseas tours and attended more than fifty committee meetings each year, often fighting the corner of the England team against more parochial arguments from the shires.

More than once, he made well-informed efforts to deflect criticism from his captains and managers by intervening with his own comments to the media. Invariably, he would find the initiative ridiculed for a remark taken out of context.

There are several things, in the past few years, he will wish he had not said and yet, until recently, he still privately conveyed an enjoyment of his position. 'It has given my life a focus,' he said once, and he will certainly not wish to lose touch again. 'I could be like a Cabinet minister retiring to the back benches,' he suggested of his future. 'I know how things work and I could be of use.'

It is possible he now regrets one of the first comments he made when the chairman's position was offered to him. 'Everything I have done in life has prepared me for this job,' he said.

He was, however, not quite prepared for the relentless, unforgiving scrutiny. When asked yesterday what qualities the board would be seeking in Dexter's successor, Alan Smith responded quickly: 'A very thick skin.'

Alan Lee, *The Times* (10 August 1993)

Malcolm Marshall

He was listening to the radio and did not believe what he had heard. Minutes later, Wesley Hall telephoned to say the same. He trembled, for he had played only one match for his native Barbados – and began to dream.

He dreamt of his hero, Sir Garfield Sobers; the languid, laughing, liquid Sobers whose style entranced a nation. All through his childhood he had mimicked Sobers, collar stiff and turned high, shoulders rolling, hips swaying, and now, suddenly, he had the chance to walk the legend's stage.

Kerry Packer had ripped the heart from the West Indies team and, shorn of their stars, the selectors searched for some young and spirited characters to tour India. One they chose was unknown but was from the most famous island in the cricket empire and destined to capture more Test match wickets than any other West Indian. This week he retired from English cricket.

Malcolm Marshall was born thirty-five years ago in St Michael, a small parish in the middle of Barbados, to a policeman father and a doting mother who spoiled him rotten. He went to school in the crispest clothes and was, the teachers say, a model pupil and a team man even then.

He did not know his father, who died in a motorcycle accident before the boy's first birthday, but he knew his grandfather, Oscar Welch, because Oscar bowled at him days and nights in the parks and on the beaches.

He loved batting and, in truth, loves it best even now. He took to bowling because he once waited four days for a knock in the school yard. The rules were clear; you batted until dismissed, and one or two could play a bit, so the tiny, frail boy started bowling, as fast as he could. By the end of break-time, he was batting.

Much of Marshall epitomizes the calypso cricketer. Much does not. The joyous grin, the incessant chatter, the flailing willow, the stumps flying, the bouncers whizzing, the shiny black face with its gleaming teeth and the wide open laugh, head thrown skywards, that accompanies the simplest of fun.

His youth was conditioned by his environment in the way of Constantine and Kanhai; Ramadhin and Richards; Worrell, Walcott and Weekes. They all, it sometimes seemed, were affected by the sun and the sand and so they performed the most outrageous of deeds and otherwise the most crazy.

Their temperament and impulse could run riot in the heat, and thereby came the charm of their brilliant, instinctive cricket that was played without inhibition.

But, today, the West Indian cricketer is not so happy-go-lucky, for he is conditioned by success and salaries, pay cheques and professionalism. Marshall is this, too, a man reared by Clive Lloyd, who played tough, uncompromising cricket in a team that no other could surely have beaten. The rules were for breaking all right, but batting and its beauty suffered as remarkable fast bowlers – collectively the best in the game's history – tore into unprepared and intimidated opposition and laid waste their defences. This was cruel, calculated cricket and Marshall was as impressive in this role as he is when playing the court jester.

He says: 'I am a fast bowler. This is my job. If I bowl dangerously and intimidate, then the umpires are empowered to stop me. I have no problem with that. I love cricket and am a keen professional. I have obligations to meet, mortgages to pay. I am a man who wants to do the best for himself and his team every time I go to work.'

This is the very key to Malcolm Marshall and his incredible success. He has never given less than everything for his team. He is self-interested in the acceptable way of top sportsmen but when it is not his day, and others are wreaking their havoc, he is as pleased as punch.

In fourteen years, I do not remember him once giving short change and, along·with Mike Procter and Sir Richard Hadlee, whom Marshall greatly admires, he has been the best overseas cricketer in English cricket. To be so, he has remained supremely fit and his sharp mind has ensured the preservation of those supple, rubbery limbs as the years have taken their toll.

His body, though chubbier now, is absurdly slight for one so powerful. He has small bones and small feet and stands no taller than 5ft 10in, yet at various times he has been the world's greatest, fastest, most skilful, and, more improbably, most lethal bowler.

Around his neck hangs a gold chain and on the pendant glows his nickname, 'Macko'. The word 'Macko' evokes joint emotions of hand-slapping glee and sinister oppression.

When Macko first played for Hampshire in 1979, there was no sign of the hand-slapping glee. The weather was appalling. It snowed and he clung to the radiator, fingers frozen and fearfully homesick. He had an awkward summer, plagued by no-balls and an unsympathetic captain, but he had talent, oodles of it, and we youngsters wanted him back, for we quickly spotted the sinister oppression.

As a boy, he had followed Hampshire from the pages of the Barbados newspapers, initially with an interest in his namesake, Roy Marshall, and then studying the career of another hero, Andy Roberts. It was natural, then, that he should go to Hampshire and he has loved the county ever since that chilly introduction.

In return, we have loved him too, for he has taught us plenty and won us matches. He has taken 823 wickets for Hampshire (1,550 in all first-class cricket and 376 in Test matches), 134 of them in 1982.

In the early days, his bowling was based on a whippy, sideways action that caused the ball to skid at its target with deadly outswing. He bowled a bouncer so evil that even the players with the quickest wit were forced back, thus leaving themselves open to his vicious movement.

As his action became more chest-on, he developed the inswinger and, of course, with age and experience came accuracy.

He is a sprinter to the crease, with light toes that barely scuff the turf. He has based his bowling on a still head, an upright body and a loose wrist which controls his swing. He is revered by umpires, who call it a joy to work with him, and feared by batsmen, who are confused by the whiplash of his fast arm and the intensity of his competition.

He commands a different field for each opponent, and takes some time over setting it, and has a memory so good that no tail-end charlie, let alone top-order optimist, can escape his examination.

At his best, he made fun by nominating dismissals, two outswingers 'watch him leave them, skipper', then an inswinger 'and now watch the off stump disappear'. Bingo! Three balls later, with the job done, he would turn to me, grinning, and make a mock yawn to the heavens.

Those who have seen him only in his twilight years can have no idea of his speed or his genius. Vivian Richards believes him to have been the greatest of all fast bowlers and adds: 'He has the biggest heart and the smartest brain.'

Marshall has memories, like all of us, of Headingley in 1984 when his thumb was double fractured and he took seven wickets in the second innings; of his bowling in India and Pakistan where the odds were against his type: of the Shell Shield and of Test match whitewashes; and of a World Cup winner's medal in 1979, though he played only one match in the tournament and was not selected for the final.

Most fondly he recalls the day when he passed Lance Gibbs's 309 wickets to become the most prolific West Indian bowler of all time.

'I was one short overnight and the radio station played a song written in my honour called "Hit It O Macko O Hit It" over and over again. We were playing India in my home town Bridgetown, and finally after lunch Dujon caught Azharuddin from an outswinger. I was overwhelmed with pride.'

This was the stuff of Boycott's 100th hundred at Headingley . . . the stuff of fiction.

His other favourite triumph came with Hampshire's victory in the Benson and Hedges Cup last summer. 'The county won two trophies while I was away touring and that day at Lord's will be my day of greatest joy in fifteen years of top-level cricket.'

He will leave us now for Natal and, next summer, the leagues. With him goes the greatest enthusiasm for cricket I have ever known.

If at times on the field he has appeared cold as an assassin it is because his devotion to the game and his team is so absolute, so whole-hearted. But it is his laughter that counts, and that grin and those dancing eyes. From Sydney to Southampton, in Barbados, Bournemouth and Bangalore, Malcolm Marshall has been a man for all seasons: a devil of a cricketer with the kick of a mule.

Thankfully, for all his modern sophistication there is still the echo of the calypso.

Mark Nicholas, Daily Telegraph (17 September, 1993)

Acknowledgements

For permission to reprint copyright material the publishers gratefully acknowledge the following sources. Extracts indicated below as being from *The Cricketer* are all reproduced by kind permission of the Managing Editor.

JONATHAN AGNEW, from *Eight Days a Week* (Ring Press, 1988). DAVID AKERS, 'Is batting all that meets the eye?', *The Cricketer*, September 1985. H. S. ALTHAM, from *A History of Cricket*; reprinted by permission of George Allen & Unwin, now Unwin Hyman, an imprint of HarperCollins Publishers Ltd. JOHN ARLOTT, from *Fred: Portrait of a Fast Bowler*; reprinted by permission of the publisher, Eyre & Spottiswoode; 'Alan Knott', 'Garfield Sobers', *The Cricketer*, June/July 1970; 'The Old Cricketer', 'To J. B. Hobbs at 70', 'Cricket at Worcester' and 'A Laker Over' from *John Arlott's Book of Cricketers* (Lutterworth, 1979); all © the Estate of John Arlott. DOUGLAS AUCHTERLONIE, 'The London Guide', *The Cricketer*, 1987. ROBIN BAILEY, 'I was Larwood and Voce' ('My Career in Cricket') from *Quick Singles* (Lennard, 1986). TREVOR BAILEY, from *The Greatest of My Time* (1968); reprinted by permission of the publisher, Eyre & Spottiswoode. BRIAN BEARSHAW, from *From the Stretford End* (Partridge Press, 1990). ERIC BEECHER, from the *Australian Cricketer*, 1978. RICHIE BENAUD, from *Willow Patterns* (Hodder & Stoughton, 1969); © Richie Benaud, 1969. SCYLD BERRY, from *A Cricket Odyssey* (Pavilion, 1988). EDMUND BLUNDEN, extract from *Cricket Country* (Collins, 1944); extract from 'Forefathers', 'The Season Opens'; reprinted by permission of Peters Fraser & Dunlop Writers' Agents on behalf of the Estate of Edmund Blunden. DON BRADMAN, from *Farewell to Cricket* (Hodder & Stoughton, 1950). MIKE BREARLEY, 'Headingley, 1981' from *Phoenix from the Ashes* (Hodder & Stoughton, 1982); 'The Captain and the Media' from *The Art of Captaincy* (Hodder & Stoughton, 1985); 'John Murray', *The Cricketer*, July 1975. GERALD BRODRIBB, from *Next Man In* (Putnam, 1952). M. BURLINSON, 'Hamlet's Lament', *The Cricketer*, 1982. NEVILLE CARDUS, extracts reproduced by kind permission of the copyright holder, Margaret Hughes. DONALD D. CHRISTIE, 'How Horatius Horace Carried His Bat', *The Cricketer*, 1986. JOHN CLEESE, extract from the introduction to *The Ashes Retained* by Mike Brearley and Dudley Doust (Hodder & Stoughton, 1979); reprinted by permission of David Wilkinson Associates. JEFF CLOVES, 'Lillee', *The Cricketer*, 1983; 'Park Players', *The Cricketer*, 1987; 'The Batsman's Betrothed', *The Cricketer*, 1986. ALFRED COCHRANE, 'The Catch' and 'The Scoreboard' from *Collected Verse* (Longman). JEREMY CONEY, from *The Playing Mantis* (Moa Publications, 1985). GEORGE COX, 'Please God, let me play for Sussex – regularly', *The Cricketer*, May 1981. J. G. W. DAVIES, 'From Harris to Cowdrey', *The Cricketer*, 1971. TONY DEANE, 'Cricket in the Hindu Kush', *The Cricketer*, June 1985. WILLIAM DEEDES, 'Stolen Hours' from *Quick Singles* (Lennard, 1986). LOUIS DUFFUS, from *Stars of Today* (Pelham Books, 1970). MATTHEW ENGEL, from *Ashes '85* (Pelham Books, 1985). JACK FINGLETON, from *Masters of Cricket* (Heinemann, 1958); reproduced by permission of the Trustee of the Estate of the late Jack Fingleton. STEPHEN FRY, from *The Liar* (Heinemann); reprinted by permission of David Higham Associates Ltd. PETER GIBB, 'The Art of Being Captained' from *Quick Singles* (Lennard, 1986). ALAN GIBSON, 'Cricket in Fiction', *The Cricketer*, 1973; ' 'Endren, 'Earne and 'Aig', *The Cricketer*, 1980; 'Colin McCool . . .', *The Cricketer International*, May 1981. TOM GRAVENEY, from *Cricket Through the Covers* (Muller, 1958). © Tom Graveney 1958. IMOGEN GROSBERG, 'See off the Shine', *The Cricketer*, 1982. LORD HARRIS, letter to *The Times*, 3 February 1931; © the Estate of Lord Harris. HUGH HUNTER, letter to *The Times*, 1938; © Hugh Hunter 1938. C. L. R. JAMES, 'George Headley', *The Manchester Guardian*, 18 April 1933. FRANK KEATING, 'Tom Graveney' from *Cricket Heroes*; reprinted by permission of Lennard Associates. J. M. KILBURN, from *Overthrow* (Stanley Paul, 1975); reprinted by permission of Random House UK Ltd.; 'Brian Close', *The Cricketer*, August 1970. ANDREW LANG, 'Ballade of Dead Cricketers' (Longmans Green). JOHN LATHAM, 'Double Wicket Maiden', *The Cricketer*, 1982. BRIAN LEVISON, 'Death of a Cricketer', *The Cricketer*, 1987. TONY LEWIS, from *A Summer of Cricket* (Pelham Books, 1975); 'MCC in the Far East', *The Cricketer*, 1985. DEREK LODGE, from *Figures on the Green* (Allen & Unwin, 1982). CHARLEE MARSHALL, 'The bomb that swung late', *The Cricketer*, January 1987. CHRISTOPHER MARTIN-JENKINS, 'Shane Warne' from the *Daily Telegraph*, 1993; © The Telegraph plc, London 1993; used with permission; 'Dennis Lillee', 'Kapil Dev', 'Derek Randall' and 'Richie Benaud' all from *Cricket Characters* (1987); reprinted by permission of Lennard Associates. RONALD MASON, from *Sing All A Green Willow*; by kind permission of The Epworth Press; 'Inside the Oval' from *Batsman's Paradise* (Hollis & Carter, 1955), © Ronald Mason. FERGUS MCKENDRICK, from *Pulpit Cricket* (Collins/Willow, 1983). TERESA MCLEAN, from *The Men in White Coats* (Stanley Paul, 1987); © Teresa McLean 1987. MICHAEL MELFORD, 'Graeme Pollock', *The Cricketer*, April 1970; 'Glenn Turner', *The Cricketer*, 1974; 'Surrey's Seven Years . . .' from *After the Interval* (Chorwood, 1990). GEOFFREY MOORHOUSE, 'Northants v Worcestershire' from *The Best Loved Game* (Hodder & Stoughton, 1979); 'An Addict from Quetta' from *To the Frontier* (Hodder & Stoughton, 1984). JOHN MULVANEY & REX HARCOURT, from *Cricket Walkabout* (Macmillan, 1967). MARK NICHOLAS, from the *Daily Telegraph*, 17 September 1993; © Mark Nicholas 1993; used by permission of the author. BARRY NORMAN, 'Bradman' from *Quick Singles* (Lennard, 1986). ERIC PARKER, from *Between the Wickets* (Philip Allan, 1926). GRAHAME PARKER, from *Gloucestershire Road* (Pelham Books, 1983). TONY PAWSON, from *Runs and Catches* (Faber, 1980); reprinted by kind permission of the author. IAN PEEBLES, from *Talking of Cricket* (Museum, 1953). TERENCE RATTIGAN, 'Mr. Merryweather Says', *The Cricketer*, September 1965. TIM RICE, 'The Epithets' from *Quick Singles* (Lennard, 1986). R. C. ROBERTSON-GLASGOW, 'Nets', *The Cricketer*, 1932; 'Oxford Cricket' from *46 Not Out* (Hollis & Carter, 1948); 'Puerilities' from *The Brighter Side of Cricket* (Barker, 1933); 'E. R. Wilson', 'L. C Braund', 'W. Bestwick', 'M. Leyland', 'C. P. Mead' and 'W. J. O'Reilly', all from *Cricket Prints* (Laurie, 1943). RAY ROBINSON, extracts from *From the Boundary* (Collins, 1950); © Ray Robinson. PETER ROEBUCK, from *Ashes to Ashes* (1987); reprinted by permission of the publisher, William Heinemann Ltd. ALAN ROSS, 'The Test' ('The Element of Time') from *The Boundary Book* (Macdonald, 1962); 'The Press Box at Sabina Park' from *Through the Caribbean* (Hamish Hamilton, 1966); and 'Cricket at Brighton' from *Blindfold Games* (Harvill, 1982); all reprinted by permission of the author. SIEGFRIED SASSOON, 'Dreamers' and 'The Extra Inch'; reprinted by permission of George Sassoon. PETER SELLERS and PETER MUNRO SMITH, from *The Boundary Book* (Macdonald, 1962). JOHN SHAWCROFT, from *The History of Derbyshire County Cricket Club* (Christopher Helm, 1989); reprinted by permission of A & C Black (Publishers) Ltd. DENNIS SILK, 'George Cox', *The Cricketer*, August 1985. PETER SMITH, 'Keith Miller' from *Cricket Heroes*; reprinted by permission of Lennard Associates. SYD SMITH, 'The Night the Selectors Came to Blows', *Australian Cricket Board of Control*, 1912. E. W. SWANTON, from *The Bedside Cricket Book*, ed. Ron Roberts (Batsford, 1966); 'The Bodyline Explosion' (Jardine and Warner), *The Cricketer*, 1981; 'Thirties Characters' from *Sort of a Cricket Person* (Collins, 1922). CHRISTOPHER SYKES, 'Hadlee's Victim', *The Cricketer*, 1986. BOB TAYLOR, 'Frozen Memory', *The Cricketer*, 1987. JOHN THICKNESSE, 'Denis Compton' from *Cricket Heroes*; reprinted by permission of Lennard Associates. LESLIE THOMAS, from *County Champions* (Heinemann, 1982); © Leslie Thomas 1982; 'Ole Blue Eyes' from *Quick Singles* (Lennard, 1986). A. A. THOMSON, from *Pavilioned in Splendour* (Museum, 1956); from *Cricket My Happiness* (Museum, 1954). BEN TRAVERS, from *94 Declared* (Hamish Hamilton, 1956). PETER WALKER, from *Cricket Conversations* (Pelham Books, 1978). SIR PELHAM WARNER, from *Lord's 1789–1945* (Harrap). JOANNE WATSON, 'Collins of Clifton' and 'Not Only a Wicketkeeper' from *Moments of Glory* (Lennard, 1990). JOHN WOODCOCK, 'Typhoon Strikes' from *The Bedside Cricket Book*, ed. Ron Roberts (Batsford,

ACKNOWLEDGEMENTS

1966); 'Cricket in the Bones' from *The Times*, 24 April 1993; © Times Newspapers Limited 1993; reprinted with permission. PETER WYNNE-THOMAS, from *The History of Nottinghamshire County Cricket Club* (Christopher Helm, 1992); reprinted by permission of A & C Black (Publishers) Ltd. JACK YOUNG, '. . . from the Nursery End', *The Cricketer*, March 1964.

Index of Contributors

Subject Index